CO-ASF-151

HUMAN SEXUALITY

SECOND EDITION

CAROLE WADE   **SARAH CIRESE**
College of Marin   College of Marin

Harcourt Brace Jovanovich, Publishers

San Diego • New York • Chicago • Austin • Washington, D.C.
London • Sydney • Tokyo • Toronto

With love, for our children,
Jessica and Jason
and
Lesley and Jeffrey

Copyright © 1991, 1982 by Harcourt Brace Jovanovich, Inc.

All rights reserved. No part of this publication may be reproduced or transmitted in any form or by any means, electronic or mechanical, including photocopy, recording, or any information storage and retrieval system, without permission in writing from the publisher.

Requests for permission to make copies of any part of the work should be mailed to: Permissions Department, Harcourt Brace Jovanovich, Inc., 8th Floor, Orlando, Florida 32887.

Cover art: Georgia O'Keeffe, *Oriental Poppies*, 1928. Collection, University Art Museum of Minnesota, Minneapolis.

ISBN: 015-540430-X

Library of Congress Catalog Card Number: 90-082360

Printed in the United States of America

Text copyrights and acknowledgments begin on page 776, which constitutes a continuation of the copyright page.

Preface

•

Human sexuality is one of those topics, like love and economics, that people may think they understand better than they do. What on earth can instructors in human sexuality courses find to talk about for an entire semester? they may ask. After all, isn't sex merely doing what comes naturally? Hasn't everything a person could possibly want to know about sex already been said a thousand times before?

One of our major purposes in writing this textbook has been to help students see that human sexuality is not so simple; that it is as intricate and challenging a topic as any other studied by biological and social scientists. A kiss is *not* just a kiss, a sigh is not just a sigh, for the *meanings* we invest in erotic and sexual acts change as time goes by. Within only a few short years, the daring may become conventional, the dangerous inviting, the romantic silly—or vice versa, depending on political, economic, social, epidemiological, and ideological forces.

In this edition of *Human Sexuality*, our goal is to offer a balanced and thoughtful account of what is known about sexuality. You will find here a broad, up-to-date survey of research, and descriptions and evaluations of representative studies. Three features distinguish this book:

■ *A resolution of the "elephant problem."* In the fable about the blind men who examined different parts of an elephant, each man arrived at a different conclusion about the animal's nature. Keeping the moral of that story in mind, we have drawn liberally on research in psychology, sociology, biology, anthropology, medicine, and health education, to better understand the "whole animal" called sexuality. But an interdisciplinary approach is not enough if one chapter emphasizes just biology, another just psychology, and so forth. Our aim is to show how different levels and types of explanations illuminate nearly every sexual issue.

Consider, for example, the problem of sexually transmitted diseases (STDs). People need to know what causes them, the symptoms, and how they are treated. But biology is only the beginning. Important psychological and sociological questions can and should be raised about STDs. Many of these diseases can be easily cured, yet STDs are on the rise. Why? What mistakes have been made in past attempts to eradicate them? How do personal and cultural attitudes hinder prevention and treatment? Why do individuals often ignore safer sex practices and fail to communicate honestly with sexual partners? How committed is our society to the elimination of STDs?

In the past decade there has been increasing appreciation of how shifting cultural and political winds influence the way individuals construct and interpret their own sexuality. Social constructionists argue that human beings, living in relationship with others, are in a constant, open-ended process of creating their own sexuality—something other species cannot do. Accordingly, we have pointed out cultural influences on sexuality throughout, rather than relegate them to an isolated section. For example, we discuss how culture affects the sex education of children, body image, attitudes toward extramarital activity, the definition of sexual problems, the prevalence of rape, the meanings of homosexuality, definitions of pornography, and the role of prostitutes. We have also included pertinent historical information to help readers see how their personal experiences fit into the continuing story of humankind.

■ *Critical thinking about sexuality.* Many college textbooks claim to promote critical thinking, but unfortunately, the concept is often reduced to a set of rhetorical questions. In our view, critical thinking has little to do with anticipating or guessing the right answer. Rather, it entails an ability and willingness to make judgements based on well-supported reasons; and it requires that a person consider evidence, analyze assumptions, and weigh alternative interpretations. Our goal has been to model these processes wherever it seems appropriate. For example, we show how popular interest about the "G spot" outpaced the meager anecdotal evidence supporting its existence. And when we discuss menopause we show how older studies of women in therapy skewed perceptions of how most women experience this "change of life."

Critical thinking also means withholding judgment and tolerating uncertainty when evidence is lacking or when professional disagreement exists. Sexology is a developing discipline in which questions are every bit as important as answers, and open questions abound. Why have all societies insisted on regulating sexual behavior? Why do women have more difficulties with orgasm than men do? How does the quality of a relationship affect sexual functioning? How does sexual orientation arise? Is there such a thing as a sexual addiction? We raise questions like these at many points, and ask what types of evidence might resolve differences of opinion. In addition, boxed inserts pose provocative issues for readers to ponder and a special supplement provides a series of critical thinking assignments coordinated with the text.

■ *Getting personal.* Findings on human sexuality are not just academic; they matter, sometimes in urgent and immediate ways, to all of us. In this edition, a new feature at the end of each chapter, *Personal Perspective*, invites readers to explore their own views, experiences, and concerns, and to apply what they have read to their own lives. For example, there are Personal Perspectives on motives for choosing, rejecting, or postponing parenthood; finding the right partner; drawing a line between erotica and pornography; facing forbidden thoughts and desires; and recalling personal sexual milestones. Some Personal Perspectives are intended only for personal use; others can be adapted for use in class assignments or group discussion.

The Second Edition is completely revised. Part I, "Sex in Perspective," includes a new introductory chapter to help readers define their goals in studying sexuality and to frame sexuality in historical and cross-cultural perspective. Chapter 2 examines the sexual legacy of Western culture and includes new material on twentieth-century changes in attitudes and behavior. Chapter 3 explains how sex research is done and what problems researchers face, so that students can evaluate and appreciate the quality of the information to follow.

Part II, "The Psychobiology of Sex," explains sexual anatomy and physiology, but in keeping with our integrative approach, it also discusses how thoughts, emotions, and "sexual scripts" influence sexual arousal and response. Chapters on reproduction and birth control are included here.

Part III, "Sexual Relationships and Behavior," shows what people do sexually and how relationships provide an emotional context for what they do. We discuss the nature of love, how and why relationships begin, the characteristics of ongoing relationships, and conflict resolution in relationships. This section includes chapters on conventional and unconventional behaviors, and on sexual problems and solutions.

Part IV, "The Origins and Development of Sexuality," examines the chronology of sexual development. We devote one chapter to childhood sexuality, including gender development and childhood sexual behavior, and one chapter to adolescent and adult sexuality. A third chapter explores the possible roots of sexual orientation.

Part V, "Social and Health Issues," focuses on psychosexual health, broadly defined. By health, we mean an individual's personal well-being and that of the society as a whole. Chapters on sexual exploitation and commercial sex raise questions about how societies encourage or discourage these expressions of sexuality. A new final chapter shows how medical, psychological, and sociocultural considerations play a part in sexual health, and it asks the reader to speculate on what a sexually healthy child, adult, and society might be like.

There is not a separate chapter on gender because we believe that gender has too profound an influence on sexuality to be compartmentalized. Instead, we integrate gender issues throughout the book, issues such as: Do gender roles learned early in life affect erotic imagery later on? Do male and female adolescents sometimes differ in their motives for sex? How does gender affect aging? How does gender affect intimacy, self-disclosure, and romanticism? Why is unconventional behavior more common among men than women?

Readers are entitled to the highest standards of scholarship in an introductory textbook, but it is our conviction that a scholarly approach need not put students to sleep. Surely a sexuality textbook ought to be as interesting as its subject matter! We have drawn on our experience as teachers and writers to make this one as engaging and as readable as possible.

This edition has been enhanced by many new, inviting illustrations. We have tried to avoid photographic cliches and to use photographs as a way of informing, reinforcing important points, and raising issues for critical thought. In addition, color has been added to anatomical illustrations to make them easier to comprehend and remember. Also, a list of key terms with page references has been added to each chapter.

Finally, an enlarged and improved supplements package accompanies this edition:

- A set of 18 *critical thinking assignments* is available free to students upon adoption of the textbook. Each assignment consists of four to six provocative items that ask students, for example, to examine assumptions, defend a position, or evaluate arguments. Instructors can use some or all of these assignments, in class or as homework, to stimulate thought about the complexities of human sexuality.

- A revised *Instructor's Manual*, written by the authors, contains several teaching aids for each chapter: a brief chapter description, specific learning objectives with relevant page numbers, a detailed chapter outline, teaching tips, lecture enhancements and class activities, issues for further discussion, and guidelines for evaluating responses to the critical thinking assignments described above. The *Instructor's Manual* includes a revised and expanded *Test Bank* with over 1,400 multiple-choice and short-answer essay questions keyed to specific learning objectives. Essay questions are accompanied by suggested points to look for in evaluating student responses. Each multiple-choice item is referenced by difficulty and by the textbook page where the answer can be found. A unique feature of this *Test Bank* is a preselected 10-item Reading Check Quiz for each chapter. We think instructors and students will find this a helpful instrument for testing initial comprehension of a chapter, before the material has been covered in depth.

- A new *Study Guide* includes an introductory section on how to use the text to best advantage and, for each chapter, learning objectives, a review outline keyed to the learning objectives, and a variety of self-tests.

Any project of this magnitude requires the talent and commitment of many people. We are grateful to the editorial and production team at Harcourt Brace Jovanovich for all their hard work. Marcus Boggs, who was executive editor when this revision was launched, provided continued enthusiasm to keep it on track. Rick Roehrich, our acquisitions editor, inspired us with his good cheer. Sandy Steiner, our marketing manager, provided consistent support and offered helpful standards for the design of the supplements package. Ruth Rominger shouldered the burden of editing the manuscript. David Watt efficiently supervised the complicated editorial process, and Mandy Van Dusen guided production through a tight schedule. Socorro P. González capably copyedited the manuscript and kept the work flowing smoothly. Paulette Russo imaginatively researched the photographs, giving us a wealth of splendid choices from which to choose. Candy Young showed unusual dedication and perseverance in assisting with the photo research. Jim Hughes developed the beautiful and elegant design of the book, including the cover.

Our thanks also go to the artists who contributed so much to this book. Elizabeth Bennett produced the handsome illustrations of sexual positions and activities. Bobbi Angel prepared the fine anatomical drawings that were carried over from the first edition; and Sandra McMahon, Fiona King, Susan Jaekel, Fred Haynes, and Bob Yochum produced the many equally fine drawings and charts that are new to this edition. We also thank Kerry Sandler and Lucille Taylor for their assistance with research and clerical support.

We are enormously grateful, too, for the constructive criticism of academic colleagues who reviewed parts or all of the manuscript, including Pauline Bart, University of Illinois at Chicago; Laura Brown; Michael Carey, Syracuse University; Sally Foster, Mira Costa College; Eliana Gil, California Graduate School of Family Psychology; Michael Godsey, College of Marin; Peggy Kleinplatz, University of Ottawa; Susan H. McFadden, University of Wisconsin Oshkosh; Neil Malamuth, UCLA; Diana E. H. Russell, Mills College; Wendy Stock, Texas A&M University; Susan Walen, Towson State University; and Sharon Wolf, California State University, Long Beach.

Special thanks go to Ellen Berscheid of the University of Minnesota, who authored a draft of the chapter on love and intimate relationships for the first edition. Many of her insights remain, and we are fortunate to have had the benefit of her scholarship and wisdom. We are also grateful to Julia Heiman, of the University of Washington, who was an invaluable consultant on the topic of sex therapy during preparation of the first edition. We wish, too, to acknowledge the important influence that Leonore Tiefer, of the Montifiore Medical Center in New York City, has had on our thinking about sexuality. And we are infinitely grateful to our colleague Carol Tavris for her intellectual insights and moral support.

Above all, we wish to thank Howard Williams and Albert Brewster, who always kept us facing forward when the light at the end of the tunnel seemed dim. They have helped us through the difficult task of revising this textbook by giving us two of life's greatest gifts, love and laughter.

Carole Wade
Sarah Cirese

Table of Contents

•

1

Sex in Perspective

2

C H A P T E R   O N E

■

Why Study Sex?

●

Amoebas at the start/Were not complex;/They tore themselves apart/And started Sex.

Arthur Guiterman

Sex. What do you think of when you read that word? A sexual act? A feeling between two people? A problem? Do you want to laugh, or sigh? To cheer, or groan? To joke, or blush?

Sex does a lot of work for such a little word. Sex can mean an activity ("I had sex last night"), or an urge or motive ("Sex interfered with my better judgment"). It can specify the genetic or anatomical status of male or female (What's the baby's sex?"). Often it is used as a synonym for **gender,** the psychological and social status associated with being biologically male or female ("By treating boys and girls differently, parents promote sex differences"). As an adjective, sex may refer to a basis of attraction ("I looked at him twice because he was so sexy") or a commercial commodity ("I finally got up the nerve to visit a sex shop"). According to some scholars, sex is a fundamental, innate instinct or drive, a source of energy that fuels most of our activities. For others, sex is a social phenomenon, created and defined by cultural rules and regulations. To make matters even more confusing, some writers use *sex* and **sexuality** as synonyms, while others (including the authors of this text) think of sexuality as a broader term, encompassing all psychological, physical, and social qualities that contribute to the subjective sense of oneself as a sexual person.

One thing is clear, though: For human beings, sex is more than a physical act that might or might not result in pregnancy. The reason: unlike amoebas, aardvarks, or antelopes, people attach meaning to sexual acts. Just as February 14 is not just another day, because it's Valentine's Day, sex is more than a biological response, *because of the meanings we give it*. Sexual encounters may be tender, intimate, friendly, playful, passionate, or romantic, depending on your purposes. They may also be routine, selfish,

When anatomy is destiny *Most animals are limited by their anatomy and physiology to certain predictable patterns of sexual behavior. But human sexuality is distinguished by its flexibility and variability.*

exploitive, or harrowing. In human beings, sexual motives range from physical release to the expression of spirituality. That is why sex is as complex as human psychology itself.

This complexity is apparent when we compare human beings with other animals. Like us, other animals often use sexual behavior to send non-sexual messages. A dominant male monkey will sexually mount a subordinate one as a way of showing who's boss. When two baboons fight, one may cry "uncle" by pointing his rump toward the other one, which is also what female baboons do to show sexual interest. But animals, as far as we know, don't use sex to win their friends' approval, rebel against parents, prove love, or make a living—only a few of the many sexual motives found in human beings.

When compared with the sex lives of human beings, the sex lives of most other animals are marked by their predictability. Furry and feathered creatures do engage in many kinds of sexual behavior, including masturbation and mouth-genital stimulation (Beach, 1977), but for most animal species the *when* of sex is determined largely by hormones, and the *how* by anatomy.

The lower a species on the evolutionary scale (the earlier it evolved), the stronger the influence of hormonal cycles on the timing of sexual responsiveness and behavior. Among most mammals, the female is usually sexually active only when she is "in heat" (in estrus), and fertile. The capacity of a male to attract a female, his attraction to females, and his ability to perform sexually are all strongly affected by sex hormones. However, among the higher mammals, the primates, there is much more flexibility. For example, the female common chimpanzee is sexually receptive even when she is not ovulating (Goodall, 1986). The female pygmy chimpanzee is sexually receptive and attractive to males nearly *all* the time (DeWaal, 1989). And human beings, the highest of the primates, can and do have sex at all phases of the female's hormonal cycle. Hormones have some influence on human sexual arousal and behavior in both sexes (see Chapter 5), but it is subtle; hormonal peaks are not the reason people have sex.

Sexual technique also depends on the evolutionary level of the species. Anatomy prevents many animals from caressing (assuming they'd want to), and most can copulate only in the rear-entry position (Tiefer, 1979). Different species have different sexual habits, some of them quite colorful from the human point of view, but within a given species sexual behavior is often stereotyped and unvarying. Within non-primate species, this behavior occurs without much learning; if you've seen one couple of the species having sex, you've pretty much seen them all. But for primates there is considerable flexibility in techniques and positions. Moreover, sex is not just doing what comes naturally. Primates require certain kinds of experiences for the development of their sexuality, and this is particularly true of those fascinating primates, the *homo sapiens*. Experience shapes what people do sexually, and how they do it.

When all is said and done, the most significant difference between us and other animals is our possession of a large, well-developed brain. The human cerebral cortex enables us to reason, evaluate, form opinions, and take off on flights of the imagination. Because of these abilities, we actively construct our own sexuality. The nature of our sexuality is profoundly shaped by culture, learning, and experience, and is not merely a biological given. We interpret and direct our biological urges and surges, and sometimes choose to ignore or resist them. For human beings, sex is not only a reproductive act, but an expression of upbringing, feelings, and outlook on life.

STUDYING HUMAN SEXUALITY

Because human sexuality is so complex, people are often perplexed by sex in their own lives. Even those of us who are completely untroubled about sex may feel a need to understand it more fully. **Sexology,** the scientific study of human sexuality, can provide some answers and insights. Sexology is an *interdisciplinary* field; it draws on the work of biologists, physiologists, medical researchers, psychologists, sociologists, anthropologists, and historians. In this book, you will discover what the various specialties have revealed about the physical, emotional, and cultural aspects of sexuality. You will also find out what mysteries remain.

Of course, sex is not a new topic for you. That makes this course unique. When students enroll in introductory computer science, organic chemistry, or French, they usually know little if anything about the subject. But before ever taking a course in human sexuality, you already know a great deal about it. You are familiar, for example, with cultural attitudes toward sex, because those attitudes are pushed at you every day from billboards and television programs, in commercials and popular songs. Having experienced puberty, you know something about the physical changes that prepare the body for sexual activity and reproduction. Having passed through adolescence, you also know about the curiosity and confusion teenagers have about themselves and the other sex. Sexual exploration is a normal consequence of these feelings. Most teenagers read sexually explicit materials (which they manage to obtain, despite the best efforts of adults to prevent it); they examine their own and other people's bodies; they "fool around"; they masturbate; and many have sex with a partner. By age twenty, most people have experienced one or more sexual relationships and know something about the joys and tribulations such relationships bring.

By the time you finish this book, however, you are likely to know many things you did not know before, even if you are quite sophisticated sexually. Much of what people believe about sex is based on unreliable evidence. Some of the "findings" reported in popular books and magazines are no more than unsupported opinions. Moreover, we all tend to overgeneralize from our own experiences, and to forget that our feelings, attitudes, and behavior are not necessarily universal.

As you begin this book, take time to consider what you want to get from it. The following are some goals you might set for yourself in order to maximize your learning.

Get Your Questions Answered

If you are like most people, you want to study human sexuality in order to gain greater insight into yourself and others. You may also need reliable information about sexuality because you are planning a career in counseling, nursing, psychotherapy, social work, or some other medical or helping profession. You may have questions that are technical ("How safe are birth control pills?" "Where does seminal fluid originate?") or personal ("Why don't I have orgasms?" "How can I communicate my sexual needs to my partner?"). This book will give you an opportunity to expand your knowledge and integrate the separate bits and pieces of information you already have.

Over the years, we have received hundreds of written queries from students, ranging from the serious ("How does early sexual abuse affect a

person's later feelings about sex?"), to the silly ("Why do fools fall in love?").
You might want to jot down any questions of your own to refer to as you read.

Clarify Your Sexual Attitudes and Values

A course in human sexuality can provide an opportunity for examining
your feelings about sex. Is your sexual experience relatively limited? You
may want to concentrate on making decisions about the sorts of experiences
you wish to have, when, and with whom to have them. Are you a parent, or
do you expect to be one? Why not work on clarifying the sexual values you
will transmit to your children. Are you currently in an intimate relationship?
You may want to compare your sexual attitudes with those of your partner.
Or, like many students, you may simply be curious about other people's feelings, and wonder whether yours are "normal."

As you evaluate your attitudes, keep in mind that although sex is a private activity, it has a way of moving from the bedroom to the ballot. In a
democracy citizens may be asked to take positions on pornography, prostitution, abortion, homosexuality, and sex education. This book cannot tell you
what to think or believe about such issues, but it can help you arrive at
informed opinions.

© 1985 Mal Ent Inc.

Become More Comfortable about Sex

You may be relatively inexperienced sexually, or you may have had
many sexual partners and experiences. You may be just starting to date, or
you may be married or divorced. You may consider yourself inhibited, or daring. But whatever your sexual history, chances are that certain sexual topics
or circumstances make you feel slightly uncomfortable. Sexual partners are
often embarrassed to discuss birth control or protection from sexually transmitted diseases with one another. Parents often fluster when a child asks
how people "do it," or what masturbation is. Lovers sometimes find themselves in a power struggle because one partner likes some sexual practice
(say, oral sex) that the other considers wrong or disgusting. Patients may fail
to ask their physicians important medical questions because they cannot
bring themselves to use words like *penis*, *vagina*, or *anus*.

Valid information about sex can be an antidote to some of the "sex-
negative" messages we have all been exposed to. As we will see in Chapter
2, our culture has a long history of guilt, shame, and anxiety about sex, as
reflected by our "dirty" sexual jokes. Even with the increased openness
about sexuality, messages about sex, both in schools and in the mass media,
often frighten and mislead people instead of informing them. Some schools
place an exclusive emphasis on disease and unwanted pregnancy (see Chapter 18). Of course, people need to know about maximizing sexual health and
reducing the chances of unwanted pregnancy, but an exclusive emphasis on
these topics implies that sex is *always* dangerous or shameful. Accentuating

Everything you wanted to know about sex? *The scientific study of sexuality can help people separate reliable information from unsupported claims, speculations, and folklore.*

the negative does not help people appreciate the place of sex in love and play, or as a form of intimate and cherished connection with another person.

A quite different image of sex is found in romantic novels, movies, soap operas, and advertisements. It says, "Sex is the magical answer to all your problems. You must constantly strive to be glamorous or handsome and sexually in demand." Paradoxically, such messages can arouse as much anxiety as the negative messages. They encourage people to make sexual "success" a barometer of self-esteem, and they set people up for disappointment when life fails to measure up to fiction. Moreover, fantasy sex in the media fails to teach sexual responsibility. The heroes and heroines of romances are almost never shown working out arrangements for birth control, taking precautions against sexually transmitted diseases, or discussing sexual needs with each other. Media fantasy images do not prepare us for dealing with real sex.

Maximize Your Sexual Health

While an exclusive emphasis on the negative may be damaging, it is a sad but true fact that sex is not always safe. Acquired immune deficiency syndrome (AIDS), a deadly disease transmitted primarily through sexual contact and the sharing of contaminated needles by drug users, is, as of this writing, incurable. Genital herpes, another incurable sexually transmitted disease, is not life-threatening to adults, but its symptoms are unpleasant and it poses a serious risk to newborns during childbirth. Other common sexually transmitted diseases can be cured, but often go undetected, causing infertility and harming health.

However, it is also a fact that certain *safe sex practices* greatly lower the chances of contracting sexually transmitted diseases. One of the simplest is the proper use of condoms. (We will examine other precautions in Chapter 17.) But maximizing your sexual health requires more than protection from disease. This book will also give you information on the safety of various birth control methods, tell you how to do a breast or testicular self-examination, and provide information that can help you keep your reproductive and sexual organs healthy.

Become a Critical Consumer of Sexual Information

It is nearly impossible today to open a newspaper or magazine without coming across some survey, study, or advice column on sex. Books on sex are almost as plentiful as those on dieting and cooking. Talk shows on television offer advice for every sexual problem. How much of this information is helpful and how much is hokum?

Recognizing the hokum requires more than finding out what a person's credentials are. Journalists are sometimes more accurate and trustworthy than people who have impressive letters after their names. Advanced degrees do not necessarily make one an expert on sexuality. Physicians, for example, are sometimes knowledgeable about sexuality and sometimes they are not. Sex education in medical schools is often poor (Matteson, Armstrong, & Kimes, 1984). Some mental health professionals are also poorly informed. Though various states require such persons to have some formal training in human sexuality, the requirement is sometimes no more than a weekend seminar.

This book will help you distinguish the facts from the fiction in what you read and hear about human sexuality.

Expand Your Understanding of Your Culture

Your sexual attitudes, feelings, and behavior say a lot about who you are. In the same way, a *society's* sexual customs and assumptions tell us something about its history, its guiding precepts, and its arrangements of power and status. When we study a culture's sexual ways, we are also studying its stance toward love, the body, the family, authority, control, personal freedom, individual responsibility, and gender roles.

For example, most parents in our society strongly encourage teenagers to remain celibate (to abstain from sex) despite the overwhelming evidence that they won't. Yet few parents require teenagers to be constantly accompanied by chaperons. In North America, boys and girls are usually free to drive around town, have parties, and go on dates without bringing an adult along. Freedoms such as these are characteristic of societies that emphasize personal choice and the internal control of impulses to which the society objects. In contrast, societies that are highly traditional and that emphasize the external (communal) control of human impulses usually require young people to have chaperons (Slater, 1990).

As you can see, sexual customs can provide a window through which to view a culture's unique "personality." However, by going beyond ourselves and our own experiences, we can also gain insight into ourselves as individuals. Our personal decisions and actions are often the result of larger social forces. As social psychologist Stanley Milgram once observed, "We are all fragile creatures entwined in a cobweb of social constraints" (Tavris, 1974). By understanding these constraints, we can better understand our own lives.

THE CULTURAL COBWEB

We can begin to understand the nature of our sexuality by noting that the "cobweb of social constraints" that Milgram spoke of consists of norms and roles. **Norms** are rules or standards that govern the way people are supposed to behave in everyday life. They make our relationships with other people orderly and predictable. Many sexual norms, such as the prohibition against incest, are encoded in law. Others are informal. For example, nowhere is it written that you shouldn't talk about your sex life in a loud voice on a crowded bus, but if you do so, you are likely to get some strange looks.

The other component of the social cobweb, **roles,** are positions in society that are governed by norms. A person usually occupies many roles in life, including child, parent, worker, and student. **Gender roles,** the roles we play as men or women, have an especially powerful impact on our sexual behavior. Traditionally, in our culture, men have been expected to initiate sex and be virile, while women have had the right to accept or reject a sexual initiative and the obligation to make themselves sexually attractive. We will examine the influence of gender roles at many points in this book.

But examining our own culture's "cobweb" is not enough. By looking at the cobwebs other cultures have spun, we can temporarily shake ourselves loose from our own pattern to get a better perspective on it. Sex as we know it is not sex as everyone knows it. Our own customs can feel so natural, so inevitable, that we are blinded to alternatives and surprised by change. As one writer notes "we continue to indulge the fantasy that our sexuality is the most innate and natural aspect of being human, and that sexual conduct . . . is predestined . . . by the dictates of human nature" (Highwater, 1990). But other people's customs seem, to them, equally natural and inevitable. Let us briefly see how people in other cultures express their sexuality.

Other Places, Other Ways

Our knowledge of other cultures comes mainly from studies by anthropologists. Such studies are extremely difficult to do. In early anthropological reports, researchers sometimes let obvious biases affect their observations of permissive societies, which they described with such pejorative terms as "licentious" and "promiscuous." Some scholars barely touched on sex, skipping over it quickly and moving on to more comfortable topics, like basket weaving or canoe building (Marshall & Suggs, 1972). Another obstacle has been winning the confidence of people who may feel uncomfortable talking about sex to an outsider, or even an insider, for that matter. And there is always the possibility that the respondents in a study were having a bit of fun with the researchers, exaggerating their exploits or concocting stories to shock the funny foreigners. For these reasons, our knowledge of other cultures is incomplete, and what we do know is tentative.

Still, we can get some picture of how diverse sexual customs are by looking at the findings. We will focus on four areas: modesty, masturbation, premarital intercourse, and homosexuality. You will find cross-cultural information on other sexual topics in later chapters.

MODESTY   Imagine that it is 1769, and you are with the crew of explorer Captain James Cook. Your ship has just dropped anchor in Tahiti, and the captain has led the crew in Christian worship. Immediately following the benediction, you and your shipmates are treated to a strange sight. Later, the captain will describe it in these words:

> A young man, near six feet high, performed the rites of Venus with a little girl about eleven or twelve years of age, before several of our people and a great number of the natives, without the least sense of its being indecent or improper, but, as it appeared, in perfect conformity to the custom of the place. Among the spectators were several women of superior rank, who may properly be said to have assisted at the ceremony; for they gave instructions to the girl how to perform her part, which, young as she was, she did not seem much to stand in need of (in Brecher, 1979, p. 9).

As a member of Captain Cook's crew, what do you conclude? That the Tahitians are immoral? That they have no sense of modesty?

Clearly the Tahitians of Cook's time viewed adolescent sexuality and public sexual activity differently than Westerners. However, the Tahitians did have a sense of modesty. In Tahiti, as in many other societies, it was taboo for brothers and sisters to eat together. Sharing food was regarded as a quasi-sexual act, something you did with someone of the other sex only in marriage. If brothers and sisters failed to turn their backs to one another while eating, they were guilty of a kind of culinary incest!

Indeed, every society has certain standards defining modesty in behavior and dress. But cultures differ in what makes them blush. In ancient Egypt, men wore a kilt-like garment that covered the buttocks but exposed the genitals. Other cultures have allowed exposure of the buttocks, but

Variations in modesty customs   *Covering the body can be sexual, and uncovering it can be nonsexual. The sexual attractiveness of the Japanese Geisha, a professional dancer, singer, and companion to men, is enhanced by an elaborate costume covering most of her body. Conversely, on Pentacost Island in the South Pacific, near nudity is not associated with sexiness.*

required that the sex organs be covered. Anthropologist Edgar Gregersen (1982) tells of a female researcher who went to a Pacific island in the late 1950s dressed in conservative western clothing. The island women, like females in many societies, were accustomed to going topless. They did not go bottomless, though; they wore wraparound skirts reaching clear to the ground. The researcher noticed that men paid little attention to the bare breasts that were everywhere to be seen, yet they continually ogled her ankles. She quickly realized that exposing the legs was not approved behavior for women. So she "went native," and fit right in.

In our culture, stripping in public is likely to be seen as a sexual invitation or a sign of derangement (with some exceptions, as on nude beaches). In some societies, however, covering up means you have something to hide. For example, the traditional Zulu of South Africa believe that sexual looseness leads to a flabby body. If you refuse to take your clothes off, you must be trying to hide the bodily signs of immorality. Certain Zulu rituals call for girls to dance clothed only in beads. Influenced by Europeans, many girls now cover their breasts during such rituals. But older Zulus do not see this as modesty; they suspect the girls are trying quite literally to cover up their sexual transgressions (Gregersen, 1982).

Cross-culturally, men conceal less of their bodies than women. There are exceptions, though. For example, on Aoriki, in the eastern Solomon Islands, females go entirely naked until they marry and have children. Even then they cover the pubic region with only a small patch of fringe. Males, on the other hand, are careful to cover their genitals after reaching puberty (Davenport, 1977).

In cultures where people go completely or almost completely naked, there are often elaborate rules about not staring at the genitals of the other sex. Both the Australian Aborigines and the Kwoma of Papua New Guinea have such rules. They also train girls to sit "modestly," with their legs close together. A Kwoman boy or man is expected to fix his eyes on the ground when in the presence of a woman, or turn with his back towards her. Girls and women who sit with their legs apart or bend over when men are present may be branded as loose and have trouble finding a marriage partner.

Whenever a part of the body is normally covered up because of modesty norms, exposure of the part can be a way to flirt or show sexual interest. In East Bay, an island society of Melanesia, women usually wear skirts that cover the thighs, because the inside of the thigh is considered highly erotic. Some women have tattoos made there, and an occasional glimpse of a tattoo is very arousing to a man. Women, of course, know this perfectly well, and use it to their advantage, "accidentally" revealing the tattoo when it suits their purposes.

Symbols of modesty can also assume political importance. Traditional Muslim societies have often required women to wear veils. The purported purpose is to protect women's chastity and to protect men from the supposedly dangerous temptations of women, which, if given rein, would threaten

the social order (Mernissi, 1975). In some places, women wear the veil from the onset of menstruation until old age, except in front of other women, children, husbands, or close male relatives. Often the wearing of veils is combined with *purdah*, the seclusion of females from the public world. In some societies the veil covers the lower part of the face, in others the entire head (with only the eyes exposed), and in yet others, most of the body. (The ancient Hebrews also used veils, and vestiges of the custom survive in Jewish and Christian bridal attire.)

In 1935, Reza Shah, the ruler of Iran, outlawed the veil as part of a westernization program. Ten years later he was forced into exile, and the veil immediately reappeared. Later it again gave way to westernization, until the late 1970s, when Iranian women, including westernized women, put on the veil to demonstrate their opposition to the Shah Mohammed Reza Pahlavi. Today the veil is a symbol of allegiance to the fundamentalist Muslim regime that rules Iran.

MASTURBATION   As we will see in the next chapter, Western societies have traditionally taken a dim view of masturbation. The Old Testament says that death is a fitting punishment for the man who "spills his seed." In nineteenth-century England and the United States, masturbation was thought to cause everything from consumption to bad breath. Many non-western cultures have worried about the practice, too. East Indians disapprove of male masturbation because they think the loss of semen makes men weak, and many African groups also share this belief (Davenport, 1977).

In fact, there seem to be few if any societies that approve of adult masturbation. Often, though, the only punishment is mild ridicule, and some societies allow for extenuating circumstances. Thus in ancient China, male masturbation was condemned as a waste of "yang," or male essence—the force associated with the sun, sky, light, and fire. But exceptions were made

Cover-up *The traditional veils worn by women in many parts of the world, from Xingiang Province in China (left) to the Lamu Island off the coast of Kenya (middle) symbolize cultural requirements for female modesty and chastity. A vestige of the ancient Hebrew custom of veiling women survives today in Western bridal attire (right).*

during prolonged absence from women, or when the semen (which embodied yang) was in danger of becoming clogged within the body and therefore losing its potency (Davies, 1984).

Masturbation sometimes even takes on a religious significance. The ancient Egyptians believed the world was created through an act of divine masturbation by the god Atum, and sometimes depicted the earth god Geb performing fellatio (oral-genital stimulation) on himself. Similarly, the Greeks thought that Zeus, the God of all Gods, occasionally masturbated. The Mohave Indians, who held extremely relaxed attitudes toward almost all forms of sexual expression, believed that the god Matavilye wanted girls to manually stimulate both themselves and each other. The god had also decreed that children should build small mounds of soft earth. Boys could thrust the penis into such mounds, and girls could rub their genitals against them (Davies, 1984).

Many cultures, even ones that condemn masturbation by adults, allow children to masturbate. In East Bay, adults believe masturbation among young boys is normal, and they encourage it. They also tolerate it among adolescent boys, though they think it is a rather childish thing for a young man to do (Davenport, 1977). In the Tahiti of Captain Cook's day, adults actively encouraged children to play sex games. When grownups became annoyed by the children's shouting, they would tell them to go off and masturbate, the equivalent of an exasperated American parent saying "Go outside and play." In such an accepting environment, many children began to masturbate almost as soon as they could talk.

PREMARITAL INTERCOURSE   As we will see in the next chapter, premarital virginity, especially female virginity, has long been an ideal in western culture. In the Old Testament, if a bride's parents could not provide bloodstained bedding to prove that her hymen had been broken by her husband during their first act of intercourse, the unfortunate young woman could be stoned to death (Deuteronomy 22:13-19). Similar tests of virginity have been reported in many parts of the world, including the Mediterranean region, eastern Europe, parts of Africa, the Far East, and Oceania. Less graphic tests have also existed. Among the eastern Achomawi of California, adults would carefully watch for signs of fatigue in boys and girls during a ritual puberty dance. Tiredness meant that the dancer's virginity had been lost (Davies, 1984).

In certain regions of the world, premarital intercourse is considered a far more grievous sin than in our culture, especially for women. Some Muslim countries punish the offense with a public lashing. But a harsh ban on premarital intercourse appears to be the exception cross-culturally, not the rule. One survey of 131 societies found that 36 required brides to be virgins, but 34 approved of girls having premarital sex and another 29 tolerated such activity if it was discreet (Broude & Greene, 1976).

The classic description of approval was published many decades ago by anthropologist Bronislaw Malinowski. Malinowski (1929) observed the

Weighty matter
*"Measuring up" sexually
is a concern in many
cultures. This fresco, from
the ancient Italian city of
Pompeii, reflects upon
the anxiety men have
often felt about penis
size.*

Trobriand Islanders of British New Guinea in 1917 and 1918, before western influences took over. He found that no Trobriand adolescent would dream of remaining a virgin. The islanders believed that the more partners a young person had before marriage, the better spouse that person would make. Boys and girls customarily paired off and lived together in special "bachelors' houses," which accommodated three or four monogamous couples at a time. These houses were furnished only with cots, but that was all they needed, for the relationships that went on in them were purely sexual, and lovers continued to take their meals with their families. Liaisons were easily started and just as easily ended. Teenagers too young to live in the bachelor's houses could use them for short sexual trysts. Young people were also permitted to indulge in sexual games during outings, picnics, and bathing parties (Davies, 1984).

Other societies, too, have viewed premarital sex as a natural and even necessary part of growing up. There are always some limitations, though, on when and with whom one may have sex. In some societies, young people are expected to choose premarital partners who also qualify as prospective spouses in terms of age, status, or kinship. In others, the opposite is true: premarital partners are never potential marriage partners. For example, an older relative may initiate and train a young person in the ways of sex, but is prohibited from marrying the "trainee" (Davenport, 1977).

HOMOSEXUALITY   All the problems of studying sex cross-culturally are magnified when it comes to homosexuality. We do have some useful information, however. In a classic survey by Clellan S. Ford and Frank A. Beach

(1951), 49 of the 76 societies on which there was information (64 percent) considered at least some homosexual acts to be "normal and socially acceptable for certain members of the community." A more recent survey of 294 societies found 59 reports that gave clear information on male homosexuality (Gregersen, 1982). Eighteen of the 59 societies (31 percent) condemned it, while 42 (69 percent) approved it in at least some instances and for some purposes. Despite the problems with the evidence, it seems clear that most societies do not fear or hate homosexuality as ours traditionally has. (Unfortunately, few anthropologists have provided data on lesbianism, and we know less about attitudes toward it than toward male homosexuality.)

Just as attitudes toward homosexuality vary, so does behavior. In some places no one will admit to engaging in homosexual behavior. But in other places, nearly all males participate openly in same-sex acts at some time in their lives. In East Bay there is no recognition of exclusive homosexuality, but practically all boys in late adolescence have same-sex relationships. By that age, a boy is expected to give up masturbation, but until he marries, anal intercourse with another boy is a perfectly acceptable substitute for heterosexual intercourse. A married man is also allowed to have anal sex with a young boy under some conditions, for example, if the man's wife has recently given birth and he cannot obtain a mistress. He must get permission from the boy's father, though.

Among the Siwans of North Africa, it was the custom for prominent men to lend their sons to each other, and men who did not have homosexual experiences were considered peculiar (Davies, 1984). In other cultures, homosexual men who were also transvestites (who dressed in women's clothes) occupied a special and respected position. This was true among the Plains Indians of North America, where the *berdache* took on female duties and activities, and sometimes became the wife of an important man. Although the Plains Indians emphasized the importance of male bravery and warrior skills, they did not ridicule or reject the berdache. On the contrary, they often gave him special privileges (Williams, 1986).

Ancient Greece was a society famed for its tolerance toward male homosexuality. Classical Greek literature is full of glowing references to homosexual love. In the *Symposium*, Plato argued that the most formidable army in the world would be one made up of male lovers, because they would inspire one another to valiant and heroic deeds. And in fact, in the fourth century B.C., Thebes was defended by an elite fighting unit called the Sacred Band that was composed of pairs of male lovers (Bullough, 1976). A common argument for male homosexuality was that females were inherently inferior, fine for breeding purposes but lacking in the spiritual qualities necessary for the higher forms of love. But strict rules governed homosexuality, and in some city-states it was a crime. In general, homosexual liaisons were permitted only between a free adult citizen and a free adolescent. Exclusive homosexuality and serious homosexual liaisons between adults were discouraged as a threat to the family.

A Tale of Two Islands

Our brief cross-cultural tour suggests that for every custom at one end of the cultural spectrum there is another at the opposite end. Anthropologists like to make this point by contrasting two societies, Mangaia, a small island in the South Pacific, and Inis Beag (not its real name), a small island off the coast of Ireland.

Three decades ago, anthropologist Donald Marshall (1971, 1972) spent a year in Mangaia. Mangaians, he reported, loved sex. No man or woman was so maimed, so ugly, so poor, or so aberrant that he or she could not find a sexual partner. Although men and women rarely socialized in public, among the young the most subtle sign of interest—a flick of the eye, a raised eyebrow—could lead to copulation. It was not necessary to feel affection for, or even to like, the other person. Most boys started having intercourse at age 13 or 14, after undergoing superincision, a painful initiation rite involving the slitting of the upper part of the penis. The superincision expert told the boy how to make love: how to kiss and suck a woman's breasts, perform oral sex on a woman, and have intercourse. The boy learned that he should give pleasure to his partner, and should wait for her to climax several times before enjoying his own orgasm. Two weeks later, he had a chance to practice these lessons by having intercourse with a mature and experienced woman. Girls, too, received instruction in the ways of sex, from an older woman. They learned they should move their hips "like a washing machine." The Mangaians believed women must learn to have orgasms, and they claimed that in Mangaia, every woman did.

During adolescence, according to Marshall, both sexes had several partners. A boy would often show his courage by sneaking into the room where a girl's entire family was sleeping to silently have intercourse with her, a custom known as *motoro*, or sleep-crawling. If her parents heard what was happening, as they were bound to, they looked the other way. Children born out of wedlock were not stigmatized. After marriage, frequent intercourse continued, although husbands and wives shared few other activities. Mangaians tended to be tolerant of extramarital sex for men who were away traveling and for women if they had been deprived for a long time of a husband's attention.

Inig Beag is a very different story. In the late 1950s and early 1960s, when anthropologist John Messenger (1972) studied them, the people there were among the most sexually naive in the world. Messenger, who lived on the island for some time, found that the residents of Inis Beag had an overwhelming fear of damnation and a preoccupation with sin. They never discussed sex when children were present. Even if they had, they wouldn't have had much to talk about. Adults seemed to be completely ignorant of deep kissing, oral-genital sex, oral stimulation by the male of the female breast, and manual stimulation by the female of the male's penis. They either had not heard of female orgasm, or doubted its existence. One middle-aged bachelor, who had sex with a tourist, was puzzled by her violent bodily reactions. When Messenger explained their cause, the man said he had not realized that women could climax.

Courtship on Inis Beag was almost nonexistent, and premarital intercourse appeared to be unknown. Most villagers married late, men at 36 on the average, women at 25. Parents arranged their children's marriages, with little regard for their offsprings' feelings. Within marriage, sex was limited to a little kissing and rough fondling, followed by a brief act of intercourse with the male on top. Women regarded sex as a duty to be endured.

The people of Inis Beag so abhorred nudity that they kept their underclothes on even during sex, always changed clothes in private (sometimes under the bedcovers), and washed only their faces, necks, lower arms, hands, lower legs, and feet. Although the men spent a great deal of time at sea in canoes, none had learned to swim; they were too modest to wear swimsuits. When Messenger and his wife inadvertently walked in on a barefooted man who had just "bathed," the man hurriedly pulled on his socks and said, with obvious relief, "Sure, it's good to get your clothes on again."

SEXUAL UNIVERSALS

Most societies fall somewhere between Mangaia and Inis Beag. And many, like our own, are sexually permissive in some respects, and restrictive in others. Indeed, from the welter of customs and behaviors on this colorful planet of ours, it is tempting to conclude that nothing about sexuality is universally true. But out of the diversity, a few generalizations do emerge.

Sexual Regulation

The most fundamental sexual universal is that *every* human society, whether "permissive" or "restrictive," regulates and controls sexual behavior. There has never been a society that has said, in effect, "What you do in the privacy of your home, hut, or palace is entirely your own business, so long as you don't harm anyone else." Every society has norms that govern what is sexy, and who can do what with whom, and how often. In many societies, there are even rules, official or unofficial, on just how people should do it (see Chapter 9). Regulations governing human sexuality may differ, but the fact of regulation is universal.

A few types of rules and behaviors also seem universal. For example, every society seems to have some sort of *incest taboo* prohibiting sexual relations between individuals related by blood, adoption, or ritual. The scope of the taboo varies: one culture might permit brother-sister marriage among royalty but not common folk; another might prohibit a man from having sex with his younger brother's wife, but not his older brother's wife. Kinship is clearly an important part of sexual regulation.

Every society also seems to understand the notion of sexual jealousy in marriage. Again, the particulars vary. Some cultures prohibit all sexual relationships outside marriage, and expect spouses to be jealous when one occurs. Others, like the Turu in Tanzania, allow husbands and wives to take outside lovers so long as they do not flaunt their affairs in public (Schneider, 1971). But whatever the nature of the rules, all cultures seem to expect jealousy when the rules are violated (Hupka, 1981; Reiss, 1986). This is as true in societies that allow polygamy—the taking of more than one spouse—as in those that require monogamy. (We will discuss incest and jealousy further in subsequent chapters.)

Double Standards

Although sexual regulations exist everywhere, they do not apply equally to everyone in a society. All societies seem to give greater sexual privileges to men than to women. A **double standard** for males and females has even existed in places where both sexes have enjoyed considerable sexual freedom. In Mangaia, for example, a "good girl" was free to take three or four partners before marriage, but boys were encouraged to find many more. A boy who had many girls was "a strong man, like a bull, going from woman to woman." A girl who chased after the boys was called a pig.

One common rationale for tight control over female sexuality is women's presumed insatiability and seductiveness. Some cultures warn men that dire things will happen to them if they yield too often to the temptations of women. They will weaken, or die; their penises will fall off; they will lose magical powers; they will lose the football game. The Manu code of India, a

One man's family *This Kenyan man has 40 wives and 349 children. Cross-culturally, polygyny, the practice of having more than one wife at a time, is far more common than polyandry, the practice of having more than one husband. Cross-culturally, many sexual privileges are granted more frequently to men than to women.*

set of laws dating from about 100 A.D., explained that "it is in the nature of women to seduce men [and] for that reason the wise are never unguarded [in the company of] females. For women are able to lead astray in this world not only a fool, but even a learned man, and to make him a slave of desire and anger."

Caste and class also determine how tightly the sexual rein is pulled. Typically the ruling class gets away with more than the common folk do. In the eastern Solomon Islands, for example, men of political and social influence are expected to show their power from time to time by violating one of the laws governing sexual behaviors, in particular adultery and rape. Rank does not always bring privilege, though, especially not for women. In Polynesia, princesses were supposed to remain virgins until they could be married off to men of equal rank. In Samoa, a chief's daughter was "deflowered" by her husband's first two fingers in front of witnesses; if no blood was visible, her relatives clubbed her to death. In contrast, commoners of both sexes were free to enjoy sex with many partners before marriage.

The Belief-Behavior Gap

Throughout the world, doctrine is one thing, while actual behavior is another. Religion, law, and custom set sexual standards, but people do not always obey. Thus the Kagaba of South America condemn male masturbation as a serious offense, yet many married men admit that masturbation is their favorite form of sexual activity (Gregersen, 1982). Masturbation "contests" among men (similar to the "circle jerks" of American boys) have been reported among American Indian groups, in Polynesia, and in West Africa, despite official disapproval of adult masturbation.

We call the discrepancy between ideology and practice the "belief-behavior gap." In Chapter 2 we will take a close look at the belief-behavior gap in Western culture.

SOME SPECULATIONS ON SEXUAL SUPPRESSION

Perhaps by now you are wondering why all societies limit or at least regulate the sexuality of their citizens. Why has no society ever affirmed the right of people to do what they please in their own bedrooms? Why not leave sex a personal matter instead of regulating it? Answering such questions is not easy. Here are four possibilities, offered in the spirit of speculation.

Sexual Control, Order, and Productivity

According to one line of thought, individuals must suppress their private desires, including their sexual ones, for the sake of social cohesiveness and the smooth functioning of society. In this view, sex is a raging instinct, and overindulgence in pleasure is a call to anarchy. If left to their own devices, people would stay at home to eat, drink, and make whoopee, rarely bestirring themselves to work, do the marketing, raise the children, fight wars, drill for oil, or buy on the installment plan. Societies must convince their members to restrain their passions and rechannel them for the greater good. Sexual control enhances social stability.

Perhaps the most eloquent spokesman for this argument was Sigmund Freud (1856-1939), who founded psychoanalysis and profoundly influenced modern American and European attitudes toward sex (see Chapter 3). Freud believed that sexual suppression could lead to personal neurosis, and, so, many people mistakenly think he was a sexual liberal. In fact, Freud was pessimistic about the consequences of loosening sexual controls. The task of every parent, he said, is to teach his or her children to redirect their primitive impulses. The parent must replace the infant's efforts to avoid all pain and experience only pleasure with the mature adult's ability to delay gratification. In the same way, said Freud, societies must redirect the sexual energy of their members toward socially productive activities. This sexual redirection, or *sublimation*, inevitably takes an emotional toll on individuals. But, according to Freud, it also makes possible organized government, business, science, art, and culture:

> We believe that civilization has been built up, under the pressure of the struggle for existence, by sacrifices in gratification of the primitive impulses, and that it is to a great extent forever being recreated, as each individual, successively joining the community, repeats the sacrifice of his instinctive pleasure for the common good. The sexual are among the most important of the instinctive forces thus utilized: they are in this way sublimated, that is to say, their energy is turned aside from its sexual goal and diverted toward other ends, no longer sexual and socially more valuable. (Freud, 1960, p. 27)

If Freud was right, individuals who sublimate should be more productive socially than those who give in to their sexual urges. In an effort to test this idea, Alfred Kinsey, who felt that sublimation was a religious concept in psychological clothing, analyzed the case histories of 170 young men who rarely had orgasms. He found no evidence that these men were rechanneling their sexual energies into creative or higher pursuits (Kinsey, Pomeroy, & Martin, 1948). This may not be a good test of Freud's ideas, though, because productivity and sublimation probably cannot be measured. A creative person who has sex three times a day may be sublimating; without sublimation, perhaps that person would indulge even more often. On the other hand, a person who has sex once a month may simply have a low sex drive.

The notion of sublimation also implies that societies whose members sublimate should be more stable and productive than those that are more permissive. Again, it is hard to test this idea. Some writers think that ancient Rome collapsed because its citizens frittered their time and energy away at orgies; most historians blame other factors. In general, it is unclear whether sexual regulation is associated with cultural stability and productivity.

Sexual Suppression and Political Power

Power is sometimes defined as the ability to enforce one's will against the opposition of others. To exercise political power, a government or ruling group can hold a gun to people's heads or send police officers or soldiers against them. But these methods are crude and in the long run ineffective, because they alter behavior without necessarily changing attitudes. Power tends to be more enduring when those who are governed comply with their rulers voluntarily, especially when they are persuaded to agree with the powerholders' policies. Control can then be maintained without force or even surveillance—and that is real power.

It follows that if ruling authorities are able to get people to obey sexual rules of conduct, they have an effective means of maintaining their own political power. Those who are ruled do not truly own their own bodies, for they are under the influence of others even in the privacy of their own homes. Sexual obedience becomes a political loyalty test, a way of saying, "You see? I can be trusted. I put social duty and allegiance before selfish pleasure."

If sexual restrictions serve political purposes, then sexual suppression should be most severe where power is centralized and authoritarian. This has sometimes been a theme in fiction. In his classic anti-utopian novel *Nineteen Eighty-Four*, George Orwell gave us a terrifying vision of a totalitarian state in which the government manipulates not only behavior but also language and thought. Sexual desire, because it is personal and private, becomes subversive. Two characters, Winston and Julia, dare to rebel by carrying on a secret love affair. When they have intercourse, it is a "battle," a "blow struck against the Party," a "political act." But the battle is all too brief. Winston and Julia are soon caught, and under torture they betray each other.

Does sexual suppression go along with political repression in real life? After the Khmer Rouge took over Cambodia in 1975, political repression was as severe as any the world has known. Mass extermination of a large portion of the population took place. Significantly, one of the first things the new authorities did was impose rigid sexual restrictions. Couples reportedly could not go for an unauthorized evening stroll without permission. Similarly, one of the first things fundamentalist leader Ayatollah Khoumeini did upon taking control of Iran in 1980 was to promulgate a set of strict sexual regulations. (His original decree required *purdah* for wives, but the protests of thousands of women succeeded in modifying the requirements.) Today Iranian women who work need not wear the veil, but they must observe a conservative dress code. Adultery is punishable by death.

In modern China, sexual rules have fluctuated with political philosophy. For many years, the People's Republic of China enforced what we would consider a severe sexual code. Adults discouraged premarital sex and

Changing customs
Political reforms during the 1980s brought a new sexual permissiveness to China. Articles and seminars on sexuality suddenly became available, and for the first time in many decades, couples felt free to express affection in public.

public displays of affection, and tried to eradicate masturbation by "correct" political thought. In the 1980s, however, as Western notions invaded China and as political reforms occurred, more liberal attitudes toward sexuality emerged. For the first time, many young people felt free to adorn themselves, to dance, and to display affection openly to members of the other sex.

Sexual suppression does not exist *only* where power is centralized or rigid. In the nineteenth century, England and America were probably more democratic than other Western societies of the time, but they were also fairly conservative sexually (see Chapter 2). Nor does an authoritarian political system *always* result in severe sexual suppression. The Soviet Union and East Germany both have an authoritarian history, yet in the 1980s East Germans were reportedly more relaxed about sex. However, political factors do seem to explain many cross-cultural differences. Power differences can also explain sexual double standards within societies. Since the upper classes have more political and social power than the lower classes, and since men have more power than women, it is not surprising that the upper classes and men generally enjoy more sexual privileges than do the lower classes and women.

Sex and the Family

According to another theory, many of the rules surrounding sex exist to protect the stability of the family. Though most societies permit at least some nonmarital sex, all restrict it in some way. Perhaps there is an underlying fear that if people were freer to form sexual attachments outside marriage, they would abandon their families in droves, causing social, emotional, and economic chaos. This theory would explain why marital jealousy is universal, and why the more importance a culture places on marriage, the stronger the jealousy within the culture (Hupka, 1981). It would also explain why even societies that encourage homosexual activity have been jittery about exclusive homosexuality between adults.

Sexual restrictions also tend to clarify how property is to be transmitted from one generation to the next. Historically, paternity has often determined inheritance; only legitimate sons could inherit. But paternity was hard to determine until very recently. Restricting sex to marriage may have been a way to ensure that a woman's offspring were fathered by her husband. This would prevent constant squabbles about who was entitled to what upon the death of a property owner. (Inheritance is not a factor in all societies, however. Some do not fully understand the relationship of sex to reproduction, and many trace descent through the mother's line, not the father's. In these cases, identifying the father is far less important.)

If sexual rules exist primarily to protect the family, then why are limits often placed on the behavior of children, or on husbands and wives *within* marriage? After all, such limits do not seem to have much to do with family stability. One possibility: cultural authorities have worried that sexual freedom before or within marriage might lead to **hedonism,** the pursuit of pleasure. People might realize, in the immortal words of Mae West, that too much of a good thing can be wonderful. Soon husbands and wives would be wanting gratification outside of marriage, too, or, would seek greater happiness with others. Better to regulate *all* sexual activity, even in marriage, than to open the door, even a crack, to personal pleasure.

Some years ago, psychoanalyst Mary Jane Sherfey (1973) proposed a variation on this theme to explain the historical suppression of female sexuality. She suggested that in prehistoric days, human females were sexually voracious, but only around the time of ovulation. This hypersexuality presumably gave human females an evolutionary advantage, because it kept them continually pregnant. But when, in the course of evolution, women became capable of sexual interest any day of the month, sexual insatiability became a problem. It would never do to have women lurking in the forest, luring unsuspecting men away from the hunt. Besides, such women would not want to stay home to care for the children or do the housework. When a stable family structure became essential to civilization, the irresistible force of female sexuality met the immovable object of the family, and something had to give. The result was sexual prohibitions that especially oppressed women—not because men were natural oppressors, but because, in Sherfey's words, "the strength of the drive determines the force required to suppress it."

Although Sherfey thought modern women deserved their sexual rights, like Freud she worried about the consequences. If the modern woman's sexual drive is still as "naturally" strong as in prehistoric times, she reasoned, and if women are unable to control this drive, family life and child care might suffer. In that case, "a return to the rigid, enforced suppression [of the past] will be inevitable and mandatory" (Sherfey, 1973, p. 140). But Sherfey's gloomy prediction rests on certain highly debatable assumptions: that "natural" human behavior resembles that of a chimpanzee, and that people cannot manage an uninhibited sex life and their family obligations, too. What do you think?

Sexual Customs and Birth Control

Behind the many religious, medical, and moral justifications for sexual restraint may lurk a simple though unspoken concern with managing the size of the population. When a society lacks a good method of birth control and has too many mouths to feed, it may seek to solve this problem by discouraging sexual activity (although the strategy may not be explicitly acknowledged). But if the society has too few people, it may do the opposite. Anthropologist Ernestine Friedl (1975) cites the example of two New Guinea tribes with remarkably different sexual customs. One tribe has been settled a long time and has little new land or resources. If the population were to grow, some people would go hungry. In this tribe, antagonism between men and women runs high. People believe that intercourse weakens men and that women are sexually dangerous. They regard sex as a mysterious force and prohibit sexual activity in the garden, believing that it will blight the crops. The other tribe, not far away, controls a great deal of uncultivated land and needs more people to garden and to defend the group against hostile neighbors. In this tribe the sexes get along pretty well. The people consider sexual intercourse fun and revitalizing. They believe sex *should* take place in gardens, because it will foster the growth of plants.

We do not know whether the need to limit or expand population can fit all the facts of sexual custom. Certainly there are exceptions. The early Christians, for example, promoted celibacy even though they were a small, embattled group that needed to grow. However, they also believed that human history would soon come to an end, and so population considerations may not have been important to them.

Historically, population control may have been less a matter of public policy than personal necessity, particularly for women. In most societies, women have married very young. The bride's family selects the groom, and may or may not consider her feelings in the matter. Once married, a woman in a traditional society is likely to bear several children in rapid succession. Given the primitive techniques available historically for delivering babies, childbirth has been a risky business. In colonial New England, for instance, the average woman bore eight or nine offspring, and an estimated one-fifth of all women died in childbirth (Demos, 1970). As late as 1915, the first year for which there are reliable records, sixty-one American women died for every ten thousand live births, compared to two per ten thousand today (Ehrenreich & English, 1973). A moral philosophy that encouraged sexual restraint might have been lifesaving for such women. This might explain why women were often the staunchest defenders of an antipleasure ethic.

Perhaps you can think of other possible reasons why all societies attempt to regulate and limit human sexuality. Remember, though, that the *particular* rules a culture adopts reflect its unique collection of ideas, values, beliefs, and needs. Sexually, no two societies are identical. In the following chapter, we will examine more closely the sexual norms of our own culture, and see how they have changed.

. . . .

PERSONAL PERSPECTIVE

SPEAKING OF SEX

When we speak of sex, we make choices about how to express ourselves. One option is to use formal or technical terms, like *coitus* (sexual intercourse), *introitus* (vaginal opening), and *ejaculation* (expulsion of seminal fluid from the penis). Such terms often have Latin origins. They are not always appropriate in an intimate setting ("Darling, how about repairing to the bedroom for a little coitus?"), but sexologists find them handy because they are precise and morally neutral. For these reasons, you will find them throughout this book.

Another option is to use *vernacular*, or slang, terms, such as *cock*, *cunt*, *fuck*, and *come*. Slang terms are colorful, lively, and rich in metaphor and imagery. When used with humor or affection, they are unsurpassed for expressing sexual meanings. But often they are vague. The word *cunt*, for example, may refer to either the vagina or the vulva (the entire external genital area in women). Moreover, many slang terms, such as *cunt* and *prick*, have negative connotations, and sometimes these terms are used to insult and demean. In one study of insults, college students who were asked for the "worst thing" one could call a man or a woman responded most frequently with sexual terms such as *cunt*, *prick*, and *faggot*. If the target was a woman, the reference was usually to sexual looseness; if the target was a man, it was usually to homosexuality (Preston & Stanley, 1987). Of course, even when no insult is intended, slang terms may offend people.

A third kind of language is *euphemistic*. Euphemisms are terms that allow you to avoid saying what you really mean. Examples are *down there*, *doing it*, and *that time of the month*. Euphemisms imply that whatever is being referred to is too nasty, unpleasant, or embarrassing for words. Ironically, euphemisms reveal a great deal about sexual feelings and attitudes, both personal and cultural.

You can examine your own use of sexual language by copying the chart below on a piece of paper. The first column gives some formal/technical terms. In the second column, fill in any corresponding vernacular/slang expressions you use. In the third column, list any euphemisms you use. Then, on each line of the chart, circle the term (formal, slang, or euphemistic) that you think you use most often. If you never refer to the body part or sexual behavior in question, put a check in the last column.

After you complete the chart, consider these questions: a) In what sorts of situations do you use the various terms on your chart? b) How hard would it be for you to use the various terms with a lover or spouse, your child, a friend of the same gender, or a friend of the other gender? c) Which terms would you feel comfortable using during a classroom discussion in your human sexuality course?

Formal/Technical	Vernacular/Slang	Euphemistic	None
vagina			
clitoris			
penis			
testicles			
pubic hair			
female breasts			
sexual intercourse			
masturbation			
oral sex			
anal sex			
orgasm			
menstruation			

IN BRIEF

1. The word *sex* can refer to an activity, a motive, or genetic or anatomical status, and is sometimes used synonymously with *gender*. *Sexuality* encompasses all those qualities that contribute to the subjective sense of oneself as a sexual person.

2. Sexual behavior is more complex in human beings than in other animals in part because of the meanings we give it. In other animals sex

has fewer motives, hormones have greater control of sex, and sexual techniques are relatively limited. Our unique mental capacity explains why human sexuality is an expression of upbringing, feelings, and outlook on life.

3. *Sexology* is the scientific study of human sexuality. Researchers in biology, physiology, medicine, psychology, sociology, anthropology, and history all contribute to this field.

4. A course in human sexuality can help you to get your questions about sex answered; to clarify your sexual attitudes and values; to become more comfortable about sex; to maximize your sexual health; to become a critical consumer of sexual information; and to expand your understanding of your culture.

5. Individual decisions and actions are often the result of social forces, a "cobweb of social constraints." These forces includes *norms* (or rules), standards that govern the way people are supposed to behave, and *roles*, social positions governed by rules. *Gender roles* have an especially powerful impact on sexual behavior.

6. By examining the "cobwebs" that other cultures have spun, we can get a better perspective on our own pattern. Cross-cultural research shows how diverse sexual customs are. For example, though every society has standards of modesty, dress customs vary from the near nudity of the traditional Zulu to the wearing of veils in traditional Muslim cultures. Few if any societies approve wholeheartedly of adult masturbation, but many permit or even encourage it in children, or allow for extenuating circumstances, and in some cultures masturbation even takes on a religious significance. Many societies have a severe ban on premarital intercourse, especially for females, but most are more tolerant, and many actively encourage it. Similarly, many societies condemn homosexuality, but most approve of it in at least some instances and for some purposes.

7. For every sexual custom at one end of the cultural spectrum there is another at the opposite end. The permissive extreme is exemplified by Mangaia, where adults teach children about sexual technique, adolescents start having intercourse early, both sexes have several premarital partners, and extramarital sex is tolerated under certain circumstances. The restrictive extreme is exemplified by Inis Beag, where adults never talk to children about sex, people are naive about sexual technique, premarital intercourse appears to be unknown, and nudity is abhorred.

8. Despite the diversity of sexual customs and behaviors, some universals do emerge. Sexual regulation exists in all societies, whether permissive or restrictive. Certain types of rules and behaviors, such as the incest taboo and marital jealousy, appear to exist everywhere, though they

take different forms. A *double standard* for men and women appears to exist virtually everywhere. Caste and class usually affect a person's sexual privileges. Finally, throughout the world, there are discrepancies between ideology and practice, a "belief-behavior gap."

9. Why do all societies limit or at least regulate the sexuality of their citizens? Possible explanations include the following: (a) Sexual restrictions may help to maintain order, stability, and productivity in society. Sigmund Freud was a spokesman for this position; (b) Authorities may use sexual suppression to establish political power; (c) Sexual rules may protect the stability of the family by encouraging fidelity to the family and making it possible to determine paternity; (d) Sexual rules may work to limit or expand the size of the population to meet a society's needs.

10. There may be other general explanations for the regulation of sexuality. But the particular rules a culture adopts reflect its unique collection of ideas, values, beliefs, and needs.

Key Terms

sex *(3)*

gender *(3)*

sexuality *(3)*

sexology *(5)*

rules (norms) *(9)*

roles *(10)*

gender roles *(10)*

berdache *(16)*

sexual regulation *(18)*

double standard *(19)*

belief-behavior gap *(20)*

sublimation *(21)*

hedonism *(24)*

C H A P T E R T W O

■

Our Sexual Legacy

•

Custom controls the sexual impulse as it controls no other.

Margaret Sanger

D o we live in sexually permissive times, or sexually repressive ones? Are most Americans relaxed about sex, or guilty and uncomfortable? Has sexual liberation arrived, or is sex still the biggest "hangup"?

In the last chapter we surveyed some sexual customs of other societies. Now let's do the same for our own. Imagine that you are an anthropologist from somewhere else—Tahiti, China, Mars—and you wish to understand the sexual ways of North Americans. Diligently you interview the natives, read their books and magazines, analyze their scientific studies, watch their television programs, and eavesdrop on their public and private habits. What do you conclude? Do you side with social critics who warn that the United States is headed the way of Sodom and Gomorrah, or with those who complain that Americans are too rigid and narrow-minded about sex?

SEXUAL AMBIVALENCE IN MODERN AMERICA

Consider what you might learn while studying the four areas we discussed in Chapter 1: modesty, masturbation, premarital sex, and homosexuality.

Modesty

The modesty rules of the United States depend a lot on place and circumstance. In many parts of the country, people wear a minimum of clothing during the summer, even on the street. In fact, partial nudity is a common sight. On most beaches, any kind of swimsuit is acceptable, no matter how scanty or seductive, so long as the genitals and the nipples of the female breast are covered. Yet a "proper" woman does not let her bra show through her blouse, or her legs show through her skirt. In non-X-rated films, male actors may appear naked from the rear, but not the front, while females may reveal their breasts and buttocks, but not their pubic hair. The rules on television are more stringent: until 1987, brassiere advertisements could not show human models.

Total public nudity is termed "indecent exposure" and is generally taboo. But there are exceptions. In the United States (in contrast to Europe), nude beaches are illegal, but sometimes law enforcement authorities look the other way. Moreover, people are free to join private nudist clubs and colonies. In some parts of the country, friends and neighbors think nothing of a friendly evening of nude bathing in a pool or hot tub. Sexually explicit films and tapes showing people stark naked do a multimillion dollar business, and many of these materials can be rented for a few dollars at the local mom and pop video store. Similarly, magazines that show the female genitals close up are easily obtainable at convenience stores and markets. Nudity in serious objects of art—in sculpture and painting—is permissible in museums, and sometimes (though not always) in public plazas and parks.

Masturbation

Many sex therapists and educators in the United States regard masturbation as an essential part of sexual development. In fact, therapists often prescribe it for people who are having trouble getting an erection or having an orgasm. Yet masturbation remains a source of embarrassment and discomfort for many Americans. Cultural hostility toward masturbation is reflected in the very word, which is thought to derive from the Latin words *manu* (hand) and *stuprare* (to defile), or possibly from *manu* and *turbare* (to disturb or agitate). Modern slang terms for masturbation are also derogatory: "frigging," "jerking off," "beating the meat," and so forth. In surveys, few people condemn masturbation outright. But just as few people talk about it the way Woody Allen did in his film *Annie Hall*, where he defined it as "having sex with someone I love."

Not surprisingly, most parents never discuss the topic with their children or teenagers. Many find it hard to think about their offspring masturbating, and some explode emotionally when they happen upon a son or daughter in the act. Yet almost all boys and many girls have masturbated by the time they leave adolescence (Kinsey, Pomeroy, & Martin, 1948; Kinsey et al., 1953; Hunt, 1974). In marriage, too, masturbation is common. According to research done in the 1970s, 70 percent of young husbands masturbate, with a median rate of twenty-four times a year. And nearly the same percentage of young wives masturbate, with about the same median rate (Hunt, 1974). Masturbation in America may be almost unmentionable, but it is also exceedingly common.

Copyright 1987, G.B. Trudeau. Reprinted with permission of Universal Press Syndicate. All rights reserved.

Premarital Intercourse

For lack of a better term, we use *premarital intercourse* for intercourse experienced by never-married people. (Keep in mind, however, that not everyone in this group eventually marries.) American attitudes toward premarital sex are a far cry from those of the Mangaians or the Tahitians, who, as you will recall from Chapter 1, thought everyone ought to give it a try—or two, or ten. Many adults refuse to acknowledge teenage sexuality. Schools often do not teach even the most fundamental facts about sexuality and birth control (Kirby, 1984). Where sex education does exist, it is likely to strongly discourage premarital sex. One organization that runs sex education in the schools promotes such slogans as "Don't be a louse, wait for your spouse" (see Chapter 18).

A few decades ago, fewer than half of all women had premarital intercourse by age nineteen (Kantner & Zelnik, 1972; Sorenson, 1973). By the 1980s, about three-fourths did (Hofferth, Kahn, & Baldwin, 1987; Wyatt, Peters, & Guthrie, 1988). (Note that these figures do *not* include women who would go on to have premarital intercourse for the first time *after* age nineteen.) Premarital intercourse rates among teenagers may have begun to level off in the late 1980s, in part, perhaps, because of concern about AIDS and other sexually transmitted diseases (Gerrard, 1987; Hofferth, Kahn, & Baldwin, 1987; Mott & Haurin, 1988), and it's possible that the rates may eventually decline. But as of this writing there is little evidence for such a decline. Moreover, teenagers are continuing to become sexually active at younger and younger ages (see Chapter 13).

Homosexuality

During the 1960s and 1970s, gay liberation groups sprang up around the country. Partly because of their efforts, homosexuality is now more acceptable as a topic in books and movies and on television talk shows and

The sexual pendulum swings   *Sexual attitudes can change surprisingly rapidly, depending on politics, social conditions, and the threat of sexually transmitted diseases.*

sitcoms. In sexually liberal communities like San Francisco, acknowledged homosexuals are running for, and winning, public office. In 1974, both the American Psychological Association and the American Psychiatric Association voted to stop treating homosexuality as a mental disorder. Today, a division of the American Psychological Association is devoted exclusively to gay and lesbian psychology.

Does all this mean that homosexuality is now accepted in the United States? Hardly. Although some public opinion polls have found a live-and-let-live attitude toward homosexuality, most of the population still does not support legalizing homosexual relations. According to the Gallup organization (1989), support for legalization fell from 45 percent in 1982 to only 33 percent in 1987 (perhaps as a reaction to the AIDS epidemic, which occurred first in the gay community). Two years later the figure rose again, to 47 percent, but over a third were definitely opposed, and the rest were not sure. Many, if not most, heterosexuals still regard homosexuality as abnormal. Voters in several cities have repealed laws that would grant homosexuals basic civil rights in housing and employment. Most homosexuals still feel pressure to stay "in the closet." Ominously, there has been a recent upswing of violence against homosexuals in major cities. In surveys, parents say they want the topic of homosexuality discussed in sex education courses—but only if young people are taught that it is morally wrong.

You can see that the American sexual scene is full of paradox. Our customs are not as easy to sum up as those of Mangaia or Inis Beag. The above examples demonstrate that modern sexual attitudes are neither entirely positive nor entirely negative; rather, they are ambivalent and contradictory. There are geographical and religious differences, and there are conflicts and contradictions within individuals. A woman who had many affairs before marriage may blow up when she discovers her daughter has a lover. A man may support "free love" for heterosexuals but want homosexuality to be a crime. Often people try to extend one foot into a sexually liberal future while keeping the other stuck firmly in a sexually conservative past.

We can gain some understanding of this ambivalence by considering Western culture's sexual history. Much of what we know about that history comes from the journals, letters, speeches, and writings of official policy makers—politicians, religious leaders, and medical authorities. This evidence reveals that official views of sex have varied from nervous suspicion to outright hostility. As we will see later in this chapter, ordinary folk probably broke the legal and moral rules as often as not. Indeed, if people had not "misbehaved," no rules would have been needed to regulate and control their behavior! But official views have an important influence; they permeate our myths, art, and literature, and undoubtedly affect the sexual feelings of average citizens. If Americans appear to both welcome and worry about the "sexual revolution," their ambivalence may be traced in part to the sex-negativism promoted for so long by the sexual rule-makers. Altering the inherited beliefs and customs of three thousand years is no small matter.

JUDAISM: THE LEGISLATION OF LUST

Since the Judeo-Christian tradition is often blamed for modern sexual anxiety, an examination of our sexual history must begin with a look at what the Bible and the ancient Hebrews had to say about sex. The Five Books of Moses, which form the core of the Old Testament, contain long lists of rules and regulations about everyday behavior, many of them about sex. For example, the laws of Leviticus and Deuteronomy prohibit adultery, male homosexuality, incest, sex during menstruation, loss of female virginity before marriage, and, indirectly, masturbation (see Table 2-1). These rules worked to promote population growth, foster social harmony, and distinguish Judaism from other Middle Eastern religions (which often permitted practices forbidden to Jews). They also established a major feature of our sexual legacy: the idea that sexual activity is wrong if it does not lead to conception and the birth of legitimate heirs. For the people of the Old Testament, the main purpose of sex and marriage was to produce babies, and the limits on sexual freedom reflect that aim.

The religious basis for emphasizing procreation comes from Genesis, in which God commands the Hebrews to be fruitful and multiply. A husband's sexual duty was to impregnate his wife, and a wife's was to bear and rear their offspring. In fact, according to later Jewish writings, if a woman remained childless after ten years of marriage it was her husband's right and even obligation to divorce her and find someone fertile. (The Hebrews were obviously unaware of male infertility.) This is not to say that procreation was supposed to be unpleasant. The Old Testament views marital intercourse positively, allowing it to continue even during pregnancy or when the wife

Temptress   *The old Testament often portrays women as sexually dangerous. Here, Delilah lulls her lover, Samson, to sleep so that her servant can cut his hair, the secret of his great strength. Delilah's betrayal renders Samson powerless against his enemies.*

. . . .

TABLE 2-1 **The Sexual Laws Of Leviticus And Deuteronomy**

Adultery

If a man commits adultery with the wife of his neighbor, both the adulterer and the adulteress shall be put to death (Lev. 20:10).

If a man is found lying with the wife of another man, both of them shall die, the man who lay with the woman, and the woman; so you shall purge the evil from Israel (Deut. 22:22).

Female Virginity

But if the thing is true, that the tokens of virginity were not found in the young woman, then they shall bring out the young woman to the door of her father's house, and the men of her city shall stone her to death with stones, because she has wrought folly in Israel by playing the harlot in her father's house (Deut. 22:20-21).

Homosexuality

You shall not lie with a male as with a woman; it is an abomination (Lev. 18:22).

If a man lies with a male as with a woman, both of them have committed an abomination; they shall be put to death, their blood is upon them (Lev. 20:13).

Incest

None of you shall approach any one near of kin to him to uncover nakedness (Lev. 18:6).

---

seems to be infertile. But the focus on procreation is reflected in a basic rule that all married couples were expected to obey: the husband must deposit his semen in his wife's vagina and nowhere else. The Hebrews seem to have been almost obsessively concerned about "spilling the seed." Genesis tells the story of Onan, who was killed by God for selfishly spilling his semen on the ground—a willful act of *coitus interruptus.*

A second major theme in the Hebrew tradition is the inequality of men and women. True, the Hebrews cherished the faithful wife and mother (her price was "above rubies") and valued the husband-wife relationship (Genesis 2:24 tells us that a man "shall cleave unto his wife: and they shall be one flesh.") But in Jewish myths and writings, men are dominant over women. Independent yet virtuous women like Esther and Deborah the Prophetess are rare.

One rationale for the domination of women was that women were sexually dangerous: "For the lips of a loose woman drip honey, and her speech is smoother than oil; but in the end she is bitter as wormwood, sharp as a two-

. . . .

The man who lies with his father's wife has uncovered his father's nakedness; both of them shall be put to death, their blood is upon them. If a man lies with his daughter-in-law, both of them shall be put to death; they have committed incest, their blood is upon them (Lev. 20:11-12).

If a man takes his sister. . .it is a shameful thing, and they shall be cut off in the sight of the children of their people (Lev. 20:17).

Sex During Menstruation

You shall not approach a woman to uncover her nakedness while she is in her menstrual uncleanness (Lev. 18:19).

If a man lies with a woman having her sickness, and uncovers her nakedness, he has made naked her fountain, and she has uncovered the fountain of her blood; both of them shall be cut off from among their people (Lev. 20:18).

Illegitimacy

No bastard shall enter the assembly of the Lord: even to the tenth generation none of his descendants shall enter the assembly of the Lord (Deut. 23:2).

Seminal Emission

And if a man has an emission of semen, he shall bathe his whole body in water, and be unclean until the evening. And every garment and every skin on which the semen comes shall be washed with water, and be unclean until the evening (Lev. 15:16-17).

---

edged sword" (Prov. 5:3-4). Among Biblical victims of female perfidy were Lot, whose two daughters plied him with liquor and seduced him; Samson, who was betrayed by the treacherous Delilah; and Joseph, who was falsely accused of rape by Potiphar's wife after he rejected her sexual advances.

The inequality of men and women found expression in a sexual double standard that punished women more severely than men for certain sexual transgressions. As we saw in Chapter 1, the Bible called for a woman who could not demonstrate virginity upon marriage to be stoned to death. But men who came to marriage without their virginity were not punished, and a man who raped a virgin maiden merely had to pay her father fifty silver shekels and make an honest woman out of his victim by marrying her (Deut. 22:28-29). Both male and female adulterers were killed, but adultery was defined as sexual intercourse between a married woman and a man other than her husband, and was considered a violation of the husband's property rights. In contrast, sex between a married man and a single woman was not adultery, but merely fornication, a lesser sin.

Still, despite the sexual restrictions and the double standard, the Hebrews' attitudes were less negative than those of many cultures that followed. Although **ascetic** Hebrew sects did exist, mainstream Jews never thought very highly of **celibacy,** the deliberate abstinence from marriage or sexual relations. On the contrary, they expected everyone to marry, the sooner the better, in order to get on with the task of being fruitful and multiplying. Any male over eighteen who remained single could be called before the elders to explain himself, and holy men were no exceptions. Widows and widowers were encouraged to remarry as quickly as possible.

Within marriage the Jews considered sex something more than a procreative duty. A good Jewish husband was supposed to make sure his wife was sexually satisfied. Talmudic scholars carefully spelled out the man's obligations: gentlemen of leisure were to have intercourse every night; laborers who worked in their own city, at least twice a week; laborers who traveled to another city, only once a week; donkey drivers once a week; camel drivers once every thirty days; sailors once in five months; and scholars once a week, customarily on Friday night, the beginning of the Jewish sabbath (Bullough, 1976).

In fact, parts of the Jewish scriptures contain outright celebrations of sexuality. Some of the most sensuous poetic imagery in Western literature can be found in *The Song of Songs,* a collection of lyric love poems attributed to Solomon but probably written by various poets over a period of some five centuries (Gordis, 1978). *The Song of Songs,* which is still read in Jewish synagogues during the holiday of Passover, celebrates the passionate love between a man and a woman—a love that is physical as well as spiritual:

> *Thy form is like a palm-tree,*
> *Thy breasts, like clusters of grapes.*
> *I said: I will climb up into my palm-tree,*
> *And take hold of its branches.*
> *Let thy breasts be as clusters of the vine,*
> *And the fragrance of thy face like apples,*
> *For thy kiss is like the finest wine*
> *That gives power to lovers,*
> *And stirs the lips of the sleepers with desire.*
>
> (Translation from Gordis, 1978, p. 71)

The two lovers of *The Song of Songs* continually praise each other's bodies, express their longing during separation, and pledge their eternal devotion. Their words are so frankly erotic that many religious scholars felt obliged to reject a literal reading. Rabbis said the songs were an allegory about the ideal relationship between God and his people Israel. Christian interpreters insisted the songs were about the relationship between Christ and his Church (Gordis, 1978). The sex-positive elements of Judaism were ignored while the legalistic prohibitions survived.

EARLY CHRISTIANITY:
THE CELEBRATION OF CELIBACY

Although we talk about a Judeo-Christian legacy, it may be more accurate to refer to a Judeo-Greco-Christian legacy, for classical Greece probably influenced the early Christians more than the Hebrew tradition did. For the most part, the Greek view of sexuality was positive. Greeks generally appreciated and even revered the human body (especially the male body), considered sex a source of pleasure, and permitted most sexual activities, at least for males. Although homosexuality was illegal in many city-states, it was often tolerated between upper-class men and young boys, and even praised, as we saw in the last chapter. But within Greek culture there was another tradition that was more hostile toward sex, and it was this tradition that appealed to the Christians.

The philosophical basis for this minority view was **dualism,** the belief that soul and body are separate and antagonistic entities. Plato (427-347 B.C.) spoke for this view when he distinguished sacred love (love of another person's mind and soul) and profane love (physical desire or infatuation). Plato believed that only by passing beyond sexual desire to spiritual love could one find true happiness. (Today we refer to nonsexual relationships as *platonic*.) Plato's ideas were so similar to those of the Christians, who lived centuries later, that one early Christian Father wondered if Plato had been versed in Christian prophecy (Bullough, 1976).

Other Greek writers claimed that intercourse was dangerous to one's health, an idea that would be taken up again in England and America over two thousand years later. The Stoics, who taught that people should strive to control their passions, discouraged affection and pleasure even in marriage.

Jesus' Views

Jesus himself had little to say about sex, but his example was to have a profound effect, for Jesus is believed to have been celibate, and this was a break with Jewish tradition. Also, Jesus seems to have considered celibacy as desirable in principle. When he told his disciples that divorce was morally wrong (another departure from the past), they wondered aloud if it might be advisable to stay single, and he replied:

> Not all men can receive this precept, but only those to whom it is given. For there are eunuchs who have been so from birth, and there are eunuchs who have been made eunuchs by men, and there are eunuchs who have made themselves eunuchs for the sake of the kingdom of heaven. He who is able to receive this, let him receive it. (Matt. 19:11-12)

A **eunuch** is a castrated man, and a few early Christians, taking Jesus literally, actually castrated themselves. But the usual interpretation of this passage is that a man can better serve God if he remains celibate.

In the Sermon on the Mount (Matt. 5:27-30), Jesus harshly condemned not only adultery, but even thoughts about it: "I say to you that everyone who looks at a woman lustfully has already committed adultery with her in his heart." Yet when the Jewish elders tested Jesus by bringing him a woman caught in the act of adultery, he showed compassion. Instead of upholding the old Mosaic penalty of death by stoning, Jesus told them, "Let him who is without sin among you be the first to throw a stone at her" (John 8:7). The elders, getting the point, melted away, one by one. Then Jesus simply warned the woman to sin no more, and sent her on her way. In other instances, too, Jesus showed himself to be a man of mercy and love. According to Episcopal writers Morton and Barbara Kelsey (1986), Jesus did not single out sexual offenses as particularly grievous. Also, unlike his predecessors or most of his followers, he seems to have valued women and treated them as equals.

Advocating Abstinence: St. Paul's Views

The Apostle Paul (A.D. ? -67) had more influence than Jesus himself did on Christian attitudes toward sex. Paul was the first Christian writer to argue explicitly that sex should be avoided and that celibacy is a preferred way of life. In his sermons he preached that although those who marry and have sex are not sinful, they tend to get wrapped up in worldly worries and are not totally free to give their lives to Christ. Paul recognized that most people are unable to live a celibate life and do marry. And he acknowledged that once married, a husband and wife have sexual obligations to one another. But marriage, in Paul's view, is basically a compromise solution to the problems of the flesh, a way to control the fires of desire, a second-best alternative to celibacy: "To the unmarried and the widows I say that it is well for them to remain single as I do. But if they cannot exercise self-control, they should marry. For it is better to marry than to be aflame with passion" (1 Cor. 7:8-9).

Like the writers of the Old Testament, Paul regarded women as the subordinate sex. After all, if Eve had not tempted Adam, there would be no need for the sacrifice of Jesus, and therefore Christian women were to regard their husbands as lords and masters. They were also to cover their hair in church so that the beauty of their hair would not seduce the angels. Some of Paul's followers held that female subordination should extend even to the marriage bed, where women ought to show respect by staying literally on the bottom—in the position that later, appropriately enough, would be dubbed the "missionary position."

Prohibiting Pleasure: St. Augustine's Views

St. Paul, like other Christians of his time, thought the Second Coming was due any day. Liberal theologians have argued that he may simply have considered earthly entanglements to be a waste of time and a distraction, since the Final Judgment was nearly at hand (see, for example, Goergen, 1975). The same cannot be said, however, of St. Augustine (A.D. 353-430), who elaborated on Paul's ideas and whose teachings profoundly influenced Church doctrine.

After struggling for years with his own sexual passions ("Give me chastity and continence," he would pray, "but not just now"), Augustine became a Christian and adopted a life of asceticism. After his conversion, he denounced sexual pleasure in principle, something that neither Jesus nor St. Paul had done. Sex, he argued, is shameful because, since the Fall of Adam and Eve, it has involved lust.

Like the Hebrews, Augustine felt that the only legitimate purpose of sex is procreation. Unlike the Hebrews, however, Augustine viewed sex as an unpleasant necessity rather than a pleasurable duty. *Every* act of intercourse is sinful, he said, and every child is conceived in the sin of his or her parents (*original sin*). It was necessary to beget children, but Augustine regretted that they could not be conceived without intercourse: "They who marry for [procreation] only, if the means could be given them of having children without intercourse with their wives, would they not with joy unspeakable embrace so great a blessing? Would they not with great delight accept it?" (quoted in Goergen, 1975). One cannot help wondering what he would have thought of "test-tube" babies.

In Augustine's view, the best way to live is in total abstinence. Next best is marital sex solely for procreation. Sexual intercourse in marriage for any other reason is a *venial sin* (one that does not necessarily deprive the soul of divine grace), while sex outside of marriage is a *mortal sin* (one that condemns the soul to everlasting hell). Augustine opposed sex during menstruation and pregnancy, after menopause, and in cases of infertility. The earlier a married couple could swear off sex, the better.

Other sex-negative features of the Augustinian code include:

1. *A distinction between natural and unnatural sexual activities.* This idea, borrowed from Greek writers, assumes that any activity not common among animals is perverse and therefore a sin against nature. Such behaviors include homosexual activity, masturbation, anal sex, and oral-genital sex. To support this argument, the Church Fathers had to ignore the many animal species in which such behaviors do occur.

2. *Contempt for the human body.* This attitude stemmed from the Greek concept of dualism and was another departure from

Self-punishment
Denigration of the human body is part of the Western religious tradition. In Medieval Europe, members of a Christian sect called the Flagellants attempted to demonstrate their piety by whipping themselves raw in public.

the Jewish viewpoint. *"Inter faeces et urinam nascimum,"* Augustine declared, "Between feces and urine we are born." (He and St. Ambrose had trouble accepting that Jesus, being born of woman, had come into contact with Mary's genitals. Eventually it was decided that as part of the miracle of his birth, Jesus had not made the usual trip down the birth canal.) Disdain for the physical nature of the human body found expression in the self-torture inflicted by early saints, who fasted, beat themselves, placed themselves on the rack, or went about in chains.

Formal Codes: The Middle Ages

Hundreds of years passed before the doctrines of Paul, Augustine, and other Christian Fathers began to have a substantial impact on people's attitudes and behavior. During these centuries, Roman customs and the traditions of the Germanic tribes of Western Europe were more influential than Christianity (Kephart & Jedlicka, 1987).

In the early years of the Roman Empire, marriage was highly valued and divorce was difficult to obtain. But as the Empire declined, social restraints gave way. Fewer people married and informal sexual relationships became common. Premarital sex, extramarital sex, and homosexuality flour-

The original hot tub
During the Middle Ages many religious writers published long lists of penances for sexual infractions. But not everyone went along with such rules. This group seems bent on satisfying all their sensual needs simultaneously—an example of the "belief-behavior" gap in action.

ished. The Germanic culture was less pleasure-oriented than the Roman, but polygyny (the practice of having more than one wife) and wife-capture were common in some tribes, and marriages were often informal—similar to the common-law marriages of today. It wasn't until the fifth to eighth centuries A.D. that Christianity took hold throughout Europe. And then, as fast as the Church made rules to limit sexual "looseness," men and women thought up ingenious ways to break the rules.

To bring people into line, many theologians, most of them members of religious orders, compiled lists of punishments, or *penances*, for various sexual offenses. A seventh-century Irish abbott wrote that those who "befoul their lips" with oral-genital contact must do penance for four years—prayer, fasting, and so forth. For habitual offenders, the penance was extended to seven years. Anal intercourse merited seven years, sex with animals a year, incest with one's mother three years. Married couples were to refrain from all sexual activity during three forty-day periods of the year, plus every Saturday and Sunday night, on Wednesday and Friday, during the wife's pregnancy, and during her menstrual period. After the wife gave birth, the couple was to abstain for thirty-three days if the child was male, sixty-six if it was female (Bullough, 1976). A few calculations show that there was little time left over for sex.

The Middle Ages are often dated from 476 A.D., when the last Roman emperor was deposed, to 1453 A.D., when the Turks conquered Constantinople. Toward the end of this period, St. Thomas Aquinas (1225-1274) systematically set down the Church's moral code in his *Summa Theologica*. Aquinas gave the Church's position on almost every aspect of sexual feeling and behavior, and tried to offer rational reasons for these views. To the Church's standard list of unnatural practices he added heterosexual intercourse in any position other than face-to-face with the female on her back. Like his predecessors, Aquinas accepted male dominance (a woman is described as a *mas occasionatus*, a "failed man") and rejected sex for pleasure as shameful. Celibacy and virginity were good, homosexuality and masturbation were unnatural, and nearly every other sexual or quasi-sexual behavior was wicked, including kissing before marriage, dancing, and dressing immodestly (Simons, 1973).

The views of Augustine and Aquinas prevailed, and continue to form the basis for official Roman Catholic doctrine to the present day. In a 1976 encyclic on sexual ethics, Pope Paul VI reaffirmed the Church's condemnation of homosexual acts, nonmarital sex, and masturbation. The Rabbinical Council of America supported the document, adding that heightened eroticism was to blame for the rising divorce rate. Pope John Paul II has since repeated on several occasions the Catholic Church's opposition to sexual permissiveness, nonprocreative sexual acts, and the selfish pursuit of pleasure. However, priests, ministers, and rabbis are often much more flexible about breaches of the sexual code than are their respective hierarchies.

"A" is for adultery
Hawthorne's heroine, Hester Prynne, was forced to wear a "scarlet letter" because of her offense.

PROTESTANT VIEWS: THE SANCTITY OF MARITAL SEX

During the sixteenth century many Christians broke from the Catholic Church, in part because they rejected the absolute authority of the Pope, and in part because they opposed certain abuses by the clergy. These protesting Christians (Protestants) challenged the Catholic notion that sexual celibacy was necessary for the religious life and eliminated compulsory celibacy for the clergy.

Martin Luther (1483-1546) was one of the leaders of the reform movement. As a Catholic priest, Luther had struggled with his own sexual feelings, finally giving up the priesthood and marrying a former nun. To expect a man or woman who is not celibate by nature to give up sex, he argued, is unrealistic. Besides, it is based on the false belief that one can win the good graces of God by performing certain tasks, or "good works." Luther believed that salvation is a matter of faith, not life style. Marriage, he said, is a splendid institution, and besides, it is the best way to keep man's sinful nature under control: "He who does not marry must misconduct himself." So long as sex is not "abused" and occurs in marriage, it is natural and good.

Another great Protestant leader, John Calvin (1509-1564), took a slightly more liberal position on sexual matters than Luther did. Intercourse within marriage, he believed, is not only honorable, but holy. Therefore, a husband and wife might feel free to enjoy themselves as long as pleasure is only a side product of their desire to procreate. But Calvin, like Luther, stopped short of accepting pleasure for its own sake, and he warned against getting too carried away by passion. He denounced sex outside of marriage (by definition for pleasure) as plainly sinful, and he tried (unsuccessfully) to get the civil authorities at Geneva, where his followers were concentrated, to enact the death penalty for adultery (Bullough, 1976). Both Calvin and Luther perpetuated the idea of female inferiority.

Although Calvin was somewhat more liberal in his views on married sexuality than Luther, he was less accepting of worldly pleasures in general. His followers in America, the Puritans, renounced the joys of this world in the interest of showing that they were among the fortunate few bound for salvation. The **puritan ethic** accepted sex but tried to limit it strictly to marriage. Punishments were decreed for all nonmarital sexual activities. An unmarried couple who had intercourse could be publicly whipped (although if they were engaged to marry, the community was likely to be tolerant). Adultery earned the offender a distinctive mark on the clothing, like Hester Prynne's red "A" in Nathaniel Hawthorne's classic novel *The Scarlet Letter*. Sex with animals was the worst sexual crime; its punishment was death.

Yet the Puritans were not prudes (D'Emilio & Freedman, 1988). For the Puritans, right living was motivated by spiritual salvation, not social propriety. They were rugged pioneers, and the conditions of frontier life discouraged drawing-room manners and extreme modesty. The Puritans allowed courting couples to *bundle* (crawl into bed with their clothes on), ostensibly to save on firewood. When preachers threatened their flocks with fire and brimstone, they named sinful acts in language that may have titillated as much as it terrified. The Puritans, in other words, looked depravity in the face without blinking. Their relatively realistic view of sexuality probably had less influence on our notions of sexuality than did the ideas of the Victorians who followed.

VICTORIANISM: THE REIGN OF RESPECTABILITY

For a brief period around 1800, Western societies became a little more relaxed about sex. This was the era of the French and American revolutions and of the intellectual movement known as the Enlightenment. Philosophers were advocating a rational, scientific approach to life, and religion lost some of its influence on daily behavior. Men went about in tight breeches; women climbed out of their corsets and exposed their arms, shoulders, and even part of their breasts (Rugoff, 1971).

But before long, the pendulum swung back. Historians argue about the reasons, but many think the Industrial Revolution was partly responsible. Industrialization strengthened the Protestant middle class, with its heritage of rectitude, male dominance, and restrictions on nonmarital sexuality and "unnatural" acts. Although the middle class was not large, it became a powerful arbiter of style and manners. The watchword of this class was respectability. During the long reign of Queen Victoria of England, which spanned roughly the last two-thirds of the nineteenth century, middle class Europeans and Americans worried less about their immortal souls than about the development of good character and the maintenance of spiritual and physical health. In the words of one writer, "The Puritans bore down on sexual pleasures with the wrath of God; the Victorians treated them with suppression, euphemism, and silence" (Rugoff, 1971).

Since politeness was as important as purity, proper Victorians set about to clean up the English language. They carefully avoided words that referred to parts of the body ordinarily covered by clothing, such as the thigh, hip, breast, navel, belly, buttocks, and even leg. They used euphemisms like self-abuse or solitary vice for masturbation, fallen woman for whore, statutory offense for rape, house of ill repute for brothel. A woman (or better, a lady) did not wear underwear, she wore lingerie; she did not get pregnant, she was in the family way; she did not give birth, she went into confinement.

Dreadful Consequences: Sex and Health

In addition to their sense of propriety, other characteristics set the Victorians apart from those who had gone before. One was an obsession with the supposed physical hazards of sex. Even medical authorities who considered themselves to be enlightened reformers were constantly warning against "excessive" or "unrestrained" sexual activity. One advised that frequent intercourse could cause paralysis and epilepsy. As to what "frequent" meant, some experts thought that once a month was ideal, although even then, sex was assumed to be dangerous if the partners made love for too long. Women were much too fragile to exert themselves more often than that. Men risked the loss of semen, which many Victorians revered as a magical substance to be hoarded jealously and dispensed stingily. The loss of one drop of semen was said to equal the loss of four, or forty, or sixty drops of blood, depending on which authority you consulted. With every ejaculation a man wasted some of his precious reserves, damaged his nervous system, and moved a little closer to death. Smart men would be sexual capitalists: they would invest cautiously (procreate) but never squander their resources.

Nothing worried the Victorians quite so much as masturbation. Every self-styled expert had his own list of its horrible effects on body and mind, ranging from bad breath to death. Parents were constantly cautioned to save their children from the masturbator's fate by watching them carefully and keeping them away from the servants, who were presumed to be a bad influence. Some doctors recommended a regimen of prayer and exercise, while others went much further. "Treatment" for boys included piercing the foreskin of the penis with wire, applying leeches to the base of the penis, or cutting the foreskin with a jagged scissors. "Treatment" for girls included applying a hot iron to the thighs or clitoris, or removing the clitoris in an operation called a *clitoridectomy*. Adults who preferred to treat themselves (or their children) could buy various commercial devices, such as metal mittens, an alarm that went off when the bed moved, rings with metal teeth or spikes to wear on the penis at night, or guards worn against the female's vulva. Some of these horrors were so popular that they were advertised in the Sears Roebuck catalog.

Views of Women: The Pedestal-Gutter Syndrome

Another feature of Victorianism was a new twist on the double standard. Since Biblical times, women had been viewed as a threat and temptation, lesser creatures whose sexuality could do men in. But many Victorians denied female sexuality and argued that women were *more* moral than men. Abstinence might be the goal for men, but everyone knew most men could not reach it. Nice women, though, could and should. And since women were men's moral superiors, they were responsible for subduing men's natural passions, and acting as the "final umpire" on the matter of coital frequency.

The most widely quoted English-language book on sex during the second half of the nineteenth century was Dr. William Acton's *The Functions and Disorders of the Reproductive Organs*. Acton assured readers that "the majority of women (happily for them) are not very much troubled with sexual feelings of any kind. . . . Love of home, children, and domestic duties are the only

passions they feel." Many writers agreed. Others did acknowledge sexual feelings and even orgasms in "good women," and some told women to go ahead and enjoy themselves. But even they considered women more delicate than men and more vulnerable to the ravages of "excess."

While people were putting women on a pedestal, they also assumed it was scandalously easy to topple them off that pedestal, smack into the gutter. Victorian literature is full of fair maidens who are seduced and then become depraved. The idea that women were somehow responsible for their own downfall made it possible to condone prostitution as an inevitable evil, one that conveniently protected those women who were still "good" from the hard-to-control sexuality of men.

Of course, like any society, Victorian society had its share of rebels and nonconformists. These individuals preached free love and sometimes even started communes where they could put their ideas into practice. Some drew huge audiences on the lecture circuit of the day and became what we would now call media personalities. But they were most definitely excluded from polite society and often were persecuted for their beliefs. For most of the

Up on a pedestal, down on her luck *Many Victorians believed that one sexual misstep led—literally—to the gutter. In a common theme in Victorian novels, an innocent young woman falls in love with a rich and worldly man and runs away with him. But he soon tires of her, and, penniless and degraded, she turns to prostitution.*

middle class, appearances were what mattered. Proper people simply closed their eyes to the real world, where most women, far from being gauze-draped angels, toiled long hours in factories or in their own homes; where most men had experience with prostitutes; and where florid pornographic books were as popular as Louisa May Alcott's *Little Women* (see Marcus, 1966). Above all, the Victorians were great pretenders.

THE BELIEF-BEHAVIOR GAP REVISITED

With so much animosity toward sex over the centuries, you may be wondering how the human race ever managed to keep going. The answer, of course, is that doctrine is one thing, actual behavior another. In Chapter 1 we saw that a belief-behavior gap characterizes human sexuality around the world. The West is no exception. For example, the Puritans adamantly opposed premarital sex, but it was a rather common transgression. In fact, in the 1680s a small path behind Wall Street in New York City was popularly known as Maiden Lane, apparently because so many young women lost their maidenhood there (Bullough, 1976).

Similarly, Victorian women were apparently far less inhibited than one would think from reading men like William Acton. In the Stanford University archives, historian Carl Degler (1974) discovered an unpublished sex survey begun in the early 1890s and completed in 1920. The researcher, Dr. Celia Duel Mosher, was a physician and medical advisor to women students. Mosher questioned forty-five women, most born before 1870. The majority of them said they enjoyed intercourse, considered sex a normal part of life, and experienced orgasms. Of course these women may have been somewhat atypical; most were highly educated, and modern studies have found that highly educated women are more likely than others to be orgasmic. Also, none of the women came from the sexually conservative south. On the other hand, such women were just the ones who were most likely to be familiar with the works of writers like Acton. From other Victorian records, we know that people then engaged in every sexual behavior that they do now, from autoeroticism (masturbation) to zoophilia (sex with animals), though perhaps in fewer numbers, and usually more discretely. Even Queen Victoria was not all that Victorian (Gay, 1984).

As we saw in Chapter 1, sexual restrictions never seem to apply equally to all levels of society. In America, whites assumed that Indians, Chinese immigrants, and black slaves were morally inferior, and they simply looked the other way when white men took liberties with nonwhite women. In Europe, the ruling class often got away with sexual adventures that the average citizen could not. During the eighteenth century, which historian T. H. White dubbed the Age of Scandal, upper-crust Englishmen cavorted in private clubs and then went out to terrorize the public. One group liked to rape women; another liked to expose themselves in public. Sexual privileges sometimes extended to the very people who promoted a strict religious morality. While many religious moralists must have been sincere, honest

Group marriage *Every era has its sexual nonconformists. In the 19th-century, the religiously-inspired Oneida community, in New York State, practiced communal marriage. Every woman was theoretically "married" to every man. This etching shows a new member being introduced to the community.*

men who followed their own advice, both Catholic and Protestant leaders sometimes practiced what they would never dare preach. During the Middle Ages and the Renaissance, even an occasional Pope was sexually fallible (Bullough, 1976).

The belief-behavior gap shows that although religious and other authorities set moral standards, they cannot always make people obey. But that does not mean such standards have no effect. For thousands of years the sexual message, though justified in different ways, was monotonously the same: sex is a dangerous force that must be controlled; pleasure is immoral; activities that do not lead to conception are unnatural; men and women do not have the same sexual rights. Such teachings must have had an impact, if not always on behavior, then at least on how people felt about what they did. Psychologists have shown that when people's beliefs fail to jibe with their actions or their true desires, they tend to feel guilty, remorseful, and uncomfortable. People may indulge in sexual pleasure despite all the stern warnings, but historically they have undoubtedly paid a price—and many still do.

SEX IN THE TWENTIETH CENTURY

We have emphasized the negativity about sex in our sexual legacy. And traditionally suspicious attitudes toward sexual freedom are still reflected in our legal codes. In many states oral-genital sex is a felony, even between a husband and wife. Some states prohibit unmarried men and women from living together or having intercourse ("fornication"), and in at least fifteen states, adultery is a crime punishable by a fine or imprisonment. Although laws restricting sexual activity between consenting adults are not often enforced, they perpetuate the assumption that government has the right to legislate personal morality. (In other chapters of this book we will examine the legal status of prostitution, pornography, homosexuality, and various sexual activities.)

Nevertheless, sexual behavior today is considerably less inhibited than it once was. Despite discomfort about specific acts, there is widespread acceptance of sexual pleasure as a legitimate goal in intimate relationships, and less Victorian reticence. Early in this century a man might have gotten a thrill from accidentally glimpsing a woman's ankle as she boarded a bus. Now it is commonplace for people to watch explicit sex on cable TV or a rented video tape. A New York telephone number that reaches a sexually explicit recording attracts more than half a million calls a day from across the country. There are even sexually explicit computer games. Sexual pleasure is no longer simply an embarrassing by-product of sexual activity: for many of us, it is the goal.

Our Victorian heritage
Until this segment of the "I Love Lucy" show in 1952, television viewers in the U.S. had never seen a pregnant actress portraying a mother-to-be. Desi Arnaz and his producer had to overcome sponsor and network resistance to incorporate Lucille Ball's pregnancy into the story line. The word "pregnancy" was never used in the script. Here Lucy tells Ricky she is "expecting."

Actually, the United States and other Western countries have gone through not one, but two sexual revolutions. The first occurred during the Roaring Twenties, an era when styles in dancing, dress, and manners were completely transformed (see Table 2-2). Young women of the 1920s were far less likely to remain virgins before marriage than their mothers had been (Kinsey et al., 1953). The second revolution occurred in the late 1960s, a period of general social upheaval. An unpopular war in Southeast Asia shook the faith of young people in their government and in established authority; racial conflicts led to violent battles in the cities; political leaders were assassinated and confrontation was the order of the day. The sixties witnessed both the growth of an idealistic social activism (the Peace Corps, Head Start, the "Great Society") and the beginning of a turning inward (the hippie movement, the widespread use of drugs, pop psychology). Amidst all this turmoil sexual mores were changing, too. The cast of the hit musical *Hair* appeared naked on stage, and in *Oh! Calcutta!* actors took off their clothes for sexually explicit skits. Ordinary folk stood in line for hours to see the X-rated film *I Am Curious, Yellow* (which is quite tame by today's standards) and flocked to nude encounter sessions where they could get in touch with more than their feelings. Beginning in the mid-1960s, there was a striking increase in the incidence of premarital sex, particularly among women.

What accounts for such a profound shift away from our sexual legacy? We cannot answer this question with certainty, but we can look at some likely explanations. Our society is different in many ways from what it was at the turn of the century. Let's look at the possible impact of these changes on sexuality.

The Growth of Science

We can begin with the growth of science, which has challenged traditional religious philosophies that promote an absolute standard of morality. Scientists assume that truth is never final, and that different viewpoints deserve a hearing. Science encourages relativism, not absolutism. This is not to say that religion is without influence on us. But religious influences today are pluralistic, and most denominations are not as sternly moralistic as the Puritans were. Many encourage people to ponder moral guidelines rather than blindly follow the dictates of authority. Some have discarded dogma previously considered sacred. Most religions continue to condemn certain activities (for example, extramarital sex) and discourage others (for example, premarital sex). But many also encourage an active, pleasurable, erotic sex life within marriage. Even a few right-wing religious people have joined this trend. For example, fundamentalist leaders Beverly and Tim LaHaye, who oppose abortion, pornography, and homosexuality, are coauthors of a marriage manual that encourages frank communication about sex, variety in sexual positions, concern for female sexual needs, and specific techniques for arousing a reluctant partner (see Paige, 1987).

TABLE 2-2

Changing times.
The twentieth century
has seen many changes
in sexual custom and
belief. Here are only a
few of the milestones
along the way. (For
historic developments in
sex research, see
Chapter 3.)

1900-1919: A time of transition between Victorianism and modernity.

- In *Three Essays on the Theory of Sexuality*, Sigmund Freud outlines a theory of personality development that gives sexuality a central place. (1905)

- Dr. Paul Ehrlich discovers Salvarsan, a treatment for syphilis. (1912)

- The first nude calendar appears. (1913)

- The first commercially produced pornographic film is distributed. (1915)

- Margaret Sanger opens the first birth-control clinic in the United States, in Brooklyn. (1916)

- World War I nurses develop the disposable sanitary napkin.

1920s: The decade of the "first sexual revolution" in the United States.

- Congress ratifies the nineteenth amendment to the Constitution, giving women the vote. (1920)

- "Flappers" rebel against Victorianism by wearing short skirts and short hair; some women also defy convention by smoking cigarettes and drinking alcohol.

- Cheek-to-cheek dancing gains popularity, along with the Charleston, the Rag, and the Tango.

- Young men and women take up the practice of dating, going off alone together unchaparoned (in a car, whenever possible).

- In *Ideal Marriage* (1926), Dutch gynecologist Theodore Van de Velde unabashedly advocates foreplay, variety in intercourse positions, and the "genital kiss" (oral sex).

1930s: A decade of depression and high unemployment, in which flamboyance gives way to concern about economic survival.

- Widespread use of the condom and diaphragm leads to a dramatic drop in the U.S. birth rate.

- The introduction of the tampon frees women to engage in all activities during menstruation; many people come to see menstruation as a normal part of life, rather than an illness.

- A U.S. District Court Judge rules that James Joyce's sexually explicit masterpiece *Ulysses* is not obscene when read "in its entirety" by "a person with average sex instincts." (1933)

- Radclyffe Hall publishes the first major modern novel about homosexuality, *The Well of Loneliness*. (1938)

- Alfred Kinsey offers the first college course on sexuality, at the University of Indiana. (1939)

1940s: A decade disrupted by World War II in its first half, and dedicated to recovery and "catching up" in its second.

- A new "miracle drug," penicillin, becomes widely available, and provides a convenient, reliable, and safe cure for syphilis and gonorrhea.

- Hollywood practices self-censorship to head off the threat of official censorship; in films, even husbands and wives sleep in separate beds.

- Women, responding to the nation's need for wartime workers, leave home for offices and factories.

- After the war, "Rosie the Riveter" loses her job to the returning G.I. Joe.

1950s: A decade of economic recovery and stability, and the celebration of family "togetherness."

- George Jorgensen undergoes the first sex-change operation, in Denmark. (1952)

- The first Playboy magazine appears. (1953)

- Elvis Presley's wild gyrations on the Ed Sullivan television show shock and disgust some, and please and delight others (but the camera stays above his waist during the entire performance).

- The Supreme Court rules that certain sexually explicit materials, such as D. H. Lawrence's *Lady Chatterly's Lover*, may be distributed in the United States. (1957)

- The first bikini bathing suits appear in the U.S. (1959)

1960s: The decade of the "second sexual revolution," marked by social and political protest and widespread experimentation with both sex and drugs.

- The Food and Drug Administration approves the oral birth control pill. (1960)

- Betty Friedan publishes *The Feminine Mystique*, a landmark event in modern feminism. (1963)

- The mini skirt dominates women's fashions.

- Homosexual men openly fight against police harassment at the Stonewall Bar in New York City. (1969)

1970s: A decade of increased openness and continuing political protest that also sees the start of a conservative backlash.

- Courses in sexuality become common in colleges and universities

- The President's Commission on Pornography concludes that adults should not be prevented from obtaining sexually explicit materials. (1971)

- *Cosmopolitan* magazine publishes the first nude male centerfold; the model is Burt Reynolds. (1972)

- Alex Comfort's *The Joy of Sex* (1972), and Nena and George O'Neill's *Open Marriage* (1972) become best sellers.

- X-rated movies like *Deep Throat* (1972) become popular entertainment, along with "topless" and "bottomless" shows.

- The Supreme Court rules that states may not restrict abortion during the first trimester of pregnancy. (1973)

- The American Psychiatric Association and American Psychological Association vote to stop regarding homosexuality as a psychological disorder. (1974)

- An organization called "Save Our Children" successfully convinces voters in Dade County, Florida, to repeal existing laws safeguarding the civil rights of homosexuals. (1977)

- The first successful "test tube" (in vitro) fertilization takes place. (1978)

- Herpes infections increase, and concern grows about sexually transmitted diseases.

1980s: A decade of increased political and religious conservatism, during which the deadly disease AIDS causes a reexamination of sexual attitudes.

- The first cases of AIDS in the United States are diagnosed (1980) and by 1982 their significance begins to be recognized.

- The Equal Rights Amendment (ERA) narrowly fails to achieve the required ratification by two thirds of the states.

- Public support increases for sex education in the schools, largely in response to high teenage pregnancy rates and concern about AIDS.

- The Supreme Court rules that the state of Georgia may outlaw homosexual sodomy. (1986)

- Attorney General Edwin Meese's Commission on Pornography attempts to link pornography and sexual violence. (1986)

- A New Jersey court rules that a surrogate mother may not reclaim her child. (1987)

- The Supreme Court allows states greater latitude in restricting access to abortion. (1989)

The shift to relativism has important roots in the nineteenth century and the evolutionary theories of Charles Darwin. The physical characteristics of human beings, Darwin showed, can be studied objectively, just like those of other animals, with whom we share common evolutionary origins. Physical characteristics are adaptations to circumstance, that is, to changes in the natural environment. Today most scientists believe that human customs, including sexual customs, can also be seen as adaptations to circumstance rather than inevitable or divinely ordained.

Science has had yet another consequence: it has tempered our notions of what *should* be by providing us with information about what *is*. Learning about human sexuality (for example, that women, like men, are sexual beings) has forced us to rethink some of our previous attitudes and alter our behavior.

Wars

Our country has participated in four major wars in this century: World War I (1914-1918), World War II (1939-1945), the Korean War (1950-1953),

Military action *War affects sexual attitudes and behaviors in many ways. For example, frequent experiences with prostitutes can affect a soldier's attitudes toward women and sex. In cultures that highly value female virginity before marriage, the prospects for women who are recruited as prostitutes are severely limited.*

and the Vietnam War (1954-1975). Wars always have an impact on sexual behavior. The loss of children, spouses, and lovers disrupts couples and families. Because of the uncertainty of the future, people refuse to postpone pleasure, sexual and otherwise: "Eat, drink, and be merry, for tomorrow we die." Women, left behind to keep the home fires burning and the economy running, take over men's jobs, and gain a new independence. Or they serve in the military or as nurses overseas, with the same result. Soldiers, cut off from loved ones and enduring great hardship, use sex as a form of rest and recreation. They frequent prostitutes, and they contract sexually transmitted diseases. In foreign wars, they come in contact with different cultures and different sexual values. They bring home war brides and leave behind war babies.

As mentioned previously, the Vietnam conflict played still another role in altering sexual attitudes because of its unpopularity.

Industrialization and Affluence

Industrialization has changed us from an agricultural society to an urban and suburban society. Most of us no longer live and die in a small village or farming community, where everyone knows us and always has.

The "good life" *In a consumer society, pleasurable experiences, including sexual ones, come to be viewed as one of the "perks" of affluence. Images like this one, in ads for hotels, airlines, and vacation resorts, tell us that erotic experiences can be purchased, like any other consumer item.*

Instead of working on a family farm or ranch, we provide goods and services in exchange for wages. We may move many times in search of a better job. Both the anonymity of the city and increased mobility can make it difficult to establish long-term friendships and commitments. One consequence is a weakening of the old influences. If we violate some of the traditional rules, who's to know or care? Anonymity and mobility may also make us more dependent on our spouses for emotional support and companionship. Few other people can offer such support, since they don't know us very well. Emotional intensity in marriage means that sex is no longer merely a procreative duty, or a commodity that women reluctantly provide for their husbands. It is a pleasure to be mutually enjoyed and a way of maintaining a close bond between marital partners.

Industrialization has also meant that young people must spend many long years preparing themselves for jobs. As long as they are in school or "in training," they are apt to remain dependent on their parents, and to postpone marriage. (Men on the average marry for the first time now at 26, women at almost 24, compared to 22.5 and 20.5 two decades ago.) As a result, adolescence in America now extends for some young people into the mid-twenties. The lengthening of adolescence may have contributed to the relaxation of prohibitions against premarital sex. It is one thing to tell a young person to wait for marriage when marriage is only two or three years away, and quite another when marriage may be ten years away.

Industrialization has had another consequence: It has brought relative affluence to millions, and the affluent can afford the pleasures of life. Affluence probably helps explain a shift in values from thrift and self-control to consumerism and self-gratification (and, some critics would say, self-indulgence). Advertisers, eager to separate us from our money, promote this ethic of pleasure. Indeed, our economy depends on an ever-increasing demand for products and experiences that define "the good life." Little wonder that having a good time, seeking excitement, and enjoying the "here and now" have become all-important to many of us (D'Emilio & Freedman, 1988). A reward in the hereafter in exchange for a life of sacrifice, hard work, and devotion to duty no longer seems enough. We want fun in our lives, and we want it *now*.

Changes in Family Life

We have suggested that mobility forces marriages to become emotionally intense. Ironically, this intensity may contribute to their instability. People used to believe that marriage was forever, no matter what. But over the past century, Americans have come to feel that marriage should bring them happiness. If they do not achieve marital bliss, they may regard their marriages as failures and end them. This is easier to do than it once was; the educational and economic functions that the family used to perform are now performed by other institutions. We marry at a somewhat higher rate than we did at the turn of the century, but our divorce rate is over seven times what it was in 1900.

Because of divorce, today the single parent household is almost as common as the two-parent household. One of every five children, and half of all black children, lives in a one-parent household (*U.S. Bureau of the Census*, 1989). Remarriages have created blended stepfamilies. Getting married, having children, being a husband or a wife—these experiences no longer have the same meanings as at the turn of the century. People may get married, only to be dating again a few years later. Children of single or divorced parents may be forced to confront their parents' sexuality in a way that they never would if their parents were married. Premarital virginity—"saving yourself for your spouse"—may not mean the same thing when that spouse may turn out to be only a temporary companion.

The Changing Roles of Men and Women

A woman's place is no longer solely in the home. Women have gradually moved toward economic and political parity with men, though they are still far from achieving it. During only the last decade or two, hundreds of changes have occurred, from the dual listings of married couples in telephone books to the retention by married women of their own last names, to the entry of women into all sorts of previously male jobs. (For a review of social, economic, and political changes affecting gender roles, see Tavris & Wade, 1984). However, changes in domestic arrangements (who tends the children, cleans the house, handles social obligations) have been much slower in coming.

The changing roles of men and women have brought complex and often unanticipated changes in sexual and intimate relationships. As women have become miners, lawyers, and world-class athletes, it has become more and more difficult to hold onto the myth that they are the "weaker" sex. Although women still earn far less than men—about 65 percent of a man's wages, on average—more and more women have their own money, which gives them a greater degree of independence and power not only in the marketplace, but at home. At the same time, "no fault" divorce, intended as a progressive reform, has eliminated most alimony, creating a class of displaced homemakers with few job skills and little experience in the work force. Indeed, divorce, along with the lower pay of women and the lack of child-care services available to them, has had a devastating financial impact on women. Half of all female-headed households with children live in poverty, and two out of three poor adults are women (Cocks, 1982; Wikler, 1982).

Sexually, the double standard is far from dead, as we will see again and again in later chapters. Dating customs have changed very little; men still feel obligated to pay, women to repay—sexually. The pedestal-gutter syndrome is alive and well in American high schools. The culture still often blames female victims of sexual exploitation: rape, incest, harassment. But most of us have long rejected the old stereotype of women as asexual and men as sexual "animals." And many of us strongly resist the notion that women's main duty is to function as sex objects. Such ideas become ludicrous and unworkable when men and women are colleagues on the job and share economic responsibilities in their families. It is not easy, but many couples are groping towards greater sexual equality (Blumstein & Schwartz, 1983).

Changes in Technology

It would be hard to exaggerate the impact of technology on our sexual lives. The automobile alone has had a radical influence. Cars give unmarried couples both mobility and privacy. The back seat, the motel, drive-in movies, and lovers' lanes are part of the cultural history of sexuality in this century.

Here are some other technological developments that have influenced sexual attitudes and behavior:

■ Effective birth control (especially the Pill) has permitted the separation of sex and reproduction. When used conscientiously, it removes an important barrier to nonmarital sex: pregnancy.

■ Reproductive technologies aimed at helping infertile couples—*artificial insemination, in vitro fertilization* ("test-tube babies"), and *embryo transplants*—have completed the process that birth control started. Birth control allowed people to have sex without reproduction; now they can reproduce without sex. Our society is just beginning to grapple with the emotional and ethical implications.

- Antibiotics have lessened the health consequences of some (though by no means all) sexually transmitted diseases. Few people die of syphilis in the United States anymore.

- Telephones have altered the way we conduct our courtships. The phone gives young people a way to talk privately. Along with the car and the jet airliner, the phone expands the arena from which we can seek friends and mates.

- The mass media (newspapers, books, magazines, and television) supply us with all we might want to know about sex, and more. Sex scandals and the messy divorces of prominent people are front page news. Films and video tapes allow us to vicariously experience every conceivable romantic and erotic fantasy, in living color. They also create and promulgate cultural images of beauty and good looks; media "sex symbols" show us what we mere mortals should aspire to. Advertisements in magazines and on television associate ordinary products with sexual success, exploiting our insecurities and creating sexual doubts. And because the media are pervasive the sexual messages they promote in films, ads, and music have a wide and immediate cultural effect.

Sexual change in the twentieth century is so rapid that it is hard to keep up with. In only the few short years since the first edition of this book, there has been increased acceptance of sex education; an apparent increase in caution about having sex with multiple partners (most likely in response to worry about AIDS and herpes); an explosion in the use of pornographic videos; and fluctuations in support for the legalization of homosexual relationships. It is hard to predict what lies ahead in the next five or ten years. Whatever happens, though, we need to keep in mind that sexual changes do not come from nowhere. They reflect our domestic arrangements, our ways of making a living, our vulnerability to disease, and our access to technology.

In the chapters that follow, we will explore more fully both the major sexual changes of the twentieth century and the contradictions that remain.

. . . .

SEX IN THE "OLDEN DAYS": WHAT WAS IT LIKE?

PERSONAL PERSPECTIVE

One way to find out what life used to be like is to ask someone who was there. We are all surrounded by eyewitnesses to history: our parents, grandparents, teachers, and older friends and co-workers. These people cannot tell us what former times were like for *everyone*, but they can share their personal memories and perceptions of the "olden days."

To do some personal historical research, why not interview someone fifteen or twenty years older than yourself about the sexual customs of previous decades? If you can find someone who is of your grandparents' generation, so much the better. Make it clear that you want to know about general customs, not your informant's personal past (unless, of course, the person wishes to share that). Be careful not to be intrusive or nosey.

The best questions are open-ended; they ask for a description, not just "yes" or "no." Some people's memories are easily jogged by the most general of queries ("How have things changed since you were young?"), but others need to be prodded for specific information. Here are a few possible queries to get you started:

1. How was sex portrayed in movies and/or television when you were younger?

2. Do you think most teenagers had sexual intercourse when you were in high school?

3. What kind of birth control was available when you were younger?

4. Where did kids go to "make out" when you were a teenager?

5. What were advertisements for personal products, such as sanitary pads, like when you were growing up?

6. What kind of sex education did young people get in school?

7. Do you recall any "sex scandals" involving movie stars, politicians, or other celebrities when you were younger? What were they about?

8. How did popular music handle topics like sex and love? How do you think song lyrics have changed since you were younger?

9. How were sexual expectations for women different when you were younger? Were they also different for men?

10. What do you consider the most important changes in sexual customs and behavior in the past few decades? Which of these changes do you regard as positive and which as negative?

You need not limit yourself to these questions, of course. Use your imagination, and ask about topics that particularly interest you. Try to get a picture of what the sexual climate was like when your interviewee was younger. How does your experience differ from that person's? Do you think there is a "generation gap" in ideas about sexuality? What appeals to you about the sexual customs of the 1930s, 1940s, 1950s, or 1960s, and what doesn't?

IN BRIEF

1. Modern American attitudes toward sex are ambivalent and contradictory. We can gain some perspective on the conflicts people feel regarding changing sexual customs by examining our sexual heritage.

2. The Judeo-Christian tradition is often blamed for modern sexual inhibitions. However, the Jewish part of the tradition is not uniformly negative. The Old Testament implies that procreation is the main purpose of sex, promotes a sexual double standard, and limits sexual freedom in many ways. However, it takes a positive view of marriage and marital intercourse. Some parts of the Jewish scriptures even celebrate sensuality. The positive elements of the Jewish tradition tended to be ignored by later Christian thinkers, while the legalistic prohibitions survived.

3. The Greek concept of dualism, the belief that soul and body are separate and antagonistic entities, made a strong impression on early Christian thinkers. So did the teachings of some Greek writers that sex is dangerous and people should control their passions.

4. Jesus himself had little to say about sex. However, he appeared to advocate celibacy for those who could exercise the necessary self-control, and he himself was probably celibate. This was a break from Jewish custom.

5. St. Paul was the first Christian writer to argue explicitly for celibacy. Paul viewed marriage as a compromise solution to the problem of sexual desire. Later St. Augustine went farther and denounced all sexual pleasure as sinful. Other features of the Augustinian code include a distinction between natural and unnatural sexual acts and contempt for the human body.

6. Toward the end of the Middle Ages, St. Thomas Aquinas set down the Catholic Church's moral code and presented a rationale for the Church's position on almost every aspect of sexuality. The writings of Paul, Augustine and Aquinas continue to influence official Roman Catholic doctrine today.

7. During the sixteenth century, Protestants challenged the notion that sexual celibacy was necessary for the religious life. Martin Luther argued that expectations of celibacy were ften unrealistic and that marriage was a good way to keep a person's sexual nature under control

John Calvin went somewhat farther, praising marital intercourse as not only honorable but holy. But both men stopped short of endorsing sexual pleasure for its own sake, and both perpetuated the notion of female inferiority.

8. Calvin's followers in America, the Puritans, enacted severe punishments for nonmarital sex. The puritan ethic renounced the joys of this world in favor of a stern morality. However, the Puritans were rugged people who were not overly modest. Their motivation was spiritual salvation, not social propriety.

9. The Victorians probably influenced our notions of sexuality more than the Puritans did. The Victorians were more concerned with propriety and respectability than with sin. They also worried about the supposedly harmful physical consequences of "excessive" sex and masturbation. Unlike those who had preceded them, they tended to regard respectable women as lacking in sexual desire, or at least as more delicate than men and more vulnerable to the ravages of excessive sex.

10. There has always been a pronounced gap between sexual belief and behavior. For example, Victorian women were undoubtedly far less inhibited than one would think from reading authorities of the time. Also, some people were able to get away with more transgressions than others. However, official teaching probably affected people's experiences by making them feel guilty, remorseful, and uncomfortable.

11. Today, despite ambivalent feelings toward sexual freedom, sexual behavior is less inhibited than it used to be and sexual pleasure is widely accepted as a legitimate goal in intimate relationships. The United States and other Western countries have experienced two revolutions in sexual customs, one in the "Roaring Twenties" and the other in the 1960s.

12. Changes in sexual roles may be a response to many factors. Science has challenged traditional religious philosophies that promote an absolute standard of morality. Wars have made people unwilling to postpone pleasure and have introduced young men to new customs and values and women to new independence. Industrialization has changed our society from agricultural to urban. Mobility and the anonymity of the city have weakened traditional influences and encouraged us to seek emotional intensity and pleasure in marriage. The need to train for many years before joining the work force has extended the period of adolescence. Affluence has helped shift values from thrift and self-control to consumerism and self-gratification. Divorce has changed our domestic arrangements and thrown middle-aged people into single life styles. The changing roles of men and women have brought complex changes in sexual and intimate relationships. Finally, technological antibiotics, telephones, automobiles, and mass media—have altered the way we conduct our courtships and how we view our sexuality.

Key Terms

Judeo-Christian tradition *(35)*

procreation *(35)*

ascetic *(38)*

celibacy *(38)*

dualism *(39)*

eunuch *(40)*

St. Paul *(40)*

St. Augustine *(41)*

venial sin *(41)*

mortal sin *(41)*

unnatural activities *(41)*

penances *(43)*

Thomas Aquinas *(43)*

Martin Luther *(44)*

John Calvin *(44)*

puritan ethic *(44)*

Victorianism *(45)*

clitoridectomy *(46)*

pedestal-gutter syndrome *(46)*

belief-behavior gap *(48)*

relativism vs. absolutism *(51)*

industrialization *(55)*

64

**CHAPTER
THREE**

■

Science Gets Down to Sex

•

. . . no aspect of human biology in our current civilization stands in more need of scientific knowledge and courageous humility than that of sex.

Alan Gregg

It was the hottest sexual topic of 1982. In a book called *The G Spot and Other Recent Discoveries About Human Sexuality*, psychologist-writer Alice K. Ladas, nurse Beverly Whipple, and psychologist John D. Perry announced the discovery of a small, sensitive area in the lower front wall of the vagina, about two inches from the entrance. When stimulated, this spot purportedly swelled and triggered a vaginal orgasm. What's more, at orgasm, some women with the spot appeared to ejaculate a fluid from the urethra, the tube that normally carries urine from the body. This fluid, the authors speculated, came from "prostate-like" tissue surrounding the urethra.

Gynecologist Ernst Grafenberg had described similar phenomena in 1950, although he located the spot along the urethra, rather than in the vaginal wall per se. Grafenberg was ignored. But timing is everything in life, and when Ladas, Perry, and Whipple resurrected the spot, now named the Grafenberg or G spot, people took notice. The public had been misled, said these authors, into thinking the clitoris was the critical organ in female sexual response. All women could (and by implication *should*) have G spot orgasms. *The G Spot* book would tell them how to locate the magic button. And if at first a woman didn't succeed, she could always try, try, again—with the help of a device available from the authors, costing several hundred dollars.

In support of their claims, the authors of *The G Spot* said they had examined 400 women and found spots in all of them. But they gave no details about these women and never published anything else about them. The rest of their evidence consisted of anecdotes, hearsay, casual observations, and a single case study. The sole scientific study of the spot, performed by a team that included Whipple, had produced disappointing results (Goldberg et al., 1983). It was not included in the book. Nonetheless, the authors became overnight celebrities. They appeared on TV talk shows and in *People* magazine. Seven book clubs, including *Cooking & Crafts* and *Better Homes and Gardens*, adopted the book. Other professionals jumped on the bandwagon; G spot "stimulation exercises" and detailed instructions for finding the spot began to appear both in popular books on sex and in college texts. Special vibrator attachments, G spotters, came on the market.

Few people stopped to ask why detailed directions and elaborate exercises were necessary to locate an area that presumably was universal among women and had been around for a few hundred thousand years (Tavris & Tiefer, unpublished paper). Gradually, however, doubts set in. In the years after *The G Spot* book was published, researchers, along with thousands of women, have been unable to confirm the existence of a specific erogenous spot on the front wall of the vagina, although some have found erotic sensitivity in the front and sometimes the back wall (see Chapter 5). One group of Czechoslovakian researchers has reported evidence for "female ejaculation" (Zaviačič, Doležalová, et al., 1988; Zaviačič, Zaviačičová, et al., 1988), but American researchers have been unable to distinguish the fluid expelled by female "ejaculators" from urine (Goldberg et al., 1983).

Today, most sexologists take a cautious position on the G spot. *Some* women *may* have something like the area that Ladas et al. described, but others—perhaps most—may not. Some women with "spots" may emit a fluid at orgasm, but "female ejaculation" may turn out to be nothing more than urinary stress incontinence, a condition that causes minor urinary leakage when a person coughs, laughs, exercises, or has sex. As for the public, it appears to have lost interest; the G spot is about as popular a topic at cocktail parties as the hula hoop, 3-D movies, and other one-time American fads.

The saga of the G spot is an object lesson in what happens when enthusiasm outpaces evidence. In our open society, it is easy to get information about sex. Do you have a penchant for percentages? Stacks of statistics describe the sexual habits of men, women, teenagers, the elderly, and the readers of various national magazines. Do you want to know how people do what they do? Multitudes of how-to manuals are ready to tell you. Given the sheer volume of written material on sex, it is tempting to conclude that ours is the age of sexual enlightenment. Tempting, but premature. Researchers have learned a lot about sex in recent years, which is why *this* book exists. But serious sex research is in its adolescence. At this stage, the consumer of information about sex may find it hard to separate sense from nonsense.

When it comes to diets, love, and sex, people are always on the lookout for something new. Sexual anxiety, a desire to be "normal," and the American desire for a quick technological fix for every problem, all make the public vulnerable to sexual fadism. We do not want *you* to be vulnerable—and that is why we have written this chapter.

SENSATIONALISM VERSUS SCIENCE

The scientific study of sexuality has its roots in the final years of the nineteenth century, when Western ideas about sex began to shift. Oddly enough, the groundwork was laid by the very same Victorian medical writers we met in Chapter 2. Whatever their errors and prejudices, these men did insist that it was permissible to talk about sex and even to write about it. Between 1897 and 1928 Henry Havelock Ellis, an English physician, published and revised a monumental seven-volume work called *Studies in the Psychology of Sex.* At about the same time, a relatively obscure Viennese neurologist named Sigmund Freud was busy constructing a sweeping theory of human development and behavior—and sex was its very cornerstone. The year before Freud's death, Alfred Kinsey, an American biologist, began to ask ordinary people some rather pointed questions about their sex lives— and the rest, as they say, is history.

Today, serious modern scholars of sex, like other scientists, depend on *empirical evidence,* evidence based on careful observation or experimentation. They are cautious. They know that a particular result may be *unreliable;* that is, it may fail to stand up to the test of further study. They do not keep secrets: they reveal exactly how they tested their ideas, so that others can *replicate* their studies and verify their findings. They are also aware of the dangers of overgeneralizing. A study of white males does not necessarily produce findings that hold for black males; a survey of teenagers tells us nothing about adults. Above all, trained scientists know that the way they conduct a study can influence its outcome, so they are careful which methods they use.

We know that for some readers methodology seems about as interesting as a television test pattern. But when people can't tell the difference between good methods and faulty ones, they often wind up with some pretty strange beliefs. Consider the case of the nineteenth-century doctors who visited mental institutions, observed the popularity of masturbation among the inmates, and concluded that masturbation must cause insanity. Being naïve

about scientific methods (or perhaps they just didn't care), the good doctors neglected to compare their findings with statistics on masturbation among the sane. They also did not bother to find out whether disturbed people masturbate as much outside of institutions as they do inside them, where there is nothing much to do to pass the time. In the same way, nineteenth-century medical authorities linked tuberculosis to hypersexuality because TB was common among prostitutes. We can learn from such errors.

Nowadays several methods are used in the scientific study of sexuality. Each has its advantages and disadvantages, and each answers questions that the others do not. In this chapter we will describe and evaluate the various approaches. Along the way we will also examine some of the landmark studies of sex.

CASE STUDIES

A **case study** is a detailed description of a selected individual. The study may include information about the person's early life, fantasies, dreams, relationships, ambitions—in fact, anything that might help the researcher understand the case. Because a case study enables the researcher to get to know the individual well, the researcher may notice subtle aspects of personality and behavior that might be missed if the person simply filled out a questionnaire or took part in an experiment. Most of us are interested in the lives of others, and case histories often make absorbing reading. Descriptions of real people make the findings of sex research come alive in a way that an abstract discussion never can.

Case studies have often been used by psychologists, psychiatrists, and other mental health professionals to study disorders or unusual behaviors. The disadvantages of this method, however, are many. The person being studied may not be typical of other people—even those in the same general socioeconomic, religious, or cultural group. If the researcher interviews the person over a long period of time and develops a close relationship with the person, scientific objectivity may get clouded. Most important, the researcher's ideas and opinions may distort his or her interpretation of the facts of the case. Indeed, researchers sometimes draw different conclusions from the same case study.

Because of these methodological problems, many scientists no longer consider case studies of much value. Yet, while the small number of observations does mean that broad generalizations are not always possible, case studies do have their place in research. For example, physiologists and psychologists would like to know whether the presence of male hormones before birth alters the brain of a developing male fetus and makes it different from a female's brain. Some evidence from animal research suggests that such changes do take place, and this evidence has heated up an ancient debate about which contributes more to sex differences, biology or learning.

Obviously one cannot ethically test the relative importance of prenatal sex hormones by taking male children (exposed to male hormones before birth) and raising them as females. But such situations sometimes occur accidentally, and under these circumstances the study of a single case can provide valuable information.

In one carefully studied case of a boy raised as a girl, researchers have followed the development of a seven-month-old boy who had his penis burned off during what was supposed to be a routine circumcision by electrocautery (Money & Ehrhardt, 1972). For ten months the parents agonized over what to do. Finally they authorized surgery to turn their little boy into a little girl. A few months later the surgery was performed, and the parents proceeded to raise him as a her. A demented scientist could not have arranged matters better as far as the study of prenatal hormones is concerned, for the child had an identical twin brother. Thus her development could be compared with that of a sibling who was genetically identical and who had the same prenatal hormone history. Within a few years it became clear that the child thought of herself as a girl, preferred different clothes and toys than her brother did and was the neater of the two children. No information is available on their adult development or adjustment. However this case and others strongly imply that upbringing can probably override any effects that prenatal hormones might have on gender identity.

Case studies also allow scientists to find out whether a particular behavior ever occurs. For example, a researcher might discover that some women can experience orgasms through fantasy alone and study their experiences. The scientist would not be able to estimate how many women are able to have orgasms in this way. But the study would demonstrate that at least *some* women do not require physical stimulation to reach orgasm. This finding would be quite interesting in itself because it draws attention to the variety in human sexual response and to the importance of what happens mentally during sexual activity.

The Case Studies of Havelock Ellis

One of the most skillful users of the case study technique was Henry Havelock Ellis (1859-1939), a man who did as much as anyone to usher in the age of sex research. Like many Victorians, Ellis suffered from various sexual anxieties. As a teenager he worried about his frequent wet dreams because his reading had him convinced that they were a sign of a dreadful disease called "spermatorrhea." Ellis's first waking orgasm occurred at age nineteen, while he was reading an erotic book, but he remained a virgin until thirty-two, when he married. Within a few years Ellis and his wife decided to discontinue sexual relations, although they remained intimate and devoted friends for life. A passionate and romantic man, Ellis then embarked on a series of affairs, but apparently he could not complete the act of intercourse with those for whom he cared most. Ellis's story has a happy ending, though;

Henry Havelock Ellis

This English scientist and man of letters used his gift for clear and graceful prose to document hundreds of sexual case histories.

at fifty-nine he began his last and longest affair and found sexual happiness (Brecher, 1979). Fortunately for the study of sexuality, Ellis was one of those people who not only surmounts personal problems but gains insight from them that he can share with others. In fact, his own sexual frustrations led him to study and write about sex in the first place.

Ellis drew upon anthropological and medical information that had been gathered by others and upon hundreds of case histories written in the first person by friends, colleagues, advice seekers, and correspondents. He made no effort to get histories that were representative of the population, so broad numerical generalizations from his findings are not possible. But he did demonstrate that more variations exist in people's sexuality than anyone had suspected. No two individuals had the same kind of history. Victorian physicians argued about whether intercourse should take place once a month or once a week, but many of Ellis's respondents reported several orgasms a day with no apparent ill effects. At the other end of the scale were people who said they had never once been sexually aroused.

Ellis addressed himself to almost all the issues with which modern researchers are concerned. Many of his specific conclusions were surprisingly accurate, while others were way off base and tinged with Victorian preconceptions. (Even Ellis worried about the poor health that might result from "excessive" masturbation.) However, the real significance of his work lies not in his findings but in the tone he set for further studies. Ellis was unabashedly enthusiastic about sex, at least so long as it was coupled with love. He extolled sex as "the chief and central function of life—ever wonderful, ever lovely." In *The Sex Researchers* (1979) writer Edward Brecher aptly dubs him "the first of the yea-sayers." Ellis's studies led him to become an ardent supporter of sexual reform. He favored sex education for males and females, trial marriages, equal sexual rights for women, legal birth control, and freedom for consenting adults to do privately whatever they want. Most contemporary sex researchers share Ellis's liberal orientation.

The Case Studies of Sigmund Freud

Four decades after his death Sigmund Freud (1856-1939) still inspires controversy. People either love him and his theories or they want to burn him in effigy; but nearly all agree that Freud was one of the towering figures of modern psychology and perhaps the most fascinating. Despite a long and painful battle with cancer, Freud wrote nonstop for forty years, producing over three and a half million words that fill more than twenty volumes. A good deal of psychological research has been devoted to trying to prove or disprove Freudian ideas.

Freud was the father of *psychoanalysis*, a theory of human development and behavior that holds that the most important human motives are buried in the deepest recesses of the mind—buried so deep that we ourselves have no conscious awareness of them. To understand human nature the psychologist must become an archaeologist of the mind, digging below the conscious surface to uncover the hidden realm of the unconscious. Just as an archaeologist finds a few fragments of pottery and reconstructs a civilization, the psychologist must use fragments of thought or behavior, including dreams, fantasies, free associations, and slips of the tongue, to reconstruct a person's innermost desires and conflicts. Inevitably, Freud believed, many of these will be sexual, because everyone is born with a sexual instinct that profoundly influences development.

Sex researchers today generally regard Freud as a sexual conservative because, like other Victorians, he viewed sex as a dangerous force that could all too easily get out of hand. Also, like other Victorians, Freud mistrusted sexual activity other than intercourse. While such activity might not be immoral or physically debilitating, it was "immature," which was almost as bad. Freud was especially conservative on the matter of women. Although he recognized that women have sexual needs and he sympathized with the fact that sexual repression takes its greatest toll on women, Freud also believed that sexual energy is "invariably and necessarily of a masculine nature, whether it occurs in men or in women" (Freud, 1905). He claimed that men are more highly sexed than women, have more "energy" available for *sublimating*, or rechanneling, into other, higher activities, and therefore are destined to be the primary creators of civilization. Freud's theories have been used by those who wish to justify the sexual double standard, to define women in terms of reproduction, and to keep females in their place, which is to say, at home.

When his views first became known, however, Freud was often condemned as a sexual radical for daring to speak frankly about sex. During a lecture series at Clark University in 1909, Freud discussed sexual impulses in children. Some members of the audience were shocked, and the *Boston Evening Transcript*, reporting on the lectures, felt obliged to leave out nearly all mention of this part of Freud's remarks (Hale, 1971). As late as 1917 some psychoanalytic texts were kept in a guarded room of the New York Public Library, where they could be seen only by those who had special permission.

Freud, like Ellis, relied on case studies, but unlike Ellis he did not gather his data from a wide variety of people. Most of his ideas originated from his analysis of a few disturbed and unhappy patients, an in-depth analysis of himself, and his voluminous knowledge of literature and history. He assumed that the dreams and free associations of his patients were the stuff of human nature—a questionable assumption still made by many clinicians. He overlooked the possibility that the psychoanalyst, in interpreting the patient's private world, could introduce distortions and biases. Because of these limitations in psychoanalytic method, some critics would like to discard Freud's theories altogether. But we ought to be careful not to throw out the baby with the bath water. Many psychologists accept the notion of unconscious conflicts rooted in childhood experiences. Freud touched on

Sigmund Freud *Freud's ideas about sexuality had a profound influence not only on psychology and psychiatry but also literature and the arts.*

issues of great importance in people's lives. We will consider his ideas about sexual development again in Chapter 12.

SURVEYS

Surveys are questionnaires or interviews that ask people about their experiences, attitudes, or opinions. Sociologists, social psychologists, and other researchers often use sex surveys to gather information on the *incidence* of a behavior or belief (how many people do certain things or feel a certain way) or the *frequency* of a behavior (how many times per week, month, or year, on the average, people do things).

Surveys can produce piles of data quickly and inexpensively, but they are hard to do well. The biggest problem is to find a **sample,** or subset, of people who are representative of the *population* in question. It is seldom possible to question everyone in a population, whether that population is all the residents of the United States or all single American men under thirty.

When samples are not representative, the results may be misleading. In 1936 a popular magazine called *The Literary Digest* predicted that Democrat Franklin D. Roosevelt would lose to Republican Alf Landon in the race for the Presidency. This prediction was based on a telephone survey of the magazine's readers. On election day Roosevelt won a smashing victory. How did the magazine make such a blunder? Because during the Depression people who (1) owned telephones and (2) subscribed to magazines tended to be well-off, and people who were well-off tended to be Republicans. Thus, the sample was not representative of the American population. The *Literary Digest* example is particularly important to us because several surveys of sexual behavior and attitudes have been conducted by popular magazines.

In the best of all worlds, a survey researcher will be able to obtain a **probability sample,** in which important characteristics are represented in proportion to their frequency in the larger population. For example, if the population in question is U.S. teenagers, then the sample should have the same racial composition as that population. The same goes for such variables as sex, age, socioeconomic status, and educational level. There are various ways to accomplish this. One is to select subjects *randomly*. In a **random sample,** (1) any member of the population has the same probability as any other of being selected; and (2) the selection of one person does not influence the selection of any other. If it is large enough, a random sample is likely to be a representative one; however the method of selecting the sample is more important than its size.

Several sex surveys have used probability samples. For example, during the 1970s, John Kantner and Melvin Zelnik studied sexual and contraceptive behavior in a national probability sample of over four thousand 15- to 19-year-old single women (Kantner & Zelnik, 1972, 1973; Zelnik &

Kantner, 1977). Because of their excellent sampling techniques, we can feel confident about using their results to generalize about late-teenage women in the 1970s. We cannot safely generalize in this way from the many surveys done of students at a particular college. If Professor Probe surveys students at Midwest University, at best his results may generalize to college students in the area where Midwest U. is located. If he surveys only students taking Human Sexuality, he cannot even generalize to all students at Midwest U.

Sometimes a probability sample is just not possible—for example, when a researcher is studying a population of people whose behavior is stigmatized by others. Suppose you want to study the behavior of gay people. Given our culture's negative attitudes toward homosexuality, you cannot just ask every fifth person at random, "Are you gay? I'm doing a survey." Many gay people are still "closeted" and do not want to be identified. Instead, researchers have had to recruit participants for surveys of homosexuals by placing ads, getting personal referrals, visiting gay bars and social clubs, and so forth. We can get useful information from studies using nonrandom samples, but we must be careful about overgeneralizing.

Even the best-done surveys may suffer from another problem, **volunteer bias.** Usually more people are approached for a study than are actually willing to take part. The minority who volunteer may differ in some significant way from the majority who hold back. In general, people who refuse to take part in surveys are older and poorer that those who participate (Fitzgerald & Fuller, 1982). When a survey questionnaire is very long, volunteers are likely to be more verbal than the average person, or more comfortable about revealing personal opinions and experiences. In sex surveys, volunteers may be less inhibited in their sex lives than other people.

There are some other problems inherent in the survey method:

1. *Subjects may not tell the truth.* Some subjects may answer yes to questions just because they want to please the researcher, or they may exaggerate to make an impression. Others may deny that they have done certain things or that they hold certain attitudes because they are afraid of appearing deviant.

2. *Memory may be inaccurate.* While researchers have ways to check for outright lying, even truthful people depend on memory for answers, and memory can play tricks. Psychoanalysts believe that some sexual experiences are beyond recall because people banish them from consciousness. And modern psychologists have shown that memories are often only reconstructions of what we figure *must* have happened and what we would *like* to have happened. For example, those embarrassing gropings in the back seat of the car during adolescence may be transformed by memory into polished lovemaking. Errors in memory occur even for fairly recent events and certainly for those that happened ten or fifteen years

ago. It is difficult, if not impossible, to control for such distortions.

3. *Survey information may be superficial.* For instance, numerous surveys designed to "count virgins" give a pretty accurate idea of changes in the incidence of premarital sex over the past few decades. But these figures miss the emotional components of the vanishing-virginity phenomenon.

4. *Survey results may be open to interpretation.* To take one example, in 1977 Anthony Pietropinto and Jacqueline Simenauer reported a survey of four thousand American men in a book titled *Beyond the Male Myth*. The book was loaded with new information about male sexuality, but the statistics did not always give strong support to their conclusions. Thus one question asked men, "How would you feel when a love affair ends?" Here were the replies:

A little sad, but adjust easily	37.3%
Quite hurt, avoid women for a while	21.5%
Quite hurt, but quickly seek a new woman	19.8%
Indifferent	9.5%
So depressed my work suffers	6.0%
No answer	4.6%
Close to a mental breakdown	2.3%

The authors observed that "more than half of all men would be significantly hurt by the breakup of a romance." (Actually, the figure came to a bit less than 50 percent.) This seems to support their general argument that most men possess qualities of depth and vulnerability. But in their conclusion they overlooked their own information on the intensity and duration of the feelings. Over two-thirds of their subjects said they adjusted easily, quickly sought a new woman, or were indifferent, while only 29.8 percent were seriously affected for any length of time.

Despite these problems, surveys are one of the best ways to get information on the sexual characteristics of a given population. You just have to know how to interpret them.

The Kinsey Survey

The benchmark research against which all sex surveys are judged was carried out by Alfred C. Kinsey (1894-1956) and his associates, Wardell B.

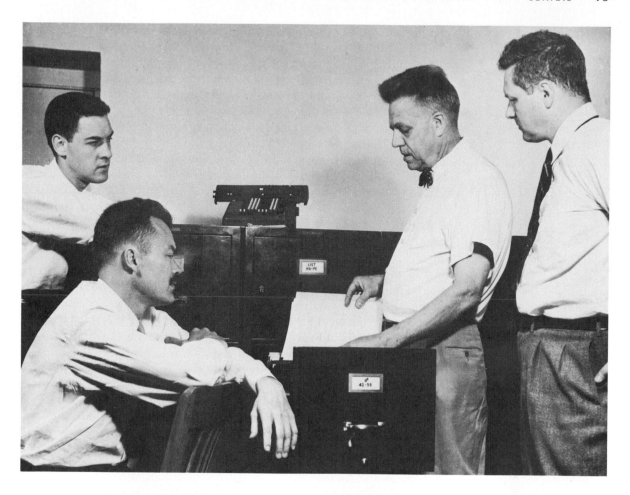

Pomeroy, Clyde E. Martin, and Paul H. Gebhard. A few decades ago Kinsey's name was a household word and his picture made the cover of *Time*. He gained fame by being the first person to use large-scale survey methods to study human sexuality. Where others had preached, moralized, or theorized, Kinsey quantified. Limited surveys had been done—he himself cited nineteen—but most reported the experiences of select groups, such as students at a particular university or women seen by a particular gynecologist. Kinsey and his associates set their scopes much more broadly, interviewing a grand total of eighteen thousand Americans from every background and geographic area. When they reported the data from twelve thousand of these interviews in two massive volumes, *Sexual Behavior in the Human Male* (Kinsey, Pomeroy, & Martin, 1948) and *Sexual Behavior in the Human Female* (Kinsey, Pomeroy, Martin, & Gebhard, 1953), they not only shattered some cherished beliefs about the bedroom behavior of the average citizen, but they established sex once and for all as a legitimate area of study.

The Kinsey Group

Kinsey and his three associates were the only persons who had access to the group's research files on sexual behavior. This 1953 photo shows (from left to right) Martin, Gebhardt, Kinsey, and Pomeroy in their guarded file room.

In appearance and manner Kinsey hardly seemed to fit the part of myth smasher. With his conservative suits, crew cut, and plain features, he might have been cast by Hollywood as an accountant—which, in a sense, he was. Unlike Ellis, he prided himself on being unromantic about sex. Unlike Freud, he was no theoretician. "What distinguished him intellectually," recalls Pomeroy, "was his doggedness, his incredible persistence" (Pomeroy, 1972). These traits served him well during the two decades preceding the sex survey, when, as a professor of zoology at Indiana University, Kinsey devoted himself to studying the gall wasp. Kinsey collected and categorized over four million specimens of the insect, which, by the way, reproduces asexually. He was also known as an avid collector of lilies, irises, classical records, and recipes for alcoholic beverages. But he was no mere collector; he had a certain knack for raising questions no one else asked. His first paper, written as a teenager, was entitled "What Do Birds Do When It Rains?".

In the summer of 1938, Indiana University decided to establish an interdisciplinary marriage course. Kinsey, with his solid academic credentials and his respected standing in the community, must have seemed a safe choice as coordinator. What the university could not have predicted was that Kinsey's enormous curiosity and his conscientiousness as a scientist would plunge the school into fifteen years of controversy. Charged with the task of lecturing on human sexuality, Kinsey consulted the university library. There he discovered, much to his surprise, that almost no reliable information existed about sex. Kinsey was not one to talk about a topic without data, so he began informally to collect sexual histories from his students and colleagues. Gradually he became more and more involved in sex research, and he collected statistics on sex with the same patience and persistence that he had used collecting gall wasps.

KINSEY'S METHODS   For the next eighteen years Kinsey talked to people about their sex lives. His ultimate goal, never reached, was to interview one hundred thousand people. You can get some feeling for the diversity of those he surveyed from this partial list: YMCA secretaries, bootleggers, a colony of castrated men, factory workers, members of the Times Square underworld, coeds at Sarah Lawrence and Vassar, members of the Yale Divinity School, a Salvation Army settlement house in Chicago, imprisoned sex offenders, the scientific staff at the American Museum of Natural History, social workers, top executives at Johnson and Johnson Company, physicians and psychiatrists, PTA groups, schoolteachers, students and professors, two Episcopal diocese groups, members of various homosexual communities, Quaker groups.

Most previous researchers had relied on questionnaires administered to groups or mailed to individuals. Questionnaires are the cheapest, quickest way to do a survey. In Kinsey's study every subject was interviewed personally, either by Kinsey or by one of his three co-workers. (Unfortunately, all the interviewers were men. This may or may not have introduced certain biases into the study.) Kinsey believed that people would be more open about their experiences if they felt some rapport with the interviewer. Anyone working on the project had to be able to put a person at ease by adapting his language according to the class, education, and race of the individual. A Kinsey interviewer had to be able to move from the standard English of college professors to the specialized vocabulary of the prostitute. He also had to be able to memorize a basic set of 350 questions that could be expanded to as many as 521, depending on a person's replies. And he had to be able to vary the order of those questions, depending on which areas an interviewee felt sensitive or defensive about. The questions covered a broad range of sexual activities and preferences, including such taboo topics as homosexuality, masturbation, and sex with animals. (However, not much was asked about anal sex, sadomasochism, or mate swapping, apparently because these were assumed to be extremely rare in the 1940s, and nothing was asked about incest, which we now know is more widespread than once supposed.)

Several other steps were taken to guard against lying:

1. The interviewer shot questions at the respondent in rapid-fire succession and jotted down the responses in a short-hand code so that there were no protracted pauses in the conversation. This gave people very little time to think up phony replies.

2. All questions were direct and to the point. According to Pomeroy (1972), "Unlike previous researchers, we did not say 'touching yourself' when we meant masturbation, or 'relations with other persons' when sexual intercourse was intended. 'Evasive terms invite dishonest answers,' was Kinsey's dictum."

3. The interviewer never asked whether a person had engaged in a particular behavior. He always began by asking *when* the person had first done it. This leading question, Kinsey felt, discouraged easy denials. In Pomeroy's words, "We had to let the subjects know there was nothing they could tell us that we did not know about, or would fail to understand."

4. Several methods were used to check for consistency, including asking interlocking questions, reinterviewing some people after at least two years had passed, and comparing one spouse's report with that of the other. Occasionally an interviewer would let a subject who was obviously lying go right through the interview and would then say, "Now give it to me straight." The surprised subject would then pour out the truth.

Much to the surprise of many people, Kinsey's surveys caused his subjects no emotional distress. Far from intimidating people, the interviewers' straightforward, no-nonsense approach seemed to make the subjects relax.

Top Secret *Kinsey and his colleagues used code marks to record their interviews. They claimed that a professional cryptographer was unable to break their code.*

Of the eighteen thousand participants, only six became visibly upset. (Interestingly, three of these were psychiatrists.) Most appeared to enjoy the interview, and many said it was therapeutic because they were free to get things off their chests that they had never dared reveal to anyone (Pomeroy, 1972).

METHODOLOGICAL PROBLEMS Kinsey boasted that "nowhere in psychological or sociological literature has there ever been a sample which approaches the adequacy of ours" (quoted in Pomeroy, 1972). He was probably right. Nonetheless his work is flawed by some statistical inadequacies that were immediately pointed out by critics. For example, Kinsey's sample of subjects was not randomly selected and was not representative of the American population as a whole. He recruited subjects wherever he could find them, and sometimes he sought out those he thought particularly intriguing. He wound up with too many mid-westerners, especially from Indiana, and too many students, well-educated people, prison inmates, homosexuals, and single women. He had too few farmers, Catholics, Jews, laborers, and older people. His sample of African-Americans was small and unrepresentative, and so he did not analyze their data or include them in his two reports. (The results for African-Americans were finally published three decades later, but only as statistical tables [Gebhard & Johnson, 1979].)

Another problem was volunteer bias, which, as we have seen, is common in survey research. Kinsey worked hard to overcome this problem, but he was not entirely successful. He would visit a group of people to recruit subjects—a PTA meeting, a college class, a prison—and instead of relying on a few volunteers, he would give a rousing talk on the need for sex research, in an attempt to get every person present to give a history. Being both persuasive and persevering, Kinsey often did get 100% cooperation.

However, only a quarter of his male sample and a seventh of his female sample were obtained in this way. And, although "100% sampling" avoided volunteer bias *within* a particular group, it did not necessarily eliminate volunteer bias in the sample as a whole. Groups willing to have Kinsey address them may have been more likely to cooperate in the study than other groups.

Kinsey was attacked repeatedly on other methodological grounds as well. Kinsey analyzed his data by age, sex, religion, and class; critics wanted to know why he had not considered intelligence, family background, personality traits, or any one of a dozen other factors. Kinsey set out to study observable behavior; psychoanalysts wanted to know why he did not explore unconscious motivations. Kinsey described sexual customs; critics of all stripes complained that he had not described love.

In retrospect, it seems clear that critics applied standards in evaluating Kinsey's study that had rarely been applied to other sociological research (although perhaps they should have been). This may have been the price Kinsey paid for being first. In addition, some of the flurry over methodology may have masked misgivings that went far deeper. Until Kinsey came along, Americans could delude themselves into thinking that homosexuality was rare or that only bad girls had sex before marriage. Kinsey proved these beliefs wrong, showing that sexual activity was more varied and widespread than most people thought. These findings upset many people. Furthermore, although he repeatedly claimed to be merely a reporter of sexual customs, with no interest at all in espousing any particular philosophy, actually he held strong liberal opinions that subtly suffused his writings and alienated traditionalists[1] (see Box 3-1). Today, despite its methodological shortcomings, Kinsey's work is generally regarded as a great milestone in sex research and is still used as a valuable source of information. We will cite many of Kinsey's findings in later chapters.

Post-Kinsey Surveys: From Hunt to Hite

Many large- and small-scale sex surveys have been done since Kinsey's. Most have looked at the sexual behavior of specific groups, such as adolescents (Zelnik & Kantner, 1977; Coles & Stokes, 1985) or homosexuals (Bell & Weinberg, 1978; McWhirter & Mattison, 1984). A few surveys have compared the responses of different groups, such as heterosexuals and homosexuals (Bell, Weinberg, & Hammersmith, 1981). It has become routine for magazines, especially women's magazines, to query their readers about their preferences and experiences. And scores of surveys have been done using the most available of all groups, college students.

---

[1]The one glaring exception to Kinsey's liberalism was his belief that the greater sexual activity of males compared to females was due to an innate difference (see Kinsey et al., 1953, pp.710-12). On this matter as well as others, Kinsey tended to overlook possible cultural explanations.

BOX 3-1   ## The Politics of Sex Research

In the first chapter of *Sexual Behavior in the Human Female* (1953), Alfred Kinsey and his colleagues wrote, "The scientist who observes and describes the reality [of sexual function] is attacked as an enemy of the faith. . ." Kinsey was soon to have firsthand experience with the kind of prejudice he described. Like Havelock Ellis, Kinsey wanted to show that there is no clear boundary between normal and abnormal behavior—in fact, no boundary at all as far as biology is concerned. He did not seem to realize that his philosophy of tolerance was in fact a moral ideology, capable, in the era of conformity and McCarthyism, of causing an uproar.

The first rumblings of that uproar had occurred after publication in 1948 of the male volume, which was an instant bestseller, even though few could get through the eight hundred or so pages of unadorned prose, technical charts, and tables. According to a Gallup poll, a majority of ordinary people thought Kinsey's research was "a good thing." But the *New York Times* at first refused to accept advertising for the book and even delayed reviewing it, although other media had reviewed it. At Wellesley College the local bookstore reportedly told students they needed written approval from a professor to buy the book. The president of Princeton University wrote, "Perhaps the undergraduate newspaper that likened the reports to the work of small boys writing dirty words on fences touched a more profound scientific truth than is revealed in the surfeit of rather trivial graphs with which the reports are loaded" (quoted in Pomeroy, 1972).

Then the volume on women appeared, and criticism in some quarters became almost hysterical. Representative Louis B. Heller of New York denounced the book as "the insult of the century" and urged that it be barred from the mails until Congress could investigate. (Like many critics, Heller had not read the book, but only press accounts.) Some respected academics worried that Kinsey was dehumanizing sex. The great anthropologist Margaret Mead, for example, hoped that the book would not become a bestseller because "the sudden removal of a

One well-known national survey, now rather old but still often cited, was commissioned by the Playboy Foundation in the early 1970s and reported by writer Morton Hunt (1974). Although commonly referred to as the Playboy study, the survey did not query *Playboy* readers. A private research organization designed and administered a questionnaire to a sample of two thousand adults in twenty-four cities around the United States. An effort was made to obtain a probability sample. Thus 10 percent of the sample was black, and other subject characteristics, such as age, education, occu-

previously guaranteed reticence has left many young people singularly defenseless in just those areas where their desire to conform was protected by a lack of knowledge of the extent of nonconformity" (quoted in Pomeroy, 1972). Translation: what they don't know won't hurt them.

It was one thing to bring male sexuality into the open; most people already knew that boys will be boys. But here was Kinsey, tearing down the entire edifice of Victorian womanhood by showing that women had orgasms, masturbated, formed homosexual relationships, and so forth. An ultra-right-wing congressman formed a committee to investigate tax-exempt foundations, with the thinly disguised purpose of pressuring the Rockefeller Foundation, the main funder of Kinsey's Institute for Sex Research. The Foundation gave in, withdrawing its support in 1954 (Pomeroy, 1972). Some people think the notoriety and personal abuse that rained down on Kinsey contributed to his death from a heart attack in 1956.

Oddly enough, less than a decade later, when William Masters and Virginia Johnson began to report their direct observations of human sexual behavior (see text), their work provoked less outrage than had Kinsey's questionnaires. Apparently, in only a few short years people had adjusted to the idea of sex research. But even today, sexology remains vulnerable to the shifting winds of politics and public opinion. In 1983, when the World Congress of Sexology met in Washington, D.C., both the White House and the Mayor's office refused to send official greetings, though this courtesy is routine for scientific meetings. As of late 1990, a long-planned, federally-funded National Survey of Health and Sexual Behavior was being blocked by congressional foes. The survey would be the first really large-scale national study of behavior and attitudes since Kinsey's was done, half a century ago. Social scientists want to use data from the survey to design better programs for reducing teenage pregnancy and fighting sexually transmitted diseases, including AIDS. But right-wing politicians have been holding up the study.

pational status, marital status, and urban-rural background, were represented in roughly the same proportion as in the larger population. Although selection of the sample was not really random and although some groups, such as very poor people and prison inmates, were not included, the sample was more balanced than most.

However, there were methodological weaknesses in the study. Potential participants were first called on the telephone, after their names were selected randomly from the phone book. They were asked to participate

Shere Hite *Hite's methods have been widely criticized, but her books vividly portray the diversity of human sexual behavior.*

anonymously in small, private panel discussions of present trends in sexual behavior, as part of a research project. At this time nothing was said about filling out a questionnaire. Only one in five people agreed to participate. Therefore volunteer bias may have existed. Also, only after the panel discussions had actually taken place were people asked to fill out a long anonymous questionnaire. By then the subjects were highly motivated, and nearly all agreed to do so. But participation in the discussions may have influenced their replies.

The Playboy study used different sampling techniques than Kinsey used. It relied primarily on questionnaires rather than interviews; only 200 people were interviewed in depth. Questions were worded differently than in Kinsey's study. All these differences need to be kept in mind when comparing results of the two studies. However, because the Playboy study (unlike most surveys) covered many of the same topics as Kinsey, it does offer an opportunity to examine changes in sexual behavior that took place in America between the 1940s and the 1970s. As we will see in later chapters, Hunt found an increase in premarital intercourse, a decrease in male-female differences, and a decrease in social-class differences.

Two other well-known surveys were done by Shere Hite. One, of women, was done for her doctoral dissertation and was published with much national fanfare as *The Hite Report* (1976). Another, of men, followed a few years later (1981). Hite's goal was not to find out how many people engaged in a particular behavior but to find out *how* people had sex and how they actually felt about their experiences. Other surveys had counted orgasms, because that approach lends itself to statistical analysis. Hite wanted to know how people achieved orgasm and what it was like for them physically and emotionally. An ardent feminist, Hite believed that previous studies had treated female sexuality as merely an inferior analogue of male sexuality, and in her first survey she aimed to correct this bias.

Many researchers have dismissed Hite's work because of her slipshod methods. Hite's samples were not even vaguely representative of the female or male populations. (Initial distribution of the female questionnaire was through mailings to women's groups, primarily feminist groups, and women's centers on college campuses.) The return rate was extremely poor, questions were changed midstream, and some questions were leading ("If you are just about to have an orgasm and then don't because of withdrawal of stimulation or some similar reason, do you feel frustrated? When does this tend to happen?"). The information gathered about respondents' characteristics (age, race, and so forth) was inadequate. For all these reasons, Hite's findings cannot be taken seriously *if what we are interested in is incidence rates*, that is, how many people are doing what.

On the other hand, like other surveys of nonrepresentative samples, Hite's findings are useful for showing the variety in human sexual behavior. Consider masturbation. Most surveys ask people if they have ever masturbated, when they started masturbating, and how often they masturbate, and stop there. Hite asked both women and men *how* they masturbated, and she asked for all the details. What did women use for stimulation: their fingers, the whole hand, the bed? Where did they touch themselves? Did they prefer to have their legs together or apart? Did they lie on their back or their stomach? How did men masturbate? Did they hold the penis with the hand and move the hand, or move the whole body, or rub against something? Did they ever add lubrication? Which part of the penis was most sensitive? Did they ever massage the testicles? How did they feel about the wetness of ejaculation?

Hite phrased many of her questions in an open-ended way, which is a bad idea if you want to do a statistical analysis later on, but a good idea if you want to learn someone's innermost feelings. Because of her methods, we can forget about Hite's figures and percentages. But Hite does provide us with two vast collections of case studies that demonstrate the astonishing diversity of human sexuality.

LABORATORY OBSERVATIONS: THE MASTERS AND JOHNSON STUDY

A survey is a good way to study attitudes and experiences, but it is not a reliable way to get information about sexual physiology. Many of the bodily changes that take place during sex occur internally, where they cannot be observed by the person in whom they are happening. Also, when people are in the throes of passions, they are neither interested in nor capable of observing what their testes, wombs, clitorises, and cervixes are doing. Even when they are not in the throes of passion, people are pretty poor at recalling even such fundamental facts as how long various responses last (Levitt, 1983). Direct **laboratory observation** and recording by an uninvolved person, though costly and time-consuming, is the only effective way to gather physiological data.

Scientists have been watching animals copulate for centuries, but they have been less willing to eavesdrop on human beings because of the strong taboos against public sex. Still, observational studies of people go back at least a century, starting with the work of a Frenchman named Felix Roubaud (Brecher, 1979). Most were reports on one or a few subjects who were clearly atypical in their responses. In 1917 the renowned American behavioral psychologist John B. Watson hooked himself and a female partner up to some instruments in an effort to study what happens physiologically during intercourse. Alas, his partner was not his wife. When the latter found out what her husband was doing down at the lab, she divorced him forthwith and destroyed his records. The judge at the divorce trial called Watson an expert in *mis*behavior. Watson's academic career was ruined (McConnell, 1977).

Although it is not generally known, Alfred Kinsey also did some observational studies. In fact, he probably witnessed more human sex (for scientific purposes) than anyone else up to that time (Pomeroy, 1972). He and his

William Masters and Virginia Johnson *This husband-and-wife team is known both for studies of sexual physiology and the development of treatments for sexual problems.*

associates observed and filmed assorted sex acts (heterosexual, homosexual, and masturbatory), both at Kinsey's Institute for Sex Research and "in the field." Some of the resulting data were used in a chapter on physiology in the female volume, but Kinsey did not say exactly how they were obtained. Given the emotional climate surrounding sex research in the early 1950s, that was undoubtedly a wise decision. At the time of his death Kinsey was planning to set up a special laboratory to study physiological responses firsthand.

Kinsey's reports set the stage for the scientific study of sexual physiology, and onto that stage strode William Masters, an obstetrician-gynecologist at the Washington University School of Medicine. Masters had already established a firm research reputation, especially in the area of hormone replacement therapy for women past menopause. By 1954 he was ready to do for sex what other scientists had done for such physiological processes as digestion and circulation: he would chart the course of human response from the beginning of the process until the end. For subjects, Masters planned to use male and female prostitutes, who were accustomed to performing on demand. However, prostitutes did not make good subjects for this kind of study: they did not stay put for long in one city, and many suffered from varying degrees of pelvic pathology. For a year the project hung in limbo. Then Masters told people that he was planning a study of sexual physiology, and to his surprise many people offered themselves as participants. At this point, Virginia Johnson joined Masters (she responded to an advertisement at the university placement bureau), and the team of Masters and Johnson was born.

During a research program that lasted for 12 years, Masters and Johnson observed the sexual responses of 694 people—312 men and 382 women—and an estimated 10,000 "response cycles." These cycles included both intercourse and masturbation, and also what Masters and Johnson called *artificial coition:* in order to observe what happens in the vagina and cervix during sexual excitement and orgasm, they asked some women volunteers to masturbate while inserting a clear plastic artificial penis containing a light and camera into the vagina. For the first time scientists could make visual observations, record internal and external changes on motion picture film, and take precise physiological measurements like heart rate, blood pressure, and vaginal acidity, all at the same time. These data were supplemented by extensive interviews with all the subjects.

The first question most people ask when they hear about the Masters and Johnson research is, Why would anyone volunteer to have sex in a laboratory? There seems to have been a variety of reasons. Most wanted to increase their own understanding of sex, while some were referred by other doctors or were Masters' former patients. Since subjects were paid, some probably took part to earn extra money. Anyone who showed signs of anxiety or psychopathology or who seemed to be looking for thrills was screened out. All the subjects were heterosexual, and all had to be able to reach orgasm, but otherwise they were a varied lot. They ranged in age from 18 to 89. Most were white, but eleven couples were black. Most were married or had been married, but some were single. Some were academics, but others had not graduated from high school. There were some pregnant women.

This is not to say that the sample was representative. How could it have been? Not all groups are equally likely to volunteer for such an experience. Also, the volunteers had to have a certain amount of free time and had to appreciate the value of the enterprise. On the whole, the sample was better educated than the average. In fact, over two hundred had attended graduate school. Since education correlates with social class, this means that upper-class people were overrepresented. Historian Paul Robinson (1976) argues that this bias could have influenced at least some findings. For example, Kinsey found that richer people masturbate more than poorer ones. If people in the Masters and Johnson study were more experienced with masturbation than the average person—more practiced, as it were—then their physiological responses during masturbation may have differed as well. The sample also contained very few young people: only two females and no males under 21. This too may have distorted the data somewhat. For example,

Masters and Johnson's female subjects come across as at least as vigorous if not more vigorous sexually than the men, but the picture might have been different if there had been more adolescent males and females (Robinson, 1976).

Of course, participants in this study did not simply walk into the laboratory and begin to masturbate or copulate in front of white-coated researchers carrying clipboards. Certain procedures were taken to overcome self-consciousness:

> The individuals considering active cooperation with the program. . .were exposed to the research quarters. All equipment was exhibited and its function explained to the uninitiated. Sexual activity first was encouraged in privacy in the research quarters and then continued with the investigative team present, until the study subjects were quite at ease in their artificial surroundings. No attempt was made to record reactions or introduce other members of the research personnel to the reacting unit, until the study subjects felt secure in their surroundings and confident of their ability to perform. (Masters & Johnson, 1966, p. 22)

Apparently these precautions worked; most subjects acclimated to the laboratory rather rapidly.

Later, critics would claim that sex in the lab must be different from sex in the bedroom, but the subjects themselves denied this. A more serious criticism is that the volunteers, because they all were able to have orgasms easily, and in surroundings where other people might not be able to, could be characterized as "high performers." Subsequent research has found that volunteers for laboratory studies tend (as you might expect) to have less sexual guilt and to be more sexually experienced than people in general (Farkas, Sine, & Evans, 1978; Wolchik, Spencer, & Lisi, 1983). It is at least possible that the physiological responses of such persons are somewhat different from those who do not have orgasms so readily or are more inhibited. Unfortunately, it is hard to know how this problem could possibly be remedied, since laboratory studies must always depend on willing volunteers.

Between 1959 and 1965, reports on the research were distributed only to doctors and scientists. Many of them disapproved, and some well-known medical journals refused to publish the findings. In 1962 Masters and Johnson made a presentation to the annual meeting of the American Psychological Association and got a warm reception, but, strangely, the public hardly reacted. In 1966 they published a book-length report, *Human Sexual Response*. Despite its tortured prose, the book sold more than 250,000 copies in the United States and was translated into 9 languages. Considerable debate followed publication, and some professionals attacked the work, especially—once again—psychiatrists (see, for example, Farber, 1966). But Masters and Johnson's direct observations were accepted with less controversy than Kinsey's questionnaire.

Masters and Johnson's studies are the source of most of what is now known about sexual physiology. Their work has had many practical applications, not only in the treatment of sexual problems but in the areas of infertility and contraceptive failure. But Masters and Johnson's work is not the last word on sexual physiology. Recent physiological research raises questions about some of their findings. Also, establishing the facts about sexual response is one thing and interpreting them is another. Not everyone agrees with all of Masters and Johnson's interpretations. Many unanswered questions remain, as we shall see, and it will take further research to clear up these issues.

Only the most recalcitrant moralist, however, would deny the magnitude of Masters and Johnson's contribution to our understanding of human sexuality. Those who find their descriptions of organs and tissues "tasteless" or "indelicate" are really saying that they find the bare facts of sex painful or disgusting. As Paul Robinson (1976) writes, Masters and Johnson force us "to confront the physical fact of our sexuality without apology or euphemism. . . . High-mindedness and decorum, the usual masks of repression, are overwhelmed by the sheer weight of physiological detail."

CLINICAL EVALUATION STUDIES

Clinical evaluation studies, or *outcome studies*, measure the success or failure of therapy. The best ones involve carefully controlled comparisons between people who received a particular treatment and people who did not. Sometimes, though, therapists simply report case histories based on their experiences with clients. Naturally, the more rigorous the procedures for evaluating outcomes, the more confidence we can have in the results.

One problem in doing evaluation studies is defining exactly what success or failure means. Suppose a man who always ejaculates prematurely undergoes sex therapy. At the completion of therapy he ejaculates prematurely 65 percent of the time. Is that a significant improvement? Or suppose a woman who does not have orgasms during intercourse seeks treatment in hopes of learning to have them. After therapy she still does not have orgasms but she says she feels more satisfied than before. Has the treatment been successful?

Masters and Johnson, so well-known for their physiological work, are just as famous for their clinical techniques. In their second book, *Human Sexual Inadequacy* (1970), they outlined a revolutionary sex therapy program based on work with several hundred patients. (Their third book, *Homosexuality in Perspective* (1979) described both physiological and clinical studies of homosexuals.) In Chapter 10 we will discuss Masters and Johnson's approach to sex therapy, and some of the problems that arise in evaluating their results.

ETHNOGRAPHIC STUDIES

In an **ethnographic study,** the researcher attempts to describe an entire sexual subculture (for example, a gay community or an organization of

Margaret Mead

Controversy about Mead's work has focused attention on some of the difficulties in doing ethnographic studies of sexuality.

"swingers") or the sexual customs of an entire society (for example, Mangaia and Inis Beag, the two contrasting societies described in Chapter 1). This method is often used by anthropologists and sociologists. Some ethnographic researchers use formal measures of behavior. Others simply immerse themselves in a group or culture and observe. Occasionally ethnographers become members of the group or culture being studied, or **participant-observers.** A researcher who belongs to the group is privy to insider information, which is particular helpful when the group is suspicious of, or hostile to, outsiders.

At their best, ethnographic studies offer vivid glimpses into the lives of others. However, ethnographic studies can be hard to replicate, especially when the procedures are informal. Participant-observers may become so integrated into the group being studied that they lose their objectivity. Or an observer may see only what he or she wants to. For these reasons, different observers sometimes come to quite different conclusions.

Consider the fate of the one of the most famous ethnographic studies ever done—a study of Samoa by anthropologist Margaret Mead. In 1925-26, when Mead was 23, she spent nine months in Samoa. As a woman, she was excluded from participating in any serious meetings of male village leaders, but she did have frequent opportunities to interview adolescent girls, the focus of her research. In the popular bestseller *Coming of Age in Samoa* (1928), Mead described a culture where the stresses and strains Westerners associate with adolescence were unknown. In Samoa, said Mead, sexual liaisons among young people were casual, numerous, and guilt-free. Competition was rare, and rape almost unknown. These findings supported Mead's conviction that culture is a far greater influence than biology on human behavior.

For decades, hardly anyone publicly questioned Mead's conclusions. Then, a few years after her death, Australian anthropologist Derek Freeman (1983) published a book arguing that Mead's description of Samoan life was, in a word, wrong. Citing research of his own going back to 1940, Freeman suggested that an inexperienced Mead, who was far from fluent in Samoan, had been taken in by fanciful tales told by her young informants. Samoa, he said, was never a "Shangri-La of Free Love." On the contrary, it had a well-developed cult of virginity that sternly forbid premarital sex. Rape, far from being unknown, was common. As you can imagine, Freeman's book caused a great stir among ethnographers. Where Mead had seen free love, placid emotions, and cooperation, Freeman saw adolescent stress, conflict, and jealousy. Scholars are still arguing about which description of Samoa is closest to the truth—or whether both may have captured a piece of it.

EXPERIMENTS

The **experiment** is the method of choice in scientific research, but only in the past few years has it come into its own in studies of human sexuality. In an experiment, the researcher systematically varies some factor of interest and studies how this variation affects people's behavior. Control over the variables in the study allows the researcher to trace sequences of events and draw conclusions about *cause and effect*.

Suppose, for example, that you wanted to know whether certain kinds of pornography can cause people to develop calloused attitudes about rape. In the real world, it would be hard to show a cause-and-effect relationship. Even if you found that people with calloused attitudes tended to have more experience than average with pornography, you would not know whether the pornography caused the attitudes or the attitudes led to increased use of pornography. An experiment, however, would allow you to *control* exposure to pornography, and thus draw conclusions about its effects on attitudes.

In one such study, researchers Edward Donnerstein, Leonard Berkowitz, and Daniel Linz showed men three different versions of a film. One version contained a scene of a woman being tied up, threatened with a gun, and raped. A second version left out the sexually explicit parts of the film and showed only the violent ones. A third version showed the sexual aspects of the rape scene, but not the violence. Then the researchers measured the men's attitudes about rape. The men who saw *only* the violence but not the explicit sex had the most callous attitudes. They were also most apt to indicate some likelihood of committing rape or using force themselves. Men who saw the sex but not the violence had the least callous attitudes and were least apt to indicate some likelihood of raping. Men who saw both sex and violence scored in between (cited in Donnerstein, Linz & Penrod, 1987). Together with many other studies, this research suggests that depictions of violence against women do not need to be sexually explicit to affect people's attitudes. It is violent imagery, rather than sexual explicitness *per se*, that contributes to acceptance of rape and violence toward women (see Chapter 16).

Sex researchers doing experiments face a number of special problems. Experiments sometimes involve deception; the researcher must disguise the real purpose of the study, because if the subjects knew the hypothesis, the experiment would be ruined. Many critics argue that such deception is unethical, because it deprives subjects of the right to give **informed consent** before they participate in the research. Also, experiments sometimes expose the participants to stress. (For example, some people might get upset when viewing violent or sexually explicit films.) Some critics object to stressful procedures on moral grounds, even when the subjects have been forewarned and have given informed consent.

In addition, most experiments are done in the laboratory, and the results may not be valid in real life. If we measure people's physiological responses to erotic films and books, for instance, we cannot know for sure that those responses would be the same while watching a pornographic videotape or reading a sexy novel at home. Finally, experimenters' results, like those of other researchers, can be skewed by poor sampling techniques and volunteer bias. Despite these drawbacks, however, the experiment is a powerful tool for understanding human behavior. It is becoming more and more common in sex research, as scientists move from describing sexual behavior to explaining its causes.

KEEPING NUMBERS IN THEIR PLACE

By now it should be obvious that no sexual statistic is etched in granite. A study may accurately describe only a restricted group of people. Also, times change and what was true ten or even five years ago may no longer be so true. Unfortunately, once a certain statistic becomes generally known (X percent of all women have multiple orgasms; Y percent of all married people have extramarital affairs), people begin to think that they ought to live up to the numbers, that statistics define what is normal or right for the sexually adjusted adult. Old restrictions collapse, but from their ashes rise phoenix-like new ones that can be every bit as coercive. The straight facts about sex, which are supposed to liberate people, can also terrify them.

Moreover, facts can mislead if they are not interpreted correctly. This is especially true of averages. An average is merely a number that summarizes a mass of data. The most commonly used average, the *arithmetic mean*, is computed by adding up all the scores or numbers in a set and dividing the sum by the number of quantities in the set. The arithmetic mean is very sensitive to extreme scores or numbers. Thus if you were computing the average frequency of sex for a group of twenty subjects, one unusual person having sex ten times a day could push the average much higher than it would otherwise be, and give a wrong impression of the group as a whole.

Even when there are no extreme scores, averages oversimplify, because they do not convey any information about variability among the people in the sample. (Statistics exist that do this, but they are hardly ever mentioned in nontechnical reports because they are hard for most people to understand.) Suppose we ask twenty people when they had their first experience with intercourse. Let's assume that all have had intercourse and that half say they were fifteen years old, while the other half say they were twenty. If we compute the average or mean age of first intercourse, we get a figure of 17.5, even though in our hypothetical sample *no one* has given that particular age in response to our question. Even when the data are not clustered in this way, the average can be deceiving. So we should keep in mind that the statistical average does not necessarily mean *typical* or *normal*.

Statistical findings called **correlations** can also be misleading. A correlation is a measure of how strongly two or more factors of interest are related to each other. For example, suppose a survey finds that the more education a woman has, the more orgasms she experiences. We would say that for women, education and the ability to have orgasms are correlated. It would be easy to conclude from this finding that education somehow increases a woman's ability to have orgasms. But in fact, the correlation tells us nothing at all about cause and effect. Highly educated women may simply have more sensitive lovers. Or the ability to have orgasms might be related to self-concept, and women with a positive self-concept might be the most likely to

Copyright 1981, Jules Feiffer. Reprinted with permission of Universal Press Syndicate. All rights reserved.

seek a higher education. Because correlations do not tell us about causation, we need to be very careful about interpreting survey results.

We need to keep in mind that all findings in science are tentative and that, in any case, questions of normality and satisfaction are basically subjective matters, not statistical ones. James Thurber and E. B. White made this point over half a century ago in a cheerfully wicked spoof of sex research entitled *Is Sex Necessary?*

> Sex is by no means everything. It varies, as a matter of fact, from only as high as 78 percent of everything to as low as 3.10 percent. The norm, in a sane, healthy person, should be between 18 and 24 percent. In these hectic days, however, it is not unusual to hear even intelligent persons say, or imply, that sex is everything. This, of course, leads to the mistaken idea that a couple who are, so to speak, emotionally compatible are

going to be compatible in every other way. "Take care of sex, and the details will look after themselves," is the rule. Nothing could be more stupid. A man and woman may be very, very happy emotionally and not get anywhere at all. (1957, p 140.)

• •

PERSONAL PERSPECTIVE

A CONSUMER'S GUIDE TO SEX QUIZZES

It is easy to mistake a phony sex quiz or a limited sex survey for science, and be intimidated by the results. Consider a widely-publicized report from a *Ladies Home Journal* survey a few years back, that the average American wife makes love with her husband three to five times a week. Lots of women—and men, too—must have felt pretty inadequate when they read that, not realizing that the question had been poorly worded or that the women who answered were not necessarily typical (or truthful).

Quizzes can be just as intimidating. Some questionnaires in the popular media are legitimate, but many are merely lists of questions thought up by a journalist on a rainy day. Recently we came across a particularly obvious example in the "style" section of our local newspaper—a "sex IQ" test (Goulart, 1987). "Don't be a dummy in bed," it exhorted. That challenge was followed by twenty-four multiple choice items that promised to measure the reader's "sex smarts." But like many other newspaper and magazine quizzes, the test actually revealed nothing about the test taker's sexual knowledge, satisfaction, or prospects.

It is hard to resist a sex quiz. They can be fun. But next time you try one, separate entertainment from information by asking some hard questions of your own. For example:

WHERE DID THE ANSWERS COME FROM?   Answers to quiz questions are not trustworthy unless they are based on strong empirical evidence from reputable sources. The "sex IQ" quiz in our paper prefaced its answers with the headline, "Scientists Reveal the Facts of Love," and claimed the answers were based on information supplied by a well-known sex therapist, two sexual dysfunction clinics, and a study by two sociologists. However, there was no way for the reader to know which answers came from which source. In the few cases where a specific source was mentioned in an answer, it was either vague ("a 1984 survey by a leading women's magazine," or suspicious (the author of a book on "foods for love"). You should not be satisfied with this sort of "evidence."

HOW WERE STATISTICS COMPUTED?   Anyone can bandy numbers about, but the numbers may be meaningless. Our sex-quiz writer claimed that "ninety-eight percent of us—men and women—rate sex as essential," but did not say where she pulled that figure from. It might have been thin air. She also mentioned a "finding," from a magazine survey, that 95 percent of married women initiate lovemaking. But how often? Three times a day? Once a month? Once every ten years? Were the women who answered the magazine survey necessarily representative of the entire female population?

WHAT DO THE ITEMS MEASURE?   Our quiz promised to test our "sex IQ" on the assumption that "the more you know, the better it [sex] gets." But the questions actually had little bearing on sexual satisfaction, and many were downright silly. Some examples:

1. Sexual intercourse burns as many calories per minute as: a) belly dancing; b) shoveling light snow; c) both

2. What is rush hour in a house of ill-repute?

3. Which beauty had ribs removed to give her a sexier waist-line? a) Raquel Welch; b) Jane Fonda; c) Sophia Loren; d) Farrah Fawcett

(We know you are dying for the "answers," so here they are: 1 c. The author claims that belly dancing, snow shoveling, and sex all burn 8 calories per minute, but she cites no reference, and makes no distinction between languid sex and encounters of the more vigorous kind. 2. Rush hour is supposedly 3 to 4 in the afternoon. The source: Xaviera Hollander, a "madam" and author of *The Happy Hooker*. 3 a. According to the quiz writer, Ms. Welch was deribbed, but there is no reference for this contribution to sexual scholarship.)

HOW ARE THE QUESTIONS WORDED?   Watch out for leading questions that push you into certain assumptions. Beware, too, of questions that are open to interpretations. For example, our quiz asked: "Eighty-two percent of American women are happy in bed. True or False?" But what does "happy in bed" mean? Supremely attracted to one's partner? Orgasmic? Satisfied with one's performance or ability to please? Able to sleep soundly?

HOW GRANDIOSE ARE THE CLAIMS?   Overblown, sensationalized claims are more attention-grabbing and circulation-boosting than carefully qualified ones, but they are untrustworthy. For instance, the claim that ninety-eight percent of all Americans rate sex as essential is implausible on the face of it, because such unanimity almost never occurs in a heterogeneous culture. The strongest, most reliable generalizations are apt to apply only to certain individuals, depending on such factors as age, gender, education, and ethnic or national identity.

Sexual statistics can be seductive. But "findings" based on unscientific surveys and quizzes produce only what one researcher has aptly called fake knowledge, or "fakelore" (Gagnon, 1989). Let the consumer beware!

IN BRIEF

1. Although books and articles on human sexuality are plentiful, many works claiming to be scientific give inaccurate or unsubstantiated information. To evaluate findings about sexuality, readers need to be familiar with methods used to carry out sex research.

2. Case studies (a) provide detailed information about individuals, (b) often enable researchers to notice subtle aspects of personality and behavior that are missed by other methods, and (c) sometimes make it possible to study phenomena that cannot be examined experimentally because of practical or ethical obstacles. However the persons studied may not be typical of other people and the interpretation of cases is quite subjective. Havelock Ellis and Sigmund Freud are two important researchers who depended primarily on case histories for their data.

3. Surveys are carried out by interviewing people or having them complete questionnaires. Surveys allow researchers to get information on the general characteristics of a given population. The validity of survey findings depends on how the sample of subjects was selected; ideally, there should be a probability sample that is representative of the larger population from which it was drawn. Problems inherent in the survey method include the following: (a) subjects may not tell the truth; (b) memory may be inaccurate; (c) the information that results may be superficial; and (d) survey results may be open to interpretation. Dependence on volunteers introduces the possibility of volunteer bias.

4. The best-known and most comprehensive sex survey was carried out by Alfred Kinsey and his associates, who interviewed eighteen thousand people and reported data on twelve thousand. Kinsey's work suffers from certain statistical inadequacies but is generally regarded as a milestone in sex research and a useful source of information about sexuality.

5. Several large- and small-scale sex surveys have followed Kinsey's. The Playboy survey, commissioned by the Playboy Foundation and reported by writer Morton Hunt, covered roughly the same topics that Kinsey did and offers an opportunity to look at changes that took place in sexual behavior in America between the 1940s and the 1970s. Two surveys conducted by Shere Hite have severe methodological problems, but are useful because they examined in detail how women and men perform certain sexual acts and what they like and dislike about sex.

6. Laboratory observations provide an effective way to gather data on the physiology of sex. This approach is exemplified by the work of William Masters and Virginia Johnson. Although Masters and Johnson's sample was not representative of the American population as a whole, their

work is the source of much of what is now known about sexual physiology. However, many unanswered questions remain.

7. Clinical evaluation studies measure the success or failure of treatment or therapy techniques. The best ones involve controlled comparisons between people who received a particular treatment and people who did not. Masters and Johnson are well-known not only for their physiological work but for their evaluation studies.

8. Ethnographic studies describe an entire subculture or society. Sometimes ethnographers become participant-observers. Formal measures of behavior may or may not be used. When they are not, different observers may come to different conclusions.

9. Experiments permit researchers to vary some factor of interest systematically to see how it affects behavior. Control over the variables in an experiment allows a researcher to draw conclusions about cause and effect. Like any research method, the experiment has some drawbacks, but it is a powerful research tool and is becoming more common in sex research.

10. We need to be careful about the numerical findings produced by sex research. They may not apply to all groups of people, and they can change over time. They can mislead if they are not interpreted carefully. Most important, they do not necessarily define what is normal, right, or satisfying.

Key Terms

empirical evidence *(67)*

replicate *(67)*

case study *(68)*

Havelock Ellis *(69)*

Sigmund Freud *(70)*

psychoanalysis *(70)*

survey *(72)*

representative sample *(72)*

population *(72)*

probability sample *(72)*

random sample *(72)*

volunteer bias *(73)*

Alfred Kinsey *(74)*

"100% sampling" *(79)*

Playboy study *(80)*

Hite report *(82)*

laboratory observation *(83)*

William Masters and Virginia Johnson *(84)*

clinical evaluation study *(87)*

ethnographic study *(87)*

participant-observer *(88)*

experiment *(88)*

informed consent *(89)*

correlations *(90)*

The Psychobiology of Sex

**CHAPTER
FOUR**

C H A P T E R   F O U R

■

The Sexual Body

●

For all the talk about sex, many people still feel uncomfortable about the physical apparatus required for it. American parents give their children dolls whose external genitals are conspicuously absent. Many women and some men who have been sexually active for years cannot bring themselves to look unblushingly at their own genitals. People who want to talk frankly about the sex organs find themselves using euphemisms like "private parts," "down there," and "you-know-where." You'd think we would all feel kindly toward the organs of the human body that afford us the pleasures of passion and physical intimacy, but for many they remain virtually uncharted territory.

Because human beings have feelings about their bodies, both positive and negative, sexual anatomy and the psychology of sex are inseparable. This does not mean that you have to be a medical authority on the structure of the penis or the anatomy of the vagina to enjoy yourself in bed. You can appreciate a good meal without knowing much about the stomach; you can jog a couple of miles before breakfast without understanding the structure of the foot; and you certainly can engage in sex without knowing the Latin name for each and every sexual part. Still, a general knowledge of sexual anatomy and an acceptance of the sex organs probably facilitates communication and forms the foundation of honest and spontaneous sexual expression.

Getting rid of negative feelings is easier said than done because these attitudes usually originate early in life. Many parents discourage their children in one way or another from exploring their own bodies. A woman now in her late thirties recalled:

Love's mysteries in souls do grow, but yet the body is his book.

John Donne

> When I was a little girl my mother instructed me to wash myself "down there" with a special washcloth. Then I had to hang the cloth on a hook below the bathroom sink. Later, when I was not around, my mother would come in to remove the cloth by lifting it off the hook with a long stick. (authors' files)

Even if a parent never actually says that the genitals are disgusting, the look on the parent's face when a child touches the genitals, accompanied by a terse order to "stop doing that," is sufficient to get the message across. No wonder so many of us go about wearing an imaginary fig leaf.

Feelings about the genitals may also be conditioned by cultural attitudes toward urinating and defecating. In males the opening at the end of the penis is the outlet for both urine and semen. In the women the opening for urine is separate from the vaginal opening but near it. In both sexes the external genitals are located just up the road from the anus. Although in many societies urinating and defecating by children is taken in stride, in our society children know by the age of two or three that to make "pee-pee" or "poo-poo" anywhere but in the toilet is to dirty themselves. By extension, anything south of the navel and north of the thighs becomes dirty, smelly, and disgusting—a case of guilt by association.

People of both sexes are more likely to be repelled by the female than the male genitals; photographs of penises may produce giggles, but they do not usually evoke the discomfort that pictures of female genitals do. Part of the reason may be relative unfamiliarity with the female genitals, which, unlike the male's, are tucked away where they can be missed unless one makes a special attempt to see them. Greater familiarity might breed increased acceptance. Feelings of repugnance toward the female genitals may also be associated with negative feelings about menstruation, normal vaginal secretions, and the moistness of the delicate female tissues. Our culture seems inordinately uncomfortable with bodily wetness of any kind.

As you can see in Figures 4–1 and 4–2, sex organs vary considerably in size and shape. They also differ in position, color, and sensitivity. Indeed,

FIGURE 4–1
Variations in the female external genitals These illustrations represent three possible variations in the appearance of the vulva, but there are many others.

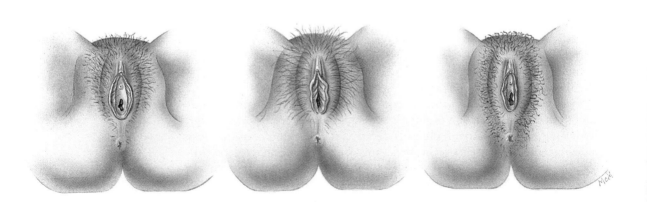

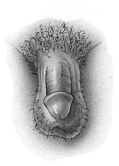 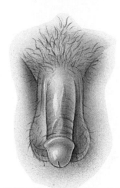 

FIGURE 4–2
Variations in the male external genitals The penis and the scrotum can vary greatly in size, shape, and color. Variations also exist in the angle of the penis when it is erect. The penis shown on the right is uncircumcised.

they are no more alike than are people's ears, noses, or feet. You may find that looking at drawings or photographs of other people's genitals is a good first step in learning about sexual anatomy, but to get to know what your own organs or those of a partner are like, you have to look. (To maximize the benefits of self-examination, see the Personal Perspective at the end of this chapter. Sexual health is covered in Chapter 18.)

In this chapter we turn first to a description of the main sexual and reproductive organs. Then we will consider some nongenital areas of the body that are sexually sensitive. Finally, we will take a brief look at the most important "sex organ" of all—the brain.

WOMEN'S GENITALS

Technically the word **genitals** applies both to internal and external sexual and reproductive organs, but in practice most people use the term to refer only to external ones. In females the external genitals are known collectively as the **vulva**, from the Latin for "covering." In medical texts, the vulva has sometimes been called the *pudendum*, from the Latin for "thing of shame"—a reflection of historical attitudes toward women's bodies (see Chapter 2). In many cultures, the vulva has been subject to ritual mutilation—without benefit of anesthesia. Even today, it is the practice in some parts of Africa, Asia, and the Middle East to remove the clitoris and/or to cut and sew up the outer lips of the vulva, leaving only a small opening for the passage of urine and the menstrual flow. Such procedures, which are performed for a variety of religious and cultural reasons, often cause serious medical and sexual problems, including hemorrhaging and infections that are sometimes fatal. In women who have undergone mutilation, severe pain during intercourse is common, and a large number never experience sexual desire or orgasm (Lightfoot-Klein, 1989).

In Western cultures, the vulva has often been described as "mysterious," for reasons that are not clear. Some people say it is because most parts of the vulva are hard to see, but then so are the tonsils, and nobody ever calls them mysterious. As we discuss the various parts of the woman's genitals, you may wish to refer to Figure 4–3.

FIGURE 4–3
External structures of the vulva This drawing illustrates the female genital structures that are visible when the major lips are parted. But no vulva looks exactly like this; the drawing is a kind of composite or average.

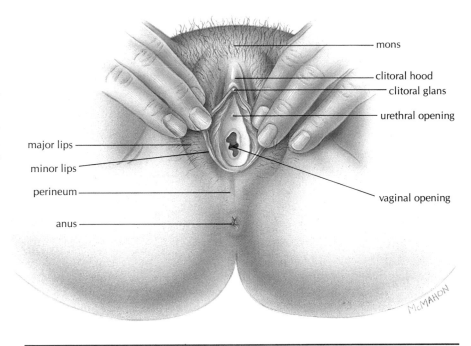

mons

clitoral hood

clitoral glans

urethral opening

major lips

minor lips

perineum

anus

vaginal opening

The Mons

When a woman stands upright with her legs together, the only part of her sexual anatomy that is visible, aside from her breasts, is a soft cushion of fatty tissue called the **mons pubis** or, more romantically, the *mons veneris*—the mount of Venus. This cushion lies about six inches below the navel and is covered with pubic hair. The hair may be sparse or thick, dark or light, long or short. Beneath the mons one can feel the pubic bone. The mons area contains many pressure receptors and is sexually quite sensitive.

The Major Lips

When a woman is sitting on the floor with her legs slightly spread, the **major lips,** or **labia majora,** also become visible. These are two fatty folds of skin that extend downward from the mons. Usually they meet to form a midline, but in women who have given birth, they may not. The skin on the outer surfaces of the major lips is darker than surrounding skin and is covered by pubic hair. The skin on the inner surfaces is smooth and hairless. Toward the **anus** (the opening to the *rectum*, or lower part of the intestine), the lips flatten out until they are no longer distinguishable from the muscular tissue—the sexually sensitive **perineum**—that separates the anus from the lower part of the vulva. The major lips provide protection for the vaginal opening and other delicate parts of the vulva. They are sexually sensitive, but usually not as sensitive as the minor lips and other underlying structures.

The Minor Lips

When the major lips are parted, another pair of skin folds, the **minor lips,** or **labia minora,** are visible. (In some women they are fairly long and hang below the outer lips.) The minor lips are moist, pinkish in color, and hairless. Sexually, they are very sensitive. Masters and Johnson call the minor lips the "sex skin" because during sexual arousal they swell and change color dramatically, becoming much darker.

On the inner surface of the minor lips, where they cannot be seen, are the outlets for two small glands, the **Bartholin's glands.** For many years physiologists thought the Bartholin's glands secreted a fluid that lubricated the opening of the vagina and made insertion of the penis easier during intercourse. Masters and Johnson (1966) proved this assumption wrong. The vagina does become wet during sexual arousal, but, as we will see in Chapter 5, the lubricant comes from blood vessels behind the vaginal walls, not from the Bartholin's glands. During sexual arousal the glands secrete only two to four drops of fluid, not nearly enough to provide effective lubrication. The fluid from the glands may produce a hospitable environment for sperm by reducing the acidity of the vagina (sperm do not do well if it is too acidic), but again, the quantity secreted seems insufficient to do the job. The function of the Bartholin's glands, like that of the appendix, remains a mystery.

The Urethral Opening

Toward the upper end of the minor lips, above the entrance to the vagina and below the clitoris, is a tiny slit-shaped opening through which urine passes. This urethral opening is so small that sometimes even doctors have a hard time finding it. A short tube, the **urethra,** runs from the bladder in the abdomen to the urethral opening. The urethral opening plays a role in *cystitis,* an infection of the bladder (see Chapter 18).

The Clitoris

Above the urethral opening, just below the mons area, is the **clitoris** (usually pronounced with the first syllable stressed, but sometimes with the second). The clitoris is cylindrical in shape, like the penis, but usually the only part that is visible is the smooth, round tip, or *glans.* In most women the glans looks like a small bump peeping out from beneath a fleshy hood of skin formed where the two minor lips join together near the mons. During sexual arousal, the clitoris swells, though it does not stand away from the body the way the penis does. But "at rest," it is sometimes hard to find. To see the glans, it may be necessary to pull the hood back a bit. If it still cannot be seen, it can easily be located by touch, because of its extreme sensitivity. The rest of the clitoral body consists of a *shaft* containing two tunnels of spongy tissue that fill with blood during sexual arousal (see Figure 4–4). The shaft remains hidden from view but can be felt beneath the clitoral hood.

At first glance, the size of the clitoris may seem unimpressive; it varies from about a quarter of an inch to an inch in length. But looks can be deceiving. Below the clitoral body itself there is additional erectile tissue that cannot be seen from outside. Indeed, the clitoral body—glans and shaft—is actually only the tip of an erogenous iceberg. At its base the clitoral shaft divides into two parts called *crura* (from the Latin for "legs"), which spread out like the sides of a wishbone. Each *crus* is about three inches long and is attached to the pelvic bone. The crura get engorged with blood during sexual arousal and double or triple in size. Erectile tissue also exists in the form of two **vestibular bulbs,** which lie beneath the minor lips on each side of the vaginal opening.

The clitoris is by far the most sensitive part of a woman's genitals. The glans especially is crowded with nerve endings—possibly as many as in the much larger penis. It is so sensitive that women often do not want to have it touched directly. Instead they prefer stimulation of the mons area or the major lips, which indirectly stimulates the clitoris lying beneath. Masters and Johnson (1966) maintain that no matter what excites a woman sexually—an erotic novel, sexual intercourse, breast stimulation, sexual fantasy—the clitoris is the main subjective focus of arousal, just as the penis is for a man. Most other sexologists agree. However, not all women are dependent on stimulation of the clitoral body for sexual arousal. Some women who undergo removal of the clitoral body (*clitoridectomy*) continue to experience arousal

FIGURE 4–4
Underlying structures of the vulva   In this drawing you can see parts of the female external genitals that lie hidden beneath the major and minor lips and the clitoral hood. Note that the clitoral glans and shaft comprise only a small part of the total volume of erectile tissue; the rest consists of the clitoral crura and the vestibular bulbs.

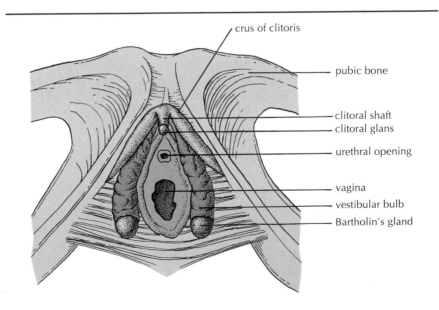

crus of clitoris
pubic bone
clitoral shaft
clitoral glans
urethral opening
vagina
vestibular bulb
Bartholin's gland

and even orgasm, perhaps because the clitoral tissue underlying the shaft remains. Moreover, as we will see in Chapter 5, recent research suggests that there is considerable variability among women both in erogenous zones and subjective experience during sex. The clitoral glans is the most sensitive part of a woman's genitals, but it is not the only sensitive part.

The importance of the clitoris has been recognized for ages. A sex manual of the eighteenth century advised men to pay attention to the clitoris so that their partners would experience greater satisfaction. Yet, if you try to think of slang expressions for the clitoris, chances are you will come up with fewer than you can for the vagina or the penis, if any at all. Even the most liberal parents usually neglect to tell their children about the clitoris (see Chapter 12). Some women, ignorant of its existence, have mistaken it for a tumor or growth. Informal surveys in our classes find that some students, male and female, have only a vague idea of where and what the clitoris is. They may wrongly locate it inside the vagina or just outside the vagina (it is actually closer to the mons than the vagina). A few confuse it with the inner lips or think it is an extension or covering of the vagina. In one class survey, many students said they had not learned the word *clitoris* until after high school.

It may be anxiety-arousing for people to talk about an organ that, unlike the penis or vagina, has no direct reproductive or other nonsexual function. The clitoris and the vestibular bulbs are the only organs in the human body whose sole function is to contribute to sexual arousal.

The Vaginal Opening

The vaginal opening is sometimes called the *introitus* (Latin for "entrance"). Some people seem to think of this opening as a gaping hole. Actually, it is not visible at all unless you spread the minor lips apart, and even then it is usually kept partially closed by a ring of muscles. If a woman is extremely nervous, she may involuntarily contract these muscles, making it difficult to insert anything into the vagina. That is one reason why girls sometimes have a hard time inserting a tampon.

If a woman has never had intercourse, the vaginal opening may be partially covered by a membrane called the **hymen.** (Some say the Greek god of marriage, Hymen, took his name from the hymen; others say it is the other way around.) As Figure 4–5 illustrates, hymens come in many forms. The opening is usually large enough for a finger or tampon to pass through easily. Sperm can also pass through, if they are deposited on the vulval lips. So, while the odds are slim, a woman who is "technically" a virgin can become pregnant.

Throughout history the hymen has been a symbol of purity and chastity. Some societies, such as the Biblical Hebrews, allowed a husband to divorce his bride forthwith, or even put her to death, if she came to the marriage bed hymenless. We now know that this was not only cruel but unfair

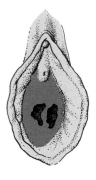

septate (divided)

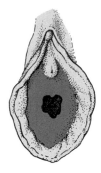

annular (ringlike)

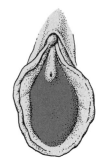

imperforate (no opening)

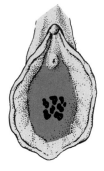

cribriform (sievelike)

FIGURE 4–5
Different types of hymens Hymens, like other genital structures, vary in appearance from woman to woman. The imperforate hymen, which completely seals off the vaginal opening, is a relatively rare variation. It often escapes notice until a girl past puberty fails to menstruate. A doctor then ruptures the hymen so the menstrual material can pass normally.

because not all virgins have an intact hymen. Often the membrane is thin enough to be ruptured inadvertently by a tampon, finger, or even active exercise. Many women who expect a painful "deflowering" are pleasantly surprised to find that the flower has already been plucked. If the hymen is not ruptured or stretched until the first intercourse, the woman may experience a little pain, especially if she is tense. The rupture may also be painful if the hymen is relatively thick and does not break or stretch easily. The pain can be avoided by having a physician rupture the hymen during an office visit or by stretching the hymen oneself with the fingers.

The hymen apparently exists only in the human female. Several writers have speculated about the reasons for its development, but none of these speculations is generally accepted. Despite all the fuss made over this little bit of tissue, no one really knows what its biological purpose is.

WOMEN'S INTERNAL SEX ORGANS

The internal sex organs in women include the vagina, the cervix, the uterus, the ovaries, and the Fallopian tubes. Figures 4–6 and 4–7 show these and other internal structures.

The Vagina

The **vagina** is a narrow, flexible canal that has several functions. It receives the penis during vaginal intercourse; the fetus passes through it during childbirth; and menstrual fluid exits through it during menstruation. Just as people tend to think of the vaginal opening as a gaping hole, they often imagine the vagina itself as a vast interior space filling up a woman's entire lower abdomen. Innumerable bad jokes about the vagina reflect a pervasive fear about its size. Some refer to getting lost in the vagina, like Alice in the rabbit's hole, others to vaginas that swallow up whole farms and villages, like some sinister monster in a grade-B science fiction film. There are also jokes about vaginas that are too tight.

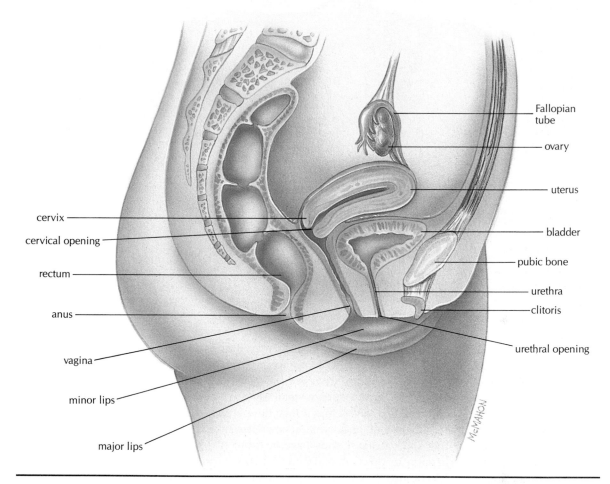

cervix

cervical opening

rectum

anus

vagina

minor lips

major lips

Fallopian tube

ovary

uterus

bladder

pubic bone

urethra

clitoris

urethral opening

McMAHON

Worries about huge vaginas are not based on anatomical fact. The word *vagina* comes from the Latin for "sheath," and it seems a good choice. When a woman is not sexually aroused, the walls of her vagina are collapsed and touching. In other words, the interior of the vagina is a potential, rather than an actual, space. If you insert a finger into the vagina you find that the walls expand just enough to accommodate it, enclosing the finger snugly. This is true even if, as occasionally happens, the muscles behind the vaginal walls are so stretched or torn by childbirth that they do not actively grip a penis as tightly as they once did. Of course, diagrams and illustrations have to show some space so you can see where the vagina is located, but they are all technically inaccurate. During sexual arousal, the interior part of the vagina does expand, but the walls surrounding the lower part of the passageway get engorged and swollen, so that there is a snug fit around the penis during intercourse.

The vagina also cannot be too tight for intercourse. The vagina is an amazingly flexible organ; after all, most of us once passed through it. As long

FIGURE 4–6
Female internal sexual and reproductive organs, cross-section The anatomy shown here is that of a relatively young woman. Among the changes that take place with age are a smoothing of the vaginal walls.

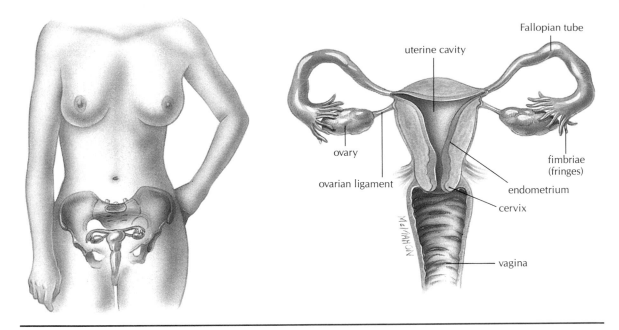

FIGURE 4–7

Female internal sexual and reproductive organs, front view   The drawing on the left shows the location of the sexual and reproductive organs within the body. In the schematic illustration on the right, the vagina, the uterus, and the cervix are shown in cross-section.

as it is well lubricated, the smallest vagina is roomy enough for the largest penis, especially if adjustments in position are made to avoid very deep penetration. When insertion is difficult it is usually because of inadequate lubrication or because the woman is tense and the muscles surrounding the entrance are contracting. Once the penis is in the vagina, it does not have to stay there any longer than its owner wants it to. Some men worry about getting stuck because they have heard of this happening to male dogs. It does happen to dogs. A male dog's penis is not fully erect when it enters the female dog's vagina. Glands on the side of the penis swell after insertion, and the male remains "stuck" until he is completely through ejaculating and loses his erection. In one study beagles stayed locked together an average of fourteen minutes (Hart, 1978). But fortunately for all of us, a human male's penis does not behave at all like a dog's.

In the unexcited state the vagina measures about three to five inches in length. It slants toward the small of the back at about a forty-five degree angle to the floor when the woman is standing. The walls of the vagina are lined with a moist, soft mucous membrane, like the inside of the mouth. Their wetness depends on whether or not a woman is sexually aroused and what stage she is at in her menstrual cycle. All women produce vaginal secretions that are either transparent or slightly milky in color. The amount varies considerably from woman to woman. Vaginal fluids are salty, and if a woman is free of vaginal infection and maintains good hygiene, they have a slight musky smell. The secretions, which have a cleansing effect, consist of mucus from glands in the cervix and moisture from the vaginal walls. They also contain cells that are continually being shed from the vaginal lining.

Harmless bacteria in the vagina help decompose these cells. In the process they produce lactic acid, which destroys potentially harmful bacteria. Frequent *douching* (washing out the vagina with water or some other liquid) can remove the good bacteria, alter the acidity of the vagina, and create conditions that foster vaginal infection. And feminine hygiene sprays, which are supposed to cover up natural vaginal odors, can cause irritation, inflammation, and infection. Acceptance of female secretions and scents makes such products totally unnecessary.

The walls of the vagina are rather wrinkled in premenopausal woman. After menopause, in a reversal of what happens to most skin of the body, they become smoother as well as thinner. Behind the walls there is a ring of muscle tissue called the **pubococcygeus (PC) muscle.** If a woman inserts a finger into the vagina and then contracts her muscles the way she would to hold in urine, she can feel the pubococcygeus muscle. Some sex therapists believe that learning to control this muscle through daily exercise increases a woman's subjective enjoyment of sex and the likelihood of being orgasmic but most studies have failed to confirm these benefits (see Chapter 11).

The lower third of the vagina is quite sensitive in many women, though usually not nearly as sensitive as the clitoris. As we saw in Chapter 3, a few researchers have reported that some women have an especially sensitive spot in or behind the anterior wall of the lower vagina (at the front in a standing woman). However, the anatomical nature of this "Grafenberg spot" has not yet been determined, and its very existence is a matter of controversy. We will return to this matter once again in the next chapter.

The rest of the vagina contains relatively few nerve endings, and if something makes light contact with the walls—for example, a tampon—a woman does not feel it. In fact, the upper or innermost part of the vagina is so insensitive to touch that sometimes doctors can perform minor surgery on it without giving an anesthetic. However, it is sensitive to stretch and pressure, and women's subjective reports about feelings inside the vagina during intercourse vary a great deal.

The Cervix

If you insert a finger deep into the vagina, toward the back you may be able to locate a bump that feels something like the end of the nose. This is the **cervix,** which is simply the lower part, or neck, of the uterus extending into the vagina. As you can see from Figure 4–6, the cervix is not quite at the back of the vagina. In the center of the cervix is a tiny opening about the size of a pencil lead. It is too small for a tampon or finger to pass through, but large enough for bacteria and sperm. Mucus from the interior of the uterus exits through the opening and becomes part of the vaginal discharge.

Like the innermost part of the vagina, the cervix is not very sensitive. Doctors can usually cauterize an eroded cervix (one with sores on the surface) without giving an anesthetic. But like the vaginal walls, the cervix does have pressure receptors, and it is probably more variable in sensitivity, at least to pressure, than is commonly thought. During intercourse, some positions allow the penis to come into contact with the cervix.

The Uterus

The **uterus,** or womb, receives a fertilized egg and becomes home to a developing fetus during the nine months of pregnancy. As you can see in the accompanying drawings, the uterus looks something like a small inverted pear and is located behind the vagina, between the bladder and the rectum. Although the uterus is often described as hollow, if a woman is not pregnant and is not using an intrauterine birth control device, the walls of the uterus stay close together, just like the walls of the vagina. Usually, the uterus tilts forward, held in place by various ligaments loosely enough so that it can shift position during sexual activity. In some women it tilts backward. A "tipped" uterus does not affect fertility.

The walls of the uterus are thick and contain extremely powerful muscles—the better to expel a baby with. These walls have a delicate mucous membrane lining, the **endometrium,** which is richly supplied with blood vessels. In pregnancy the fertilized egg embeds itself into this tissue. Otherwise, about once a month, the lining partially sloughs off and exits through the vaginal opening as menstrual fluid. After menstruation the uterine lining gradually renews itself. Menstruation, conception, and pregnancy are all described more fully in Chapter 6.

The Ovaries

The **ovaries** are small organs about the size and shape of unshelled walnuts, lying on either side of the uterus and connected to it by ligaments. Like the testes, they are **gonads:** glands that produce cells that are able to unite with other cells to start a new organism. In women the reproductive cells are called *ova*, or "eggs." The ovaries also produce the hormones *estrogen* and *progesterone*.

When a female is born, her ovaries contain all the eggs she will ever have (some 400,000 of them), but they are not mature. After puberty eggs mature at the rate of one every twenty-eight days or so. The mature egg pops out of the capsule in which it is housed, on the surface of the ovary, and for a brief time simply floats free. For some eggs, that may be the end of the line. Most, however, soon find what they are looking for: one of the Fallopian tubes.

The Fallopian Tubes

The **Fallopian tubes** are oddly shaped ducts whose appearance has been compared to rams' horns, saxophones, and funnels. Like the ovaries, they are attached to the uterus on either side. Since an egg can float but not swim, and since the Fallopian tubes are not attached to the ovaries (see Figures 4–6 and 4–7), no one is quite sure how an egg ever finds its way into a tube. One likely explanation: the ends of the tubes are fringed, and as they move, they make waves in the abdominal fluid that draw the egg in, like some predatory South African flower entrapping an unsuspecting fly. Once inside, it takes a few days for the egg to travel down the four-inch tube to the tiny opening that leads from the tube to the uterus. Fertilization, if it occurs, takes place in the Fallopian tube.

MEN'S GENITALS

We hear all the time that a male's sexual anatomy, compared to a female's, is simpler and more straightforward. As therapist Bernie Zilbergeld puts it, "A man's sexuality is [thought to be] concentrated in one place and there it is, hanging out for all the world to see" (Zilbergeld, 1978). In truth, a male's sexuality is physically every bit as complicated as a female's. There are as many male as female organs, and their structure is equally complex.

In fact, many female and male organs are **homologous**—that is, they develop from the same embryonic tissue (see Table 4–1). Until an embryo is about six weeks old, there is no way to tell whether it will become male or female without examining the chromosomes in its cells. Each embryo contains (a) two undifferentiated gonads that develop into either testes or ovaries; (b) a rounded projection of tissue that develops into either male or female external genitals; and (c) two sets of ducts, one that develops into the

• •

Members of each pair of organs on this list develop from the same embryonic tissue. They are similar in structure and, in some cases, function.

TABLE 4–1
Homologous sexual organs

Male	Female
testes	ovaries
glans of penis	glans of clitoris
spongy body of penis	vestibular bulbs (possibly)
penile shaft	clitoral shaft
foreskin of penis	hood of clitoris
underside of penile shaft	minor lips
scrotum	major lips
prostate gland	Skene's ducts
Cowper's glands	Bartholin's glands

FIGURE 4–8
Prenatal differentia-
tion of the male and
female internal sexual
organs This schematic
drawing shows two
stages in the
differentiation of the
internal duct systems of
male and female fetuses.
In genetic males, the
Wolffian ducts become
the vas deferens, the
epididymis, and the
seminal vesicles. In
genetic females, the
Müllerian ducts become
the Fallopian tubes, the
uterus, and the inner
two-thirds of the vagina.
Internal sexual structures
form during the second
and third month of fetal
development.

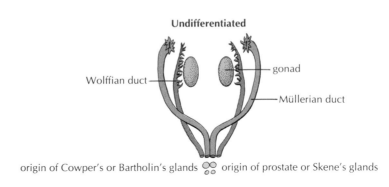

Undifferentiated

Wolffian duct — gonad — Müllerian duct

origin of Cowper's or Bartholin's glands   origin of prostate or Skene's glands

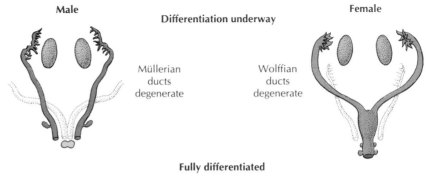

Male

Differentiation underway

Female

Müllerian ducts degenerate

Wolffian ducts degenerate

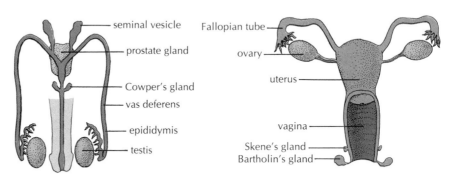

Fully differentiated

seminal vesicle
prostate gland
Cowper's gland
vas deferens
epididymis
testis

Fallopian tube
ovary
uterus
vagina
Skene's gland
Bartholin's gland

internal structures appropriate to the embryo's genetic sex and another that
eventually degenerates (see Figures 4–8 and 4–9). The development of
male or female sex organs depends on the presence or absence of the hormone testosterone, which the gonadal tissues in male embryos begin to
secrete at about the sixth week of development. If testosterone is present,
the embryo will become anatomically male in appearance; if it is absent, the
embryo will become anatomically female. We will discuss sexual differentiation further in Chapter 12.

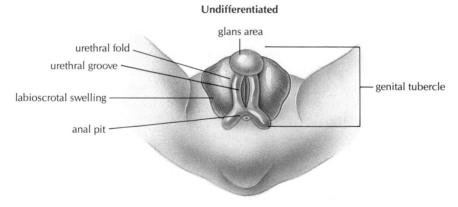

Undifferentiated

glans area

urethral fold

urethral groove

labioscrotal swelling

anal pit

genital tubercle

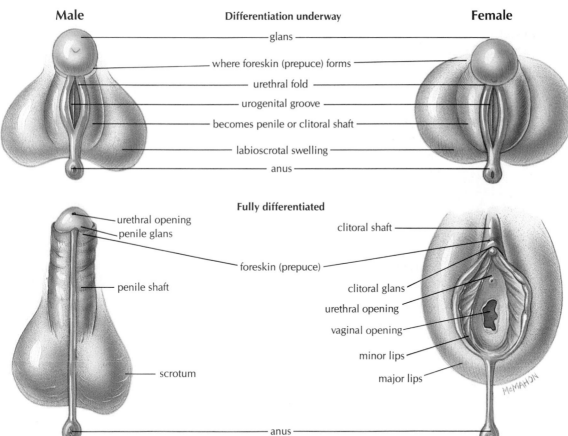

Male

Differentiation underway

Female

glans

where foreskin (prepuce) forms

urethral fold

urogenital groove

becomes penile or clitoral shaft

labioscrotal swelling

anus

Fully differentiated

urethral opening

penile glans

foreskin (prepuce)

penile shaft

scrotum

clitoral shaft

clitoral glans

urethral opening

vaginal opening

minor lips

major lips

anus

FIGURE 4–9

Prenatal differentiation of the male and female external genitals   This schematic drawing shows two stages of change in male and female fetuses as the genital tubercle develops into fully differentiated external organs. The external organs form a month or two after the internal ones.

The Penis

The **penis,** the most sexually sensitive part of a male's sexual anatomy, is the organ through which both urine and semen leave the body. Like the clitoris, it consists of a *shaft* and a *glans*. As you can see in Figure 4–10, the shaft is covered by loose, hairless skin. This skin contains so many blood vessels that sometimes the penis has a slightly bluish cast when erect. The glans is the smooth tip, or head, of the penis. Its name in Latin means "acorn," and, with its small fissure at the very end, that is a little what it looks like. If a man has not been circumcised, a fold of skin called the **foreskin,** or *prepuce,* extends from the shaft and covers or partially covers the glans, and you have to pull it back to see the entire glans. **Circumcision** surgically removes the foreskin, leaving the glans permanently exposed. (Box 4–1 discusses the controversy surrounding this operation.) The glans is crowded with nerve endings and in most men is far more sensitive than the shaft. Two areas are especially sensitive: the **frenulum** (or *frenum*), a thin strip of skin connecting the glans to the shaft, and the **corona** (crown), a ridge that slightly overhangs the shaft.

The penis extends deep into the body, almost to the rectum. You can feel this part during an erection by pressing your fingers up into the area behind the scrotum. It is called the base, or root, of the penis and is surrounded by the same kinds of muscles that encircle the lower part of the vagina in women. *Crura* at the base of the penis connect to the pelvic bone, just as they do in the clitoris.

Muscles at the base of the penis help to eject semen and urine, but they do not produce an erection. A man may be able to jerk his penis slightly, using these muscles, but he cannot call his penis to attention voluntarily because the penis itself has no muscles capable of accomplishing the task, nor does the penis contain a bone. Instead of muscle or bone, inside the penis there are three chambers of spongy tissue (see Figure 4–11). The two larger ones are called the **cavernous bodies,** or **corpora cavernosa,** and are

FIGURE 4–10

External structure of the penis   This drawing illustrates the structures that are visible in an uncircumcised man, with the foreskin pulled back. In circumcision the foreskin is removed.

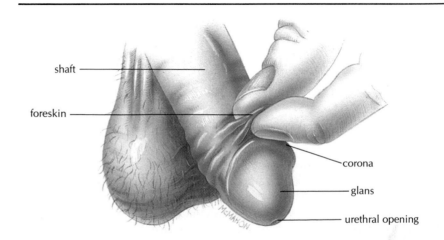

shaft

foreskin

corona

glans

urethral opening

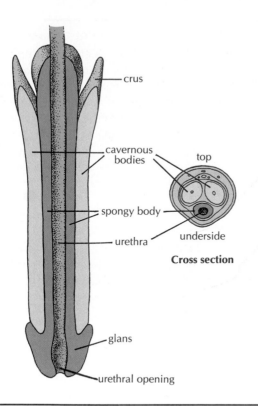

FIGURE 4–11
Internal structure of the penis The illustration on the left shows the internal chambers of spongy tissue that run along the length of the penis. The drawing on the right gives a cross-sectional view of the same structures.

crus

cavernous bodies

top

spongy body

urethra

underside

glans

urethral opening

Cross section

analogous to the chambers in the clitoris; below them is the third, the **spongy body,** or **corpus spongiosum.** The glans of the penis is actually the end of the spongy body. The little slit in the glans, the urethral opening, is the outlet for the urethral tube, which runs down the center of the spongy body and carries both urine and semen. If a man examines his penis when it is not erect, he will be unable to feel any of its internal structures; if his penis is erect, he can feel the spongy body as a ridge on the underside.

A penis goes from flaccid (limp) to erect when the many arteries leading to the three chambers of the penis bring in more blood than the veins drain away. Blood gets trapped inside the penis, so it expands and gets hard, just as a balloon does if you fill it with air or water. Erections usually occur when a man is sexually aroused, although fatigue or anxiety about performance can keep the penis from rising to the occasion. An erection can also occur in the absence of sexual arousal, while lifting an unusually heavy load, straining during a bowel movement, or simply getting worked up. All men, except those who have erection problems with physiological origins, have partial erections several times a night. These erections occur while they are dreaming, whether their dreams are sexy or not, for reasons that are not yet understood.

What most men want to know about their own penis is whether it looks and acts like everyone else's does. Let's end the suspense: the answer is no.

BOX 4–1

The Circumcision Debate: To Cut or Not to Cut?

Circumcision is an ancient and widespread practice. Cultures as diverse as the aborigines of Australia, the Hottentots of Africa, and the Kazakh of Russia circumcise their male children. An Egyptian inscription from about 4000 B.C. refers to the operation, and male mummies have been found to be circumcised. According to the Old Testament, God commanded Abraham to circumcise all the males of his household as a sign of his special covenant with God. Ever since, Jews have circumcised their sons on the eighth day of life, in a ceremony called the *Brit Milah*, or *bris*. Circumcision is also a religious tradition in the Muslim world.

Such a common custom must surely fill some sort of basic human need, but scholars cannot agree on what it is. Students of the Bible have long assumed that circumcision served not only as a religious covenant but as a sign of group identity and solidarity. The problem with this interpretation is that the Jews were not the only people in the Middle East to practice the custom. Some anthropologists say circumcision functions as a rite of passage that symbolically turns boys into men. But boys are circumcised at different ages in different cultures, and often well before they can understand the notion of masculinity. Psychoanalysts tend to focus on unconscious sexual rivalry between fathers and sons; in this view fathers circumcise sons to show just who is boss. But in most cultures, the operation is handled not by a father but by an uncle, chief, doctor, or professional circumciser.

Others speculate that the practice originated among early peoples as a way of ensuring the good will of fertility gods and warding off evil spirits that threatened man's procreative powers. In the words of one writer, "It was like a fee paid in advance for one's reproductive activities" (Brasch, 1973). Circumcision may also be a political act. A study of circumcision in 114 tribal societies suggests that the custom is performed for the benefit of the group as a whole. A man who allows his son to undergo it is saying, in effect, "I promise to be loyal to this group, and by symbolically sacrificing my son, I'm proving it. You can trust me" (Paige & Paige, 1981).

When circumcision first caught on among non-Jews in Western countries in the late nineteenth century, it was not meant to please fertility gods or to prove allegiance to the group. It was an attempt to wipe out masturbation. You will recall from Chapter 2 that the Victorians blamed "self-abuse" for ills ranging from insomnia to insanity. Doctors thought that cutting off the foreskin would reduce the sensitivity of the penis and thus the temptation to play with it. (Historically the opposite claim has also been made—that circumcision increases penile sensitivity. Modern studies do not support either belief.)

Circumcision grew in popularity after World War I. By the end of the 1930s about three-fourths of all American middle-class families and one-fourth of lower-class families were having their sons circumcised. Then, after World War II, the antimasturbation frenzy passed, and European countries stopped performing the operation. (When Britain's National Health Service stopped paying for it, the number of English babies undergoing circumcision dropped to less than 1 percent.) Only in the United States did the operation remain routine. Today the United States is the only country in the world where a majority of baby boys are circumcised for nonreligious reasons.

Since the 1970s, however, there has been active opposition to the operation. Critics point out that circumcision is not as safe as it has been made out to be. If it is not done properly, too much skin may be removed or the tip of the penis may be injured. The overall complication rate is only about 1 percent, but that means that for every one million circumcisions there are ten thousand complications, including two deaths (Paige, 1978).

Another concern is pain. For years doctors assumed that a newborn's immature nervous system did not register pain, but several studies now show that this is false (e.g., Chamberlain 1989; Porter, Miller, & Marshall, 1986; Tyler, 1988). Although an anesthetic can be given by injection (it's called a dorsal penile nerve block), the anesthetic itself poses a small risk, and not all doctors support its use. Research is being done to test the effectiveness of topical creams (Mudge & Younger, 1989).

Are there any medical justifications for circumcision? In 1971, the American Academy of Pediatrics (AAP) concluded that "there are no valid medical indications for circumcision in the neonatal period." The Academy reaffirmed this statement in 1975, and three years later the American College of Obstetricians and Gynecologists issued a similar one. In the 1980s some hospitals stopped performing routine circumcisions on newborns and some insurers stopped paying for them. The percentage of newborn males having the operation fell, from a high of perhaps 90 to 95 percent in the 1960s to an estimated 60 to 70 percent today.

Recently, however, the AAP reconsidered its position. In 1989, it concluded that circumcision does have "potential medical benefits and advantages," after all. Uncircumcised male infants have eleven times more urinary tract infections than other infants, and such infections can be serious (Wiswell et al., 1987; Wiswell & Geschke, 1989). New studies reviewed by the AAP also suggest that circumcision reduces the risk of penile cancer (a form of cancer rare in the United States) and possibly of sexually transmitted diseases and of cervical cancer in women (although studies so far have been inconclusive). But the AAP has stopped short of actually recommending the operation. Instead, it suggests that parents make their own decisions after considering medical, aesthetic, religious, and cultural factors.

Some of the apparent medical benefits associated with circumcision may be related to hygiene. On the underside of the penile glans are small glands that secrete a pungent waxy material called **smegma.** This material can collect between the foreskin and the glans, become rancid, promote irritation, and possibly harbor bacteria and viruses. Some uncircumcised men who do not practice good hygiene must be circumcised later in life to counteract bacterial infection or inflammation of the glans. Cutting off the foreskin in infancy destroys the smegma's hiding place. But teaching boys proper care of the penis—how to wash under the foreskin—may accomplish the same thing. A pamphlet describing proper penile hygiene, produced by the American Academy of Pediatrics, is available through pediatricians.

At present, the circumcision debate leaves many parents in a bind. They may not want to subject an infant to even a small risk if the operation is not absolutely necessary from a medical point of view, but at the same time, they want Junior to look just like Dad and the majority of other American boys. Because sexual aesthetics, personal hygiene practices, and parental versus children's rights are all at issue, it is not surprising that such a tiny snippet of skin can produce so much anxiety. All we can recommend is that you become as well-informed as possible *before* your child is born, and that you make your decision based on personal values and your assessment of the risks and benefits.

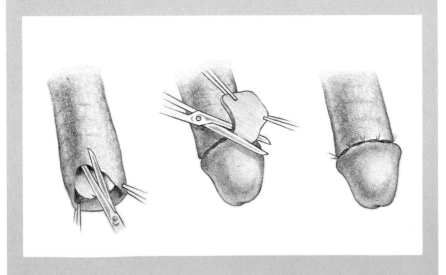

Of course there are statistically average penises (three or four inches when flaccid, with a diameter of about one and one-fourth inches), but statistics can be misleading, given the great variation from the "norm," which, after all, is just a number you get by measuring a lot of penises, adding up all the figures, and dividing by the number of men. This variation does not correlate with race, body size, virility, or anything else. There is also variation in the way penises look when erect. Some jut out at a forty-five degree angle from the rest of the body, while others assume angles slightly higher or slightly lower.

Still, many men worry about their penises. In *Male Sexuality* Bernie Zilbergeld writes:

> Penises come in a variety of shapes and sizes. . .and about the only thing most penises have in common is that they are the wrong size or shape as far as their owners are concerned. In the many hours we have spent talking to men in and out of therapy, we have heard every conceivable complaint about penises. They are too small (the most common complaint), too large, too thin, too thick, stand up at too small (or great) an angle when erect, bend too much to the right, or left, or in the middle, or don't get hard enough when they erect. (Zilbergeld, 1978, p. 113)

Zilbergeld points out that in America a fantasy model of the penis and its abilities dominates sexual humor, pornography, and sexually explicit fiction: "It's two feet long, hard as steel, and can go all night." In pulp novels off the drugstore rack and classics of erotic literature such as D. H. Lawrence's *Lady Chatterley's Lover,* you can find many such depictions. In fantasy land, says Zilbergeld, penises come in only three sizes: large, gigantic, and so big you can barely get them through the doorway. In real life, though, penises are more modest in their dimensions, and they are rarely as unflaggingly active as fictional ones.

Two facts may help put the issue of penis size into perspective. One is that flaccid penises vary more in size than erect ones because smaller penises tend to expand proportionately more in size than larger ones. Because most heterosexual men only see other men's penises when they are flaccid, they probably have an unrealistic notion of size differences. The other point, perhaps more important, is that most women seem perfectly satisfied with penises the way they are. When Zilbergeld and Lynn Stanton asked over 400 women, aged 18 to 63, to say on a questionnaire what they liked and did not like in sex, not one woman spontaneously mentioned penis size (reported in Zilbergeld, 1978). (What they did say they wanted was equal treatment, understanding, sensitivity, open communication, and emotional sharing.) This is not to say that women never have a preference in such matters. When the researchers talked personally to some of the respondents, some women said they liked long, thin penises; some said they preferred short, thick ones; and some voiced still different opinions. But these were not strong preferences and they certainly did not influence a woman's choice of man.

Zilbergeld calls such preferences "druthers"—something you'd like to have if you could have anything you wanted, but not a high priority.

The Scrotum

The **scrotum** is a muscular sac that hangs loosely behind the penis and contains the testes. Its skin is darker than the rest of the body and is covered sparsely with pubic hair. A seam-like line, the *raphe* (ray-fee) divides the scrotum into two halves.

The scrotum may seem like a pretty vulnerable place to house the testes, but Nature had her reasons. Sperm, which are manufactured in the testes, do not take to hot temperatures. In fact, they cannot be produced and will not survive for very long at the normal body temperature of 98.6°F. They do just fine, though, in the scrotum because it is a few degrees cooler. The scrotum acts like a sort of weather vane. When the weather is cool, the muscles from which it is suspended contract, pulling it closer to the body where it is warmed. (When this happens, the smooth skin of the scrotum gets wrinkled.) When the weather is hot, the muscles relax so that the testes are suspended farther from the body, where they can cool off. A man can observe this phenomenon by varying the temperature of his bath or shower water. The scrotum also rises during sexual arousal.

According to Masters and Johnson (1966), the scrotum is not as sexually sensitive as the female's vulval lips or vaginal opening. In fact, Masters and Johnson claim that sexual sensations for the male are "limited primarily to the penile shaft and glans." But this generalization seems much too strong. Many men in Hite's male sample (1981) said they liked a sexual partner to caress or play with the scrotum, and over a third said that during masturbation they themselves stroked it. Her data do not make clear, however, whether these men were enjoying the sensations that came from stroking or stretching the scrotal skin, or pressure on the testes within the scrotum—or both.

MEN'S INTERNAL SEX ORGANS

The internal sex organs in men include the testes, the epididymis, the vas deferens, the seminal vesicles, the prostate, and the Cowper's glands. These organs form a system for producing, storing, and transporting *sperm*, the male reproductive cells. The internal sex organs are shown in Figures 4–12 and 4–13.

The Testes

The word **testis**, or its synonym **testicle**, comes from the Latin word for "witness." In Biblical days men would take an oath by placing a hand on the genitals of the person to whom they were making it. This gesture, which seems so peculiar today, may have symbolized an understanding that if the

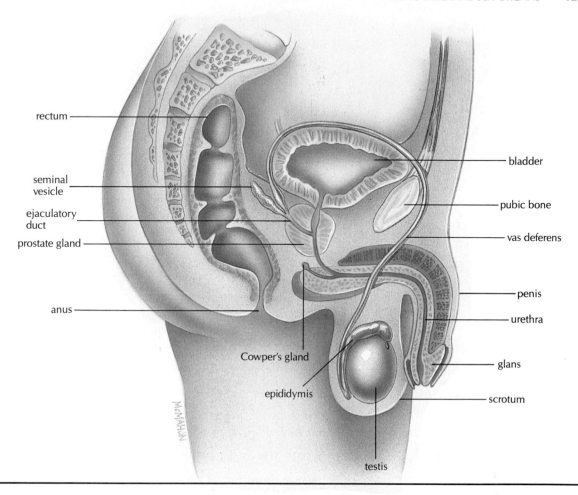

rectum

seminal vesicle

ejaculatory duct

prostate gland

anus

Cowper's gland

epididymis

McMAHON

testis

bladder

pubic bone

vas deferens

penis

urethra

glans

scrotum

FIGURE 4–12

Male internal sexual and reproductive organs, cross-section This drawing is a kind of composite or average and illustrates the anatomy of a relatively young man. Changes that occur with age include shrinking of the testes and growth of the prostate.

oath-taker broke his vow, the other man's unborn children had the right to punish him (Brasch, 1973). The ancient Romans apparently modified the custom; they put their hands on their own testes. Words like "testify," "testimonial," and "testament" all bear witness to the ancient method of taking an oath.

The testes are the male gonads. If you gently squeeze the scrotum, you can feel them: they are egg-shaped and about one and a half to two inches long. Each testis is suspended in a separate sac within the scrotum. The left testis usually hangs a little lower than the right one. After puberty, the process of *spermatogenesis* (sperm production) takes place within the testes, in thin convoluted tubes called **seminiferous** (sperm-bearing) **tubules** (see Figure 4–14). The seminiferous tubules, if stretched out end-to-end, would have a total length of about 700 feet. The tubules produce billions of sperm each month. The other major function of the testes is to produce the male sex hormone *testosterone*. This takes place in the **interstitial,** or **Leydig's cells,** located in the tissue between the seminiferous tubules.

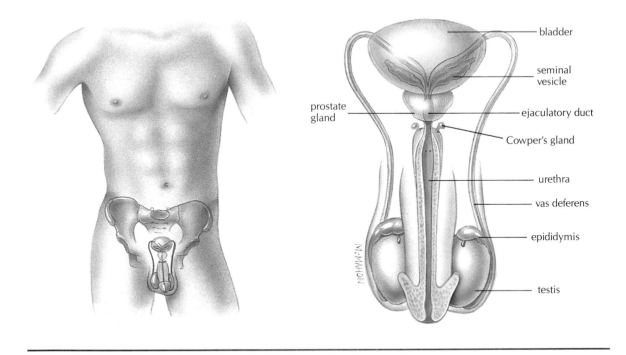

McMAHON

FIGURE 4–13

Male internal sexual and reproductive organs, front view   The drawing on the left shows the location of the organs relative to the rest of the body. The schematic illustration on the right shows the penis in cross-section and indicates the position of the seminal vesicles behind the bladder.

Contrary to common belief, the testes do not contain any **seminal fluid** (the fluid ejaculated, along with sperm, when a man has an orgasm).

The Epididymis and the Vas Deferens

Once formed, sperm move out of the seminiferous tubules into a C-shaped tube called the **epididymis** (from the Greek for "above the testes"). There are two of these, one per testis. Each epididymis is long—about twenty feet—but is coiled so tightly that it can perch atop the testis to which it is attached. Sperm mature there and can be stored for up to six weeks before being ejaculated or reabsorbed by the body.

You would think that after their stopover in the epididymis, the sperm would move right on to the penis for ejaculation, but life for sperm is not easy. First they have to take a long detour through the abdomen to pick up some seminal fluid. At the peak of sexual arousal they leave the scrotum through the **vas deferens,** a duct that is a continuation of the epididymis. (Again, there are two of them.) The part of the vas deferens that is in the scrotum is encased in a rubberlike tube called the **spermatic cord,** which also contains blood vessels and nerves. You may be able to feel this cord above each testicle with your fingers. Because the vas deferens is so easy to locate, the best way to sterilize a man is to cut or tie it off, in a simple operation called a *vasectomy* (see Chapter 7). After a vasectomy, a man can ejaculate just as before, but his semen contains no sperm.

After entering the abdomen, each vas deferens loops behind the bladder and turns downward toward the prostate gland.

The Seminal Vesicles

Next to each vas deferens, above the prostate and behind the bladder, is a structure called a **seminal vesicle.** At one time physiologists thought that the function of the seminal vesicles was to store sperm, but we now know that to be false. The vesicles are actually glands that produce a sticky, alkaline secretion that comprises over two-thirds of the seminal fluid. Seminal vesicle secretions contain fructose, a sugar that appears to contribute to the nutrition of sperm and makes them capable of movement. Until the sperm merge with these secretions, they have only a limited ability to travel on their own. In the epididymis and the vas deferens, they are probably propelled by contractions of the ducts and the movement of tiny hairlike structures called *cilia*, which line the inner walls of these ducts. Once the sperm are activated by seminal fluid, however, they can move on their own by whipping their tails back and forth.

The opening of each seminal vesicle joins with the vas deferens to form a short tube called the **ejaculatory duct.** The two ejaculatory ducts are entirely surrounded by the prostate gland.

The Prostate

The **prostate** is a gland about the size and shape of a chestnut that lies just below the urinary bladder. In the interior of the prostate the ejaculatory ducts meet and open into the urethra. The urethra is the last duct the sperm

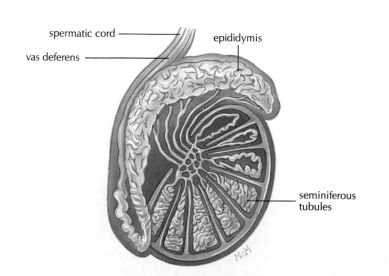

FIGURE 4–14
Internal structure of the testis This cross-section shows the highly complex set of coiled tubes in which sperm production takes place. Testosterone is produced in cells that are located in tissue between the tubules.

ever see, for it leads through the spongy body of the penis to the outside world. Before the sperm can exit, however, they must mix with the seminal fluid. As we saw above, much of this fluid comes from the seminal vesicles, which secrete directly into the ejaculatory ducts. The rest comes from the prostate, which produces a thin, milky fluid containing many nutrients. The sperm-seminal fluid mixture, called **semen** (pronounced "sea-men") or **ejaculate** (rhymes with "immaculate"), is a sticky, off-white substance that has the consistency of a balsam cream rinse. During ejaculation, about a teaspoonful of semen is expelled through the urethral opening.

The prostate is prey to a variety of health problems. The one most frequently encountered by younger men is *prostatitis*, an inflammation caused by various kinds of infection, including gonorrhea (see Chapter 18).

The Cowper's Glands

The **Cowper's glands,** or *bulbourethral glands*, are two small pea-shaped glands on either side of the urethra that secrete a clear, sticky fluid during sexual arousal but before ejaculation. Cowper's gland fluid probably helps to neutralize the acidic environment of the urethra, which is harmful to sperm. During sexual arousal a drop or two of Cowper's gland fluid may ooze out of the tip of the penis. Although this fluid is not semen, it does sometimes contain stray sperm that can enter the vagina and fertilize an egg. That is one reason why withdrawing the penis before ejaculation is an unreliable method of birth control.

To recap, sperm travel a long, circuitous route from the seminiferous tubules in the testes to the epididymis to the vas deferens to the ejaculatory duct in the prostate and into the urethra, which leads out through the penis. Seminal fluid originates in the prostate and the seminal vesicles and mixes with sperm in the ejaculatory ducts to form semen.

And they say that the sexual anatomy of men is simple and straightforward!

SKIN-DEEP SEX: OTHER EROGENOUS ZONES

Other areas of the body besides the genitals are erotically sensitive, and some go through marked physiological changes during sexual arousal. A Frenchman once called love "the harmony of two souls and the contact of two epidermes," and in a sense, the entire skin surface can be thought of as a sex organ. It contains 7 to 135 nerve endings per square centimeter that respond to touch and well over half a million sensory fibers that convey nerve impulses to the spinal cord and brain. Sex is a touching experience, and although the skin has many nonsexual functions—sensing hot and cold, protecting our innards, alerting us to danger through the pain receptors—it also serves as a conductor of erotic feeling. Besides giving us physical gratification, it affords us a way to communicate with a partner nonverbally. The noted anthropologist Ashley Montagu speculated that the skin may even register "vibes" that pass between one person and another:

> The "electricity" that is. . .said to pass between people when touching one another, may be something more than a mere metaphor. The skin is an especially good electrical conductor. . . .There can be little doubt that in tactile stimulation electrical charges are transmitted from one individual to the other. (Montagu, 1971, p. 148)

Although the entire skin surface is sensitive, certain nongenital areas are more erotically sensitive than others and together with the genitals are referred to as **erogenous zones.** Among the most sensitive are the breasts. Breasts are neither external nor internal sex organs; like beards and deep voices, they are **secondary sexual characteristics** (nongenital characteristics that distinguish males from females). In our culture the female breast is considered sexually alluring.

Until puberty the breasts of boys and girls are much alike, but from puberty on girls' breasts develop in response to the release of estrogen. The breasts of mature women contain milk-producing (*mammary*) glands that become active after childbirth, and ducts that lead from these glands to the *nipples*, or tips of the breasts. Breasts also contain fat tissue, which affects the size and shape of the breast. Normal female breasts may be small or large, firm or soft, rigid or pendulous, and they may or may not have hair around the *areola* (the darker skin surrounding the nipple). The nipple may point outward, be flat, or be inverted. Typically, one breast is slightly larger than the other.

Many women worry about the size or shape of their breasts, in much the same way that men worry about the size or appearance of their penis. Because our culture associates a full breast with sex appeal, the small-breasted woman may feel inadequate. Her larger-breasted sister, on the other hand, may wish she were smaller so she could look more like the slender, flat-chested models in fashion magazines. Older women may wonder if their sexual partners will be less attracted to breasts that have lost some of their firmness. Actually, very few women have the kind of large yet firm breasts seen in erotic films and magazines.

The size or appearance of the breasts has nothing whatever to do with their erotic sensitivity. This is an individual matter. Some women do not particularly enjoy breast stimulation; others say the nipples of the breasts are the most sexually sensitive nongenital area; and a few (2 percent in Masters and Johnson's sample [1966]) reach orgasm from breast stimulation alone. Many men also have sexually sensitive nipples.

Another erogenous zone is the mouth. An English poet once wrote, "What is a kiss? Why this, as some approve: The sure wet cement, glue, and lime of love." Kissing is also a good way to rub erogenous zones. The lips are so sensitive that the brain area devoted to them, like the area devoted to the tips of the fingers, is disproportionately large compared with areas associated with other parts of the body. The tongue and the entire inside of the mouth are also erogenous, and some people enjoy a leisurely exploration of their partner's mouth (the "French kiss"). When people perform cunnilingus (oral stimulation of a woman's genitals) or fellatio (oral stimulation of a man's genitals), they give not only genital gratification to their partner but oral gratification to themselves.

Besides the mouth and the breasts, there are other erogenous zones, such as the earlobes, the buttocks, the anus, and the inner thighs. Indeed, any part of the skin surface may be erogenous, or may not be, depending on an individual's unique physiology and personal history. A concentration of nerve endings does not always spell sexual ecstasy; different folks need different strokes. A physical message from the skin must be interpreted as erotic before it can be experienced that way. There are no nerves leading from the skin that are reserved just for sexual pleasure, and the impulses that travel from the lips to the brain travel the same route whether they are initiated by a lover's tongue or a ham sandwich. Even the nerve endings in the genital organs are no different from those in the rest of the body. Sex is more than a skin game. Indeed, it is a cliché among sexologists that the most erogenous zone in the body is not the penis or the clitoris or the vagina or anything else below the neck: it is the brain.

SEX AND THE BRAIN

When people say that sex is "all in your head," they usually are referring to the *cerebral cortex*, the wrinkled, densely packed surface layer of cells ("gray matter") covering the huge, mushrooming cerebrum (see Figure 4–

FIGURE 4–15

Brain areas important in sex and reproduction
These structures are involved in the mental, hormonal, and emotional aspects of sexuality, as described in the text.

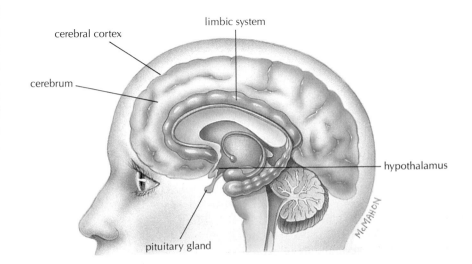

cerebral cortex

limbic system

cerebrum

hypothalamus

pituitary gland

15). The cerebral cortex of lower animals is relatively small and smooth. In higher animals capable of complex thinking and behavior, the cortex is larger in comparison with other brain areas, and its surface is more wrinkled. When we think about sex, talk about it, or write a passionate poem to a lover, we use the cerebral cortex. As yet scientists know little about these processes. Most of our scientific knowledge about the brain's role in human sexuality comes from studies of subcortical parts of the brain—areas that developed much earlier in our evolution as a species. These brain areas play two important roles in sexuality: they regulate various hormones important in sex and reproduction, and they are active in sexual arousal and functioning.

The Neuroendocrine System

We have already come across the sex hormones in our discussion of the testes and the ovaries. It is now time to take a brief but closer look at what these substances are and where they come from.

Hormones are chemical messengers that are manufactured in structures called **endocrine glands.** Hormones travel through the body to various target organs, whose tissues they affect. Unlike other glands mentioned in this chapter, such as the mammary glands and the seminal vesicles, endocrine glands are *ductless.* That is, they release their secretions directly into the bloodstream instead of into ducts that connect with other organs. The *neuroendocrine system*—the nervous system together with the endocrine glands—regulates many bodily processes, including growth and metabolism. But here we are interested only in those parts of the system that are relevant for sex and reproduction (see Figure 4–16).

Think of the neuroendocrine system as consisting of a boss, a supervisor, and various employees. The boss is a small area of the brain called the **hypothalamus.** The supervisor is the **pituitary gland,** a small structure about the size of a cherry that is attached to the lower surface of the brain, right beneath the hypothalamus. The employees are the gonads and the **adrenal glands**—two endocrine glands located above the kidneys. The hypothalamus, the pituitary, and the adrenal glands have many functions, but we will confine our attention here to their role in sex and reproduction.

The job of the hypothalamus is to send orders to the pituitary gland by releasing chemical messengers that travel through a network of tiny blood vessels connecting the two organs. (The pituitary has two lobes, or roundish divisions, but the sex-related messages only go to the front [anterior] lobes.) The chemical messengers tell the pituitary to produce **gonadotropins**—hormones that travel through the bloodstream to the ovaries and the testes.

Then it is the pituitary's turn; it sends out two kinds of gonadotropins. One of these is called **follicle-stimulating hormone (FSH).** In women, FSH has the job of stimulating the growth of hollow, podlike clusters of cells in the ovaries called *follicles.* An ovum (egg) develops in each ovarian follicle. Follicles also secrete the female hormone *estrogen.* In men, FSH stimulates

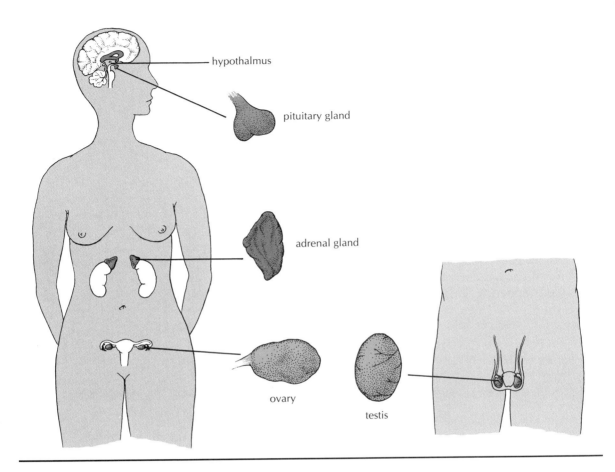

hypothalmus

pituitary gland

adrenal gland

ovary

testis

FIGURE 4–16

Glands important in sex and reproduction   The glands in this drawing discharge their secretions directly into the bloodstream, which carries the hormones to target organs.

sperm production. Men have no follicles. Unfortunately, FSH got its name before anyone realized that the same hormone operates in both males and females.

The name of the other gonadotropin depends on whether it is produced by the pituitary of a male or a female. In women it is called **luteinizing hormone (LH),** and its job is to bring on **ovulation**—the release of a mature egg from the follicle. It also causes the ruptured follicle to secrete the female hormone progesterone, and some estrogen. In men, it is called **interstitial-cell-stimulating hormone** (ICSH), and it stimulates the production of the male hormone testosterone.

That's a lot of complicated terms, but the basic plan is simple (see Figure 4–17): by way of hormones, the hypothalamus tells the pituitary what to do and the pituitary tells the gonads what to do. The hormones produced by the gonads are the ones we usually mean when we say "sex hormones." There are three main types of sex hormones, and they are chemically quite similar. Calling them male and female sex hormones is really a misnomer

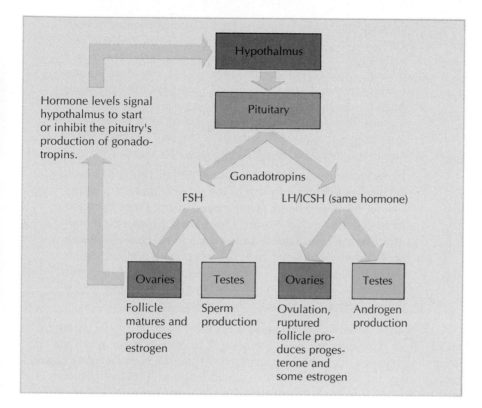

FIGURE 4–17
The way the neuroendocrine system works   Note that the system is self-regulating: when sex hormones reach certain levels in the bloodstream, the hypothalamus signals the pituitary's to start or stop producing gonadotropins.

because all three are produced by both males and females, though in different amounts:

1. **Androgens** are masculinizing hormones. The most important androgen is **testosterone.** Androgens are produced mainly in the testes, but small amounts are also produced in the female's ovaries and the *adrenal cortices* (outer part of the adrenal glands) in both sexes. (The adrenal glands, like the gonads, are controlled by hormonal messages from the pituitary.) The overall quantity of androgens in a man's bloodstream is much greater than in a woman's—somewhere between five and twenty times as great in various studies. Androgens are responsible for instigating and maintaining the physical changes that occur in males at puberty and for the development of pubic and underarm hair in girls. They are critical in the development of male fetuses (see Chapter 12) and can influence sexual arousal (see Chapter 5.)

2. **Estrogens** are feminizing hormones. The most important estrogen is *estradiol.* Estrogens are manufactured primarily in the ovaries, but small amounts are also produced in the

male's testes, in fat cells, and in the adrenal cortices of both sexes. Men have only half as much estradiol as premenopausal women do at the low point of the hormone's monthly cycle (Hawkins & Oakey, 1974). But after women reach menopause and their estradiol levels fall sharply, men actually produce more of this hormone. Estrogens are responsible for instigating and maintaining most of the physical changes that occur in females at puberty and they play a role in the menstrual cycle (see Chapter 6).

3. **Progesterone** is a hormone whose main function is to stimulate and maintain the growth of the uterine lining in preparation for the implantation of a fertilized ovum. Progesterone is produced mainly in the ovaries, but smaller amounts are produced in the male's testes and in the adrenal cortices of both sexes (Money & Ehrhardt, 1972). Measuring progesterone is difficult, but one group of investigators estimated that men have about the same amount as women do at the lowest point in the hormone's monthly cycle (Tea et al., 1975).

You may have wondered what keeps the gonads (and the adrenal glands) from producing too much hormone. The answer is that when the sex hormones reach a certain level in the blood stream, the hypothalamus signals the pituitary to stop manufacturing gonadotropins. This control system, which operates in both sexes, is called a *negative feedback loop*. For example, when testosterone reaches a certain level in men, the hypothalamus tells the pituitary to stop manufacturing ICSH. Then, when testosterone falls to a certain low level, the hypothalamus again starts the production cycle.

Table 4–2 summarizes the information covered in this section.

The Brain and Sexual Response

The part of the brain that seems to be most directly involved in sexual responsivity is called the **limbic system.** It takes its name from the Latin for "border" because it forms a sort of border on the underside of the cerebrum. The limbic system is not one well-defined area of the brain but is a network of areas, not all of them contiguous. Some anatomists include at least parts of the hypothalamus in the limbic system. The limbic system seems to be responsible for various emotional responses involved in self-preservation, including anger, fear, and affection. It transmits signals between the higher brain centers—those that control thought—and the lower ones, which handle stereotyped behavior and certain glandular responses.

Physiologists began to recognize the role of the limbic system in sexual response over five decades ago, when Heinrich Klüver and Paul Bucy (1939) discovered that rhesus monkeys underwent profound personality changes when a part of the system was destroyed. Rhesus monkeys are ordinarily mean and surly, but the experimental monkeys became extremely tame.

TABLE 4–2
The main reproductive hormones
Note that these substances are found in both men and women.

Type of hormone	Where produced	Main functions	Comment
Follicle-stimulating hormone (FSH)	Pituitary gland.	In females: stimulates growth of ovarian follicles (where ova mature), and estrogen production. In males: stimulates sperm production.	
Luteinizing hormone (LH)	Pituitary gland.	Induces ovulation and stimulates ruptured ovarian follicle to produce progesterone.	Identical to ICSH in men.
Interstitial-cell-stimulating hormone (ICSH)	Pituitary gland.	Stimulates androgen production in testes.	Identical to LH in women.
Androgens	Primarily in testes; lesser amounts in ovaries and adrenal cortices.	Stimulate fetal development of male sex organs. Influence development of male secondary sex characteristics. Can affect sexual arousal and functioning.	The most important androgen is testosterone.
Estrogens	Primarily in ovaries; lesser amounts in testes and adrenal cortices.	Influence development of female secondary sex characteristics, help regulate menstrual cycle.	The most important estrogen is estradiol.
Progesterone	Primarily in ovaries; lesser amounts in testes and adrenal cortices.	Helps regulate menstrual cycle; stimulates growth of uterine lining in preparation for implantation of fertilized egg.	

They had difficulty recognizing objects and compulsively placed both food and non-food objects in their mouths. In addition, they behaved sexually toward both animate and inanimate objects; females would even proposition a water faucet.

Nowadays, instead of destroying parts of the brain, a common method for probing brain-behavior relationships is electrical stimulation of the brain (ESB). In a typical experiment an animal sits in a restraining device, and an electric current is applied to specific brain areas through needlelike electrodes. The researchers observe any behavior that occurs during stimulation. The procedure is painless because the brain itself has no pain receptors. No significant damage is done to the brain because the electrodes are extremely thin and pass through very few cells.

Electrical stimulation studies with monkeys have located various sex centers in the brain. Erection centers have been found in the limbic system of male monkeys, and one study found that a female squirrel monkey will have a clitoral erection if similar sites are electrically stimulated (Maurus, Mitra, & Ploog, 1965). Stimulation of another limbic region will cause a male monkey to have a seminal discharge, sometimes before an erection (MacLean, 1962).

ESB researchers have established that pleasure centers exist in the limbic systems of all mammals, including human beings, and some of these centers produce pleasure that is distinctly sexual. But before anyone runs out to patent an "orgasm machine" like the one in Woody Allen's film *Sleeper*, we should point out that most human subjects do not get orgasms from ESB. They enjoy the sensation, but they also say that it is unlike the sensations of actual sex. Unlike laboratory rats, they will not starve themselves or cross electrified grids to have their brains electronically zapped. That is not surprising. The richness and diversity of human sexual pleasure cannot be traced to any one "sexual center" in the brain. Because our sexuality emerges from our thoughts, memories, perceptions, and beliefs, the entire human brain is a sexual organ.

Female self-examination
Many women are unfamiliar with their own external genitals. Self-examination can reduce the anxiety that may be associated with sexual anatomy and teach a woman what her sexual organs should look like when they are healthy.

. . . .

PERSONAL PERSPECTIVE

DOING A SEXUAL SELF-EXAM

A picture may be worth a thousand words, but direct experience is worth a thousand pictures. Although we have tried to make the various drawings in this chapter as realistic as possible, even the most accurate depiction is stylized and abstract. Nor can photographs capture the variations in size, shape, symmetry, position, color, odor, texture, and sensitivity that characterize people's genitals. Our bodies are no more alike than our faces. Therefore the best—in fact, the *only*—way to know what *your* sexual anatomy is like is. . .to look.

A personal tour of your genitals will increase self-knowledge and self-awareness. It will make the information in this chapter "real" and help you retain it. If you are not altogether comfortable with your own body, it may increase your comfort—or at least tell you which parts make you most uneasy, and why. Another benefit to self-examination: people sometimes miss signs of infection or disease in the sexual and reproductive organs because they are not sure what *healthy* organs are supposed to look like. A self-exam will tell you. (Signs of disease are covered in Chapters 17 and 18.)

Here are some suggestions for making your self-examination a rewarding one:

- Provide yourself with the right setting. You will need a hand mirror, a good light, and privacy. Take the phone off the hook and find a pleasant, comfortable place where you will not be interrupted. Give yourself plenty of time.

- Start by sitting with your back against a pillow, with your knees up and feet on the floor. Then be creative about positions so that you can see yourself from varying angles. You may want to squat over the mirror, put one leg up on a chair, lie on your back, or back up to a full-length mirror on your hands and legs. No one can see you, so forget about looking ridiculous.

- You can use the figures in this chapter as guides. If you are a woman, identify visually or by touch the mons, major lips, minor lips, vaginal opening, hood of the clitoris, clitoral glans and shaft, urethral opening (if possible), perineum, and anus. (Spread the lips of the vulva apart to see the underlying structures. Don't worry if you can't find the clitoris; in some women it is entirely hidden beneath its hood.) If you are a man, identify the penile glans and shaft, urethral opening, foreskin (if you are uncircumcised), corona, frenulum, raphe of the scrotum, testes, perineum, and anus.

- Use your hands. Move parts, stretch skin, stroke sensitive areas. How do parts change in appearance when you do this? Where do you find a light touch more pleasant than a firm one, or vice versa? How sensitive to temperature are your genitals?

- Women can insert a finger into the vagina to see what the vaginal walls feel like. Both men and women can gently insert a finger into the anus. (Fingernails should be short, and a lubricant can help. If you are not relaxed, the strong sphincter muscles surrounding the anus can make insertion somewhat uncomfortable. Also, do not touch the vulva or vagina afterwards without washing your hands first.) What happens when you contract your pelvic muscles? How strong do these muscles seem?

Male self-examination Although men are probably more familiar with their own genitals than women are, they, too, can benefit from self-examination. Like women, they may become more comfortable with their sexual organs and learn to recognize signs of infection or disease.

- If you are a woman, try moving the hood of the clitoris back and forth over the clitoral glans. If you are an uncircumcised man, try moving the foreskin back and forth over the penile glans. (If this is uncomfortable, or the foreskin does not move easily, you may need to see a physician.)

- If some parts seem too dry, try wetting them with a water-soluble oil or cream (not a petroleum-based one), saliva, or (if you are a woman) vaginal secretions.

- If you like, let art imitate life: try drawing your own genital pictures, based on what *you* look like. What colors would you choose? How would your pictures differ from those in this chapter?

- Notice any positive or negative thoughts you have about your genitals, but don't censure them. If you have a negative reaction, think up some positive or humorous ways to describe the parts in question. (For example, if you are a woman, you might compare the vulva to a beautiful, dewy flower, with the major and minor lips the "petals.") What kinds of metaphors do you use when thinking about a sexual organ; is it an appendage, a friend, a weapon, or a tool? (Some men think of the penis as a "buddy," and even give it a nickname.) Or is it simply another part of you?

Self-examination is still a strange idea to some, but many of those who have tried it say it helped them become more relaxed about genital anatomy and more appreciative of the clever, if sometimes complicated, way the human body is put together.

IN BRIEF

1. Self-examination is a good way to learn about one's unique sexual anatomy and overcome negative feelings about the genitals. It also increases the probability of recognizing signs of disease or infection in the sexual and reproductive organs.

2. The female external genitals, or *vulva*, include the mons, the major lips, the minor lips, the Bartholin's glands, the urethral opening, the clitoris, and the vaginal opening. The *mons* is a soft cushion of fatty tissue, covered by pubic hair. The *major lips* provide protection for the vaginal opening and other delicate parts of the vulva. The *minor lips* are sexually very sensitive and swell and change color dramatically during sexual arousal. The *Bartholin's glands* secrete a small amount of fluid during sexual arousal but not enough to provide effective lubrication; their

function remains unknown. The *urethral opening* is the outlet for urine. The *clitoris*, located below the mons area and above the urethral opening, is an extremely sensitive organ consisting of a *glans* and a *shaft* that divides at its base into two *crura*, or legs. Most writers on sexuality agree with Masters and Johnson that the clitoris is the main subjective focus of arousal, just as the penis is for a man. The vaginal opening is usually kept partially closed by a ring of muscles. In a woman who has never had intercourse, it may be partially covered by a *hymen*.

3. The female internal sex organs include the vagina, the uterus, the ovaries, and the Fallopian tubes. Worries about the *vagina* being too large or small for sexual intercourse are not based on anatomical fact. The lower third of the vagina is sexually sensitive, but the upper two-thirds has few nerve endings that respond to touch. The *cervix* is the lower part of the uterus extending into the vagina; it contains a small opening through which sperm can pass. The *uterus* is located behind the vagina, between the bladder and the rectum, and is lined with tissue in which a fertilized egg embeds itself. The *ovaries* are the female gonads; they produce ova (eggs) and the hormones estrogen and progesterone. The *Fallopian tubes* are ducts through which ova pass after being released from the ovaries and are the site of fertilization.

4. The male external genitals include the penis and the scrotum. Like the clitoris, the *penis* consists of a *glans* and a *shaft* and is connected to the pubic bone by *crura*. In uncircumcised men, a *foreskin*, or prepuce, covers or partially covers the glans. The glans is the most sensitive part of the penis, The penis contains no muscle or bone; erection occurs when internal chambers of spongy tissue fill with blood. Many men are concerned about the size of their penis, and these concerns are reinforced by exaggerated images of the penis in humor and fiction. Controversy exists about whether *circumcision* of the penis is justifiable. The *scrotum* is a muscular sac that hangs loosely behind the penis and contains the testes.

5. The male internal sex organs include the testes, the epididymis, the vas deferens, the seminal vesicles, the prostate, and the Cowper's glands. The *testes* are the male gonads; they manufacture *sperm* and produce the hormone testosterone. Contrary to common belief, they do not contain any seminal fluid. An *epididymis* is attached to each testis and provides a storage place for sperm. The *vas deferens* is a duct through which sperm leave the scrotum; it enters the abdomen and loops around the bladder. The *seminal vesicles* are glands that produce most of the seminal fluid. The *prostate* is a gland lying just below the bladder that produces the rest of the seminal fluid. The prostate surrounds two *ejaculatory ducts* formed by the joining of each seminal vesicle with the end of a vas deferens. In the prostate, the ejaculatory ducts meet and open into the *urethra*, which leads out of the penis. The Cowper's glands are small glands on either side of the urethra that secrete a clear, sticky fluid prior to ejaculation.

6.   The entire skin can respond to sexual stimulation, but certain areas, called *erogenous zones*, are particularly sensitive. Their sensitivity is influenced by an individual's unique physiology and personal history.

7.   The breasts are secondary sexual characteristics that are sensitive to erotic stimulation. Our culture considers female breasts sexually alluring, and many women worry about the size or shape of their own breasts. Breast appearance is unrelated to erotic sensitivity.

8.   It is often said that the brain is the most important erogenous zone in the body. The cerebral cortex of the brain enables us to think, write, and talk about sex. But most scientific knowledge about the brain's role in human sexuality comes from studies of subcortical areas that regulate various hormones and are active in sexual arousal and functioning. Hormonal regulation is a function of the *neuroendocrine system*. The *hypothalamus* of the brain sends chemical messages to the *pituitary gland*, which in turn produces hormones that direct the activity of the ovaries and the testes. In women, *FSH* from the pituitary stimulates ovarian follicle development and secretion of *estrogen* by the developing follicle. In men, FSH stimulates sperm production. In women, *LH* from the pituitary brings on ovulation and stimulates the ruptured follicle to produce progesterone and some estrogen. In men, ICSH, which is identical to LH, stimulates *androgen* production. The *limbic system* of the brain is involved in sexual responsivity. It contains centers for erection, ejaculation, and the experience of sexual pleasure. However, the richness of human sexuality cannot be traced to subcortical "sexual centers"; it emerges from our thoughts, memories, perceptions, and beliefs.

Key Terms

genitals *(101)*

vulva *(101)*

mons pubis *(102)*

major lips/labia majora *(102)*

anus *(102)*

rectum *(102)*

perineum *(102)*

minor lips/labia minora *(103)*

Bartholin's glands *(103)*

clitoris *(103)*

clitoral glans *(103)*

clitoral shaft *(103)*

crura of the clitoris *(103)*

vestibular bulbs *(103)*

vaginal opening/ introitus *(105)*

hymen *(105)*

vagina *(106)*

pubococcygeus muscle *(109)*

cervix *(109)*

homologous organs *(111)*

uterus *(110)*

endometrium *(110)*

ovaries *(110)*

gonads *(110)*

ova *(110)*

Fallopian tubes *(110)*

penis *(114)*

penile shaft *(114)*

penile glans *(114)*

138

CHAPTER
FIVE

C H A P T E R   F I V E

■

The Physiology Of Sex

•

. . . sex, as it is woven into the whole texture of our . . . body, is the pattern of all the process of life.

Havelock Ellis

he relationship of sexual anatomy to sexual physiology is something like the relationship of a violin to music. Just as the ability to name all the parts of a violin is of limited value in making music, a knowledge of sexual anatomy is not sufficient for understanding how we function sexually. The study of anatomy describes the "apparatus" necessary for sexual experience, but tells us little about what sets this apparatus in motion or what makes its various parts work together harmoniously. Physiology, the study of bodily processes, together with psychology, fills this gap by helping us understand the sequence of bodily reactions known collectively as the **sexual response cycle.** In this chapter we will take a careful look at what happens physically before, during, and after sexual arousal and then consider how reflexes, hormones, and mental events all contribute to these changes.

THE SEXUAL RESPONSE CYCLE

As we saw in Chapter 3, much of what is known about sexual physiology is due to the work of Masters and Johnson (1966), researchers who brought sex from the bedroom to the laboratory, where it could be measured and quantified. Masters and Johnson discovered that although men and women differ anatomically, their bodies undergo some similar changes during sexual excitement and orgasm. Nearly all of these changes can be traced to two fundamental processes: (1) **vasocongestion,** or *engorgement* of bodily organs and tissues with blood, and (2) **myotonia,** or muscular tension, throughout the body and especially in the genital area. In addition, during sexual response the heart speeds up, blood pressure rises, and breathing grows heavy. A measles-like rash (**sex flush**) may appear on the upper abdomen and spread to the chest. At the height of passion, both men and women may become relatively insensitive to pain and noise. Of course, individuals vary in the way they respond. Some are easily aroused; others take longer. Some cry out and move around a lot; others stay quiet and barely budge. And the way someone responds one time may not be the way he or she responds the next.

In order to organize their data, Masters and Johnson divided sexual response for both sexes into four stages: **excitement,** the beginning of arousal; **plateau,** essentially an advanced stage of excitement; **orgasm,** the release of sexual tension; and **resolution,** the return to the unaroused state. Although these stages may vary in duration for different people, and with different types of sexual activities, their *sequence* is the same whether a person is masturbating, having intercourse, or responding to oral or manual stimulation. But the stages are not like the cycles of an automatic washing machine; we are not programmed to move mechanically from one stage to another. Progress through the sexual response cycle depends on continued and effective stimulation, both physical and psychological. At times, the cycle may consist only of excitement, plateau, and resolution. At other times it may be limited to excitement and resolution. A complex combination of physical, psychological, and situational factors determines how sexual responses unfold.

Moreover, recent research shows that physical measurements in the laboratory do not always agree with what subjects say they are experiencing. In fact, subjective reports of the intensity and duration of response sometimes bear little resemblance to monitored physical changes. What a sexual response *looks* like may not be what it *feels* like (Gallagher, 1986).

With these points in mind, we will look at the primary characteristics of each stage of the sexual response cycle. The stages are summarized in Figures 5–1 (males) and 5–2 (females). You may wish to refer to these illustrations as you read the following descriptions.

Excitement

It is hardly a secret that the first observable sign of arousal in men is an **erection.** As we saw in Chapter 4, during erection blood flows into the penis faster than it flows out, so the penis becomes *tumescent* (swollen), hardens, and begins to protrude from the body. In younger men an erection may occur

Excitement

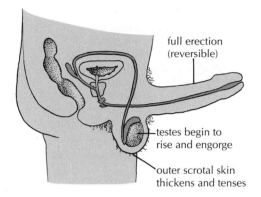

full erection
(reversible)

testes begin to
rise and engorge

outer scrotal skin
thickens and tenses

Plateau

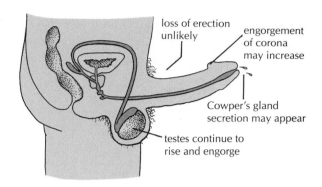

loss of erection
unlikely

engorgement
of corona
may increase

Cowper's gland
secretion may appear

testes continue to
rise and engorge

Orgasm: Emission

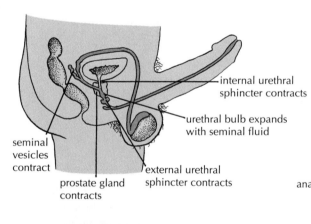

internal urethral
sphincter contracts

urethral bulb expands
with seminal fluid

seminal
vesicles
contract

external urethral
sphincter contracts

prostate gland
contracts

Orgasm: Expulsion

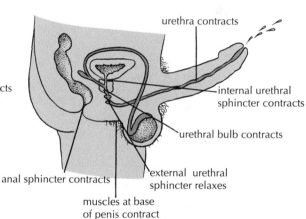

urethra contracts

internal urethral
sphincter contracts

urethral bulb contracts

anal sphincter contracts

external urethral
sphincter relaxes

muscles at base
of penis contract

Resolution

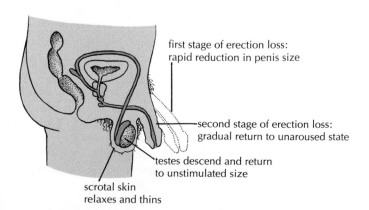

first stage of erection loss:
rapid reduction in penis size

second stage of erection loss:
gradual return to unaroused state

testes descend and return
to unstimulated size

scrotal skin
relaxes and thins

FIGURE 5–1

Changes in male sexual and reproductive anatomy during the sexual response cycle *This diagram shows changes in the penis, the scrotum, and the testes, and other internal organs during the four stages of the sexual response cycle. Note the two phases of ejaculation.*

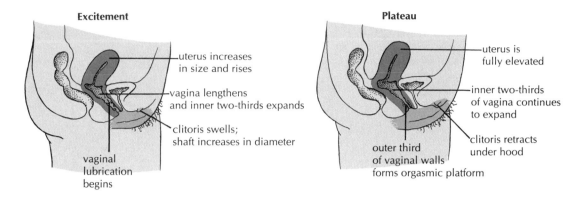

Excitement

uterus increases in size and rises

vagina lengthens and inner two-thirds expands

clitoris swells; shaft increases in diameter

vaginal lubrication begins

Plateau

uterus is fully elevated

inner two-thirds of vagina continues to expand

clitoris retracts under hood

outer third of vaginal walls forms orgasmic platform

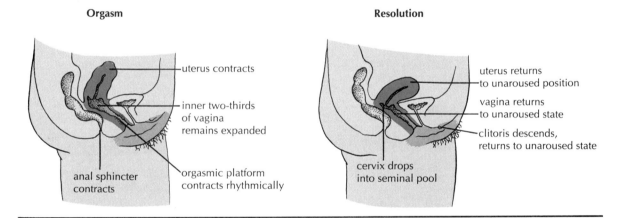

Orgasm

uterus contracts

inner two-thirds of vagina remains expanded

anal sphincter contracts

orgasmic platform contracts rhythmically

Resolution

uterus returns to unaroused position

vagina returns to unaroused state

clitoris descends, returns to unaroused state

cervix drops into seminal pool

FIGURE 5–2
Changes in female sexual and reproductive anatomy during the sexual response cycle *This diagram shows how the uterus, vagina, and clitoris expand and contract during the four stages of sexual response.*

within a few seconds of arousal; in older men the response is often slower. (Other factors, such as fatigue and use of alcohol, can also lengthen the time between stimulation and erection.) Meanwhile, the skin of the scrotum begins to pull up toward the body, and the spermatic cords get shorter, causing the testes to rise. During excitement, a man is somewhat vulnerable to losing his erection if he becomes distracted.

In women the first sign of arousal is *vaginal lubrication*, which occurs within ten to thirty seconds. Masters and Johnson's camera-rigged artificial penis revealed that the walls of the vagina appear to be "sweating." The vaginal secretions that produce this effect consist of highly filtered blood plasma. When the vagina becomes engorged this clear blood fluid seeps from blood vessels surrounding the vagina through the vaginal walls (see Figure 5–3). In intercourse, lubrication prepares the way for insertion of the penis into the vagina. In women who have not yet gone through menopause, the most common cause of insufficient lubrication is simply insufficient sexual arousal.

Other changes take place when a woman is sexually excited. Vasocongestion causes her clitoris to swell (though not always noticeably) and its shaft to increase in diameter (see Figure 5–2). The cervix and uterus move up and back, creating a "tenting" or ballooning of the upper two-thirds of the vagina. The minor lips swell and open up, and the major lips move apart a bit and become flatter. The nipples become erect (as they do in some men), but this may not be obvious because the entire breast becomes somewhat larger.

In both sexes voluntary and involuntary myotonia occurs. Heart rate increases and blood pressure rises.

Plateau

The changes that occur in men during excitement continue during the plateau stage. In fact, one critic of Masters and Johnson, Paul Robinson (1976), argued that there really is no good reason to distinguish plateau from excitement in males. Robinson suggested that Masters and Johnson did so in part because they were intent on showing how similar men and women are. If women had a plateau stage, then men had better have one, too. In any event, during this stage—or nonstage—the man achieves a full erection and

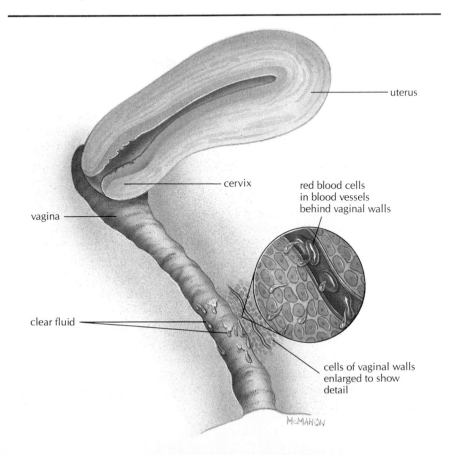

uterus

cervix

vagina

red blood cells
in blood vessels
behind vaginal walls

clear fluid

cells of vaginal walls
enlarged to show
detail

McMAHON

FIGURE 5–3 **Vaginal lubrication** *This drawing shows how droplets of clear, colorless fluid are released from congested blood vessels surrounding the vagina. The droplets pass through the semipermeable vaginal walls and coalesce to form a slippery film on the interior of the vagina.*

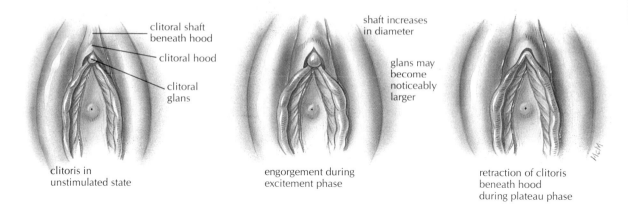

clitoral shaft
beneath hood

clitoral hood

clitoral
glans

clitoris in
unstimulated state

shaft increases
in diameter

glans may
become
noticeably
larger

engorgement during
excitement phase

retraction of clitoris
beneath hood
during plateau phase

FIGURE 5–4   Clitoral changes during sexual arousal   *Note the retraction of the clitoris beneath its hood during the plateau phase. After retraction the clitoris can no longer be seen, but it remains sensitive to indirect stimulation.*

is no longer so vulnerable to distraction. The corona of the penis becomes further engorged and may deepen in color. The Cowper's glands become active, and some fluid from them may appear at the tip of the glans. The testes continue to elevate, and vasocongestion causes them to enlarge by as much as 50 percent over their original size. During plateau, the testes also rotate forward about ninety degrees so that the back surfaces are against the perineum. The full elevation and rotation of the testes always precede orgasm and indicate that orgasm is imminent.

In women, the excitement and plateau stages are more distinct. During plateau, the walls of the lower third of the vagina become congested and swell, forming what Masters and Johnson (1966) call the **orgasmic platform.** The swelling causes the passageway through the lower part of the vagina to narrow by as much as 50 percent (see Figure 5–5). This permits some gripping of the penis by the lower part of the vagina, which enhances the pleasure of a male partner. However, the upper two-thirds of the vagina is not involved in this gripping, and it continues to balloon out. According to Masters and Johnson, the orgasmic platform is a necessary precursor of female orgasm; that is, orgasm does not occur without its full development.

At this point in the response cycle, a strange thing happens to the clitoris, which by now is fully engorged: it suddenly retracts toward the body and seems to disappear (see Figure 5–4). Before Masters and Johnson's observations, this response was unknown to science. Writers of sex and marriage manuals advised men to maintain constant manual contact with the clitoris until they inserted the penis into the vagina. Since direct contact is virtually impossible after a woman reaches the plateau stage, millions of men must have wondered what they were doing wrong. They need not have worried. Although the shy clitoris retracts into the body, it remains extremely sensitive. Indirect contact, accomplished, for example, by stimulating the minor and major lips and the clitoral hood, is usually sufficient to maintain a high degree of arousal.

During plateau, vaginal lubrication tends to decrease, and if this phase is protracted, further production of vaginal fluid may cease altogether.

One other change deserves mention. During plateau, the minor lips change color—from pink to bright red in a woman who has not borne children, from bright red to a deep burgundy in one who has. This change, brought on by vasocongestion, is a sign that the woman is very close to orgasm.

For both sexes, muscle tension, heart rate, and blood pressure continue to increase. Hyperventilation and a sex flush on the abdomen and chest may appear late in plateau.

Orgasm

Orgasm, or sexual climax, involves the entire body and is a major physiological and psychological event. For several seconds intense feelings emanate from (but are not necessarily confined to) the genitals. Muscles throughout the body tense and a person may look like he or she is in the throes of excruciating pain instead of orgasmic ecstasy. Muscle tension may cause the face to grimace, the teeth to clench, and the hands and feet to contract in spasms. The intensity may be so overwhelming that the person is oblivious to all else—children knocking on the door, music blaring from the stereo, a telephone ringing in the next room. Then it is over, and there is a great sense of physical release usually accompanied by a feeling of both physical and psychological well-being.

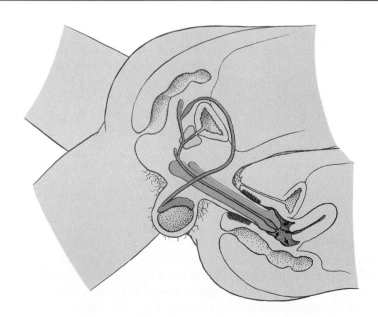

FIGURE 5–5 The sexual organs during heterosexual intercourse *When the lower vaginal walls swell to form the orgasmic platform, they tighten around the penis and create a gripping sensation. During orgasm, contractions of muscles behind the vaginal walls cause the orgasmic platform to pulsate.*

Men and women usually describe the experience of orgasm in similar terms (Vance & Wagner, 1977):

> I really think it defies description by words. Combinations of waves of very pleasurable sensations and mounting of tensions culminating in a fantastic sensation and release of tension. (male)

> Tension builds to an extremely high level—muscles are tense, etc. There is a sudden expanding feeling in the pelvis and muscle spasms throughout the body followed by release of tension. Muscles relax and consciousness returns. (female)

In men, orgasm is marked physiologically by contractions of several sets of muscles in the pelvis. The rate at which these contractions occur is a matter of debate. According to Masters and Johnson (1966), one contraction occurs every 0.8 seconds. But another group of researchers (Bohlen, Held, & Sanderson, 1980), using different methods, report that the initial contractions are 0.6 seconds apart and subsequent ones are farther apart. The researchers also disagree on when orgasm is first noticed subjectively. Masters and Johnson think it is noticed just before the rhythmic contractions begin. Bohlen and his colleagues report that some men subjectively experience the start of orgasm with the first contraction, but others perceive it before or after the first regular contraction. Finally, Masters and Johnson say that the first three or four contractions are the strongest, while Bohlen and his associates say that contractions tend to get stronger until the seventh or eighth one.

Ejaculation, the discharge of semen from the penis, occurs in two stages. (You may wish to review Figure 5–1 on page 141 before reading this description.) In the first, called **emission,** the seminal vesicles, the vas deferens, and the prostate gland contract and secrete their contents into the urethra, via the ejaculatory ducts. A circular band of muscle, or *sphincter,* located below the prostate gland, closes, as does a similar band of muscle located where the urethra exits from the bladder. As a result, the part of the urethra that goes through the prostate is closed off, and the fluid that pours in causes this part to swell to two or three times its usual size, forming the **urethral bulb** (see Figure 5–1). At this stage, the man feels that ejaculation is inevitable, and he is apt to be right.

In the second stage of ejaculation, called **expulsion,** the urethral bulb, the penile urethra, muscles at the base of the penis, and other genital muscles all contract. The sphincter between the bladder and the prostate remains closed (so urine cannot escape), but the other sphincter opens to allow the release of semen. Muscular contractions then propel the semen out through the tip of the penis.

Although ejaculation is usually a sign of orgasm, it can occur without orgasmic sensations. For instance, if emission occurs but the contractions of expulsion do not, semen may simply seep out of the penis. Conversely, a male can have an orgasm without ejaculating. Orgasms before puberty are always "dry." In **retrograde ejaculation,** the sphincters described above do not work properly; the one that usually closes to prevent urine from leaving the bladder opens instead, and the one that usually opens to let seminal fluid pass through the penis, closes. Consequently, seminal fluid enters the bladder instead of being forced out through the penis. Retrograde ejaculation can be caused by various illnesses, prostate surgery, and certain therapeutic drugs. It is not harmful—the seminal fluid simply exits later with the urine.

If a man does not have an orgasm after reaching plateau, he may be left temporarily with a full, tense feeling in his genitals, commonly known as "blue balls." This condition is not caused by a buildup of seminal fluid, but by vasocongestion and sustained muscular tension. The feeling can be uncomfortable, but it is not harmful and will eventually go away.

According to Masters and Johnson, women, like men, subjectively perceive the onset of orgasm just before rhythmic contractions begin. Orgasm starts with a spasm in the orgasmic platform. The contractions, in the pelvic area, occur every 0.8 seconds. Particularly strong ones occur in the muscles behind the lower vaginal walls, and these cause the orgasmic platform to move in and out. Other muscles contract as well, most notably in the uterus, while the upper part of the vagina continues to expand. If pelvic congestion is not relieved by orgasm, women, like men, may feel uncomfortable; but nobody has thought up a slang term yet for the female version of "blue balls."

Masters and Johnson reported a relationship between the number and duration of contractions and the perceived intensity of an orgasm. A mild orgasm might involve three to five contractions, an intense one, eight to twelve. In the most intense orgasm observed by Masters and Johnson, twenty-five contractions of the orgasmic platform took place over a period of forty-three seconds. However, subsequent research has found women's orgasms to be more variable in length than Masters and Johnson reported. In one study, they ranged in duration from 7.4 to 104.6 seconds (Bohlen, Held, Sanderson & Ahlgren, 1982). Still other research (Levin & Wagner, 1985) has found that the relationship between contractions and subjective experience is less direct than Masters and Johnson claimed. The measured duration of women's orgasms averaged 26 seconds but the women's estimates of length averaged only 12.2 seconds. There was no relationship between how long an orgasm lasted and how intense it felt.

A major difference between the orgasmic experiences of men and women is that women do not seem to ejaculate—or at least most women. Some reports (Alzate, 1985; Goldberg et al., 1983; Addiego et al., 1981; Perry & Whipple, 1981) have suggested that at least some women may expel a fluid through the urinary opening during orgasm. But at present, no one knows how many women do so. In a recent survey, 40 percent of women reported experiencing such a spurt (Darling, Davidson, & Conway-Welch, 1990). But caution is in order. All the respondents in this study were employed in nursing, sex education, sex therapy, or counseling. They had read and heard about "female ejaculation" and discussed it with friends and colleagues, and therefore may not have been unbiased about the phenomenon. Moreover, there was little agreement among the women about the source of the fluid or about when and how it was released. Other researchers think that "female ejaculation," if it exists, is uncommon. Masters and Johnson say that in the years they have spent studying sex both physiologically and clinically, they have found only a handful of women who expelled a fluid at orgasm (Masters, Johnson & Kolodny, 1986).

Disagreement also exists about what the fluid in "female ejaculation" is. Chemical analysis in one case (Alzate, 1985) found the fluid to be indistinguishable from urine, indicating that it might result from a urinary leakage triggered at orgasm. Other researchers speculate that the fluid originates from a system of glands and ducts surrounding the urethra. Further research is required to determine what female "ejaculation" is and whether it is more common than previously thought, or a rare physiological anomaly.

In both sexes, blood pressure, heart rate, and breathing rate all reach a peak at orgasm. Involuntary muscle spasms occur, including pelvic and anal contractions, and voluntary muscle control is lost.

Resolution

After orgasm, muscular tension subsides and all bodily functions return to "start." Men lose their erections in two stages, a rapid one in which the penis loses about 50 percent of its tumescence, and a more gradual stage in which the penis returns finally to its unaroused state. The scrotum and testes return to their original state rapidly in some men, more slowly (in one to two hours) in others. In women, the clitoris returns to its unaroused position in five to ten seconds but may remain extremely sensitive to touch for several minutes. The clitoral glans and shaft return to their original size within minutes after orgasm, but this may take several hours if the woman has not had an orgasm. Both men and women may experience a film of perspiration on the body during resolution. Many people—of both sexes—feel tired after sexual activity and want to rest or sleep. Others prefer to continue lovemaking for a while longer, and some bound out of bed with renewed energy.

Alternative Models

Without a doubt, Masters and Johnson have made a remarkable contribution to our knowledge of human sexual response. However, as critics have pointed out, and as you may have perceived, their picture of sexual response might be characterized as a little dry and clinical—in a word, unsexy. Sex is not just between our legs; a complete depiction of human sexual response must include the role of emotions, thoughts, and perceptions.

Several experts have proposed alternative models of sexual response that include subjective psychological phases along with objective physiological events. Helen Singer Kaplan (1974, 1979) proposes a three-phase model

Sexual Satisfaction
Erotic pleasure and gratification have as much to do with psychological responses as with physiological ones.

that includes a *desire* phase, a *vasocongestion* phase (engorgement of the genitals), and a *muscular contractions* (orgasm) phase. Bernie Zilbergeld and Carol Ellison (1980) have proposed a five-component model. The first component is sexual *interest* or *desire* (that is, how frequently a person wants to have sex). The second component is *arousal*, which refers to how excited or turned on one gets during sex. These are purely subjective phenomena. The third component is *physiological readiness* (vaginal lubrication/swelling and erection) and the fourth is *orgasm*. The last component is *satisfaction*, the subjective evaluation of the experience. Both Kaplan's model and Zilbergeld and Ellison's model recognize the role of psychological processes in sexual response, but neither is as well-developed as Masters and Johnson's model.

MULTIPLE ORGASMS: FOR WOMEN ONLY?

We come now to what Masters and Johnson (1966) consider a genuine sex difference. They believe that after a man ejaculates he is unable to get another full erection for at least a certain length of time, no matter how much he is stimulated. They call this interval the **refractory period.** (It's worth noting that in everyday speech *refractory* means obstinate, intractable, or stubbornly disobedient.) According to Masters and Johnson, the refractory period continues until sexual tension subsides to the level of early stages of excitement. For some men the refractory period is quite short; one young fellow in the Masters and Johnson laboratory had three orgasms with ejaculation (essentially three complete cycles) in the space of ten minutes. For others the period may stretch out to several hours or as much as a day. Generally, the refractory period lengthens with age. But women, according to Masters and Johnson, have no refractory period. If a woman is regularly orgasmic, and if effective stimulation continues, she may then continue to climax without dropping below plateau-phase levels of arousal. Her orgasms may come a few seconds or a few minutes apart, or may seem to follow one after the other. There seems to be no limit—apart from physical exhaustion—to the number of orgasms a woman may have. During masturbation (especially with a vibrator, which requires less physical effort than does manual stimulation), some women can have as many as fifty or more consecutive orgasms. In Masters and Johnson's studies, the orgasms following the first have been physiologically identical to the first, but often have been reported as more intense.

Masters and Johnson are not the first sex researchers to discuss multiple orgasms in women. Alfred Kinsey described them in his book on females in 1953, although many contemporary physicians and psychoanalysts refused to believe him. Two psychiatrists (Bergler & Kroger, 1954) proclaimed the multiple orgasm a physical impossibility. Kinsey's volunteers, they said, must have been "vaginally frigid" nymphomaniacs who could not tell an orgasm from a hiccup. Their final word on multiply-orgasmic women: "Briefly, such women don't exist."

But when Masters and Johnson (1966) actually recorded multiple orgasms in the laboratory, their existence could no longer be denied. The scientific documentation of multiple orgasms in women forced people to revise their ideas about female sexuality. Clearly, the old stereotype of female orgasm as purely "emotional" was wrong; women, too, could enjoy physical gratification in sex. A few writers went so far as to say that women, not men, are the turned-on sex. One theorist, Mary Jane Sherfey (1973), suggested that because women are capable of multiple orgasms that are successively stronger and more pleasurable, women's sexual appetites are, by definition, insatiable.

When people talk as if the two sexes are contestants in some sort of sexual Olympics and only one can emerge the winner, we are in the realm of sexual politics. Objective research, however, cautions us to avoid extreme claims and conclusions. Researchers using sophisticated measures of engorgement have failed to substantiate claims that women's multiple orgasms are successively stronger either physiologically or subjectively (Amberson & Hoon, 1985). Furthermore, it is not clear that *all* orgasmic women can have multiples, as Masters and Johnson implied. Kinsey's estimate of the number of women who had multiples was only 14 percent. (Kinsey asked only about orgasms during coitus, however.) To complicate the issue, different researchers have defined "multiple orgasm" differently. For Kinsey, multiple orgasms were simply orgasms in rapid succession. Others use the term to refer to one long, continuous orgasm or to a series of rapidly recurring orgasms without a return to the plateau phase. Still others, such as Shere Hite (1976), make a distinction between sequential orgasms (which include pauses between orgasmic responses and require a restimulation of the genitals every few minutes) and multiple orgasms, which are the result of continued stimulation without a break.

Perhaps multiple orgasms of one sort or another are within the capacity of most or all women. However, this conclusion goes beyond currently available evidence. In any case, Masters and Johnson were describing a potential capacity, not some sort of mandatory performance goal. Nowhere did they say that a single isolated orgasm is inferior to or less satisfying than a hundred consecutive ones. As far as orgasms are concerned, no two women are exactly alike. One may insist that for her, "once is not enough." Another may have an exceptional orgasm that brings her down to prearousal levels and leaves her feeling so terrific—and exhausted—that she doesn't care to try for more. A third woman may be completely satisfied by a single, comparatively mild orgasm. And a woman who has the capacity for multiple orgasms may at times be perfectly happy without even one.

As for the supposed "superiority" of women because they have multiple orgasms, some researchers question the dogma that males never have them (that is, that they must return to the excitement phase and repeat the entire cycle if they want to climax again). One interview study done in the 1970s suggested that there is a capacity for "dry" multiple orgasms in men leading to a final orgasm with ejaculation—a capacity that does not necessarily decline with age (Robbins and Jensen, 1978). In a more recent study, 21 men, ranging in age from 25 to 69, reported experiencing several types of multiple orgasms, with little or no loss of erection between orgasms (Dunn & Trost, 1989). Three men said they had one or more dry orgasms and then a final, intense orgasm. Two ejaculated on the first orgasm and went on to have one or more dry orgasms. Sixteen men reported varying patterns: two or more orgasms with full, partial, or no ejaculation at various points in the sequence of arousal and release. About half the men in the study had female partners who corroborated their reports. Most of the men reported that ejaculation and the intensity of an orgasm were unrelated. Most said that having multiple orgasms required a familiar, responsive, sexually interested partner with whom the man was emotionally close.

Further study is needed to clarify the physiology of multiple orgasms in men and to find out what proportion of men may have this capacity. Keep in mind, though, that for men, as for women, more is not always merrier. Sexual happiness cannot be gauged by an orgasmic score sheet.

THE VAGINAL VS. CLITORAL ORGASM DEBATE

Where do women "feel" their orgasms and which organ, the clitoris or the vagina, is the most effective source of erotic arousal? For years, experts claimed there were two distinct kinds of female orgasms, clitoral and vaginal, and held that the vaginal variety was the hallmark of the sexually mature-woman. Freud made this distinction a major tenet of his psychosexual theory. Most of his followers also insisted on the superiority of the vaginal orgasm. For example, psychoanalyst Helen Deutsch (quoted in Moore, 1961) described the clitoral orgasm as a convulsive, "anti-motherly" response to irritation, something like a sneeze. In contrast, she believed, a mature vaginal orgasm was more like a relaxed, ladylike sniff. Despite the total absence of physiological evidence, Deutsch presumed to speak for the "vast majority" of women. Late in life, however, she did begin to have doubts. So many women were unable to have vaginal orgasms; could they all be disturbed?

One critic of the vaginal orgasm was Alfred Kinsey. If the vagina was where sexual pleasure happened, he reasoned, then it ought to be a very sensitive organ (Kinsey et al., 1953). In his usual methodical way, Kinsey tested this proposition by having five gynecologists touch 879 women on various parts of their genital anatomy. Few women were even aware of a touch on the vaginal lining or the cervix, but almost all knew when the clitoris was touched. This was hardly surprising, since the upper vagina contains few nerve endings (see Chapter 4). But there were problems with Kinsey's approach. For example, the examined women were not sexually aroused, and critics pointed out that the vagina might be more sensitive during intercourse. In any case, many physicians and psychiatrists ignored Kinsey's findings on vaginal orgasms, just as they ignored his findings on multiple orgasms.

Masters and Johnson (1966) hoped to put an end to the vaginal-clitoral debate. Based on their observations of both the vagina and the clitoris, they concluded that the clitoris is the focus of subjective sensation, whatever the source of erotic arousal. They pointed out, however, that the vagina is by no means a passive organ. After all, the contractions associated with orgasm occur in the muscles that encircle the lower vaginal walls. Therefore, they argued, it makes little sense to talk about either a vaginal or a clitoral orgasm. An orgasm is an orgasm is an orgasm.

For a while it appeared as though the debate was over, with the winner being one "all-purpose" orgasm. But during the early 1980s interest in vaginal orgasms was rekindled. Reports appeared of an erogenous zone located on the anterior (front) wall of the vagina, the so-called **Grafenberg spot** ("G spot") (Ladas, Whipple, & Perry, 1982). Possession of the G spot was thought to be associated (although not always) with "female ejaculation." As we saw in Chapters 3 and 4, most researchers have been unable to verify that women generally have such an anatomically discrete structure in the vagina. However, the debate about the sensitivity of various parts of the vagina continues. Many women do report a "sensitive area" somewhere in the vagina (Darling, Davidson, & Conway-Welch, 1990). In one replicated study of a group of prostitutes, all appeared responsive to manual stimulation of *either* the back or front vaginal wall (Alzate & Londoño, 1984; Alzate, 1985). There are problems with this study, but the vagina may not always be as insensitive an organ as Kinsey thought it was.

So what difference does it make whether a woman has a "vaginal" or a "clitoral" orgasm? After all, we don't make a fuss about whether a man has a "glans" or a "shaft" orgasm. Why the continuing efforts to establish one or another kind of orgasm as the best type for women? One answer may be that "clitoral" orgasms are often associated with masturbation and "vaginal" ones with heterosexual intercourse, even though vaginal stimulation can be produced without a partner (by using a finger, dildo, or other object), and clitoral stimulation can be produced with the aid of a partner. The false equation of "clitoral" with "masturbatory" clouds the entire issue. People who are uncomfortable with female masturbation may reject the notion of the clitoral orgasm for that reason. Another explanation may be a tendency to view relationships as symmetrical. Because the vagina provides sexual pleasure for the penis, people may simply assume that the penis must provide equal sexual pleasure for the vagina—which after all would be the simplest, most "efficient" arrangement. People may cling to the idea that a vaginal orgasm is best because they can't believe what's good for the gander isn't always good for the goose.

The effort to construct a good-better-best hierarchy for female orgasms reveals common assumptions about what sex "ought" to be. If all orgasms were considered equal, people would be ready to agree with Barbara Seaman (1972), who wrote, "The liberated orgasm is any orgasm a woman likes."

THE PSYCHOBIOLOGY OF SEXUAL AROUSAL

We have reviewed the basic physiology of the human sexual response cycle. But what gets the cycle going in the first place and what keeps it going? Why and how do we get turned on? To understand the complexities of sexual arousal we must venture beyond the confines of physiology into the area of **psychobiology,** the field that integrates mind and body, and examine the neurological, chemical, and mental bases for sexual response.

Reflexes: The Neural Connections

As we saw in Chapter 1, for human beings, social and psychological factors are the strongest determinants of sexual behavior and custom. However, biology also plays its part. In fact, unromantic as it may seem, some aspects of sexual arousal are merely sequences of *reflexes*—simple, automatic, unlearned responses that take place without any conscious effort or motivation. The nervous systems of all animals exhibit reflexive behavior. In a reflex, nerve impulses from a receptor travel to a center in the spinal cord, which in turn sends out nerve impulses to some bodily tissue (usually a muscle or a gland), which then responds in some way. Sexual reflexes are similar to the knee jerk a doctor produces by hitting your knee with a hammer, although they are somewhat more complex neurologically. While the knee jerk is elicited by a single tap, sexual reflexes rely on continuous stimulation.

Consider penile erection. When skin on or near the penis is stroked, a message travels through a man's nervous system to an erection center located in the lowest part of his spinal cord—the *sacral* area. This center then sends a message back to the tiny valve-like channels that lead from the arteries of the penis to the spaces in the penis's spongy tissues, telling them to relax. As

FIGURE 5–6 **The erection and ejaculation reflexes** *In these drawings, arrows indicate the direction of nerve impulses. The erection reflex (a) may be triggered either by direct genital stimulation or by messages from the brain regarding erotic thoughts, sights, and sounds. The ejaculation reflex (b) cannot be consciously willed, but most men can control its onset to some extent by reducing the level of mental or physical stimulation, as indicated by the dotted arrow.*

a consequence, blood rushes into the chambers of the penis. Expansion of the tissue in the penis causes veins (which carry blood back to the heart) to become compressed, so that blood cannot flow out very rapidly. As a result, the penis becomes distended and erect. At the same time, a separate sensory message is traveling up to the brain; this message lets the man know that something is happening in his genitals. (For a schematic illustration of this process, see Figure 5–6.) In Chapter 4, we likened erection to what happens when you fill a balloon with air or water. The capacity for erectile response is innate. Apparently, so is the pleasure felt when sensory nerves signal the brain about an erection; even infants seem to enjoy genital stimulation.

Of course, direct stimulation of the penis is not the only way to get an erection. Erotic thoughts accomplish the same thing via neural pathways leading from the brain to the spinal cord (apparently to a second erection center, located higher up in the cord than the one involved in a physically produced reflex). But strictly speaking, an erection can occur without the brain being involved. A man whose spinal cord has been severed above the erection center can have reflexive erections if his penis is physically stimulated, even though he cannot get an erection from sexual thoughts and cannot feel the erection occurring (see Chapter 18).

Ejaculation is also a reflex. When erection occurs, changes in the part of the urethra that runs through the prostate excite adjacent sensory nerves, and a message travels to ejaculation centers in the sacral and lumbar sections of the spinal cord (the latter is somewhat higher up). These centers in turn

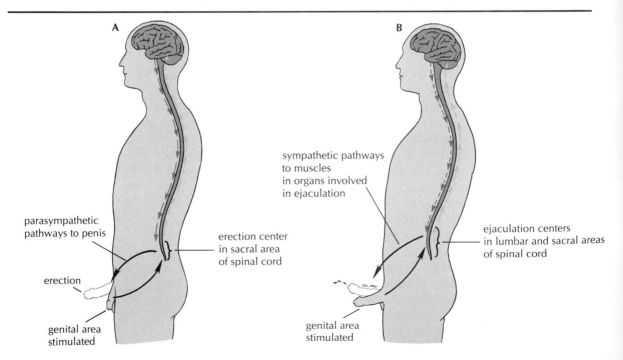

A

B

sympathetic pathways
to muscles
in organs involved
in ejaculation

parasympathetic
pathways to penis

erection center
in sacral area
of spinal cord

ejaculation centers
in lumbar and sacral areas
of spinal cord

erection

genital area
stimulated

genital area
stimulated

send out messages that produce contractions in the vas deferens, the seminal vesicles, and the prostate gland, contractions that cause them to empty their contents into the urethra. Then, when stimulation reaches a peak, other pelvic contractions force the ejaculate through the urethral opening. Most men are able to exercise some voluntary control over the ejaculatory reflex.

What about sexual reflexes in females? There has been little laboratory research on the matter. We know that in female dogs and cats, the posture that signals readiness for intercourse can be provoked reflexively when the animal's spinal cord has been cut. In addition, stimulation of a female dog's clitoris causes reflexive contractions in vaginal muscles that are analogous to the muscles that aid ejaculation in male dogs. Clinical reports on women with spinal cord injuries suggest the existence of reflexive vaginal lubrication and clitoral swelling in the human female. All this suggests that both sexes possess essentially the same sexual reflexes, involving the same spinal centers, even though their genital anatomy is different (Hart, 1978). That is not surprising, since the same basic sexual processes, vasocongestion and myotonia, occur in both males and females, and since the male and female sex organs develop from the same fetal tissue (see Chapter 4).

The above description of sexual reflexes leaves out one important piece of information. The nerves that run to and from the spinal cord, and that control sexual responses, are part of the **autonomic nervous system (ANS),** which is generally responsible for *autonomous*, or involuntary, bodily functions (heartbeat, salivation, and so forth). The ANS consists of two subsystems, the **sympathetic nervous system** and the **parasympathetic nervous system.** Generally, these two subsystems work together to adjust the body to changing circumstances, particularly those that are emotional and stressful. The sympathetic nervous system, to simplify somewhat, gears you up for action. When your heart is pounding, your pupils are dilated, your stomach is churning, your mouth is dry, and you are perspiring, the sympathetic nervous system is responsible. The parasympathetic nervous system, in contrast, is generally responsible for conserving energy and keeping your bodily processes functioning at a nice, steady rate. After exertion, it slows the heart down and increases salivation. Thus, the two subsystems interact to adjust the body to meet environmental demands.

Each subsystem dominates at a different part of the sexual response cycle. Initial arousal (erection in males and vaginal lubrication in females) is controlled by the parasympathetic nervous system. (It may seem paradoxical that sexual excitement is mediated by a system ordinarily devoted to slowing down physiological processes. But remember that relaxation of tissue in the arteries is necessary for blood to flow into the genital region.) The internal muscular contractions involved in ejaculation and orgasm are triggered by the sympathetic nervous system. Because separate nervous systems are associated with different phases of sexual response, initial arousal is not necessarily related to the ease with which a person reaches orgasm. For example, a man who has difficulty getting an erection may have no problem ejaculating once he is erect. A man who gets an erection quickly could have trouble ejaculating.

The dominance of the two separate subsystems during different phases of a person's sexual response has some other interesting implications. Sex therapists commonly observe that stress and strong negative emotions, such as anger or anxiety, can kill sexual desire. One reason may be that stress and strong emotions are characterized by sympathetic nervous system activity (as evidenced by an increased heartbeat, perspiration, and so forth). But initial arousal requires *parasympathetic* activity, not sympathetic. Thus, stress and negative emotions may not only block conscious interest in sex, but may actually decrease the body's ability to respond, whether the person wants to or not. Sexual responses are complicated processes, vulnerable to inhibition by both psychological and physiological factors.

Hormones: The Chemical Connections

Another way in which biology influences arousal is through hormones. As we saw in Chapter 4, hormones are chemical messengers that travel through the bloodstream to tissues in various parts of the body. Sex hormones help keep the reproductive "machinery" in good working order, primarily by regulating sperm production and ovulation. Both sexes produce testosterone, the most potent "male" sex hormone, and estrogen, the most important "female" sex hormone, but in different amounts. The question to be considered here is whether either of these hormones affects sexual arousal or performance. The short answer is that in both sexes, a certain level of testosterone is probably necessary for the maintenance of sexual interest and motivation. The full answer is more complicated.

Hormone specialists refer to the influences of adult hormones on sexual behaviors as **activating effects** (Feder, 1984). (For the effects of prenatal hormones on postnatal behavior, see Chapter 12.) Because altering hormones can be risky, experiments in this area have been conducted mostly on animals. Activating effects in animals depend on the species and strain of animal used, the dosage and form of the hormone administered, the state of the animal's hormones around the time of its birth, the type of behavior measured, the sex of other animals in the cage, an animal's previous sexual experiences, and other factors that are part of the experimental procedure. In some species testosterone injections typically produce, in males, sexual behavior characteristic of males, such as mounting another animal, and estrogen injections (combined with progesterone in specific ratios) typically produce, in females, sexual behavior characteristic of females, such as assuming a receptive posture. But that is only the beginning. Two hormones (estrogen and testosterone), two sexes (male and female), and two classes of behavior (masculine and feminine) can logically combine in eight different ways. At one time or another *each* of these possible combinations has been observed in one species or another (see Young, 1961). That is, testosterone sometimes produces female behavior in females, estrogen sometimes brings on female behavior in males, and so forth.

As we explore the relationship between hormones and sexual arousal in human beings it is important to keep in mind that there is still a great deal to learn about what hormones do and how they do it.

TESTOSTERONE AND MALE SEXUALITY   One way to explore the influence of testosterone on sexual arousal in men is to study individuals who have been **castrated,** that is, who have had their testes surgically removed. These males, who are sometimes called **eunuchs,** produce much less androgen than other men (some is still produced in the adrenal cortex). Historically, castration has been used for punishment or revenge. Rulers also castrated men they wanted to employ as harem attendants, to make them "safe." (The word *eunuch* comes from the Greek for "chamberlain," or "keeper of the bedchamber.") As late as the eighteenth century, boys with high voices were castrated so that they could continue to sing soprano parts in all-male choirs and operas. Unfortunately, little historical evidence exists to tell us whether any of these males had sex lives. It was assumed that they did not, but there were plenty of rumors about harem attendants who behaved like roosters in a chicken coop.

There are a few modern castration studies, mostly European, that describe the sexual behavior of men who were castrated either because they were criminal sex offenders or because they had unusual sexual habits, and it was thought that castration would cure them. A study of 224 Norwegian cases found that two-thirds of the men lost sexual interest and ceased sexual activity within a year after castration (Bremer, 1959). Other studies have yielded similar results.

Findings from castration studies do not conclusively show that hormones influence sexual behavior. A castrated man might lose interest in sex not because he lacks the necessary hormones, but because he considers himself to be mutilated and desexed. The results are bolstered, however, by studies of men being treated with synthetic hormones that achieve the effects of castration without altering anatomy. These substances either suppress male sex-hormone production or interfere with the use of androgens by the body. Sex offenders, sexual "deviates," and "hypersexual" (oversexed) men who are chemically castrated with these synthetic hormones tend to show reduced sexual behavior and ability. In one study (Laschet, 1973), subjects were treated over a long period of time with cyproterone acetate, a progestin-type substance that seems to block the body's use of its own androgens. The men in the study tended to lose their sexual urges, their ability to get an erection, and their capacity for orgasm, in that order. In some cases the effects continued even after hormone treatment stopped.

So far, the case for testosterone being the sexual arousal hormone in males seems fairly strong. However, surgical and chemical castration do not inevitably lead to loss of sexual ability and desire. Some men who are castrated for medical reasons, such as cancer in both testes, rapidly lose all interest

Royal eunuchs
Historically, eunuchs have played many roles. In China, they once served as royal attendants and advisors. This photograph of the Empress Dowager Tz'u-hsi of China, taken in 1903, shows her flanked by two of her court's most powerful eunuchs.

in sex as well as the ability to "perform," but others continue to lead a normal sex life for years.

A second way to study the testosterone–sexuality link is to do research on males with *hypogonadism*, a condition caused by various diseases of the endocrine system and characterized by an abnormally low testosterone level. When hypogonadism occurs before puberty, the body does not develop the usual adult sexual characteristics and the person is unlikely to develop a sexual interest. If the condition occurs during adulthood, the consequences are less predictable, but a loss of sexual interest is characteristic. When androgens are increased to normal levels through hormone replacement therapy, sexual interest and behavior are often restored (Carey, Howards, & Vance, 1988; Findlay, Place, & Snyder, 1989). However, even when hormone levels remain low, some aspects of sexual functioning are unaffected; in the laboratory, men with hypogonadism may experience erections while watching erotic films (Bancroft, 1984).

A third way to study testosterone and male sexuality is to look for a relationship between hormonal fluctuations and sexual arousal in normal, healthy men. One such study, of 33 young men, found that men with high blood testosterone levels had more orgasms than men with lower levels (Knussmann, Christiansen & Couwenbergs, 1986). But the researchers didn't stop there. They examined the relationship between the men's hormone levels and their exposure to sexual stimulation (fantasies and erotic materials) a day or two *before* the hormone measurements were taken. They also looked at the relationship between hormone levels and sexual activity (masturbation, petting, intercourse) *after* the assessment of hormone levels. Sophisticated statistical analysis of these data suggest that cause and effect are complicated. A high testosterone level can precipitate sexual activity. But being sexually stimulated can also increase testosterone levels.

Taken as a whole, the evidence suggests that although testosterone alone cannot account for male sexual behavior, it does play an important role. In real life, however, many factors can affect the hormone-behavior link. For example, exercise may increase testosterone, so if levels go up during intercourse, or if sexually active men have higher than average levels, there is no way to tell whether the result is due to the sheer activity involved or to sex per se. Similarly, stress seems to make testosterone levels fall; soldiers in battle, who are typically more fearful than ferocious, show a decline in testosterone. Therefore, if a man with sexual problems has a low testosterone level, his difficulties could be due to lack of the hormone, or the stress of the problem could be causing the low hormone level.

HORMONES AND FEMALE SEXUALITY   When most people think of hormones and female sexuality, they think of estrogen. But research on the possible activating effects of estrogen has produced mostly negative results. A few studies have reported increased sexual interest in women who have had estrogen replacement therapy after natural menopause or removal of the ovaries, but many find no effects. Most women do not experience a decline in sexual interest after menopause, even though estrogen drops off dramatically. In studies of the menstrual cycle, some women say they feel most aroused midway between periods, when estrogen reaches its peak; but others insist the sexiest time is right before or after menstruation, when estrogen is at its lowest point, and still others report no particular preference for one part of the cycle over another. Our best guess, at present, is that estrogen does not significantly affect a woman's sexual desire.

If there is a "libido hormone" in women, it is likely to be testosterone, just as it is in men. For decades there have been anecdotal reports of increased sexual interest in women receiving androgen therapy for various medical problems. Recent, controlled research seems to confirm these reports. Barbara Sherwin and Morrie Gelfand, of McGill University, studied women who had their ovaries removed. Some of the women received estrogen therapy, some received an estrogen-androgen preparation, and some remained untreated. Women who received the hormone combination reported higher rates of sexual desire and arousal and more sexual fantasies than women in the other two groups. Moreover, changes in these measures tended to correlate with changes in testosterone levels but not with changes in estrogen levels during the course of the study (Sherwin & Gelfand, 1987).

In a different kind of study, a team of researchers headed by Harold Persky (1978) interviewed eleven healthy young married couples who were not using birth control pills (which are composed of synthetic hormones.) Over a three-month period, data were collected about the couples' sexual behaviors, including the wives' sexual interest, sexual arousal, and masturbation. Blood samples determined the women's testosterone levels. One of the major findings: women with generally high testosterone levels reported greater sexual gratification than those with low levels. Average testosterone production did not correlate with actual frequency of intercourse, but the level of testosterone around the time of ovulation—when testosterone in women usually peaks—did correlate with frequency. Recently, another team of researchers (Morris, Udry, Khan-Dawood, & Dawood, 1987) replicated the Persky et al. study using forty-three couples and more refined methods. Again, the levels of the women's testosterone at midcycle correlated with the frequency of intercourse. However, the researchers stopped short of concluding that high levels of testosterone directly *cause* high levels of sexual activity. Rather, they speculate that testosterone indirectly increases sexual motivation, for example by increasing sensitivity to sexual stimulation.

If testosterone is related to sexual desire in women, does that mean that women, who have much lower levels than men, are biologically less lusty than men? Not at all. Hormones work by acting on special receptors in nerve cells in the brain and other parts of the nervous system; women could have more of these receptors. There is also evidence that sexual functioning requires a certain minimum amount of testosterone but quantities over the basic threshold do not increase arousal in either sex (Sherwin, 1988). That would explain why giving testosterone to people with normal levels does not boost their sexual interest. In any case, most women seem to have as much testosterone as they need!

To sum up: Although there is more evidence at present on men than on women, research indicates that testosterone affects sexual interest and arousability in both men and women. As we noted in Chapter 1, however, hormones have a far less predictable impact on human sexuality than on the sexuality of other species. In the castration and other studies we reviewed, low testosterone levels did not *inevitably* reduce sexual interest or responsiveness. In Chapter 12 we will see that at least some children are capable of experiencing orgasm even in infancy, long before maturation of the sex glands. In adulthood, individuals may differ in their sensitivity to the effects of testosterone and the extent to which their sexuality depends on it. Future research may clarify how hormone levels interact with psychological, social, and neurological influences in sexual functioning, and what their precise effects are on specific parts of the brain and sexual anatomy.

Awareness of Arousal: The Cognitive Connection

The reflexes and hormones involved in sexual arousal and response operate at a fairly involuntary level; choice and decision making play little or no part. However, for human beings, sexual arousal is not automatic: it depends on thoughts, feelings, and judgments—the processes associated with the cerebral cortex of the brain. The *cognitive*, or mental, elements in arousal have a profound impact on the *visceral* ones (those that occur in the internal organs of the body). As we saw earlier, even when researchers extensively monitor the sexual response cycle from beginning to end with the most sophisticated of devices, their recordings do not always correspond to what people report they are experiencing. Many researchers think orgasm is more of a perceptual (i.e., mental) than a genital event. Expectation is also a critical mental ingredient in the experience of orgasm. If an orgasm is anticipated, it is more likely to occur (Gallagher, 1986).

Expectancies, perceptions, fantasies, sense memories, emotions—all these cognitive events are critical to human sexual functioning. Sociologists William Gagnon and John Simon (1973, 1986) have pointed out that a

Why isn't anyone here having sex? *Despite the close physical proximity and the availability of potential partners, few people would get intimate with someone in a crowded subway car. We have all learned culturally-determined sexual "scripts" that tell us where, when, and with whom we may be sexual—and we know that public places are off-limits.*

situation is not erotic unless people perceive it that way. We learn which situations are erotic from **sexual scripts** that embody our culture's behavioral norms. (In Chapters 12 and 13 we will see how such scripts are acquired.) Scripts tell us not only *what* is erotic, but *when, where, why,* and *with whom* to be sexual. They operate at an *interpersonal* level by guiding our behavior in specific situations with individual people. They also work at an *intrapsychic* (in our heads) level by telling us how to interpret what we are feeling and how to manage our desires (Simon & Gagnon, 1986). For example, sexual scripts guide a woman to distinguish the difference in meaning between a lover's touch and a similar touch during a gynecological exam.

Sexual scripts solve two problems for us, according to Simon and Gagnon. They give us permission to engage in certain forms of sexual behavior and they tell us how to interpret the resulting experiences. Thus, like most people in this society, you probably find it easier to become aroused and sexual in private than in public; your scripts give you permission for the former but not the latter. Scripts also direct your attention and help you recognize that what you are feeling is sexual. People are not automatically aware of their sexual responses, as we saw in studies of perceived and measured orgasms. Scripts mediate between bodily responses and subjective experience; they are the cognitive connections that help us not only to attain experience, but also to be aware of its meaning.

If sexual arousal depends on both physiological arousal and a cognitive interpretation, then two people experiencing exactly the same sort of physiological arousal may report their experiences differently (Berscheid & Walster, 1974). In the past, many women may have used the label "romantic love" for physiological reactions that a man would have called "sexual arousal," because women were expected to fall in love easily but feel sexual

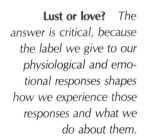

Lust or love?   *The answer is critical, because the label we give to our physiological and emotional responses shapes how we experience those responses and what we do about them.*

desire only in marriage, if then. Perhaps this is still true for some couples: he calls it lust and she calls it love, yet physiologically it is exactly the same thing. The consequences for the relationship and for the individuals' future actions can be profound. The label we choose for an experience is critical: sometimes a rose by any other name does *not* smell as sweet.

By now you can appreciate that turning on sexually isn't as simple as starting a car. Little wonder that since the dawn of time, people have searched for ways to make it easier. Often they have seized on some drug or food as the key to instant passion. So it is fitting that we close this chapter with a discussion of substances that affect sexual functioning.

SEXUAL UPPERS AND DOWNERS: APHRODISIACS AND ANAPHRODISIACS

Substances reputed to arouse sexual passion or enhance performance are called **aphrodisiacs.** (The word derives from the name of Aphrodite, the Greek goddess of love.) Across the centuries, suspected aphrodisiacs have included ordinary foods like potatoes, onions, oysters, asparagus, mint, garlic, radishes, pepper, fish, chocolate, licorice, sarsaparilla, eggs, nutmeg, and betel and litchi nuts, as well as rarer substances, including bulls' testicles, powdered rhinoceros horns, and ginseng roots (Jarvik & Brecher, 1977). None of these has any proven physiological effect on sexual desire or performance. (One unfortunate ecological effect, however, has been the threatened extinction of the black rhinoceros.)

In their pursuit of the perfect love potion, people have sometimes been willing to risk their health. Dangerous (and ineffective) substances used in the past include Spanish fly (cantharides), a preparation made from powdered blister beetles found in abundance in Spain. Spanish fly is a skin irritant that causes an inflammation of the urinary tract. It can produce **priapism,** an uncomfortable erection that won't go away. It can also cause death. The same is true of belladonna and strychnine, poisons that have also been tried as aphrodisiacs. (On the other hand, saltpeter [potassium nitrate], which was once given to schoolboys and prisoners to make them less interested in sex, has no direct effect. If it works at all, it is probably because it is a diuretic that keeps people so busy going to the bathroom that they have no time to think about sex.)

The search for the perfect "love potion" continues today; see Box 5–1. Hopes keep rising, only to be dashed. One recent candidate has been an ancient drug called yohimbine, a psychoactive alkaloid contained in the inner bark of a West African tree. Experiments in the early 1980s with rats suggested that injections of yohimbine could increase sexual arousal and enhance sexual performance, but subsequent studies with human beings have produced conflicting results (Danjou et al., 1988; Susset et al., 1989).

Mandragora mas.
Mandragore.

Don't waste your money

The ginseng (left) root and the mandrake (right) root are just two of the many substances that have been falsely labeled as aphrodisiacs. The reputations of these plants may derive from the fact that their shapes somewhat resemble the human form (that is, if you really use your imagination). Neither one "works," and the mandrake root actually reduces desire, *because it irritates the urinary tract.*

Many people believe that recreational drugs can boost sexual arousal and functioning—by relaxing the body, lowering inhibitions, increasing energy, or enhancing sensual perceptions. These claims have been hard to prove. It is clear, though, that some recreational drugs are **anaphrodisiacs,** that is, they *depress* sexual functioning or desire, either by slowing down or chemically altering brain activity, or by interfering with normal sympathetic and parasympathetic nervous system functions.

One drug that enjoys an undeserved reputation as an aphrodisiac is alcohol, the most widely used recreational drug in the United States. In the media (especially in advertising) alcohol is closely associated with sexual success, so it comes as a surprise to many that alcohol is actually a sexual downer. The first drink or two can make a person feel less inhibited because alcohol depresses neuron activity in the "higher" centers of the brain that regulate social behavior. Also, alcohol provides a convenient rationalization for behavior a person might otherwise feel guilty about. However, subsequent drinks can interfere with the ability to follow through. Researchers, using dogs and rats, have shown that alcohol affects the spinal reflexes necessary for sexual response (Hart, 1978). Recent studies with men show that alcohol substantially lowers testosterone levels in the blood, by blocking the synthesis of testosterone in the testes and accelerating its breakdown in the liver (Cohen, 1981, 1985).

Shakespeare summed up alcohol's effects concisely in *Macbeth:* "It provokes the desire, but it takes away the performance." Psychologists Gary Farkas and Ray Rosen documented the depressing effects of alcohol in the human male (Farkas, 1977). They showed sexually arousing films to sixteen college men who imbibed varying amounts of 100-proof liquor. The volunteers were hooked up to devices that measured heart rate and penis diameter. When the men had nothing to drink, watching the films produced an average nine-millimeter increase in penis diameter; after a single one-ounce drink, they showed almost a ten-millimeter increase. But after three drinks there was a reduction to just over seven and a half millimeters. Furthermore, after only two drinks, the men took longer to get an erection. Other research shows that alcohol also inhibits physiological arousal in women, although some women may say that they are actually more aroused (Wilson & Lawson, 1978). Humorist Ogden Nash gave us the immortal line, "Candy is dandy, but liquor is quicker." The findings on sex and alcohol suggest a new aphorism: What desire can inspire, drink will shrink.

Most other central nervous system *depressants* (sedatives, tranquilizers, and barbiturates) act in much the same way as alcohol. Any positive effect they may have on sexual interest is due to the relaxing of inhibitions. Sexual performance is apt to suffer, however, particularly if the dose induces sleep! One possible exception is methaqualone (Quaalude), an addictive (and dangerous) drug that is sometimes called "heroin for lovers." According to drug expert Sidney Cohen (1985), Quaalude may possess some as yet undetermined aphrodisiac quality. Heroin itself, as well as other *opiates* (such as opium and morphine), may initially promote sexual activity by lowering anxiety. But with continued use, all motives, including sexual ones, are reduced. Heroin addiction is commonly accompanied by loss of sexual ability

Do alcohol and sex mix?
People often use alcohol and other central nervous system depressants to lower social and sexual inhibitions, but these drugs can interfere with sexual responses.

BOX 5–1

The Secret Smells Of Sex

Sex is a sensual experience. For most people, stimulation of skin surfaces is the basic sensory source of arousal (see Chapter 4). Through association with tactile pleasure and through cultural learning, other senses also become avenues of erotic stimulation. The importance of vision is obvious—witness the demand for erotic photographs, films, and live sex shows, and the effect that certain clothing styles and body types have on people's sexual interest. Sounds—certain types of music, rhythms, and the groans, sighs, and heavy breathing of love-making—can also be sexually stimulating.

What about smell? Most of us are aware of the power certain odors have to turn us *off*, emotionally as well as sexually. But are there airborne chemical molecules with the strength to stimulate lustful desires? What should we make of an ad that trumpets, "Scientists Discover Mystery Chemical That Seems to Drive Women Wild!" (*Los Angeles Times*, May 11, 1986.) Could it be that even before we consciously know that we want to have sex, the nose knows?

The answer lies in the study of chemicals called **pheromones,** from the Greek *pherein* ("to transfer") and *hormone* ("to excite"). Pheromones are airborne substances secreted and released by one member of a species that affect the physiology or behavior of other members. These chemicals, many of them carrying sexual messages, were discovered early in the 1950s and have since been found in hundreds of species from insects to mice to monkeys. A female moth can send a sexual invitation to male moths miles away. The scent of a female dog in heat will draw all the unneutered male dogs in the neighborhood. In laboratory mammals (mice, rats, and monkeys) pheromones are linked to the level of the animals' sex hormones and signal both male and female fertility.

It would be logical (and lucrative) to find pheromones in human beings but, until recently, the search was disappointing. Not one study established beyond a doubt that human pheromones exist. Then, in 1986, chemist George Preti and biologist Winnifred B. Cutler, working at the University of Pennsylvania and the Monell Chemical Senses

and interest in both males and females. Some addicts in methadone maintenance programs report improved functioning, but others do not (Cohen, 1981, 1985).

In surveys, about half of all *marijuana* users report that this drug increases sexual desire and adds to sexual enjoyment. But as many as a third

Center, announced that people produce underarm pheromones that can influence women's menstrual cycles. One of Preti and Cutler's studies used a "male essence" collected from men's underarm secretions to normalize the menstrual cycles of seven women with unusually long or short cycles. The underarm secretions, diluted in alcohol, were swabbed on the women's upper lips three times a week for 14 weeks. A control group was treated with plain alcohol. In the control group, women's cycles did not change, but in the treatment group their cycles became more regular, averaging 29.5 days (Cutler et al., 1986).

A second study used underarm secretions from other *women* to synchronize women's menstrual cycles (Preti et al., 1986). The phenomenon of menstrual cycle synchrony among women who live in close quarters, such as a college dorm, had been suspected for years but never explained. Preti and Cutler hypothesize that the explanation may be a steroid called *androstenol*, which is present in human sweat.

It seems a safe bet that there are human chemical secretions that have subtle effects on other human beings. But let's not leap to conclusions about *sexual* behavior. There is no evidence that human pheromones are involved in the so-called "chemistry" that exists between people who are attracted to each other, or that human pheromones affect sexual activity (as opposed to reproductive system functioning). Smell is the most underused sense in human beings and our reactions to smells are strongly affected by learning—as witnessed by the trouble adults in our culture take to disguise their natural body odors. It's true that the smell of a male pig's saliva (which contains a substance similar to androstenol) may induce a sow in heat to assume a mating stance, but we cannot conclude that a man wearing a fragrance containing androstenol, advertised as the "mystery chemical that seems to drive women wild," will have the same effect on a woman.

And think about it. A sure-fire chemical sexual attractant that would work no matter what you look like or what your personality might seem to be worth a lot—but would you really want everyone within smelling distance panting after you?

report no effect (Cohen, 1981). Marijuana may lower sexual inhibitions or help people focus mentally on sexual stimulation. And, since it often makes time seem to pass more slowly than usual, sensations may appear to last longer than they otherwise would. Much seems to depend on what the user believes marijuana will do, with "true believers" experiencing the greatest effects. Recent studies show that marijuana use can cause a decrease in testosterone in male humans and animals and a decrease in LH and FSH in female animals. Heavy use in human males has also resulted in lowered sperm counts (Cohen, 1985).

Hallucinogens, both natural psychedelics (mushrooms, mescaline, peyote) and synthetic ones (LSD or lysergic acid diethylamide and PCP or phencyclidine, for example) have not been promoted as "sex drugs." Their mind-altering properties seem to produce essentially asexual, nonerotic experiences. However, the amphetamine-psychedelic MDA (methylenedioxyamphetamine), known as "speed for lovers," does not produce as depersonalized a state as other psychedelics, encouraging emotional closeness instead (Kowl, 1978). A milder version of MDA, the so-called "designer drug" MDMA (methylenedioxymethamphetamine), popularly known as "Ecstasy" and "Adam," enhances sensory and emotional awareness. The immediate reaction to taking MDMA is a rush of anxiety that is replaced in an hour or so with relaxation, euphoria, and feelings of enhanced emotional insight (Buchanan, 1985).

Amyl nitrite is a powerful drug that has long been used in the medical treatment of chest pain arising from coronary disease. It dilates arteries that supply the heart, the brain, and other organs, including those in the genital region. Its vascular effects in the brain can produce euphoria and giddiness, and those in the pelvic area can create a sense of warmth. Amyl nitrite usually comes in small glass ampules that are crushed for use; hence the popular terms "poppers" and "snappers." A derivative of this drug can also be obtained in the guise of a "room deodorizer" with such labels as "Rush," "Locker Room," and "Climax." A whiff just before orgasm is reputed to intensify the experience or bring on orgasm in people who do not usually have one. But carefully controlled research on such reported effects have not been done. Amyl nitrite has several negative side effects, including dizziness, headaches, and fainting; it is dangerous unless taken under medical supervision.

As part of their general arousal effects, central nervous system *stimulants* are often reported to increase sex drives. *Amphetamines* ("uppers" or "speed") may increase sexual energy and stamina, and some speed users report orgasms during the intravenous injection of the drug (Cohen, 1981). However, with long-term use, some men report difficulty in having orgasms. *Cocaine* is both a stimulant and a potent local anesthetic. Animals dependent on cocaine will pass up sex and food and endure electric shock to get the drug. In one study, monkeys pressed a bar 12,800 times in order to get a single dose (Cohen, 1985). The increased energy and "rush" produced by cocaine are said by some to enhance the intensity and frequency of orgasm. Conversely, its numbing properties can supposedly delay orgasm if it is applied to the penis. Frequent use may, however, reduce vaginal lubrication and interfere with erections (Cocores & Gold, 1989; Siegel, 1982). As cocaine use becomes a career, enhanced sexuality is replaced by a complete disinterest in sex (Cohen, 1985). This drug creates a powerful dependence in users, especially if it is injected or is smoked in the highly refined form called "crack," rather than inhaled, or "snorted".

The most widely used recreational stimulant of all is *nicotine*. In advertisements, cigarettes are supposed to increase sex appeal or create a romantic atmosphere. But in fact, they reduce sexual motivation and arousal (Glina et al., 1988; Gilbert, Hagen & D'Agostino, 1986). Nicotine constricts blood vessels and reduces circulation, and can therefore interfere with vasocongestion, which, as we have seen, is necessary for erection, vaginal lubrication, and other sexual responses.

Unfortunately, much of our information about the sexual effects of recreational drugs comes from users' reports. Such reports may not be reliable, and we can never be sure what caused the reported effect. Most street drugs are diluted or mixed with impurities and other drugs, and many drug users habitually use several substances at once. In addition, the *reputation* of a drug as a "love drug" may be the cause of most, if not all, of the experienced effects. Even in well-controlled studies, it is hard to generalize about drug effects because (1) people vary in their responsiveness and (2) a drug that enhances one area of sexual functioning, such as desire, may have little effect on another, such as intensity of orgasm. Finally, drugs have general effects on a person's mood and sense of well-being, and these feelings are hard to separate from specifically sexual effects.

Even if it turns out to be true that some recreational drugs enhance sexual functioning or experience, we might ask, "Is it worth it?" Consider the following:

1. Many people are prone to drug abuse. Abuse of any drug is physically and mentally unhealthy and tends to interfere with motivation and personal relationships and therefore sexual functioning.

2. The sharing of contaminated needles for injecting drugs spreads the HIV virus, which causes AIDS. (For more on this topic, see Chapter 17.)

3. Recreational drugs often affect judgment adversely and can lead to carelessness about contraception and protection from disease. Because they impair judgment, drugs and alcohol are also often associated with date and marital rape (see Chapter 15).

4. It is extremely unwise for a pregnant woman to use *any* non-prescribed drugs, including alcohol and nicotine, because of risks to the developing fetus.

We have been discussing recreational drugs, but what about sexual side effects of prescription drugs and over-the-counter medications? Some of these substances do influence sexual functioning through their effects on the nervous system or hormone levels, but in most cases the impact is negative or unpleasant. A few years ago there were reports that L-dopa (levodopa), which is used to treat Parkinson's disease, sexually revitalized older men who were taking the drug. But subsequent studies failed to confirm those findings. More recently, a controlled clinical study found that an antidepressant, buproprion hydrochloride (Wellbutrin) increased sexual interest in men and women with a variety of sexual problems (Crenshaw, Goldberg, & Stern, 1987). However, in light of the history of such reports—initial enthusiasm, followed by lack of confirmation—it seems wise to refrain from drawing any conclusions until more research is done.

To sum up, although many substances are rumored to be aphrodisiacs, there is no good evidence at present that any of them really work. Even if a drug does seem to boost arousal, the person may simply be experiencing the excitement of taking a forbidden drug or responding to expectations. At least two legal recreational drugs, alcohol and nicotine, and several commonly-used medications, can interfere with sexual performance.

The hope for a better sex life through chemistry, the search for super-sensitive spots, preoccupation with numbers and types of orgasms—all of these may reflect our culture's competitiveness (Am I having as many orgasms as my best friend? Will I be the first on my block to have the latest style orgasms?), dependence on technology (Maybe a machine will make me more orgasmic.), obsession with "normalcy" (Are my responses like everyone else's? I love my orgasms, but are they the right kind?), and desire for simple answers (If I could just find that spot!). Emotions, motives, and psychological context are *complicated*. It can be tempting to pin one's hopes for sexual satisfaction on passion pills or magic biological buttons. Sex therapist Avodah Offit writes, "Men watch and count their partners' peaks and have begun to tabulate their own. Women throw their heads back, try hard, and agonize to reach yet another climax. . .[people] dwell on quantity rather than quality, success rather than meaning, sensation rather than emotion" (1981).

An understanding of sexual physiology can help us feel more comfortable with our bodies and our erotic responses. But it cannot solve the difficult problems of passion, desire, fear, and choice. Analyzing sex in terms of physiology alone is like trying to understand Mozart by naming the notes he used in his compositions. Physiological facts are most useful when they are integrated with what we know about human psychology and culture.

. . . .

PERSONAL PERSPECTIVE

WHAT TURNS YOU ON?

Your body, regularly infused with a bit of testosterone, is ready for sexual stimulation even when you are asleep. But not all situations, people, or thoughts have the power to interest or arouse you. Human beings are selective about what attracts them—or repels them. It may seem that external events are controlling erotic response, but the truth is, we do it ourselves, guided by our cultural and personal scripts.

This exercise invites you to become more aware of your own sexual scripts and to take an inventory of what is apt to launch you into the excitement phase of sexual arousal.

First, what are the situations in which you are most apt to become sexually aroused? What are the dominant senses you rely on in sexual situations? What specific sights, sounds, smells, or touches seem erotic or exciting? What kinds of thoughts and mental images turn you on?

Next, think about some situations in the past when sexual arousal was unanticipated. (Most of us, at one time or another, feel erotic when it doesn't seem "appropriate.") What was going on in these situations that might have been sexually stimulating?

Finally, how would you answer the following questions?

1. What impact do the media and advertising have on your sexual scripts?

2. How aware do you think you are of your body's signs of sexual arousal? When are you apt to pay most attention? Least attention?

3. How do you feel about being sexually aroused? Is it always comfortable? Do you sometimes feel you shouldn't be aroused? When? Why? Do you ever avoid situations in which you think you might be aroused? Which ones?

4. What fears have you experienced about becoming sexually aroused? Have you ever worried about loss of control? Pain? Interruptions? Discovery? Embarrassment? Pregnancy? An "inappropriate" response, such as getting an erection in public?

5. How do stress and worry affect you sexually? Do they reduce sexual interest? Or, do you use sex to relieve every-day tensions?

IN BRIEF

1. Although men and women differ anatomically, their bodies undergo many similar changes during sexual excitement and orgasm, most of them attributable to *vasocongestion* and *myotonia*. For ease of description, Masters and Johnson have divided the sexual response cycle into four stages.

2. The *excitement stage* begins for men with penile erection and for women with vaginal lubrication. Both responses are caused by vasocongestion.

In men, the skin of the scrotum thickens and the testes elevate. In women, the clitoris swells and the uterus moves up and back, causing the upper two-thirds of the vagina to balloon out.

3. The *plateau stage* is more distinct in women than in men. The lower third of the vagina becomes congested and forms the *orgasmic platform*, without which an orgasm does not occur. The clitoris retracts and the minor lips deepen in color. Vaginal lubrication slows. In men, the penis becomes fully erect and the testes enlarge, continue to elevate, and rotate.

4. In both sexes *orgasm* is marked by strong rhythmic contractions in pelvic muscles. *Ejaculation* in men occurs in two stages: emission and expulsion. In women, muscle contractions cause the orgasmic platform to move in and out. Some women (no one knows how many) may expel a fluid at orgasm, but the existence and nature of the fluid are controversial.

5. In the *resolution stage*, muscular tensions subside and body organs return to their unstimulated state. This stage is prolonged, particularly in women, if orgasm has not occurred.

6. Alternative models of sexual response proposed by Kaplan and by Zilbergeld and Ellison include psychological responses as well as physiological ones.

7. Masters and Johnson report that during resolution men experience a *refractory period*, when further stimulation is ineffective in triggering orgasm, while women can go on to have additional (multiple) orgasms without dropping below plateau-stage levels of sexual tension. But recent research suggests that some men may also be able to have multiple orgasms.

8. For years experts, influenced by Freud, claimed that women had two different kinds of orgasms, clitoral and vaginal, and that vaginal orgasms were more mature. Masters and Johnson showed that both organs are important in sexual response and all orgasms are physiologically the same: clitoral sensations trigger orgasm and contractions of the orgasmic platform mark orgasm. However, recent findings have renewed the debate. Women's reports of orgasm differ and women may differ in vaginal sensitivity.

9. Some aspects of sexual arousal are reflexive. Specific spinal cord centers control erection and ejaculation reflexes in men and, in all probability, lubrication and orgasm in women. The *parasympathetic nervous system* is dominant during early stages of arousal; the *sympathetic nervous system* is dominant during later stages.

10. The relationship between hormones and sexual arousal is complex. Studies suggest that testosterone has an *activating effect* in both males and females. Many (but not all) men deprived of testosterone lose sexual interest and the ability to respond. In normal, healthy men there is

a positive relationship between levels of testosterone in the blood and sexual activity. In women, mid-cycle levels of testosterone are related to their arousability; apparently testosterone affects female sexual motivation. However, it is difficult to specify cause and effect; hormones can influence behavior, but behavior can also influence hormone levels. Hormonal effects are not automatic, inevitable, or simple in either sex.

11. Cognitive factors such as emotions, perceptions, memories, fantasies, and expectancies are in large measure responsible for our sexual experiences. Subjective experiences do not always correspond to their monitored bodily responses. William Simon and John Gagnon suggest that cultural *scripts*, embodying social roles and norms, enable us to interpret physical changes. Such scripts give us permission to be sexual in certain ways and circumstances, and give meaning to our experiences.

12. So far no substance has been clearly established as an *aphrodisiac*. Certain recreational drugs may affect sexual functioning by inducing relaxation, lowering inhibitions, increasing energy, or altering perceptions. However, there are good reasons for remaining cautious regarding users' reports. Many drugs, including alcohol, nicotine, and a number of medications, are *anaphrodisiacs*.

13. Physiological facts about sexuality are most useful when they are integrated with what we know about human psychology and culture.

Key Terms

sexual response cycle *(139)*

vasocongestion *(140)*

engorgement *(140)*

myotonia *(140)*

sex flush *(140)*

excitement phase *(140)*

plateau phase *(140)*

orgasm *(140)*

resolution phase *(140)*

erection *(140)*

tumescence *(140)*

vaginal lubrication *(142)*

orgasmic platform *(144)*

emission *(146)*

urethral bulb *(146)*

expulsion *(146)*

retrograde ejaculation *(147)*

multiple orgasm *(149)*

refractory period *(149)*

vaginal orgasm *(151)*

clitoral orgasm *(151)*

reflexes *(153)*

autonomic nervous system *(155)*

sympathetic nervous system *(155)*

parasympathetic nervous system *(155)*

activating effects *(156)*

castrate *(157)*

sexual scripts *(162)*

aphrodisiac *(163)*

priapism *(163)*

anaphrodisiac *(164)*

pheromone *(166)*

C H A P T E R   S I X

■

Conception and Pregnancy

•

Children should [not]
thank their parents for
conceiving them.
[But] surely they may
hope that the original
coming together was a
matter of pleasure
and satisfaction.

D.W. Winnicott

There are all sorts of reasons for having sexual intercourse, and one of them is procreation. True, having a baby is not the main goal of sex for most people most of the time. But still, sex and reproduction are intimately related in most people's minds. When parents sit down to tell children the facts of life, they often confine the discussion to "where babies come from." Until recently, sex education for adolescents has also consisted largely of reproductive biology. Sex "quizzes" and surveys in the popular press often cover conception and pregnancy as well as sexual behavior.

It is not hard to see why "sex" so often means "reproduction." At one time, having a child was a nearly inevitable consequence of sexual intercourse. People got married, in part, because they assumed they would reproduce, and they were usually right. If love and marriage went together like a horse and carriage, so did babies and marriage.

Today, however, modern birth control methods have made parenthood optional. The social consequences of this change are profound. If parenthood is no longer inevitable, then neither is marriage (though, of course, there are other reasons to marry besides having children, and a person can have a child without marrying). Most people do eventually "tie the knot," but the number of permanently single people is growing. The timing of marriage has also been affected. Postponing having children frequently means putting off marriage. In 1970, only 9.4 percent of men and 6.2 percent of women aged 30–34 had never married. By 1987 the figures had jumped to

23.1 percent for men and 14.6 percent for women (U.S. Bureau of the Census, 1989). Nowadays, we hear of couples who live together for years and marry only after deciding that the time has come for the pitter-patter of little feet.

These changes mean that sex is no longer linked to procreation in the way it once was. Yet any discussion of human sexuality would be incomplete without a discussion of conception and pregnancy. It is not just that babies can result from sexual activity. A knowledge of reproduction is also important because the desire either to achieve pregnancy or avoid it can affect the quality of a particular sexual experience or even an entire sexual relationship; and so can getting pregnant and having a child. Moreover, since the timing of parenthood is now controllable, it is also negotiable, and disagreement about when and whether to have children can become a source of friction and resentment in an intimate relationship.

Before actually examining the process of reproduction, we might ask ourselves *why* people reproduce. Sociobiologists answer this question by saying that evolution has bred into each of us a desire to pass along our genes. In fact, say the sociobiologists, most, if not all, of human behavior is motivated by each individual's need—not necessarily conscious—to see his or her personal genetic code survive (Wilson, 1975). But this theory, which is based primarily on evidence from animals, does not seem to fit all the facts of human parenthood. Many people show no interest whatsoever in passing along their genes to the next generation. Others, who are unable to transmit their genes because of infertility or because medical problems make pregnancy dangerous, choose to adopt the biological offspring of others. Some individuals who are biologically able to reproduce also choose to adopt. They may be concerned about problems of overpopulation, may wish to experience the satisfaction of providing a home to a child who might not otherwise have one, may want to avoid the inconveniences of pregnancy, or may desire to be single parents (many adoption agencies now accept unmarried people

Parenthood *Being a parent brings special experiences, joys, and responsibilities.*

as clients). The number of people hoping to adopt a healthy newborn far exceeds the number of infants available, because most unmarried mothers now keep their babies. Yet many prospective parents are willing to wait for years or travel long distances to get a child. For them, genes have nothing to do with it.

Personal motives for choosing parenthood are myriad. An individual or couple may love and value children and want to experience the unique rewards and challenges of raising them. They may feel they are suited for the task of childrearing and choose parenthood for the same reasons that they would choose any occupation—to gain a sense of accomplishment from a job well done. They may want to re-create the sense of family that they themselves enjoyed while growing up. They may find children entertaining, may view parenthood as an experience that enhances personal growth and maturity, or see childrearing as a contribution to society. (In the *Personal Perspective* at the end of this chapter, we explore these and other motives for becoming a parent, and give you an opportunity to find out which ones do or do not apply to you.)

Whatever the reasons for having a child, the experience is always a milestone in a person's life. In this chapter, we will examine the biological processes that lead to parenthood and some of their psychological consequences. We will also look at new strategies for overcoming fertility problems and their implications for parents, children, and society. Our concern will be with ways to achieve conception; in Chapter 7, we will describe ways to avoid it.

CONCEPTION: THE MARRIAGE OF OVUM AND SPERM

Until fairly recently in human history, people had no idea how babies got started, although they realized that sexual intercourse must have something to do with it. The Greek philosopher Aristotle thought that the female supplied raw material to be shaped into a child, but the male's "seed" actually got the baby going. Thomas Aquinas agreed that "the power of the female generative virtue provides the substance but the active male virtue makes it into the finished product." An eighteenth-century naturalist wrote, "The male semen is the sculptor, the menstrual blood is the block of marble, and the foetus is the figure which is fashioned out of the combination" (cited in Stannard, 1970).

When Anton van Leeuwenhoek, a Dutch microscopist, observed sperm in male semen in 1677, his findings were interpreted as a victory of male supremacy. Leeuwenhoek and others assumed that each sperm was a miniature embryo; the woman, they said, merely provided temporary room and board for nine months until the embryo was able to live on its own. One scientist gazed through his microscope and said he saw a completely formed miniature horse in the semen of a horse. Others thought they could tell male and female sperm apart, and a few even claimed to see male and female sperm copulating and giving birth to baby sperm (Bullough, 1976).

Although scientists knew for centuries that other female animals produced eggs, for a long time they refused to believe that mammalian eggs existed. Even Regnier de Graaf, who discovered the ovarian pockets that hold the female eggs, thought an egg only provided nutrition and could not leave the ovary until activated by semen. A few "ovists" believed that the egg, not the sperm, was a completely formed embryo, but they agreed with the general view that the sperm provided the vital spark that gave the ovum life. The existence of the mammalian egg was established in 1827, but the process of **conception** (the inception of pregnancy) was not really understood until near the end of the nineteenth century, when scientists finally realized that **sperm** and **ovum** must play equal roles.

The Female Role in Conception: Menstruation and Ovulation

A human female is born with over four hundred thousand immature egg cells, or *oocytes*, in her ovaries. As we saw in Chapter 4, each of these cells is enclosed in a tiny sac, or **follicle.** Since only about four hundred eggs will reach maturity and leave the ovaries during the woman's potential childbearing years, the supply is obviously far more than she needs. Apparently the overabundance is Nature's way of ensuring that enough eggs will make it to maturity, though why the surplus should be so great is something of a mystery.

The process of **ovulation,** the release of an egg from the ovary, is illustrated in Figure 6–1. It begins with the release of follicle-stimulating hormone, or FSH, into the bloodstream by the pituitary (see Chapter 4). FSH causes follicles surrounding several of the oocytes to grow. Usually only one follicle and one ovum mature fully each month. The mature follicle, with its ripened egg, gradually moves to the surface of the ovary, where it resembles a tiny bubble. The other follicles and the eggs they enclose shrink, are reabsorbed into the ovary, and are replaced by small scars. But sometimes two or even more eggs mature and get fertilized by sperm, resulting in fraternal (nonidentical) twins, triplets, and so forth.

As the ovarian follicles grow, they begin to secrete the female hormone estrogen. The estrogen has two effects: first, it causes the lining of the uterus—the **endometrium**—to start to grow and thicken, in preparation for implantation of a fertilized egg; and second, when it reaches a peak level, it triggers the release by the pituitary of luteinizing hormone, or LH. You will recall from Chapter 4 that LH brings on ovulation, the release from the follicle of the mature egg; this ordinarily occurs about midway between menstrual periods. Some women feel a slight cramp or mild abdominal pressure at ovulation.

Once it is released, the tiny egg—it is only about five-thousandths of an inch in diameter—floats in the woman's abdominal fluid. Its destination

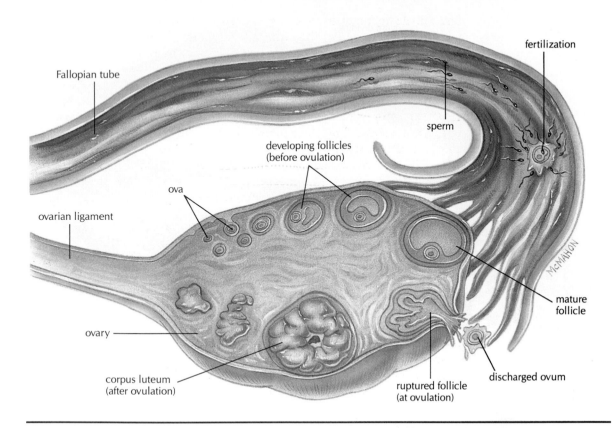

fertilization

Fallopian tube

developing follicles
(before ovulation)

sperm

ova

ovarian ligament

mature
follicle

ovary

corpus luteum
(after ovulation)

ruptured follicle
(at ovulation)

discharged ovum

FIGURE 6–1
Ovulation and
fertilization *This*
drawing shows the stages
of development of an egg
and follicle within the
ovary and the fertilization
of the mature egg in the
Fallopian tube.

is the nearby Fallopian tube, which leads to the uterus. The fringed ends of the tube may help pull the egg in (see Chapter 4). Once inside, the egg descends toward the uterus. During the trip, which takes three or four days, the egg is probably propelled by contractions of the tube or by the waving motion of the hairlike projections (*cilia*) that line the tube. **Fertilization,** the union of ovum and sperm, is most likely to occur within one day of ovulation, when the egg is in the first third of the tube, closest to the ovary. (The unfertilized ovum lives for only one, or at most, two days.) If the Fallopian tube is partially blocked by scar tissue from an infection or inflammation, a sperm may be able to reach the egg and fertilize it, but the larger fertilized egg may be unable to pass through the tube to the uterus. The result is a *tubal pregnancy*, which can be life-threatening. Tubal pregnancies must be terminated surgically (see Box 6–1).

Figure 6–2 shows the changes that take place in the fertilized egg, or **zygote.** By the time it enters the uterus, it has developed into a round, hollow cluster of about a hundred cells, called a **blastocyst.** About seven days after leaving the ovary, the egg snuggles into the uterine lining and begins to grow. Meanwhile, in the ovary, LH has caused the ruptured follicle to change into a lump-like structure called the **corpus luteum** (literally "yellow

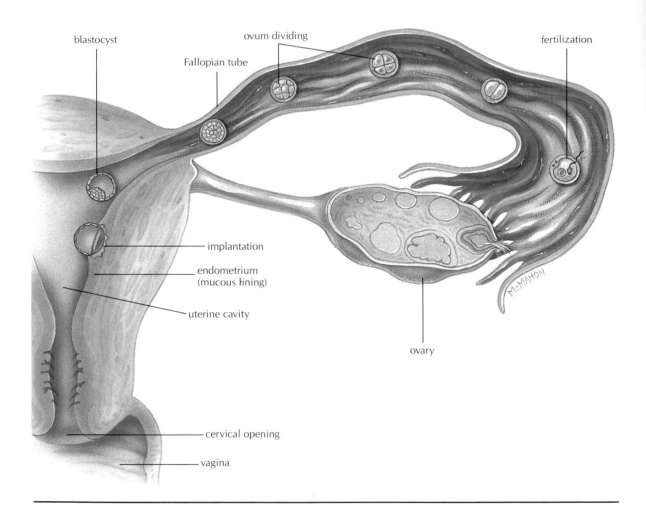

FIGURE 6–2   The ovum, from fertilization to implantation *This drawing shows the changes that take place in the egg during the seven days or so between fertilization and implantation in the uterine wall.*

body"). It has begun secreting progesterone and will continue doing so for about twelve weeks. Progesterone is essential in the development of the uterine lining and the maintenance of the pregnancy once the egg is implanted.

If fertilization does not take place, the egg simply disintegrates in the uterus. The corpus luteum gradually shrivels into a small indented scar, and estrogen and progesterone levels plummet. The blood vessels in the uterus pinch off, preventing nourishment from reaching the thick endometrium, part of which then breaks down, sloughs off, and exits from the body as the menstrual flow, along with blood, and cervical and vaginal mucus. (The menstrual and ovulatory cycles are shown in Figure 6–3.) An average flow consists of one to three ounces of fluid. The flow is odorless until it makes contact with bacteria in the air and begins to decompose.

The entire monthly reproductive cycle in women takes about twenty-eight days to run its course (see Figures 6–3 and 6–4), but there is considerable variation from woman to woman, and from month to month for any particular woman. The first day of the menstrual flow is counted as Day 1 because it is easy to identify. The cycle is usually described as having four phases: (1) **menstruation,** the sloughing off of endometrial cells, blood, and mucus, which lasts an average of five days; (2) a *proliferative phase*, between the end of menstruation and the onset of ovulation, during which cells in the uterine lining multiply; (3) a *secretory phase*, between ovulation and the day or

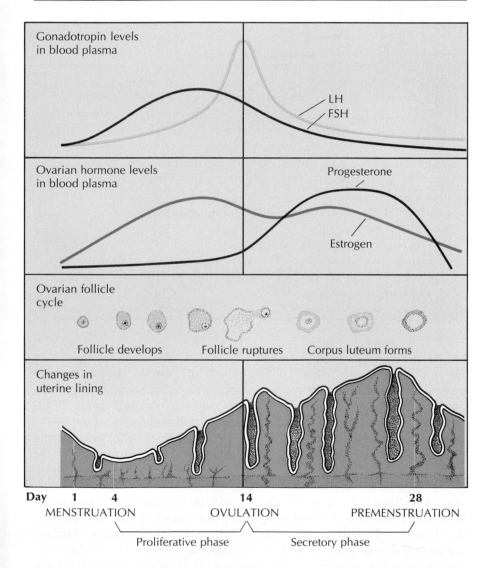

FIGURE 6–3   The menstrual and ovulatory cycles   *This figure shows average patterns of growth and change in the ovarian follicle and the lining of the uterus, and related changes in women's hormone levels. Note that both estrogen and progesterone are at their lowest point right before and during menstruation.*

BOX 6–1

Tubal Pregnancy

A fetus, as we all know, is supposed to grow in the uterus. But sometimes a fertilized egg implants in tissue outside the womb, resulting in an **ectopic,** or displaced, pregnancy. In rare cases, part of the uterine lining breaks free, along with the egg, and attaches to an ovary or another abdominal organ. Far more commonly, the egg lodges in the middle portion of the Fallopian tube, where it would normally make only a brief stop on its way to the womb. The result is a **tubal pregnancy.** Tubal pregnancies can occur when an irritation of the uterine lining causes the uterus to "reject" the egg and it drifts back into the tube. The usual cause, however, is scar tissue or unusual twisting in the tube, which blocks the egg's passage or interferes with normal tubal contractions. Tubal pregnancies are sharply on the rise. One major reason: increased rates of undiagnosed gonorrhea, chlamydia, and other sexually transmitted diseases that cause tubal scarring.

Sometimes a tubal pregnancy ends on its own when the woman's immune system dissolves the embryo or the embryo spontaneously aborts. But if the embryo continues to grow, by the eighth week or so it may enlarge enough to tear or even rupture the tube. The woman may then go into shock or begin to hemorrhage. This is a life-threatening emergency, and the pregnancy must be terminated surgically without delay. Tubal pregnancies are a leading cause of maternal deaths in the United States.

The first symptoms of an ectopic pregnancy are the same as for any pregnancy. (As we discuss in the text, though, not all women have such symptoms.) But as the pregnancy progresses, there is likely to be pain or cramping because of increased pressure in the tube. The pain may

two preceding menstruation, during which the corpus luteum secretes progesterone; and (4) *premenstruation*, during which the uterine lining breaks down. Individual variation in the length of the cycle is mainly due to differences in the length of its first half. The second half of the cycle, from ovulation to menstruation, is always fourteen days, give or take two. During menstruation, the level of LH falls, FSH is once again secreted, and the entire cycle begins anew.

Some women experience severe abdominal cramps during menstruation. They may also have backache, pain in the inner thighs, nausea, headaches, and other physical symptoms. The causes of painful menstruation (*dysmenorrhea*) are usually physical rather than psychological. Medical researchers believe that women with dysmenorrhea tend to overproduce certain hormonelike substances called *prostaglandins*, which bring on uterine

be sharp and stabbing or dull and aching. There may also be menstrual-like bleeding or spotting. A woman should call her doctor or go to a hospital immediately if she has 1) sudden or persistent abdominal pain; 2) irregular bleeding or spotting after an unusually light or a skipped period; or 3) fainting or dizziness, which can signal internal bleeding.

To avoid the life-threatening complications of an ectopic pregnancy a woman should get *any* suspected pregnancy confirmed by a medical practitioner as soon as possible. If an examination reveals that one of her tubes is enlarged, if her uterus is smaller than it should be given other signs of pregnancy, or if her medical history places her at special risk, tests will be done to determine whether the pregnancy is ectopic. These tests may include an ultrasound scan or a laparoscopy (direct examination of the Fallopian tube through a lighted tube inserted through a small incision in the abdomen). Women should also be sure to give the clinician all pertinent medical or sexual facts, including current or past use of an intrauterine device or birth control pills (see Chapter 7). These contraceptive methods protect more effectively against uterine pregnancy than ectopic pregnancy, so if a woman conceives while using one of them there is a higher-than-usual chance that the pregnancy will be ectopic. Previous tubal pregnancies and tubal surgery to overcome an infertility problem also increase the risk.

When a tubal pregnancy is caught early, a surgeon can often save the tube. In other cases, however, part or all of the tube must be removed, reducing the chances of a future pregnancy. Prevention, of course, is the best cure. Although some cases of ectopic pregnancy are unavoidable, women can lower the risk by protecting themselves against sexually transmitted diseases (see Chapter 17) and by getting frequent gynecological examinations (see Chapter 18).

contractions. Various drugs can counteract the effects of prostaglandins. Dysmenorrhea can also be caused by pelvic infection, the use of an intrauterine birth control device, and **endometriosis** (the abnormal growth of endometrial tissue outside the uterus). Any woman with severe menstrual pain should see a doctor to determine the cause.

Various other physical changes sometimes accompany menstruation. For example, water retention may cause a feeling of heaviness, and the breasts may become swollen and tender. Some women also report depression, irritability, and anxiety just before menstruation. These symptoms, along with various physical ones, are often called the *"premenstrual syndrome" (PMS)*. But evidence for a distinct emotional "syndrome" before menstruation is much weaker than most people realize. Researchers have been trying for decades to link emotional changes to the hormonal changes of the female

FIGURE 6–4   The menstrual cycle *This time line shows an average menstrual cycle, but women vary considerably in the length of the cycle and in the length of the interval between menstruation and ovulation. Also, although the probability is low, conception has occurred just before and even during the menstrual period.*

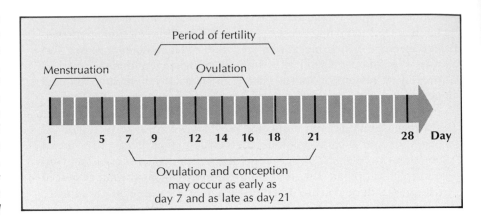

reproductive cycle. Several have tried to show that low progesterone levels or an estrogen progesterone imbalance has a negative psychological effect. Others have proposed other hormones as the cause, such as prolactin (associated with water, sodium, and potassium retention) or aldosterone (associated with sodium retention). But to date, *no* causal relationship has been established between emotional complaints and any particular hormone change (Rolker-Dolinsky, 1987). Further, there is great disagreement about how to define PMS, how many women experience it, how severe it is, and even whether or not it actually exists, except in people's minds. Expectations seem to play a big role in women's reports of negative emotional changes before or during menstruation. Several well-controlled psychological studies of "PMS" find that when subjects don't know the purpose of the study, the "syndrome" tends to disappear (e.g., McFarlane, Martin, & Williams, 1988). We will discuss this research in more detail in Chapter 18.

The Male Role in Conception: Sperm Production and Insemination

Unlike women, men manufacture their reproductive cells—in this case, sperm—continuously throughout their adult lives. **Spermatogenesis** (sperm production) occurs in the seminiferous tubules of the testes (see Chapter 4). You may recall that it is stimulated by the follicle-stimulating hormone (FSH). The sperm can be stored in the epididymis for up to six weeks, before being ejaculated or absorbed back into the body. An average ejaculation contains some three hundred to five hundred million sperm.

Each individual sperm is very tiny—much smaller than the ovum, which can be seen with the naked eye. As you can see in Figure 6–5, a sperm looks like a little tadpole; it consists of a head, neck, and long tail. The short life of a sperm is not an easy one. After they are deposited into the vagina, sperm become contestants in a race to the Fallopian tubes. Few of the contestants make it to the last lap. Some lack the ability to swim and are left floundering at the starting line. Many more succumb within the first few minutes to the acidic secretions of the vagina, even though seminal fluid has considerable buffering, or neutralizing, power. Only a small percentage make it to the opening of the cervix and manage to pass through the carpet of mucus that covers it. Once the survivors get into the uterus, the race gets a little easier. The secretions of the uterus are more alkaline than those of the vagina. Also, some scientists suspect that uterine contractions help the sperm along. But they must still pass through a tiny opening leading to each Fallopian tube. About half swim up the wrong Fallopian tube. Those that make it to the right one find themselves swimming, like salmon, upstream, against the current that is sweeping the egg toward the uterus.

Within a few hours, two thousand or so of the original three to five hundred million sperm have reached the Fallopian tube in which there is an egg. But sometimes sperm get there much faster, despite all the obstacles. In fact, sperm have been found in the tubes within five minutes after their deposit in the vagina (Fordney-Settlage et al., 1973). Since sperm only swim about an inch an hour, such unusually rapid journeys are a mystery.

FIGURE 6–5   A sperm   *The diagram shows the parts of a sperm. In the greatly magnified electron microscope photo, sperm float around an egg. Note the difference in size between egg and sperm. The egg's actual size is about the same as that of the head of a pin.*

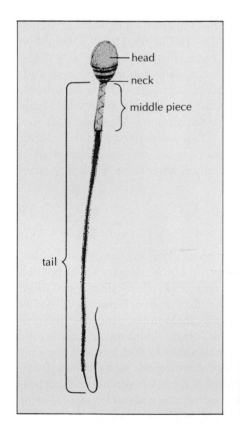

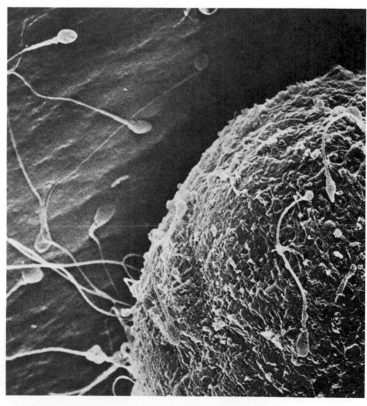

Only one sperm can fertilize the egg, but that one gets a little help from its friends. The egg is surrounded by a gelatinlike protective layer of cells. Sperm swarm around the egg, ramming blindly into it and at the same time releasing a chemical that dissolves the cell barrier. Although several sperm may penetrate the outermost part of the cell, only one finally plunges into the center and merges with it. At once a membrane forms around the egg, preventing any more sperm from entering. This is the moment of conception.

A Conceptual Note

The preceding description is probably fairly familiar to most readers. Indeed, hardly anyone over the age of twelve has not heard the saga of the sperm and the egg. Thus it is easy to overlook the fact that much of the process of conception remains mysterious. How do sperm arrive in the Fallopian tubes so quickly? What causes the various contractions that facilitate the journey of both the sperm and the egg? Why does only one egg usually mature? What causes the fertilized egg to form the membrane that keeps other sperm out?

The greatest mystery of all, of course, is how a single cell, weighing only five-thousandths of a milligram, is able to develop into a complex thinking organism composed of billions and billions of cells. "The mere existence of that cell," wrote biologist and essayist Lewis Thomas (1979), "should be one of the greatest astonishments of the earth. People ought to be walking around all day, all through their waking hours, calling to each other in endless wonderment, talking of nothing except that cell." If his sentiments seem exaggerated, consider how complex the process must be and how little is known about it beyond the level of mere description. "If anyone does succeed in explaining it, within my lifetime," Thomas promises, "I will charter a skywriting airplaine, maybe a whole fleet of them, and send them aloft to write one great exclamation point after another, around the whole sky, until all my money runs out."

PREGNANCY

Bells do not ring to announce that conception has occurred. In fact, usually a woman has no sign that anything out of the ordinary has happened until she misses her first period, about two weeks or so after conception. Then, within a few days or weeks, she may notice some other bodily changes: her breasts may swell and they may feel tender, especially the nipples; she may feel nauseated and want to vomit ("morning sickness"); she may need to urinate more often than usual; she may feel bloated; she may experience a change in appetite, become constipated, or have heartburn. However, many pregnant women have none of these symptoms, and it is possible to have all of them, including a skipped period, without being pregnant.

The site where the egg is implanted in the uterus secretes a hormone called **human chorionic gonadotropin (HCG)**. It is HCG that signals the corpus luteum to keep producing progesterone. Breakdown products of HCG can be found in a pregnant woman's urine and are therefore used in various pregnancy tests. At one time, such tests were done by injecting a woman's urine into a laboratory animal, such as a female rat or rabbit. If certain telltale changes occurred in the animal's ovaries after a day or two, the woman was pregnant. But today's tests are done without animals and give much faster results.

In a *urine slide test,* a drop of urine is mixed with certain chemicals on a slide. If the woman is pregnant (that is, if HCG is in her urine), the mixture will fail to coagulate, or clump. This test takes only two minutes and is usually accurate at about twenty-seven days after conception, when the woman's period is about thirteen days late. In a *urine tube test,* urine is mixed with HCG in a test tube, and if the woman is pregnant, cells sink to the bottom of the tube in a donut-shaped ring. This test takes an hour or two, and is usually accurate a few days earlier than a slide test. Other recently developed, more expensive urine tests may be accurate as early as fourteen days after conception. Several *blood serum tests* are also available. They are more sensitive than urine tests and give accurate results even before the first period is missed, but because they are more expensive and require sophisticated equipment, they are not used as routinely as urine tests. They are advised, however, for women with health problems that might be affected by pregnancy and for the detection of a tubal pregnancy.

Some women like to do the first test for pregnancy themselves at home, using a kit that can be purchased without a prescription at the drugstore. The kit may use the tube procedure described above, or a new procedure that causes a color bead to change color if the woman is pregnant. The manufacturers of home pregnancy tests claim accuracy rates similar to those of laboratory tests if the tests are used properly. However, some researchers dispute this claim (e.g., Doshi, 1986).

Any pregnancy test, even the most accurate, can be wrong, especially if it is done too early or two late in the pregnancy (HCG levels fall off after three or four months). *False negatives* (the test says you are not pregnant, but you are) can happen with urine tests if the urine is too warm, gets contaminated, or it is not concentrated enough. Some pregnancies never do test positive. A woman who suspects she is pregnant should always see a medical practitioner for a pelvic examination. Both a positive laboratory test and a positive examination are necessary to confirm a pregnancy. The practitioner will examine the tip of the cervix and lower part of the uterus. By the sixth or eighth week of pregnancy, the uterus and cervix usually become softer, the cervix changes from pale pink to bluish in color, and the size and shape of the uterus change. Confirming a suspected pregnancy as early as possible is important, so that the woman can get proper care or, if it is necessary, safely terminate the pregnancy.

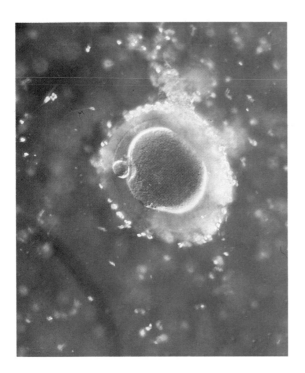

Development of the conceptus *These photos show a fertilized egg (left) and a week old embryo (right), in which the limbs are beginning to form.*

Embryonic and Fetal Development

Gestation, the period from conception until delivery, lasts, on average, nine and a half lunar months. (A lunar month is 28 days.) This works out to 38 weeks, or 266 days. By convention, however, doctors often date a pregnancy from the last menstrual period (LMP), because it is relatively easy to establish that date accurately. On average, the "due date" will be approximately 280 days after the LMP. But as you may recall from Chapter 3, "average" does not necessarily mean typical. Most babies do *not* arrive exactly on the due date. In fact, the odds are less than fifty-fifty that a child will be born within a week of that date (Kogan, 1980).

During the first two months of pregnancy, the developing organism is known as an embryo; after that it is called a **fetus.** At any stage of development it may be referred to as a conceptus. Not all of the fertilized egg is destined to become part of the embryo. Some cells form additional structures necessary to support the life of the embryo. One of these structures is the **placenta,** a network of tissues that surrounds the embryo early in development, but later moves to the side. Maternal tissue from the uterine lining also contributes to formation of the placenta. The placenta produces estrogen and progesterone and serves as a link between the woman and the conceptus. Oxygen and nutrients pass from the mother's bloodstream to that of the conceptus, while carbon dioxide and other waste products pass in the

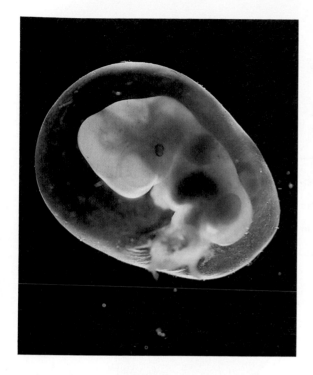
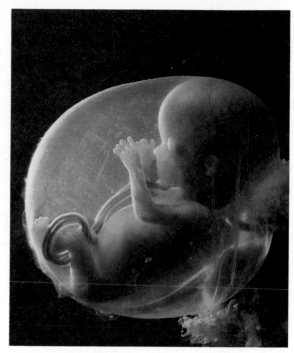

other direction. The two bloodstreams never actually mix. Within the placenta, the fetal blood circulates in tiny branchlike structures; the mother's blood circulates around these structures but does not enter them. Substances pass through the membrane that separates the mother's blood from that of the fetus.

One side of the placenta becomes attached to the uterine lining. By about the fifth week of development, the other side is connected to the embryo by the **umbilical cord** (see Figure 6–6), which contains two arteries and a vein. At birth the umbilical cord is cut and tied off to form the navel. Shortly after birth the placenta and other membranes exit from the mother's body as the **afterbirth.**

Another important life-support structure is the **amniotic sac,** or *amnion*, the innermost membrane surrounding the conceptus. It is filled with **amniotic fluid,** which maintains a constant temperature and provides a comfortable, protective, weightless environment for the fetus. The amniotic sac usually ruptures during birth; if it does not, the attending health practitioner must rupture it. The fetus floating in amniotic fluid has often been compared to an astronaut floating in space.

The gestation period is arbitrarily divided into three *trimesters*, or three-month phases, for purposes of description. The following is a brief review of some of the embryonic and fetal developments during each trimester.

From embryo to fetus
These photos of a six-week-old embryo (left) and a twelve-week-old fetus (right). By the end of the first trimester of fetal development, all major organ systems have begun to form.

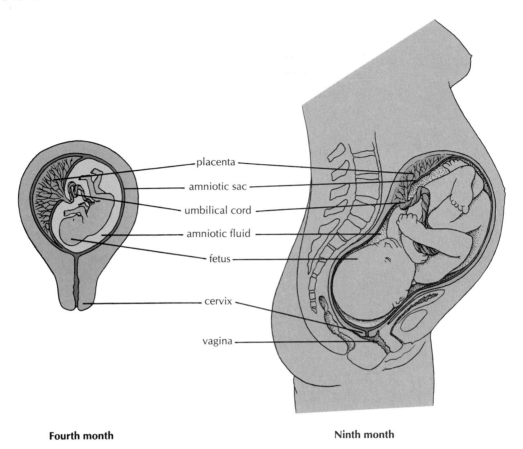

placenta

amniotic sac

umbilical cord

amniotic fluid

fetus

cervix

vagina

Fourth month

Ninth month

FIGURE 6–6 The conceptus at two stages of development *In this illustration you can see the organs that develop to support the fetus.*

FIRST TRIMESTER During the first three months of gestation, all of the basic organ systems develop. The conceptus is particularly vulnerable during this period to malformations caused by environmental factors, such as drugs, alcohol, and certain viruses that can cross the placental barrier.

At the end of the first month the embryo is about a quarter of an inch long. At this point it looks more like a sea urchin than a human child. It is folded in on itself and its head nearly touches its tail. A rudimentary central nervous system has begun to appear, followed by the beginnings of a circulatory system and a digestive tract. Buds that will eventually become arms and legs can be seen. By the end of the second lunar month, the embryo has grown another quarter inch, and limbs are recognizable, as are pawlike hands. A brain is developing in a head that is disproportionately large. A nose, lidless eyes, ears, and a mouth are visible. The tail has become smaller. All the internal organs have begun to develop. By the end of the third month the fetus is three inches long and weighs about an ounce. Lids have formed and are closed over the eyes. The skeleton is forming. Soft nails can be seen on well-formed fingers and toes. The development of sex organs makes determination of gender possible. Rudimentary kidneys excrete small amounts of urine into the amniotic fluid. The tail is gone. The fetus is recognizably human. From this point on, development will consist mainly of further differentiation and the growth of existing structures.

SECOND TRIMESTER   By the end of the fourth lunar month the fetus is almost seven inches long and weighs about four ounces. It may have a few hairs on its head. The pregnant woman may feel some subtle reflexive movements (the *quickening*), though usually that does not happen until the fifth month. By that time the fetus is quite active, and one can detect its heartbeat through a stethoscope. However, it is not yet capable of survival outside the womb for more than a few minutes. By the end of the sixth month the fetus weighs a pound and a half and is about a foot long. It is covered with fine hair, most of which it will soon shed. It sucks its thumb, swallows some amniotic fluid, startles in response to noise, and may move about actively. However, the vast majority of fetuses born at the end of the second trimester cannot survive, even with specialized medical care.

THIRD TRIMESTER   This is a period when the fetus grows rapidly in size, and fatty tissue forms beneath the skin. By the end of the seventh month the fetus is about fifteen inches long and weighs about two and a half pounds. Its eyes are open and sensitive to light. If it is male, its testicles have usually descended into the scrotum. Brain cells are still forming, and the lungs and intestinal system are still developing. Chances of survival outside the womb are only fair, but they are getting better with each passing day. By the end of the eighth lunar month the fetus weighs about four pounds and is about sixteen and a half inches long. With expert care, a majority of babies born at this time can survive. From now on, growth is dramatic; in fact, the fetus gains about half a pound a week. At birth a full-term baby weighs between seven and seven and a half pounds and measures twenty inches in length, though of course there is much variation.

The final trimester can be somewhat trying for the pregnant woman. Her uterus has expanded enormously (see Figure 6–7), and her protruding belly may cause her to walk in an awkward waddling fashion. She may suffer some back pain, and the enlarged uterus, pressing on other organs, may cause some discomfort. Pressure on the lungs may cause shortness of breath, pressure on the bladder may make it necessary to urinate frequently, and pressure on the stomach and intestines may cause gas, indigestion, and constipation. These problems do not occur in all pregnant women, however.

Detecting Fetal Problems

Unfortunately, the normal process of embryonic and fetal development just described sometimes goes awry. **Congenital diseases** (diseases present

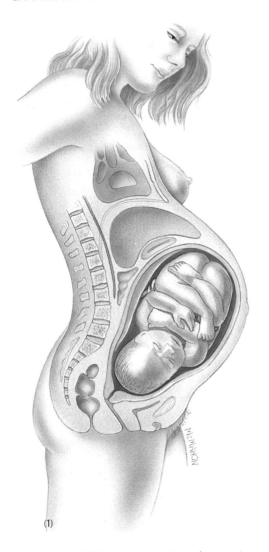

(1)

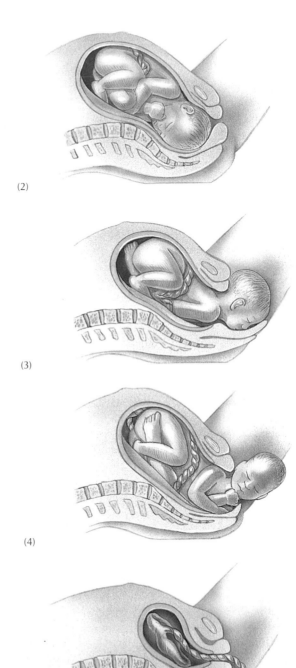

(2)

(3)

(4)

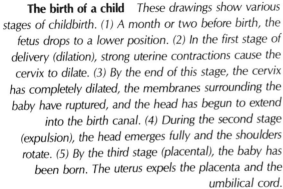

(5)

The birth of a child   *These drawings show various stages of childbirth. (1) A month or two before birth, the fetus drops to a lower position. (2) In the first stage of delivery (dilation), strong uterine contractions cause the cervix to dilate. (3) By the end of this stage, the cervix has completely dilated, the membranes surrounding the baby have ruptured, and the head has begun to extend into the birth canal. (4) During the second stage (expulsion), the head emerges fully and the shoulders rotate. (5) By the third stage (placental), the baby has been born. The uterus expels the placenta and the umbilical cord.*

at birth), as well as diseases that become apparent later in life, can get their start during the prenatal period, as can various problems in physical or mental development. The causes include maternal illness, hereditary disorders, and environmental conditions. If a pregnant woman gets rubella (German measles), the fetus's eyes, ears, or heart may be affected. If she has been exposed to the HIV virus, she may transmit it to the fetus. (The U.S. Surgeon General recommends that a woman have the AIDS antibody test before becoming pregnant. A test is especially important if she has risk factors such as IV drug use or has not been in a mutually monogamous long-term relationship.) Other sexually transmitted diseases, X-rays, toxic chemicals, cigarette smoking, alcohol use, and various drugs are all dangerous to the fetus. And increasing evidence suggests that not only the mother's, but also the *father's*

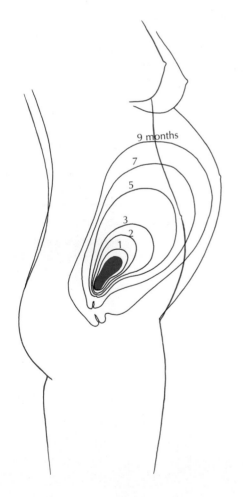

9 months
7
5
3
2
1

FIGURE 6–7   Changes in the uterus during pregnancy *During pregnancy the uterus expands to about 16 times its normal size and increases in weight from about an ounce to 2.2 pounds. Within a short time after delivery, it returns almost to its normal size.*

health affects the fetus. For example, one study has found a statistical link between alcohol consumption by the father in the month before conception and lowered birth weight in his offspring, independent of other factors (Little & Sing, 1987). Low birth weight is associated with many physical and mental problems in children, and with increased risk of death in the first year of life.

Age of the parents is also a factor in fetal problems. For example, after the age of thirty-five a woman's chances of bearing a child with *Down's Syndrome* (mental retardation caused by an extra chromosome) increase considerably. When a women is twenty-five her chances of having a Down's syndrome child are about 1 in 2,000; when she is forty-five, the chances are one in fifty. The reason for the increased risk with age is not clear. Possibly the older woman is less likely to provide the hormonal environment necessary for proper development (Kogan, 1980). Again, the father may also play a role. In a fourth of all cases, the extra chromosome appears to come from the father (Holmes, 1978).

Persons who suspect that they carry genes for an inherited disease can determine the risk of passing the condition along to their offspring by talking with a genetic counselor. These specialists can often be located through medical schools, hospitals, and local medical societies. They study the family medical history and when possible collect cell and blood samples from close relatives.

Once a pregnancy has begun, genetic and other kinds of fetal disorders can frequently be detected through a process called **amniocentesis** (see Fig-

FIGURE 6–8

Amniocentesis *During this diagnostic procedure, a hypodermic needle is used to withdraw fluid from the amniotic sac. Laboratory analysis of the fluid enables doctors to test for genetic and other abnormalities in the fetus. The photo shows an ultrasound scan of an actual amniocentesis.*

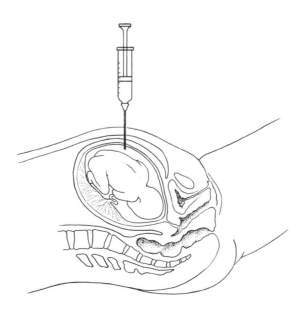

ure 6–8). In this procedure, which is usually performed during the second trimester, a physician inserts a needle through the abdominal wall into the uterus and withdraws a small quantity of amniotic fluid. There is some risk to the fetus, but it is small. Amniotic fluid contains cells from the amniotic sac and from the fetal skin, the urine, the digestive tract, and the bronchial system. The cells are grown in the laboratory and then examined for chromosomal abnormalities and the presence of certain enzymes, amino acids, and other substances that reveal the condition of the fetus.

Ultrasound scans, or *sonograms*, are also sometimes used to detect fetal malformation and other abnormalities. High frequency sound waves are passed through the woman's abdomen, and a computer uses the speed with which the waves are reflected to construct a video image of the woman's and the fetus's interior organs. The procedure is noninvasive, gives immediate information, and has never been proven harmful to human beings. However, high frequency waves generate heat, which some researchers say could potentially damage fetal cells. A panel of experts has discouraged use of the technique for frivolous reasons, such as curiosity or to check the sex of the fetus (Franklin, 1984).

In still another procedure, **chorionic villi sampling (CVS),** a physician inserts a long, thin tube through a pregnant woman's cervix, or sometimes through an incision in the abdomen. Guided by an ultrasound monitor, the physician then suctions out some of the thread-like projections of tissue (villi) on the outermost membrane surrounding the fetus (the chorion). Chorionic villi tissue is destined to form the placenta, but since it contains the

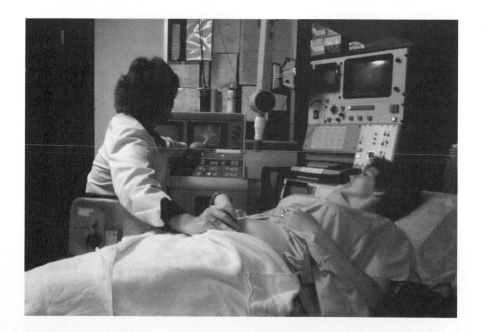

An ultrasound procedure
Ultrasound scans, or sonograms, produce an image of the fetus in the womb.

same cells as the fetus, it can be analyzed for genetic abnormalities. (CVS cannot detect spina bifida and certain other defects, but a maternal blood test in mid-pregnancy can identify a genetic marker for these problems.) CVS is done earlier than amniocentesis, between nine and twelve weeks, and the results are also available faster. The risk of a spontaneous abortion is a little higher with CVS than for amniocentesis, but as physicians get more experience with the procedure, the risk may fall. CVS originated in China several years ago. Many physicians believe it may replace amniocentesis as the preferred method of genetic diagnosis.

Amniocentesis, ultrasound scans, and chorionic villi sampling are diagnostic techniques. While they can detect the presence of problems, they do not solve them. Progress is being made in techniques to treat fetuses while they are still in the womb, including fetal surgery. But most problems are not yet curable, so if a defect does turn up, the prospective parents must usually decide whether to abort the fetus or continue the pregnancy. One advantage of CVS over amniocentesis is that since it is done early, prospective parents can avoid long, anxious months of not knowing whether the fetus is developing properly. Then, if an abortion is desired, it can be done using a simpler, safer procedure than would be possible later on.

Reactions to Pregnancy

For an expectant mother and father, a woman's pregnancy can be the best of all times. They may view the child-to-be as a tangible sign of their love for and commitment to each other. They may be just plain excited over the tremendous change about to take place in their lives:

> It gave me a sense that I was actually a woman. I had never felt sexy before. I went through a lot of changes. It was a very sexual thing. I felt very voluptuous.

> It meant I could get pregnant finally after a lot of trying, that I could do something I wanted to do. It meant going into a new stage of life. I felt filled up. (Quoted in The Boston Women's Health Book Collective, 1984, p. 344)

> My desire to be a father and have a family was one reason I got married. So I was elated when Ann got pregnant, and couldn't wait to tell everybody. (authors' files)

But pregnancy can also be the worst of all times. If the pregnancy is unexpected or unwanted, the initial reaction may be panic or depression. If the prospective parents were having problems in their relationship before pregnancy, those problems may loom larger with a baby on the way. As the pregnancy advances, the woman may feel dismay at some of the physical changes happening to her body. She is supposed to look as content and graceful as the women in the diaper and formula commercials, but she feels like Humpty Dumpty. In addition, she may worry about the pain of childbirth and wonder if her baby will be physically and mentally normal:

> When I was about six months pregnant and Dick was starting school again, I was home alone, isolated for days at a time. My nightmares and daydreams started around then. Really terrible fears of the baby being deformed. All my life I've always been the good girl. I knew I wasn't really good. I knew I had bad thoughts, but I was never allowed to express them. So I thought that my baby's deformities would be the living proof of the ugliness and badness in me. (quoted in The Boston Women's Health Book Collective, 1984, p. 347)

Changes of any sort, even happy ones, can be stressful. If the baby is a couple's first, both the mother and the father have to come to terms with the fact that they are about to become responsible for another, very helpless human being—and they may not feel quite ready.

On top of all this, many men and women worry about how pregnancy will affect their sex lives. They wonder whether the contractions of the woman's orgasm will bring on labor. They worry that the thrusting of the penis will damage the fetus or cause a miscarriage. They may hear from others that once a woman gets pregnant, she develops an obsessive interest in things maternal and loses all interest in sex. What are the facts?

Expecting   *It's normal to have a mixture of different feelings about being pregnant.*

Sexuality and Intimacy During Pregnancy

We know a great deal more about sex and pregnancy than we once did. Some of this information comes from the work of Masters and Johnson (1966), who interviewed 101 women at the end of the second month of their pregnancies, during the sixth, at the end of the eighth, and three months after delivery. Masters and Johnson also conducted detailed physiological tests on six pregnant women, using the same techniques as in their other studies of sexual physiology. Although the women in these studies were not necessarily representative of all women, the findings do show that many beliefs about sex and pregnancy are way off-track.

Based on their findings, Masters and Johnson (1966) state that sex during pregnancy, intercourse included, is usually quite safe up to the due date, or very shortly before. Some doctors still advise couples to refrain from intercourse for at least a month and a half before birth, believing that penile thrusting or uterine contractions can induce premature labor or that intercourse increases the risk of infection in the amniotic fluid. But these assumptions do not seem warranted by the evidence: well-controlled studies have failed to find that sex puts pregnant women or their fetuses at increased risk (Georgakopoulos, Dodos, & Mechleris, 1984; Walbroehl, 1984). In reported cases where the uterine contractions of orgasm appeared to have started labor, the women were extremely close to the expected delivery date anyway.

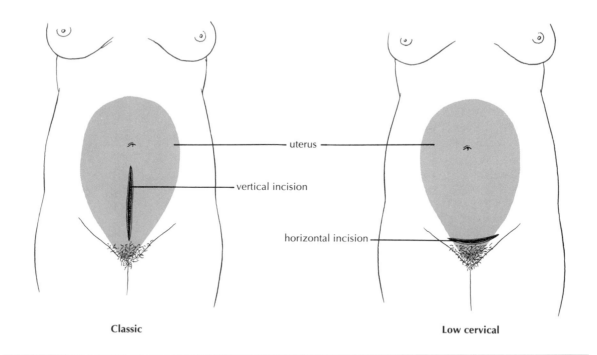

uterus

vertical incision

horizontal incision

Classic

Low cervical

Caesarian section *This procedure, which is major surgery, is used when difficult or prolonged labor threatens the survival of the fetus. After making either of the incisions illustrated, the surgeon removes the infant through the abdominal wall. Caesarian sections have tripled in frequency over the past thirty years, and despite their usefulness, critics argue that they are sometimes done unnecessarily.*

This green light for sex applies only to problem-free pregnancies. If there is vaginal or uterine bleeding, a history of previous miscarriages, or a known danger of miscarriage, all sexual activity leading to orgasm should be avoided, unless a physician gives medical approval. For most women, however, sex can continue.

Of course, as her abdomen swells, a pregnant woman may find it uncomfortable to have heterosexual intercourse with the man on top. Any pressure on her midsection may literally take her breath away. This problem is easily solved by choosing positions that take weight off the woman's body; for example, lying side-by-side or with the woman on top (see Chapter 9). Many couples also use pregnancy as an opportunity to experiment with noncoital techniques like mutual masturbation or oral-genital sex. A pregnant woman's partner should not blow air into the vagina during oral sex, however; air bubbles can enter the bloodstream and bring on a life-threatening stroke (although this is very rare).

But will an expectant woman or couple *want* to have sex? During pregnancy, some women feel more sensuous than ever before. Others notice no change, or experience a decline in sexual interest. Often sexual response fluctuates over the course of the pregnancy. During the first trimester, nausea and fatigue may understandably reduce desire. But according to Masters and Johnson (1966), during the second trimester, most women feel sexier and are more responsive than before the pregnancy. Then, during the last trimester, the desire for sexual intercourse may drop off (Calhoun, Selby, & King, 1981; White & Reamy, 1982). As you might expect, a woman's sexual responsiveness during pregnancy depends on how she felt about sex *before* getting pregnant. "Erotophilic" women—those who are disposed toward having positive attitudes and feelings about sex—report more sexual interest, activity, and satisfaction during late pregnancy than do "erotophobic" women (Fisher & Gray, 1988).

Prospective fathers (or lesbian partners) also have varying feelings about sex. Some feel closer than ever to their partner and are fascinated by the changes in her body. Others are repelled, or threatened by the profound change in the couple's life. A partner's feelings may vacillate:

> Sometimes I thought you were very beautiful and your belly was beautiful. And sometimes you looked like a ridiculous pregnant insect. Your navel bulging out looked strange (quoted in Boston Women's Health Book Collective, 1984, p. 348).

In their physiological study, Masters and Johnson were able to interview 79 husbands of the women participating in their research. Thirty-one men said they gradually lost sexual interest in their wives toward the end of the second or the beginning of the third trimester. Some claimed they were worried about the effect of intercourse on their wives or the fetus. Others said they "didn't know why." Only five men mentioned a wife's appearance. This result is surprising. Given our culture's emphasis on being slim and trim, we might expect the husband of a pregnant woman to feel at least ambivalent about his partner's expanded waist, swollen ankles, or waddling walk. But again, a person's sexual responses are likely to depend in part on pre-existing attitudes and feelings about sexuality. Men who are "erotophilic" tend to report more sexual activity and better communication with their partners than do men who are "erotophobic" (Fisher & Gray, 1988).

In sum, a pregnancy has the potential for drawing partners closer together, but it can also put distance between them. Knowing this allows a couple to anticipate the possibility of ambivalent or negative sexual feelings and take steps to deal with them. They can discuss the influence conventional notions of beauty have on their feelings. They can make sure that they set time aside for intimacy and sensuality. And they can share the excitement of pregnancy itself. When Masters and Johnson did their 1966 study, it was unusual for a man to be involved in the birth of his child. Today, pregnancy and birth have become experiences that a couple can accomplish together. Men (and lesbian partners) attend childbirth classes along with prospective mothers. They help during labor by timing contractions and encourage the woman to relax by massaging her back or guiding her through various breathing exercises. Fathers and other partners are often present at the birth itself, comforting and encouraging the woman, and they may help hold and clean the baby immediately after delivery. Couples who experience this kind of birth process often say they discover a new intimacy.

Sexuality and Intimacy After Pregnancy

Many doctors recommend avoiding sexual intercourse for about six weeks after delivery—and many women are happy to take the advice, although they may enjoy other forms of sexual expression. Giving birth is hard work. During delivery a woman's body undergoes tremendous stress, whether or not she has severe pain. If the delivering physician performs an *episiotomy* (an incision in the perineum, which some doctors feel is necessary to prevent ragged tearing of the tissues), the stitches may be uncomfortable. Vaginal lubrication during this period is typically less than normal.

There are other stresses as well. Childbirth can be an emotional ordeal. Immediately afterward, happiness may be mixed with helplessness. Within two or three days some women experience the postpartum blues: they feel scared and depressed, and they begin to doubt that they have "normal" maternal feelings. Some doctors blame the blues on biological factors, especially the sudden drop in estrogen and progesterone right after delivery, when the hormone-producing placenta is expelled. But the causes may also be situational, psychological, or cultural. New fathers often feel depressed after the birth of the baby, too (Zaslow et al., 1985).

If postpartum depression occurs, it is usually quite brief. Still, life is not the same as before the delivery, and a woman and her mate must make some fundamental adjustments. If the child is their first, they must get used to being three instead of two (or, if the woman is single, she must get used to being two instead of one). They may get little sleep. To an infant, three in the morning can seem like a perfectly good time for breakfast. Some women are somewhat anemic for a few weeks, which reduces their stamina.

New parents may also experience some resentment towards one another. If the mother does most of the baby-tending (which is usually the case), her partner may feel neglected and shut out. The mother, for her part, may feel that she doesn't have enough time and energy to meet the demands of both her child and partner. Sexual intimacy may suffer. According to a study of several thousand couples, in such cases, women are likely to see the impact of the child as "a temporary sexual inconvenience" or attribute sexual problems to other factors, such as fatigue. Husbands, in contrast, often view children as a serious disruption of their sex lives. After the birth of his child, one man, a graduate student in his late twenties, complained:

> We are so tired, we just think of it too late to do anything about it. She is also tender, she tells me. But I am afraid that she is also less interested. It's been four months and she puts so much into the kid that I feel she's more maternal than sexy. I am waiting because I do feel that it will get better (quoted in Blumstein & Schwartz, 1983, p. 204).

The birth of a child may also bring on disagreements about whether a wife should work and about who should do which domestic chores. Increasingly, women are returning to work shortly after the birth of a child. In 1970, only about 31 percent of women who had had a child in the previous year were in the labor force. By 1987, over half of new mothers were employed. In response to these changes, some men are doing more housework and childcare, but most wives still bear almost full responsibility in these areas, whether they work outside the home or not (Hochschild, 1989; Tavris & Wade, 1984). Even *unemployed* husbands do less at home than wives who put in a forty-hour work week (Blumstein & Schwartz, 1983). Husbands often say they *should* do more, but they don't; or if they do, they grumble about the loss of leisure or time to devote to a career. The result is that women often find themselves with two jobs, not just one. Naturally, this can breed resentment and dissatisfaction, not to mention sheer exhaustion.

Prospective parents need to recognize that the joys of having a baby are tempered by the need to balance the roles of parent, lover, and student or worker. Moments of increased intimacy may alternate with moments of jealousy and anger. But mutual support can make parenting easier. And an arm around the shoulder, a kiss, a good back rub—all can express sexual caring and interest.

Xs, Ys, AND SEX SELECTION

Throughout this chapter we have referred to "the embryo," "the fetus," or "the baby," sex unspecified. But of course, from the moment of conception an embryo is either male or female. The human ovum and the human sperm each contains twenty-three **chromosomes,** rod-shaped structures within each cell nucleus that give the genetic directions determining a person's inherited characteristics. When ovum and sperm merge to form a fertilized egg, the resulting forty-six chromosomes form twenty-three pairs. One pair is responsible for the embryo's genetic sex. In consists of two **sex chromosomes,** one called an X, from the ovum, and the other either an X or a Y, from the sperm. The father's contribution is the determining one: if he contributes an X-bearing sperm, the child will have two Xs and be a girl; if he contributes a Y-bearing sperm, the child will have an X and a Y, and be a boy. (We will have more to say about the prenatal development of sexual anatomy in Chapter 12.)

Male-producing, or Y-bearing, sperm and female-producing, or X-bearing, sperm do not look exactly alike. In the early 1960s, microbiologist Landrum B. Shettles discovered that X-bearing sperm have large oval heads while Y-bearing ones have smaller, round heads. Y-bearing sperm are also lighter and have longer tails, so they can swim faster. A man's seminal fluid does not contain equal numbers of Y- and X-bearing sperm. There are wide individual variations among men, with an overall ratio of about two Y-bearing sperm to every one X-bearing sperm.

Because Y-bearing sperm outnumber X-bearing sperm and swim faster, they have an advantage in the race to fertilize the ovum. This advantage is partly offset by the fact that X-bearing sperm are hardier and less vulnerable to the acidic environment of the vagina. Still, there may be as many as 160 males conceived for every 100 females. If all these embryos completed development and were born, males would greatly outnumber females on this planet. As it happens, male embryos (like male-producing sperm) are less likely to survive, so at birth the sex ratio is more nearly balanced: about 106 males for every 100 females.

At least, that is Nature's plan. But long before anyone knew about Xs and Ys, people were trying to alter the plan. Hippocrates, the father of medicine, advised tying a string around the right testicle to stimulate the production of "male seed," or the left testicle to produce a daughter. In the Middle Ages, alchemists prescribed a drink of lion's blood and intercourse under a full moon if a son was desired (Wallis, 1984). From ancient times to modern ones, men have divorced their wives for failing to bear them male offspring, ignorant of the facts of human genetics and their own critical role in the determination of sex.

In the 1960s, Landrum Shettles proposed several steps that couples could take on their own to determine the sex of their offspring. His plan made use of the physical characteristics of Y-bearing and X-bearing sperm. Shettles noted that cervical mucus is more acidic before ovulation than when ovulation occurs, and that acidity, although harmful to all sperm, is especially harmful to Y-bearing ones. Thus if a couple wanted a girl, he advised, they should have intercourse up to two or three days before ovulation, then abstain or use a condom or diaphragm to prevent conception. (Methods of estimating ovulation are described in Chapter 7.) Many of the tough X-bearing sperm would survive in the woman's reproductive tract for a few days and be there to meet the egg when it was released from the ovary. But most of the weaker Y-bearing sperm would die by then. If the couple wanted a boy, said Shettles, they should have intercourse without contraception as close to ovulation as possible and not before. Since the woman's reproductive tract would be relatively alkaline, the agility of the Y-bearing sperm would give them the advantage. To tilt the odds in favor of a girl, Shettles also recommended douching before intercourse with a solution of two tablespoons of white vinegar in a quart of warm water, and using shallow penetration (which lengthens the trip the sperm must take through the acidic vagina). If the goal was to conceive a boy, he suggested douching with a solution of two tablespoons of baking soda in a quart of warm water, and using deep penetration (Rorvik & Shettles, 1970).

Shettle's ideas created quite a stir, but controlled studies failed to confirm them (Carson, 1988). Today, interest centers instead on techniques that separate X-bearing and Y-bearing sperm in the laboratory. In one such method, sperm run a sort of race through a glass column filled with a sticky protein called albumin. The quicker Y-bearing sperm make it first to the bottom of the column. Then the prospective mother is artificially inseminated with the desired sperm type. Sperm separation techniques are being marketed in clinics in many countries, including the United States (Jancin, 1989) and reported success rates run as high as 80 percent, although some researchers are skeptical (Wallis, 1984).

Presently, the only sure-fire method of sex selection is to identify the sex of the fetus with one of the prenatal diagnostic techniques described in the previous section, and then abort a fetus of the "wrong" sex. But, arguments over abortion aside, is it wise, or ethical, to fool with Nature in this way? Traditionally, parents in most cultures have valued male offspring more than females. In the United States, surveys consistently find that although people generally hope for a sex-balanced family (a boy for you, a girl for me), both men and women generally prefer their firstborn to be male and say that if they could have only one child, they would want a boy. With the trend toward smaller families, sex selection could well lead to an overabundance of males (Warren, 1985). Already there are signs of a shift in that direction in Korea and the People's Republic of China, where many parents have aborted female fetuses after detecting fetal sex through amniocentesis or ultrasound. In one study done in China, pregnant women were offered early abortion after being told the sex of their fetuses. Only 1 of the 53 women carrying males chose to abort, but 29 of the 49 women carrying females did so (Campbell, 1976).

Future technology will probably make sex selection a reality even without selective abortion. No one can be sure what the social consequences might be if the practice becomes widespread and causes an imbalance in the sex ratio, but some social critics predict the worst. For example, some psychological studies find that firstborns have intellectual advantages relative to secondborns. With sex selection, males would be more likely than females to be firstborns and to have such advantages. Moreover, since crime and other forms of antisocial behavior are much more common among males than among females, these problems might grow more serious. But defenders of sex selection argue that after an initial boom in boys, the law of supply and demand would lead to a desire for more girls, and the sex ratio would even out again. And they point to some potentially positive outcomes. Sex selection could help eliminate certain sex-linked inherited diseases, such as hemophilia. It might encourage population control, since people would not keep having children simply to produce a child of a particular sex.

Sex selection raises other difficult questions (see Minden, 1986). Will the ability to choose a child's sex encourage parents to view their offspring as products to be designed rather than blessings to be cherished? Will parents express disappointment or anger if their sex-selected children fail to fulfill their expectations of what boys and girls are "supposed" to be like?

Of course, the entire debate might be academic if gender were less salient in people's lives. Often, the first question one hears when a child is born is not "Is it healthy?" but "Is it a boy or a girl?" The answer determines the way parents and others hold the child, talk to it, play with it (Tavris & Wade, 1984). In a truly egalitarian society, choosing the sex of one's offspring might seem like more trouble than it is worth.

INFERTILITY

In an age when millions of people are using birth control to prevent pregnancy, it is easy to forget that millions of others would like to achieve pregnancy but cannot. **Infertility** is defined medically as the inability to conceive after a year or more of having intercourse without birth control, *or* an inability to maintain a pregnancy long enough for the fetus to live on its own outside the mother's womb. Infertility may be either temporary or permanent. The permanent absence of fertility is referred to as **sterility.**

A Growing Problem

U.S. infertility rates have skyrocketed in the past few decades. Recent studies find that about one out of every six married couples of childbearing age has difficulty starting or maintaining a pregnancy. That amounts to about three and a half million couples. Some estimates are even higher.

Certain researchers believe the increased rate in recent years is misleading—a matter of better reporting and a greater willingness of couples to seek help. They note that legalized abortion and the tendency of single mothers to keep their children have reduced the number of babies available for adoption and lengthened the waiting period, in some cases to many years. And at the same time, techniques for treating infertility have vastly improved. Therefore, many infertile couples who at one time might have opted to adopt or given up hopes for having a child are now trying to achieve fertility instead—and are becoming part of the infertility statistics.

Most experts, however, believe the increase is real. As we will see, infertility and difficulties in conceiving are caused by various physiological problems. Certain social and environmental changes have probably made these problems more common. For example:

■ The incidence of sexually transmitted diseases has increased. When undiagnosed, many of these diseases, gonorrhea and chlamydia in particular, can lead to a condition known as **pelvic inflammatory disease (PID).** Pelvic inflammatory disease can cause scarring of the reproductive organs, including the uterus and the Fallopian tubes. Such scarring can prevent sperm from reaching the egg or from implanting properly.

- Certain intrauterine devices (IUDs) used for birth control have also been linked to pelvic inflammatory disease and resultant scarring of the reproductive organs.

- More and more couples are postponing pregnancy until their thirties or even beyond. Fertility in women (and possibly to a lesser extent in men) declines with age, especially after the mid-thirties, although experts disagree on just how great the decline is (Menken, Trussell & Larsen, 1986).

- Exposure to environmental and industrial toxins has increased, and as we will see, such toxins are harmful to the reproductive organs, especially the testes, where sperm are manufactured.

Fertility rites   *Ancient peoples prayed to fertility goddesses like this one when they wanted children. Today, couples with fertility problems turn to modern medicine.*

The diagnosis and treatment of infertility can be a lengthy, nerve-racking, and expensive procedure. A couple must think about their reproductive organs all the time, and may become obsessed with achieving pregnancy. They must subject the most private aspects of their lives to scrutiny. Infertile people may feel angry and envious of people with children. They may believe on some level that they are being punished. They may put other plans for their lives on hold, and allow themselves to drift in their jobs or careers. Lovemaking may become a reproductive chore instead of a pleasurable and spontaneous act (Hatcher et al., 1988).

Psychiatrist Miriam D. Mazor, who had a fertility problem herself and now counsels others, recalls: "Suddenly my getting pregnant became the major focus of our lives. We learned what it felt like to chart my basal body temperature each morning [to estimate the arrival of ovulation], have sexual relations on schedule, plan vacations and time off around medical and surgical procedures" (Mazor, 1979). Some infertile couples go through considerable trauma because they feel "defective." Women sometimes describe themselves as empty; men complain that they only "shoot blanks." Parents and friends may reinforce such negative self-perceptions. The partner with the diagnosed physical problem may start to feel sexually undesirable and may worry about being rejected. Sometimes the stress of it all leads to temporary problems with erection or orgasm.

However, these reactions are far from universal. In fact, one study failed to find any overall differences in the coping ability of fertile versus infertile people (Adler & Boxley, 1985). Individuals' reactions to infertility may reflect in part their general ability to cope with stress. Sex roles may also have an influence. In the same study, infertile men and women who scored high in masculinity on a sex-typing test, or who were *androgynous* (high in both masculinity and femininity), appeared to have fewer difficulties than those who were highly feminine or "undifferentiated" (low in both masculinity and femininity.) These findings may not apply to all infertile people, however; participants in the study were all white and all affluent, and the sample was fairly small.

Causes and Treatments

Because human reproduction is so complex, many things can go wrong. In about 40 percent of all cases, the problem is primarily the woman's. In another 40 percent, the problem is primarily the man's. In the remaining cases, the cause is unknown or each partner contributes (Hatcher et al., 1988).

Some of the causes of female infertility are:

1. *Scarring of reproductive organs.* As mentioned above, untreated sexually transmitted diseases and pelvic inflammatory disease can lead to blocking of reproductive organs by scar tissue. A previous surgery can have the same result. One of the most common causes of infertility is blockage of the Fallopian tubes, which prevents sperm from reaching the egg and fertilizing it. The tubes can sometimes be cleared surgically, using advanced techniques such as microsurgery and laser surgery.

2. *Hormonal problems.* Problems in the production of various hormones can prevent normal ovulation, implantation of the egg in the uterus, or maintenance of the pregnancy. The malfunction may occur at various locations in the reproductive system, including the ovaries, the pituitary gland, the hypothalamus, and the adrenal glands. Hormone therapy is often successful in such cases. For example, fertility drugs containing certain hormones often successfully induce ovulation. In fact, sometimes they are more successful than planned: several eggs are released, and the woman gives birth to twins, triplets, or even quadruplets.

3. *Endometriosis.* As mentioned earlier in this chapter, this is a condition in which tissue from the endometrial lining of the uterus grows in another part of the abdomen. Because the tissue does not shed during menstruation, it can scar pelvic organs or cause them to adhere to each other. Endometriosis tends to get worse with time, so it is more likely to prevent pregnancy in older than in younger women. Sometimes it can be treated successfully with hormones or surgery.

4. *The "lethal factor."* Masters and Johnson (1966) found that the cervical mucus in the vaginas of some women contains a "lethal factor" that kills or inactivates sperm within a matter of seconds. In a fascinating experiment, they placed the semen of a man married to a woman with this problem under a microscope. The sperm were alive and well. Then they placed his semen in another woman's vagina, after capping the cervix to prevent pregnancy. Again, the sperm looked fine. But as soon as semen was placed in his wife's vagina,

the sperm became immobile. We now know that some women produce antibodies that immobilize their partner's sperm. One treatment strategy is to use condoms for six months to prevent contact with sperm. During this period, the antibody level may drop and pregnancy may then be possible.

5. *Structural problems.* Infertility can result if there are structural abnormalities in the uterus or cervix. Some of these abnormalities are congenital. Women whose mothers took diethylstilbestrol (DES) during pregnancy (because it was thought to prevent miscarriage) are at increased risk of having structural problems.

This list is far from exhaustive. Among the many other causes of female infertility are excessive exercise, which can reduce body fat to levels that interfere with the production of reproductive hormones; exposure to various toxins; and cervical mucus that is too thick to permit the passage of sperm or that has a pH (acid/alkaline balance) harmful to sperm.

Most cases of male infertility can be traced to problems in the production or maturation of sperm. Often the problem is an abnormally low sperm count. But experts disagree on just how low is low. The American Fertility Society says that there must be at least sixty to one hundred million sperm in a man's ejaculate for conception to take place, yet men with far fewer sperm—as few as ten million—have been known to father children. Other infertile men produce plenty of sperm, but the sperm are poor swimmers. Or the sperm are shaped abnormally, which probably means they contain defective chromosomes; even if fertilization takes place, the embryo does not develop. Causes of poor sperm production or maturation include:

1. *Past or present infections.* Several kinds of infection can reduce male fertility. For example, after puberty, mumps can cause tissues in the testes to swell, crushing the delicate seminiferous tubules where sperm are produced. Certain bacterial infections can also reduce sperm production.

2. *Varicocele.* A **varicocele,** or varicose vein in the scrotum, can cause poor sperm production. The reason is not well-understood; possibly an excess of blood causes the temperature around the seminiferous tubules of the testes to rise, or is in some other way damaging or toxic to sperm. Fortunately, surgery can often correct the condition.

3. *Drugs.* Certain therapeutic drugs (such as Tagamet, a widely-used ulcer medication) can reduce fertility in men, typically by lowering sperm counts or causing abnormalities in sperm. Heavy use of alcohol or tobacco can cause poor sperm quality, and marijuana use may lower sperm counts or reduce sperm motility (Hatcher et al., 1988).

BOX 6–2   **Upping the Odds of Conception**

A couple trying to make a baby can take certain steps to increase the chances. One obvious step is to have intercourse when the woman is ovulating. The trick, though, is identifying exactly when ovulation occurs. Although at present no foolproof method exists for doing this, some procedures are fairly accurate. We will discuss them in the next chapter, when we look at the "rhythm" method for preventing conception. Since sperm usually can live in the woman's genital tract for forty-eight to seventy-two hours, the ideal days for intercourse are the day of ovulation and the two days preceding it.

The position a couple uses for intercourse also affects the probability of conception. When a woman is on her back in the missionary position, gravity, together with the ballooning out of the upper two-thirds of the vagina, causes semen to pool at the back of the vagina (Masters & Johnson, 1966). The longer this pool of semen exists, the better the chances for sperm to enter the cervix opening. As sexual tension decreases, the cervix actually dips into the pool. (The cervix does not suck the semen into the uterus, as many people think.) In a woman who has never given birth, the vaginal opening is usually tight enough to prevent much leakage to the outside for some time. In women who have given birth, the tissues at the vaginal opening are sometimes flattened out and the semen runs out faster. If conception is the goal, it makes sense for the woman to continue to lie on her back for a while after her partner ejaculates, perhaps with a pillow propped under her buttocks.

4. *Toxins.* Concern is growing about the effects of lead, radiation, pesticides, herbicides, and industrial chemicals on male fertility (Castleman, 1985; Weaver, 1986). The testes are particularly sensitive to environmental or industrial toxins. Some of these substances have been linked not only to low sperm counts and sperm abnormalities, but to increased rates of miscarriages, stillbirths, and newborn deaths.

5. *Autoimmune response.* Some men produce antibodies against their own sperm. This condition can sometimes be treated successfully with drugs that suppress this immune system response.

Again, this list is not exhaustive. In some men, an obstruction in the testis, caused by infection or an untreated STD, prevents sperm from leav-

Folklore has it that a woman who denies herself an orgasm lowers the chances of pregnancy. If anything, just the opposite is true. You will recall that during the plateau phase of the sexual response cycle, the tissues in the lower part of the vagina swell to form the orgasmic platform, narrowing the entrance to (or outlet from) the vagina. According to Masters and Johnson, the orgasmic platform acts like a stopper, trapping semen inside. Masters and Johnson say that if a woman reaches plateau but not orgasm, the platform will disappear at a much slower rate, and semen will be dammed up inside the vagina for a longer period of time—up to twenty or thirty minutes. Fortunately, most women find it easy enough to get pregnant while having orgasms. But in difficult cases, a woman might want to try stopping at plateau. In addition, after the man ejaculates he should stop thrusting right away. During thrusting, the weight of the penis can flatten the bottom wall in the lower part of the vagina, allowing semen to escape.

Frequency of intercourse seems to have some influence, too. But again, the folklore hypothesis—the more you do it, the greater the chances of conception—is, well, a misconception. As noted in the text, a man needs a certain minimum number of sperm to be fertile. Once he ejaculates, a day and sometimes longer must pass before he produces another complete batch. So if you are trying to achieve conception you should probably limit intercourse to no more than once every day or two when ovulation is expected.

ing. Even such a mundane thing as high temperatures can impair fertility. If a couple is trying to conceive, the man should stay out of hot tubs, avoid tight pants and jockstraps, and try to keep the scrotal area cool.

Fortunately, the causes of infertility can be identified in about 90–95 percent of all cases, and when a thorough medical workup is done, about half of these cases can be helped. (At present, male problems are easier to diagnose, but harder to treat.) Sometimes, "infertile" couples conceive without any treatment (Collins et al., 1983). Because of increased awareness of fertility problems, people may panic if they don't conceive after five or six months of trying, and seek treatment for problems they do not have (Menken, Trussell, & Larsen, 1986). Before spending time and money on a specialist, a couple may want to try certain self-help measures to increase the chances of conception (described in Box 6–2), especially if they are young and there are no signs of a medical problem.

NEW WAYS OF MAKING BABIES

If the standard treatments for infertility fail, a couple has several options. One is to adjust to life without children. Another is to adopt a child. (Incidentally, contrary to popular opinion, adoption does not cure infertility. Sometimes a couple diagnosed as infertile does conceive after adopting, but this is just as likely to happen to couples that do not adopt.) One woman wrote of the relief and satisfaction she and her husband experienced when, after years of trying to get and then stay pregnant, she had her tubes surgically removed and turned to the raising of two adopted children:

> We plan trips, without fearing that I might be pregnant. I can accept assignments and long-term projects. . .We're making the most of the life we have now, and have stopped worrying about the life we would have if only . . .
>
> We're a family, which is what we were aiming for in the first place.
> (Bouton, 1987)

Increasingly, however, couples are taking a third course: they are turning to non-coital reproductive technologies.

Artificial Insemination

When a man has a low sperm count, or when there are physical or psychological barriers to sexual intercourse, a couple may try **artificial insemi-**

En route *A sperm passes through a Fallopian tube, waved on by tiny filaments called cilia.*

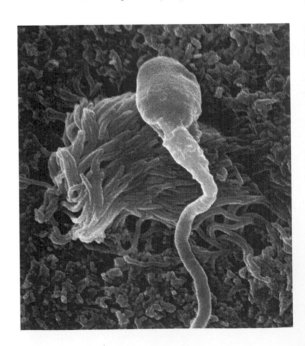

nation (AI). The man masturbates, and then his semen is collected and injected into the woman's vagina, or sometimes directly into the uterus, with a syringe or similar device. The first few drops of the ejaculate, which contain most of the active sperm, are often collected separately for this purpose. The procedure is simple, and has been used by some people without the assistance of a doctor (see Boston Women's Health Book Collective [1984] for details).

Artificial insemination has been around for many decades, and has resulted in hundreds of thousands of conceptions. It has been in the news of late, however, because of the increased use of semen donated by someone other than a woman's husband. In **donor insemination (DI),** also known as *artificial insemination by donor*, or *AID*, sperm are taken from a volunteer or paid donor shortly before insemination or are collected and then stored at extremely low temperatures in sperm repositories, or "banks," for up to several years. Sperm banks sell vials of sperm to physicians or directly to prospective parents. They also rent storage facilities to men who are planning to have a vasectomy or who must undergo radiation treatments for cancer, as well as to women who have found their own private donors.

Donor insemination is being used not only by women whose male partners are infertile, but also by single heterosexual women and single and coupled lesbians. The donor may be a friend, an acquaintance, or an anonymous stranger who has been paid a small fee by a sperm bank for his services. (Traditionally, a high proportion of donors have been medical students.) Most banks screen donors for genetic problems and HIV infection, but rely heavily on the donor's honesty in answering questions about his background. Banks generally allow prospective mothers to specify physical traits they want the anonymous donor to have.

In Vitro Fertilization

In 1978, British researchers Patrick Steptoe and Robert Edwards accomplished the world's first birth resulting from **in vitro fertilization (IVF)**—literally, fertilization in glass. Their client was Lesley Brown, a woman who had a Fallopian tube problem that could not be corrected surgically. Attempts to unblock her tubes had left her with mere remnants, and the outlook for having children was bleak until Steptoe and Edwards tried their revolutionary new technique.

In a procedure that has since become widely used, the researchers gave Ms. Brown hormones to stimulate maturation of several eggs at once. Then they inserted a long, thin optical instrument called a *laparoscope* through a small incision in her abdomen and located the ovary. Carefully, they drew out a mature egg, no larger than the dot made by a sharp pencil, through a small hollow needle. Then they placed the egg in a petri dish, along with blood serum, nutrients, salts, and some of Mr. Brown's sperm. The sperm had been bathed in a salt solution to remove certain chemical inhibitors on

Afloat   *An egg drifts just outside the opening of a Fallopian tube; the fringes at the end of the tube will soon draw it in.*

their surface that would ordinarily be removed in Ms. Brown's body. The environment in the dish was similar enough to the one in Ms. Brown's body for fertilization to take place.

After the egg was fertilized, the scientists incubated it for a few days while it underwent three cell divisions. Then they carefully placed it in Ms. Brown's uterus, which had been prepared with hormones to receive it. The egg burrowed into the uterine wall, and from that point on, development proceeded just as it would with an ordinary conception. On July 25, 1978, Lesley Brown gave birth to a healthy baby girl, the first child ever conceived outside its mother's body.

Since then, thousands of "test-tube" babies (or, more accurately, petri-dish babies) have been born in countries around the world. Certain refinements of technique have been made. In one procedure, the doctor removes eggs from the woman's ovaries by guiding a needle through the wall of the vagina, assisted by ultrasound; this is cheaper and easier than the laparoscopic procedure, and does not require general anesthesia. In most clinics, more than one egg is fertilized and implanted in order to increase the odds of success. (The odds of multiple births also increase). Some IVF embryos have been frozen and stored for later insertion into a woman's uterus; this procedure allows doctors to keep "leftover" embryos for subsequent attempts at impregnation, without requiring the woman to undergo repeated egg extractions. But in vitro fertilization remains a costly, complicated, and uncertain procedure; success rates are only about 10 to 25 percent in most clinics. A recent survey of 135 U.S. clinics found the overall pregnancy rate for IVF to be only 15 percent and the live delivery rate to be only 12 percent (Medical Research International et al., 1990).

In a related technique, called gamete intrafallopian transfer (GIFT), sperm and ova are placed directly into the woman's Fallopian tubes for fertilization. Again, because more than one egg is used, the chances of producing twins or triplets is higher than normal if fertilization takes place. Like IVF, GIFT is expensive; the chances of success per procedure are about one in five.

Donor-egg Techniques

What if a woman is infertile because her ovaries do not function, or have been removed? One solution, pioneered in Australia, is to obtain an egg from a fertile woman (ovum donor), fertilize the egg in a petri dish with the prospective father's sperm, then insert the embryo into the infertile woman's womb. The recipient can be given hormones to help her maintain the pregnancy (Lutjen et al., 1984). Another approach is **embryo transfer,** first carried out successfully in California (Buster et al., 1983). Doctors artificially inseminate an ovum donor with the prospective father's sperm. Then, a few days later, they wash the fertilized egg out of the woman's uterus through a soft plastic tube and place it in the uterus of the infertile woman. If implantation occurs, the recipient carries the fetus and gives birth to it. Unlike IVF, embryo transfer does not require surgery or prolonged exposure of the embryo to the outside world. But it does require the egg donor to have a brief pregnancy.

Donor egg techniques, though still not in widespread use, raise an intriguing possibility. They could enable women to have children even after menopause, and make the notion of a reproductive "biological clock" obsolete.

Surrogate Mothers

A **surrogate mother** is a woman who volunteers to bear a child for someone else, usually a woman who cannot conceive, cannot carry a pregnancy to term, or has had her uterus removed. The surrogate signs a contract obligating her to give up the baby after birth. In most of the hundreds of cases to date, the surrogate has been artificially inseminated with the prospective father's sperm, and then the man and his wife have formally adopted the baby. However, the use of surrogates has also been combined with in vitro fertilization.

Some couples have arranged privately for a friend or relative to act as a surrogate. (In South Africa, a 48-year-old grandmother gave birth to her daughter's triplets, conceived through in vitro fertilization of the daughter's eggs by the son-in-law's sperm.) Sometimes when a friend or relative is involved, all the parties concerned agree to play a role in the child's upbringing. But most surrogate arrangements are set up between strangers by a for-profit agency, a doctor, or an attorney. Agencies screen the surrogate for possible emotional or physical problems. The surrogate agrees to relinquish

Parenthood by proxy
Shown here are an unmarried surrogate mother (on the right), the biological father of her children, and the man's wife, all of whom are living together and rearing the children. The surrogate mother offered to bear a baby for the wife (her best friend) when the wife found she could not become pregnant. Cases like this one have raised many difficult legal and ethical questions.

the child, and in exchange she gets her expenses paid and usually receives a substantial fee. Many surrogates undoubtedly volunteer because they need the money, but some simply wish to help another woman, or have the experience of pregnancy. Most are married and have children. At the time of this writing, a few states have passed laws that regulate the use of surrogates, for example by prohibiting payments.

Brave New World: Ethical and Legal Dilemmas

— A man in Marseille, France, deposits his sperm at a sperm bank for later use, then dies of cancer. His wife requests the sperm so that she can be impregnated with them, but the bank refuses because the man has left no instructions regarding the matter. The sperm, argues the bank, are a part of the man's body, like a leg or ear, and cannot be given away. The wife sues and gets the sperm.

— At an Australian clinic, a wealthy Los Angeles couple arranges for IVF using a donor's sperm. An attempt at implantation results in a miscarriage, so two spare embryos, clusters of six and eight cells, are frozen for a later try. Unfortunately, the couple dies in a plane crash before the embryos can be implanted in the woman's womb. After some debate about what to do, the clinic destroys the "orphan embryos." Right-to-life advocates are furious.

— In a celebrated incident that will come to be known as the "Baby M. Case," a New Jersey woman, married with two children, contracts to act as a surrogate mother for an affluent couple that does not want the wife to get pregnant because of health problems. The surrogate is artificially inseminated with the man's sperm. When the baby is born, however, she changes her mind, refuses the fee, and flees with the child and her family to another state. After several months, she is found and brought back. There is a lengthy custody hearing, and a judge rules that the biological father and his wife will make better parents than the surrogate and her husband. He strips the surrogate of all parental rights, but she later regains rights of visitation.

As you can see, the new reproductive technologies now available raise some serious dilemmas. Each one poses unique legal and ethical questions. For example:

- *Donor Insemination:* What are the legal rights, if any, of a sperm donor who decides he would like to know the child he has fathered and take part in its rearing? What right, if any, does the child conceived by DI have to know its biological father? Does the recipient have the right to sue the donor, the sperm bank, or a physician if the donor lies about his health or genetic background and the child is born with a disability? How should sperm banks be regulated? There is already one clinic that uses DI to try to breed geniuses (no clear results have emerged), and most sperm banks give recipients a choice of the characteristics they want donors to have. Will this lead to a view of children as products to be manufactured according to specifications, or to the elitist position that only smart or good-looking people deserve to be parents?

- *In Vitro Fertilization:* What should be done with fertilized eggs that are not used? Should they be sold? Given to someone else? Destroyed? Used for research? The American Fertility Society approves of experimentation on or the discarding of unused embryos, but these practices are controversial, and for that reason the U.S. government currently has a moratorium on all funding of IVF. The Australian case raises yet another issue: if a frozen embryo survives its parents and is implanted in a surrogate or another woman, does it have any rights as an "heir" of its deceased parents?

- *Donor-egg techniques:* What rights, if any, does the egg donor have to know the child that is genetically half hers? What right, if any, does the child have to know who its genetic mother is? What happens in the unlikely event that the fertilized egg fails to flush out properly, and the donor continues to be pregnant? Can she opt for an abortion? Can she be forced to have an abortion?

- *Surrogate mothers.* Probably no reproductive method raises as many questions as this one. Will poor women be exploited by prosperous couples who would rather rent a womb than go through the bother of pregnancy or adoption? Does surrogacy amount to baby-selling, which is illegal in all states? Should a surrogate be allowed to change her mind and keep her baby after it is born, so long as she gives up the fee? Does she have a right to play any role in her biological child's life? What if she smokes or drinks too much while pregnant and her child is born with physical or mental problems? If the infertile couple divorces or has a change of mind, can the surrogate be forced to have an abortion? What if the surrogate does not want to go through with the pregnancy; does she have the same right that other women have to an abortion? What about the surrogate's previous children: do they have a right to know their half-sibling?

To make matters even more complex, the various methods we have covered can be combined in various ways (see Table 6–1). For instance, suppose that a married woman's eggs are fertilized in vitro with a donor's sperm and then implanted in a surrogate mother. After birth the child is reared by the first woman (the egg donor). The child will then have four kinds of parents: a genetic father (the sperm donor); a genetic and "rearing" mother (the egg donor, who rears the child); a rearing father (the egg donor's husband); and a birth mother (the surrogate).

What all the reproductive technologies have in common is that they complete the separation of sex and procreation. First, birth control made it possible to have sex without pregnancy. Now it is possible to reproduce without having sex. Critics of this separation worry that human beings are playing God without being able to predict the long-range consequences. They cite Goethe's version of the Faust legend, in which the vain Faust fulfills his need for power by creating a test-tube man, Homunculus, and winds up paying with his soul. They also draw analogies to Aldous Huxley's classic anti-utopian novel, *Brave New World*, which describes a futuristic society in which babies are made, not born. Some religious authorities, in particular, consider the new practices "unnatural" and dehumanizing. As a spokesman

In this table, "mother" and "father" refer to the woman and man who will act as the child's parents; AI = artificial insemination, DI = donor insemination, IVF = in vitro fertilization, GIFT = gamete intrafallopian transfer, and ET = embryo transfer. As an exercise, you might try to imagine the circumstances in which each option might be used.

TABLE 6–1
Some noncoital ways to make babies.

Source of ovum	Source of sperm	Identity of birth mother	Applicable techniques
mother	father	mother	AI, IVF, GIFT
mother	father	surrogate	IVF, GIFT
donor	father	mother	IVF, GIFT, AI + ET
donor	father	surrogate	IVF, GIFT, AI (if donor is the surrogate), AI + ET (if donor is not the surrogate)
mother	donor	mother	DI, IVF/GIFT
mother	donor	surrogate	IVF/GIFT to surrogate
donor	donor	mother	AI + ET to mother, IVF, GIFT
donor	donor	surrogate	DI of surrogate, IVF

for the Archdiocese of New York remarked after the birth of Lesley Brown's baby, "It's the contraception argument backward. Pius XII talked about not wanting to change the home into a laboratory. I call it switching the marital bed into a chemistry set" (quoted in *Time*, July 31, 1978). And some feminists think the new technologies give doctors too much control over conception and birth (Boston Women's Health Book Collective, 1984).

Defenders of the new methods point out that their purpose, after all, is to help couples fulfill the biblical commandment to procreate, and God helps those who help themselves. They object to the attitude that says procreation is the only "humanizing" motive for sex. What about love, commitment, and the giving and receiving of pleasure? In fact, they say, the insistence on linking sex to procreation can be viewed as dehumanizing, since it seems to equate sex with mere breeding. Protechnology feminists point out that techniques such as donor insemination give single women and lesbians the option of motherhood without dependence on a male partner for fertilization (Brown, 1983). Supporters also observe that the new techniques permit people who carry a genetic disorder, such as sickle cell anemia, Tay-Sachs disease, or hemophilia, to have healthy offspring by using the sperm or eggs of donors instead of their own.

Many medical advances that have vastly improved the quality of life initially met the same sort of skepticism that in vitro fertilization and other reproductive technologies have encountered. For example, when pain-relievers were first used in childbirth, some people objected that they were unnatural and violated God's plan for women to suffer while bringing forth children (Gen. 3:16). When heart transplants were first performed, some people called the surgeons involved modern Dr. Frankensteins. We should keep in mind that science only offers us discoveries; society has to decide whether or not to use them, and if so, how to use them wisely.

. . . .

PERSONAL PERSPECTIVE

WHY PARENTHOOD? EXPLORING YOUR MOTIVES

Two old friends meet after not seeing each other for many years. Ned tells Steve he's married, owns a business, and has three beautiful children. Steve tells Ned he's married, a successful lawyer, a jogger, and a member of the local orchestra. Ned is shocked: "You mean you have no children?" "No," says Steve. "My God!" Ned exclaims. "What do you do for aggravation?"

Most parents can appreciate this joke. Yet people often drift into parenthood with little thought about reasons or readiness. Only after the fact do they become aware that parenthood changes one's life forever. The bundle of joy that comes home from the hospital is also a bundle of responsibilities. The sweet baby whose laughter makes everyone coo and cluck also cries and complains, demanding attention. An older child may give its parents cause for pride and satisfaction, but it may also disappoint. Children give much, but they come with both an emotional and a financial price tag. And they make their parents forever vulnerable to the most profound loss and grief—for as every mother and father knows, the possibility of someday losing a beloved child is a dreaded sword over every parent's head.

With all the responsibilities that children bring with them, it behooves prospective parents to understand what they expect to get by begetting. Below you will find some reasons people have for becoming parents. Which ones apply to you? If you have not yet had children, you can use this exercise to gain self-knowledge before you make a decision about childbearing or adoption. If you are already a parent, you can explore your past decisions (or lack thereof), or the reasons you might have for wanting another child.

1. I love being around or taking care of children and want to have the pleasure of rearing my own.

2. I think I have the right qualities for being a good parent and would gain a sense of accomplishment for doing the job well.

3. Having children would give me a sense of immortality; I would know I was leaving a part of myself behind after my death.

4. Having a child would give me the satisfaction of perpetuating the family name.

5. I want someone I can nurture: someone to love and care for.

6. A child would give me an unconditional kind of love that others do not.

7. My parents or other relatives want me to have kids and I don't want to disappoint them.

8. I had a good family life when I was young and I want to recreate the sense of family I enjoyed by having children of my own.

9. Children are entertaining; I think they would make my life interesting and fun.

10. A child would be able to help me in my business or line of work.

11. Children would be a comfort to me in my old age; I could look to them for emotional and, if necessary, financial help.

12. The challenge of rearing a child would enhance my personal growth and contribute to my own maturity.

13. I want to have a child because I think people who never have children miss out on one of life's most profound experiences.

14. Fatherhood or motherhood would be a fulfillment of my masculinity or femininity.

15. Having a child would give me a sense of identity and would give my life a purpose.

16. A child would be a symbol of the love that exists between me and my spouse or partner.

17. Having a child would improve the quality of my relationship with my spouse or partner.

18. Having a child would bring me the respect of others.

19. I think having a child would be fascinating because I could watch another person develop and grow.

20. I want to have children because I believe people can contribute to society by helping to raise the next generation.

21. I feel a duty to help increase the size of my religious, ethnic, or racial group by having children.

22. Having children would broaden me because I would learn things and have experiences I otherwise would not.

23. Other: _____.

As you go over this list, ask yourself whether your reasons for wanting children are realistic. Are you expecting something from a child that it can't deliver? For example, sometimes people have a child as a way to shore up a sagging relationship or prevent a divorce. But the result is usually more problems, not fewer. Parents of young children report feeling more stress than any other group (Feshbach, 1985). New parents, particularly mothers, generally report a dip in happiness and satisfaction with their lives. Although most people enjoy their children, the increased noise and interruptions, demands on the parents' time and energy, and loss of privacy children bring are not likely to help a relationship that is in trouble. Children may contribute to an already strong marriage, but they can't turn straw into gold.

In evaluating your reasons for parenthood, explore, too, the possible consequences for the child. If, in your heart of hearts, you believe a baby will give you unconditional love, how are you likely to react when the child doesn't "come through"? If you look forward to feeling proud of your child's accomplishments, how will you feel if the child is only average or below average in achievement, or if he or she has physical or intellectual disabilities?

Which of the reasons on the list seems like good ones to you, and which do not? Perhaps none of the reasons on our list applies to you. Does this mean that you don't want children, or that you want them, but don't know why?

IN BRIEF

1. Although reproducing is not the main goal of sex for most people, the link between sex and reproduction is an important one. Concerns about achieving or avoiding pregnancy can affect the quality of a sexual relationship and decisions about marriage.

2. An accurate understanding of *conception* is a relatively recent historical development. It was not until the late nineteenth-century that scientists understood that the sperm and the ovum must play equally important roles.

3. The female role in conception involves a predictable sequence of events that occur over a cycle lasting 28 days on average. During this cycle, an ovarian *follicle* matures, ruptures, and releases an *ovum*, or egg

(*ovulation*). Estrogen and progesterone cause the lining of the uterus to thicken in preparation for implantation of a fertilized egg. If *fertilization* occurs, the egg embeds into the uterine lining. Otherwise it disintegrates and part of the uterine lining sloughs off and exits the body, along with blood and mucus, as the menstrual flow. Controversy exists about negative emotional symptoms reported by some women before menstruation (the "premenstrual syndrome"); controlled research has failed to confirm such symptoms in most women.

4. If a fertilized egg embeds somewhere other than in the uterine lining, the result is an *ectopic pregnancy*. The most common type of ectopic pregnancy is a *tubal pregnancy*, which can be life-threatening.

5. Whereas women are born with all the eggs they will ever have (in an immature form), men manufacture *sperm* throughout their adult lives. A single ejaculation contains several hundred million sperm, but only two thousand or so reach the egg in the Fallopian tube. When one sperm penetrates and merges with an egg, fertilization has occurred.

6. A missed menstrual period is usually the first sign of pregnancy, followed by various other bodily changes (although not all women have all the symptoms). Various laboratory and home pregnancy tests are available to test for the presence of *human chorionic gonadotropin (HCG)* in a woman's urine or blood, which is a sign of pregnancy, but a woman who suspects she is pregnant should always see a medical practitioner for a pelvic examination as well.

7. *Gestation* lasts about nine and a half lunar months. During the first two months the conceptus is called an *embryo;* after that it is known as a *fetus*. The first trimester of gestation is when the basic organ systems develop. During the second trimester, the fetus becomes active and its heartbeat is detectable but it cannot usually survive outside the womb. The third trimester is a time of rapid growth. By the end of the eighth month, the fetus can usually survive outside the woman's body.

8. A variety of genetic and environmental factors can cause birth defects and congenital diseases. Genetic counseling is available for prospective parents who wish to determine the risk of transmitting a hereditary condition. *Amniocentesis, ultrasound scans*, and *chorionic villi sampling (CVS)* can detect many fetal problems at various stages of pregnancy.

9. Sexual intercourse is usually safe throughout pregnancy, unless there are special problems such as vaginal bleeding or a history of miscarriages. Interest in sex sometimes fluctuates over the course of the pregnancy and will depend, in part, on a person's previous attitudes and feelings about sexuality. Many doctors recommend avoiding sexual intercourse for about six weeks after delivery or until a woman is fully recovered from the physical and emotional ordeal of giving birth. The challenges and stresses of new parenthood sometimes interfere with sexual motivation or opportunity.

10. An embryo's genetic sex is determined by the sex chromosomes. If both the mother and the father contribute an X chromosome, the result is a girl. If the mother contributes an X but the father contributes a Y, the result is a boy. Genetically, then, the father determines the sex of the child. Various laboratory methods for influencing the odds of having a boy or girl are now being used. Some observers believe that if sex selection became widespread, it would result in an overabundance of males, which could have some negative social consequences.

11. About one out of every six married couples in America has difficulty starting or maintaining a pregnancy. *Infertility* is caused by a variety of physical problems. Certain social and environmental changes, such as an increase in sexually transmitted diseases and the postponement of pregnancy by many couples, have probably increased the incidence of such problems. Male and female fertility problems are equally common. The causes of infertility can usually be identified and can often be treated.

12. Many non-coital reproductive technologies are now available for achieving conception, pregnancy, and parenthood, including *artificial insemination, in vitro fertilization, embryo transfer,* and the use of *surrogate mothers.* Critics of these procedures object to them on various ethical and religious grounds. Defenders point to the help such procedures offer to infertile couples, people who carry a genetic disorder, and single people who wish to become parents. All the new reproductive technologies raise difficult legal and ethical dilemmas. Science can only offer us discoveries; society must decide how to use them.

Key Terms

conception *(178)*

oocytes *(178)*

ovarian follicle *(178)*

endometrium *(178)*

fertilization *(179)*

ectopic pregnancy *(182)*

tubal pregnancy *(182)*

zygote *(179)*

blastocyst *(179)*

corpus luteum *(179)*

menstruation *(181)*

proliferative phase *(181)*

secretory phase *(181)*

premenstruation *(182)*

dysmenorrhea *(182)*

prostaglandins *(182)*

endometriosis *(183)*

"premenstrual syndrome" *(183)*

spermatogenesis *(184)*

human chorionic gonadotropin *(187)*

pregnancy tests *(187)*

gestation *(188)*

embryo *(188)*

fetus *(188)*

conceptus *(188)*

placenta *(188)*

umbilical cord *(189)*

afterbirth *(189)*

amniotic sac *(189)*

amniotic fluid *(189)*

trimesters of pregnancy *(189)*

congenital diseases *(191)*

amniocentesis *(194)*

ultrasound scans *(195)*

chorionic villi sampling (CVS) *(195)*

chromosomes *(201)*

sex chromosomes *(201)*

sex selection *(202)*

infertility *(204)*

sterility *(204)*

pelvic inflammatory disease (PID) *(204)*

varicocele *(207)*

artificial insemination (AI) *(210)*

donor insemination (DI) *(211)*

in vitro fertilization (IVF) *(211)*

gamete intrafallopian transfer (GIFT) *(213)*

embryo transfer *(213)*

surrogate mother *(213)*

**CHAPTER
SEVEN**

CHAPTER SEVEN

■

Birth Control

●

There was an old woman and she lived in a shoe. She had so many children, she didn't know what to do.

Anonymous

E ffective, reliable **birth control** is a product of modern technology. But women and men have been trying to control their fertility for at least the past three thousand years. Before there was a birth control pill, or a diaphragm, or a condom, or even a rhythm method, there was . . . crocodile dung. Ancient papyri describe the women of ancient Egypt stuffing the stuff up their vaginas—presumably in hopes of preventing conception. Since crocodile dung is rather alkaline, and sperm thrive in an alkaline environment, this method probably did not work too well, although it may have blocked the route of at least a few sperm. When African and Indian women later substituted elephant dung, which is more acidic than crocodile dung, it was undoubtedly an improvement.

Other birth control approaches of the past were just as imaginative and somewhat more aesthetic (Hardin, 1970; Himes, 1970; Mermey, 1975.) In Greece, women made contraceptive tampons out of honey and cedarwood oil mixed with fig pulp. In Persia, patients who visited the great ninth-century physician Rhazes of Baghdad came away with a paste made of colocynth pulp, pomegranate, animal earwax, whitewash, and elephant dung. Some of the authors of the Jewish Talmud believed that in certain cases it was permissible for women to insert vaginal sponges that absorbed seminal fluid. The women of Sumatra came close to inventing the diaphragm when they shaped opium into a cup that fit over the cervix. In Martinique women douched with a liquid produced by boiling husks of mahogany with lemon juice. In addition to using crocodile dung, Egyptian women tried to fumigate their insides by squatting over a charcoal burner. As for men, in most societies they practiced withdrawal. In India men were also advised to press firmly on the base of the penis during intercourse to prevent ejaculation; pressure against the urethra probably forced sperm into the bladder.

Although official policy in most Western societies promoted procreation, grass-roots movements, supported by some physicians and scholars, pushed for birth control. In nineteenth- and early twentieth-century America, the two opposing attitudes met head-on. Reformers published books and pamphlets describing withdrawal, vaginal sponges, condoms, and, by the end of the nineteenth-century, early versions of the diaphragm. But conservative forces, including the American Medical Association, staunchly opposed research on more effective birth control methods and fought to limit the distribution of information to the masses. Local medical societies lobbied against the establishment of neighborhood birth control clinics, possibly in part because they were usually staffed by volunteers instead of doctors (Reed, 1978).

Moralists during the Victorian era worried that once the threat of pregnancy was removed, people would turn into sex-crazed perverts. Theodore Roosevelt, early in his political career, called anyone who purposely remained childless "a criminal against the race." He said, "Willful sterility inevitably produces and accentuates every hideous form of vice. . . . It is itself worse, more debasing, more destructive, than ordinary vice. I rank celibate profligacy as not one whit better than polygamy" (quoted in Rugoff, 1971).

THE BIRTH OF MODERN BIRTH CONTROL

Despite such attitudes, during the nineteenth century the birth rate in the United States gradually declined. If **contraception,** the prevention of conception, was not available, abortion was. Newspapers and magazines were full of thinly disguised advertisements for abortion information and drugs that supposedly caused abortion (Mohr, 1978). Poor women, who could not always afford the five dollars for an abortionist, often tried to end their pregnancies themselves, using such crude devices as knitting needles inserted into the uterus. Thousands of women died of illicit or self-induced abortions every year.

One of these deaths made a deep impression on Margaret Sanger, the founder of Planned Parenthood. In 1912, Sanger was working as a nurse in a crowded tenement district on New York's Lower East Side. One hot July day she was summoned to the bedside of a twenty-eight-year-old woman named Sadie Sachs. Mrs. Sachs, who was the mother of three small children, had tried to end her fourth pregnancy herself and had become critically ill. Day and night Sanger and a physician struggled to save her, and finally they succeeded. But the patient seemed anxious and despondent. Timidly she asked the doctor how she might prevent another pregnancy. Later, in her autobiography, Sanger recalled his response:

> The doctor was a kindly man. . .but such incidents had become so familiar to him that he had long since lost whatever delicacy he might once have had. He laughed good-naturedly. "You want to have your cake and eat it too, do you? Well, it can't be done."
>
> Then picking up his hat and bag to depart he said, "Tell Jake to sleep on the roof." (Sanger, 1938, p. 91)

Jake did not sleep on the roof. Three months later Sanger watched Sadie Sachs die from another abortion attempt. Shortly afterwards, Sanger gave up nursing and launched a fifty-year campaign for the distribution of birth control—a term, incidentally, that she coined.

A few years after Sadie Sachs' death, Sanger and her sister opened a birth control clinic in a poor section of Brooklyn. The clinic did not provide contraceptives, only information. Yet on opening day 100 women and 40 men passed through its doors, and many others were still waiting when the clinic closed at 7:00 p.m. During the next few days, people came from as far away as Pennsylvania, Massachusetts, and New Jersey. Within ten days Sanger was arrested by the Vice Squad, under a New York law that made it a misdemeanor for anyone to disseminate contraceptive devices or information. She was sentenced to thirty days in jail for distributing birth control information and maintaining a public nuisance. Sanger was neither the first nor the last birth control advocate to spend time behind bars. The last state law forbidding the sale or distribution of contraceptive devices—in Massachusetts—did not fall until 1972.

Eventually, though, the pendulum swung the other way. In 1936 a Gallup poll revealed that almost two-thirds of all Americans felt birth control information should be available to those who wanted it. By 1960 the percentage in favor had risen to 72 percent, and in 1965 it was up to 81 percent. Social acceptance of birth control was possibly due not so much to the efforts of reformers as to changes in attitudes toward sexuality and the role of women, as well as growing concern about the population explosion (Reed, 1978). In any case, by the end of the 1970s widespread use of birth control had affected the birth rate dramatically. From the end of World War II to about 1957, the "baby boom" years, American couples had an average of 3.5 babies each. Then the boom collapsed (see Figure 7–1). By 1972, the rate had decreased to only 2.08 babies, and in 1977 it was only 1.8, falling below replacement (since couples were not producing enough children to take their place when they died). Fertility fell in all classes and ethnic groups, but the decline was especially striking among educated women (Wolfe, 1977). The U.S. population continued to grow because of immigration and because people of childbearing age outnumbered other age groups. Also, during the late 1980s a "baby boomlet" occurred, as many people who had postponed pregnancy started to have children. However, there has been no sign in recent years of a return to the high birth rates of the 1950s.

Margaret Sanger
Sanger, who initiated the birth control movement and founded Planned Parenthood, is shown here testifying before a Senate committee in the 1930s.

FIGURE 7-1

Fewer mothers, fewer babies *Except for a period following World War II (the "baby boom"), this century has seen a steady decline in U.S. fertility rates. In the mid-1980s, the rate was the lowest ever recorded. But by the end of the decade, the rate had begun to increase, suggesting the occurrence of a "baby boomlet."*

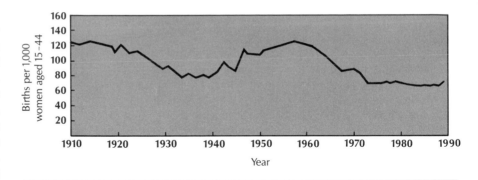

Source: National Center for Health Statistics, U.S. Department of Health and Human Services, 1990.

Financial support for the development and use of contraception peaked in the mid-1970s. The government issued a postage stamp honoring family planning and was supporting contraceptive research to the tune of some $200 million a year (Selden, 1979). By the end of the decade, though, some clouds had darkened the horizon. Studies suggested that the birth control pill increased the risk of stroke and heart attack, and there were also reports of complications from another method, the intrauterine device. These developments did not lead to a search for new, safer methods. Instead, faced with the threat of liability suits and a slow government approval process (it takes about $45 million and 15 years to win FDA approval for a new method), all but one company stopped doing contraceptive research. Government funding for such research dropped from $200 million a year in 1975 to only $20 million in 1985—or 25 cents per taxpayer per year (Wilbur, 1986). As a result, the United States has fallen far behind other countries in contraceptive research; in fact, its research efforts have ground to a virtual halt (National Academy of Sciences, 1990). According to Carl Djerassi, who helped develop the first birth control pill, "The U.S. is the only country other than Iran in which the birth control clock has been set backward" (quoted in *Time*, February 26, 1990).

The demand and need for effective and safe family planning methods have certainly not lessened, however. There are almost 58 million women of child-bearing age in the United States. Three-fifths of them use contraception. Of those, 27.5 percent have chosen female sterilization and 11.7 percent have a partner who has been sterilized; 30.7 percent use the Pill; 14.6 percent use condoms; 5.7 percent use the diaphragm; 2 percent use an intrauterine device; and 7.7 percent use some other method, such as spermicides or "rhythm" (Mosher & Pratt, 1990). But at least eight percent of sexually active women who do not want to become pregnant use no birth control at all (Forrest & Henshaw, 1983). There are over three million unintended pregnancies each year; half are the result of not using any contraception (Sweet, 1988). Attitudes toward sexuality and pregnancy, worries about the safety of various methods, and the kind of relationship a person has with his or her partner, as well as social policies regarding the distribution of contraceptives, all contribute to the decision to use or not use birth control. In the following section we will review the various methods available, noting the advantages and disadvantages of each. Then we will discuss some of the reasons that people sometimes fail to use them.

BIRTH CONTROL METHODS: PROS AND CONS

Although several birth control methods are available, the perfect method—safe, effective, cheap, easy to use, and aesthetically pleasing—still does not exist. Couples wanting to avoid pregnancy must choose the best method for them; no one method suits everyone. Making an informed choice requires knowledge of the methods themselves and awareness of how personal characteristics (such as motivation, the frequency with which one has sexual intercourse, and comfort with procedures for use) can influence the success of a particular method. Table 7–1 shows the optimum effectiveness of methods now available in the U.S. and how effective each method is in typical usage. Most methods are not as effective in practice as they could be because many people do not use them correctly or consistently.

Oral Contraceptives (The Pill)

For about 10 million women in the United States, birth control is practically synonymous with "the Pill." When Dr. Alan Guttmacher, a president of Planned Parenthood, remarked in 1958 that "we are on the threshold of a new era in birth control," he was right. Since their introduction in the early 1960s, **oral contraceptives (OCs)** have become the most popular temporary method of contraception in many Western countries. The Pill's popularity is due primarily to its high success rate: when used correctly it has an effectiveness rate of 99 percent. In actual practice, users make mistakes: a typical first-year failure rate for the pill is 3 percent, and for users under the age of 22 the first-year failure rate is 4.7 percent (Hatcher et al., 1988). Pregnancy can occur when a woman forgets to take two or more pills in a row or stops taking her pills.

There are currently more than 30 different brands of OCs but basically only three different kinds: combination, phasic, and mini-pill:

1. The combination pill contains two hormones, synthetic estrogen and synthetic progesterone **(progestin)**, which are more potent than the hormones normally produced in the body. While a woman is on the combination pill, secretion of estrogen and progesterone by her ovaries is suppressed.

2. The **phasic pill** (there are biphasic and triphasic varieties) is a combination pill that keeps the level of estrogen constant throughout the pill cycle but delivers progestin in two (or

TABLE 7–1

Contraceptive methods: How well do they work? These figures indicate the approximate number of pregnancies that can be expected for each method during the first year of use by 100 fertile users. The first column gives the lowest observed failure rates; the second shows failure rates in typical users. Note that the figures are derived from several studies, not all of which used the same methods or obtained the same figures.

Method	Lowest Observed Failure Rate (%)	Failure Rate in Typical Users (%)
Tubal sterilization	0.2	0.4
Vasectomy	0.1	0.15
Combined birth control pills	0.1	3
Mini-pill	0.5	3
IUD	0.8–2.0	3
Condom	2	12
Diaphragm (with spermicide)	6	18
Sponge	6–9	18–28
Cervical cap	6	18
Foams, creams, jellies, and vaginal suppositories	3	21
Withdrawal	4	18
Fertility awareness techniques: (basal body temperature, mucus, calendar, and "rhythm"methods)	1–9	20
Chance (no method used)	85	85

Source: Adapted from Hatcher, Robert A.; Stewart, Felicia; Trussell, James; Kowal, Deborah et al. Contraceptive Technology, *1990–1992 (15th rev. ed.) N.Y. Irvington (p. 134, Tab. 8.2)*

three) different dosages. Progestin levels are lowest during the first few days of the cycle and higher later on. The overall level of progestin in the phasic pill is less than in the conventional combination pill, and this lower level helps reduce side effects.

3. The mini-pill is not a tiny pill; it is one that contains only a low dose of progestin and no estrogen. Because the mini-pill is less reliable than the other types and may cause irregular menstrual periods or bleeding between periods, it is usually prescribed only to women who cannot tolerate estrogen.

Since OCs were first introduced, there has been a dramatic lowering of the amount of hormone used in them. Lower doses have proven to be as effective as higher ones and are associated with far fewer side effects. The precise hormone levels in all three kinds of pills vary with the brand.

The major contraceptive effect of the combination and the phasic pills is to override a woman's natural hormone cycle. It works like this. Normally, low estrogen levels after menstruation signal the hypothalamus to send a chemical message to the pituitary gland, directing it to produce follicle-stimulating hormone (FSH). As you will recall from the previous chapter, FSH production causes several ovarian follicles to grow, and one of them, containing a "ripened" egg, moves to the surface of the ovary. Estrogen secreted by the follicles then triggers the release by the pituitary of luteinizing hormone (LH), which in turn brings on ovulation. But when a woman takes the Pill, her estrogen level after menstruation stays higher than normal, so the pituitary fails to send out FSH. Follicles do not mature, and she does not ovulate, so there is no egg to be fertilized. Combination and phasic pills also may directly prevent production of luteinizing hormone. The progestin in the Pill provides further protection by increasing the thickness of the mucus at the opening of the cervix, which makes it hard for sperm to get through. Artificial levels of estrogen and progestin also interfere with normal development of the rich lining of the uterus; should ovulation and fertilization take place, it will be difficult for the fertilized egg to implant.

The mini-pill appears to work by changing the cervical mucus so that it is unfavorable for sperm movement. Ovulation is also inhibited in some cycles, and development of the uterine lining is disturbed. The minimum failure rate of the mini-pill is 0.5 percent and the typical failure rate is 3 percent.

A woman who uses the mini-pill takes one each day. A woman using the combination or the phasic pill takes twenty-one pills and then either stops for seven days or takes placebos (blanks) that have no hormone in them. During the off-week she menstruates. (Actually, doctors call the bleeding that occurs *withdrawal bleeding* because the mechanism is different than in ordinary menstruation.)

What happens if a woman forgets to take her pill? She probably won't get pregnant if she takes the forgotten pill as soon as she remembers it. If she forgets two days in a row, she should double up for the next two days and use a backup method of birth control for the rest of the month (Hatcher et al., 1988). Because the pill must be absorbed through the digestive system, stomach upsets such as diarrhea and vomiting may interfere with effectiveness. Therefore pill users should have a backup method to turn to when they are ill. (The Pill is not a good choice for women who have bulimia, an eating disorder accompanied by self-induced vomiting.) Pill users also need to know that when OCs (particularly those containing estrogen) are taken in combination with certain other medications the effectiveness of the OC or of the other medicine may be altered. Much more research is necessary to confirm which drug interactions are significant (Hatcher et al., 1988).

THE RISKS OF ORAL CONTRACEPTIVES   For the first few years of its use, the Pill seemed almost too good to be true. Although some women did experience such side effects as headaches, breakthrough bleeding, and weight gain, these problems were generally minor. Then the bubble burst. A few studies gave the Pill a clean bill of health, but others suggested it was dangerous. Deaths due to blood clots, heart attacks, and strokes were reported. Some researchers voiced suspicions that the Pill caused cancer. Manufacturers began to include long lists of potential dangers and side effects with their products. And in the 1970's, Pill use fell.

Today, however, many concerns about the Pill's safety have subsided. Most important, reduced hormone dosages have greatly lowered the risk of pill-related cardiovascular problems (blood clots, heart attacks, and strokes), and the overall probability of death from such problems is now small or nonexistent for most women (see Table 7–2). In fact, the Food and Drug Administration now advises that nonsmoking women without a history of cardiovascular problems and without risk factors for such problems can continue to take the Pill into their forties without increasing their risk. But for smokers, the story is different. The mortality rate for Pill users aged 35 to 44 who smoke is 84 per 100,000 women, versus 23 per 100,000 for nonsmokers in the same age range (Dr. Louella Klein, quoted in Rasky, 1985). Between 200 and 400 actual deaths a year (almost all from cardiovascular problems) occur among the millions of Pill users, and almost all of them involve older smokers (Wilbur, 1986). Women who smoke should not take the Pill past age 35. (Better yet: they should give up smoking.)

Besides decreased concern about cardiovascular problems (except for smokers), there is other good news. Several studies have found a *lower* incidence of ovarian and endometrial (uterine) cancers in Pill users than in nonusers, and a lower incidence of benign breast disease and ovarian cysts as well (Hatcher et al., 1988). Oral contraceptives may also offer some protection against pelvic inflammatory disease caused by chlamydia (although not gonorrhea) (Wolner-Hanssen et al., 1990a).

The evidence regarding breast cancer, however, is conflicting and contradictory. Several studies in the 1980s found no increased risk. However, a handful of recent studies suggest that this conclusion may be premature for certain users. For example, one study (Kay & Hannaford, 1988) found a three-fold increase in breast cancer in women aged 30 to 34 who had taken the Pill. Another (Schlesselman, 1989) found no overall increase in risk, but for women under age 45 who did not have children, had started menstruating before age 13, and had taken the Pill for at least eight years, there was a risk four times that of non-users. Further research is necessary to reconcile the different findings. At present, the FDA feels that the evidence on breast cancer is not strong enough to require a change in warning labels or in the use of the Pill.

In sum, for nonsmoking women whose health is good and who do not have risk factors for cardiovascular disease (e.g., high blood pressure, diabetes, obesity, and high cholesterol levels), the Pill appears to be relatively safe. However, if a user experiences severe abdominal pain, severe chest

Risk	Chance of Death in a Year (U.S.)
Motorcycling	1 in 1,000
Automobile driving	1 in 6,000
Power boating	1 in 6,000
Rock climbing	1 in 7,500
Playing football	1 in 25,000
Canoeing	1 in 100,000
Preventing pregnancy:	
Oral contraception—nonsmoker	1 in 63,000
Oral contraception—smoker	1 in 16,000
Using IUDs	1 in 100,000
Using barrier methods	None
Using natural methods	None
Undergoing sterilization:	
Laparoscopic tubal ligation	1 in 67,000
Hysterectomy	1 in 1,600
Vasectomy	1 in 300,000
Deciding About Pregnancy:	
Continuing pregnancy	1 in 14,300
Terminating pregnancy:	
Nonlegal abortion	1 in 3,000
Legal abortion:	
Before 9 weeks	1 in 500,000
Between 9–12 weeks	1 in 67,000
Between 13–15 weeks	1 in 23,000
After 15 weeks	1 in 8,700

TABLE 7–2
Putting Voluntary Risks into Perspective   One of the most important questions about a contraceptive method is, How risky is it? This table compares the mortality risks associated with various birth control methods, various activities of daily life, and pregnancy.

Source: Adapted from Hatcher et al., 1990 (p. 146, Tab. 8.4)

pain, shortness of breath, severe headaches, eye problems, or severe leg pain, she should stop taking her pills and should see a doctor at once. Even women who can safely take the Pill may experience certain less serious side-effects, including acne or oily skin, breast fullness or tenderness, break-through bleeding and spotting (especially likely with the mini-pill), headaches, nausea, or weight gain due to fluid retention. Often these side effects go away on their own, or can be eliminated by switching brands.

AN ALTERNATE HORMONAL APPROACH: SUBDERMAL IM-PLANTS   As this book goes to press in 1990, a hormonal alternative to oral contraceptives appears close to winning approval for marketing in the United States. *Norplant* is a birth control product that the Population Council has been developing since 1967. Already in use in several other countries, it consists of rod-shaped silicone capsules that are implanted just beneath the skin of a woman's upper arm—in one version two capsules, in another six. The capsules, a little over an inch in length, can be felt but usually not seen. They contain a progestin that is released at a slow, steady rate into the bloodstream. Because the hormone does not enter through the digestive tract and administration is continuous, the dose can be low. As a result, many of the side effects associated with oral contraceptives are absent. (An exception is irregular menstrual bleeding, which can occur both with *Norplant* and with the mini-pill.) Contraceptive protection is better than with any other reversible method of birth control; reported first year failure rates range from only 0.2 to 1.0 (Hatcher et al., 1988). Moreover, protection lasts for at least three or five years, depending on the number of capsules implanted. When a woman wants to become pregnant, the capsules are simply removed; fertility returns almost immediately. Thus far, *Norplant* appears to be a safe, inconspicuous, convenient, and effective method of birth control (Beckelman, 1986).

Intrauterine Devices (IUDs)

According to an old story, Arab nomads used to keep their female camels from getting pregnant on long journeys by placing pebbles in the animals' uteruses. Thus was the intrauterine device (IUD) born. The modern version of the IUD is a small object, usually made of plastic, that is inserted into a woman's uterus and left there. The Arabs who put pebbles in their camels probably had no idea why they worked, and today we are not quite sure why IUDs in human females are effective, either. The most commonly accepted theory is that the device causes an irritation in the lining of the uterus that interferes with implantation of a fertilized egg. Strictly speaking then, the IUD is probably an *inter*ceptive, not a *contra*ceptive. Whatever the mechanics, the device's effect is limited to the uterus. Ovulation occurs as usual, and hormone production does not change. The optimum first year failure rate for IUDs is 1.5 percent; the typical rate is 3 percent.

IUDs have been made in a variety of sizes and shapes, including a ring, a double coil, a double "S," a "7," and a "T" (see Figure 7–2). Some have stems encircled by fine copper wire; the release of tiny amounts of copper into the uterus increases protection against implantation. Others release minute amounts of progestin, which reduces the cramping and erratic bleeding that troubles some IUD users. An IUD must be inserted by a medically trained and experienced person. He or she places the device in a long, straw-like plunger and injects it through the opening of the cervix. The IUD is stretched out in the inserter but snaps back to its original shape once it is in the uterus. One or two threads attached to the device hang down through the cervical opening, into the vagina.

Besides being effective, the IUD appeals to some women because once it is in place, it can be forgotten (although it should be checked by the

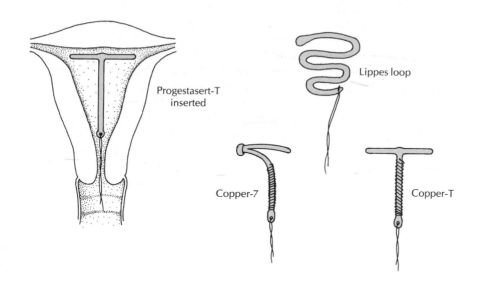

FIGURE 7–2
The IUD   *Intrauterine devices come in several shapes and sizes. At present, only the Progestasert-T and the Copper-T 380A are made and distributed in the United States, but some American women are still wearing other types, and other models are in wide use outside the U.S.*

wearer monthly by feeling for the thread hanging down through the cervical opening). A woman need not think about contraception every day, as she must with the Pill. And when she wants to get pregnant or switch to a different method, she simply has her physician remove the device.

IUDs are not without complications, however. Some women experience excessive menstrual bleeding, cramping, and lower back pain. A few users spontaneously expel their IUDs within the first year. A small percentage of IUDs will either become embedded in or perforate the wall of the uterus.

Another serious side-effect, particularly with one type of IUD, the Dalkon Shield, has been pelvic inflammatory disease (PID). When the Dalkon Shield was introduced in 1971, the A. H. Robins Company touted it as the safest and most effective IUD ever. Sales soon hit 4.5 million. But this particular IUD was eventually reported not to be safe. Its multi-filamented tail apparently acted like a ladder for bacteria from the vagina to climb into the uterus. Thousands of cases of pelvic inflammatory disease and sterility, and over a dozen deaths, were suspected of being caused by the device. The Robins Company stopped selling the Dalkon Shield in 1974, but it was not until 1984 that the company, under the threat of some 10,000 personal-injury lawsuits (most eventually settled out of court), issued a public notice advising women wearing the device to have it removed.

By 1986, all the major manufacturers of IUDs in the United States had withdrawn their products from the U.S. market (but not from markets in other countries; an estimated 60 to 70 million women still use the IUD worldwide). Their decisions were based not on medical arguments but rather economic ones: the manufacturers felt they could no longer afford product liability insurance, or even obtain it (Wilbur, 1986). Today, however, two new IUDs are again being made and sold in the United States. One, the Progestasert-T, is a progestin-releasing model that is expensive and must be replaced annually. The other, the Copper-T 380A, can be left in place for four years. An American Medical Association study panel recently reported that both these devices are safe and effective in appropriate patients (DATTA Panel, 1989). "Appropriate" means women who are in a stable monogamous relationship (and therefore at low risk for sexually transmitted diseases, a major cause of pelvic inflammatory disease), unable to take the Pill, and with no history of pelvic infections, bleeding disorders, or ectopic pregnancies. Women who have given birth are most likely to be able to tolerate the devices.

Condoms

Condoms, also know as *rubbers*, *prophylactics*, and *safes*, are thin sheaths that fit over the penis. Condoms keep sperm from getting into the vagina. In addition to providing contraception, they provide protection for both partners against sexually transmitted diseases, including some protection from HIV infection, which causes AIDS.

Men have been encasing their penises in condom-like coverings for millennia. Historically, sheaths were worn as a decoration; as protection against injury, insect bites, and attacks by demons; as a fertility charm; and even as a badge of rank, with different colors denoting different statuses (Brasch, 1973). A sixteenth-century Italian anatomist claimed to be the inventor of a linen sheath that protected the wearer from venereal disease. But the first use of the condom as a contraceptive is, you might say, sheathed in mystery. One story attributes its invention to a seventeenth-century English physician named Condom. Others say the good doctor was French. Still others say the condom actually got its name from a French village named Condom. In any case, by the eighteenth century condoms made from animal intestines were being used as contraceptives, and after 1837, when Charles Goodyear discovered vulcanization (the process of making rubber more flexible and durable), condoms went into mass production.

Today 95 percent of American models are made of latex rubber, with a rubber ring around the open end to help keep the condom on the penis. The other five percent are made from lamb intestines ("skins"). Skin condoms are strong—stronger than latex condoms in airburst testing—but their ability to block the transmission of the AIDS virus and other viruses is uncertain, and at present the FDA does not allow their packages to carry disease-prevention claims.

In the U.S., both domestic and imported condoms must meet national quality-control standards. If more than 4 per 1000 condoms in a production run leak when filled with water, the entire lot must be destroyed. In actual usage, the probability of breakage or leakage is low, although both problems do occasionally occur. According to testing by *Consumer Reports*, some brands are more reliable than others. (If you are interested in the *Consumer Reports* brand ratings, and details on the features of various brands, see the article "Can you rely on condoms?" in the March 1989 issue of that magazine, pages 135–141. Most public libraries will have it.)

Condoms come in various sizes, and there is at least one brand advertised as "20 percent larger." They can be bought in packages of three to twelve without a prescription and come with all sorts of special features. Many have a nipple tip to catch semen when the man ejaculates. (If there is no such tip, the user should leave half an inch or so of collapsed space at the tip; otherwise, the force of ejaculation may burst the rubber.) Some condoms are colored, and some even sport designs or are textured.

A condom may or may not be prelubricated. Lubrication is important; not only does it make entry of the penis into the vagina easier and increase comfort, but it also reduces the probability of tearing. Some condoms are lubricated on both the inside and the outside with a spermicidal (sperm-killing) substance. Users of nonlubricated condoms should use a lubricant such as water, a sterile jelly, or, preferably, a spermicidal foam, cream, or jelly. (DO NOT use petroleum jelly, hand lotion, shortening, or any other oil-based product as a lubricant: these products will rapidly disintegrate the rubber.)

Most condoms come rolled up in an airtight package that keeps out dirt. A man, or his partner, puts on a condom by unrolling it over the shaft of the erect penis, starting with the glans (see Figure 7–3). If the man is uncircumcised, the foreskin should first be pulled back. It is important to put the condom on before there is any contact whatsoever between a man's penis and his female partner's genitals because, as we saw in Chapter 4, pre-ejaculatory fluid can contain sperm. After ejaculation, the man or his partner should hold on to the base of the condom while the man withdraws his penis from the vagina, to be sure no fluid spills. Withdrawal should take place while the penis is still erect. After use, the condom should be checked for tears. If one is found, a spermicidal foam or cream should be inserted into the vagina as a backup precaution. Condoms should be used only one time and then discarded. Always store condoms in a dry, cool, dark place, and throw them away if there are any signs of deterioration.

When condoms are used carefully and consistently, the failure rate is only one to two percent; when they are combined with spermicides, or with the sponge or diaphragm, they are nearly 100 percent effective—on a par with the Pill. Condoms are the preferred method of contraception in Japan, England, and Sweden—countries that have very low birth rates (Seaman & Seaman, 1977). However, American couples do not always use them carefully and consistently; hence the typical failure rate of twelve percent. Common errors include waiting until the moment before ejaculation to put them on, failing to use adequate lubrication (or, if counting on the woman's natural lubrication, inserting the sheathed penis too soon), or forgetting to hold on to the base of the condom as the man withdraws.

FIGURE 7–3

Putting on a condom   *The condom is a reliable form of birth control, but its reliability depends on proper use. Air should be squeezed out of the tip of the condom before it is put on. It's a good idea to practice the technique of donning a condom alone, before using one for the first time with a partner.*

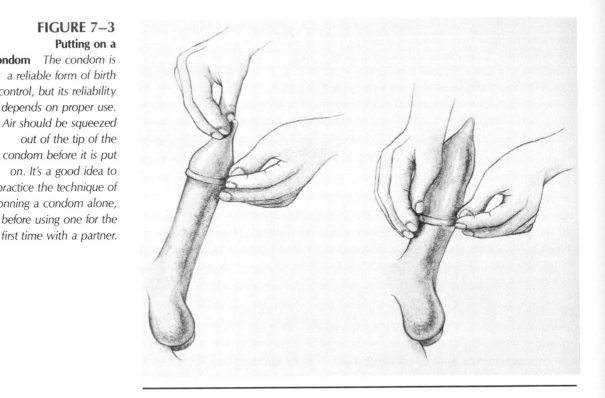

A few people (only one or two percent) are allergic to the latex in condoms. Sometimes the allergy is really to a chemical used on certain latex condoms, and switching brands solves the problem. In other cases, a skin condom can be used. (For protection from disease, one might wear a skin condom under a latex one.) Otherwise, condoms are completely safe—with one possible exception. A recent study found that if they conceive, women who use barrier methods of birth control are at increased risk for developing a dangerous condition called *preeclampsia* ("toxic pregnancy") (Klonoff-Cohen et al., 1989). This life-threatening illness is caused by an incompatibility between the mother's immune system and the developing fetus. Repeated prior exposure to a partner's sperm and semen seems to have a protective effect in some women, apparently because the sperm contain antigens that prevent the mother's system from rejecting fetal tissue. Further research needs to be done, but a woman who has been using a barrier method and then decides to conceive might be well advised to switch to a nonbarrier method of birth control for several months before attempting to get pregnant.

Besides their general safety, condoms have many advantages. They are easy to use and relatively cheap. They provide excellent protection against HIV infection and other sexually transmitted diseases for a man, his partner, and, should the woman be already pregnant, the unborn child. For these reasons, condoms, which were once shunned by most Americans, have become much more popular over the last few years. In fact, condoms are now the third most popular contraceptive choice in the U.S., after sterilization and the Pill. Rates of reported condom use at last intercourse for males aged 17 to 19 more than doubled between 1979 and 1988 (Sonenstein, Pleck, & Ku, 1989). In one study, almost two-thirds of sexually active teenage males reported experience with condoms (Kegeles, Adler, & Irwin, 1989). Women, too, have become more enthusiastic; 40 to 50 percent of all condom sales are thought to be to women.

Despite all their advantages, though, condoms are not accepted by everyone. Some men complain that condoms reduce sensitivity—that sex with a condom is like "taking a shower with a raincoat on." (Note, however, that according to *Consumer Reports*, users say some brands allow more sensitivity than others. Also, for men who tend to climax too quickly, reduced sensitivity could be an *advantage*.) Couples who do not make placing the condom on the penis part of their lovemaking often object to the interruption it causes. Some people object to the way condoms look. Some associate condoms with prostitution because prostitutes and their customers often use them. Some think (mistakenly) that condoms are uncomfortable. Finally, the advent of the Pill has encouraged some people to think of protection as a woman's job, not a man's. Nevertheless, increasing numbers of sexually active people are putting aside these objections in order to benefit from all that condoms have to offer.

The Diaphragm

A **diaphragm** is a soft, dome-shaped rubber cup with a flexible rim. Spermicidal cream or jelly is placed in the cup before insertion, so one function of the diaphragm is as a spermicide holder. Since the diaphragm fits over the cervix during intercourse, the other function is as a barrier to sperm.

The diaphragm has a rather checkered past. It was invented back in 1838. During the 1880s diaphragms made of rubber were popularized by a German physician who used a phony name to protect his reputation. But diaphragms were not manufactured in the United States until the 1920s because of the Comstock Laws, which prohibited the mailing, transporting, or importation of "obscene, lewd, or lascivious" materials, including birth control devices.

Once available, the diaphragm became a contraceptive bestseller. During the 1930s a third of American couples who practiced birth control used the diaphragm (Peel & Potts, 1969). Apparently it worked pretty well, for the birth rate during that period was the lowest achieved until the legalization of abortion in 1973 (Seaman & Seaman, 1977). Then the Pill and the IUD came along, and almost overnight the diaphragm became unfashionable. For several years, during the 1960s, medical schools did not even teach diaphragm fitting (although it takes only one day to learn), and women some-times had trouble finding a physician who could properly prescribe one (Sea-man & Seaman, 1977). But although the diaphragm was down, it was not out. In the early 1970s, reports of side effects and health risks from the Pill and the IUD mounted, and some women began to return to the diaphragm. By the 1980s the diaphragm had definitely come back from the brink of extinction.

Diaphragms come in a range of sizes, with diameters ranging from about two inches to over three and a half inches. Because a proper fit is criti-cal to its effectiveness, the diaphragm is available only by prescription. The physician or health practitioner who fits a woman for her diaphragm also instructs her on how to use it. The first step in using a diaphragm is to put about a tablespoon of spermicidal cream or jelly in its cup and spread a bit on the rim. The woman then squeezes the sides of the rim together, spreads apart the lips of the vagina with one hand, and slides the diaphragm into the vagina, cream- or jelly-side up. Then she pushes on the lower rim, which causes the diaphragm to press against the cervix and lock into place behind the pubic bone. Finally, she checks with a finger to be sure the diaphragm is in place. This procedure is illustrated in Figure 7–4.

Until recently, it was thought that the diaphragm could be inserted up to six hours before intercourse. Now there are some recommendations that it be inserted no more than one or two hours before—different manufacturers supply different recommendations. If a woman's partner ejaculates into her vagina more than once during a session of lovemaking, she must put in some more spermicide (cream, jelly, or foam). She *cannot* remove the diaphragm and remain protected. It must stay in place for at least six hours after the last act of intercourse, because sperm can live for that long inside the vagina. To remove the diaphragm, the woman simply hooks a finger under the rim and pulls it out.

When used properly and consistently, the diaphragm is relatively effective, with a failure rate of six percent. When the diaphragm is used with a condom, the rate is much lower. However, the typical failure rate is much higher—18 percent. A certain number of failures are probably inevitable, because the diaphragm sometimes shifts a bit during intercourse as the interior of the vagina balloons out. (Slippage seems especially likely when the woman is on top.) But the main reason for failure is that many women simply do not use their diaphragm with each and every act of intercourse.

The reasons are not hard to fathom. For one thing, a woman has to have both the diaphragm and a supply of spermicide with her when she wants to have intercourse—and single women, who may have sex sporadi-cally, do not always plan ahead for it. Also, some couples, carried away by the passion of a moment for which they have not prepared, hate to stop to put in the diaphragm. Many women dislike inserting the diaphragm, even though it is usually easy to do, and find the spermicides messy and unaes-

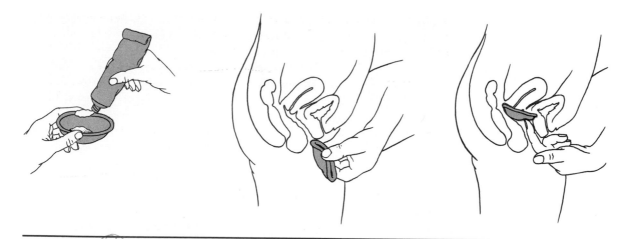

thetic. Finally, the spermicide required for diaphragm use can make oral sex unappealing.

What about health considerations? As with condoms, a few users may be allergic to the latex. And our previous remarks about the risk of "toxic pregnancy" if conception occurs after a period of consistent condom use also apply to diaphragm use. In addition, some users may experience recurrent urinary tract infections, for reasons that are not yet clear (Hatcher et al., 1988). Some cases of *toxic shock syndrome* (TSS), a potentially life-threatening illness, have been associated with diaphragm use, but the risk of death from TSS associated with the diaphragm is extremely low (0.3 per 100,000), far lower than that associated with complications of pregnancy among women using no contraception (8.3 per 100,000). In fact, it is not certain that the TSS risk is greater than for women who do not use diaphragms. However, just in case, women are cautioned against leaving a diaphragm in place longer than 24 hours, which could potentially increase the chances of infection. (For more on TSS, see Chapter 18.)

On the plus side, the diaphragm is very safe compared with other methods, and because it is used with spermicide, it offers some protection against sexually transmitted diseases. It cannot be felt by either the woman or her partner once it is in place, and it does not affect a woman's hormones. This method seems especially suitable for women who are used to sex and comfortable with their bodies, who have sex regularly (as opposed to unpredictably), and who have partners with whom they can talk about birth control. The problem of interruption can be overcome by making insertion part of lovemaking.

The Sponge

Since antiquity, natural sea sponges have been used for contraception. But it wasn't until 1983 that the FDA approved the first **contraceptive**

FIGURE 7–4

How to use a diaphragm Before inserting the diaphragm, a woman places at least a teaspoonful of spermicidal cream or jelly in its dome and around its rim. She then squeezes the edges of the diaphragm together, spreads apart the major lips of the vulva, and inserts the device—spermicide up—into the vagina, pushing it upward until it covers the neck of the cervix and its edges rest against the vaginal walls. Finally, she checks with her finger to make sure the diaphragm is properly in place.

The contraceptive sponge *This device releases a concentrated spermicide into the vagina.*

sponge, the *Today Sponge,* for marketing. It is a small, pillow-shaped polyurethane device that contains one gram of nonoxynol-9 spermicide. (As of this writing a new sponge with another spermicide, benzalkonium chloride, is being tested in the United States.) It comes in only one size. One side has a concave hollow designed to fit up against the cervix. The other side has a fabric loop attached to it to facilitate removal. Prior to use, the woman moistens the sponge with tap water; then she inserts it deep into the vagina (see Figure 7–5). Once in place, the sponge provides up to twenty-four hours of protection. Like the diaphragm, the sponge must be left in place for at least six hours after the last act of intercourse. It is discarded after use.

Because the *Today* sponge is a new product, its track record for effectiveness is still short. Existing studies find that its effectiveness is not as good as that of the other methods we have discussed so far. The best first-year failure rates are around six to nine percent while the typical rates range from 18 to 28 percent. But these figures may not be a fair estimate for women who have never given birth: failure rates for women who have given birth are over twice as high as for those who have not (McIntyre & Higgens, 1986). For all women, of course, effectiveness is greatly improved when a condom is used along with the sponge.

The sponge offers some definite advantages over the diaphragm for some users: it doesn't require a visit to a doctor or clinic; it contains its own spermicide; it's disposable; and one insertion will do for a whole day. In addition, the spermicide in the sponge protects women against chlamydial infection and gonorrhea, both associated with tubal infertility (Rosenberg et al., 1987).

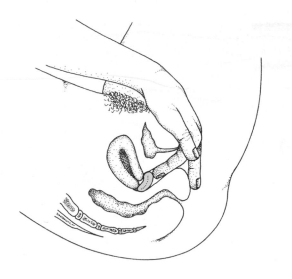

FIGURE 7–5
Inserting the sponge
*After moistening the
sponge with water, the
woman inserts it into the
upper part of the vagina,
so that it rests against the
cervix. She removes the
sponge by pulling on the
fabric loop attached to it.*

On the other hand, some women have had difficulty removing the sponge and some report irritation or allergic reactions to the spermicide. Another complaint has been that the sponge causes vaginal dryness. The major concern, however, has been the risk of infections. Use of the sponge may increase the risk of vaginal yeast infection (Rosenberg et al., 1987) and, toxic shock syndrome (TSS). In 1984, 13 cases of TSS, none of them fatal, had been linked to sponge use, out of 600,000 users and some 16 million sponges (Faich et al., 1986). But because of problems in interpreting these statistics, it is still unclear how much, or even whether, the sponge increases the risk of TSS. Another unknown is whether the large amount of the nonoxynol-9 spermicide in the sponge (far larger than in other spermicide products) has any long-term health consequences. In any case, women using the sponge should follow the directions on the package carefully, in order to maximize safety.

The Cervical Cap

The **cervical cap** is similar to the diaphragm, but is smaller in diameter and is shaped more like a thimble (see Figure 7–6). It is also held in place differently than a diaphragm. One part of a diaphragm's rim rests in the back of the vagina while the other is held firmly in place behind the pubic bone. The cervical cap stays in place at least partly because of suction between its rim and the surface or border of the cervix.

Cervical caps have existed for a century and a half and are popular in Europe, where they are sometimes called *pessaries*. Caps available in the United States 20 to 40 years ago were made of silver or copper and were left

FIGURE 7–6

The cervical cap *The cervical cap and the diaphragm work in similar ways, but, as you can see in this figure, the thimble-shaped cap fits snugly over the neck of the uterus, rather than resting against the vaginal walls as the diaphragm does. The cap is kept in place largely by suction.*

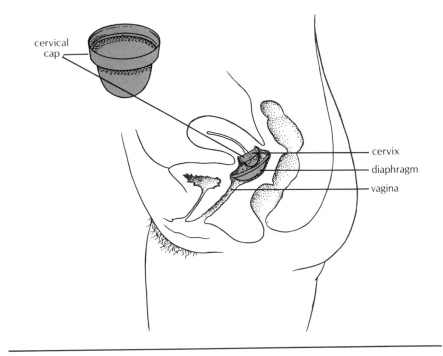

in place for as long as three to four weeks. In the mid-1970s a cervical cap with a one-way valve designed to release menstrual fluid was developed. It was custom-fitted and intended for continuous wear, but proved to have an unacceptably high failure rate. Today's caps, made of soft rubber, are not suitable for prolonged wear because of odor problems and a possible increased risk of toxic shock syndrome. The time guidelines for insertion and removal are similar to those for the diaphragm. Spermicide, about one-third capful, should be placed in the cervical cap prior to insertion.

Cervical caps were approved for marketing in the United States in 1988. As of this writing, information on effectiveness and safety is still limited. In theory, failure rates can be as low as six percent, but initial evidence indicates that in practice the typical failure rate is about 18 percent, the same as for the diaphragm. The health risks associated with the cap also appear to be similar to those for the diaphragm, but in addition, some researchers are concerned about possible acceleration of certain precancerous cervical abnormalities. A recent study failed to confirm such a risk (Richwald et al., 1989), but until more information is available, users are advised to have a Pap smear before getting the cap fitted, and again after three months, to test for such abnormalities (see Chapter 18).

The cap can be more difficult to insert and, particularly, to remove, than the diaphragm. However, some women who want to use a female barrier method and have had difficulty getting a diaphragm properly fitted may be able to use the cap successfully.

Spermicides

For thousands of years, people have known that contraception is improved by using substances that kill sperm. Today, **spermicides,** chemicals that destroy or immobilize sperm, are available without prescription in several forms, including creams, jellies, foams, suppositories, and tablets (see Figure 7–7). A recent variation is a thin 2″x2″ piece of "film" inserted on a finger tip into the vagina. As we have discussed, spermicides are also found in the sponge and are used to prelubricate some condoms.

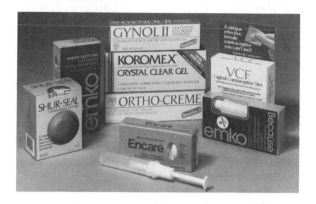

FIGURE 7–7
Spermicides
Spermicidal foams, creams, jellies, and films are available without a prescription. These products are most effective when used with a barrier method such as the diaphragm or the condom. The illustration here shows insertion of foam into the vagina.

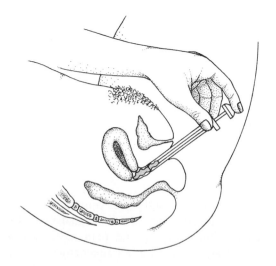

The active ingredient in spermicides is usually nonoxynol-9. Whether used alone or in combination with the diaphragm, cap, or condom, the aim of spermicides is to destroy sperm before they get into the uterus. Used alone, spermicides can have failure rates as low as three percent, but the more typical failure rate is 21 percent (Hatcher et al., 1988). The major reason for this higher rate is failure to use the substances consistently with every act of intercourse and to use them correctly. When used faithfully, according to directions and in combination with other methods, spermicides can provide good protection.

The foams, jellies, and creams are loaded into the barrel of an applicator which then is inserted into the vagina. Pushing the plunger of the applicator presses the spermicide right up near the cervix. Users of foams should be sure to shake the can twenty times or more before filling the applicator, and it is advisable to use two applicators full before each act of intercourse. Application should take place no more than 30 minutes before intercourse for maximum effectiveness. After application, intercourse can take place immediately. Spermicidal suppositories and tablets are manually inserted and must dissolve after placement in the vagina prior to sexual intercourse. This takes a period of ten to 30 minutes, depending on the brand. The "film" should be inserted no sooner than five minutes before intercourse.

In addition to being lethal for sperm, in the laboratory nonoxynol-9 kills many organisms responsible for gonorrhea, herpes, chlamydia, and AIDS. Further, women who use spermicides have a lower rate of pelvic inflammatory disease (Hatcher et al., 1988). Major drawbacks of spermicides are that they must be inserted very close to the time of intercourse, they are messy, and they have an unpleasant taste. A few years ago, a study raised concerns about a possible link between spermicide use and subsequent birth defects in babies born to users (Jick et al., 1981). The study found that rates of defects among children born to women who had purchased spermicides within 600 days before delivery were higher than for children of non-users. The researchers did not establish that any of the women had actually *used* the products at or near the time of conception, however. Also, birth defect rates among the offspring of users were not higher than national rates. Other studies, both before and since, have failed to find any relationship between spermicide use and birth defects. But the issue remains somewhat controversial, and one may want to avoid spermicides if a pregnancy may already exist (Hatcher et al., 1988).

Fertility Awareness

During the menstrual cycle, a woman's body goes through a recurring pattern—or rhythm—of fertile and infertile phases. The goal of **fertility awareness methods** is to predict these phases and plan sexual activity accordingly. Because it is "natural"—that is, neither mechanical nor hormonal—fertility awareness is the only approach to contraception currently approved by the Roman Catholic Church, which endorsed it in 1951. Catholics who wish to avoid conception are supposed to abstain from sex entirely during the period when the woman is most likely to be fertile. However, some users of fertility awareness, both Catholic and non-Catholic, rely on a condom or diaphragm during the fertile time, or use manual or oral techniques of lovemaking during that period.

Many people assume that modern "natural" methods of birth control have ancient roots. Not so. Until about 1930, many medical authorities believed the most fertile time in a woman's cycle was right after menstruation. Any advice they gave about "safe" versus "unsafe" days was likely to be wrong. But once medicine got the facts straight, natural methods began to catch on. At one time, more than a fifth of all American couples used them (Seaman & Seaman, 1977).

As we have seen, an egg can be fertilized only during the brief period (about twenty-four hours) when it is in the upper part of the Fallopian tube. But sperm can live in a woman's reproductive tract for 48 or possibly even 72 hours, so sperm deposited two or three days before the woman ovulates may fertilize an egg after ovulation occurs. This means that the actual fertile period is at most about four days, three days before ovulation and one day after. The trick is to predict ovulation correctly. If every woman's menstrual cycle were perfectly regular, that would be fairly easy. But the twenty-eight-day cycle is only a statistical average. Not only do women vary in the length of their cycles, but over 90 percent of all women have cycles that vary in length from one month to the next. To account for the variations, fertility awareness methods extend the "unsafe" period several days beyond the minimum fertile period, just to be sure.

There are three different means of trying to predict ovulation, each the basis of a different fertility awareness technique. A fourth technique combines approaches.

1. *The rhythm or calendar method.* The rhythm method has been around since the 1930s. The woman must keep a record of her menstrual cycle for six to twelve consecutive months. Counting the first day of menstruation as Day 1, she calculates the number of days in the shortest and longest cycles. A formula is used to estimate the unsafe phase: subtract eighteen from the number of days in the shortest cycle, and eleven from the number of days in the longest cycle. For example, if a woman had an absolutely regular twenty-eight-day cycle (highly unlikely), her fertile phase would start on Day 10 (28 minus 18), and extend through Day 17 (28 minus 11), for a total of eight days. But if her cycles ranged from 26 to 30 days in length (fairly typical), her fertile phase would start on Day 8 and extend through Day 19, a total of 12 days

during which she would abstain from sexual intercourse or use a barrier method of birth control. A woman with highly variable cycles cannot use the rhythm method.

2. *The basal body temperature method*, also known as the *BBT method*, takes advantage of changes in body temperature during the cycle. Just before ovulation a woman's temperature dips slightly. After a peak at ovulation, progesterone in her system maintains an increase of about half a degree (Fahrenheit), which lasts until just before menstruation (see Figure 7–8). To use the temperature method, the woman buys a thermometer that records tenths of a degree and takes her *basal* (resting) body temperature in the morning before getting out of bed or doing anything else. By recording her daily temperature readings on a chart, she can tell when she has ovulated. The safe period follows ovulation and extends from three or four days after the rise is first noticed until her period starts—a total of about ten days.

   Unfortunately, this technique is not very dependable. Illness, stress, and even lack of sleep can affect basal body temperature and throw the estimate of safe days off. Women who are not ovulating regularly (for instance during puberty or just before menopause) cannot use this method. The method is of no use if a woman doesn't take her temperature conscientiously every morning. And the method does not determine the safe days *before* ovulation, only those after.

3. *The cervical mucus method*, also known as the *ovulation* or *Billings* method, was developed in the early 1960s. Two Aus-

FIGURE 7–8

Basal body temperature (BBT) over the menstrual cycle   *A woman using the BBT method of birth control measures her temperature every morning before getting out of bed, in order to determine when she has ovulated. This graph shows a characteristic cycle, but since many factors influence basal body temperature, an actual chart can be difficult to interpret.*

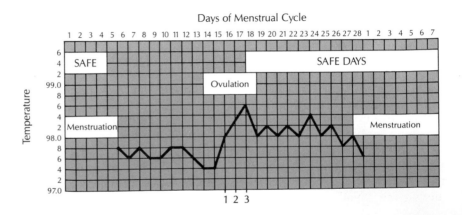

tralian doctors, Evelyn and John Billings, based the technique on the fact that a woman's vaginal discharge and her cervical mucus change in appearance and consistency during the menstrual cycle, due to the rise and fall of estrogen (Billings, Billings & Catarinich, 1974). Right after menstruation there are usually a few "dry" days, without any noticeable discharge. These days are considered safe. Then there is a discharge of mucus that is whitish or cloudy in color, and tacky or sticky in consistency. This discharge gradually increases in quantity and becomes clearer in color until one to two peak days, when it is clear, slippery, and stringy, with the consistency of raw egg white. Within 24 hours after the last peak day, ovulation occurs. The mucus then usually resumes a cloudy or whitish appearance. The period from the first sign of mucus until the fourth day after the peak—seven to 14 days total—is considered unsafe.

To use the cervical mucus method, a woman must be willing to examine her vaginal secretions. The best way to do this is to insert a finger into the vagina. The method works best when a couple abstains from intercourse during the unsafe days, because seminal fluid, jellies, creams, and foam can affect the way the mucus looks. As many as a third of all women cannot use this method because they do not have the typical mucus pattern.

4.   *The sympto-thermal method*. This approach combines the mucus and the temperature methods. Intercourse can safely resume only on the fourth day following peak mucus and the third day following the thermal rise. If one occurs without the other, a woman cannot assume she is infertile; she must wait for the occurrence of the second event.

Fertility awareness methods are safe and free, but they are among the least effective of the methods described so far. Optimal failure rates range from one to nine percent, but typically almost one in five women using these methods will get pregnant within a year. Of the four options, the sympto-thermal has the best chance of success because it relies on two signs rather than only one. As with all methods, effectiveness depends mainly on motivation. The best results seem to be achieved by women who have permanent, cooperative partners and who definitely do not want children. Fertility awareness methods demand great commitment. If a couple abstains during the unsafe period, which averages ten days, and also during menstruation, as many people choose to do, they will be able to have intercourse for only half the month. Completely spontaneous intercourse is ruled out; you always have to ask yourself, "Wait, what day is this?" This is definitely not a good method of birth control for men and women who "can't" say, or have difficulty saying, "No."

Sterilization

Sterilization, the surgical creation of infertility, is by far the most popular method of birth control in the United States and worldwide. In the U.S., over a million sterilization procedures are done each year.

The decision to have surgery to prevent having children (or any more children) is not a trivial one. Many doctors are cautious about performing such an operation on young people, who might regret the decision later; on those who seem unsure about the decision; on those who have permanent partners who do not agree fully with the decision; or on those who think they might possibly, later in life, want to start another family with a different partner.[1] Even the strongest advocates of sterilization advise people to ask themselves whether they will be happy with the decision if, later on, they divorce, or their spouse dies and they remarry, or if one or more of their children die. For those who can answer yes to such questions, sterilization has the advantage of being permanent and, over the long run, one of the cheapest methods of birth control, especially if an insurance policy covers the operation.

FEMALE STERILIZATION   Until the second half of this century, the most common method of permanent contraception for women was removal of the uterus, in an operation called a *hysterectomy*. Healthy uteruses are still sometimes removed solely for the purpose of contraception, but the practice can be likened to cutting off one's hand to cure a hang nail. Good reasons exist for performing a hysterectomy, most notably the presence of uterine cancer. But a hysterectomy is a major operation with significant complication and mortality rates (see Chapter 18), and much easier and safer methods of female sterilization are now available.

The preferred method of female sterilization is **tubal sterilization,** which involves the cutting, cauterizing (burning), clamping, or tying off (ligation) of the Fallopian tubes. The tubes are reached either through abdominal surgery or by going up through the vagina. After the operation, sperm can still get into the lower part of the tube—the part near the uterus—and an egg can still enter the upper part, but sperm and egg never meet. The procedure does not affect a woman's hormones or any organ other than her tubes, so she ovulates and menstruates normally. The blocked eggs simply disintegrate. There is no physical effect on sexual desire. Within a week or so after the operation, sexual intercourse can be resumed and no contraception is necessary.

Over 100 variations of abdominal sterilization have been developed, but currently the two major methods are the **minilaparotomy** and the **laparoscopy.** The minilaparotomy is a simple procedure often accomplished

---

[1]At least when the patient is white, middle-class, and married. There have been many shocking cases of involuntary sterilization in this country. Usually the woman has been black or Latina. Such women have sometimes been pressured to sign consent forms during childbirth and have been falsely assured that the operation is easily reversible. Involuntary sterilization of women with below normal intelligence has also been reported.

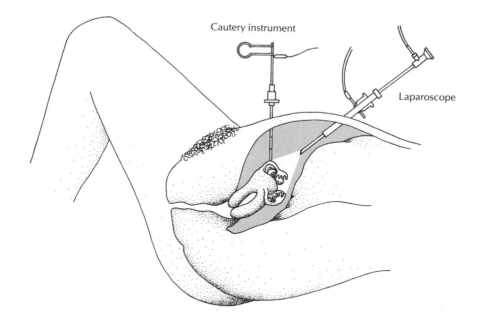

Cautery instrument

Laparoscope

with a local anesthetic. The doctor makes an incision about an inch long just above the pubic hair, finds the Fallopian tubes, grasps them with an instrument, and uses one of several methods of tying, cutting or clamping them. The laparoscopy is usually performed under a general anesthetic, but it is typically "walk-in" surgery, that is, it does not require an overnight hospitalization. This technique uses a laparoscope, a slender, hollow instrument equipped with a mirror and light source and used to examine the interior of body cavities. The laparoscope allows the doctor to locate the Fallopian tubes visually, then burn or clamp them. A common procedure is for the surgeon to make a very small abdominal incision just below the naval for the insertion of the laparoscope and another small incision above the pubis for inserting the instrument to locate and cut or cauterize the Fallopian tubes, as illustrated in Figure 7–9.

Another way to reach the Fallopian tubes is through the vagina, using a procedure called a **colpotomy.** Using either general, spinal, or local anesthesia, the physician makes a small incision in the vaginal wall. An advantage of this procedure is the absence of visible scars; a disadvantage is a higher rate of complications than experienced with abdominal procedures.

As can be seen in Table 7–2, tubal sterilization has a far lower mortality rate than continuing a pregnancy. However, a woman considering sterilization should be aware that, as with all operations, there are risks, including infection, hemorrhage, and reactions to the anesthetic. On rare occasions a "sterilized" woman may become pregnant, either because her tubes somehow heal and grow back together or because the doctor made an error. As for

laparoscopic sterilization   *In this procedure, described in the text, carbon dioxide is pumped into the abdominal cavity to separate the internal organs so that the Fallopian tubes are easy to locate.*

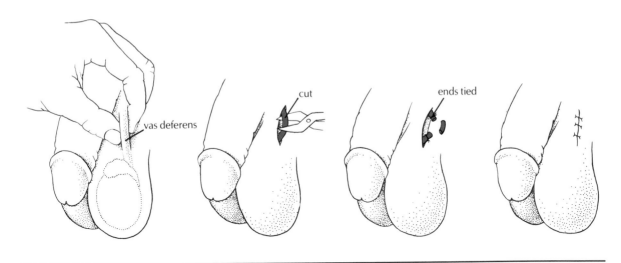

FIGURE 7–10

A vasectomy   In this simple surgical technique, each vas deferens is located and cut, and the ends are clamped or tied off. The operation has no effect on either erection or ejaculation.

intentional reversals, women are advised to consider this operation permanent. Surgeons can sometimes repair the severed tubes layer by layer, using a surgical microscope, but only a few specialists are qualified to attempt this complicated and expensive operation, and a pregnancy is not guaranteed.

MALE STERILIZATION   Vasectomy, the male form of sterilization, has been around for years, but did not become popular in the United States until the late 1960s. Then, in the 1970s, the procedure became, in some circles, almost fashionable; celebrities appeared on television talk shows to tell about their operations and to spread the word. Today vasectomy is almost as popular as female sterilization. Yet misconceptions about it still abound. Some men think a vasectomy will prevent them from getting an erection, having an orgasm, or ejaculating. Such beliefs are based on ignorance about male sexual anatomy and a tendency to confuse reproductive ability with sexual ability.

As you can see in Figure 7–10, a vasectomy is a much simpler procedure than a tubal sterilization. It is usually done in a doctor's office or at a clinic, and takes only ten to thirty minutes. The doctor injects a local anesthetic into the scrotum, makes either one or two small incisions, locates each vas deferens, and then removes a piece of each one and ties or clamps the ends. Sperm production continues as before, but the sperm cannot leave the epididymis, and they disintegrate. Since seminal fluid comes from the seminal vesicles and the prostate, which are in the interior of the body, its production is not affected. (You may want to review the illustrations of the male sexual and reproductive anatomy in Chapter 4.)

Sperm constitute only a tiny fraction of the volume of semen, so a man is not likely to notice any difference in his ejaculate. The sperm are gone, but most men never miss them. In fact, many say their sexual desire is greater for a while after the operation because they do not have to worry about their partner becoming pregnant.

After the vasectomy, a man (or his partner) has to use another method of contraception temporarily because it takes ten or fifteen ejaculations to get rid of the sperm remaining in the man's system above the blockage. After a few weeks, the man masturbates and brings some ejaculate to the doctor for analysis. If there are no more sperm, he gets the green light to go ahead with intercourse without contraception.

Among the advantages of vasectomies are their high effectiveness (see Table 7–1) and their safety (see Table 7–2). Aside from some post-operative swelling or bruising, and occasional post-operative infection or inflammation, a vasectomy is hazard-free. About one-half to two-thirds of men will develop sperm antibodies following a vasectomy, but there seem to be no health consequences. Several years ago questions were raised, based on studies in monkeys, about the possibility that these antibodies might lead to increased risk of cardiovascular disease, but four large studies have failed to find any link in men (Hatcher et al., 1988). No long-term health hazards in human males have ever been verified.

As for psychological consequences, most men seem to be as happy with their operations as women are with theirs (McCormick et al., 1977). But problems sometimes develop in men who are insecure about their masculinity. These men, and men who feel pressured by a partner into getting a vasectomy, are not good candidates for the operation.

Chances of reversing a vasectomy are not much better than those of reversing a laparoscopy. Again, the procedure requires a specialist and sophisticated equipment. Rejoining the ends of the vas is one thing, but making a man fertile again is another. Even if sperm get into the ejaculate, they may be incapable of fertilizing the egg (Hatcher et al., 1988). This problem may be due to the production of antibodies.

Two Tried and Untrue Methods

Two other means of attempting contraception deserve mention. Both are old and undependable. One is **withdrawal,** or, to use the fancier name, *coitus interruptus*. The male simply pulls his penis out of the female's vagina before ejaculating and ejaculates somewhere else. It sounds simple enough. But, as you will recall from Chapter 4, stray semen can make their way into the Cowper's glands secretions that precede ejaculation, so the woman may get pregnant anyway. Also, since withdrawal taxes a man's self-control to the limit, there are bound to be times when he does not quite make it out in time and deposits sperm in the vagina. Not surprisingly, withdrawal has a rather unimpressive failure rate of 18 percent. Psychologically, too, withdrawal has several drawbacks. The man has to concentrate on when he is going to ejaculate, instead of on the pleasure in getting there. The woman may feel pressured to get her orgasm "out of the way" quickly, or anxiety may prevent her

Unplanned parenthood
Men may not get pregnant, but they do become fathers. Posters like this one are aimed at helping young people see that birth control is a human concern, and not just a "women's issue."

Would you be more careful if it was you that got pregnant?

See your pharmacist for free information on family planning, venereal disease and other communicable diseases.

© *PPSI PO Box 1336, Sausalito, CA 94966*

from having an orgasm at all. Habitual use of withdrawal sometimes leads to premature ejaculation problems in men. The best you can say for withdrawal is that it is free, and better than nothing.

Another old but unreliable method is **douching** immediately after intercourse—washing the vagina out with water or a special douching solution. With a typical failure rate of 40 percent, douching should not be considered a form of birth control. Even if the woman sprints into the bathroom (not a very romantic way to end lovemaking), she won't have a chance to beat the tiny, aggressive sperm, who can be through the cervical opening within seconds after ejaculation. And in fact, douching may actually push some sperm toward the cervix. Douching has been statistically associated with PID (Wolner-Hanssen et al., 1990b).

After the Fact

"As long as condoms break, inclination and opportunity unexpectedly converge, men rape women, diaphragms and cervical caps are dislodged, people are so ambivalent about sex that they need to feel 'swept away,' IUDs are expelled, and Pills are lost or forgotten, we will need morning-after birth control," say the authors of *Contraceptive Technology*, the "bible" of birth control (Hatcher et al., 1988). Although the FDA has not approved any drugs specifically for use as morning-after birth control, some drugs approved for other purposes can also function as postcoital contraception. Physicians in the United States have been using these drugs for several years, especially for rape victims (Hatcher et al., 1988). However, postcoital methods of contraception are not recommended as a regular form of birth control; at this time, they are used only as emergency techniques.

Since the 1960s, a massive dose of the strong estrogen **DES (diethyl-stilbestrol) has been used as a morning-after pill.** (This is the same drug that was used in the 1950s, in a different dosage, to treat women who had difficulty maintaining pregnancies; it has been connected with the development of a type of vaginal-cervical cancer in the daughters of these women and is no longer used for this purpose.) Other high-dose estrogens have also been used. Morning-after pills probably work by preventing implantation of the fertilized egg. They all seem to share the undesirable side effects of nausea and vomiting.

Fewer adverse side effects result from using a particular combination birth control pill, called *Ovral*, as a morning-after pill. Two Ovral pills taken within 72 hours of unprotected intercourse, followed by two additional pills 12 hours after that, are highly effective in preventing pregnancy (though less than 100 percent effective). Timing is a critical factor in Ovral's effectiveness as a morning-after pill, and side effects can occur, so use for this purpose should always be under a doctor's supervision.

An alternative postcoital method, a French pill called *RU-486*, blocks the action of progesterone, the hormone that maintains the stability of the uterine lining. When RU-486 is given within the first seven to nine weeks of conception, it induces menstruation. As a result, if conception has occurred, the fertilized egg will fail to implant or will slough off. When taken along with the hormone-like substance prostaglandin, RU-486 is 96 percent effective (Silvestre, 1990). It must be used under a doctor's supervision.

Although RU-486 has been available in France since 1988, and appears to be quite safe, as of this writing little testing has occurred in the United States. Why? Like other postcoital methods, RU-486 does not actually prevent conception, but *intercepts* it. For this reason, it can be considered an extremely early abortion method. As such, it is adamantly opposed by antiabortion activists in the U.S. American companies, fearing boycotts and also liability problems, have shown little interest as yet in producing or distributing the product, despite a potentially huge market. Still, many observers believe that RU-486 will eventually be available in the U.S., and will take the place of many surgical abortions.

ABORTION

Abortion: the very word can raise people's blood pressure and turn friends into enemies. Abortion opponents believe that an embryo or fetus has an inalienable right to life. Supporters insist that every woman has an inalienable right to control her body without interference by others. In recent years, the abortion debate has turned into a highly charged and even violent political battle.

The conflict is a relatively modern development. Historically, abortion was tolerated in most Western societies until the *quickening,* the time during the fifth month or so when a pregnant woman first feels the fetus move. The Roman Catholic Church held that a fetus did not become a person until the soul entered the body; only then did abortion become a serious crime. The cut-off point was forty days after conception for boys and eighty days for girls, because female souls, which supposedly fell somewhere on a scale between man and beast, were thought to be weaker and thus slower to develop. However, it was not clear how a woman was to know whether she was carrying a male or female fetus (Boston Women's Health Book Collective, 1984).

In 1869, Pope Pius IX declared all abortions to be murder. Shortly thereafter, in America, states began to pass the first antiabortion laws. But the motives were not religious. In those days, abortion was a primitive and risky undertaking, and many reformers were concerned for women's health. Physicians supported these efforts, not only out of concern for women's lives but, according to historian James C. Mohr (1978), because abortion was often done by midwives and other nonphysicians. Governments and social planners at the time were interested in promoting population growth, not reduction, because the industrial revolution demanded an increased supply of laborers for the factories. In addition, Victorian morality tended to regard an unwanted pregnancy as a just punishment for illicit—or even licit—sexual pleasure.

Severely restricting abortion did not abolish it, however. Women continued to seek illegal abortions, often delivering themselves into the unwashed hands of unscrupulous opportunists who preyed on those not wealthy or knowledgeable enough to find cooperative doctors. Or, like Margaret Sanger's patient, Sadie Sachs, they tried to perform their own abortions by inserting hooks, coat hangers, and knitting needles into their wombs, douching with disinfectants, or hurling themselves down a flight of stairs.

Until January 1973, only a few states in the U.S. permitted abortion, and then only under certain conditions. Then the United States Supreme Court ruled seven to two, in *Roe v. Wade*, that any state restricting or prohibiting abortion during the first trimester of pregnancy was infringing on the right of a woman and her physician to privacy. The court also ruled that after the twelfth week, a state could regulate where and by whom the operation was to be performed and that after the twenty-fourth week (when the fetus has a chance of living on its own outside the woman's body) a state could prohibit most abortions—but not those necessary to preserve the life or health of the woman.

The Supreme Court reaffirmed *Roe v. Wade* in 1983 and again in 1986. But in 1989, in a case brought by the state of Missouri (*Webster v. Reproductive*

Health Services), the Supreme Court ruled that states could impose three types of restrictions not allowed by *Roe v. Wade*. The Court said that Missouri could bar public employees from performing abortions that were not necessary to save a woman's life; prohibit the use of public buildings for performing abortions; and require doctors to perform tests to determine the fetus' ability to live outside the womb if the woman was at least 20 weeks pregnant. Ironically, this ruling, much criticized by pro-choice advocates, seemed to mobilize public opinion in favor of abortion rights.

About one in three pregnancies each year in the U.S. ends in abortion. That translates into about a million and a half abortions each year—about a third of these to teenagers (Henshaw, 1986). The U.S. rate is lower than the rate in the Soviet Union and Eastern Europe, and also the worldwide rate, but is higher than that of any other Western industrialized nation. The reason is that the U.S. has more unwanted and unplanned pregnancies than does any other developed country; over half of all pregnancies are mistimed or unwanted.

Although both history and research show that abortion has always been a common response to unwanted pregnancy, a coalition of religious and politically conservative groups, the "Pro-Life" movement, has been seeking for several years to make abortion illegal again in the United States. Because they feel that human life begins in a meaningful sense at conception, and should always be protected, they regard abortion as murder. Opposition to abortion in the last decade has focused on successful efforts to restrict public funding for abortion; pressure on Congress to pass a constitutional amendment banning or severely restricting abortion; and efforts to pass legislation requiring minors to get parental consent for an abortion. Frustrated by their relative lack of success in the legal arena, some abortion opponents have tried to blockade the entrances to facilities that provide abortions by sitting in front of the doors until arrested. Extremists have even bombed abortion clinics. In response to antiabortion forces, "Pro-Choice" groups have rallied to oppose any changes that would prevent a pregnant woman from having an abortion if she so chooses.

Abortion Methods

There are various methods for terminating a pregnancy, depending on how long it has existed:

1. The **vacuum curettage** method (also called *vacuum aspiration*) is the simplest and most widely used abortion procedure. It can be done up to the sixteenth week, counting from the last menstrual period. After giving a local anesthetic, the physician inserts a rigid metal or plastic instrument into the uterus. The instrument is hollow and is connected to a long tube that is in turn connected to an electric or mechanical

FIGURE 7–11
The vacuum curettage method of abortion *This procedure, described in the text, is the safest and simplest abortion method, and the most widely used in the United States.*

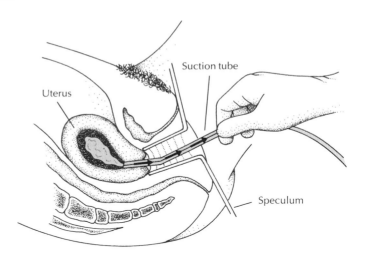

pump. The vacuum produced by the pump gently draws out the fetal material (see Figure 7–11). The procedure takes less than ten minutes and is done in a doctor's office or clinic. The more advanced the pregnancy (from about eight weeks on), the more likely it is that the cervix will need to be dilated (opened) prior to the extraction. This may be accomplished by placing progressively larger rod-shaped instruments, called dilators, through the cervical opening, or by using a natural material called laminaria. Laminaria, a kind of seaweed, is compressed into a small stick that is inserted into the cervix 6 to 24 hours prior to the abortion. Because it absorbs cervical secretions, the laminaria expands slowly, gradually dilating the cervix with less discomfort than the dilator procedure.

2. **Dilation and evacuation (D and E)** is the most widely used method between the thirteenth and sixteenth weeks and is often used up through the twentieth week. Because the pregnancy is more advanced and the conceptus is larger, the cervix requires more dilation than in a vacuum curettage procedure. After dilation, the uterine contents are removed with a combination of suction equipment, special forceps, and a scraping instrument called a curette. A general anesthetic may be given.

3. **Instillation procedures** are sometimes used between the sixteenth and twenty-fourth week. They involve injecting a substance into the amniotic sac or introducing it through the woman's vagina, to bring on uterine contractions. Usually

the cervix opens and the fetus and placenta are expelled, as in a normal delivery. The process takes from twelve to thirty-six hours. The substance used is usually a saline (salt) solution or a prostaglandin. Sometimes a hormone called oxytocin is given to speed the contractions. Instillation methods of abortion entail about six times more risk than the instrumental evacuation methods described above. The major complications are due to infection, embolism, reactions to the anesthesia, and hemorrhage. If induced labor does not begin after saline solution or prostaglandin injection, a final alternative is a *hysterotomy* (not to be confused with a hysterectomy), in which the fetus is removed through an abdominal incision. Hysterotomy involves a risk 74 times that of the evacuation methods and so it is rarely used (Hatcher et al., 1988).

As can be seen in Table 7–2, early abortions are safer than late ones and much safer than childbirth. Legal abortions are safer by far than illegal ones.

Many people assume that abortion is always a traumatic experience, but studies fail to support this assumption, at least for early abortions (which is to say, most abortions). A recent review of the research literature concluded that a) abortion is no more closely linked with depression than are other significant life events for women, including having a baby; b) the rate of post-abortion depression is similar to the rate for the general population of adult women; and c) negative emotions tend to decrease following abortion, with most women reporting feelings of relief (Wilmoth & Adelstein, 1988). Cases of prolonged or severe guilt, regret, or disturbance are rare. In 1989, a government draft report drew a similar conclusion: that there is little scientific evidence that abortion causes women significant physical or emotional harm. (Then-Surgeon General C. Everett Koop, a staunch opponent of abortion, decided not to issue the report.) The same year, a working group of the American Psychological Association, after analyzing the 21 most methodologically sound studies on the topic, concluded that severe reactions are rare, and that the time of greatest distress is likely to be *before* the abortion (Adler et al., 1990).

This is not to say that the decision to abort or the experience of having an abortion is easy. Before the abortion, a woman may feel angry at her partner, herself, a birth control method that failed, or parents and friends who pressure her either to have or not have the abortion. Afterward she may feel lonely and alienated because no one really understands the crisis she has gone through. The American Psychological Association review found that women are most likely to suffer negative reactions if they initially desired a child, lacked support from partner or parents, or were unsure of their decisions and delayed the abortion until the second trimester of pregnancy (Adler et al., 1990).

Late abortions are typically more stressful than early ones for several reasons. The woman may have felt the fetus move and may have begun to visualize it mentally as a baby. She may have trouble finding a doctor and a hospital that will perform the abortion, and when she does, she may find herself on a ward with expectant mothers. If the method is an instillation procedure, the woman must go through a complete delivery, just as she would if she were carrying the fetus full term. Medical people are sometimes disturbed by the delivery of a dead fetus and may respond by acting distant and aloof. After a late abortion, the woman may find relief mixed with grief.

For their part, the men involved do not always have an easy time with an abortion. In the view of sociologist Arthur Shostak, abortion is an unrecognized trauma for some men. In a survey of male "abortion veterans," he found that the majority of men supported the woman's choice and her right to abort but, hidden underneath, they had ambivalent, angry, or resentful feelings (Shostak, McLouth & Seng, 1984).

There is conflicting research on the long-term effects of abortion on a woman's subsequent ability to get pregnant and have a healthy baby, but increasing evidence indicates that legal, early abortions cause few, if any, long-term fertility problems (Hatcher et al., 1988).

WHY PEOPLE DO NOT USE BIRTH CONTROL

Most heterosexuals use birth control at some time in their lives. Their reasons may be personal (they want few or no children, or they wish to postpone having children so they can devote their energy to other activities); philosophical or ethical (for example, they may be concerned about population growth); economic (they are not financially able or willing to raise children, or they wish to space out their children and spread out the costs); or related to health concerns.

People reject birth control for as many reasons as they use it. Some people, of course, consciously want and intend to have a child. Others, some psychologists believe, fail to use birth control because they have an *unconscious* desire for pregnancy. And sometimes people are simply uninformed about their contraceptive options. After all, how many parents discuss specific methods of birth control with their offspring or help them obtain contraceptives if they become sexually active? Young people often grow up relying on friends for information and often get misinformation instead. Many adolescents mistakenly believe that they are too young to get pregnant or that one must have intercourse frequently or a certain number of times for conception to take place. Some think that maximum fertility occurs just before, during, or after menstruation, rather than at midcycle (Kantner & Zelnik, 1972).

Often contraceptive failure (that is, the inception of a pregnancy that was unintended and is unwanted) is the outcome of conflict and ambivalence about sexuality or birth control. Not only are individuals of two minds about contraception, but our society is currently struggling with several birth control issues that influence how we think and behave.

Psychological Conflict

Sociologist Kristin Luker (1975) has suggested that unwanted pregnancies are the result of a decision-making process in which a woman weighs the costs and benefits involved in both contraception and pregnancy, and assesses the likelihood of pregnancy. (While the discussion that follows focuses on *women's* conflicts about contraception, we do not intend to neglect the man's role. As has been pointed out, maternity never takes place without paternity. However, most research in this area has concentrated only on females, perhaps because, although making a baby takes two bodies, the pregnancy ends up in only one.)

Generally, Luker believes, women decide that the pregnancy risk is low. (In truth, of course, it is sometimes low and sometimes high.) If the costs associated with contraception are numerous, or there are many benefits associated with pregnancy, then the woman begins to take risks. What are some of the costs of contraception? Planning to use, and using, contraception requires an acknowledgement that one is sexually active, and this is not always easy, especially for young, single women. Being prepared for intercourse, say by taking the Pill, indicates to oneself and others that one is sexually available. People often perceive a decrease in spontaneity as a cost of using such methods as the diaphragm, spermicides, and condoms. There is also the cost of obtaining the method in the first place. Prescription methods require making an appointment with a doctor or a clinic, waiting, getting there and back, and, often, getting to a pharmacy. Over-the-counter methods involve going into a store and openly acknowledging—at least to people in the store—that one is a sexual person. For many, a contraceptive cost is the necessity to talk about birth control with a partner. Another cost for some is concern about the safety of the IUD and the Pill or about potential side effects.

A woman might also perceive some benefits of pregnancy. Pregnancy is proof of fertility and, for some women, of womanhood. It can enhance a woman's sense of self-worth and importance. Getting pregnant can also be a way of trying to alter a relationship. A teenager, for example, may see pregnancy and motherhood as a way to rebel against her parents or gain her independence. Pregnancy may be used in an attempt to get a man to commit himself to the relationship. And, finally, the sheer excitement of risk-taking may prompt some people, male and female, to be careless or nonchalant about birth control.

People are not always fully aware of the various pros and cons that go into their decision making. The costs and benefits will vary from one person to the next, and from one time of life to another. Contraception is more "costly" at the beginning of a relationship (when insecurity makes it more difficult to be assertive) and, often, at the end of a relationship (when strong emotions or futile attempts to get back together are apt to cloud one's judgment). Risk taking, if it is successful (as it will sometimes be, on the basis of probability alone) promotes further risk taking. When a woman thinks she might be pregnant, she may swear she will always be careful in the future. But if her pregnancy fears are unfounded, she may figure she got away with it once, so why not again?

Luker feels that the more aware we are of our decision-making process, the more control we will be able to exert over our contraceptive behavior.

Religious Considerations

When birth control became more effective, many members of religions that oppose contraception experienced conflict between their faith and their wish to avoid pregnancy. Religion, however, is not nearly as powerful an influence on contraceptive behavior as most people think. Consider the Catholic Church's condemnation of all "artificial" methods, which Pope Paul VI reaffirmed in a 1968 encyclic entitled *Humanae Vitae* (Of Human Life). Studies show that despite the ban, Catholic and non-Catholic Americans scarcely differ in their birth control practices. A national survey taken in 1975

"Mr. Contraceptive"
Some countries have made an all-out effort to encourage birth control. In Thailand, Mechai Viravardya uses public relations techniques to promote contraception. A national hero, he has sponsored balloon-blowing contests using condoms and given prizes to people who promise to use birth control. His efforts have contributed to Thailand's highly successful campaign to lower its birth rate.

found that 76.4 percent of all married Catholic couples in which the wife was under 45 practiced some form of birth control, compared with 79.9 percent of non-Catholic couples (Westoff & Jones, 1977). A little less than six percent of the Catholics used rhythm, down from about 32 percent in 1965, and the rest used an "artificial" method. The same proportions of Catholics and non-Catholics used the Pill, and almost as many Catholics as non-Catholics used the IUD. About a third of non-Catholics had chosen sterilization, compared with a little more than a fourth of the Catholics. In nearly two-fifths of the Catholic couples who were "contraceptors" and had all the children they wanted, one partner had been sterilized.

The data also showed that the longer a Catholic woman was married, the less likely she was to rely on abstinence or rhythm. This was true for both religious and nonreligious women; only about four percent of devout women married five to nine years followed official Catholic doctrine. The researchers estimated that soon the birth control practices of Catholics and non-Catholics in this country would not differ at all, and their prediction seems to have been borne out. A more recent study, using a large sample of women, found 88.7 percent of Protestants and 88.3 percent of Catholics using some method of birth control (Bachrach, 1984). The "belief-behavior gap" (see Chapters 1 and 2) applies even to abortion; among women reporting a religious affiliation, Catholic women are about as likely as non-Catholics to have an abortion, and about one-sixth of women who have abortions are born-again or evangelical Christians (Henshaw & Silverman, 1988).

Health Concerns

Uncertainty about the safety of the Pill and worry about other IUDs, after the established danger of the Dalkon Shield, have caused some women to shy away from these methods out of concern for their health. Some have turned to less effective means or have given up contraception altogether (without giving up sex, however). There is a built-in Catch-22 here, for pregnancy is even more dangerous to one's health than birth control is (see Table 7–2). To be sure, when a woman wants a child, the risks of pregnancy and childbirth seem small. But when she does not want to be pregnant, avoiding birth control because of the health hazards involved may be like cutting off her nose to spite her face. (Ironically, other health concerns, about the hazards of sexually transmitted diseases, may be contributing to better use of condoms and spermicides.)

A Research Quagmire

It is a given in the field of contraception that no one method of protection is perfect for everyone; the more choices, the better. But, as we saw at the start of this chapter, instead of more choices, the trend is toward fewer choices. A number of safe, effective methods are not available because they are bogged down in a stalemate involving the Federal Drug Administration (FDA), researchers, pharmaceutical companies, and the insurance industry. The FDA, severely criticized for inadequate research prior to approving the Dalkon Shield, now takes extreme care that the methods it approves are safe. At the same time, as we noted earlier, research funding has dropped and, due to product-liability issues, the insurance necessary to begin and continue human trials is unavailable. Drug manufacturers are unwilling to take any risks or foot any bills without assurance that they will make a profit. Interest in one-time and long-acting methods is low because, compared with the Pill, they generate a poor profit. Hence, it is uncertain how many more methods will be available in the near future. (New ideas and possibilities abound, however. For a discussion of what *could* be and what *might* be in the field of contraception, see Box 7–1.)

The Advertising Controversy

There is a general trend in our society to "play now, pay later." A credit-card culture cannot be too concerned about the future. It is romantic to be carefree and spontaneous. Such values are reflected in the media. Each year, thousands of sexual scenes are depicted on prime-time network television, but rarely is there a mention of the possible consequences or the need for protection. On television and in movies, the most desirable, sexy people have abundant sex but never worry about contraception, and don't get pregnant. These models give us implicit approval not to think or talk about birth control. Moreover, as of mid-1990 the major networks still had not accepted advertisements for contraception, arguing that such ads would be in "bad taste." This policy reflects a desire to avoid political controversy. Many groups support the availability of contraceptive information, including the American Civil Liberties Union, Planned Parenthood Federation of America, the American College of Obstetrics and Gynecology, the Population Institute, and the National Council of Churches of Christ. But some politically powerful groups oppose it, including Morality in Media, the National Right to Life Association (an antiabortion group), and the National Conference of Catholic Bishops.

An individual's ambivalence about birth control occurs in the context of cultural ambivalence about sex and contraception. (For more on cultural influences, see Chapter 13.)

WHAT HATH BIRTH CONTROL WROUGHT?

People whose sexual histories predate the early 1960s can appreciate the profound difference that effective birth control can make in a person's sex life. Without birth control, each and every act of intercourse may be marred by the fear of conception. But the consequences of birth control extend beyond the individual to society as a whole. Think of it: for the first time in all of history, ordinary people can decide when and if they will procreate. Because we are participants in this revolutionary development, evaluating it is difficult. But we can speculate about some of the implications.

One possible consequence of reliable birth control is an increase in the incidence of premarital sex. In fact, some people give full credit (or blame) to the Pill for the "sexual revolution" of the 1960s. As we saw in Chapter 2, the percentage of people having sex before marriage did soar in the late 1960s and early 1970s, only a few years after the Pill became widely available. However, that fact alone does not prove that the Pill and other effective methods *caused* premarital sex to be more common. A causal connection is hard to establish. Thus, while studies find that teenagers who use the Pill have sex more frequently, on the average, than users of other methods, it could be that having frequent sex makes people more likely to turn to reliable methods, rather than the other way around. Also, as we saw in Chapter 2, many other events occurred during the late 1960s and early 1970s that might have influenced sexual behavior. For example, the Vietnam War and the Watergate scandal probably led to disillusionment with established authority and social conventions of all kinds, including sexual ones.

Many social observers feel that improvements in birth control contributed to the rise of the modern feminist movement; it can even be argued that without it, the movement would never have made the gains it did. In a society that makes childcare a female responsibility, a woman who cannot predict when she will bear children is in no position to make serious plans about anything else. Even if a woman wants children and cherishes the role of mother, without birth control she lacks true control over the course of her life. For women, birth control means control of one's personal destiny. New options open up, including the option to take a long-term job or make a career commitment. As new possibilities become available, women's self-concepts and relationships with men are bound to change. (But, of course, birth control is not the only explanation for the changing role of women; inflation—which makes two-paycheck families an economic necessity—is another factor that comes to mind.)

Choice, however, is a double-edged sword, for men as well as women. Having a number of options can be exhilarating, but how does one decide which one to take? Deciding if and when to have children may be the toughest decision people ever make. (If you have not gone through the process, perhaps you gained a feeling for the issues while working on the *Personal Perspective* exercise in Chapter 6.) Birth control not only liberates us to make choices but forces us to confront our alternatives. Unfortunately, none of us can try out all of life's possible paths. As French statesman Leon Blum once wrote, "Life does not give itself to one who tries to keep all its advantages at once. . . . Morality may perhaps consist solely in the courage of making a choice."

BOX 7–1

Contraceptives Of The Future

In the short span of thirty years we have seen a great improvement in contraceptive effectiveness. But the "perfect" birth control method, one that is 100 percent effective, easy to use, absolutely safe, and readily reversible, still does not exist. As we have noted in the text, as of 1990, funding in the United States for contraceptive research and development had slowed to a trickle. Still, eventually we are likely to see some new alternatives.

One such alternative, a controversial one, is *Depo-Provera,* a progestin currently used by women in 90 countries. Depo-Provera is administered by injection four times a year, and is highly effective, with reported failure rates typically less than 1.0 (Hatcher et al., 1988). But it has failed several times to get FDA approval as a contraceptive. Critics are primarily concerned about the occurrence of breast tumors in beagles treated in the laboratory with the drug. However, a study of human users has found no increased risk of breast cancer among Depo-Provera users (Liskin & Blackburn, 1987). Other injectable hormones are also being used in certain countries. One, combining estrogen and progestin, is administered monthly and is expected to undergo improvements in the near future.

Another hormonal approach uses a silicone vaginal ring to release either a progestin or an estrogen-progestin combination. The ring can be left in place for three months, except for temporary removal during intercourse if desired. Some of the side effects of oral contraceptives are eliminated with this method. The ring can be inserted or withdrawn without the aid of a medical practitioner.

Yet another hormonal method uses biodegradable subdermal implants containing progestin. Unlike Norplant (described in the text), these implants dissolve eventually, and therefore do not need to be removed by a doctor. Biodegradable implants remain effective for at least 12 or 18 months, depending on the type of progestin used.

Estrogen and progestin are not the only hormones that might be used for contraception. Another contender is an agonist (inhibitor) of *gonadotropin releasing factor* (GnRF), the substance which, when released by the hypothalamus, signals the pituitary gland to release luteinizing hormone (LH) in women and interstitial-cell-stimulating hormone (ICSH) in men. Giving GnRF agonist to women disrupts the hormonal cycle and prevents ovulation. There appear to be no serious short-term side effects, and effectiveness rates are good (Hatcher et al., 1988).

A new barrier approach for women is another possibility. One, the "vaginal sheath," or "intravaginal pouch," is already in existence. Misleadingly called by some "the female condom," it consists of a soft polyurethane sheath attached at each end to a flexible ring. The sheath is inserted like a tampon into the vagina, with the ring at the closed end of the sheath covering the cervix and the other one staying outside, over the labia. After use, it is simply pulled out gently. As of 1990, the sheath was not yet generally available in the U.S., although that could change. Critics want more testing, to make sure the sheath stays in place properly during intercourse and the penis cannot enter the vagina alongside the device, instead of within it.

A different idea, being tested on animals, is an *anti-fertility vaccine*. One approach would alter the protective coating on the egg in such a way that sperm could not penetrate for fertilization. Another would stimulate the production of antibodies against sperm (Franklin, 1989). In addition, genetic engineering techniques are being used to develop a vaccine from a fragment of *human chorionic gonadotropin* (HCG), the hormone released after an egg has been fertilized. HCG stimulates the production of progesterone, which primes the uterus for the egg's implantation. A woman vaccinated with the HCG fragment would produce antibodies against HCG, and so implantation could not occur (Wilbur, 1986). However, there are several problems with this method, including nonreversibility, and it is not expected to be generally available for many years.

Another radically new approach involves a tiny battery placed in the cervical canal. The very small electrical fields it creates in the cervical mucus paralyze sperm so they cannot enter the uterus. This device is being tested on baboons with great success, but human tests are years away *(Contraceptive Technology Update,* February, 1987).

Female sterilization without surgery is also under investigation. A *chemical sterilant* (methyl cyanoacrylate), a "super-glue-like" substance, is squirted into a woman's Fallopian tubes with a special device. The chemical causes an inflammation in the tubes, resulting in scarring that closes them off. Initial tests in women show it to be more effective than the IUD but not as effective as surgical sterilization *(Contraceptive Technology Update,* July, 1987).

What about something for men? Interest in male contraception has lagged far behind interest in female methods, but there are some possibilities. One is *gossypol,* a derivative of cottonseed oil, taken orally by thousands of men in China. This substance reduces sperm production without suppressing male sexual desire. However, a substantial percentage of men do not regain their fertility when they stop taking gossypol and the chemical can cause a potassium deficiency (Hatcher et al., 1988).

Another contender, as for women, is a GnRF agonist. A pump implanted under the skin that constantly infuses GnRF agonist into the

**BOX 7–1
CONTINUED**

man's system will effectively suppress sperm production. Unfortunately, this method suppresses testosterone production so much that sexual desire and erectile ability may also decline. Maintaining testosterone levels while destroying fertility in men has been a major stumbling block. One effort at a solution has been to deliver GnRF agonist in a nasal spray; another has been to give testosterone supplements along with it. It is unclear how long sperm production remains suppressed, but this method may be improved enough to be usable within a few years.

Finally, a nonhormonal approach for men is to inject a synthetic "plug" into the vas deferens. This method also lowers the pH of the tubal cavity, which inhibits the ability of sperm to move. Later, if fertility is desired, the plug can be removed. This method has been shown to be effective for longer than a year in monkeys (Guha, 1985).

Time will tell which of these many inventive approaches to contraception will actually become a reality.

. . . .

**PERSONAL
PERSPECTIVE**

MAKING YOUR CONTRACEPTIVE CHOICE

If you have already made your choice about birth control, and it is not a permanent method, this exercise will give you a chance to review and reassess. Most people use several methods of contraception over their lifetimes, adjusting to the changing circumstances of their sex lives.

If you have *not* chosen a method, now is the time (unless, of course, you are exclusively gay or lesbian or have chosen life-long celibacy.) If you have not yet had your first experience with sexual intercourse, take this opportunity to think through the personal issues involved, so that you will know what you want and will be better prepared to talk candidly with your partner about the options. (Discussing birth control for the first time with a new partner may be terribly hard, but often there is no other way to be sure you are protected.) If, like many of our students, you have had unprotected intercourse or have used unreliable methods for a time, or you have already experienced an unwanted conception, this exercise may help you to take more control over your sex life.

In thinking about birth control, remember:

■ Birth control is a *trade-off*. You must do something, give up something, or put up with something to get contraceptive protection. What you give up, put up with, or do is your choice, within the limits of the currently available methods. The object is to choose wisely and select a method you will use willingly.

■ A woman and a man are equally involved in conception, so both have a stake in contraception. If the woman is taking the Pill, that's the man's birth control, too. If the man is using a condom, that's also the woman's contraception. Do not leave what should be a joint responsibility for contraception up to only one partner.

■ Two methods are always more reliable than one (unless the one is sterilization).

■ No method is a good method if it is not used carefully and consistently.

Now, consider the following questions:

1. *Do you need a permanent method* (are you *sure* you don't want any [more] children?) *or a reversible one?*

2. *How frequently do you have sex?* If not often, you may not be motivated enough to use a daily method. You may prefer a "for the occasion" method such as the diaphragm, the sponge, or condoms.

3. *Do you have one committed partner or several partners?* Contraception is much more likely to be a joint decision for a committed couple. Couples can and should talk together and agree to support each other in their decision. A person who is not involved in a relationship is often on his or her own to make sure conception does not occur. Anyone who has multiple partners should take account of the fact that latex condoms and spermicides provide protection from sexually transmitted diseases, including AIDS. The Pill decreases a woman's chances of getting chlamydia-related pelvic inflammatory disease.

4. *What about side effects?* Of the unwanted side effects that pertain to you, which are intolerable and which are ones you can live with because the method is effective or convenient, or the risks are relatively low.

5. *Are you a woman who smokes and is over 35?* If so, you should not use the Pill. What are your alternatives? (Would you consider giving up smoking?)

6. *If you have chosen the Pill, are you taking any medications that might result in an undesirable drug interaction?* A number of drugs (in particular, certain anticonvulsants and antibiotics) may reduce the effectiveness of the Pill. Check with your medical practitioner or birth control clinic.

7. *If money is a factor for you, what is the best protection you can get for the least cost?* Condoms and sponges are not expensive per package, but the cumulative cost is high if you have sex frequently.

8. *How important is spontaneity to you?* If you feel awkward about taking time to put on a condom or use spermicides, they may not be for

you, despite their advantages. But remember, you can learn to incorporate the "interruption" into your love-play.

9. *Do you have trouble with the idea of planning ahead and being prepared for sex?* Would you feel funny about taking your diaphragm or some condoms or sponges with you just in case? You may want to come to grips with a discrepancy between your feelings and your behavior.

10. *What does your religion say regarding contraception?* How important is this for you personally?

11. *What will you do if you experience a contraceptive failure?* What is your choice for a backup method?

12. *How do you feel about enjoying "outercourse" (activities like hugging, snuggling, mutual masturbation, and oral-genital sex) instead of intercourse?* For some people, the best form of birth control is to abstain from sexual intercourse and use other sexual techniques.

13. *What might be some "benefits" of pregnancy (yours or your partner's)?* Are these expectations realistic? Think about a pregnancy now as compared with one in the future. Contrast the meaning of an unplanned and unwanted pregnancy with a planned and wanted baby.

IN BRIEF

1. Throughout history, regardless of official policies against birth control, people have searched for ways to prevent pregnancy. During the nineteenth and early twentieth centuries, pro- and anti-birth control forces in Western societies clashed. Reformers like Margaret Sanger were prosecuted for illegally distributing birth control information. But by the 1930s, birth control was accepted, and by the 1970s its use had caused the birth rate in the United States to fall dramatically.

2. Concern mounted in the mid-70s that the Pill might not be safe. Also, cases of pelvic inflammatory disease (PID) were associated with the intrauterine device, especially the Dalkon Shield. Concerned about liability, all the major distributors of IUDs in the United States withdrew them from the market. Funding for contraceptive research diminished drastically, and today the United States lags behind other countries in contraceptive research and development. However, demand for effective contraception has not decreased.

3. *Oral contraceptives* (the Pill) are at present the most effective reversible method of birth control; they are nearly 100 percent effective when used correctly. They work mainly by preventing ovulation. *Combination pills* contain both synthetic estrogen and progestin. *Phasic pills* deliver a

constant amount of estrogen, but the level of progestin varies over the cycle. The *mini-pill* contains only progestin. Drastically lowered hormone levels have made the Pill safer than it used to be, and some health benefits have even been established. However, there are still some risks, and the Pill is not recommended for women over 35 who smoke, because of the possibility of cardiovascular problems.

4. As this book went to press, an alternative hormonal approach, *Norplant,* was nearing approval for marketing in the U.S. It consists of subdermal implants that slowly release progestin into the bloodstream. Protection lasts for a number of years. Norplant is even more effective in preventing conception than the Pill.

5. *Intrauterine devices (IUDs)* are small objects placed in the uterus and left there. They appear to work by interfering with implantation of a fertilized egg, and thus are probably "interceptives" rather than contraceptives. Only two models are currently marketed in the United States. They are relatively safe and effective in monogamous women at low risk for PID or ectopic pregnancies.

6. *Condoms* are sheaths that fit over the penis. During heterosexual intercourse they keep sperm from entering the vagina. When used carefully and consistently they are very effective, and they also have the advantage of reducing the risk of contracting a sexually transmitted disease. For these reasons, and because they are generally safe, condoms have increased in popularity in recent years.

7. *Diaphragms* are soft rubber cups that cover the cervix during sexual intercourse, acting as a barrier against sperm and as a means of holding spermicide close to the cervix. When used properly they are extremely effective. They are generally very safe, although there is concern about a possible increased risk of urinary tract infections.

8. *The contraceptive sponge* is a disposable spermicide holder placed high in the vagina prior to intercourse. Like the condom, it is available without a prescription. Because it can be inserted several hours before intercourse, its use need not interrupt lovemaking. The sponge is not as effective when used alone as are the methods described above, especially for women who have already given birth.

9. *Cervical caps* are thimble-shaped cups that fit snugly over the cervix, held in place at least in part by suction. They work in the same way as the diaphragm and appear to be similar to the diaphragm in effectiveness and safety, although information is still somewhat limited.

10. *Spermicides* are chemicals that kill sperm. They are available in several forms without a prescription and are most effective when used in conjunction with other methods. The nonoxynol-9 in most spermicides has been shown in the laboratory to kill many organisms responsible for sexually transmitted diseases. Some people object to them because they are messy and unpleasant tasting.

11. *Fertility awareness methods* rely on the prediction of fertile and infertile phases of a woman's menstrual cycle. During the fertile phase a couple must use a barrier method of birth control or non-coital techniques of lovemaking. Ovulation is predicted using the rhythm or calendar method, the basal body temperature (BBT) method, the cervical mucus method, or the sympto-thermal method. Fertility awareness has a poor reputation for effectiveness, but highly motivated couples who cannot or will not use any other method may be able to use it successfully. It is completely safe.

12. *Sterilization* is now by far the most popular form of birth control in the United States. The standard method for women is *tubal sterilization;* the standard method for men is *vasectomy*. Both methods leave sexual functioning and desire unaffected. Sterilization should be considered permanent, since reversals cannot be counted on.

13. *Withdrawal* is a relatively undependable method of contraception. *Douching* is not only ineffective, but may actually push some sperm toward the cervix.

14. *Morning-after* birth control should not be considered for use on a regular basis. One morning-after pill, containing DES, has undesirable side effects. Ovral, a birth control pill sometimes used as a post-coital method, has fewer such effects. RU-486, a French pill that brings on menstruation by blocking the action of progesterone, may eventually be available in the United States, but remains controversial because, like other post-coital methods, it can be considered an early abortion method.

15. *Abortion* is a source of heated controversy in the United States. Methods include *vacuum curettage, dilation and evacuation (D and E),* and *instillation techniques*. Legal, early abortions are better than late or illegal ones, from both a physiological and a psychological standpoint. Early abortions do not appear to affect fertility or have adverse psychological consequences in most women.

16. People may reject or fail to use birth control because they unconsciously wish for pregnancy to occur, are uninformed about available methods, or have conflicts about sexuality and contraception. According to one theory, a woman's contraceptive risk-tasking depends on the perceived probability of pregnancy, the costs involved in using contraception, and the possible benefits of pregnancy. Religious considerations may be salient for some people, although studies find that religion is not as powerful an influence on contraceptive behavior as many people think. Health concerns may also be a factor; however, the risks of the various methods should be weighed against the much higher health risks involved in pregnancy and childbirth.

17. Cultural ambivalence about contraception is apparent in the media. Television depicts thousands of sexual scenes annually in which birth control is never mentioned or even implied, and the major networks have for years refused to accept ads for contraceptives.

18. Birth control has profound consequences for individuals and for society as a whole. Its availability may affect the incidence of premarital sexual activity, although a cause-and-effect relationship is hard to prove. It may also have been a contributing factor in the rise of the modern feminist movement and changes in the role of women. The availability of contraceptive choices requires that people make difficult decisions and face some perplexing existential questions.

Key Terms

birth control *(225)*

contraception *(226)*

oral contraceptives (OCs) *(229)*

combination pill *(229)*

progestin *(229)*

phasic pill *(229)*

mini-pill *(230)*

intrauterine device (IUD) *(234)*

condom *(236)*

diaphragm *(239)*

contraceptive sponge *(242)*

cervical cap *(243)*

spermicide *(245)*

fertility awareness methods *(246)*

rhythm method *(247)*

basal body temperature method *(248)*

cervical mucus method *(248)*

ovulation method *(248)*

sympto-thermal method *(249)*

sterilization *(250)*

hysterectomy *(250)*

tubal sterilization *(250)*

minilaparotomy *(250)*

laparoscopy *(250)*

colpotomy *(251)*

vasectomy *(252)*

withdrawal *(253)*

douching *(254)*

DES (diethylstilbestrol) *(255)*

morning-after pill *(255)*

abortion *(255)*

vacuum curettage *(257)*

vacuum aspiration *(257)*

dilation and evacuation (D&E) *(258)*

instillation procedure *(258)*

prostaglandins *(259)*

hysterotomy *(259)*

Sexual
Relationships
and Behavior

**CHAPTER
EIGHT**

C H A P T E R   E I G H T

■

Love And Intimate Relationships

●

In love there are two things: bodies and words.

Joyce Carol Oates

Sex with a partner usually involves a relationship between two people. This relationship may be casual or deep, permanent or temporary, boring or exciting, pleasant or painful. The particular quality of the relationship inevitably permeates the physical act of sex and imbues it with a particular meaning. In old-time movies, romantic Romeos had a line about getting together "to make beautiful music"; the nature of the relationship between sexual partners determines, in large part, whether the music they make is the erotic equivalent of a ballad, a symphony, a rock concert, an "oldie but goodie," an advertising jingle—or, perhaps, silence.

To understand how people experience their sexuality, therefore, we must understand the nature of intimate relationships. What brings two potential lovers together in the first place? Why are some people attracted to each other, and others not? What happens as the novelty of a new relationship wears off and people get to know each other better? What does it mean to be close to another person? Does intimacy mean the same thing for men and women? Is love eternal, or does it carry the seeds of its own destruction? What is love, anyway?

Poets, novelists, philosophers, and song writers have always had plenty to say about such matters. So have psychotherapists. But in this chapter we will focus on the work of behavioral scientists, particularly social psychologists. Although behavioral scientists have been studying the joys and pitfalls of close relationships systematically for only a few decades, their findings have greatly increased our understanding of attraction, intimacy, and separation. Most researchers have focused on heterosexual relationships, and therefore, so will we, but many and perhaps most of the findings apply to homosexual relationships as well. (For more on homosexual relationships, see Chapter 14.) Since this is a sexuality text, we will concentrate on romantic and sexual liaisons, rather than other types of close relationships.

First we will define what we mean by closeness, and discuss different types of love that people experience in their close relationships. Then we will look at how and why relationships begin, how they change over time, and some of the reasons they dissolve.

THE NATURE OF CLOSE RELATIONSHIPS

Why do you call your relationship with a spouse or lover close, but not your relationship with a neighbor—or vice versa? Is closeness a feeling? A commitment? An attitude?

Social scientists have given considerable thought to identifying the common denominator that differentiates "real" relationships from mere acquaintanceships. When all the possible definitions are boiled down, the essential ingredient turns out to be **interdependence** (Kelley and Thibaut, 1978; Kelley et al., 1983). Interdependence refers to the ability of two people to influence each other's thoughts, plans, actions, and emotions. The degree of closeness in a relationship depends on how often people influence each other, how many areas of their lives they influence each other in, and how strongly they affect each other. If contacts are *frequent, diverse,* and *intense,* the relationship is close; otherwise it is not. Thus Maria and Joe may play tennis together every day, but if that is *all* they do, their relationship is not close, because their contacts are neither diverse nor intense. Even sex does not guarantee closeness if partners never share opinions or problems and rarely see each other except in bed.

Although closeness is a quality of a relationship, the *perception* of closeness can differ for the two partners. Suppose Joe greatly affects Maria's behavior; for example, when he mentions that he enjoys photography, she immediately enrolls in a photography course. But Joe takes no steps to adapt his behavior to Maria's interests. She may view their relationship as close, but he may say they are scarcely more than acquaintances. Such extremely asymmetrical relationships are unlikely to last long because of their potential for causing pain. In the usual course of events, people monitor their growing reliance on others in order to avoid being exploited (Thibaut & Kelley, 1959). Still, some differences in reliance or dependency are to be expected. Two people's perceptions of a relationship may be similar, but they are probably never identical, and sometimes they are quite different.

Perhaps you are wondering why our definition of closeness says nothing about happiness, love, respect, or other warm, cozy feelings. The reason

MEN AND WOMEN by Mel Calman © Dist. Field Newspaper Syndicate

is that although some of the most positive emotions people ever experience take place in their close relationships, so do some of the most negative. Spouses or romantic partners are more likely than most other people to make us angry or depressed (Berscheid & Fei, 1977; Fitz & Gerstenzang, 1978; Mandler, 1984). We feel close with people not because they bring us unremitting joy, but because they are important to us and have an impact on our lives. Hostility, impatience, and jealousy may threaten a relationship, but the greatest enemy of closeness is indifference.

THE NATURE OF LOVE

Of all the emotions associated with close relationships, love is the most central for people in our culture (as you can easily verify by turning the radio dial to any popular music station). But the word *love* can describe a wide variety of thoughts, feelings, and behaviors, including, among others, fondness, passion, adoration, admiration, enchantment, desire, longing, attachment, and yearning. Two people who say they love each other may not mean the same thing; they may be experiencing love in different ways.

Social psychologists often draw a distinction between **passionate love,** characterized by a turmoil of intense emotions, and **companionate love,** characterized by affection, trust, and loyalty (Brehm, 1985; Hatfield, 1988; Walster & Walster, 1978). Passionate love is emotionally intense, unstable,

BOX 8–1

Styles of Loving

Love is a many splendored thing, but different people tend to focus on different splendors. Sociologist John Alan Lee (1973, 1988) has expanded the four-fold division of love discussed in this chapter into six independent categories, which he labels with Greek names. His categories include: 1) *eros*, or romantic, passionate love; 2) *ludus*, or game-playing love; 3) *storge*, or friendship love; 4) *mania*, or possessive, dependent love; 5) *pragma*, or practical love; and 6) *agape*, or selfless love. People, says Lee, often prefer one "style" over the others. Lee's theory was recently supported by two studies involving over 1300 students (Hendrick & Hendrick, 1986). The students were asked to rate their agreement or disagreement with a series of statements about love. Statistical analysis showed that their responses tended to cluster into six groupings that corresponded nicely to Lee's categories. Here are some examples of statements associated with each "style":

Eros:
My lover and I were attracted to each other immediately after we first met.
My lover and I have the right physical "chemistry" between us.
I feel that my lover and I were meant for each other.
Ludus:
I have sometimes had to keep two of my lovers from finding out about each other.
I enjoy playing the "game of love" with a number of different partners.
I try to keep my lover a little uncertain about my commitment to him/her.
Storge:
It is hard to say exactly when my lover and I fell in love.
The best kind of love grows out of a long friendship.
Genuine love first requires caring for awhile.

fragile, and highly sexualized. The lovers lack familiarity with one another and fear rejection. Companionate love is emotionally calm, stable, reliable, and not necessarily sexualized. The lovers know each other well and trust one another.

Behavioral scientists trying to classify types of love have also borrowed some notions from the ancient Greeks. The Greeks had separate words for four kinds of love: **agape**, or unselfish love; **storge**, or attachment; **philia**, or friendship; and **eros**, or romantic love. Modern researchers have tried to pin down the determinants and characteristics of these varieties of love

Mania:

Sometimes I get so excited about being in love that I can't sleep.

I cannot relax if I suspect that my lover is with someone else.

When my lover doesn't pay attention to me, I feel sick all over.

Pragma:

It is best to love someone with a similar background.

I try to plan my life carefully before choosing a lover.

I consider what a person is going to become in life before I commit
myself to him/her.

Agape:

I would rather suffer myself than let my lover suffer.

I cannot be happy unless I place my lover's happiness before my own.

I am usually willing to sacrifice my own wishes to let my lover achieve
his/hers.

Women and men did not differ in their endorsement of statements
reflecting eros or agape. However on the average men were more ludic
than women, while women were more pragmatic, storgic, and manic
than men. These findings are in agreement with those of other studies
(see text). Some ethnic differences also emerged. For example, Asian-
Americans were more likely than whites, Hispanics, or African-Americans to be pragmatic and storgic, and less likely to be romantic. And in
one of the studies, Hispanic students appeared to be more ludic than
nonHispanics.

The success of a relationship may depend in part on whether love
means the same thing for both partners. If Herman sees love as the
excitement of the chase (ludus) while Harriet defines it as attachment
growing gradually out of friendship (storge), they are likely to be navi-
gating troubled waters before long. Similarity in "styles of loving" may
be as important as the level or intensity of love.

Which style do you think describes you?

(Berscheid, 1985). Most assume that a couple may experience different types
at different stages of a relationship, and that sometimes two or more types
can exist at the same time. Let us examine each type more closely. (For
another, somewhat finer set of distinctions, see Box 8–1.)

Altruistic Love

People who love each other often care strongly about each other's welfare. Because they care, they do things that promote their partner's well-
being, sometimes even at the expense of their own. In most religious

traditions, this type of love, altruistic and unselfish, is the ideal. When St. Paul told the Corinthians that they should love others whether or not those others deserved it, he used the Greek word *agape*. Psychiatrist M. Scott Peck, writing from a religious and spiritual perspective, but broadening the notion of care to include oneself, is in the same vein when he defines love as "the will to extend one's self for the purpose of nurturing one's own or another's spiritual growth" (Peck, 1978). By this definition, much that passes for love—dependency, possessiveness, overprotectiveness—is not love at all.

Strong feeling is not strictly necessary for unselfish love to exist in close relationships. Neither is erotic attraction. Agape is love in action rather than an emotional response. It is what people promise each other when they commit themselves for better or for worse. If the future turns out to be worse rather than better, agape may involve self-sacrifice, as when one partner nurses another who is ill or depressed, not merely out of duty but out of genuine commitment. In its purest form, agape can mean giving up a relationship if that is in the best interest of the other person. The rewards of such altruism are subtle: the knowledge that you are living according to your principles, growing spiritually, and contributing to another person's life. In literature (and occasionally in real life), lovers sometimes make the supreme sacrifice: their own lives. In Dickens' *A Tale of Two Cities*, the hero, Sidney Carton, goes to the guillotine for the sake of the woman he loves, proclaiming: "It is a far, far better thing that I do, than I have ever done; it is a far, far better rest that I go to, than I have ever known."

Agape is the kind of love that psychoanalyst Erich Fromm discussed in his classic book *The Art of Loving* (1956). It is also the kind that humanist psychologist Abraham Maslow (1968) dubbed "B-love," or love for another's being. According to Maslow, B-love can occur only between two independent, self-sufficient people. In contrast, D-love, or deficiency love, is based on neediness and the hope or expectation that another person will satisfy one's desires. Maslow believed that few people are capable of B-love, and it does seem rather rare. One researcher who studied various types of love and lovers found he could not locate a single unqualified example of agape (Lee, 1974). Most people, it seems, seek out and continue relationships in order to get their own needs met. Still, many of us would like to be capable of agape, and some of us, on occasion, are.

Attachment

If agape is lofty and rare, *attachment* is mundane and commonplace. In attachment, people feel bound to one another, desire to be together, and experience distress and anxiety when separated, even when the separation is voluntary. Attachment begins in infancy, with the bond between parent and child. It is especially noticeable when people are sick or find themselves in frightening or threatening situations, where they need the aid, comfort, and protection of others. The rewards of attachment include predictability in a relationship and a feeling of belonging and connection.

Attachment is often associated with feelings of fondness, affection, and devotion. But the object of one's attachment may or may not have endearing or lovable qualities. Attachment depends primarily on familiarity, and mere exposure over time is enough to generate it (Hill, 1978). People can become attached to someone whom they neither like nor respect. In fact, the positive pull of the familiar is so strong that it can breed strong bonds of attachment even when the other person brings pain, not pleasure. The attachment of an abused child to a cruel parent, a battered wife to a violent husband, or a puppy to an abusive owner, are poignant reminders that attachments can and do persist in the face of harsh treatment.

Close couple *As they share interests and activities over a period of time, couples who are lovers also become friends.*

Friendship

Friendship occurs when two people think highly of each other and provide each other with emotional or tangible rewards. Our friends generally see the world in a similar way, enjoy the same activities, like and dislike the same people, and value the same goals. They know our flaws and accept us anyway. Because they like us, we can generally count on them to help us and support us in various ways. They share good times and bad, and worry about us when we are in trouble.

Friends are important throughout life. But a person who always seems to be surrounded by people may feel miserably lonely if he or she has no significant emotional attachment. Many years ago, sociologist Robert Weiss (1973) distinguished *emotional isolation*, which results from the absence of a close, stable emotional attachment, from *social isolation*, which occurs when a person lacks a supportive social network. A person can belong to a dozen clubs, yet be emotionally isolated. Conversely, when people marry, they often assume their spouse will solve their loneliness problems forever, and are disappointed when this does not happen, having failed to recognize that a husband or wife cannot rescue them from social isolation.

Age, gender, and culture all affect the number and kinds of friends people have. Teenagers, for example, often seem to run in packs, yet national surveys find that adolescents and young adults are more vulnerable to loneliness than any other age group. Contrary to stereotype, elderly people tend to have more close friends than younger adults do and feel less lonely (Rubenstein & Shaver, 1982). Women tend to report having more close friends than men do; married men often say their only close friend is their spouse, while women can usually name other close friends as well (Rubenstein & Shaver, 1982). Culture affects not only the number of friends you have, but the kind you need. For example, Mexican-Americans often rely on their extended families for emotional support more than Anglo-Americans do. Anglos, in contrast, tend to rely on more casual networks, even listing fellow workers as people they depend on (Griffith, 1983).

Romantic Love

Romantic love, or erotic passion, is what people refer to when they say that they are *in* love. Romantic love, more than any other kind, has been praised by philosophers and playwrights, songsters and sonneteers. But it has also been viewed with a more jaundiced eye. Plato called it "a grave mental disease." Lord DeWar dubbed it "an ocean of emotions, entirely surrounded by expenses." And American humorist H. L. Mencken regarded it as "the triumph of imagination over intelligence." Any emotion that can elicit such opposing evaluations must be powerful, indeed.

Romantic love differs from *liking* in a host of ways (Berscheid & Walster, 1974). In romantic love there is often strong—even urgent—sexual desire. Liking can also involve sexual desire, but the feelings are typically less intense and insistent. Romantic lovers fantasize a great deal about the anticipated rewards of a relationship; their love is full of visions of tomorrow. Liking depends more on rewards already received; it is rooted in today. Romantic love is sometimes accompanied by insecurity, frustration, or jealousy; liking brings pleasure and contentment.

Psychologist Zick Rubin (1973) was one of the first to show empirically that loving and liking are horses of a different color. Rubin devised two questionnaires, a liking scale and a love scale, to differentiate between the two. The love scale includes items such as "I would do almost anything for___" and "I feel very possessive toward___." The liking scale includes items such as "I would highly recommend___for a responsible job" and "In my opinion,___is an exceptionally mature person." A person rates each item on a scale of 1 to 9 to indicate agreement or disagreement, answering with regard to someone with whom the subject has a relationship.

People who say they are in love with the individual in question generally answer differently than those who say they simply like the person. For example, lovers are more intimate and interdependent than friends, while mutual respect seems a more important component of liking than of loving. People "in love" may or may not like each other. Using Rubin's questionnaires, several researchers have found that young women tend to like their romantic partners more than young men do (Brehm, 1985). This may be one reason why young women, after a breakup, are more likely than young men to want to remain friends with their former lovers (Akert, 1984).

FALLING IN LOVE   Romantic love is a strong emotion that often develops quickly. Like other emotions, it involves both physiological arousal (for example, a pounding heart or trembling hands) and a mental interpretation of that arousal ("I'm all worked up; it must be love!") (Berscheid & Walster, 1974). People learn which situations deserve the label "love" in the same way they learn all emotional labels: from parents, peers, and cultural symbols. When, as adolescents, we find ourselves tongue-tied, flush-faced and shaky-kneed in the presence of the boy or girl next door, we look to songs, movies, magazines, and other people to tell us what we are feeling.

A person who "falls" in love perceives the object of his or her desire as someone who can provide pleasure (often sexual) and promote well-being. It follows that the less well-off and the less satisfied with life we are, the more likely we are to fall "head over heels" in love. Prince or Princess Charming seems able to give us something we lack, and holds out the promise of changing our lives and helping us to reach otherwise unattainable goals. This may explain why people are especially vulnerable to romantic love when they are on the "rebound" from another relationship. At times of emotional need, people tend to fantasize about and idealize those who they think can satisfy their needs (Shaver & Hazan, 1987; Stephan, Berscheid, & Walster, 1971). Thus the experience of falling in love seems to depend as much on the needs of the faller as it does on the qualities of the loved one—even though a person in love is likely to attribute his or her emotional state solely to the appeal of the other person.

Love is grand *Love can be shown in many ways and in many places not usually defined as "romantic."*

ROMANTIC LOVE AS A BASIS FOR MARRIAGE   Romantic love is not a modern invention; stories about impassioned lovers are as old as history itself. Romanticism reached a high point during the Middle Ages, when the doctrine of *courtly love* idealized relationships between adoring, devoted young men and unapproachable, older, married noblewomen. A young man in such a relationship passionately dedicated himself to the service of his lady, living for the day when she would at last bestow on him a kiss or an embrace. (In some cases the lady eventually bestowed sexual favors of a more daring sort.)

However, passion has rarely been a prerequisite for marriage. In many non-Western cultures, people look on marriage as a contractual arrangement that has nothing whatsoever to do with love. In Western societies, romantic love was not widely accepted as the basis for marriage until the nineteenth century. In colonial America, romance implied irrationality, which was to be avoided within marriage (Rothman, 1984). Even during the period of courtly love, marriage was regarded as a business arrangement or an institution for producing heirs, not only by aristocrats but by people of all classes. Love was considered entirely inappropriate as a motive for marrying. In 1174, the Countess of Champagne, the "Miss Manners" of her day, issued the following proclamation:

> We declare and we hold as firmly established that love cannot exert its powers between two people who are married to each other. For lovers give each other everything freely, under no compulsion of necessity, but married people are in duty bound to give in to each other's desires and deny themselves to each other in nothing. (quoted in Hunt, 1967, pp. 143–44)

Today, in contrast, most Americans believe that being in love should precede marriage. If anything, this belief has increased among young people in recent years, especially among women. Back in the 1960s, William M. Kephart (1967) asked a mostly white sample of college men and women, "If

S-o-o-o-o romantic *We get many of our notions about love from images in books, films, and video, but are those images realistic? In the many wonderful movies they made together, Fred Astaire and Ginger Rogers epitomized the cultural ideal of romantic love. What their films never showed is how Fred and Ginger fared once they settled down with a mortgage and kids.*

a man (or a woman) had all the other qualities you desire, would you marry this person if you were not in love with him (or her)?" About two-thirds of the men said "No," versus only about a fourth of the women. Kephart and others concluded that while men could afford the luxury of marrying solely for love, women had to be more practical; their financial security and that of their children depended on it. In 1976 and again in 1984, Jeffry Simpson, Bruce Campbell, and Ellen Berscheid replicated Kephart's research, again with a mostly white sample. In both studies, they found that the vast majority of both sexes had come to view romantic love as a prerequisite for marriage: 80 and 86 percent of the women and men, respectively, in 1976, and about 85 percent of both sexes in 1984. (Most of the remaining subjects were undecided.) The researchers speculated that the especially large change in women's responses was probably due in part to their increased economic, legal, and social independence, which freed them to marry for romantic rather than purely practical reasons (Simpson, Campbell, & Berscheid, 1986).

Our feelings about love, then, and the kind of love we feel, are influenced more strongly than most of us would guess by economic and social factors. And they are also influenced by the kind of culture we live in. Psychological anthropologist Francis L. K. Hsu (1981) has argued that romantic love is valued as a basis for marriage in "individual-centered" cultures like that of North America. In contrast, "situation-centered" cultures like that of China place less importance on matters of the heart. In fact, for a traditional Chinese, "love" as applied to male-female relationships might imply an illicit liaison rather than a respectable relationship. He quotes a Chinese woman who described her developing relationship with her fiancé: "We never talked about the word love when we saw each other; therefore I trust him deeply and respect him very much."

Is the romantic ideology of Western culture a realistic one, or does it create expectations that cannot possibly be met? Since most people enter marriage hoping that it will be permanent, the belief that romantic love should be the basis for marriage seems to rest on an assumption that romantic love can last forever, or at least for a long, long time. Let us examine this assumption more closely.

THE COURSE OF ROMANTIC LOVE OVER TIME We do not usually expect strong emotions other than love to persist for any length of time. We know that no matter how angry we are, eventually our tempers will cool. No matter how frustrated we may feel when we cannot achieve a goal, eventually we will find a new goal and our frustration will fade. No matter how elated we are by some achievement, soon we will once again be absorbed in everyday problems. This is all to the good: permanently intense emotions would threaten our survival by tiring the body and distracting the mind.

It follows that romantic passion, being a strong emotion, must decline with time, even though people may wish it otherwise—and this is what research finds (Berscheid, 1985; Botwin, 1985). In a classic study, Robert O. Blood (1967) compared Japanese arranged marriages with American "love matches." He found that American marriages started out with a high level of love, as measured by expressions of affection, sexual interest, and marital satisfaction. Japanese arranged marriages started out relatively low in love, compared with American marriages, but then love increased. Most significantly, as the years passed, love decreased in both groups until after ten years there were no differences. Blood concluded that "the corrosive effect of time. . .is unambiguously confirmed by our international comparisons." (Of course, some couples were more emotionally satisfied after ten years than others. We will discuss some attributes of successful relationships later in this chapter.)

A traditional Japanese wedding   *As the years pass, couples in arranged marriages and love matches have similar levels of marital satisfaction.*

Most social psychologists believe that because romantic love is based largely on fantasies about the other person, it actually carries the seeds of its own destruction. What lovers want most is to be together, but once this wish is fulfilled they are exposed to accurate information about one another, and reality intrudes upon fantasy. The knight in shining armor or the girl of one's dreams is not so glamorous when he or she is belching, snoring, or criticizing one's mother. Passion subsides, and may be replaced with disappointment or even despair. (This situation was portrayed some years ago in the movie "10," in which the hero madly pursues and ultimately wins the girl of his dreams, only to find to his dismay that she has the mind and morals of a mosquito.) According to psychologist Robert Sternberg (1985), "The divorce rate is so high not because people make foolish choices, but because they are drawn together for reasons that matter less as time goes on."

Romantic love is doomed to be ephemeral for other reasons as well. Even if a lover were to meet all expectations and fulfill every need, he or she could not continually arouse strong emotion. As time goes by, a lover's qualities and behavior become familiar, and familiarity, as you will recall, breeds affection and attachment, not passion. Of course, a lover may rearouse strong passion by threatening to withhold what the partner has come to expect—for example, by moving to end the relationship. Then once again, the stage is set for a strong emotion, but it will not be a pleasant one.

All this may seem like bad news to romantics. But there is also good news. Although romantic passion is usually short-lived, it can serve as the spark that ignites a relationship and as a precursor of other types of love: of friendship, attachment, and even altruistic love. With the passage of time, a couple may become companions in the adventure of life, with fond memories, perhaps, of the exhilaration of courtship. To some, the after-glow may seem pallid compared with the flame of the original fire, but to most it is probably a satisfying source of warmth and security.

Moreover, people can and do behave in romantic ways without experiencing earth-moving passion. They continue to enjoy romantic evenings in front of the fireplace, bring each other unexpected gifts, flirt with each other, tease and act sexy. We like to call the erotic and affectionate behavior of such couples, which seems more enduring than grand passion and more exciting than simple attachment, *romantic sentiment*. To our knowledge, no one has studied this variety of love. Our suspicion, though, is that it is most likely to flower between partners who continue to grow as individuals, bringing new ideas, experiences, and interests to the relationship.

First, however, the relationship must get started. How does this happen?

GETTING TOGETHER: HOW AND WHY RELATIONSHIPS BEGIN

A relationship begins when person A causes some change in the behavior of person B, or when B first notices A (noticing is a behavior). The earliest stage of a relationship is a time for examining the other person's physical, social, and mental attributes, judging the potential profitability of an association, and assessing the attractiveness of one's own attributes to the other person. Social psychologists have discovered several factors that help determine which relationships blossom and which ones get nipped in the bud. In general, they find, people are drawn to those who are 1) geographically available; 2) socially "appropriate"; 3) physically appealing; 4) similar to themselves; and 5) likely to respond in kind.

Physical Proximity

Some people think that relationships are made in heaven and that waiting somewhere is a one-and-only whom the gods have chosen expressly for them. If this is true, then the gods must be making up college course

A closed field setting
The setting is an important determinant of friendship when people have little choice but to interact, as they do at their place of work.

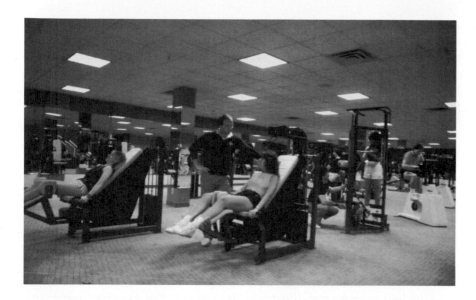

An open field setting
Personal characteristics play an important role in the formation of relationships in settings where people have many choices about whom to interact with—as at parties, singles bars, and health clubs.

requirements and setting up seating arrangements in Geology 101. Numerous studies show that one of the strongest determinants of whom we notice and form relationships with is simple **proximity:** being in the same place at the same time as the other person (see Berscheid & Walster, 1978, for a review). Both friendships and romantic relationships are most likely to develop between persons who, for one reason or another, frequently cross each other's paths. They may live in the same neighborhood, work at the same place, belong to the same groups, or take similar courses in school.

Proximity is especially powerful in situations known as **closed field settings,** where people have little choice about interacting. Examples include study groups, offices, and dormitories where roommates are selected by chance. Closed fields make certain people available for relationships and reduce the costs of pursuing and maintaining those relationships. If you have to show up at your history class every day, interacting with Sam on the right or Sue on the left costs little in terms of time or effort. But trudging two miles across campus through sleet and snow to exchange a word with Howard in Forestry 201 is a different story—and Howard had better be worth it.

In **open field settings,** in contrast, there are many opportunities to form relationships but the physical environment does not dictate an interaction with any particular individual. Bars, parties, and dances are open field settings. To predict which individuals get together in an open field setting, you must know something about their personal characteristics.

Social Eligibility

Although the physical environment is a major determinant of who is available for relationships, the social environment—our friends, relatives, and society in general—also influences us. It exerts this influence in part through cultural *norms*, or standards, that tell us who is "appropriate" for various types of relationships. Robert Winch (1958) coined the term **field of eligibles** to describe the set of people our culture considers appropriate for a given individual to date or marry. The field of eligibles generally includes those who are similar to oneself in age, socioeconomic status, religious background, intelligence, and education. Traditionally, however, the field has been defined somewhat differently for males than females. Men have been free to marry women who are younger, less educated, less affluent, and lower in power and status than themselves. Women have been encouraged to "marry up" in order to increase their own social status and financial security. Thus, no eyebrows are raised if a man marries his secretary, but people may gossip if a professional woman dates her male clerk.

The influence of social norms is sometimes subtle, and sometimes not. The woman who decides to marry a man who is much younger than herself, or the man who selects a woman taller than himself, may be questioned or even ridiculed by friends about the choice. Social norms often limit our relationship opportunities, cutting us off from people who might be well worth knowing and even loving. But norms do change. For example, interracial and interreligious marriages are much more socially accepted than they once were, and are growing in number (Murstein, 1982). The same is true for matches between older women and younger men, although a double standard in such "May-December" matches still exists (Cowan, 1984).

We should also note that sometimes the opposition of others backfires, and *increases* attraction between two people, once a relationship begins. Driscoll, Davis, & Lipitz (1972) studied this "Romeo and Juliet effect" by interviewing committed dating couples and married couples about interference from their parents. They discovered that the greater the interference, the stronger the love felt by a couple. Several months after the initial interviews, couples whose parents had become resigned and were interfering less were starting to cool off in their feelings. But those whose parents had stiffened their resistance to the relationship were even more deeply in love. This seems to be an example of what social psychologists call *reactance*, the tendency of people to react against the loss of freedom of choice.

Physical Attractiveness

People sometimes deny that physical attractiveness is important to them in choosing a partner. "Beauty is only skin deep," they protest, or "You can't judge a book by its cover." But what people say does not necessarily predict what they do. In reality, physical appearance has a major impact on the initiation of most types of relationships.

Of course, different cultures have different notions about what constitutes beauty. In some, women are supposed to be pleasingly plump, in others svelte and slender. Some cultures admire well-developed muscles in men; others do not. Even within a culture, standards of beauty change over time and differ for various ethnic and racial subcultures. But the majority generally has great power to impose its own standards of the moment, and people's self-acceptance and acceptance by others often depend on how well they meet those standards. (Sadly, one result is that minority members may have difficulty accepting their own attributes if these are not valued by the majority.)

The first major study of the role of attractiveness in the development of heterosexual relationships was conducted by Elaine Walster [Hatfield] and her associates (1966). They randomly paired 752 students with dates for a college "computer dance." Before the dance, the researchers assessed each student's intelligence, social skills, personality traits, and physical attractiveness. Then, during an intermission at the dance, the researchers asked the students individually how much they liked their dates. To their surprise, the researchers found that *only* physical attractiveness significantly influenced the ratings: the more attractive a person was, the more he or she was liked. Other attributes mattered little in comparison. Later studies found attractiveness to be important not only on first dates but on subsequent ones as well (Mathes, 1975).

Our society has traditionally considered physical attractiveness to be more essential for women than men. When people are asked what they want

Hey, good looking! *In surveys, men have traditionally placed more importance on the physical attractiveness of a date or mate than women have, but when given a choice, both sexes tend to be influenced by physical appearance.*

in a date or romantic partner, both sexes tend to put personal qualities before attractiveness. However, men typically place more importance on attractiveness than women do (Nevid, 1984). They are also more likely to stress looks when placing a "personal ad" (Deaux & Hanna, 1984). But that may be because women are more embarrassed to admit that looks count with them. What happens when they actually "size up" a potential date? To answer that question, researchers have asked college women to rate their interest in dating men after viewing pictures of candidates or after meeting potential dates. In general, when given a *choice* in the matter, women are about as influenced by a prospective date's appearance as men are (Crouse & Mehrabian, 1977; Nida & Williams, 1977; Stretch & Figley, 1980).

One reason that people prefer those who are attractive is that they accept a **physical attractiveness stereotype,** assuming that good-looking people have other desirable traits as well. When asked to rate strangers on several dimensions based solely on their photographs, people tend to guess that the attractive individuals are more sensitive, kinder, more interesting, stronger, more poised, more outgoing, happier, and more sexually responsive than the unattractive ones. They also assume that the attractive individuals have better jobs and marriages, and lead more fulfilling lives (Dion, 1986; Dion, Berscheid, & Walster, 1972; Hatfield & Sprecher, 1986).

The physical attractiveness stereotype does seem to contain at least a kernal of truth. Physical attractiveness does correlate with a positive self-concept, good mental health, self-confidence, and other positive qualities (e.g., Adams, 1981; Dion & Stein, 1978; Lerner & Karabenick, 1974). This may be the result, though, of a self-fulfilling prophecy. People tend to treat attractive persons well, and this preferential treatment may turn expectation into reality by increasing the social skills, self-confidence, and opportunities of attractive individuals. Laboratory studies support this conclusion. In one study, men talked on the telephone with a woman they had been led to believe was either attractive or unattractive. Those men who thought their phone mates were attractive were friendlier, funnier, and more animated. Their behavior, in turn, seemed to affect the woman herself (who did not know the purpose of the study). She became friendlier, more outgoing, and more self-confident (Snyder, Tanke, & Berscheid, 1977).

Some theorists believe that physical appearance is becoming more important than ever in dating and mating choices (Berscheid, 1980, 1981). As noted earlier, with increasing economic and legal independence, many women can now make choices based on personal attraction rather than practical considerations. Other social changes, including increased geographic and occupational mobility and high rates of divorce, require both men and women to establish many new relationships over a lifetime. One's co-workers, neighbors, lawyer, doctor, car mechanic, and even spouse may not stay the same for very long. The result, according to Ellen Berscheid (1980), is a society in which "one is constantly assessed very quickly by others simply on

In the eye of the beholder   *Fashions in beauty change. Slimness was not considered attractive when Peter Paul Rubens painted* The Three Graces *in 1630. Most women who are today thought to be beautiful would have been seen by Rubens and his contemporaries as in need of a good meal.*

the basis of one's appearance rather than upon one's record of actual behavior and other characteristics." This pressure may be one reason for the growing appeal of plastic surgery among both women and men.

The importance of physical appearance in our society may be depressing for those of us who are not beautiful (most of us) or those who believe that judging a book by its cover keeps people from some worthwhile "reading." But exceptional beauty also has some drawbacks. Very attractive people are sometimes viewed by others as vain, egocentric, materialistic, or snobbish (Dermer & Thiel, 1975). Although moderate attractiveness can enhance one's social standing, great beauty sometimes arouses envy and resentment. Good-looking people are sometimes perceived as unavailable for dating when in reality they are dying to be asked.

Further, as important as physical appearance is, a person does not have to be a "knock-out" to attract acceptable social and sexual partners. At the computer dance described earlier, people did not have to worry about rejection; their dates were chosen for them. But when acceptance is less certain, as it is in the real world, people avoid "aiming too high." They temper their admiration for good looks with a preference for those whose attractiveness roughly matches their own (Price & Vandenberg, 1979; White, 1980). This preference for partners who are similar to oneself extends to other qualities as well—which brings us to our fourth factor.

Similarity

In general, people seeking relationships conform to the **matching principle,** which holds that like attracts like. They tend to prefer dating and marriage partners who are similar to themselves in interests, intelligence, attractiveness, affiliations, age, family background, religious attitudes, and habits (Burgess & Wallin, 1943; Murstein, 1982). Research shows that birds of a feather not only flock together, they are more likely than others to stay together as well (Rubin, Peplau, & Hill, 1981). It is hardly surprising that most of us associate with those who resemble us; such people are likely to be doing what we are doing, and fall within our field of eligibles.

But what about that old saying, "Opposites attract"? Isn't too much similarity boring? Three decades ago, Robert Winch (1958) suggested that in mate selection, a certain amount of **complementarity** is necessary. According to Winch, in complementary relationships, one partner completes the other by bringing qualities and talents to the relationship that the other lacks. The idea that complementarity enhances a relationship is captured in the old nursery rhyme, "Jack Sprat could eat no fat/ His wife could eat no lean/ And so between the two of them/ They licked the platter clean." Yet so far, research has not supported this idea (Antill, 1983; Meyer & Pepper, 1977; Murstein, 1976).

Having said this, however, we should note that psychologists may have overlooked characteristics for which complementarity does count. Similarity clearly matters a great deal in such fundamental areas as interests or beliefs. If you love to spend your leisure time outdoors, you probably will not want to get deeply involved with someone who spends most of the weekend playing bridge or watching television. If you are a political conservative, you may have trouble living with a liberal. But in daily life, we suspect, complementarity in certain traits and skills may be valuable. If you like to be the life of the party, you may not want to marry someone who competes with you; instead you may prefer a good listener. If you love to vacuum but hate gardening, someone with the opposite preference might be appealing. We feel that further research is needed to find out what role, if any, complementarity actually plays in attraction and successful relationships.

Reciprocity of Liking

Suppose that the physical environment is right for the start of a relationship: you have frequent contact with a person you would like to date. Suppose, too, that this person falls within your field of eligibles, is attractive, and seems to share your views and interests. Are you likely to try to arrange a date? Perhaps, as long as one additional criterion is met: you have reason to believe the person wants to pursue a relationship with you. No one likes to be rejected. Therefore we are usually not attracted to others unless the feeling seems *reciprocal,* or two-way. In considering a relationship, we look for signs that the other person sincerely likes us (or is apt to like us once he or she gets to know us) before we extend ourselves. The *reciprocity rule* may be the strongest rule of attraction in human relationships (Berscheid & Walster, 1978).

The reciprocity rule contains a moral: If you wish to be attractive to others, you should develop an acceptance of and interest in others. Or, as the second-century philosopher Hecato put it, "I will show you a love potion without drug or herb or any witch's spell; if you wish to be loved, love."

Interactions

Perhaps, while reading the preceding sections, you thought of some exceptions to our various rules of attraction. You may know a woman who looks like a model yet married a homely man. Or perhaps you knows a devoutly religious person who lives contentedly with an atheist, or a couple that managed to get their relationship off the ground even though one of them had to get in an airplane every weekend to do it.

The tall and short of it
Not everyone feels constrained by cultural norms about whom they should marry. This bride didn't feel she had to "marry up."

These apparent exceptions are explained in part by the fact that people weigh the various determinants of attraction differently, depending on their particular circumstances and needs. The homely man may offer the model something she greatly desires, such as money or kindness. A devoutly religious person may put up with a partner's atheism because that partner is emotionally supportive or fun to be with. A "commuter couple" may feel that their relationship's potential rewards offset their lack of proximity.

Moreover, the determinants of attraction interact with people's individual characteristics. Consider one such characteristic, a personality trait called *self-monitoring*. People who score high on this trait tend to monitor their own behavior and modify it depending on the social situation in which they find themselves. Those who score low are less self-conscious and behave more consistently across various situations. Self-monitoring people seem to be especially concerned about a partner's physical appearance. In one study, men who were high or low in self-monitoring received file folders on two prospective dates, "Kristen" and "Jennifer." Kristen's folder indicated that she was plain looking but outgoing and friendly. Jennifer's indicated that she was good-looking but self-centered and moody. Most of the high self-monitoring men chose good-looking Jennifer, despite her negative personality traits. Most of the low self-monitoring men chose Kristen (Snyder, Berscheid, & Glick, 1985). It seems, then, that men who care about their own image are more likely than other men to care about a date's appearance. Those who are low in self-monitoring care more about a date's inner qualities.

Finally, context may promote or squelch a relationship. For example, two people who meet on vacation might embark on a romance that neither would consider back home. Conversely, two people who work together and wish to preserve their professional relationship may take pains to avoid a romance that might otherwise flower.

The Social Exchange Theory

Much of what we have discussed so far about attraction and love can be explained by a popular theory of relationships called the **social exchange theory** (Homans, 1961; Thibaut & Kelley, 1959). According to this theory, the decision to begin or continue a relationship depends on the same kinds of factors that operate in the economic marketplace: rewards, costs, and available alternatives. When two people meet, they begin to explore the contribution the other can make to their lives. They mentally construct a ledger of love, entering on one side the potential rewards each brings to the relationship (such as praise, affection, sex, practical help, good company, and insurance against loneliness) and on the other side the costs (such as loss of freedom, financial obligations, or the other person's annoying habits). If the benefits are great and the costs few, people are likely to pursue the relationship.

©1987 United Features Syndicate, Inc.

Be patient. I'm calculating the risk-benefit ratio.

Here are some ways in which our five determinants of attraction affect the "bottom line" of the relational balance sheet:

- *Proximity* reduces the costs of pursuing a relationship in terms of time, effort, and money. It increases rewards by promoting familiarity, which leads to comfort and attachment. Also, people we see often tend to be predictable, and so we feel safer around them than with others.

- *Social desirability* maximizes rewards by eliciting the approval of our friends and relatives. It reduces costs by allowing us to avoid criticism and social embarrassment.

- *Physical attractiveness* in a partner brings a person the esteem of others. A study by Sigall and Landy (1973) demonstrated this quite clearly. Some of their subjects had to evaluate a man who was seated with (and was said to be associated with) an attractive woman. Others evaluated the same man when he was with an unattractive woman or when he was alone. The man got more favorable ratings when he was with the attractive woman than when he was with the unattractive one. His evaluations when he was with the unattractive woman were actually lower than those he received when he was alone.

- *Similarity* prevents us from "aiming too high" and courting rejection. Those with similar attitudes also validate our own attitudes and reassure us that our view of the world is correct. They are predictable, and reduce our uncertainty in social situations. Since they resemble us, they are likely to want to do the things we enjoy doing.

- *Reciprocity of liking* minimizes the chances of rejection and protects self-esteem. It signals that the other person is willing to bestow rewards if a relationship begins.

According to social exchange theory, when we assess the rewards of a relationship, we compare them to what we have learned to expect or think we deserve, a standard that is sometimes called a *comparison level* (Thibaut & Kelley, 1959). This standard evolves from past experiences, observations of other people's relationships, and information obtained from reading or listening to others. If a relationship compares favorably with our expectations, we will probably go ahead with it. Some people have sadly low expectations, while other have unrealistically high ones.

People also weigh the potential rewards of a relationship against the rewards available from other relationships. The lowest level of rewards a person will accept, given the alternatives available, is that person's *comparison level for alternatives*. If Willie has few opportunities to date but he doesn't want to be alone, he is likely to respond to Althea when she shows an interest in him, even if the potential rewards are modest and the costs are high. But if droves of desirable women want to go out with him, he might pursue someone else instead, even if Althea is bright and good-natured.

THE GROWTH OF RELATIONSHIPS

We have seen that people's opportunities to form relationships, romantic or otherwise, are constrained in certain ways. Many relationships that the "gods" might consider fulfilling never have a chance to begin, and others die quickly because the obstacles to their growth are too great.

If a close relationship is to survive, the people in the relationship must adapt to certain changes in its character. According to psychologist Robert Sternberg's **triangular theory of love** (1988), love in close relationships has three components: *passion*, which is a motivational component (because it is the drive that brings people together); *intimacy*, which is an emotional component (because it involves feelings of bonding and connection); and *commitment*, which is a cognitive component (because it involves a decision). Passion, as we have seen, is destined to decline over time. Intimacy, says Sternberg, tends to increase steadily, then grow at a slower rate, and finally level off. Commitment is gradual at first, then speeds up, and finally, if the relationship continues for a long time, usually levels off (or declines, if the relationship flags).

True closeness in a relationship does not occur overnight (even if the night was very pleasant). It develops gradually, as partners begin to spend more and more time together, and share activities, thoughts, plans, and goals. In romantic relationships, it is associated with increased self-disclosure, sexual sharing, the establishment of equity, and, eventually, a decision to stop "shopping around."

Self-Disclosure

The potential rewards of a relationship are hard to judge unless two people have information about each other. Much of this information comes from **self-disclosure,** the revelation of one's needs, values, emotions, and feelings to the other person. Early in a relationship, disclosing private information too quickly can put the other person off. But in very close relationships, the personality of each partner has been "penetrated" or made known to the other in its most complete sense (Altman & Taylor, 1973; Altman, 1974). Self-disclosure is a sign of trust, and complete self-disclosure is often taken as the hallmark of a fully developed relationship (Levinger, 1977).

An unspoken rule in the ongoing process of self-disclosure is that if one person reveals some information, the other should do the same at about the same level of intimacy. As Richard Archer (1980) has observed, "Disclosure from another is a thing of value that must be paid back." If Sheila tells Larry about her previous relationships and her secret ambitions, he is not supposed to reciprocate with his views on who will win the World Series. This social rule sets the stage for a common source of friction in heterosexual relationships, for research shows that women are generally more comfortable than men are with self-disclosure. Men tend to reveal their strengths or talk about relatively impersonal matters, such as cars, sports, work, and politics. Women are more likely to reveal their weaknesses, or talk about their feelings, fears, and relationships (Rubin et al., 1980; Hacker, 1981). In marriage, when one partner discloses more, it is usually the wife (Burke, Weir, & Harrison, 1976; Hendrick, 1981). In general, men tend to want "side-by-side" relationships, defining intimacy in terms of shared activity, while women prefer "face-to-face" relationships, defining intimacy as self-revelation (Brehm, 1985). This last sex difference seems to appear early. A study of 300 eighth graders found that boys achieved feelings of closeness with each other through group activities, such as football, while girls depended on one-to-one conversations (Camarena & Sarigiani, 1985).

Some writers believe that male and female attitudes toward self-disclosure reflect different levels of comfort with intimacy. Women, they say, tend to view intimacy as a haven from lonelines. Men are more ambivalent, anticipating the danger of entrapment or betrayal (Gilligan, 1982; Rubenstein & Shaver, 1982). Others are not so sure this is true. Not all studies find men to be more ambivalent (Benton et al., 1983), and in those that do, the difference is small (Helgeson & Sharpsteen, 1987). But whatever their source, sex differences in self-disclosure are maintained and encouraged by the attitudes and responses of others. Americans tend to like women who reveal their feelings, especially feelings of love, weakness, or concern, but they dislike men who do the same. Conversely, Americans tend to like men who reveal their achievements, but view women who do so as pushy or aggressive (Brehm, 1985; Petty & Mirels, 1981).

Until recently, most writers praised the female style of intimacy and admonished men to be more emotionally expressive. Now, however, some psychologists are arguing that the female pattern has both pluses and minuses. On the plus side, self-disclosure is a bridge across the sea of differences that arise in any relationship. It reduces feelings of separation and

I'll be loving you, always
One of the secrets of a long-term, successful relationship is a commitment to commitment.

CATHY/Cathy Guisewite

Cathy, *Copyright Cathy Guisewite. Reprinted with permission of Universal Press Syndicate. All rights reserved.*

wards off loneliness. During dating and in marriage, couples who self-disclose the most also tend to express the greatest satisfaction with their relationship (Shea & Adams, 1984; Rubin et al., 1980; Hendrick, 1981). On the minus side, talking about problems can sometimes be a substitute for action, and may increase negative emotions instead of getting rid of them. Moreover, opening yourself up to another person poses certain dangers. Psychologist Elaine Hatfield (1984) observes that when people reveal their foibles and flaws, they risk betrayal, abandonment, and the arousal of anger or contempt. They also risk losing their sense of privacy and individuality. One of the greatest challenges in any close relationship is to balance the "urge to merge" and the desire to be known with one's need for autonomy and a sense of privacy.

Sexual Sharing

A relationship can be close without sexual sharing. Conversely, sex does not necessarily make a relationship close. For some people, sex is simply a form of play or recreation. They seek sex for fun, not for the establishment of deep emotional rapport (Lee, 1974). But for most people in our culture, sex is ideally an expression of love as well as a physical pleasure. As psychiatrist Robert Coles observes, sex can be a way of searching for meaning, revealing the private recesses of one's imagination and enduring the boring, demanding, and puzzling aspects of life. It is "the oasis that nourishes the progress of the journey" (Coles, in Coles & Stokes, 1985).

At one time there were fairly clear (though unstated) rules about how much sexual activity was permitted as a relationship developed. "Necking" was all right on a casual date, light petting with a steady, and heavy petting or intercourse with a fiancé. But today, the official status of the relationship seems less important in determining sexual activity than the quality of the relationship. What matters is whether two people feel affection, consider themselves a couple, and are emotionally committed (D'Augelli & D'Augelli, 1979).

Couples vary in the meaning they attribute to sex in the development of a relationship. Some have sex early, before they are actually "going together" or feel much affection for each other. Some begin sexual activity after becoming emotionally involved. And some put off sex, or at least intercourse, until they have made a permanent commitment. Degree and timing of sexual involvement do not seem to predict either satisfaction in dating relationships or the likelihood of breaking up (Peplau, Rubin, & Hill, 1977). Agreement between the partners on the place of sex in the relationship is probably more important than whether or not they "do it," or how often. The same seems true in marriage. Happily married couples usually say they have a good sex life (Hunt, 1974; Lauer & Lauer, 1986). But married life can be satisfying for some people with little or even no sex, or miserable with lots of it. People may master sexual technique, yet remain novices in matters of the heart. Long-married couples tend to view sex as just one component of marriage, along with friendship, understanding, and respect. They rarely credit sex with keeping the marriage going (Lauer & Lauer, 1986).

It probably will not surprise you that among young people, men and women differ somewhat in their attitudes toward sexual involvement, with women generally linking sex more closely to love (Leigh, 1989; Whitley, 1988). In one study, when college students were asked to rank various reasons for getting into their current dating relationship, both sexes placed the greatest value on having a good time with someone and having a friend of the other sex, and lowest priority on finding a marriage partner or having a guaranteed date. Sexual activity and falling in love were in the middle of their scale of priorities. But men as a group rated sex more highly than love, while women as a group rated love more highly than sex (Peplau, 1984). Sex differences exist in behavior as well as attitudes. Decades of studies show that although both sexes *prefer* having sex with someone they love, on the average men are more likely than women to experience casual sex, including during their first sexual experience. We will discuss these and other sex differences in sexual attitudes and courtship further in Chapter 13.

Equity

Earlier we said that when people begin relationships, they tend to balance the costs and benefits. But many social psychologists believe that as a relationship deepens, partners are likely to become less concerned with strict equality in the "transaction" and more concerned with **equity,** or fairness. Equity exists when each partner's benefits are proportional to what he or she contributes to the relationship (Walster, Walster & Berscheid, 1978). If one person is seen as contributing more, then that person is usually seen as entitled to more benefits. Suppose, for example, that one partner works full time and pays all a couple's bills while the other has quit a paying job in order to write the Great American Novel. If the employed person has to do all the laundry and cooking, or even half of it, that person is likely to view the relationship as inequitable.

Equitable relationships seem to be more satisfying than inequitable ones. Partners who are "underbenefited" tend to feel angry, while those who are "overbenefited" sometimes feel guilty (though the latter are more likely to be satisfied than the former). In the absence of fairness, the chances of one partner ending the relationship increase. But equity does not necessarily mean constant account keeping ("Let's see, I took out the garbage this week, so I deserve an extra hug tonight"). With the growth of the relationship, trust increases, and the goal becomes fairness over the long haul. People often agree to put up with inequity for a period of time with the understanding that it will eventually be restored (Traupmann & Hatfield, 1983). Moreover, a person may experience the fulfillment of the other person's needs as subjectively rewarding, despite the objective "costs" involved (Clark & Reis, 1988).

Commitment

Commitment can be defined as "an avowed or inferred intent of a person to maintain a relationship" (Rosenblatt, 1977). Committed partners stop comparing the rewards they are obtaining with those that might be available from others. Usually they have decided that the present rewards exceed those they can reasonably expect to get elsewhere. Though no one can predict his or her future feelings, commitment implies a strong desire for the

When all is said and done . . . *Love has its risks, but for most of us, those risks are outweighed by the promise of intimacy and shared joys.*

relationship to continue. For most people in our culture, it implies sexual monogamy (although behavior does not always follow belief).

Commitment is essentially an agreement, and, like other agreements, it tends to reduce costs for each participant (Berscheid & Campbell, 1981). In particular, it saves both partners the effort, time, and money that would otherwise be spent on seeking other partners. Commitment also reduces feelings of insecurity about the relationship. Once a commitment is made, a person can relax and enjoy the relationship without constantly worrying about the other partner's intentions. Commitment also serves as a safeguard for the future, when one or the other partner may not be able to provide the rewards he or she once did. In the traditional marriage vow, the bride and groom promise to love and cherish one another for better or for worse, in sickness and in health, and for richer or for poorer. In return for these promises, each partner gets the same insurance against future personal disasters.

Of course, the "insurance" is not a real guarantee of security. A partner can always back out of the agreement, and many do. But a commitment to the idea of commitment seems to enhance the chances that a relationship will survive. Two researchers studied 351 couples who had been married for at least 15 years, most of them happily. When asked what accounted for the permanence of their relationship, most men and women put the belief that marriage is a long-term commitment near the top of the list. These people had been willing to endure some temporary troubles and work through their problems. One man, married for twenty years, said, "I wouldn't go on for years and years being wretched in my marriage. But you can't avoid troubled times. . . . That's when commitment is really important" (Lauer & Lauer, 1986).

Why are some people able to make and keep a commitment while others are not? Researchers are just beginning to probe this question. Life circumstances are part of the answer. For example, when people think the time is right for marriage, courtship is likely to be relatively brief and commitment leading to marriage, rapid; but when they have educational or career priorities that interfere with commitment to a relationship, serious dating is likely to last for a long time before wedding bells ring (Surra & Huston, 1987). Personality traits also play a role. For example, there is evidence that people high in self-monitoring, which we described earlier, tend to resist commitment in dating and are willing to end a current relationship if another appealing one comes along. Intimacy also tends to develop more slowly in their relationships than in those of low self-monitoring people (Snyder & Simpson, 1987). The reasons for this await further research.

CONFLICT IN RELATIONSHIPS

"And they lived happily ever after." That is how fairy tales end. In real life, though, even the best relationships are marked by at least occasional

BOX 8–2

The Green-Eyed Monster: Jealousy

If you have ever been involved in a romantic relationship, you have probably felt at least a twinge of jealously at one time or another. Most people feel jealous when a valued relationship seems threatened by a real or imagined rival. People sometimes get jealous about a loved one's former partners, or the possibility of a future competitor. A jealous person feels threatened by actual or potential losses, including loss of face, loss of equality or fairness in the relationship, loss of self-esteem, loss of a feeling of specialness, and, of course, loss of the partner (Buunk & Bringle, 1987).

Most people who write on jealousy regard it as a complex experience involving several different emotions. Fear and anger seem to predominate, but anxiety, resentment, humiliation, depression, vulnerability, and sorrow may also occur, either in combination or sequentially. Like many negative emotional experiences, jealousy is often accompanied by uncomfortable bodily responses and obsessive thoughts. It is also associated with negative behaviors, such as brooding, nagging, aggressiveness, and even criminal assault or murder. No wonder Shakespeare, in *Othello*, called jealousy "the green-eyed monster which doth mock the meat it feeds on."

Researchers have had to rely largely on questionnaire studies to find out what sorts of people experience the greatest jealousy. The results are mostly correlational, and must be interpreted with caution. Nonetheless, many psychologists believe that certain individuals are more disposed to jealousy than others. Highly jealous people tend to have lower self-esteem than others and to be less happy and satisfied with life and with their partners (Bringle et al., 1977; Pines & Aronson, 1983). People who have traditional beliefs regarding sex roles tend to be the most jealous (Hansen, 1985). The tendency to become jealous declines with age, perhaps because as people gain more experience, they become more secure and self-confident and so are less easily threatened by real or imagined rivals (Pines & Aronson, 1983).

There is no consistent evidence that one sex is more vulnerable to jealousy than the other, but men and women may respond to jealousy somewhat differently. In one study, women said that in jealousy-arousing situations they would try to repair the damaged relationship—for example, by making themselves more attractive. Men were more apt to say they would try to repair their damaged self-esteem or save face—for example, by going out with others (Bryson, 1977).

conflicts. The more interdependent two people become, the more they have to disagree about, and the more opportunities there are for disappointment and hurt feelings. (One common source of friction is jealousy, as discussed in

The way a person interprets a partner's behavior affects the intensity of the jealousy felt (Buunk & Bringle, 1987). Research suggests that you are most likely to feel threatened when you think your partner's jealousy-arousing behavior is due to your own inadequacies or to weaknesses in the relationship, as opposed to your partner's traits or to circumstances. You are also likely to feel most threatened if you think the cause is a stable one, unlikely to change (for example, your partner's habitual lack of self-control), as opposed to an unstable one, such as an unusual situation or temporary mood.

Some writers treat jealousy as a pathological response, and often, when it is based on inaccurate perceptions of reality, it is. But because people everywhere value their close relationships and see the loss of these relationships as a threat, jealousy appears to be universal. The way people experience and express their jealousy, however, and the circumstances in which they feel threatened, depend on the particular culture. Anthropologist Ralph B. Hupka (1981) has argued that "jealousy situations" are seen as most threatening in societies that value personal ownership of property, require marriage for guilt-free sex, place a premium on personal descendants, and require marriage for economic security and social recognition. In contrast, reactions to a sexual rival or interloper are relatively mild in societies where people are not possessive about things or each other, sexual gratification is easily available, and the group is more important to a person's welfare than are children or a spouse. Thus Toda husbands and wives in turn-of-the-century India allowed each other to take lovers, and women could even have several husbands. (However, both spouses might feel angry if the other had a *secret* affair, without revealing it publicly.)

Utopian experiments in our own culture have sometimes tried to eliminate jealousy by minimizing personal possessions and competition, and abolishing romantic love and monogamy. But because jealousy is cultural as well as personal, most of us probably cannot rid ourselves entirely of jealousy without also devaluing the importance of our romantic, marital, or sexual partners. Still there are some steps that we can take to reduce the destructive impact of jealousy. We can strive to manage our jealousy gracefully. We can be careful to distinguish reasonable jealousy from overreactions. We can attempt to balance togetherness with a recognition that each partner in a relationship needs some autonomy and freedom. Above all, we can work to build communication, security, and trust in our intimate relationships.

Box 8–2.) Conflict does not mean two people have stopped loving each other, or that their relationship is doomed. In fact, the degree of love that couples report is unrelated to their reports of conflict (Braiker & Kelley,

1979). The result of conflict depends in part on the strategies the partners use to get their way, the balance of power in the relationship, and how each partner interprets the behavior of the other.

Influence Strategies

Relationship partners often have different strategies for getting their way, and the clash of influence "styles" can create tension and miscommunication. A couple may even wind up fighting over how to fight.

Some influence strategies are *direct;* that is, they involve saying what you want. Others are *indirect.* Some strategies are *bilateral*, requiring interaction between the partners; these include bargaining, asking, or reasoning ("It's silly to buy that car; it has a terrible repair record"). Others are *unilateral*, requiring only your own action; they include pouting, dropping hints, and making suggestions ("Uh, do you think perhaps we should read up a bit more on that car before we buy it?"). Table 8–1 gives examples of the various types of influence strategies.

In heterosexual couples, by their own accounts, men are more likely than women to use influence strategies that are direct and bilateral and women are more likely than men to use strategies that are indirect and unilateral (Falbo & Peplau, 1980). Men also depend more than women do on what psychologists call "hard" strategies, such as demanding, shouting, or acting assertively, while women depend more than men on "soft" strategies, such as acting affectionate or saying nice things about the other person (although women are not always "nicer" in relationships) (Kipnis & Schmidt, 1985). These sex differences, however, are not necessarily *caused* directly by gender. As we will see in the next section, in many relationships men have more power than women do. The strategies favored by men are exactly those used by people who have power and influence, whatever their sex. Those favored by women are exactly those used by people who lack power and influence, whatever their sex (Falbo & Peplau, 1980). People who have power can afford to be direct. Those without it are afraid to challenge the status quo or make the other person angry.

Both "hard" and "soft" strategies have drawbacks. People who use hard strategies often hurt their partners and arouse resentment. Those who use soft ones can lose self-respect. Sadly, in all too many cases, arguments escalate into violence. One national study found that 1 in 8 married couples had attacked each other physically during the past year (Straus, Gelles, & Steinmetz, 1981). Estimates of the overall incidence of husband-wife violence in the United States range from 25 to 60 percent of all couples (Pagelow, 1984). Physical abuse seems to be high, too, among dating and co-habitating couples (Pirog-Good & Stets, 1989; Stets & Straus, 1989). Women are as likely as men to engage in "lower level" violence—pushing, shoving, throwing things—but their actions are often in self-defense, and when they strike out, they are more likely than men to be struck back. Men are far more

Strategy	Example
Asking	"I ask him/her to do what I want."
Bargaining	"We negotiate and compromise."
Laissez-faire	"I just do it by myself."
Negative affect	"I pout or threaten to cry if I don't get my way."
Persistence	"I keep reminding him/her of what I want until he/she gives in."
Persuasion	"I try to persuade him/her my way is right."
Positive affect	"I smile a lot and am especially affectionate."
Reasoning	"I reason with him/her and argue my point logically."
Stating importance	"I tell him/her how important it is to me."
Suggesting	"I drop hints and make suggestions."
Talking	"We talk about it and discuss our differences and needs."
Telling	"I tell her/him what I want. I state my needs."
Withdrawal	"I clam up. I become silent."

TABLE 8–1
Influence strategies in relationships   These are some of the strategies people in close relationships use to try to get their way. Which strategies do *you* rely on most often?

Adapted from Falbo & Peplau, 1980, page 621.

likely to use fists, guns, and knives, and to seriously injure their partners (Makepeace, 1986; Mason & Blankenship, 1987).

There is an alternative, however. Couples who share power tend to bargain rationally, discuss their disagreements, and make compromises. They avoid hurting or alienating each other, but they also express their separate viewpoints openly and honestly. They stick to the issues instead of attacking, bullying, hurling insults—or simply caving in. Couples who are able to do this are the most satisfied with their relationships (Kipnis & Schmidt, 1985; Pruitt & Rubin, 1986). Let us look more closely, then, at the role of power in relationships.

Power

In a loving relationship, *power* may seem like a dirty word. Most young adults in this society feel that when people love each other they should share power equally, or power should not be an issue at all. But reality often differs from the ideal. A study of dating couples found that despite their own professed egalitarianism, fewer than half considered their own relationship "exactly equal" in power. When one person had more influence on decisions, it was usually the man (Peplau, 1984).

Why is this so? Your first answer might be that boys and girls learn different ways of influencing people while growing up. And that is correct—up to a point (see Chapter 12). But social psychologists have found that power in relationships is also closely tied to the education, income, and occupational prestige of those involved. People who have more of these "resources" have more power. And despite great gains by women, men often still have an advantage in these areas. In general, the greater a man's resources, the more power and status he has both outside and inside the home.

Ironically, the ideal of equity (discussed earlier) can actually reduce women's power in relationships. As you will recall, in close relationships people's notions of fairness depend on what the two partners are contributing. In the United States, people tend to assess others largely in terms of their economic worth (Crosby, 1986). Often we apply this standard both at work and at home. Because domestic work in the home is unsalaried, its true financial worth to the family tends to go unrecognized. Thus the person who "brings home the bacon" has more say in family matters than the one who cooks it (or brings less of it home).

Traditionally, these facts have favored husbands and boyfriends over wives and girl friends. There is nothing inevitable, however, about sex differences in power. Since resources can change, so can the amount of power a person has. Studies have consistently found that when wives work outside the home, their power in the family rises (Blood & Wolfe, 1960; Blumstein & Schwartz, 1983). And when men stay home to raise children while their wives go to work, the wives tend to have greater power than the husbands (Beer, 1984). But such changes in the power balance within a relationship are not always apparent to the outside world. We conduct our relationships in a context of cultural assumptions about what is legitimate and "normal" in them—so much so, that when a man and a woman do share power in a relationship, they may conspire to hide the fact from relatives and friends (Lips, 1991).

The trouble with power differences—whomever they favor—is that they often lead to power struggles. In married couples, when one spouse has most of the power, we are much more likely to find quarreling, and even violence, than when both spouses feel they have an influence on decisions (McElfresh, 1982; Yllo, 1983). Most studies find that satisfaction and stability in marriage are associated with roughly equal power in decision making (Gray-Little & Burks, 1983).

Attributions

Lovers and spouses quarrel about all sorts of things, from money to music. The way they resolve their conflicts depends a great deal on how they explain their partner's behavior. For example, when people in happy marriages or dating relationships are irritated by a partner's behavior, they tend to attribute the behavior to some temporary situation outside the relationship ("He's under a lot of pressure at work"). Discontented people, in contrast, tend to blame what they see as unchanging, general features of the partner's personality ("He only thinks of himself"). There is some evidence that the opposite is true, though, when the partner does something nice. Then contented people give the partner's personality all the credit ("She's so thoughtful") while discontented ones write the behavior off as situational ("Her girl friend probably told her to do that") (Grigg, Fletcher, & Fitness, 1989; Holtzworth-Munroe & Jacobson, 1985).

These results do not mean you should excuse or overlook a partner's abusive or obnoxious behavior. Sometimes an explanation that blames the other person is correct! In general, however, the normal tensions that arise in everyday life between lovers and spouses are more likely to get resolved if both partners resist blaming the other person's rotten personality or making personal attacks ("You're such a slob"; "You've always been lazy, just like your father"). It is far more constructuve to look at problems as something to work through together. If he is neat and orderly and she is messy and disorganized, for example, the couple can try for a compromise that makes both partners reasonably happy (she keeps all her junk in one room, with the door closed). Negotiation provides an opportunity for greater understanding and increased intimacy between the partners.

Breaking Up

Sometimes all the sweet reason in the world cannot save a relationship. Boredom, emotional problems of one or both partners, attraction of a partner to someone else, incompatible interests or goals—all can cause a relationship to crumble. One partner looks at the ledger of love and decides that a better bargain can be struck elsewhere, or that being single is better than remaining in an unhappy situation. Or the two partners mutually decide that their differences are irreconcilable and that a parting of the ways would be best for both.

Breaking up, as everyone knows, is hard to do. It is not always equally hard for both partners, though. Initiating the breakup is less upsetting and stressful than being left. "Breakers" may feel guilty and somewhat unhappy, but they remain in control. Negative feelings may be balanced by positive ones, such as relief or a sense of renewed independence. In contrast, "breakees" often feel a loss of control and experience psychological pain that can lead to physical symptoms, such as eating and sleeping problems. Couples who together arrive at the decision to split up fall somewhere in the middle; they are not as upset and heartbroken as breakees, and they retain a sense of control, but they do experience considerable stress which may be expressed in physical symptoms (Akert, 1984).

Does one sex tend to suffer more than the other when relationships crumble? So far, the findings are contradictory (Akert, 1984; Hill, Rubin, &

Hard times   *In every close relationship, there will be at least occasional feelings of hurt and anger. Successful couples learn constructive ways to negotiate their differences.*

Peplau, 1976). Age and situation are probably at least as important as gender in predicting who will experience more grief. There is some evidence, however, that for divorcing couples, the *timing* of grief tends to differ for men and women. In one study, divorced women said the worst time for them was before the separation, while the decision was still being made; divorced men, in contrast, said the worst time was afterwards (Hagestad & Smyer, 1982).

This finding supports the suggestion by some psychologists that men and women differ in their awareness of their own emotional dependence in a relationship (Brehm, 1985; Rubin, 1983). Women tend to closely monitor their relationships, whereas men often do not think much about them until something goes wrong (Holtzworth-Munroe & Jacobson, 1985). Thus men may be less aware than women of how much they depend on their partners for psychological and practical support. And they may also have less opportunity to deal with the possibility of loss before it actually occurs. After the divorce, a man's grief may be compounded by his surprise and dismay at the depth of his own feelings. (Men, we should note, also tend to have less support available to them from friends and relatives after a separation, and this may also contribute to their suffering.)

Whatever their degree of grief, men and women often have different problems to deal with after divorce. For example, women are likely to retain physical custody of their children, and that may soften the blow of separation somewhat by providing them with company and a reason for living. On the other hand, after divorce, women are far more likely than men to suffer financially, because they usually make less money and because most divorced fathers do not pay regular child support.

Breaking up, whether from a marriage, a live-in relationship, or a dating relationship, can be traumatic. It can also be liberating, freeing a person to go on to a more rewarding, healthier life. The trick, of course, is how to judge wisely whether the costs of a troubled relationship are too high to justify its continuation. As Ellen Berscheid and Bruce Campbell (1981) have noted, the freedom to stay or go has a price: it means we continually expend time and energy evaluating and reevaluating our alternatives. As behavioral scientists learn more about what causes relationships to develop and deteriorate, their findings may be able to help people make wiser choices.

THE FUTURE OF INTIMACY

Most of us think of our intimate relationships as private affairs that have little to do with the outside world. In fact, however, shifting economic conditions, social norms, and even health considerations (e.g., the threat of AIDS) affect the way we begin, conduct, and end relationships. As these conditions, norms, and considerations change, so do the ways we experience intimacy and love. As we end this chapter, we encourage you to think about how close relationships may change in the future.

As we have noted, the most intense feelings of passion seem to arise when people have strong needs that they look to others to satisfy. In the past, traditional sex roles made each sex dependent on the other in certain ways. Men needed women because they created a secure nest and provided nurturance and emotional support. Women needed men because they conferred status and provided financial security. As sex roles become more flexible, are the sexes becoming less dependent on each other for these needs? Will men and women become better friends because of increasingly similar interests on the job and in the home? Or will they become competitors? Will older woman/younger man matches become more accepted? How will the availability of jobs and the nation's need for workers affect the balance of power in families and between lovers?

And what about attraction and love? Will the aging of the baby boom generation, now in its thirties and forties, alter our standards of beauty and reduce the social value of a youthful appearance? Will love come to be seen as something people choose to do rather than as an emotion over which they have no control? Will romantic dreams continue to fuel our hopes and expectations about marriage, or will people marry for nonromantic reasons and be less disappointed when the notoriously fickle muse of romantic love decides to move on?

The answers to these questions, of course, must await the passage of time. In the meantime, we hope the information in this chapter will help you think about how to weather the inevitable storms that arise in close relationships, and enjoy the rewards that make them so precious.

. . . .

**PERSONAL
PERSPECTIVE**

FINDING THE RIGHT PARTNER—AND BEING ONE

This exercise (adapted from Cirese, 1985) asks you to think about your priorities in intimate relationships. You can never get everything you want from a relationship or lover, but you may be able to get what you want *most*. First, though, you must be clear about what that is; love that lasts is not blind.

Start by listing all the qualities you want in a lover or mate. Consider such areas as: family background, age, physical attractiveness, occupation, intelligence, financial status, emotionality, temperament, social skills, kindness, interest in sex, lovemaking style, ability to display affection, interests, housekeeping skills, personal habits, sociability, romantic inclinations, flexibility, sense of humor, political opinions, race, religion, attitudes toward children, independence, ethical beliefs. . .or anything else you think is important. Try not to include a quality merely because it is culturally or socially valued; be honest and list the attributes that really matter to *you*. This part of the exercise should take some time if you do it thoughtfully.

When you finish your list, examine what you have written. What does the list tell you about your "window of acceptance"? Is it open wide, making many potential partners available to you? Or is it narrow, letting in only those who meet certain high standards? How are the qualities on your list influenced by your gender, background, or past experiences?

Now rank the five qualities on your list that are of greatest importance to you, the ones that are essential to your well-being. If you are currently in a relationship, how well are your top five priorities being met? Do you generally seek out people with these qualities, or do you tend to "fall into" relationships with individuals who lack them. Have you ever found yourself attracted to people with characteristics that you know will cause you unhappiness or pain? If so, why do you think this has happened?

One of our students once wisely noted that people tend to think more about finding a good lover than about being one. Keeping this in mind, we now ask you to make another list, this time with the attributes you think *you* ought to bring to a relationship. You can use the categories on your first list as a guide, but feel free to delete or add items. When you are done, again rank the five qualities that seem most essential.

Are the qualities you listed for yourself similar to or different from those you want in a partner? At this point in your life, how well have you met your own standards? Are there some qualities you would like to bring to a relationship but do not? If so, what obstacles prevent you from doing so? Are you satisfied with yourself as a partner in an intimate relationship? Do you expect too much from yourself in relationships—or too little?

IN BRIEF

1. The defining characteristic of close relationships is *interdependence*, the ability of those involved to influence each other's thoughts, plans, actions, and emotions. The closeness of a relationship depends on the frequency, diversity, and intensity of contact between the two people.

2. Social psychologists often distinguish *passionate love*, characterized by intense emotion, from *companionate love*, which is calmer and more stable. Another classification is based on the Greek concepts of *agape, storge, philia,* and *eros*. Even finer distinctions are possible, as in John Alan Lee's descriptions of "styles of loving."

3. *Altruistic love* involves a desire to care for and promote the welfare of another person. It does not require strong feeling or erotic attraction.

4. *Attachment* involves a feeling of being bound to another person and is often associated with feelings of fondness, affection, and devotion. People tend to become attached to those they know well, even when those individuals are unkind and abusive.

5. *Friendship* occurs when two people think highly of each other and provide each other with emotional or tangible rewards. Friends are important throughout life, but knowing a lot of people does not necessarily protect a person from loneliness. Age, gender, and culture all affect the number and kinds of friends people have.

6. *Romantic love* is a powerful emotion that often develops quickly. The notion that romantic love is a prerequisite for marriage is not universal, and did not take hold in Western societies until the nineteenth century. Today, however, most Americans believe that one should be in love before marrying. This belief may raise expectations that cannot be met and lead to disappointment, because romantic love is based largely on fantasy and therefore carries the seeds of its own destruction. But romantic love may also set the stage for other, more permanent forms of love, including what the authors have called "romantic sentiment."

7. Five factors influence the likelihood that a relationship will begin. a) Relationships are most likely to get started in settings that encourage physical *proximity*, especially *closed field settings*. b) Social and cultural norms define others as socially desirable or undesirable partners. One's *field of eligibles* generally includes those who are similar to oneself in age, socioeconomic status, religious background, intelligence, and education. c) Physical attractiveness affects perceptions of desirability, in part because of the *physical attractiveness stereotype*. Some theorists believe physical appearance is becoming more important than ever in dating and mating choices, although most people tend to avoid rejection by not "aiming too high." d) People generally gravitate toward those who are similar to themselves in terms of interests, intelligence,

attractiveness, age, and various other qualities. e) Relationships are most likely to begin when people perceive that the other person will reciprocate their feelings.

8. The influence of the various factors involved in attraction will depend in part on particular circumstances, needs, and personality characteristics. According to *social exchange theory,* a relationship is likely to begin if the people involved perceive the benefits as great and the costs few. But a relatively rewarding relationship may be abandoned if an alternative offers even more rewards, while an unhappy relationship may continue if no better alternatives seem to be available.

9. According to Robert Sternberg's *triangular theory of love,* the survival of a relationship depends on the ability of those involved to adapt to changes in the strength of three relationship components: passion, intimacy, and commitment.

10. As a relationship grows, so does *self-disclosure.* Studies find that women tend to define intimacy largely in terms of self-disclosure, while men tend to define it in terms of shared activity. Some psychologists have argued that both male and female styles of intimacy have advantages and disadvantages.

11. Most people in our culture see sex ideally as an expression of love as well as a physical pleasure. But among young people, women tend to link sex more closely to love than men do. Agreement between partners on the role and meaning of sex in their relationship is probably more important than how or how often they "do it."

12. *Equity* exists in a relationship when each partner's benefits are proportional to what he or she contributes. Equitable relationships are likely to be more satisfying than inequitable ones.

13. *Commitment* characterizes most close relationships. Commitment reduces the costs for each participant in a relationship. A commitment to the idea of commitment seems to enhance the chances that a relationship will survive. Both life circumstances and personality traits can influence the degree of commitment a person is willing to make.

14. Even the best relationships are marked by at least occasional conflicts. During a conflict, people may use different *influence strategies* to try to get their way. In heterosexual relationships, men are more likely than women to use *direct, bilateral,* and "hard" strategies, and women are more likely than men to use *indirect, unilateral,* and "soft" strategies. These gender differences appear to stem from (power) differences. Unfortunately, in America, many people try to resolve their problems with physical violence.

15. When one person has more influence on decisions than another in a relationship, it is most often the man. Power in relationships is related

to the resources each person possesses, including education, income, and occupational prestige. Power differences often lead to power struggles; satisfaction in marriage is associated with roughly equal power in decision making.

16. The attributions people make about each other's behavior can influence how differences in a relationship are resolved. In happy relationships, people generally attribute negative behavior by a partner to a temporary situation rather than an undesirable personality trait. Successful couples view problems as something to work through together.

17. The breakup of a relationship is likely to be more stressful for the person being left than for the initiator. Both sexes suffer when a relationship breaks up, but there is some evidence that men suffer more after a divorce, and women before. Some psychologists have suggested that women are more likely than men to recognize their own emotional dependence on the relationship and to deal with their feelings before the actual separation.

18. As economic conditions and social norms shift, so will the ways we experience intimacy and love. Close relationships are private affairs, but they are influenced by the outside world.

Key Terms

interdependence *(278)*

passionate vs. companionate love *(279)*

agape *(280)*

storge *(280)*

philia *(280)*

eros *(280)*

"B-love" and "D-love" *(282)*

attachment *(282)*

"styles of loving" *(280)*

emotional vs. social isolation *(283)*

courtly love *(285)*

"romantic sentiment" *(288)*

proximity *(289)*

closed vs. open field settings *(289)*

field of eligibles *(290)*

Romeo and Juliet effect *(290)*

reactance *(290)*

physical attractiveness stereotype *(292)*

matching principle *(294)*

complementarity *(294)*

reciprocity *(295)*

self-monitoring *(296)*

social exchange theory *(296)*

comparison level *(298)*

comparison level for alternatives *(298)*

triangular theory of love *(298)*

self-disclosure *(299)*

intimacy *(299)*

equity *(301)*

commitment *(302)*

influence strategies *(306)*

attributions *(312)*

**CHAPTER
NINE**

C H A P T E R   N I N E

Sexual Activities

*Familiar acts are
beautiful through
love.*

Percy Bysshe Shelley

hapter 5 began with a musical analogy that compared sexual anatomy to a violin and sexual physiology to an explanation of how the violin works. But we left out a very important element in our analogy: the composition to be played. Just as music may take many different forms, from a march to a mazurka, sexuality can be expressed in many different ways. Intercourse is what most of us first think of when we hear the word *sex,* but erotic fantasy, masturbation, caressing, oral-genital techniques, and anal stimulation can also form part of a person's sexual repertoire.

In this chapter we are going to discuss all these techniques of sexual arousal and behavior. Before we begin, though, a few cautionary words are in order. The vocabulary we use when talking about sex reveals certain conscious or unconscious assumptions about the functions and attributes of sexual activities. In Chapter 2 we saw that the Victorian values of thrift, self-control, and prudent investment spilled over into the sexual arena. People talked about "squandering" their sexual resources and "depleting" their sexual reserves. In fact, in those days the slang expression for having an orgasm was "to spend." Contemporary use of terms like *technique* and *performance* reveal a new set of values. People in today's society often assume that technical solutions are the key to most problems, that people ought to work to improve themselves, and that sex is a skill like any other, to be mastered by following certain well-defined steps.

This is the age of how-to books. Technical manuals offer instruction on everything from raising vegetables to filing for divorce to making love. Information on how to perform sexually can be very useful, of course. One way or

another we have to *learn* how to perform sexually, and sometimes trial and error is not enough. But no matter how much information is available, sexual activity is more than merely learning the right "moves." If we return to our musical analogy, we might compare sexual technique to hitting all the right keys or plucking all the right strings. With practice, most people can develop a certain competence. But a real musician has something more—an elusive quality that we might call *inspiration*. In lovemaking, such qualities, including a capacity for psychological intimacy, honesty, a concern for the partner's feelings, an ability to abandon oneself to passion, and a healthy respect for one's own desires and needs are as important as assembling the right apparatus and performing the right acts.

Having said this, we turn now to the acts themselves. We will use the term *sexual act* to mean any activity that can give oneself or another person sexual pleasure. We begin with those acts that do not necessarily require the presence of another person and then consider those that, like the tango, take two to perform.

SEXUAL FANTASY

One of the most common sexual behaviors, and certainly the most effortless, is simply thinking about sex. Sexual fantasies, either fleeting or elaborate, can occur in any setting at any time—even during sleep, in which case they are called sexual dreams. Much of the research on sexual fantasy has focused on those that occur during masturbation. Kinsey and his colleagues (1948) found that some 89 percent of all males who had masturbated (which was most males) had used fantasies as a source of stimulation during masturbation, and some 72 percent had more or less always done so. The figures for females were somewhat lower: 64 percent of those who had ever masturbated had fantasized, but only 50 percent had done so regularly (Kinsey et al., 1953).

These findings have led some sexologists to argue that men are more easily aroused than women by erotic thoughts and visual images. That was Kinsey's own view; he believed women were dependent on actual physical contact. But not everyone agrees. William Masters, Virginia Johnson, and Robert Kolodny (1986) report that in a sample of 300 women aged eighteen to thirty-five, 86 percent had erotic fantasies at various times. In another study, 97 percent of Canadian college women responding to a questionnaire reported having experienced sexual fantasies. Although daydreaming fantasies were the most common, only 27 percent of women who had experienced intercourse said they never fantasized during intercourse, and only 13 percent of those who had masturbated said they had never fantasized during masturbation (Pelletier & Herold, 1988). Still other research has found that the frequency of fantasy during daydreams, masturbation, and lovemaking is similar for men and women (Knafo & Jaffe, 1984). In at least one study, women actually reported fantasizing somewhat more often than men during intercourse (Hessellund, 1976). For many women, fantasies supplement the physical stimulation, boost arousal, and increase the probability of orgasm (Sholty et al., 1984).

Fantasy Themes

Sexual fantasies can sometimes cause considerable anxiety, and the reason is not hard to find: more often than not they involve some sort of forbidden or unusual behavior. In fantasy, a person can safely "try out" all sorts of things that he or she has never done—for example, doing a striptease or having public sex. Heterosexuals, although they usually fantasize about other-sex partners, sometimes imagine same-sex partners. Similarly, homosexuals will sometimes fantasize about other-sex partners.

Sexual reveries can range from elaborate "stories" to brief visual images. In general the most common themes include the following:

- sex with a different partner, such as an anonymous stranger, an acquaintance, a previous lover, or a famous person;

- sex with more than one person at a time;

- forcing or seducing someone into having sex or being forced or seduced by someone else;

- techniques or acts a person would not ordinarily engage in, ranging from common ones, such as oral sex, to highly taboo ones, such as sex with animals;

- sadism (enjoying inflicting pain) and/or masochism (enjoying receiving pain or being tied up);

- watching other people having sex;

- enjoying a romantic interlude with a partner who behaves exactly as the fantasizer would like.

In addition to allowing us to do daring or forbidden things in perfect safety, fantasies also permit us to enjoy, in our imagination, perfect sex, unmarred by bras that won't unlatch, dragon breath, or annoying interruptions. In her novel *Fear of Flying* (1974), author Erica Jong had her heroine rhapsodize about one such fantasy, which she called the "zipless fuck": "The zipless fuck was more than a fuck. It was a platonic ideal. . .when you came together, zippers flew away like rose petals, underwear blew off in one breath like dandelion fluff. . . ."

Studies done during the 1970s found that certain themes were more characteristic of one sex than the other. Not surprisingly, the differences tended to reflect cultural stereotypes about powerful, aggressive males and sought-after females. Men were somewhat more likely than women to imagine impersonal sex with a stranger, group sex, forcing someone to have sex, or overcoming a woman's initial resistance (Hunt, 1974; Sue, 1979). On the other hand, women seemed more likely to visualize romantic situations (Shope, 1975) or being overpowered or forced to have sex (Hunt, 1974; Sue, 1979). But Masters, Johnson, and Kolodny (1986) believe sex differences in fantasy themes have been exaggerated. In recent years, they say, they have been finding women's sexual fantasies to be quite explicit and sexually detailed: "Our impression is that men and women are more similar than different in their sexual fantasy patterns."

Fantasy versus Reality

Perhaps you have heard that sexual fantasies have nothing to do with reality. That is not quite right. Many fantasies have little or nothing to do with a person's preferences in real life, but others are closer to actual wishes. The relationship of fantasy to reality depends on the person and the nature of the fantasy.

Consider, first, female "rape" fantasies. This label is a misnomer. Rape is a scary, degrading, humiliating experience. But in fantasies about forced sex, the force is under the woman's own control, and the imagined experience is self-enhancing rather than humiliating. For example, a woman may imagine herself as a harem slave seduced by an irresistibly attractive sultan, or she may fantasize about before forced into intercourse by several men who adore her body and cannot contain their desire for her. Many psychologists and psychiatrists believe that fantasies of this sort allow women to let go and enjoy the thought of engaging in sex without taking responsibility or feeling guilty. Such fantasies often begin in adolescence, when a girl is still ambivalent about her sexual feelings. If the fantasy occurs during masturbation, the resulting pleasure is reinforcing and the fantasy tends to persist. But the fantasy need have nothing to do with reality. A woman who enjoys being dominated in fantasy often has a forceful, independent personality and is successful in her personal and professional life (Singer & Switzer, 1980).

Other "taboo" themes may also be quite unlike anything a person would actually want to have happen. As Masters and Johnson (1986) point out, a person who daydreams about robbing a bank does not necessarily have a criminal mind, nor does daydreaming about being a war hero necessarily mean you want to go to war. Similarly, daydreaming about other partners does not necessarily mean you want to be unfaithful to your partner, nor does thinking about group sex mean you wish to try it.

Sometimes, though, people do "try out" their fantasies——with a willing partner, with "swingers" groups, with prostitutes. There may possibly be a sex difference in this regard. Masters and Johnson (1986) say that most women they have studied have no interest in acting out taboo fantasies about rape, incest, sex with animals, or sadomasochistic sex. In contrast, many men say they might be willing to try out such taboo acts under the right circumstances.

Psychologists are just starting to study the interactions between personality, fantasy, and actual behavior. In one study, men filled out questionnaires that measured their aggressive tendencies, their likelihood to commit rape in the future, and their actual coercive sexual behavior in the past. The men also reported the frequency of coercive sexual fantasies. Both aggressive tendencies and coercive sexual fantasies were associated with the likelihood to rape and with past coercive behavior. Although these results are only correlational, the authors of the study speculate that at least in some men, seeing aggressive images (for example, in violent pornography) may stimulate aggressive sexual fantasies that may then lead to sexually coercive behavior (Greendlinger & Bryne, 1987). (In Chapter 16 we will discuss more direct evidence for a link between the viewing or reading of violent pornography and anti-woman attitudes and behavior.)

In sum, the relationship of fantasy to reality is a complicated one. It is wrong to assume that a sexual fantasy must reflect a real wish. It is just as wrong, however, to assume that fantasies *never* have any connection with reality. Moreover, if fantasies do sometimes "lower the threshold" for certain acts, that may be either good or bad, depending on the act. For example, if a person wants to participate in oral sex, but feels inhibited about it, fantasizing about it may make the actual act more acceptable or enjoyable, which is a desirable outcome. One friend of ours notes that fantasies can be "undress rehearsals" for things you've never had the chance (or nerve) to try.

Is Fantasy "Healthy"?

Just as the relationship of fantasy to reality is complex, so is the issue of fantasy's role in a healthy sex life. For many years, the only mental health professionals to discuss sexual fantasies in any depth were psychoanalysts, and they generally took a gloomy view. Fantasies about anything but ordinary sex with one's regular partner were deemed to be immature and a sign of pathology. Such thoughts, according to the psychoanalysts, were a way of avoiding sexual anxiety, escaping from the reality of sex with an unloved partner, or punishing a partner by disengaging emotionally.

Today, however, most sexologists take quite a different view. Obsessional fantasies *can* be a sign of psychological problems. However, studies show that most people who fantasize are ordinary men and women who show no signs whatever of psychological disturbance (Hariton, 1973; Campagna, cited in Singer & Switzer, 1980). And while some fantasy themes may be upsetting to the fantasizer, most people enjoy their sexual dreams and daydreams. Fantasy adds variety to their sex lives and increases their sexual pleasure. For this reason, most therapists advise people to simply go ahead and enjoy their sexual thoughts. Some therapists even suggest that partners turn each other on by sharing their fantasies. Such sharing, they say, is not only a form of sex play but an intimate means of communication: "Infantile, symbolic, fetishistic and generally wild fantasies are part of love, and only a problem if they take up too much time and start spoiling the full reciprocity of sex. . . ." (Comfort, 1986).

MASTURBATION

Masturbation, which is also called self-stimulation and autoeroticism, is probably practiced by at least some members of every human society. As we saw in Chapter 1, cultural attitudes range from bemused tolerance to total condemnation backed up by the threat of physical punishment.

Views in our own society fall toward the hostile end of the continuum. For centuries the rationale for denouncing masturbation was the Biblical injunction against "wasting seed," but in the nineteenth century people began to consider masturbation a danger not only to the soul but to physical and emotional health (see Chapter 2). Vestiges of this belief remain. When Masters and Johnson did their laboratory studies in the 1950s and 1960s, every man questioned believed that "excessive" masturbation could bring on mental problems. (None could define precisely what "excessive" meant, but each was certain that it was more often than he himself masturbated—whether the frequency was once a month or three times a day.)

In his analysis of the Playboy survey, Morton Hunt (1974) found that masturbation was one of the few remaining unmentionables, even for men and women who considered themselves sexually liberated. Almost none of Hunt's respondents could bring themselves to tell lovers or mates that they still occasionally masturbated. Although only about a third of those older than thirty-five agreed with the statement "Masturbation is wrong," and only about a sixth of those younger than thirty-five agreed with it, the in-depth interviews that supplemented the questionnaire data revealed that guilt and shame about one's *own* masturbation were still common and had roots in adolescence:

MALE MASTURBATION

When I was an adolescent and would get an erection, I'd want to grab it and do things to it—I'd be almost sick with wanting to—but I felt too terrified. (Male, 38)

I worried and held back, and fought it, but finally I gave in. The worry didn't stop me, and doing it didn't stop my worrying. (Male, 25)

. . .I tried not to, and wept and prayed, but I did it anyway. But that was only for a little while. As soon as I fell in love with a boy, at the age of sixteen, I got the strength to stop, and I felt clean and decent again—until the next time. And then I stopped again—and so it went. (Female, 38) (Hunt, 1974, pp. 78, 79, 95)

Our own informal classroom surveys find that uneasiness about masturbation is still common. Students who will anonymously answer questions about premarital intercourse, orgasm, oral sex, and homosexuality will sometimes refuse to respond at all to queries about their masturbation experiences and practices.

Is Masturbation "Healthy"?

Although people today are probably better informed than they once were, enough misconceptions remain to make it worth saying that masturbation, in and of itself, does not cause any sort of physical or mental problem. Naturally, if someone did nothing else all day but sit around and masturbate, we would suspect that person of having some sort of emotional problem, but the compulsiveness of the behavior and the person's isolation from other people would be the proper focus of our concern, not the act of masturbation per se.

Over the years, the attitudes of psychologists and psychiatrists toward masturbation have changed considerably. At one time most mental health professionals went along with the traditional psychoanalytic view, which held that masturbation in adulthood prevented a person from developing "true genital heterosexuality." Masturbation was supposedly immature, and, at best, a crutch to be used when intercourse was either unavailable or inappropriate.

Today, however, the prevailing view is that masturbation is a perfectly valid way to get rid of sexual tension and an excellent way to get in touch with one's own body—literally. Some theorists have pointed out that during adolescence, learning to be sexual *solely* through masturbation can have certain drawbacks. For instance it may promote a sexuality that is too genitally focused or impersonal (see Chapter 13). But mental health professionals see masturbation in a generally positive light. They do not regard it as a substitute for anything, but simply as one sexual alternative among many.

In fact, in only a few decades, masturbation has been transformed from a symptom into a treatment. Sex therapists often prescribe it for women who have never experienced orgasm, as a way of learning how (see Chapter 11). Some therapists also advise men to masturbate in order to develop ejaculatory control and explore new sensations without the pressure that can occur when a partner is present (Zilbergeld, 1978).

Masturbation Techniques

By far the most common way men masturbate is by encircling the penis with one hand and moving the hand rhythmically back and forth across the glans and shaft. Men differ considerably, though, in how much of the penis they touch while stroking it, how much of the hand they use (for example, full fist or thumb and two fingers), and in the rhythm and pressure they use. In Hite's study of male sexuality (1981), many men said that they accompanied penile stimulation with stimulation of other body parts as well, most notably the testes and the anus. Interestingly, thrusting was almost never reported. Many men like to use some type of lubricant to reduce irritation from too much friction. Common ones are hand and body lotions, massage oils, sterile jelly, saliva, and soap and water. A few men masturbate by

squeezing the penis, rubbing it between both hands, or rubbing it against a bed or other object. According to sex therapist Bernie Zilbergeld (1978), occasionally these atypical methods, if used exclusively, can cause problems during intercourse with a partner because the stimulation is so different in the two activities. Zilbergeld suggests that men who use atypical methods also try to learn the usual stroking technique.

Female masturbation techniques seem to vary even more than do male techniques. Kinsey reported that 84 percent of all women who had ever masturbated stimulated the clitoris or the minor lips or both, but they did so in very different ways. Some used a single finger, others several fingers, and still others the entire hand. Some women pulled on the lips instead of stroking them. Another technique was to rub the major lips, usually by applying general pressure to the whole area. Nearly 10 percent of Kinsey's females had masturbated at times by crossing their legs and pressing them together, which causes pressure on the entire genital area. A few women masturbated to orgasm by developing muscular tension throughout the body, usually while lying face-down on a bed and sometimes while pressing the genitals against the bed, a pillow, or some other object. About 11 percent of the women in the sample stimulated their breasts, usually while stimulating the genitals as well. A very small percentage could reach orgasm from breast stimulation alone.

Kinsey also found that only about 20 percent of the women in the sample had ever inserted something into the vagina while masturbating. When they did, the insertion most often consisted of placing a finger just beyond the muscular ring surrounding the vaginal entrance to anchor the hand while

FEMALE MASTURBATION

it stimulated the outer part of the genitals. Many women stopped inserting things into the vagina once they became more experienced with masturbation and more familiar with their own anatomy and sexual response.

Finally, about 11 percent of Kinsey's female sample depended on a miscellaneous assortment of techniques, including rubbing the genitals against a pillow, clothing, a chair, or some other object: applying a stream of running water to the genitals; douching; using a vibrator (probably more common now than in Kinsey's day); administration of enemas; and even urethral insertions. Two percent of the women reached orgasm through erotic fantasy alone, without touching any part of the body.

In her study of female sexuality, Hite (1976) also asked about masturbatory techniques. The majority of her sample preferred clitoral or vulval stimulation while lying on the back. However, some preferred to lie on their stomachs. Most women stimulated the clitoral area, but not the clitoral glans itself. Only a few inserted something into the vagina, even occasionally. Women differed in the leg position they preferred. Some needed to have their legs apart, others preferred them together, or bent, or up in the air.

Incidence of Masturbation

Someone once said that if masturbation really caused hairy palms and nearsightedness, as the Victorians thought it did, we would be a nation of hirsute myopes. Kinsey and his colleagues (1948) found that virtually all the men they surveyed—92 percent—masturbated at some time in their lives, and most did so frequently. And they found that 62 percent of all women masturbated at some time in their lives, most of them to the point of orgasm (Kinsey et al., 1953). (The onset of masturbation was different for men than for women. Most men masturbated by the end of adolescence but many women did not discover masturbation until their twenties, thirties, or forties. We will have more to say on this sex difference in Chapter 13.)

Figures from the Playboy sample (Hunt, 1974) are similar to Kinsey's but were computed in a different way. Kinsey's figures are statistical estimates of cumulative, lifetime figures. They indicate the percentage of the total sample that would eventually masturbate during their lifetimes, whether they already had or not. The Playboy figures simply reflect what had happened in the subjects' lives up to that point. Morton Hunt, in his report of the Playboy results, concluded that masturbation had become at least slightly more common than it was in Kinsey's day. Hunt also reported that people—especially females—were starting to masturbate at an earlier age than Kinsey's subjects, and they also masturbated more frequently. (See also Atwood & Gagnon, 1987.)

Another difference between the Kinsey findings and the Playboy findings is in the frequency of masturbation among married people. In Kinsey's study about 40 percent of husbands in their twenties and thirties masturbated, with a median rate of about six times a year; in the Playboy study more than 70 percent of young husbands masturbated, with a median rate of twenty-four times a year. Similarly, in Kinsey's study about 30 percent of young wives masturbated, with a median rate of ten times a year; in the Playboy study almost 70 percent of young wives masturbated, with about the same median rate.

What all these numbers suggest is that masturbation is not merely a substitute for intercourse, as the traditional psychoanalysts contended. Hunt found that among both married and unmarried people intercourse had become more frequent, but so had masturbation. Moreover, people who have frequent intercourse seem no less likely to masturbate than those who have intercourse only rarely (Abramson, 1973). Intercourse and masturbation, then, are *not* mutually exclusive.

KISSING, CARESSING, AND STROKING

The entire skin is a sexually sensitive organ, and people generally like to be kissed and touched, whether these activities lead to genital sex or not. Sex between two people typically begins with whole-body stimulation; the partners may simply lie together for a few moments, enjoying the sensation of skin on skin. People usually then proceed to manual or oral stimulation of specific erogenous areas, such as the breasts, the inside of the thighs, and the genitals. Traditionally, these activities have been lumped together in a single category called **foreplay.** The word is revealing. It reflects the common view that manual and oral activities are merely warm-up exercises in preparation for the main event, which in the case of heterosexual sex is assumed to

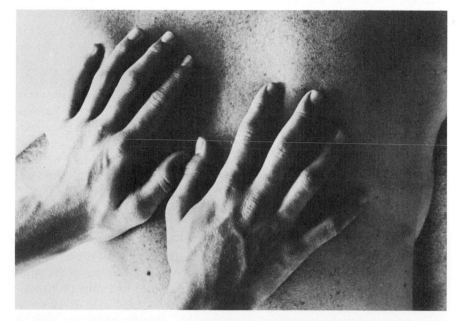

Skin on Skin   *Sex is first and foremost a touching experience.*

be vaginal-penile intercourse. Yet non-coital activities can also occur during and after intercourse, and good sex can take place without the occurrence of intercourse.

There are no simple rules for how to touch another person, because different people have different preferences. For example, one woman may have sensitive breasts and want her partner to stimulate them lightly. Another may like more vigorous stimulation that goes on for quite a while. People also differ in the way they like their genitals touched. Most men seem to prefer firm pressure, and most women prefer a gentler hand, at least in the earlier stages of arousal, but there are many exceptions. Part of getting to know another person sexually is learning which techniques the person favors.

Men and women today seem to spend more time on sexual caressing than their parents and grandparents did. In Kinsey's study (1948) college-educated men reported that foreplay lasted from five to fifteen minutes or more, while those with less education reported that it was much briefer. But in the Playboy survey Hunt found that the median for both college and non-college men was fifteen minutes. He also found that young people spent more time than older people.

Yet sex therapists say that many people still rush through foreplay or perform it in a stereotyped and utterly predictable way. For heterosexuals the script goes something like this. Step one: male and female kiss. Step two: male stimulates female's breasts manually or orally for a few seconds, or perhaps a couple of minutes. Step three: male proceeds directly to the female's clitoris, while the female simultaneously strokes the male's penis. Step four: as soon as vaginal lubrication begins, the male inserts his penis. Like any script that is followed without variation, this one can destroy spontaneity and lead to monotony. There is some evidence that homosexuals in committed relationships understand this somewhat better than heterosexual couples, and go about their lovemaking in a more leisurely, less stereotyped fashion (see Box 9–1).

It seems clear that men and women are not always on the same wavelength during love-making (Denny, Field, & Quadagno, 1984). Women often say that they would like more emphasis on touching, especially whole-body touching, both before and after coitus. Men, too, have their complaints. When we ask our students to write down their sexual problems anonymously, men sometimes say they wish their female partners would initiate more often and take a more active role during lovemaking.

ORAL-GENITAL SEX

In oral-genital sex, one partner stimulates the genitals of the other with the tongue or lips. In **fellatio** (rhymes with Horatio) the recipient of the stimulation is male. Although the word comes from the Latin *fellare*, "to suck" (slang expressions include "to blow," "to give a blow job," and "to go down on"), many variations in technique are possible. Besides gently sucking on

the penis, one may slide the lips up and down over the glans and shaft, lick the penis, or use a feathering motion with the tongue. In **cunnilingus** (pronounced as it is spelled, with stress on the third syllable) the recipient is female. The word comes from the Latin *cunnus*, for "vulva," and *lingere*, "to lick," and slang expressions include "to eat," "to eat someone out," and "to go down on someone." Again, many variations in technique are possible. The partner may gently suck the clitoris, use the tongue to massage the clitoris or the area around it, or insert the tongue into the opening of the vagina. (One should not blow air into the vagina, however; it could get into the blood stream and cause a life-threatening embolism [obstruction] in a blood vessel, although this is rare.) In both fellatio and cunnilingus, individuals need to communicate clearly which kinds of stimulation they find most effective.

SEXUAL CARESSING

Simultaneous performance of oral sex by both partners is called *sixty-nine* (or sometimes "soixante-neuf," which simply means sixty-nine in French), because of the numerals that are vaguely suggested when two people lie next to each other, head-to-tail. Some couples like "sixty-nining" because they feel it permits total involvement. Others find it less satisfactory, because they find it hard to concentrate fully on both giving and receiving pleasure. They say it is a little like trying to rub your stomach and pat your head at the same time.

Incidence of Oral-Genital Sex

Half of all states still have laws banning "sodomy," which is a catch-all term covering not only anal but also oral sex (Morosco, 1987). Yet surveys show that most Americans today approve of oral sex. In the Playboy survey,

BOX 9–1   ## Are Gays And Lesbians Better Lovers?

In 1979 Masters and Johnson published *Homosexuality in Perspective,* which supplemented their original report on heterosexual sex in the laboratory (1966) with one focusing on gay men and lesbians. The book offers an impressionistic account of homosexual-heterosexual differences in lovemaking—an account that clearly favors homosexuals. According to Masters and Johnson, homosexual couples in their sample who had lived together for at least a year tended to take a more free-flowing, relaxed approach to sex than did married heterosexual couples. The homosexuals, they say, treated each sexual activity as something to be appreciated in and of itself, with orgasm just one more step in the exchange of sexual pleasure. In contrast, heterosexuals were performance-centered and seemed to be in a hurry to "get the job done." "At times," reported Masters and Johnson, "they [the heterosexuals] created the impression that the objective experience of goal attainment was valued almost as much as the subjective experience of orgasmic release."

Masters and Johnson describe specific differences between homosexuals and heterosexuals. For example, lesbians spent considerable time holding, kissing, and caressing a partner's total body before touching the breasts and genitals. Heterosexual men rarely spent more than a minute on these activities before stimulating the partner's breasts or genitals. When the lesbians did get to breast play, the approach was nondemanding and devoted to enhancing the experience of the moment. Heterosexual men, in contrast, spent less time on breast play and seemed less concerned about the partner's responses. Lesbian women were aware that at certain times in the menstrual cycle (usually before menstruation) a woman's breasts may be so tender that sexual stimulation causes pain, and they often asked their partners if there was any discomfort. Most men were unaware of this problem, apparently because their partners had never told them about it. Finally, lesbians usually stimulated a partner's vulval lips, mons, inner thighs, and

three-fourths of the men and four-fifths of the women disagreed—most of them strongly—with the statement, "It is wrong for a man to stimulate a woman's genitals with his lips or tongue." Even more men and nearly as many women disagreed that it was wrong for a woman to stimulate the male genitals with her lips or tongue (Hunt, 1974). Although there are no statistics from the Kinsey survey that permit a comparison, it seems clear that attitudes have become much more tolerant in the past generation or two. Where oral sex was once nearly unmentionable, today ordinary movies depict it

vaginal opening before stimulating the clitoris. Men were likely to stimulate only the clitoris.

Gay men, like lesbians, tended to spend more time on whole-body contact than did heterosexuals. After initial kissing and caressing, most moved on to nipple stimulation, either oral or manual. In contrast, only three or four wives out of a hundred stimulated their husband's nipples, and the heterosexual men were less responsive to this stimulation than were the homosexuals. When homosexual men stimulated a partner's genital area they tended to included the anus, thighs, perineum, scrotum, and lower abdomen. Heterosexual women typically confined their attention to the penis and scrotum. Gay men often stimulated the frenulum, the area just below the corona that is one of the most sensitive parts of the penis. Women usually concentrated on the shaft of the penis, rarely paying special attention to the frenulum. Finally, gay men tended to watch their partners closely to gauge the level of sexual excitement and then purposely prolong the partner's excitement without bringing on an orgasm. Women rarely did this.

Masters and Johnson do not come right out and say that homosexuals are better lovers, but that is their implication (see also Masters, Johnson, & Kolodny, 1986). They point out that homosexuals have the advantage of "intragender empathy," which is a fancy way of saying that a homosexual person knows what a partner's subjective experience is like because it is similar to his or her own. Hetereosexuals, who do not have this advantage, must rely on verbal communication. Masters and Johnson note that most of the heterosexuals who performed sexually in their laboratory did not communicate their sexual needs and preferences well, even though they were all sexually experienced and were obviously not shy.

One caution: Masters and Johnson do not say precisely how many couples in each group fit their general description. Their findings are thought-provoking, but they need to be replicated by other researchers.

(though not explicitly) or refer to it in dialogue. (In Alan Alda's film *The Seduction of Joe Tynan*, Alda says to actress Meryl Streep as he sucks on a grape, "I'm very oral." She replies slyly, "Yes, so I've noticed. . . .")

As for actual behavior, the changes since Kinsey's day are truly startling. In Kinsey's study only about two-fifths of married males said their wives had ever performed fellatio for them; in the Playboy survey nearly three-fifths had had it performed by their wives in just the past year. Similarly, in Kinsey's study only two-fifths of married men had *ever* kissed or tongued their

ORAL-GENITAL STIMULATION: FELLATIO

wives' genitals; in the Playboy survey nearly two-thirds had done so in just the past year.

The greatest changes have occurred among men without college educations. In Kinsey's day very few had oral sex with their wives, although they might have had it with prostitutes. But differences between college educated and non-college educated men have disappeared. Among young married people, experience with oral-genital sex is almost universal (Hunt, 1974). It has also become part of the "sexual scripts" of many young, single people who are just beginning their sex lives (Gagnon & Simon, 1987). In fact, teenagers today often have oral sex before they experience intercourse, a reversal of the pattern that used to hold. In one study, over half of the teenage boys and two-fifths of the teenage girls interviewed had had oral sex (Newcomer & Udry, 1985). One of the attractions of oral sex for young people may be that it allows them sexual pleasure without the need for birth control.

Behavior Versus Feelings

Numbers do not tell us how people feel about performing oral sex, only how many do it. We cannot assume that because most people now perform fellatio and cunnilingus, they all feel entirely comfortable about it. As sociologist Lillian Rubin (1976) has observed, "When, in the course of a single lifetime, the forbidden becomes commonplace, people may do new things, but they don't necessarily like them." During the 1970s, Rubin interviewed fifty white, working-class couples in the San Francisco area about all aspects of their lives, including sex. She reported her findings in an absorbing book called *Worlds of Pain: Life in the Working-Class Family* (1976). Among other things, Rubin learned that although 70 percent of the couples had engaged in oral sex, many of the women had reservations about it. One woman said:

> I let him do it, but I hate it. He says I'm old-fashioned about sex and maybe I am. But I was brought up that there's just one way you're supposed to do it. I still believe that way, even though he keeps trying to convince me of his way. How can I change when I wasn't brought up that way? (With a pained sigh.) I wish I could make him understand. (p. 138)

When a woman like this had oral sex, it was because she wanted to please her husband, felt a sense of duty, was afraid of losing him, was resigned to her fate, or used compliance as a bribe or payment for good behavior from him.

ORAL-GENITAL STIMULATION: CUNNILINGUS

Women are not the only ones who sometimes have trouble with oral sex. One woman in the Hite survey (1976) reported that after cunnilingus her husband always brushed his teeth and washed his face. Another said her man gagged whenever he tried to perform cunnilingus. And a third sometimes caught her partner watching television out of the corner of his eye. In Hite's survey of men (1981), almost all said they enjoyed fellatio, but some were uneasy about being the passive recipient of pleasure or felt the act was degrading to the woman. Similarly, most men were enthusiastic about cunnilingus, but some did have qualms about it.

Even young, supposedly liberal people may feel uncomfortable with some aspects of oral sex. A comprehensive survey of teenagers from forty-nine states found that two-thirds of 17- and 18-year-old girls had performed fellatio, but many did so more for their partner's pleasure than their own—and the boys often knew it. Though most boys got over any initial negative feeling about cunnilingus, many girls felt their boyfriends were reluctant to perform it (Coles and Stokes, 1985).

When our students write about their sexual problems, oral sex frequently crops up. Sometimes people like to receive it but not to give it; sometimes it is just the opposite. Some people complain that their partner does not do it very well. Some love oral sex but express disappointment that their partner is not as enthusiastic. When our students articulate exactly what bothers them about oral sex, they bring up issues that rarely appear in the pages of sex manuals.

One such issue is whether or not the man ejaculates in the partner's mouth during fellatio. Semen has a salty, not unpleasant taste and is completely harmless if swallowed. But many women find the idea of taking semen into the mouth quite revolting. One woman wrote, "I can't swallow his semen! Choke! Choke!" Another wrote, "I always want to say 'Well, would you like me to blow my nose in your mouth?' That's how I feel about it; I'm not trying to be rude." If the male insists on ejaculating, these women are likely to become angry and resentful. And, of course, if a woman is worrying about ejaculation, she is not going to enjoy the experience too much. Ejaculation needs to be discussed forthrightly between the partners. If the woman (or the male homosexual partner) does not want to take semen into the mouth, the recipient of fellatio can ejaculate elsewhere.

Another source of concern, particularly for males, is odor. Although the vagina is a naturally clean organ, containing fewer bacteria than the mouth, if a woman has not washed for some time the accumulated secretions can smell unpleasant. The same is true for men. Under these circumstances, suggesting tactfully that a partner bathe is better than suffering in silence.

People sometimes complain that performing fellatio can be tiring to the jaw muscles and lips. Also, if the penis touches the back of the throat, it may activate the involuntary gag reflex. To some extent, these problems can be handled by learning to use the tongue and lips more effectively and by switching off between oral and manual stimulation. Finally, some positions for oral sex can be uncomfortable or seem impersonal. This problem, too, can be solved if the partners are willing to communicate and experiment a little. (A caution should be added: although the chance is thought to be very low, there may be some risk of transmitting the HIV virus that causes AIDS through oral-genital contact. Therefore, only monogamous couples who are definitely free of infection are entirely free from risk.)

Despite the various concerns some people have about oral sex, cunnilingus and fellatio provide some special pleasures in lovemaking. During cunnilingus the sensitive clitoris can be stimulated both gently and precisely, with the natural lubrication of saliva preventing irritation. During fellatio, the active partner can vary rhythm, pressure, and type of stimulation by using not only the lips but also the tongue and interior surfaces of the mouth. Many women in Hite's first study said that cunnilingus was the best (or only) way they had orgasms. And as noted earlier, most men in the second study were enthusiastic about the special sensations of fellatio.

Perhaps most important, both sexes often experience oral-genital sex as a uniquely intimate expression of their feeling for the other person. The active partner shows that he or she accepts and cherishes the lover's entire body, including its tastes and smells, while the recipient exhibits trust and a willingess to expose even the most private parts of the physical self.

ANAL STIMULATION

Many people find stimulation of the anus to be sexually gratifying. The most common techniques include fingering of the anal area; insertion of a finger or fingers into the rectum; kissing or tonguing of the anal area (*anilingus*, or "rimming"); and anal intercourse (insertion of the penis into the partner's rectum). Unlike the vagina, the anus and rectum do not lubricate in response to sexual excitement. Therefore it is usually necessary to use saliva, sterile jelly, or some other water-soluble substance (petroleum jelly is not water soluble) as a lubricant during anal intercourse. Even then, anal intercourse can be painful, especially if the muscles surrounding the anus are tensed. With increasing relaxation, however, the pain often disappears.

A generation ago few scientific studies referred to any kind of anal sex. Even Kinsey did not collect any publishable data on the practice. He was not a prude: he simply regarded it as too rare to study in a survey. But by the early 1970s attitudes had evidently changed. Hunt (1974) wrote that when he analyzed the Playboy results on anal sex, he expected to find some measure of tolerance for it but was "unprepared for the results that came out of the computer."

What came out of Hunt's computer was this: most people were tolerant of anal intercourse, and many had tried it. Only a little over a quarter of all males and females agreed with the statement "Anal intercourse between a man and woman is wrong," with a majority disagreeing and the rest holding no opinion. Young people were especially accepting. Despite the illegality of anal intercourse in many states, about a fourth of married couples under thirty-five said they incorporated anal intercourse into their lovemaking at least now and then, and over a sixth of single people under twenty-five who had ever had coitus had also tried anal intercourse. As for other anal practices, well over half the married men and women under thirty-five had tried manual stimulation, and over a fourth had tried anilingus.

Of course, these incidence figures, like those for oral sex, do not tell us how people feel when they try out techniques once considered taboo. This is an issue that has been studied very little. In her book on male sexuality, Hite (1981) reported that most men who had been anally penetrated by a finger (almost a third of the heterosexuals and most of the homosexuals) said they had enjoyed it, and many—it is not clear how many—who had been penetrated by a penis or a penis-sized object also said they enjoyed it. But as we have noted, Hite's sample was not scientifically selected. In Hite's female questionnaire (1976) there was an ambiguously worded item on "rectal contact," but it is not discussed in her book. So we still do not know how enthusiastic people generally are after trying anal techniques.

Anal practices pose certain health hazards, some of them extremely serious. When practiced by heterosexuals, bacteria that are harmless in the rectum may cause infection if they reach the vagina, and such infection may spread to other parts of the reproductive tract. For this reason, anal intercourse should never be followed directly by vaginal intercourse. Similarly, a finger should never be inserted into the vagina if it has just been inserted in the anus. Another risk is intestinal infection. Organisms that are harmless in the lower part of the gastrointestinal tract enter the mouth during anilingus and can then cause serious illness.

The greatest danger of anal intercourse is increased vulnerability to blood-borne viruses like the HIV virus, the one that causes AIDS (see Chapter 17). The rectum is lined with fragile, easily damaged cells. It also contains an abundance of blood vessels. Anal intercourse causes tears and abrasions in the lining, and so the HIV virus can easily get into the receiving partner's bloodstream. "Fisting" (insertion of the entire hand) or insertion of dildos or other objects severely traumatizes the rectum and increases the risk even more. Even when the rectum is not traumatized, there are likely to be tiny tears in its lining. The high rate among gay men of hepatitis B, another blood-borne viral disease, is apparently related to frequent use of anal intercourse. Unless it is certain that both partners are uninfected and have been monogamous in their relationship with each other, they should abstain from anal sex, or should have it only with a condom and practice withdrawal before ejaculation.

COITUS

The word *intercourse* is understood by most people to mean heterosexual, vaginal-penile intercourse, but technically it refers to any sort of sexual

coupling, including oral or anal. The word **coitus** refers specifically to vaginal-penile intercourse. It derives from the Latin *coitio*, meaning "a coming together" or "uniting," which is a rather nice way of describing what happens during the act. Traditionally, coitus has been regarded as *the* sex act; if one did not have coitus, one did not really have sex. Several writers, though, have argued that coitus should be viewed as just one sexual activity among many and that it does not need to occur in every heterosexual encounter for people to enjoy themselves and feel satisfied (see Hite, 1976, 1981). Nevertheless, for most heterosexual men and women, coitus sill holds a special place of honor among sexual acts, for psychological if not for physical reasons.

Coital Positions

Elizabeth Barrett Browning wrote to Robert Browning, "How do I love thee? Let me count the ways." In coitus counting all the ways is difficult, because there are so many of them. The male's penis enters the female's vagina, but all else is variable. The partners may be lying down, standing up, sitting, or kneeling. They may be face-to-face, or the woman may have her back to the man. One partner may be on top, or the two may lie side-by-side. Still, we can distinguish four general positions, with most of the others essentially variations on these themes.

FACE-TO-FACE, MALE ON TOP   This is the standard position in our culture, but it has not always been preferred. The ancient Romans reputedly believed that the woman should be on top. The Polynesians traditionally preferred a squatting stance. When the Polynesians found out how the strange Europeans who sought to convert them to Christianity did it, they promptly dubbed the male-on-top posture the "missionary position."

When a couple uses this position, the penis usually fits easily into the vagina, especially if the woman or man guides it manually and the woman keeps her legs apart with the knees bent. Once **intromission,** insertion of the penis, is accomplished, the woman's legs can assume a variety of positions; they may be bent or straight, apart (with the man's legs between them) or together (with the man's legs on the outside). Penetration is usually deeper if the female's legs are apart and up, but some women report less pressure against the clitoris in this position than when the legs are closer together. The woman may also rest her legs on her partner's shoulders or wrap them around his body.

The male-on-top position has the advantage of being suitable for different moods. Penetration can be shallow or deep; thrusting can be vigorous or gentle. On the minus side, a woman may find it hard to move freely, especially if her partner is heavy or fails to support himself on his elbows or forearms. Also, some men find it difficult to delay orgasm as long as they would like to in this position.

FACE-TO-FACE, FEMALE ON TOP   Probably the best way to accomplish intromission with the female on top is for the woman to squat over the man on her knees and guide the penis into her vagina as she slowly lowers herself onto it. This works best when the male has a stiff erection. Once the penis is in the vagina, the woman may continue to squat or may lean slightly forward and carefully stretch out her legs so that her body is on top of his.

Many women like to be on top so that they can control the contact between the base of the penis or the male's pubic bone and the clitoris. The female can also move more freely than when she is on the bottom and can regulate the depth of penetration. Males often find that they can "last" longer in this position than when they are on top because less muscle tension builds up. However, in this position the male may be unable to thrust as vigorously as he would like to.

The female-on-top position is more popular than it used to be. In Kinsey's survey only a little more than a third of all married people had tried it, but in the Playboy survey nearly three-quarters had done so. Still, there are some couples who feel psychologically uncomfortable in this position because they are used to thinking of the male as the more active or assertive partner in sex.

SIDE-BY-SIDE   In the side-by-side, or lateral, position the man and woman face each other with their legs entwined in one way or another. Getting the penis into the vagina can be a bit tricky in this position. It usually helps if one of the woman's legs is hooked over her partner's torso. This position is not very taxing physically. Because penetration is fairly shallow, a man can delay orgasm more easily than in other positions. This is a good position

to use during pregnancy, since it puts no weight on the woman's abdomen. The main drawback is that it may not allow movement to be as vigorous as the partners like.

In Kinsey's study only a little more than a quarter of married couples had tried the side-by-side position, but in the Playboy survey the figure was over 50 percent.

REAR-ENTRY   In rear-entry coitus (not to be confused with anal intercourse) the partners face in the same direction, with the male behind the female. Both may lie on their sides, in the "spoons" position. Or the woman may sit on the man's lap with her back to him, kneel with her knees drawn up beneath her, or lie on a bed either flat or with the hips raised. Like the side-by-side position, the rear-entry position is useful during pregnancy or when the male is much heavier than the female. Also, rear-entry leaves a man's hands free to caress his partner's body. When the woman kneels or raises her hips, penetration can be very deep because the vagina is shortened. (But for some women this may be painful.) Some people dislike rear-entry because they cannot see their partner's face.

FACE-TO-FACE COITUS: FEMALE ON TOP

SIDE-BY-SIDE COITUS   A generation ago Kinsey found that only a little over one-tenth of all married couples had used a rear-entry position. In contrast, the Playboy survey found that two-fifths of married couples had tried rear-entry, and about a fifth of all couples under twenty-five used it often.

This brief description of possible positions barely scratches the surface. Coital positions are limited only by the imagination and flexibility of the partners and certain physical laws. It is possible, for example, to have coitus standing up, or with one partner perched on the edge of a bed, or with the male lying beneath the female and both facing the ceiling, or face-to-foot with the female on top and each partner between the other's legs—the X position. Many people like to shift from one position to another.

Duration of Coitus

People often wonder how long coitus should last. The answer is that it should last as long as the partners want it to last. Sometimes a "quickie" is just fine for both. At other times, a couple may want to take a leisurely approach. In general, Americans seem to be spending more time on intercourse than they used to. Kinsey estimated that about three-quarters of all

married males ejaculated within two minutes after intromission, and many finished even faster. However, according to the Playboy survey, married people in the 1970s took an average of about ten minutes, and couples under twenty-five took thirteen.

The duration of intercourse is related to the probability that a woman will experience an orgasm during intercourse. When Paul Gebhard (1966) interviewed over a thousand married women, he found that few of them could reach orgasm regularly when intercourse lasted less than a minute. But when it lasted one to eleven minutes, half the wives reported having orgasms almost all the time. And when it lasted sixteen or more minutes, two-thirds reached orgasm almost all of the time. Other studies estimate the percentage of women who regularly have coital orgasms to be considerably lower. The point, though, is that some women probably do not have coital orgasms because intercourse is too brief.

On the other hand, prolonged intercourse does not *guarantee* that a woman will reach orgasm. In fact, our female students often complain that when intercourse goes on for too long, they get sore, bored, numb, or tired, rather than more orgasmic. Also, duration of stimulation cannot in itself be the key to female orgasm, because during masturbation women generally

COITUS IN A SITTING POSITION

reach orgasm as quickly as men—a male-female time difference turns up only in coitus. Kinsey (1953) found that 45 percent of women who masturbated climaxed in only one to three minutes, and only 12 percent of the women took longer than ten minutes. The inescapable conclusion is that there is something about coitus, as opposed to masturbation, that causes women to respond more slowly than men and prevents many women from experiencing orgasm at all.

Coitus and the Elusive Female Orgasm

To understand why coitus often fails to produce orgasm in women, or produces it irregularly or slowly, we must go back to our discussion of anatomy. You will recall that the upper two-thirds of the vagina is relatively insensitive. Although some women may have more sensitivity in the lower vagina, the primary locus of sexual sensation in women is usually the clitoris. This means that deep thrusting is not what brings on an orgasm in most females.

Well then, what does? On this the experts disagree. First let us consider what Masters and Johnson have to say. Masters and Johnson (1966) note that as the penis moves in and out of the woman's vagina, it pulls on the minor lips. These lips are attached to the hood of the clitoris; in fact, the clitoral hood is really an extension of the lips. Traction on the lips tends to pull the hood back and forth over the clitoris. Masters and Johnson believe that the resulting friction against the clitoral glans is sufficient to produce orgasm.

Many sexologists have accepted this explanation on faith, even though Masters and Johnson do not say how they arrived at it, since they were unable to observe the clitoris in their subjects once it retracted. But there are certain problems with the theory, the most important being that if it were true, we would not expect so many women to have difficulty with orgasms during coitus.

Masters and Johnson's most outspoken critic on this issue has been Shere Hite (1976). Hite agrees that the female orgasm depends on friction between the clitoral hood and the clitoral glans, but she does not think the thrusting of a penis is sufficient to produce this friction in most women. Hite points out that no one expects most men to reach orgasm merely from the stretching of penile skin that results from pressure against the base of the penis or the scrotum. Similarly, she says, we should not expect most women to reach orgasm merely from the stretching of the labial skin. Masters and Johnson's model, said Hite, "sounds more like a Rube Goldberg scheme than a reliable way to orgasm." (Hite's reference is to the work of a cartoonist who drew complicated machines, full of levers and pulleys, that didn't actually accomplish anything.)

When a man rubs his penis against a woman's vaginal walls, he gets stimulation that is similar to what he would get during masturbation. Women, says Hite, also need to duplicate the stimulation that works for them during masturbation. That is, they must consciously try to obtain sufficient clitoral contact. For the women in Hite's survey who were able to experience orgasm during intercourse without any manual stimulation, clitoral stimulation usually involved contact with the male's pubic area or the base of the penis.

According to Masters and Johnson, women, unlike men, need continuous, uninterrupted stimulation in order to reach orgasm. An interruption at any time, even in the middle of an orgasm, immediately lowers the level of arousal. Some women in Hite's study said continuity of stimulation was best achieved with a "grinding" motion, rather than the more conventional thrusting. And when there was thrusting, women often preferred a slow, definite rhythm.

> There is a particular rhythm I find most helpful. It is that when the man pushes in, he stays pressed against me for a few seconds, instead of backing up right away. Also that he does not back away as soon as I press against him, which some men have a tendency to do. (Hite, 1976, p. 279)

Sometimes women wanted movement to stop altogether at the moment of orgasm.

However, there was no unanimity among the women in Hite's sample about what was the most reliable way to have a coital orgasm. Some liked to be on top, but others preferred the male-on-top or one of the other coital positions. Some liked full penetration, but others wanted only partial penetration. Some liked to lift their legs during intercourse, but others insisted that they had to have their legs pressed tightly together. No one knows what determines such differences. A woman's preferences during coitus may be related to how she originally learned to masturbate or to the size or position of a woman's clitoris. Or perhaps different bodies fit together in different ways, so that what is optimal with one partner may not be with another.

A more recent study of twenty-eight orgasmic women confirms the striking variation in the way women have coital orgasms. In interviews, most of the women said that an orgasm did not just happen to them; rather, they had to do something to help bring it about. Almost all reported "some level of conscious control" over their orgasmic response, and almost all said it was important to concentrate or focus on reaching orgasm. But the mental and physical techniques the women used to facilitate their own orgasms varied, ranging from getting into the "right" position (the one that "worked" reliably for the individual woman) to breathing faster (Sholty et al., 1984).

One coital "technique" that women may overlook is the use of manual stimulation of the clitoris or vulva during intercourse. Such stimulation can be provided either by the woman herself or by her partner. Although this technique can be very effective, unfortunately some people reject it as "second best," believing that there is only one "correct" way to have an orgasm. We would like to argue that there is no one "correct" way. Intercourse, after all, is not soccer: you get to use your hands!

Finally, while we are on the topic of individual variation, we should point out that men, too, have their preferences regarding coital position, depth of thrusting, and so forth (Hite, 1981). For one man, orgasm might depend on rubbing the tip of the penis against the wall of the vagina; for another, the critical factor might be friction of the penis against the vaginal opening during thrusting; for a third, pressure on the scrotum and testes might be effective. However, it is not clear whether individual preferences in coital stimulation are as important to men as to women.

CONCLUSION: FROM THE JOB OF SEX TO THE JOY OF SEX

No two people are alike in their sexual needs. Some people like frequent sexual activity, others only occasional, and still others none at all (see Box 9–2). A particular sexual activity will appeal to only some of the people some of the time. Open-minded experimentation can help people find out what they do and do not like, and frank communication can help them share what they learn with their partners.

The list of sexual activities in this chapter can be a guide to experimentation. But note: it is not intended as a checklist or a prescription for success. Pressure to experience all forms of sex can be as coercive as pressure to perform sex for procreation only.

Sociologist Philip Slater, in an article published in the early seventies but still relevant today, argued that the Protestant ethic, with its emphasis on worldly success, too often causes people to turn sexual play into work and to seek objective criteria for measuring sexual success or failure. We speak of "achieving" orgasm, and we put an imaginary notch in our belt every time that we succeed in "doing it." According to Slater, the focus on orgasm in our culture reflects a general inclination to emphasize the product of an activity at the expense of the process:

> The term "climax" expresses not only the idea of a peak or zenith but also the idea of termination or completion. Discussions of the sexual act in our society are thus primarily concerned with how it *ends*. Leisurely pleasure-seeking is brushed aside, as all acts and all thoughts are directed toward the creation of a successful finale. The better the orgasm, the more enjoyable the whole encounter is retrospectively defined as having been. . . .In such a system you can find out how much you're enjoying yourself only after it's all over, just as many Americans traveling abroad don't know what they've experienced until they've had their films developed. (Slater, 1973, pp. 19–20)

BOX 9–2

Choosing Celibacy

For most people, sexual liberation means the freedom to choose from among the smorgasbord of possible sexual activities according to one's personal inclinations and values. But having a menu set before you does not mean you have to order. A few people express their freedom of choice by opting for permanent celibacy, the deliberate avoidance of sex. This choice takes various forms. It may entail a withdrawal from sexual relationships (the word *celibate* comes from the Latin for "single"), but permit sexual fantasy and masturbation. Or it may mean total abstinence from all forms of sexual stimulation.

Most people go through celibate periods in their lives. Sometimes their celibacy is not by choice. A person might experience temporary celibacy when a spouse or lover is away—for example, on military duty. Or an individual may abstain from sex because of illness or because he or she is unable to find an acceptable sexual partner. The result can be loneliness and depression. But a period of abstinence can also be viewed as an opportunity, as in the case of a divorced, middle-aged woman who was sexually active for many years but suddenly found herself going through a "dry spell":

> The longer I am celibate, the less I seem to crave a sexual relationship. I am enjoying having my own "space," both physically and emotionally. I'm content to put all my energy into the development of my career. I would like to be involved with a man again one of these days, but right now I don't feel like making the effort required to find one. (authors' files)

At other times, celibacy is deliberate. Reasons for purposely choosing temporary or permanent celibacy include the following:

Religious convictions Many of the world's religions encourage or require celibacy for the clergy or for those wishing to lead a spiritual life. Roman Catholic priests and nuns take a vow of lifelong celibacy and commit themselves completely to church service. Hinduism encourages celibacy during youth for those who want to study and pursue the growth of consciousness, and in old age as part of a renunciation of social ties and the material world.

Desire to wait for a serious relationship A person may feel that sex is appropriate or meaningful only in the context of a truly intimate rela-

In place of achievement-oriented sex, Slater envisions sex in which orgasm is "a delightful interruption in an otherwise continuous process of generating pleasurable sensations." People would no longer use orgasms as units for counting the number of times they made love, and the term *sex*

tionship and may choose to wait for such a relationship to develop. For some this means marriage; for others it simply means a loving and committed relationship.

Need for an emotional rest A person may withdraw temporarily from sex after the end of a sexual relationship because he or she is not emotionally ready to undertake another one and has no desire for casual sex. The time off from sex may be used to "get in touch" with innermost feelings and sort out personal goals and needs, or strengthen nonsexual friendships.

Absorption in other activities Sex itself need not take much time or energy, but intimate relationships usually make a demand on both. Sometimes people choose to forego such relationships so they can concentrate fully on other priorities. For example, one student of ours who was working night and day to start his own business confided that he had not had sex for months because he had no current girl friend, and he did not want to take time to cultivate a new relationship. He said he did not miss sex much because he was thoroughly enjoying the total immersion in his work.

A desire to experiment A person who has been sexually active may decide to try celibacy simply to see what it is like. The period of abstinence may be a time for finding out just how important or unimportant sexual relationships are in one's life, or how dependent one is on them for happiness.

The exploration of other types of loving. Sometimes couples, as well as individuals, put sex aside for a while in order to focus on other ways of expressing closeness or sensuality. Or sexual partners may decide to "disengage" temporarily, in order to develop individual strengths or gain a sense of autonomy. (It is important, of course, that partners come to an agreement in this matter.)

Finally, some people are simply asexual. This is not surprising. People differ in their enthusiasm for work and social life, and in the intensity of their physical appetites. Some live to eat, while others only eat to live. Why shouldn't the same hold true for sex? Most people find that sex enhances their intimate love relationships, but for some, such relationships may be more gratifying without it.

would encompass interludes that do not culminate in orgasm.

This view of sex does not mean that people should not enjoy their orgasms. Nor does it mean that they should set a clock by the bed to be sure they are spending enough time in non-goal-oriented lovemaking. That would just set up a new sexual mandate in place of the old one and would create new opportunities for "failure." For Slater and others who take a similar position, true sexual liberation is not a matter of living up to someone else's definition of good sex, but the freedom to make one's own sexual choices.

- -

YOUR SEXUAL "DRUTHERS"

Most people in our society consider the sexual activities covered in this chapter to be conventional adult behavior. Not all of these acts appeal to everyone, however, and most of us have some decided preferences about the way in which particular acts should be carried out. For instance, although most people like to kiss, some of us prefer "wet" kisses while others like "dry" ones.

This exercise is a guide for exploring your personal preferences regarding sexual activities. It gives you an opportunity to clarify what you like (or dislike) about each of the activities you have read about, and how you want (or might want) an activity performed.

Consider the following list:

- Fantasy

- Masturbation

- Kissing

- Caressing, hugging, stroking, and other mutual manual activities

- Fellatio

- Cunnilingus

- Anal stimulation

- Sexual intercourse

Take a sheet of paper, and for each of these activities write your answers to the questions below. There are no "right" or "wrong" answers; you do not have to like what other people like, nor do you have to please anyone else. The focus is solely on what *you* prefer.

1. What precisely about this act appeals, or would probably appeal, to you? Write down as many gratifying or pleasant aspects of this activity as you can think of.

2. What are your preferences about how this activity should be performed? For example, do you prefer a slow tempo or a fast one? A light touch or a firm one? Do you like to be active or

passive—or both? What positions work best for you, and why? What else affects your sexual arousal or how you respond to this activity?

3. What sort of setting do you prefer, or might you prefer, for this activity? How great a difference does setting make to you?

4. What about this act concerns or worries you? What, if anything, about this act arouses some anxieties or fears?

5. What about this act, or about how it is carried out, is distinctly unappealing to you? Is there anything so distasteful about the act that you are (or would be) quite uncomfortable taking part in it?

Now look at the list of activities again. Which ones would you select from a "menu" of sexual activities? Are there any that you have not tried but think you might enjoy? If you have a permanent partner, you might consider asking him or her to try this *Personal Perspective* with you. (Do not pressure your partner though; not everyone feels a need to analyze their sexual preferences or share them with someone else.) If your partner is interested in doing the exercise, the two of you can respond separately and then share your answers. Remember to be tactful, nonaccusing, and respectful of the other person's individuality. When you are done, ask yourself what you have learned about each other. What, if anything, do you disagree about? How might you resolve your differences?

IN BRIEF

1. Sexual fantasies, masturbation, caressing, oral-genital techniques, anal stimulation, and coitus may all be part of a person's sexual repertoire.

2. *Sexual fantasies* are a common source of sexual arousal for both women and men. They often involve forbidden activities, permitting people to enjoy in imagination what they might not want or be able to do in reality. Sometimes, however, people do eventually "try out" their fantasies; the consequences may be positive or negative, depending on the act in question, and the results. Traditional psychoanalysts have viewed sexual fantasizing as immature or a sign of pathology, but today most sexologists regard it, in most people, as a harmless source of sexual pleasure.

3. *Masturbation* is more widely accepted than it once was, but is still often a source of uneasiness or guilt. Traditional psychoanalysts regarded it as immature in adults or as a second-rate substitute for coitus, but today the prevailing view is that it is a perfectly valid way to relieve sexual tension and a good way to learn about and enjoy one's own body. Techniques

vary considerably, especially among women. Kinsey found that almost all men and about two-thirds of all women had masturbated at some time; Hunt's incidence rates were somewhat higher. Masturbation does not cease when people marry.

4. The use of the term *foreplay* to refer to kissing, caressing, and stroking reflects a widespread view of these activities as merely warm-up exercises for the "main event." However, all these activities can be enjoyed during, after, and without intercourse. Americans seem to spend more time on sexual play than they did when the Kinsey study was done. Still, many people rush through foreplay in a predictable sequence, and men and women are sometimes on a different "wavelength" regarding erotic touch. According to Masters and Johnson, the married heterosexual couples they have studied have been less skilled at foreplay than committed gay and lesbian couples.

5. In *oral-genital sex*, one partner stimulates the genitals of the other with tongue or lips. In *fellatio* the recipient is male; in *cunnilingus* the recipient is female. Most Americans find oral-genital sex acceptable and a majority have tried it; this represents a change since Kinsey's day. Not everyone feels entirely comfortable with oral-genital sex; some people worry about ejaculation during fellatio or have other concerns. But for many people, oral sex provides special pleasures in lovemaking.

6. *Anal stimulation* includes manual and oral stimulation of the anus, and anal intercourse. Attitudes toward anal techniques have changed markedly since the Kinsey study, and a sizable number of people have tried them. Anal practices, however, pose certain health hazards, some of them quite serious, including the transmission of the virus that causes AIDS.

7. *Coitus*, or vaginal-penile intercourse, has traditionally been regarded as *the* sex act. The four basic coital positions are: face-to-face, male on top; face-to-face, female on top; side-by-side; and rear entry. Women often do not experience orgasm during coitus because the stimulation they receive is inadequate. Those women who do experience coital orgasm vary in the rhythms, positions, and motions that they say "work" reliably for them. One coital "technique" that women (and their partners) may overlook is the use of manual stimulation of the clitoris or vulva during intercourse.

8. Because individuals differ in their sexual responses and preferences, frank communication and a willingness to experiment are important to the success of a sexual relationship. Sexual liberation is not a matter of living up to someone else's definitions of good sex, but the freedom to make one's own sexual choices.

Key Terms

sexual fantasy *(318)*

masturbation *(322)*

foreplay *(327)*

fellatio *(328)*

cunnilingus *(329)*

coitus *(336)*

intromission *(338)*

celibacy *(346)*

**CHAPTER
TEN**

C H A P T E R   T E N

■

Unconventional Sexual Behavior

●

One half of the world cannot understand the pleasures of the other.

Jane Austen

Sex researcher John Money (1977) once wrote that problems of human sexuality can generally be classified as "too little, too much, or too peculiar." The behaviors discussed in this chapter have traditionally fallen into the third category. Known technically as **paraphilias** (from the Greek *para*, meaning "beside, near, beyond, or amiss," and *philia*, meaning "love"), these unconventional sexual behaviors share two central characteristics: they tend to be performed compulsively and they are viewed by most people as strange.

Until recently, psychiatric writers commonly referred to paraphilias as "perversions" and "deviations." These terms supposedly had objective clinical meanings but were frequently code words for immoral, distasteful, or offensive. Today professional use of such pejorative labels is rare. However, most mental health professionals still consider paraphilias to be abnormal.

In practice, judgments of abnormality are not always easy to make. The line between the unusual and the pathological is not always clear. Also, such judgments occur within a particular cultural and social context, and so they can change. A century ago, most people, including medical authorities, viewed both masturbation and oral-genital sex as abnormal. Today these activities are commonplace, and most authorities consider them to be completely normal. Abnormality, including sexual abnormality, is to a large extent a function of time and place.

Recognizing this fact, some writers have tried to banish the concept of sexual abnormality altogether, calling those who practice unconventional sexual behaviors "sexual minorities." Others, taking a more clinical approach, have retained the term *abnormal*, but have tried to define it in a morally and culturally neutral way. For example, one way to decide whether a behavior is abnormal or not is to ask whether it is harmful or destructive to the person practicing it. By this criterion, paraphilias are often abnormal. At least one, masochism, can bring physical harm on oneself. Others, because they are illegal, can lead to arrest and imprisonment. Many unusual sexual behaviors cut a person off from affectionate relationships with others, and cause guilt, shame, and a sense of isolation. Typically, a person practicing a paraphilia is dependent on the behavior, and unable to achieve sexual arousal or gratification in other ways. An act that for other people might be just one component of a sexual interaction becomes instead an end in itself. The act is irresistible and involuntary—a compulsion (American Psychiatric Association, 1987).

A related criterion for abnormality is the consent, or lack of consent, of a person's sexual partners (Money, 1977). According to this criterion, the behavior of a man who cannot get an erection unless his partner urinates on him is not pathological unless the partner does not want to cooperate. The

Classified information
People with unconventional sexual interests may seek partners or paraphernalia by responding to ads in sexually oriented newspapers.

$10.95. Info/samp $3; NYWC, 59 W. 10 St., NYC, NY 10011.

Sexual Identity

For your copy send $1 and legal SASE to: Identity #4, Box 878, Metuchen, NJ 08840 (270 Wood-bridge).

Gay Porno Books

12 different novels—$15
25 different novels—$30
50 different novels—$60
Over 21, postpd. Fields, 81-13A Bdwy., Elmhurst, NY 11373.

Wrestling stories, photos, newsletter, illus & now bxing mat. Free details: BG, 7985 Sta. Monica Blvd., #109-81, W. Hwd., CA 90046. Second big year.

Hot and Horny?

Then get on LE SALON's redhot mailing list! LE SALON'll rush you their latest brochures on the very newest male mags, films, aromas, video-cassettes & adult novelties/rubber goods! Don't wait . . . just send $3 (check, $, & or m.o.) and a signature you're over 21 to: LE SALON, 30 Sheridan St., Dept. AC, S.F., CA 94103.

DISABLED PEN-PALING newsltr w/free ads: Para-Imps, Box 515, South Beloit, IL 1080 (805 Church). SASE fr info

Free ads on our scenes lists! Lists are cheap! SASE + sign over 21. Our World, Box 803, Santa Ana, CA 92702. Nationvide

for details.
Box 2402 Z, Sepulveda, CA 91343.

Pocket size KY—$3. T.J. Inc.; Box 50227, Wash., DC 20004 (330-14th Pl.).

Tattooing technics manual, 83-pps, illus—$30 ppd. Temporary-"Hotline" tattoo ink pkt—$15. ppd. Offer void where prohibited by law. A. Lemes MD 6615 Franklin Ave., #211, L.A., CA 90028.

Replica Cock Kit

Now you can make a realistic flexible rubber replica of your cock. For free brochure on product and trading club, send your name and address to:
"Replica," Box 472,
Santee, CA 92071 with B stamp.

"IMMORAL MINORITY" Buttons 5/8'' diam red/wh $1 ea. Reality Developmentals, Box 191, E. Lansing, MI 48823. Large orders write: K. Fraske, 519 Forest, E. Lans., MI 48823. Call (517) 332-2606 aft 7PM

Ex-Cop Selling

used jockey shorts, dirt cheap. Limited #. Send $9: Nick Manbrino, 54 E. 4th, NYC, NY 10003.

For free leather catalog deal send SASE: MBE, Box 99429 A4, S.F., CA 94109 (3110 Clay).

Make extra money. Part time. 2 or 3 hours a week. Great potential. Catalogue names. For full details send SASE to:
Creative Artists,
Box 26072

Orientals & Othrs

Gdlkg W/m, 6'2'', 35, seeks friends. Chuck, (213) 380-9799.

BONDAGE SLAVE WANTED SEND "RESUME" TO: TIM, BX 27736, L.A., CA 90027

USAF manholes. (213) 760-3600.

Hunky 23-yr-old bodybuilder seeks hot White men (18-30). Bob, (213) 652-7699.

W/m, 37, 5'5'', 118#, into B&D, Fr & Gr. (213) 650-4269.

PALM SPRINGS EXPENSE PAID VACATION OFFER TO CLN-SHAVEN SMOOTH-CHESTED SENSUAL W/M BY FUN-LOVING EROTIC W/M EARLY 40'S. PHOTO ETC: H. MANLY, 303 EAST ARENAS ROAD, SUITE 101, PALM SPRINGS, CA 92262

• SPANKING SCENES • for guys 18-30. Al Tanum, Box 7305, Long Beach, CA 90807.

18-30? Lean/trim & Fr pass? Bob, (213) 782-7797 eve/wkend.

W/m—52, 6'2'', 165#—seeks affect, vers, active, any-age pal (over 18) under 170#. Box 57366, L.A., CA 90057.

Super built hot yng men esp USMC—hot times/place to stay. BJ, (714) 575-1711.

Musc smth v hndsm top 29, 6', 165. You must be yng musc smth tight sm waist. (213) 662-6830.

3-WAY GR ACTION 2 gdlkg hung Gr act & vers studs, early 30's, seek gdlkg vers Wh or Oriental guys 18-28 for hot

bizarreness of the behavior is not the issue. The existence or absence of consent often determines whether a particular sexual behavior is regarded as a crime. It is perfectly legal for a man to gaze at a woman as she undresses if she permits him to do so; it is a crime (and considered pathological) if he spies on her through a window. Similarly, nudity is fine in the bedroom but is banned in public, where passersby may have to view it unwillingly. The criterion of consent recognizes that the social context in which a behavior occurs affects its normality or abnormality.

In practice, however, if a sexual behavior seems odd, people are apt to call it abnormal even though it causes no harm to either the practitioner or to others. For example, some clinicians regard habitual dressing in the clothes of the other sex as abnormal even when it occurs in complete privacy and causes no distress. Conversely, a socially accepted behavior is likely to be viewed as normal even when one of the usual criteria for abnormality is met. Thus a desire for oral sex is considered normal even when this desire happens to upset a sexually conservative partner.

Because judgments of abnormality are bound up with personal and cultural notions of what is bizarre, professional opinions about the behaviors in this chapter vary and are subject to modification. At present, there is nearly universal consensus about some of these behaviors. For example, no sexologist or mental health professional argues that sexual attraction to a dead body is ever normal. But for other behaviors, controversy exists about both their abnormality and the necessity for treatment. In some cases, a judgment of abnormality may depend on the particular circumstances.

As you read through the following sections, you will find that paraphilias are far more common in men than in women. One possible reason is that gender roles encourage men, but not women, to be sexually assertive. Even if she wants to, a woman may hesitate to spy on a man while he undresses for the same reason that she does not publicly ogle men or make an overt sexual pass at a man: women are expected to respond to sexual behaviors, not start them. In addition, paraphilias are often motivated by hostility or a desire to exploit or humiliate another person. Women are certainly capable of experiencing hostility and anger, but it is socially less acceptable for women than for men to express these feelings sexually. Differences in the socialization of the sexes may also make women more conventional and willing to abide by social rules than men are. Many unconventional sexual behaviors are illegal, and women are much less likely than men to break the law.

As you read, you will also find that most theories about paraphilias have been either psychoanalytic or behavioral. Psychoanalysts believe that these behaviors reflect a failure to progress beyond certain childish stages of sexual development or to resolve early emotional conflicts. In this view, paraphilias function as defense mechanisms that protect a person's distorted sense of reality (Limentani, 1987). In contrast, behaviorists view paraphilias as behaviors acquired through a process of accidental conditioning. However, some writers are now focusing less on the individual and more on social conditions that might encourage paraphilias. In these *sociological* approaches, the question is not "Why do some people practice such behaviors?" but rather, "What social conditions encourage such behaviors?" For example, one writer has argued that sexual sadism may develop when societies foster dominance-submission relationships, value aggression, and support an unequal distribution of power (Weinberg, 1987). Of course, such explanations still leave the question of why some individuals develop paraphilias and most do not.

Finally, before we turn to specific behaviors, we want to point out that the information in this chapter is based largely on observations of people in therapy and studies of people who have run afoul of the law. We do not know how well these individuals represent the total population of those engaging in unconventional practices. Most people who do things that are socially unacceptable are not eager to offer themselves as research subjects. Those people who have been studied may have characteristics that are not shared by those who have managed to keep their activities and preferences hidden.

VOYEURISM

Voyeurism is the act of covertly observing, for the purpose of sexual gratification, others who are nude, in the act of undressing, or engaged in sexual activity. The colloquial term for a voyeur is *peeping Tom*. According to legend, during the eleventh century the husband of Lady Godiva agreed to lift a burdensome tax on his tenants if his wife would ride naked through Coventry, England, on a white horse. She accepted the challenge, and in deference to her bravery the townspeople stayed indoors—except for Tom the Tailor, who peeped at her and promptly went blind. Virtually all voyeurs who come to the attention of the law are, like Tom, male.

In voyeurism, it is the situation in which the behavior occurs that is considered unusual, not the behavior itself. Our society tolerates and even encourages looking in many forms (Tollison & Adams, 1979). Most people probably would not use the label *voyeur* for a man who noticed a female neighbor undressing in front of a window and stopped to look. Opportunities for socially approved "voyeurism" abound: in men's (and more recently women's) magazines, in pornography, at topless bars and burlesque shows, and at beauty contests and performances by cheerleaders at football games.

What sets voyeurism apart from ordinary looking is that the voyeur favors looking over any other sexual activity and prefers to watch someone who is unaware that she is being observed. Usually she is a stranger. The behavior is often compulsive, and the voyeur may spend hours in great discomfort in order to have a chance to peep:

> Typical of the voyeur's willingness to take risks and wait patiently for a
> view is a 27–year–old man who was caught spying on women and couples in a small motel. A clerk on the evening shift, he said he took this

job in order to put his carefully laid out plan into operation. When alone in the motel office he would use a straightened paper clip to bore holes in the walls separating the motel office from three adjoining guest rooms. He took as long as a month to bore each hole with this primitive tool, being careful that it was small enough not to be detectable. Once his three peep holes were completed he assigned attractive women and couples to these rooms and watched them. When he was finally apprehended he had engaged in the behavior for almost a year, often patiently waiting for hours for a view and running to the different walls to check the view in each of the rooms. When he could see a woman undress or was lucky enough to watch a couple having intercourse, he would masturbate while viewing the arousing scene. (Tollison & Adams, 1979, pp. 229–30)

Risk may be what makes the voyeur's activities so exciting to him. Most voyeurs show little interest in nudist camps or the kind of socially approved occasions for sexual looking mentioned above.

The typical voyeur is a young male adult. According to Tollison and Adams (1979), about two-thirds are single, a quarter are married, and the rest are divorced, widowed, or separated. Most voyeurs are not dangerous, although there are exceptions. Also, most are not seriously mentally disturbed. Many, however, have had only limited and unsatisfactory sexual experiences and are deficient in sexual and social skills.

Many psychoanalysts believe that voyeurs are motivated by fear of women and that this fear results from failure to resolve early emotional conflicts. Looking at a female may be far less threatening than actually approaching her or making physical contact. In fact, looking at an unsuspecting victim may give the voyeur a feeling of power and superiority.

Behaviorists, in contrast, believe that voyeurism develops when looking somehow becomes associated early in life with sexual arousal. But such an association, which must be common, does not always lead to voyeurism. Perhaps the association becomes significant for later sexuality only when it is repeated on several occasions. Or the association may assume special significance for those who are immature and socially inept. Small children are normally curious about sexual anatomy and often try to peep at their elders; people with immature personalities may never outgrow this behavior and be able to move on to satisfying relations with other persons.

EXHIBITIONISM

Exhibitionism is the exposure of one's genitals to an unsuspecting person as a way of experiencing sexual arousal. Like looking, exposing one's body to another person is an intrinsic part of ordinary sexual encounters. Most of us find it extremely gratifying, and even sexually arousing, to have our bodies admired, so in a sense we can all be considered exhibitionists. Clinicians reserve the term, however, for those who compulsively expose

Is this exhibitionism?
Where is the line between being seductive—which our culture encourages in women—and being an exhibitionist? How does the setting and the gender of those involved affect your answer?

their sex organs in an inappropriate situation—for example, in public. Virtually all those arrested for exhibitionism are men. Exhibiting ("flashing") can take various forms. The exhibitionist may simply expose a flaccid penis, or he may expose an erect penis, or he may masturbate.

Exhibitionism seems to involve more than just a desire to achieve sexual arousal or gratification. Typically, there is also a need to shock the viewer or express contempt and hostility. Consider these words of an exhibitionist who preferred victims of a certain age and social class:

> Middle-aged women, smartly dressed, no one else. Someone who reminds me of my mother, a doctor said once, he pointed that out to me, and I think that might be right, that I'm still trying to insult her. No, it's not a prelude to a sexual assault, there's never anything like that in my mind. Just to shock. If a woman looks disgusted and turns away, then I'm satisfied. A woman smiled at me once and came towards me instead; I ran away from her as hard as I could. . . .
>
> I can't tell you why I do it; when it's happening I'm not conscious of anything except this feeling of being contemptuous towards women and wanting to try and give one a shock. (quoted in Parker, 1969, p. 171)

Exhibitionism seems to be fairly common in our society. This activity accounts for 35 percent of arrests for sexual offenses (Freese, 1972). In a recent study, a third of the undergraduate women surveyed reported having encountered an exhibitionist, and over half knew other women who had had such encounters. Although most of the women said the experience was only slightly or not at all upsetting, one in five found it severely distressing (Cox, 1988).

The typical exhibitionist is in his twenties, single, and emotionally immature. He is likely to be lonely, timid, inhibited, and puritanical. Usually he is not dangerous. Occasionally, however, an exhibitionist may be intent on terrorizing his victim and may even become assaultive. Those exhibitionists who come close to their victims are most likely to be a serious threat.

Psychoanalytic explanations of exhibitionism focus on the exhibitionist's attempts to ward off "castration anxiety." In this view, the victim's response of fear or shock reassures the exhibitionist that he really does have a permanent penis. Exhibiting may also express unconscious feelings of defiance toward the mother, as suggested in the previous quote. (See also Box 10–1.) In contrast, behaviorists argue that exhibitionism develops when exposing the genitals becomes associated with sexual arousal and then later is relived in fantasy. Because arousal is extremely rewarding, the person may repeat the exhibiting.

Other psychological theories emphasize the exhibitionist's need to express contempt for authority by performing an antisocial act. Exposing the genitals is analogous to thumbing one's nose or "giving the finger." Not only is exhibiting contemptuous, but it gives the person a feeling of power and potency, traits traditionally associated with an erect penis.

OBSCENE TELEPHONE CALLING

Many mental health experts consider **obscene telephone calling** to be a kind of subtle exhibitionism (Matek, 1988). Like exhibitionism, it is an invasion of another person's privacy. The caller gets a sexual thrill from shocking, embarrassing, or manipulating the person at the other end of the line.

Obscene calls are quite common; in 1982 AT&T received reports of 1.3 million such calls (Newmark, 1984). Some of these calls, no doubt, are by teenagers playing pranks. Usually, however, the caller is an insecure adult male who has difficulty establishing intimate relations. The anonymity of the phone allows him to have an erotic experience without making face-to-face contact. Most callers phone their victims at random, but some select a particular person for harassment. Some callers say nothing; they merely breathe heavily. Some "talk dirty." Some boast about their sexual powers or

BOX 10–1

Exhibitionism: A Case History

Lance Rentzel seemed to have everything. He was prosperous, handsome, and a professional football star with the Dallas Cowboys, and he was married to actress Joey Heatherton. But on November 19, 1970, when, as he puts it, the Cowboys were again "blowing their chance" to be champions of the National Football League, he exposed himself to a ten-year-old girl. Rentzel recalled that it was like thumbing his nose at a teacher when her back was turned. In the ensuing public uproar, it was revealed that he had done the same thing in front of two girls four years earlier in Minneapolis while playing for the Minnesota Vikings, at a time when he was depressed, worried about his mother's health, and not playing well. The humorists had a field day with comments such as "trades to the Montreal Expos," "can really handle the fly pattern," "will be playing only during the exhibition season." He was out of football for a year, his marriage was in trouble (it was later dissolved), his whole life seemed to be going down the drain, and he considered suicide. How did "Golden Boy" Lance Rentzel come to such a state?

Rentzel grew up the winner, the center of attention, the mischievous but polite boy who couldn't say no, and the bearer of all his family's ideals. He believes his supermasculine strivings were attempts to escape from his overprotective mother and to win the approval of his successful father, who was away most of the time. He developed two immature needs that were all but invisible to him and everyone else: to prove his masculinity over and over and to avoid a meaningful adult relationship with a woman for fear she would smother him and he would not then be a man. Winning in football before thousands or millions of fans and conquests of women became major ways of handling these needs and whatever "furies" developed inside him. When he or his team wasn't winning, he resorted to a childish way of "proving" his masculinity, which may also have been one way of avoiding intimacy with his wife or with anyone else.

In his autobiography Lance said, and his psychiatrist affirmed, that he was learning in psychotherapy to be a man without having to prove it, and to separate his value as a person from winning in football.

Summarized and adapted from Rentzel, 1972.

describe their sexual behavior (usually masturbation) in detail. Some make threats ("I know where you live"). Still others trick their target into revealing sexual information about herself by pretending to be conducting a sex survey or selling lingerie. One woman we know was maneuvered into a discussion of her breasts by a man posing as a doctor from the hospital where she had recently given birth.

Although obscene callers are more pathetic than dangerous, their calls can be extremely upsetting. Phone companies say the best response is to hang up immediately. If the calls persist, you can either get an unlisted number or ask the police to have the phone company use an electronic "trap" to find out where the calls are originating.

FETISHISM

In its general sense, a *fetish* is an object that is regarded as having magical power, and fetishism is belief in or use of fetishes. However, in psychiatry and psychology the term **fetishism** refers to sexual arousal in response to a particular part of the body or an inanimate object. The body part may be sexual, such as the breasts, or nonsexual, such as the feet. The inanimate object most often is an article of clothing, such as underwear or shoes. For some fetishists the form and shape of the object is important, while others respond to the material from which the fetish is made. Fetishists are nearly always male.

Of course, many people are aroused at the sight of certain features of the body (large breasts, small rear ends), by certain articles of clothing (garter belts, lacy bras), or by certain settings. This response is perfectly normal and in the view of most psychiatrists and psychologists does not make a person a fetishist. The true fetishist has a compulsive attachment to his fetish and typically cannot achieve sexual arousal or gratification in its absence.

What the fetishist does with the object varies from person to person and depends, in part, on the nature of the object. Some fetishists masturbate against it or fantasize about it or fondle it while masturbating. If the object is an article of clothing, the fetishist may insist that a partner wear it during intercourse. Sometimes a fetishist is able to find a partner who is nonjudgmental and will cooperate with him:

> The husband was fascinated by elbow-length gloves. Unless his wife wore white kid gloves during intercourse he was practically impotent. As soon as she drew them on, however, he was powerfully stimulated. They kept a number of pairs of gloves in a special drawer. It was ceremoniously unlocked before going to bed as though beginning a sacred rite. This preliminary was a kind of symbolic love-play. (Chesser, 1971, p. 116)

Since fetishists come to the attention of legal authorities much less often than voyeurs and exhibitionists do, it is not clear how numerous they are or what motivates them. Mild fetishism is probably common among people who are not considered disturbed, especially if one includes objects or body parts that are merely fantasized about during sexual relations.

Psychoanalysts have proposed many theories to explain fetishism. Freud claimed that the fetish was a substitute for the penis, which the fetishist, as a child, believed his mother possessed. According to Freud, as a fetishist grows up he comes to realize, at a conscious level, that the mother does not have an actual penis. But at an unconscious level he persists in the belief that she has some sort of mysterious male organ. Non-Freudians find such explanations fanciful, however. Instead of providing a penis substitute, fetishism, like other unusual sexual behaviors, may simply give an immature or anxious person a way to obtain sexual gratification in a socially undemanding situation (at least in cases where the fetish is used for masturbation). Or, for the person who is afraid of an emotionally intimate relationship with another human being, it may put emotional distance between the person and his partner.

Behaviorists explain fetishism in the same way they explain exhibitionism and voyeurism: as accidental conditioning. At some early point in development, usually before adolescence, arousal happens to occur in the presence of an object or body part. This pleasurable event is then repeated in fantasy, and the fetishist eventually becomes dependent on the object or body part for arousal. For example, Tollison and Adams (1979) cite the case of a man who developed a fetish for plaster casts. At age eleven he broke his leg. An attractive nurse held the bare leg so that the cast could be set, stimulating his thigh and producing an erection. Later he masturbated while thinking about the incident. Eventually he amassed a collection of actual casts to use during masturbation and heterosexual intercourse.

In an intriguing experiment, S. Rachman (1966) demonstrated just how sexual arousal to inanimate objects can develop through conditioning. Rachman showed pictures of women's boots to clinical psychology graduate students, pairing these pictures with photographs of nude females. After many such pairings, sexual arousal (as measured by changes in penile blood volume) occurred in response to pictures of the boots alone. In fact, arousal generalized to pictures of other types of women's shoes as well!

TRANSVESTISM

Transvestism (often abbreviated as TV) is dressing in the clothing of the other sex for the purpose of sexual arousal and gratification. The term is usually applied only to heterosexual males. It should not be confused with *transsexualism*, which is discussed in the next section and in Chapter 12. Transvestism is similar to fetishism, except that instead of using one article of clothing for sexual arousal, the transvestite uses a whole costume, and he wears the clothing.

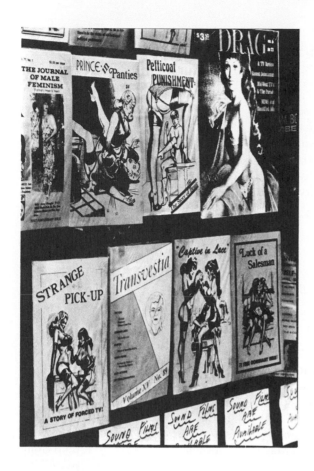

Transvestite magazines
Some kinds of pornography appeal to unconventional sexual interests. Several different magazines cater to transvestites.

Most people who cross-dress are *not* transvestites. Women who cross-dress do so to be comfortable, to make a political statement, or to be fashionable, not to get sexually excited (although there are some rare exceptions). Female impersonators cross-dress to entertain other people. Some gay men cross-dress—dress in "drag"—in order to be outrageous, get attention, or parody gender roles. Many of us cross-dress on Halloween. Some men simply experiment with cross-dressing once or twice to see what it is like. Cross-dressing is transvestism, however, only when it is sexually stimulating to the cross-dresser.

How the transvestite uses cross-sex clothing varies from person to person (see Table 10–1). He might masturbate while observing himself in a mirror, cross-dress during heterosexual relations, cross-dress in public and attempt to pass as the other sex, wear garments of the other sex under his regular clothing, or masturbate to memories or fantasies of public excursions. Some men identify with a transvestite subculture. When not "dressed," transvestites are as masculine-looking as the next man.

	Feature	Type I	Type II	Type III
TABLE 10–1 **Types of Transvestism** Not all transvestites (TVs) have the same degree of interest in cross-dressing, nor do they necessarily share the same motivations or styles. This table compares three different types of transvestites.	Life Style	Lives as a man. Gets occasional "kick" out of "dressing" or fantasizing about this activity.	Lives as a man. "Dresses" periodically or part of the time. "Dresses" underneath male clothes.	"Dresses" as often as possible. May live and be accepted as a woman. May "dress" underneath male clothes, if no other chance.
	Gender Identity	Masculine	Masculine	Masculine (but with less conviction)
	Sex Life	Masturbation fantasies may include "dressing" and "sex change" themes. May enjoy TV literature.	Masturbation with fetish. Guilt feelings. Tries to refrain from "dressing" but relapses.	"Dressing" gives sexual satisfaction and gratification. May try to refrain from "dressing," but relapses.
	Psychotherapy?	Not wanted. Unnecessary.	May be successful.	Usually not successful.
	Remarks	Interest in "dressing" is only sporadic.	May try out double (masculine and feminine) personality with male and female names.	May assume double personality. A few become transsexuals.

Adapted from The Transsexual Phenomenon *by Benjamin, Harry. New York: Warner, 1966.*

For transvestites who cross-dress in public, fooling people may be as exciting as the dressing. In the words of one man:

> It is the challenge of being so much like a woman that no one knows I'm a man that turns me on. The combination of doing something that I want to, that everyone says is impossible and is forbidden anyway, produces in me an arousal which. . .becomes sexual arousal. (Gosselin & Wilson, 1980, p. 267)

In a survey of subscribers to a magazine called *Transvestia*, over three-fourths of the respondents were either married or divorced (Prince & Bentler, 1972). Some wives of transvestites are very supportive of their husbands, even helping them choose clothes and make-up. Some wives dislike the cross-dressing, but tolerate it. And some are greatly upset by their spouse's behavior, insisting he go for treatment if he wants to stay married.

Transvestites usually report cross-dressing before the age of ten (Croughan et al., 1981). The development of transvestism is poorly understood. There is a folklore among transvestites that says cross-dressing begins with a "petticoat punishment," when parents humiliate their son by dressing him in girl's clothing. But other stories attribute transvestism to encouragement of cross-dressing by parents who wanted a girl instead of a boy. Some psychoanalysts believe that transvestism is an attempt to conquer the fear of castration. The person reassures himself that females are no different from males—that women do possess a penis—by making himself into a "phallic woman." In contrast, behaviorists believe that transvestism occurs for the same reason that fetishism does: the clothing of the other sex is associated early in life with sexual arousal or behavior and thus becomes capable of eliciting sexual responses.

TRANSSEXUALISM

Transsexuals are persons who believe that nature has trapped them in bodies that are at odds with their true psychological gender. Their belief causes them great discomfort and may drive them to seek sex-change surgery and to live as a member of the other sex. Many transsexuals cross-dress, but their motive is not sexual arousal, as it is for the transvestite. They simply want to make their appearance congruent with what they perceive to be their gender. Some writers on sexuality classify transsexualism with the paraphilias, but we feel this is a mistake, because transsexualism involves a person's entire sense of identity rather than specifically sexual behavior. For that reason, we discuss transsexualism in detail in Chapter 12, where we cover the development of gender identity.

SADOMASOCHISM

Sadism is the infliction of pain or abuse for one's own pleasure. It can occur in any kind of relationship, sexual or nonsexual. Here our concern is

Free to be me

Demonstrations for civil rights are common in the United States. It's not so common to see a rally for transvestite rights, though—or to see participants as good-natured as these.

with the infliction of suffering, humiliation, or pain as a preferred or necessary element of sexual excitement. The term sadism derives from the name of the Marquis de Sade (1740–1814), a French novelist and soldier who wrote about such brutal exploits as hanging women from the ceiling and whipping them as his servant manually stimulated the Marquis' genitals. De Sade was eventually committed to an insane asylum.

Masochism is the enjoyment of self-denial, submissiveness, or suffering. Like sadism, it can occur in any kind of relationship. Here our focus is on the need or desire to experience suffering, pain, or humiliation to achieve sexual excitement. The term masochism comes from the name of the Austrian novelist Leopold von Sacher-Masoch (1835–1895), who wrote about people who obtained sexual gratification from pain, and who was himself a masochist.

The term **sadomasochism** (SM) is used for the combination of sadism and masochism. Images of sadomasochism in fashion and popular music have become commonplace over the last decade. Such images raise, once again, the thorny issue of where to draw the line between normal experience and disordered activities. Many people have masochistic or sadistic fantasies (although they do not necessarily want their fantasies realized). Many people enjoy being bitten, scratched, or pinched, or having their hair pulled or their arms pinned down during intercourse. Morton Hunt (1974) reported small but noteworthy proportions (ranging from 2 to 10 percent) of men and women who obtained sexual pleasure from either inflicting or receiving pain. (In his sample men were more likely to inflict, women to receive.) Kinsey (1948, 1953) found that roughly half of both the men and women in his study reported at least some erotic response to being bitten during sex.

Some people enjoy playing mock sadomasochistic games in which both partners agree that the activities will cease if either genuinely protests. For example, one partner might tie the other to the bed with scarves and pretend to inflict a flogging. In enactments of this sort, the pain is usually feigned. The appeal of mock sadomasochism is probably not pain but the idea of overcoming resistance, or, for the "victim," of having one's resistance overcome. Many psychologists and psychiatrists consider activities of this sort perfectly normal and harmless. One psychoanalyst, Robert J. Stoller (1979), has argued that even in conventional sex, a bit of hostility or tension enhances sexual excitement, while its complete absence leads to apathy and boredom. But for most professionals, the line is drawn when erotic gratification and pain are repeatedly or exclusively fused in sexual activity with a nonconsenting or even with a consenting partner.

Recent research has examined sadomasochism as a social phenomenon. A sizable subculture of sadomasochism exists in the United States. According to a review by Thomas Weinberg (1987), within this subculture, sadomasochistic activity has certain shared meanings: it is erotic, consensual, and recreational. Play-like SM scenarios often involve elaborately staged fantasies and expensive props, sets, and costumes. The essential elements seem to be the illusion of violence and the ritualization of dominance and submission. Terms such as "master," "mistress," and "tops" for the dominant partner and "slave" or "bottom" for the submissive one are used. Typically both partners collaborate in developing the scenario. Together they agree on what acts will occur, when they will occur, and even the dialogue to be used. It is not unusual for partners to switch roles.

Some writers distinguish the heterosexual SM "scene" (often called "D&S" for dominance and submission) from homosexual SM subcultures. The different groups have their own organizations, sexual signals, and preferred attire. For example, sadomasochistic gay men are more likely than heterosexuals to wear leather. Among both heterosexuals and homosexuals there are more male practitioners of both sadism and masochism. Sadomasochistic acts vary from verbal humiliation and the suggestion of pain to

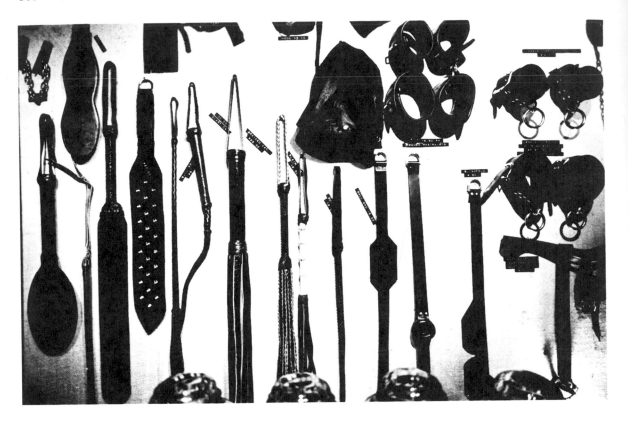

"The pleasure chest"

This photograph of sadomasochistic paraphernalia was taken at a store located on an avenue lined with office buildings in the middle of New York City.

more dangerous activities, such as trampling, whipping, and strangulation. Some individuals have a specific preference for bondage and discipline ("B&D"), in which one partner ties up and whips or spanks the other. Some get sexual stimulation from enemas, having one partner urinate on the other ("water sports"), having one partner defecate on the other, or cross-dressing. Special interests are emphasized in ads, such as the following, placed in underground and sexually oriented publications:

> Dominant male looking for single females, couples and submissive TS's. Fully equipped dungeon, training in all arts. [TS stands for "toilet slave," one who receives the excrement of the "mistress" or "master."]

> Young male submissive seeks to serve a beautiful, well shaped Mistress as your personal toilet slave. I enjoy cock and ball torture. (Weinberg, 1987, p. 62)

Some heterosexual male masochists patronize prostitutes who specialize in sadistic services. There are houses of prostitution with special "torture chambers" stocked with whips, chains, ropes, enema bottles, and the like. The prostitute and her client may engage in elaborate role-playing, in which the prostitute acts the part of the mistress and the client the part of a slave.

Psychoanalysts suggest that sadism, like exhibitionism, provides relief from sexual anxiety by making someone else powerless. The goal is to "do unto others before they do unto you" (Tollison & Adams, 1979). In this view, sadism by a male against a female may also express rage unconsciously felt toward the sadist's mother. Psychoanalysts regard masochism as sadism turned inward toward the self or as fixation at an early state of psychosexual development when the person felt helpless and overpowered. Behaviorists usually see both sadism and masochism as resulting from the past association of orgasm with pain. For example, masochism might develop in a person who was spanked while being simultaneously caressed on the genitals by a disturbed parent. However, one study of self-defined sadomasochists (Moser, 1979) found that over 80 percent of the sample did not recall having received erotic enjoyment from being punished as a child.

Other explanations of sadomasochism see it as emerging from a social context. Sexologist Paul Gebhard (1969) has noted the importance of dominance-submissiveness relationships in the organization of our culture. The male sadist's motives may be similar to those of the rapist: to establish a sense of power and prove masculinity by dominating, humiliating, and overwhelming another (Johnson, 1972). Perhaps masochism is particularly attractive to individuals who lead lives governed by great self-control or responsibility; they may enjoy the novelty of feeling helpless and putting themselves at the mercy of another person.

Many questions regarding sadomasochism remain unanswered. Why are most men in the United States SM subculture submissives? How interchangeable are the roles? How is it that the rate of injuries and deaths attributed to SM practices is not excessive? And how does pain become eroticized in the first place?

PEDOPHILIA

Pedophilia (from the Greek for "love of children") is a primary sexual attraction to children. Sometimes the terms "pedophilia" and "child molester" are used synonymously, but not all **child molesters** are pedophiles. A child molester is anyone who sexually approaches or has sexual contact with a child. The hallmark of pedophilia is a strong or exclusive orientation toward children as sexual objects. This description does not fit all child molesters. For example, in incest cases, the adult may have sexual contact with a daughter or son, but not be sexually attracted to children in general. (We discuss incest at length in Chapter 15.) Psychiatric and psychological opinion is that most people who engage in isolated acts of child molestation are not pedophiles (American Psychiatric Association, 1987).

Pedophiles are usually male and may be either heterosexual or homosexual. Pedophiles vary considerably in their personal characteristics. They may be young or old, although most often pedophilia begins in adolescence. Some individuals have criminal records but others are to all appearances, upstanding citizens—teachers, scout leaders, and others who have frequent contact with children. All studies find that a pedophile is more apt to be a friend or an acquaintance of the victim than a stranger. In most cases, just one child and one adult are involved but sometimes a group of adults may, together, operate a ring of molesters. Some pedophiles are involved in the production and consumption of child pornography.

Attempts have been made to classify molesters according to various psychological characteristics. For instance, Cohen, Seghorn, and Calmas (1969) distinguished three general categories, according to motive. The *personally immature* pedophile is uncomfortable with adults. He feels safer and more in control with children. He is usually drawn to children he knows, befriending them and spending a lot of time with them. The *regressed* pedophile approaches children after experiencing problems in adult relationships that threaten his sense of masculinity or make him feel sexually inadequate. Usually he acts impulsively and approaches children he does not know. *Aggressive* pedophiles—the rarest category—are antisocial and hostile. Their motives resemble those of rapists and they may physically assault their victims.

Pedophiles are oriented toward female children twice as often as to male children, but many are attracted to both boys and girls (American Psychiatric Association, 1987). Those oriented mainly to girls tend to prefer eight- to ten-year-olds while those attracted to boys tend to prefer slightly older children. Some people who act on pedophilic urges limit their activities to undressing and looking at the child, exposing themselves to the child, or masturbating in the child's presence. Some go farther, touching and fondling the child or performing oral-genital acts. And some perform anal acts, using fingers, objects, or the penis, with varying degrees of force. Perpetrators commonly rationalize their behavior by telling themselves that the child enjoys it, that they are giving the child valuable "sex education," or that the child has been sexually provocative (American Psychiatric Association, 1987). In reality, however, children are never responsible for adult-child sex, and they often suffer devastating consequences lasting well into adulthood. We discuss these consequences further in Chapter 15.

HYPERSEXUALITY

The term **hypersexuality** is used to describe a state of sexual insatiability. A hypersexual individual experiences more or less continual sexual desire and arousal, focuses his or her life around sexual activities, and is unable to establish satisfying personal relationships or make other life adjustments because of the sexual compulsion (Tollison & Adams, 1979).

Certain other terms have been used to refer to hypersexual individuals. *Nymphomaniac* (from the Greek *nymph*, meaning "maiden" or "bride," and *mania*, meaning "madness") is the traditional word for a woman with an excessive sexual craving. A less well-known term, *satyr*, is sometimes applied to a man with an excessive sexual craving. (In classical mythology, a satyr was a woodland deity—part human and part goat—who attended Bacchus, the god of wine and fertility. Satyrs were noted for riotousness and wanton lustfulness.) Another label for male hypersexuality is *Don Juanism*, derived from the name of a legendary Spanish nobleman and libertine. In recent years all these labels have fallen out of favor with psychologists and sex researchers because of their moralistic connotations and because they are frequently used indiscriminately to label people who are normal and healthy but are simply more sexually active than the average person.

Sex and sexual conquest dominate and run the hypersexual person's life, but ultimately, sexual experiences are emotionally shallow and disappointing. The compulsive quality of the hypersexual's behavior has led some to think of hypersexuality as an "addiction" to sex (see Box 10–2).

While some researchers believe that hypersexuality can result from disease or injury to the limbic system of the brain (see Chapter 4), most cases probably have a psychological explanation. For example, the person may have an unusually strong need for love and affection but be unwilling or unable to make the emotional investment necessary for true intimacy. Instead, he or she may go from one sexual partner to another in the vain hope that the next one will magically bestow emotional or sexual satisfaction. Or, hypersexuality may be a way of expressing hostility toward others—a way of saying that the partner is only one among many and therefore of little value (Altrocchi, 1980). Hypersexuality sometimes characterizes antisocial people who pride themselves on using others for their own needs while remaining emotionally detached themselves.

In many cases, compulsive sexuality may be symptomatic of a problem that is not really sexual at all. According to sex therapist Helen Singer Kaplan (1979), many individuals who appear to be preoccupied with sex do not have an unusually strong sex drive. They are simply anxious and tense persons who try to relieve their discomfort by having sex. The sexual obsession serves as a smoke screen to obscure whatever it is that is really bothering the person. In such cases, says Kaplan, the person needs long-term psychotherapy to uncover the hidden source of the distress.

OTHER PARAPHILIAS

In addition to the unconventional behaviors already discussed, people engage in a variety of exotic paraphilias. The following are some of the more unusual ones:

- *Autoerotic asphyxia* refers to the practice of cutting off one's oxygen, usually by means of a noose around the neck, in an

BOX 10–2

Sex Junkies Anonymous

Many of us know someone who is an alcoholic. Some of us have friends we call workaholics. But can a person be a "sexaholic"? Can people be "addicted" to sex just as they are to alcohol and drugs? Some psychologists and psychiatrists think so.

Patrick Carnes, author of *The Sexual Addiction* (1983), was one of the first people to call attention to this question. Carnes observes that some people use sex the same way others use alcohol and drugs, in a compulsive attempt to relieve psychological pain, manage anxieties and tensions, or escape feelings of isolation. Sex "addicts" are hypersexual: they are obsessed with sex, but unable to enjoy it for either recreation or the expression of affection. Some use casual sex as a way to be physically close while avoiding emotional closeness. Some compulsively engage in exhibitionism or voyeurism. Some, says Carnes, get hooked on orgasms in the same way that drug addicts get hooked on drug-induced highs.

According to Carnes, compulsive sexual behavior is always secret, abusive of oneself or others, a source of painful feelings or a way of avoiding feelings, and unrelated to a caring, committed relationship. Carnes describes a four-phase cycle that typifies the "addict's" behavior. It begins with an intense preoccupation with thoughts of sex. This phase is followed by the performance of a sexual ritual or routine that intensifies the preoccupation and adds arousal and excitement—for example "cruising" for partners in some habitual place. Neither the preoccupying thoughts nor the sexual ritual is necessarily obvious to others. In the third phase, the person engages in some compulsive, uncontrollable sexual act. Finally, there is despair, the feeling of utter helplessness addicts have about their behaviors. But this despair is soon numbed by thoughts of sex—and so, the cycle starts all over again. According to Carnes, like other addicts, "sex addicts" find that a "fix" (in this case, sex) does not end their craving.

attempt to heighten sexual excitement or orgasm while masturbating. Unlike many other paraphilias, this is a private, solitary activity and is extremely dangerous. Autoerotic asphyxia results in an estimated 500 to 1,000 deaths a year in the United States, a good percentage of them misdiagnosed as suicide or homicide or covered up by the family because of embarrassment (Brody, 1984). Almost all the victims of auto-

Mark Schwartz, a specialist in sex therapy at Tulane University, has also developed a set of criteria to recognize "sexual addiction." They include: a willingness to take inordinate risks to engage in sexual encounters; a sexual preoccupation that interferes with a normal sexual relationship with one's spouse or lover; a compulsion to have repeated sexual relations in a short period of time; a need to keep sexual behavior secret from others; habitually taking large amounts of time away from work or family in order to engage in sex or look for sexual adventure; and routinely feeling anxious and depressed or guilty and ashamed after engaging in sexual behaviors (Schwartz & Masters, 1988).

Not everyone agrees, however, that the concept of sexual addiction is a useful one. The term *addiction* has traditionally been used in medicine and physiology for conditions in which brain chemistry is modified by some substance, without which the person experiences physical withdrawal symptoms. To extend the word to any activity that people overdo, including sex, say the critics, deprives it of its meaning. Moreover, the term "addict" could easily be used to label as pathological anyone whose behavior one disapproves of on moral grounds. Neither sexual addiction nor hyperactive sexuality is currently included in the *Diagnostic and Statistical Manual* (DSM III-R) of the American Psychiatric Association, the official guide to diagnosis for both psychiatrists and psychologists.

However, while the professional debate continues, a self-help movement is growing. Most major U.S. cities now have groups, modeled after the Twelve Step program of Alcoholics Anonymous, for people who believe themselves to be sexually compulsive. Begun in the late 1970s, such groups include Sex and Love Addicts Anonymous, Sexaholics Anonymous, Sexual Compulsives Anonymous, and Sex Addicts Anonymous. Their members come together to offer each other support and compassion for a problem others may find funny, but which, for them, is no joke. Research, however, is needed to evaluate the outcomes of such programs.

erotic asphyxia are adolescent and young adult males who inadvertently lose consciousness and hang to death. Often the victim is found with pornographic materials and is partly or totally undressed or wearing women's underclothes (Hazelwood, Deitz & Burgess, 1983). Autoerotic asphyxia can be combined with sadomasochism, transvestism or festishism (Sarason & Sarason, 1987).

BLOOM COUNTY   By Berke Breathed

Bloom County, COPYRIGHT, 1983, Berke Breathed Reprinted with permission of Universal Press Syndicate. All rights reserved.

Water fowl?!   *In all cultures, certain sexual preferences are considered strange and shocking.*

- *Coprophilia* is sexual interest in and arousal to excrement. The person may watch others defecate, defecate on others, or ask to be defecated on. Sexual excitement preferentially or exclusively from the use of enemas is called *klismaphilia*. Sexual gratification from eating feces is known as *coprophagia*.

- *Frottage* (or *frotteurism*) is the practice of obtaining sexual arousal by touching or rubbing against a nonconsenting person. In its most common form, a man rubs his penis against a fully clothed woman. Frottage sometimes occurs in crowded public situations, such as on a bus or in a subway. Frotteurs are usually unable to maintain an erection in more conventional sexual situations.

- *Necrophilia* is sexual interest in corpses. The necrophiliac either looks at the corpse for sexual stimulation or has intercourse with it (although the word *intercourse* seems something of a misnomer, since it implies two participants). Necrophiliacs are usually psychotic.

- *Urophilia* is sexual interest in and arousal to urine. The urophiliac may watch others urinate, urinate on others, ask to be urinated on, or even drink urine. The urination is often referred to colloquially as "golden showers." The famous nineteenth-century sex researcher Havelock Ellis reputedly had a mild form of urophilia.

- *Zoophilia* (or *bestiality*) is a sexual interest in animals. It may involve intercourse with an animal, the licking or rubbing of a person's genitals by an animal, the masturbation of an animal, or the performance of oral sex on an animal. Some people engage in sex with animals out of curiosity or when human partners are unavailable. Such temporary behavior is not considered a paraphilia. Kinsey and his associates (1948) reported that 17 percent of male adolescents who grew up on farms had sexual contact with animals to the point of orgasm, and perhaps as many had relations that did not lead to orgasm. Overall, almost eight percent of adult males reported having sexual contact with an animal at some point in their lives. For females the corresponding figure was four percent (Kinsey et al., 1953). Few of the females had contact that led to orgasm.

Two other behaviors, *pyromania* (a compulsion to start fires) and *kleptomania* (an obsessive impulse to steal), may at times have sexual significance. Indeed, any behavior can be eroticized and constitute a paraphilia.

TREATING PARAPHILIAS

Throughout this chapter we have emphasized that engaging in an unconventional form of sexual expression does not automatically mean a person is abnormal. Experimental or occasional involvement in certain forms of sexual variation may be completely harmless, both to the person and to others. But when a behavior becomes compulsive or threatens someone's happiness or welfare, then treatment may be appropriate. The major approach in treating paraphilias is behavioral. At times psychotherapeutic or medical treatments are also used.

Behavioral treatment focuses on two goals, the elimination of sexually inappropriate behaviors and the promotion of desirable ones. *Aversive conditioning* has often been used to eliminate unwanted behavior or thoughts. This method consists of systematically pairing an unpleasant stimulus, such as electric shock or a nausea-inducing chemical, with the inappropriate behavior or thought. For example, a transvestite might receive a shock each time he imagines dressing up in a woman's clothing, or while he actually cross-dresses and watches himself in a mirror. A voyeur might receive a shock while watching slides showing the kind of woman he likes to "peep" at. Or shock might be paired with verbal descriptions of peeping.

A technique called *aversive behavior rehearsal (ABR)*, which associates shame with the person's behavior, has been used in the treatment of exhibitionism (Sue, Sue & Sue, 1990). The exhibitionist is required to carry out his usual exposure routine in front of a preselected audience of women who stare at him impassively. During the session, which is videotaped, he verbalizes his thoughts and feelings. Since he cannot hide behind anonymity, he experiences humiliation. Later, while watching the tape, he can see how his behavior looks to others.

Some therapists use a behavioral technique called *covert sensitization*, in which the patient thinks about his behavior while including negative elements in his fantasy. For example, a sadist might be encouraged to imagine being discovered, arrested, ridiculed, and imprisoned for his acts (Hayes, Brownell & Barlow, 1978). Or an exhibitionist might imagine being caught by the police in the act of exhibiting, or getting sick and vomiting as he starts to exhibit.

In addition to eliminating unwanted behaviors, behaviorists usually attempt to foster appropriate sexual responses. One technique involves pairing images or thoughts of appropriate behaviors with a pleasant stimulus or experience. For example, an exhibitionist who has orgasms only while exposing himself in public might be encouraged to masturbate while fantasizing about ordinary heterosexual intercourse. In *orgasmic reconditioning*, an appropriate sexual stimulus, such as the image of a woman, is substituted for the inappropriate stimulus. A sadomasochist, for example, might be asked to masturbate while imagining an SM scene. Just before ejaculation, he substitutes the image of a woman, then continues to masturbate to orgasm. This process is repeated over and over, with the image substitution occurring a little earlier in the sequence on each successive occasion (Sue, Sue, & Sue, 1990). Sometimes this positive approach is combined with aversion therapy. For example, a fetishist might inhale strong smelling salts whenever he starts to think about his fetish and also be encouraged to masturbate while looking at photographs of nude women (Tollison & Adams, 1979).

An important therapeutic process for many paraphiliacs is learning how to manage the anxiety they experience in ordinary sexual encounters. *Desensitization* first teaches a person to cope with situations that are only slightly threatening; then he moves on to progressively more anxiety-provoking ones. For example, a man might first master the anxiety aroused when he is in the same room with a woman, then learn how to comfortably introduce himself to a woman, and later learn how to relax while carrying on a casual conversation. A total treatment program may include assertiveness training and other methods of teaching social and sexual skills. Treatment for married men may include couples therapy.

Psychoanalysis, which involves the long-term exploration of unconscious motivations and feelings, and other long-term therapies, are not used as often in the treatment of paraphilias as are behavioral therapies, in part because of the time and expense required. Opinion is divided on the ultimate effectiveness of psychoanalysis for these conditions. Insight oriented group therapy has been tried with men incarcerated for sexual crimes such as indecent exposure and child molestation, with unclear results.

Medical approaches rely mainly on the administration of antiandrogens to reduce the level of the person's sexual excitation (see Chapter 5). When the patient's feelings of sexual urgency are reduced, other forms of therapy may be more effective.

At present it is difficult to say how effective any of these treatment techniques are in producing long-term changes in unconventional behavior. Most research reports are case studies that do not include a control group, so effectiveness is hard to assess (Sue, Sue & Sue, 1990). A critical factor in any program is the motivation of the individual undergoing treatment. If the person is satisfied with the way things are and has no serious adjustment problems, therapy may not only be a waste of time but may be unjustified from an ethical point of view. (As Mark Twain once wryly observed, "Nothing so needs reforming as *other* people's habits" [emphasis added].) But when the person or the person's sexual partner suffers because of the behavior and there is a willingness to change, then attempts to alter or eliminate the behavior are justified.

. . . .

FACING THE FORBIDDEN

PERSONAL PERSPECTIVE

Students often tell us that the information in this chapter brings up strong feelings, most of them negative. Some of the behaviors described, like voyeurism, exhibitionism, and obscene telephone calling, are not only unconventional but involve a nonconsenting target who may experience the behavior as abuse. Abusive behavior is so common in our society that this chapter often triggers recollections of negative personal experiences.

Another reason this chapter can make people uncomfortable is that paraphilias are socially taboo. In the process of being socialized, we learn to label these acts as "weird," "kinky," "sick," "deviant," and "perverted." But, as Adam and Eve found in the Garden of Eden, the forbidden can have a seductive appeal. Images of acts we publicly abhor may creep into our dreams and fantasies. Our feelings about prohibited behaviors may reflect a basic conflict between our socialization and our hidden desires.

We do not all have the same reactions to the same behaviors, however. This exercise can help you become more aware of *your* feelings.

Rate your reactions to the acts in the list below according to the following scale:

+ + Positive, one of my preferred activities.
+   Accepting, though I am unlikely to engage in this behavior.
+ − Mixed. I have both positive and negative feelings.
−   Unaccepting. I feel uncomfortable about this act.
− − Negative. This act is disgusting.
0   Neutral. I don't have any feelings one way or the other.

_____ 1. Watching a partner undress
_____ 2. With binoculars, watching a neighbor undress
_____ 3. Being watched, unawares, by a stranger while undressing
_____ 4. Undressing for a partner
_____ 5. Displaying one's genitals to a stranger
_____ 6. Being sexually seductive with a lover on the telephone
_____ 7. Talking "dirty" to a stranger on the telephone

_____ 8. Receiving an obscene phone call
_____ 9. Regarding shoes as "sexy" (literally)
_____ 10. Being sexually attracted only to women with large breasts, or men with small buttocks
_____ 11. Saving mementos (ticket stubs, letters, pictures, etc.) as reminders of special dates or partners
_____ 12. Dressing in the clothes of the other sex in order to be sexually aroused
_____ 13. Dressing in the clothes of the other sex on Halloween
_____ 14. Being overwhelmed and overpowered by a lover during lovemaking
_____ 15. Participating in mock sadomasochistic games as part of lovemaking
_____ 16. Including some biting, scratching, or pinching during lovemaking
_____ 17. Spanking or whipping a sex partner or lover
_____ 18. Being spanked or whipped by a sex partner or lover
_____ 19. French-kissing (tongue kissing) a young child
_____ 20. Kissing a young child goodnight
_____ 21. Going nude in front of a child in your home.
_____ 22. Caressing and fondling a child out of sexual desire
_____ 23. Enjoying sex and sexual fantasies more than most other recreational activities
_____ 24. Constantly thinking about sex to the exclusion of all other activities
_____ 25. Masturbating a dog

Remember:
  a) Some people, try as they may, cannot identify their gut feelings.
  b) It is not uncommon to have feelings about our feelings. We are comfortable with some of our reactions, but there are others we would just as soon ignore.
  c) Feelings are not immutable, though we don't change them as easily or as frequently as we change our clothes.
  d) The first step in changing an unwanted feeling is to acknowledge it.
  e) Feelings and actions are *not* the same. Unconventional feelings and fantasies are probably more common than most people realize.

IN BRIEF

1. *Paraphilias* are unconventional sexual behaviors that are viewed by most people as bizarre and abnormal. Such judgments occur in a social

and cultural context and are therefore subject to modification. Most mental health professionals consider paraphilic behaviors to be abnormal, although in specific cases judgments of abnormality are not always easy to make. Paraphilic behaviors are often compulsive, may be harmful or destructive to those who practice them, and may affect a nonconsenting partner. Men are more likely to engage in these behaviors than women are, possibly because of certain features of male and female gender roles.

2. Most theories regarding paraphilias have been either psychoanalytic or behavioral. Psychoanalysts attribute these behaviors to psychosexual immaturity or emotional conflict and see them as defense mechanisms. Behaviorists emphasize accidental conditioning. Recently, some writers have focused on the social conditions that might encourage paraphilias. Much of what we currently know about paraphilias is based on clinical observation and studies of convicted sex offenders.

3. *Voyeurism* is the achievement of sexual gratification through covert observation of people who are nude, in the act of undressing, or engaged in sexual activity. Voyeurs show little interest in socially approved opportunities for sexual looking, preferring instead situations that have an element of risk.

4. *Exhibitionism* is the exposure of one's genitals to an unsuspecting person as a way of experiencing sexual arousal. It accounts for a high proportion of arrests for sexual offenses. The exhibitionist may have a need to shock the viewer or express contempt and hostility.

5. *Obscene telephone calling* is also quite common. The caller gets a sexual thrill from shocking, upsetting, and manipulating the recipient of the call.

6. *Fetishism* is a compulsive sexual attachment to some inanimate object or body part. The person cannot obtain sexual gratification in the absence of the fetish, and uses it in masturbation or in relations with a partner.

7. *Transvestism* is cross-dressing for the purpose of sexual arousal and gratification. Transvestism is similar to fetishism except that instead of using one article of clothing to achieve arousal, the transvestite wears an entire outfit. Most transvestites are heterosexual males.

8. *Transsexuals* are people who believe that nature has trapped them in the body of the wrong sex. Because transsexualism involves a person's entire sense of gender identity rather than a specific sexual behavior, the authors do not consider it to be a paraphilia. It is discussed in detail in Chapter 12.

9. Sexual *sadism* is the infliction of pain, suffering, or humiliation for the purpose of sexual excitement. Sexual *masochism* is the need or desire to experience pain, suffering, or humiliation for the purpose of sexual

excitement. The term *sadomasochism* (SM) refers to the combination of the two behaviors. Mildly sadistic activities, such as biting and pinching, as well as mock sadistic games, sometimes occur during "normal" sexual relations and seem to be harmless. But when erotic gratification and pain are repeatedly or exclusively fused, real physical or mental violence may take place. Recent research has examined the SM subculture, which ritualizes dominance and submission according to elaborate scenarios. Many questions remain about the meaning and safety of sadomasochistic behavior.

10. *Pedophilia* is a strong or exclusive orientation toward children as sexual objects. Pedophiles vary considerably, but have been classified according to motive as personally immature, regressed, and aggressive. Pedophiles are usually men and are usually heterosexual. They are oriented toward female children more often than male children, but many are attracted to both boys and girls. Pedophiles commonly rationalize their behavior and deny the devastating consequences it will have for their victims.

11. *Hypersexuality* is compulsive sexuality that interferes with satisfying personal relationships. The person may be unable or unwilling to make the emotional investment necessary for intimacy with a partner, or may use sex to express hostility toward others. In many cases, hypersexual behavior may be an attempt to relieve anxiety caused by nonsexual problems. Some clinicians think of hypersexuality as an addiction to sex, but this view is controversial.

12. A number of other paraphilias exist, including autoerotic asphyxia, coprophilia, frottage, necrophilia, urophilia, and zoophilia.

13. Several behavioral techniques have been used to treat paraphilias, including aversive conditioning, aversive behavioral rehearsal, covert sensitization, orgasmic reconditioning, and desensitization. Psychoanalysis and other long-term therapies have also been used, although less frequently. At present it is difficult to say how effective treatment has been in producing long-term changes in behavior.

Key Terms

paraphilias *(353)*	transvestism *(362)*	child molester *(369)*
voyeurism *(356)*	sadism *(365)*	hypersexuality *(370)*
exhibitionism *(357)*	masochism *(366)*	autoerotic asphyxia *(371)*
obscene telephone calling *(359)*	sadomasochism (SM) *(367)*	coprophilia *(374)*
fetishism *(361)*	pedophilia *(369)*	frottage *(374)*

necrophilia *(374)*

urophilia *(374)*

zoophilia *(374)*

aversive
conditioning *(375)*

aversive behavior
rehearsal *(375)*

covert
sensitization *(375)*

orgasmic
reconditioning *(376)*

desensitization *(376)*

CHAPTER   ELEVEN

■

Sexual Problems and Solutions

•

The source of sexual anxiety relates intimately to the wellsprings of life's other difficulties.

Avodah K. Offit

S exual problems are not new to the human race, and neither is sex therapy. Efforts to help people with sexual difficulties date back at least as far as the Greek physician Galen of Pergamon (A.D. 129–199). John Hunter (1728–1793), a personal physician to King George III of England, noted that "nothing hurts the mind of a man so much as the idea of inability to perform well the duty of sex." One direct but apparently effective approach used by Hunter in treating erection problems was to advise a man to abstain from sex for a while:

> I told [one patient] that he was to go to bed [with] this woman but first promise himself that he would not have any connection with her for six nights, let his inclinations and powers be what they would: which he engaged to do. About a fortnight after, he told me that this resolution had produced such a total alteration in the state of his mind that the power [to get an erection] soon took place, for instead of going to bed with fear of inability, he went with fears that he should be possessed with too much desire. And when he had once broken the spell, the mind and powers went on together. (quoted in Zilbergeld & Evans, 1980, p. 29)

Although Hunter's method was simple, it was thoroughly modern in its recognition of the role that anxiety and fear of failure can play in sexual problems. However by contemporary standards, past approaches to sexual problems have often been less enlightened than Hunter's. Just as definitions of "abnormal" sexual behavior have varied from era to era and place to place (see Chapter 10), so have definitions of more conventional problems in sexual functioning. A sexual problem today was not necessarily a sexual problem yesterday—and vice versa. For example, in the nineteenth century, when many writers considered a "good" woman to be an asexual creature who had sex with her husband only out of a sense of duty and a desire to procreate, authorities were concerned with excessive desire in women. If a husband wanted to have sex once every two months and his wife wanted it twice a week, she might be suspected of having the "disease" of nymphomania. But today, with increasing recognition of women's potential for sexual arousal and orgasm, the diagnosis for such a couple would probably be low sexual desire in the man. In short, the way one defines a sexual problem depends on one's model of normal or healthy sexual functioning.

WHAT ARE SEXUAL PROBLEMS AND HOW COMMON ARE THEY?

A sexual problem is any difficulty associated with sexual desire, arousal, performance, or pleasure. Sexologists sometimes refer to such problems as sexual "dysfunctions." But to us, that word seems cold, more appropriate for a malfunctioning machine than a troubled human being. Another common term, *sexual disorder*, implies pathology, but not all sexual difficulties are due to pathology. So in this chapter we simply use "problem."

A sexual problem may be *primary* (lifelong), in existence since a person began sexual relations, or *secondary*, one that did not always exist. Thus a man who experienced erections in the past but now has trouble getting or keeping one is said to have a secondary erection problem. Secondary sexual problems are much more common than primary ones. Sexologists also distinguish between *global* problems, which are experienced in all sexual situations, and *situational* ones, which occur only in certain activities or contexts, or with a particular partner. A third distinction is sometimes made between a *total* problem, which occurs invariably (at least in particular situations), and a *partial* one, which occurs often but not always.

Most contemporary sex therapists would say that a person's sexual functioning is healthy when his or her physiology, behavior, attitudes, and feelings are in harmony. When one or more of these components of sexuality is out of phase with the others, a problem exists. For example, a person may want to perform a particular sexual activity—say, intercourse—but his or her body may not respond appropriately. Or a person may be able to perform some activity—say, oral-genital stimulation—but may hate it.

When we talk about sexual problems, we are not just talking about the ability or inability to perform sexual acts or experience sexual pleasure. People's sexual functioning both reflects and contributes to who they are: how they view themselves, how they relate to other people, and their capacity for happiness and contentment. As one West German sex therapist has noted,

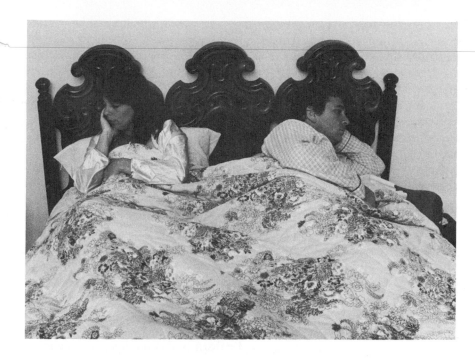

Impasse *Sexual problems are not simple "malfunctions." They can both feed and reflect feelings of hurt, shame, anger, and alienation.*

"Sexual problems often harbor. . .a fear of not being loved, of being abandoned, and of loneliness; a deep-rooted insecurity in one's sense of self-esteem; feelings of humiliated and mistreated masculinity or femininity" (Schmidt, 1983).

How common are sex problems? Most people probably go through one or more periods in their lives when they are uninterested in sex, find it difficult to become aroused, or have specific problems performing sexually. For example, a man who is exhausted from working too hard at his job may have a temporary problem getting an erection. Sexuality is a sensitive barometer of how one's life is going at the moment, so it is hardly surprising that disappointments, crises, and life changes can affect a person's sexual needs and sexual expression.

Masters and Johnson (1970) believe that about half of all married couples are either presently experiencing a sexual problem or will in the future, and they consider this number to be on the conservative side. Others have made estimates that are either lower or higher. But no one really knows the true incidence of sexual problems in the general population because research on a national random sample has yet to be done. All current estimates are essentially guesses, based on limited samples of subjects, typically married people seeking help from therapists.

Any researcher who tries to find out how common sex problems are must first decide how narrowly or broadly to interpret the term *problem*. If you use the word broadly, then just about everyone has a sex problem; after all, almost anyone can probably think of some way in which his or her sex life could be improved. But if you use the term narrowly, you might overlook certain subtle difficulties that are worth considering. For example, a woman might have orgasms in intercourse with her partner but wish for more variety in their activities.

Interestingly, subjective reports of sexual satisfaction do not always correlate well with the existence of what clinicians would label a problem. Some people who do not appear to have any specific or easily identified problems say they are dissatisfied with their sex lives. On the other hand, people who appear to have very definite sex problems often say they are perfectly content (Frank et al., 1978). Why? Perhaps they have low expectations for sexual happiness. Perhaps they are unconcerned about the limits on their sexual satisfaction because they are continuing to enjoy the cuddling and hugging of intimate physical contact, or because they are satisfied with the level of psychological intimacy in their relationships. Or perhaps they actually *are* unhappy but are afraid to admit it, even to themselves.

The subjective nature of sexual problems means that sex therapists cannot diagnose this kind of difficulty as easily as physicians diagnose diseases. A man who ejaculates within three minutes after the start of intercourse may be too slow for some partners, too fast for others, and just right for still others. The man himself may be distressed about his performance or perfectly happy with it.

As you can see, sexual problems are not easy to define. Sexual therapists do agree, however, that sexually healthy people are comfortable with their sexual functioning, feel free to experiment with different techniques if they wish, and are able to enjoy their participation in sex.

THE ORIGINS OF SEXUAL PROBLEMS

Over the years researchers and clinicians have identified many factors that contribute to sexual problems. These can be classified as organic (physiological), psychological, interpersonal, and cultural.

Organic Factors

Until recently, most experts thought sexual problems were almost always psychological in origin. That view has changed, however, as evidence accumulates about the way in which physical disorders affect sexual functioning, particularly arousal. The fatigue, pain, or discomfort of any illness can inhibit sexual desire and disrupt a person's sexual response. More specific organic causes of sexual problems fall into five general categories:

1. *Neurological disorders* Any trauma to the central nervous system can interfere with sexual functioning. A head injury, tumor, or stroke may damage brain areas involved in sexual

feeling and response. Direct injury to the spinal cord can interfere with sensation and sexual reflexes. Illnesses such as multiple sclerosis and diabetes can interfere with sexual arousal or release.

2. *Vascular disorders* Disorders that affect the vascular (blood vessel) system can interfere with vasocongestion of the genitals. One such disorder is arteriosclerosis ("hardening of the arteries"). Heavy smoking can also affect the vascular system, by constricting smooth muscles in artery walls and restricting blood flow. Vascular disorders do not reduce desire, but the responses associated with arousal may go awry.

3. *Hormonal disorders* Most researchers believe that testosterone must remain at some minimal level in the bloodstream for normal sexual response to occur (see Chapter 5). An individual's hormone balance can be affected by various diseases (such as thyroid infection and diabetes), by surgical injury or removal of endocrine glands, by radiation therapy, and by the administration of hormone preparations.

4. *Genital disorders* In women, vaginal infections may cause burning and itching, making intercourse uncomfortable and reducing the desire for sex. In men, genital deformities or traumas may make sex painful or impossible.

5. *Side effects of drugs* Various drugs prescribed routinely for medical conditions can influence sexual response. And, as we saw in Chapter 5, certain recreational drugs, including alcohol, also interfere with arousal and/or sexual release.

Because sexual problems sometimes have organic causes, a reputable sex therapist will be certain that a person seeking treatment undergoes a complete physical examination. Even if the cause is a physical one, however, psychological counseling may be useful in helping the person adjust to the physical disorder by modifying his or her sexual practices.

Psychological Factors

Therapists believe that sexual problems are often attributable to such psychological factors as an individual's attitudes, feelings, personality traits, and outlook on life—all of which can be influenced by current or past circumstances in a person's life. An example of a current psychological factor is worry about pregnancy or a sexually transmitted disease. An example of a historical factor would be guilt about sex traceable to childhood experiences. Other psychological factors include depression, low self-esteem and lack of confidence, anger and hostility, guilt, unrealistic expectations about sex, a poor body image, and negative attitudes due to unpleasant past experiences or antisexual religious training.

It has become almost a cliché to say that anxiety underlies many sexual problems. Anxiety is psychological tension due to the conscious or unconscious perception of danger or threat. Because it is associated with sympathetic nervous system activity, anxiety is thought to interfere with parasympathetic nervous system responses necessary for initial sexual arousal (see Chapter 5). Sexual anxiety may originate in a traumatic episode in an individual's past, such as rape, incest, or an extremely unpleasant first sexual experience. But it may also be a long-standing personality trait in someone with low self-esteem and fear of rejection. Some therapists believe anxiety often reflects a fear of attachment and closeness, or insecurity about one's gender identity. In such cases, they say, sex becomes threatening, and the sexual problem provides an excuse for avoiding sexual contact (Schmidt & Arentewicz, 1983a).

Anxiety may also reflect a person's fear of losing control. Sexual response—and especially orgasm—usually requires an ability to abandon oneself to the sexual experience. People who are worried about looking ridiculous, or about being too loud, or about perspiring too much, may have difficulty letting go:

> I cannot seem to get into sex with my boyfriend. I find myself thinking all the time about how my butt is jiggling. This keeps me from moving very much when I'm on top. (woman in her mid-twenties, authors' files)

Sometimes anxiety is due to a fear of failure. People who have been unable to respond sexually in the past often continue to worry about their performance in every sexual situation. This sets up a vicious cycle in which sexual pleasure is replaced by sexual pressure. Fear of failure leads to anxiety, anxiety leads to failure, and failure leads to increased anxiety. The effects of anxiety are more obvious in men, but worries about performance can and do occur in both sexes. Men are usually concerned about getting and keeping an erection, or ejaculating too soon; women are usually concerned about their ability to have an orgasm.

People who fear failure often become harsh critics of their own performance. Instead of allowing themselves simply to experience the sexual situation, they mentally watch and evaluate every response. Masters and Johnson (1970) call this self-monitoring **spectatoring.** A person who is "spectatoring" may be so busy grading how he or she looks, moves, and sounds, that sexual arousal and enjoyment become impossible.

Yet despite the importance therapists place on the role of anxiety, anxiety does not *always* reduce arousal or interfere with performance. In fact, in certain people or certain situations, it may enhance arousal (Barlow et al., 1983; Beck et al., 1984; Beggs, Calhoun, & Wolchik, 1987). Perhaps anxiety interferes with arousal only when it is distracting (Norton & Jehu, 1984). Or perhaps, in certain situations, people interpret the physiological arousal of

Togetherness? *If people are bored with their lives, or are not connecting emotionally in a relationship, they may not "connect" sexually.*

anxiety as sexual in nature, and so perceive themselves to be sexually excited. Further research is necessary to clarify exactly when anxiety helps arousal and when it hinders it.

Relationship Factors

The emotional quality of the interaction between sexual partners can affect the quality of a sexual experience in profound ways. People can easily lose sight of this fact. Couples sometimes go for sex therapy when their basic problem seems to be that they don't like each other. These people may believe that sexual arousal is something they can turn on and off automatically, like a light switch or a television set, and they may be genuinely puzzled by the fact that their sexual relationship has fizzled. Although some couples may be able to have a satisfying sex life even when most everything else between them is going wrong, the majority probably cannot.

Therapists have noted certain patterns that are especially destructive to a sexual relationship. (These patterns may be more relevant to long-term than short-term relationships, since therapists see more of the former.) They include the following:

1. *Anger and hostility* A certain amount of dissension and conflict is inevitable in a close relationship. Any couple that has been together for any length of time is bound to experience minor disagreements and periodic quarrels. These won't necessarily affect their love life. Long-term resentments, however, are another matter. They tend to color the way in which a person views a partner and can sour erotic feelings. Resentments often arise from serious disputes about money, child-rearing, assignment of responsibilities, friends, use of leisure time, and other basic issues. Anger may also stem from a power struggle: one partner tries to dominate the other, or both constantly vie for control of the relationship. Sometimes one partner attempts to get even with another partner in bed:

> My husband and I were always arguing over his participation in the care of our home and in family activities. I'd nag, and he'd agree to help more around the house, or to take the kids off my hands for a few hours, but then he wouldn't do it. He'd come home, wolf down his dinner, and disappear into the den for three hours, with hardly a word to me. Yet at bedtime he was ready to screw. I was so angry I'd just go limp and passive. There was no way I was going to have an orgasm, or even show arousal. My lack of enthusiasm was a way of hurting him back. (authors' files)

Anger and hostility sometimes cause a partner to withdraw from sex altogether or to consciously or unconsciously sabotage it. For example, people may pick fights or bring up problems just as sex is about to begin. They may find a million excuses not to have sex (I have to call my mother, clean the bathroom, go to the market, watch the late news, make a telephone call, walk the parakeet, etc.). They may initiate sex only when the partner is clearly in a hurry to get somewhere else, about to fall asleep, ill, preoccupied or worried about work, or too drunk to perform. Or they may keep the partner at a distance by letting their appearance become slovenly and unattractive, or deliberately behaving in as unsensual a manner as possible. Human beings are, if nothing else, resourceful.

Although we often regard a person who is chronically angry or hostile as having an emotional problem, in certain circumstances anger and hostility may be quite justified. People in close relationships often take each other for granted, behave inconsiderately, take out their frustrations on each other, abuse each other, and try to manipulate each other to fit some ideal and unrealistic image. In such cases the real threat to the relationship may not be the anger, but the underlying cause of the anger.

2. *Boredom* Boredom is usually associated with long-term relationships, but it can occur even in relatively new relationships, once the initial romantic glow has faded. Boredom may be strictly sexual—for example, when sex always takes place at the same time, at the same place, and in the same way—or it may indicate a general disinterest in the partner. Some people probably have a higher need than others for novelty. But even when people do not have such a need and have realistic expectations of a relationship, boredom can occur. The two partners may become so used to each other, and so comfortable with each other, that they no longer take any pains to make themselves interesting or stimulating. The problem of sexual monotony and some suggestions for dealing with it are discussed more fully in Chapter 13.

3. *Conflicting sexual expectations* If two people have conflicting sexual beliefs or values, and therefore different expectations, sexual problems may arise. On the other hand, if a couple has similar expectations, they may do fine together, even when those expectations seem restrictive or unenlightened to others. For example, suppose that Max and Lisa agree that Max should do most of the initiating in sex, that intercourse should be part of every sexual contact, and that oral sex is revolting. Their sex life may not be terribly creative, yet it may be thoroughly satisfying to both. In contrast, suppose Max likes manual and oral sex more than intercourse, while Lisa loves intercourse but finds oral sex impersonal. Max would like Lisa to initiate lovemaking as often as he does, and he is tender and sensitive in his sexual play. Many women would be delighted with such a man, but Lisa expects her sexual partner to be domineering and forceful because that is what makes her feel desirable. As a result, she finds Max's tenderness soothing but not arousing. You can see how the incompatability of Max's and Lisa's goals and sexual styles might lead to sexual problems.

4. *Poor communication* Most people in reasonably happy relationships can talk about practical everyday problems, but when it comes to sex, they get completely tongue-tied. Instead of coming right out and saying that they need more kissing and hugging before intercourse or that they'd like to

What's the real problem?

Sometimes sex therapists see couples who believe they have a specific sexual problem when the real issue is a problem not directly related to sex.

be touched in a particular place or that they'd like intercourse more often, they resort to covert, subtle, nonverbal strategies for making their feelings known. Unfortunately, such strategies often lend themselves to misinterpretation. Then the person may get angry and strike out verbally at the partner ("You don't love me anymore," "You never do the right things to arouse me; all you care about is yourself"). Because communication about sex is so difficult, some people respond to a partner's attempts to communicate by denying that there is a problem, even when sex has become about as much fun as weeding the lawn. But the problem may continue to fester. Some suggestions for communicating about sex in a clear but tactful way are offered in Box 11–1.

Cultural Factors

In Chapters 1 and 2 we saw that many cultures traditionally have been sex-negative, and although attitudes are changing, negative attitudes still often affect the way people feel about sex. These attitudes may take root in childhood, when people hear their parents equate sex with sin, or notice their parents' embarrassment when a sexual topic is brought up, or learn that the genitals are dirty and that it is wrong to touch them. Even if no overtly negative messages are transmitted by the parents, a conspiracy of silence about sex may result in ignorance about sexual anatomy and even about the basic ways in which sexual acts take place.

Sexual difficulties can also arise from rigid cultural ideas about the proper roles of males and females. In the U.S., some people still believe that men are more sexual than women, that they are always ready for sex, that they should always initiate and orchestrate sex, and that they should not express certain feelings too openly (weakness, fear, vulnerability, tenderness, sensitivity). In contrast, women are expected to be seductive but not directly sexual, to accept but not initiate sex, and to repress anger and aggressiveness. As noted at many points in this book, such inflexible expectations fail to take personal characteristics and styles into account and can put distance between the sexes, hinder communication, and lead to resentment.

Having said that culture can influence sexual functioning, we must point out that the connection between a person's cultural background and beliefs and the person's sexual satisfaction is not always direct and simple. For example, sex therapists have noted that many of their clients come from sexually restrictive family backgrounds (LoPiccolo & LoPiccolo, 1978; Masters & Johnson, 1970). In many of these cases, the person was exposed to religious training that equated sex with sin and damnation. However, saying that people with sexual problems often come from a restrictive or religiously orthodox background is not the same as saying that people with such backgrounds are likely to wind up with a sexual problem. At least one survey, by *Redbook* magazine, has found religious women to be as orgasmic and sexually satisfied as nonreligious women (Tavris & Sadd, 1977). The survey did not use a random sample, but it seems clear that religious orthodoxy does not *necessarily* lead to sexual problems. Social scientists are still a long way from understanding why some people from a particular religious or cultural background develop problems while others do not.

The Real World: Interacting Causes

Occasionally it is possible to show a direct causal path from one of the factors we have discussed to a specific sexual problem. Usually, however, that is not the case. The same problem can have different origins in different people, and in any particular instance, there may be several contributing factors that interact in complicated ways.

As a case in point, consider the effects of alcoholism on sexual functioning. Alcohol abuse can interfere with sex by damaging the nervous system, the vascular system, or the liver (which is involved in sex hormone production). For these reasons, alcoholism is often classified as an "organic"

BOX 11–1

Pillow Talk: Communicating About Sex

Robert and Rita care about each other a lot and enjoy their sexual relationship. But Robert has one complaint: during sex Rita rarely touches his genitals, and on the rare occasions when she does, her approach is too tentative. Robert has tried to ignore this, but it really bothers him. He would like to tell Rita that he would appreciate more frequent and forceful manual stimulation. How should he tell her?

When we present such situations in class, our usually voluble students often respond with embarrassed silence. Or they giggle, or shake their heads and sigh. For many people, talking with a partner about sex seems more difficult than doing it. Even sexually experienced and sophisticated people may have trouble expressing their sexual needs to a partner. No wonder that many sex therapy techniques, such as the exercises prescribed by Masters and Johnson, are aimed at improving communication.

There are many reasons why an otherwise assertive person might become tongue-tied at the prospect of informing a sexual partner about personal likes and dislikes. Many of us grow up without any model whatsoever for effective sexual communication. As adults we must figure out how to communicate entirely on our own. Often we find ourselves with a very inadequate vocabulary for making our thoughts and feelings known. Technical words and Latinisms may seem cold and clinical. Slang expressions may seem crude or may be associated with feelings of hostility.

Other more subtle barriers also interfere with sexual communication. For example, some people accept a romantic ideology that says that if someone *really* loves you, he or she should be able to read your thoughts. ("Their eyes met, and without a single word being spoken, they knew. . . .") Some people think that disclosing sexual information will make them seem selfish or overly critical. Some fear the self-revelation that sexual communication entails. Some women may worry about seeming too forward if they make a specific request or ask a partner what he wants. Some men may think they must protect the image of the "strong, silent type"; others may avoid asking about a partner's needs because they feel they are supposed to seem like sexual experts.

For those who find it hard to talk about sex, nonverbal communication is often helpful. A lot can be said with a gesture or a change of facial expression. But nonverbal communication alone is inadequate for many issues that arise between sexual partners. Nonverbal messages are easy to ignore or misinterpret. A touch on the shoulder, for example, may mean either "I'm feeling tender toward you" or "Let's have sex." People often need to talk about when and how often they like to have sex, which positions and techniques they favor, which body parts are most sensitive, and so forth.

Sex therapists have no pat formulas for ensuring good sexual communication. The script must be varied to suit the partners and the circumstances. Some specific suggestions that can be helpful include the following:

1. *Try to keep the message short and to the point* Although serious problems may call for marathon communication sessions, most issues do not.

2. *Be specific* Do not expect a partner to read your mind or "get" your vaguely worded hint. "I'd love for you to give me a backrub" is better than "Oh boy, does my back ever ache." "I'd like for us to spend more time kissing and hugging" is better than "I need more affection."

3. *Devote as much energy listening as you do talking* All too often people fail to hear what someone is saying because they are busy planning their own reply. Some therapists suggest that the listener paraphrase what the speaker has said so that both partners can be certain that the message was accurately understood.

4. *Be tactful* It is one thing to be assertive about your sexual desires and needs, and quite another to be aggressive, rude, and hurtful. Even a rejection can be phrased in a considerate manner.

5. *Start sentences with "I"* People who train others to be more assertive recommend frequent use of the pronoun *I*. This may seem strange, and even egocentric, but it has many advantages. It encourages the speaker to express his or her own feelings ("I'd like to make love more often") instead of placing blame and putting the listener on the defensive ("You don't make love to me enough"). It helps the speaker stick to what he or she knows best—the speaker's own thoughts and feelings. And it can help to keep the communication focused on concrete issues instead of abstract arguments.

6. *Accentuate the positive* People tend to associate sexual communication with the expression of complaints and problems. But praise is also important. Kind words can soften a criticism and make a positive response from one's partner more likely. ("I love when you touch me there, and I'd love

it even more if you'd do it more often.") Praise also provides the partner with information about what he or she is doing *right*.

Sexual communication alone cannot guarantee that a couple will solve their sexual problems or have a more fulfilling sex life. Two people may communicate effectively, only to find that bitter disagreement and conflict remain. And if sexual partners basically dislike one another—if their relationship is characterized by distrust and hostility—all the talking in the world probably will not help them sexually. But when a relationship is basically healthy, communication can enhance sexual functioning, increase emotional intimacy—and in the process, make sex more fun.

factor in sexual problems. But alcoholism also reduces motivation, lowers self-esteem, interferes with social skills, and causes tension in close relationships—and all of these consequences can also cause problems with sex. Thus it is difficult to separate alcohol's physical impact from its effects on a person's emotional well-being and relationships with others. For this reason, we cannot assume that becoming sober will automatically clear up the sexual problem. Indeed, in one study, problems with erection, loss of sexual desire, and premature ejaculation continued in male alcoholics nine months after they had completed an inpatient alcoholism program (Fahrner, 1987).

In real life, different causes of sexual problems often merge, or one factor leads to another (Schmidt & Arentewicz, 1983a). Suppose that Donald has problems with erection because he has a fear of intimacy. As a child, he coped with the pain of being abused and rejected by learning to stay aloof from others. Today he is uncomfortable with the self-revelation and honesty required in a close relationship, and is unwilling to make himself vulnerable by trusting his partner and exposing his true self. Donald's sexual "dysfunction" actually serves a psychological function: it gives him a reason to avoid situations in which his partner expects intimacy. According to our previous discussion, the cause of Donald's problem can be classified as psychological. But what began as Donald's personal problem is likely to lead to relationship problems, as Donald's partner responds with anger, frustration, or hurt. These relationship problems are likely, in turn, to make Donald's sexual difficulties worse. At that point, psychological and relationship factors will be intertwined.

In the real-life diagnosis of sexual problems, it is hard to separate cause from effect for other reasons, as well. Depression can cause sexual problems, but sexual problems can also cause depression. Anger toward a partner can

CATHY/Cathy Guisewite

Cathy, Copyright Cathy Guisewite. Reprinted with permission of Universal Press Syndicate. All rights reserved.

cause sexual problems, but sexual problems can also cause anger toward a partner. Because causation can go in either direction—or in both at once— the exact causes of a particular sexual difficulty are frequently unclear.

Saved by the bell
Communication is not always easy.

SOME GENERAL PRINCIPLES OF SEX THERAPY

Sex therapy as an independent specialty has existed for about two decades. The predominant twentieth-century approach to the treatment of sexual problems before 1970 was psychoanalysis. Psychoanalysts have traditionally viewed sexual problems as symptoms of deep-seated personality conflicts. They believe these conflicts originate in childhood and can be resolved only through intensive exploration of all aspects of a person's life. Psychoanalysis is expensive, and its effectiveness in treating sexual problems has been, and still is, a matter of controversy.

The shift away from psychoanalysis occurred in 1970. In that year, Masters and Johnson published *Human Sexual Inadequacy,* which described their therapeutic work with 790 couples at the Reproductive Biology Research Foundation in St. Louis. Masters and Johnson reported new techniques and impressive success rates. Their methods were immediately lauded as revolutionary and adopted by many mental health practitioners. It is no exaggeration to say that Masters and Johnson put sex therapy on the map. Today there are thousands of sex therapists, and several journals devoted to reporting research on sex therapy.

Actually, Masters and Johnson's approach was not entirely new. It borrowed from and modified behavioral methods that were around during the 1950s and 1960s but were not widely known. These action-oriented techniques tackled a patient's anxiety about sex directly instead of dwelling on unconscious sources of the anxiety. The goals were to educate, change negative attitudes, improve communication, and build sexual skills. Masters and

Johnson's contribution was to spell out a detailed program for achieving these goals with couples.

The Masters and Johnson approach begins with the taking of a thorough *sexual history* from each partner, as well as complete medical evaluations. Then the couple is assigned "homework"—a series of well-defined exercises to carry out in private. The first task is one that Masters and Johnson call **sensate focus.** The partners are instructed to touch and massage any part of each other's unclothed bodies, *except* for the genitals and the woman's breasts. While they do this, they are expected to talk about what they do or do not like. One partner is arbitrarily selected to start out as the giver of stimulation; the other is the receiver. The receiver simply responds verbally to the physical contact. Then the partners change roles. Specific sexual activities, such as intercourse, and specific goals, such as orgasm, are ruled out of bounds. (You can see a certain similarity to Hunter's treatment, described at the beginning of this chapter.)

Sensate focus exercises give people an opportunity to be sensual—to learn to give and accept pleasure without guilt and without feeling pressured to perform sexually. Sexually experienced and well-adjusted couples probably do this without being told; they rub each other's backs, run their fingers through each other's hair, and so forth. But some couples do not know how to caress each other in a manner that is not goal-directed. As Masters and Johnson noted,

> For most women [in therapy], and for many men, the sensate focus sessions represent the first opportunity they have ever had to "think and feel" sensuously and at leisure without intrusion upon the experience by the demand for end-point release [orgasm]. . .without the need to explain their sensate preferences, without the demand for personal reassurance, or without a sense of need to rush to "return the favor." (Masters & Johnson, 1970, p. 73)

Once a couple feels comfortable with nonerotic touching and pleasure, they are instructed to move on to stimulation of the genitals and the woman's breasts. Again, these exercises are to be done in a non-goal-oriented way, in order to eliminate performance pressure. Verbal communication during this phase is encouraged but not required. The exercises are supplemented with discussions in the office between the therapists and the patients and with informational talks about sexual anatomy and physiology. Finally, the couple is given specific exercises tailored to the problem that has brought them into therapy. The organization of the tasks encourages "success" at each stage— and nothing succeeds like success.

Masters and Johnson's therapy was, and still is limited to couples, even when only one of the partners reports a problem. Their decision to counsel only couples reflects their belief that "there is no such thing as an uninvolved partner in any marriage in which there is some form of sexual inadequacy"

(Masters & Johnson, 1970). Working with an individual alone, they argue, "ignores the fundamental fact that sexual response represents (either symbolically or in reality) interaction between two people." They point out that when only one partner is treated, the other may undermine some or all of the progress made in therapy because of ignorance or insensitivity about the problem. Masters and Johnson insist that the patient in therapy is not the person with the specific complaint, but a relationship.

But what happens when the patient is single or does not have a partner willing to cooperate in therapy? In the years before publication of their book, Masters and Johnson overcame this obstacle in a straightforward way: they provided the patient with a **sexual surrogate**—a stranger who served as a temporary sexual partner during the course of therapy. (In every case, the patient was an unmarried male and the surrogate a female.) Surrogates were not professional prostitutes but paid volunteers who offered to play the role for a variety of reasons. Their job was not only to engage in sex but to provide psychological support. Master and Johnson stopped using surrogates in 1970. However some other therapists still use them with success (e.g., Dauw, 1988), although the ethics of the practice remain controversial.

Today most sex therapists have adapted Masters and Johnson's basic approach of assigning an ordered series of exercises, but there are many variations on the basic theme. Several new behavioral techniques and "homework exercises" have been developed. Many therapists work with individuals, who then "practice" what they learn with a partner who is not directly involved in the therapy. Unlike Masters and Johnson, who have always worked as a team, many (perhaps most) therapists work alone. Many combine graded tasks with more traditional methods of psychotherapy and marriage counseling, in order to resolve underlying personal and relationship difficulties (Kaplan, 1974). Some therapists work with small groups comprised of individuals or couples who share a common problem. In groups, people can talk about their common experiences, offer each other insights, develop social skills, discuss the results of their homework, and give one another emotional support. Finally, some therapists now use a *systems approach*, which examines the hidden functions that a sexual problem may be serving in a relationship (Verhulst & Heiman, 1988).

Whatever the exact approach, however, the basic goals of sex therapy remain the same: to provide education and information, facilitate open and honest communication, relieve anxiety about sexual feelings and performance, and help people change behavior to enhance sex functioning. (For some suggestions on how to locate a sex therapist, see Box 11–2.)

In non-problematic sex, sexual desire leads to sexual arousal; sexual arousal (if there is continuing stimulation) often leads to orgasm; and orgasm is followed by feelings of release and satisfaction. As Table 11–1 indicates, difficulties can occur at any point in the process. We are now ready to examine some of the specific problems treated by sex therapists.

BOX 11–2

How to Find A Sex Therapist

A man has an ejaculation problem. A woman has difficulty reaching orgasm. Self-help efforts have not worked, and the individual, perhaps with a partner, decides to seek professional assistance. But how does one find a competent therapist?

The answer is far from easy. Most states have not yet enacted licensing requirements for sex therapists, so nearly anyone can hang out a shingle that says "sex therapist." On the other hand, many mental health professionals who use other titles are well-qualified to do sex therapy by virtue of their education and experience. They include certain clinical psychologists, psychiatrists, social workers, psychiatric nurses, marriage and family counselors, and pastoral counselors.

When looking for a sex therapist, one thing to consider is the person's basic approach. This chapter describes standard techniques used by most sex therapists, but many practitioners supplement these with more general methods of psychotherapy. Most draw flexibly from five approaches: psychoanalytic, humanistic, behavioral, cognitive, and family systems. But there may be an emphasis on one or another of these methods, and different emphases are suitable for different people. An extremely inarticulate person is likely to feel frustrated in psychoanalysis, which requires constant verbalization. A person whose underlying problem is hostility toward the other sex might find a behavioral approach superficial.

A first step in seeking sex therapy, then, might be to read up on the various types of psychotherapy. College textbooks in general psychology, abnormal psychology, and personal adjustment can be helpful. The next step is to get the name of one or more therapists. A family doctor, religious counselor, or human sexuality instructor may be a good source of referrals. Friends and relatives who have had a positive experience with a therapist may be willing to recommend that person. Community hospitals, university medical centers, and student health services sometimes have clinics specializing in sex therapy. Other sources of referrals include local mental health associations, medical societies, psychological associations, or associations of marriage and family counselors. The local chapter of the National Organization for Women may have a list of therapists it considers nonsexist, and gay centers may be able to recommend therapists they consider supportive of homosexuality. Crisis centers and hotlines sometimes make referrals, too.

The first appointment with a sex therapist is usually an interview. The therapist needs to be sure that the problem is one that he or she is qualified to treat. If the interview (or a subsequent assessment) reveals a physical disorder, psychological problem, or complex relationship issue that the therapist is not trained to deal with, the therapist should refer the client(s) to an appropriate specialist. For example, a physical problem might call for a referral to a urologist or gynecologist.

The interview also gives clients a chance to ask questions and assess the therapist. One question should be about fees, which vary widely and are generally higher for private therapy than for treatment offered through publicly supported clinics and agencies. Psychiatrists, who are medical doctors and can prescribe drugs, generally charge more than clinical psychologists, who in turn generally charge more than social workers and other therapists.

You should also inquire about the therapist's training, experience, and credentials. The American Association of Sex Educators, Counselors, and Therapists (AASECT) certifies sex therapists after they meet specified training and experience requirements; you can get the names of certified therapists in your area by writing AASECT at 435 North Michigan Ave. Suite 1717, Chicago, IL 60611. Note, though, that many licensed professionals who are not certified as sex therapists are perfectly well-qualified to do sex therapy. Also, degrees and certification alone do not a good therapist make. The personality of the therapist is critical. Is he or she empathic? Nonjudgmental? Friendly? Do you feel comfortable with and trust this person? Be suspicious if the therapist guarantees success, but do ask for some idea about the projected length of treatment. If you do not like the therapist, try another.

Finally, there is the matter of nonstandard techniques, such as the use of surrogates (see text). Find out about any special techniques, and if you have objections, voice them. Be aware that any type of sexual contact between therapist and client may be harmful and is always highly unethical. Licensed professionals can lose their right to practice if they engage in such behavior. (We discuss this matter further in Chapter 15.)

Whatever therapist is chosen, the client should understand that results are rarely immediate. Consider the therapist a guide to the process of problem solving. Be patient, and give the therapy a chance. And remember, a therapist cannot "cure" a sex problem by waving a magic wand. In therapy, as in life, growth and well-being are ultimately the responsibility of the individual.

Phase	Men	Women	Both sexes
Desire			Inhibited sexual desire; sexual desire discrepancies; sexual aversion
Arousal	Inhibited erection	Low arousal, insufficient vaginal lubrication	
Penile insertion		Vaginismus	Painful intercourse (dyspareunia)
Orgasm	Premature ejaculation; ejaculatory inhibition	Orgasmic difficulties (anorgasmia)	
Satisfaction			Lack of physical and/or emotional gratification

TABLE 11–1

Different phases, different problems As this table shows, sexual difficulties can be classified according to the stage at which they occur during sexual activity. Each is defined and described in the text.

PROBLEMS OF SEXUAL DESIRE

Inhibited sexual desire (ISD) is essentially lack of sexual appetite (Kaplan, 1979). People with ISD have little or no interest in sexual fantasy or activity. Some do respond physically and psychologically once they are having sex; others do not.

A common misconception is that low sexual desire is always a problem. This belief is based on the assumption that people *ought* to want sex, and that if they do not, there is something wrong with them. It also assumes that there is an agreed upon standard of what a "normal" or "acceptable" level of sexual appetite is, when in fact, there is not (Leiblum & Rosen, 1988). In diagnosing ISD, most therapists take into account a person's own dissatisfaction with his or her level of interest in sex. Some therapists consider low desire a problem for couples only when there is a **sexual desire discrepancy,** that is, a marked difference between partners in sexual desire, leading to disagreement about how frequent sex should be (Zilbergeld & Ellison, 1980; Kilmann & Mills, 1983). If both partners agree that sex twice a year is enough, that may be statistically unusual but they do not have a problem. The problem occurs when one partner wants sex twice a year and the other wants it twice a week or twice a month.

Inhibited sexual desire and discrepancies in sexual desire are probably the most common of all sexual complaints. These problems can occur for a wide range of physical, psychological, and interpersonal reasons:

- *Physical causes* include chronic illness, the use of certain medications, abnormally low levels of testosterone, and drug and alcohol abuse.

- *Psychological causes* include fear of failure (particularly in men); depression; fear of intimacy and commitment; sexual guilt; a poor sexual self-image; and nonsexual stress and worry. (For more on sex and stress, see the *Personal Perspective* at the end of this chapter.)

- *Interpersonal causes* include virtually any relationship issue, with power struggles being common. In one study, researchers found that some women with sexual appetites before marriage had lost their desire after marriage. The husbands of these women rarely listened to them, conflicts were not resolved, and there was little closeness between partners. According to the researchers, the women had been "robbed of the original stimulants of their sexual desire" (Stuart, Hammond, & Pett, 1987).

A lack of interest in sex may also occur simply because a person has never experienced much pleasure in sex. It's not necessarily that the person suffered a traumatic episode; it may simply be that he or she never enjoyed many satisfying experiences. For example, suppose a woman never masturbated to orgasm, never experimented much with sexual techniques, and failed to get the stimulation she needed during coitus to have an orgasm. And suppose that most of her experiences with sex had been brief, with little erotic touching. Then she would have had little opportunity to learn about the satisfactions of sex. Her response to sex might not be "Yuck" but rather "Who cares?"

Treatment of low desire begins with an attempt by the therapist to gain insight into the specific causes. Therapy typically focuses on 1) facilitating erotic responses, for instance, by encouraging sexual fantasies and the use of sex as a way to relax after a hard day; 2) developing increased sensory awareness, for example through sensate focus; 3) finding ways to improve the quality of sex; and 4) overcoming psychological barriers to sexual enjoyment, such as fear of intimacy. (When there is a serious long-standing psychological disorder, such as depression, it usually must be treated first, before the desire problem is considered.)

When treating couples, most therapists focus on both partners and work for compromise. If the person with the higher desire is using sex to get nonsexual needs met (for self-esteem, say, or entertainment) the therapist may help that person find other avenues to satisfy those needs.

In mild cases, desire may increase after only brief treatment. For example, consider this case:

> Tony was a 55-year-old restaurant owner who had been married for five years to Theresa, a woman who claimed to be 38 but who was probably older. Theresa complained that Tony showed no sexual interest in her, which he confirmed and blamed on the pressures of business. The couple had sexual intercourse about once a month. Tony typically climaxed rapidly, which depressed and agitated his wife. . . . In treatment, Theresa was reassured about Tony's feelings for her. The couple was assigned nondemanding pleasure exercises. The therapist emphasized the positive elements of their relationship. Tony revealed that he needed direct stimulation of his penis in order to have an erection and said that he had been ashamed to tell his wife this. As it turned out, she loved to provide this stimulation, and his performance anxieties disappeared. Theresa also learned to express her desire for reassurance verbally instead of demanding sexual performance. After ten sessions once a week his desire had returned and the couple was having intercourse every weekend, which both found satisfactory. (adapted and abridged from Kaplan, 1979, pp. 105–106).

In general, however, desire problems seem harder to treat than other kinds of sexual difficulties (Kaplan, 1977; LoPiccolo, 1980; Zilbergeld & Hammond, 1988). Probably the most difficult cases are those in which relationship problems are the source. Relationships, as we all know, are complicated. Moreover, once a discrepancy in desire exists, it tends to create new frictions. Often the partner with the higher desire keeps trying to initiate sex, gets rebuffed, and winds up feeling rejected and unloved. The partner who wants less sex comes to see the other person as overly demanding and selfish, and feels used and unappreciated. Treatment is usually aimed at interrupting this vicious cycle.

The difficulties we have been describing should be distinguished from a more extreme desire problem, **sexual aversion,** in which a person experiences persistent or intense feelings of anxiety and even panic in sexual situations and avoids sexual contact (Kilmann & Mills, 1983). The causes of sexual aversion are not well understood, but traumatic sexual experiences, such as rape, incest, and other forms of sexual abuse or humiliation often play a role (see Chapter 15). Treatment typically focuses on working through feelings about prior negative experiences and reducing current anxiety. One common approach is *systematic desensitization*, a procedure that has long been used to eliminate nonsexual fears and phobias. The client first constructs a list of desirable sexual situations, ordered from least to most anxiety-provoking. A typical list might begin with being hugged and end with intercourse. The person is then instructed in the use of relaxation techniques, and told to imagine the first situation while completely relaxed. As the person's panic subsides, each successive situation is imagined in this way. "Homework" consists of actually trying out a situation that has already been imagined without panic. Eventually the person is able not only to imagine but to take part in all the situations on the list.

PROBLEMS OF SEXUAL AROUSAL

Desire is not the same as arousal. Arousal refers to how sexually excited a person actually gets, both subjectively and objectively, in response to sexual stimulation. A person may want to have sex, but be unable to get aroused.

Female Arousal Difficulties

If a woman fails to become sexually aroused in a sexual situation, her genital area will not become engorged with blood, and her vagina will not become well lubricated. In some cases, the woman may simply be tired or may not be getting effective stimulation. In others, she may be sexually inhibited because of the psychological, interpersonal, or cultural factors discussed earlier. A lack of physiological arousal does not necessarily prevent a woman from enjoying the tactile satisfactions of sex and the feelings of emotional intimacy it brings. And it does not necessarily prevent her from having and enjoying intercourse, although, if the vagina is very dry, there is likely to be discomfort or pain during insertion of the penis unless a lubricant is used. Treatment of arousal problems in women is similar to the treatment of problems with orgasm, which will be discussed in a later section.

Erection Difficulties

Because arousal problems in men interfere with erection, they are hard to overlook or ignore. A man cannot fake an erection or have intercourse without one. Of course, if intercourse and the man's orgasm are not the couple's goal, then **erectile inhibition**—a persistent inability to get or maintain an erection, in response to sexual stimulation—need not be a problem. An erect penis is not absolutely essential to a happy, fulfilling sex life. Men with spinal cord injuries that prevent them from having erections can continue to enjoy the closeness and intimacy of sex and can be sensitive and effective lovers. So can able-bodied men who do not get erections. Yet most people tend to view the angle of a man's penis as the measure of his sexual prowess. As one man with an erection problem said,

> I want to feel like a whole man again. If I could just function normally at least some of the time when I'm with a woman, that would do it. I know I can use my hand or tongue to satisfy them, and that's fine some of the time, but I'm not going to feel good about myself until I can get a good hard-on and use it. I feel so useless when that thing just hangs limp between my legs. (quoted in Zilbergeld, 1978, p. 291)

The emphasis people place on erection and intercourse is reflected in the traditional term for an erection problem: impotence. According to the dictionary, *impotent* means lacking in power or ability, without force or effectiveness, or physically helpless. A label like that can cause a man with an erection problem to feel sexually disabled, and the resulting anxiety can only add to his problem. That is one reason many therapists now avoid the term. (Another is that it is often misinterpreted to mean sterile or infertile.)

Kaplan (1974) believes that half of all men occasionally find that they cannot get an erection or that they lose an erection during sex, and her estimate is probably too conservative. Probably this happens to most men at least once in a while. Stress, fatigue, worry, anger, or too much alcohol can all interfere with the erectile response. If such incidents are simply taken in stride, they are usually short-lived. Sex therapists do not consider them a problem; after all, tomorrow is another day.

Well then, when can we say that a man has an erection problem? Therapists disagree about the answer. Some try to use some sort of precise quantitative criterion. For example, Masters and Johnson say that a problem exists if a man has difficulty with erection in 25 percent or more of his sexual encounters. Others set the criterion as high as 75 percent (Kilmann & Mills, 1983). But any numerical approach is arbitrary. Why not use 20 percent, or 30, or 57.5, as the cut-off point? The critical issue, in the opinion of many therapists, is not numbers but the person's subjective response to his own performance and his partner's response. If a man and his partner are satisfied with their mutual sex life, it doesn't matter how many erections he gets. And if a lack of erection occurs often enough to bother the man or his partner, then he has a problem.

CAUSES   What causes a penis to remain soft when its owner would prefer it to get hard? Until recently most therapists assumed that the vast majority of erection problems were caused by psychological factors. But there is growing evidence that in a substantial number of cases the cause is primarily physical. In one study of men with erection difficulties, 30 percent of the subjects were found to have a physical condition that could have been related to the sexual problem. Some had an illness, like diabetes, vascular disease, or high blood pressure, and some were using prescription drugs known to interfere with erection (Shrom, Lief, & Wein, 1979). Some medical authorities believe that as many as half of all erection problems are caused primarily by physical factors (Shabsigh, Fishman, & Scott, 1988), but no one knows the exact percentage yet.

Psychological causes of erection problems include shame, anxiety about failure, an inability to let go emotionally, a history of punishment for sexual arousal, and stress. Many men with erection problems originally start out with a premature ejaculation problem: apparently, anxiety about ejaculating leads to an inability to get an erection (Masters & Johnson, 1970). Sometimes a man with an erection problem has experienced a traumatic initial or early sexual encounter—for example, incest or an encounter with a partner who ridiculed his performance. Occasionally a man who complains of erection problems with a female partner is trying to suppress a homosexual orientation.

Often what begins as a purely situational problem (for example, the man is exhausted from too much work) turns into a chronic one when the man panics and tries to force an erection in the absence of sexual arousal. He thinks that a temporarily soft penis equals a lack of masculinity and feels so pressured to perform that the next time he has an opportunity to do so, he cannot. As Bernie Zilbergeld (1978) puts it, "Because so much is at stake, the absence of an erection is greeted with the same degree of calmness as would be the announcement that someone in the neighborhood had the bubonic plague." Fear leads to failure which leads to fear which leads to failure. . .and a vicious cycle is set in motion. It doesn't help any if a partner overreacts to the man's lack of an erection and says—or more likely, communicates nonverbally—that he is "over the hill," or a great disappointment in bed. Although this is most likely to happen in a hostile relationship, according to Kaplan (1974) it can also occur when the partner cares for the man. The partner may feel rejected or threatened by the man's inability to get an erection and may try to get reassurance by pressuring him to perform.

TREATMENT   The first step in treatment of an erection problem is (or should be) a thorough examination by a physician to determine whether the cause is physical. One easy test measures the erection reflex during sleep. Normally a man will have partial erections during REM (rapid-eye-movement) sleep, the state of sleep associated with dreaming. This type of erection is known as **nocturnal penile tumescence (NPT).** NPTs can be checked at home by encircling the penis with a strip of stamps before retiring; if the strip is broken in the morning, the man has probably had an erection. A more sophisticated approach is to use a strain gauge—a flexible device that encircles the penis—to measure changes in the circumference of the penis throughout the night. If there are difficulties doing these tests, an alternative is for the man to spend a few nights in a sleep laboratory, where the strain gauge test can be supplemented by an electroencephalogram (EEG) to identify brain waves characteristic of REM sleep.

When a man does not have REM erections, his problem is likely to be physical; when he has them, it is psychological. If the problem is physical, further tests must be done to pinpoint the exact cause. For example, a special instrument that measures blood pressue in the penis can be used to diagnose vascular disease, and blood tests can be done to identify hormonal disorders. The treatment of a physical problem depends on the exact cause. An abnormally low hormone level may call for hormone therapy. Undiagnosed diabetes may call for insulin treatments. Some problems with blood flow to the penis can be corrected by surgery.

When irreversible damage to nerves or blood vessels has occurred, some men elect to undergo the surgical implantation in the penis of a device that permits them to experience mechanically produced erections. There are

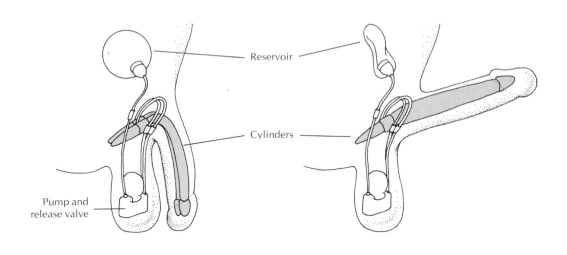

Reservoir

Cylinders

Pump and
release valve

Penile implant *This
device consists of two
cylinders, one in each
cavernous body of the
penis, a pump and release
valve in the scrotum, and
a fluid-filled reservoir in
the pelvis. When the
pump is squeezed, the
fluid inflates the cylinders,
producing a mechanical
erection. When the valve
is released, the fluid
returns to the reservoir.*

two types of **penile implant:** a semi-rigid rod-shaped device that produces a permanent erection, and a more popular inflatable device that permits complete relaxation of the penis between erections (see Figure 11–1). If a man was able to become aroused and to ejaculate before the onset of his problem, there is a good chance he will be able to do so after he gets an implant.

Some urologists are very enthusiastic about penile implants and recommend them often. However, most sex therapists are more cautious, and consider an implant a last resort. Some argue that patients are not always given adequate information about treatment options before getting an implant, and that the procedure has sometimes been done when it was unnecessary or inappropriate (Shaw, 1989). These devices destroy much of the interior of the penis, and the decision to have one implanted is irreversible. While many men who get the implant are delighted to have their erections restored, some report dissatisfaction with the subjective sensations of sex or the stiffness of their erections (Steege, Stout, & Carson, 1986). Recipients also often find that mechanical devices do not magically solve relationship problems that are interfering with sexual enjoyment. And critics observe that the presence of a physical disorder does not automatically mean that a sex problem is physical in origin or requires a physical solution. In one six-year follow-up study of 101 diabetic men and women who had received no treatment at all for sexual problems, 8 men and 6 women recovered from their problem anyway (Jensen, 1986).

Recently, a new medical treatment has emerged as an alternative to penile implants. Erection is induced by injecting a smooth muscle relaxant called *papaverine* directly into the penis (Althof et al., 1987). In some men with vascular or neurological problems, this brings on an erection within a few minutes that lasts about two hours (Levine et al., 1989). However, some complications have been reported, including infection and difficulties with orgasm, and long-term effects have not yet been studied (Malloy & Wein, 1988). At present, it is too soon to know how widespread this technique will become.

Having looked at physical treatments, let us consider some psychological ones. As you might guess, psychological approaches are aimed at improving communication and reducing anxiety. They may begin with the sensate-focus exercises mentioned previously. At first, intercourse and ejaculation are specifically prohibited. If an erection happens to occur, the partners are instructed to ignore it. The man is not expected to become aroused. The idea is to remove fear, reduce spectatoring, and set up the kind of non-pressured situation where arousal and erection can take place naturally. As the couple gradually moves on to manual and oral stimulation of the genitals, the man has an opportunity to show his partner which kind of stimulation works best for him. Even then, however, the couple is told not to try to accomplish anything. Under these conditions, erection often occurs spontaneously and without fanfare.

Once the man is having full erections, the partner may be instructed to "tease" him by stopping all stimulation as soon as an erection occurs and deliberately allowing the erection to subside. Then the partner resumes stimulation and the teasing technique. Men with erection problems typically feel that they must use an erection immediately, since they may never get one again. The teasing technique reassures a man that what goes down will eventually come up once again.

The final stage of treatment for heterosexual couples often has the woman initiate sexual play as she sits astride the man, who is on his back. If he gets a full erection, she inserts his penis into her vagina in an unhurried, nondemanding manner. This relieves him of any responsibility for accomplishing insertion, which can be a distraction. This step, like manual stimulation, is repeated several times in a teasing way. Then the woman begins to move slowly up and down on the shaft of the penis. If the penis softens, fine. If it stays hard, then the man may take his turn at slow pelvic thrusting, concentrating all the while on his own erotic pleasure. If one or the other partner has an orgasm, it should be "by happenstance." Once the couple has a few "successful" sexual episodes, the problem may be resolved.

PAINFUL SEX AND VAGINISMUS

One of the most distressing sexual problems a person can have is pain or discomfort during sex. Pain during or right after intercourse is known medically as **dyspareunia.** It may take the form of burning, tearing, aching, or pressure. It may be prolonged or only momentary. Typically intercourse is always painful and therefore unpleasant and frustrating.

Most cases of pain during intercourse are probably caused by physical problems. In women these causes include (among others): insufficient vaginal lubrication, irritation of or damage to the clitoris, vaginal infections, thinning of the vaginal walls with age (see Chapter 13), urinary tract infections, pelvic infections, endometriosis (abnormal growth of uterine tissue outside the uterus), tumors and cysts in the reproductive organs, and tears in the ligaments supporting the uterus as a result of childbirth or rape.

In men physical causes include (among others): irritation of the foreskin in uncircumcised men (easily solved by improved hygiene), phimosis (a tight foreskin that is difficult to retract), Peyronie's disease (a condition in which excess fibrotic tissue causes the penis to assume an unusual angle), penile chordee (a downward bowing of the penis usually caused by direct trauma to the erect penis), prostate problems, urinary tract infections, scars left by gonorrhea, and extended or repeated erections without ejaculation (Masters & Johnson, 1970). Both men and women can also have an allergic reaction to spermicides, semen, or the partner's sexual fluids, though fortunately this is rare.

If the cause is physical, it may be possible to correct the condition by medication, surgery, or use of a lubricant during intercourse. If the problem is not physical, the therapist will explore possible psychological factors. For example, the discomfort may have been conditioned by a past association of pain with intercourse, as in rape or some other traumatic experience. Sometimes coital pain seems to be associated with a poor relationship—as if the body is speaking out against a situation that the person does not want to face. A person who feels resentful toward a partner may unconsciously be using the pain to put the partner in a difficult position ("You see what you're doing to me for the sake of your own pleasure?"). Therapy usually focuses on increasing a person's sense of control during sexual interactions, decreasing fear and guilt, and improving trust and communication in the person's relationship with the partner.

Vaginismus also causes discomfort or pain—but before intercourse can even begin. In this condition, muscles around the lower third of the vagina contract spasmodically and involuntarily. These contractions make penetration by the penis (and even gynecological examination) difficult and sometimes impossible. A woman with vaginismus may be unable to have intercourse for months or even years. In some cases vaginismus has prevented married couples from ever having sex. Although women with this problem may be unresponsive sexually, it can also occur in a woman who becomes aroused, experiences vaginal lubrication, and has orgasms through manual or oral stimulation.

Vaginismus may be associated with a past sexual trauma, fear of pregnancy, severe conflict about sex, hostility toward the partner, or a homosexual orientation in a woman with a male partner. It may also be a reaction to physically caused dyspareunia. Whatever the cause, the woman does not purposely contract her muscles. The spasms are a conditioned response beyond her conscious control.

Treatment consists of relaxation exercises and gradual dilation of the vagina. One approach to dilation is to have the woman gently insert a finger

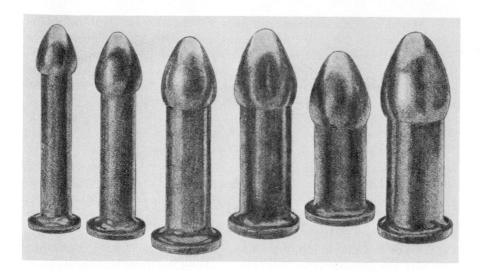

into her vagina, using an external lubricant, such as sterile jelly. Once she can do this without discomfort (and it may take a while), she inserts two, then three fingers. Another method is to have her use plastic dilators that are graduated in size and cylindrical in shape. She starts with a very small dilator, but eventually she is able to insert one the size of a penis. This procedure often solves the problem and permits the couple to have intercourse (Masters & Johnson, 1970). Some therapists supplement vaginal dilation with anxiety-reducing techniques, behavior modification, and corrections of misconceptions (for example, that sex is supposed to hurt) (Kessler, 1988).

PROBLEMS WITH ORGASM

Orgasmic Problems in Women

The traditional term for orgasmic problems in women is *frigidity*, but, like the term *impotence*, it is now avoided by many if not most sex therapists. The word implies that a woman who does not have orgasms is an emotional icicle, when typically this is not the case. Some women who have difficulty with orgasm have little feeling in their genital area, but enjoy the physical and emotional closeness of sex. Others become very aroused—in fact they reach the plateau stage—but do not make it "over the hump" to orgasm. Therefore therapists now prefer to use the term **anorgasmia** for an inability to have orgasms. Some, following a suggestion by therapist Lonnie Barbach (1975), use the term *preorgasmic* for women with a primary orgasmic problem (they have never had an orgasm). This reflects an assumption that all women are capable of eventually learning to be orgasmic, though not necessarily in coitus.

As with erection problems, numbers of "successes" or "failures" do not adequately define the problem. Once again, the desires and expectations of the individual woman are crucial. Many women say that they have a satisfying and fulfilling sex life without any orgasms. Others feel cheated and angry or are left feeling tense and unsatisfied after experiencing high levels of arousal. Orgasm is certainly not the only reason to have sex—perhaps not even the primary reason for many people—but it is an extremely pleasurable and rewarding experience.

Sex therapists and sex researchers disagree about how common orgasmic problems in women are. Research studies have tended to focus solely on coital orgasms. One review of such studies concluded that 40 to 50 percent of sexually experienced women under forty always or almost always have coital orgasms; 20 to 30 percent often have them; 20 to 25 percent occasionally have them; and 5 to 10 percent never have them (Schmidt & Arentewicz, 1983b). But it is hard to interpret these numbers, because researchers often fail to say whether they are counting as coital orgasms those brought about by simultaneous manual stimulation. Shere Hite (1976) is an exception, and she found that only 30 percent of her female respondents had orgasms routinely during intercourse without additional manual stimulation. (But as noted in Chapter 3, Hite's sample may not be representative.)

Because of these ambiguities, about all that can be said with certainty is that many women have never had an orgasm from any form of stimulation. Millions more—perhaps the majority—have orgasms manually or during oral sex, but not in intercourse unless they also get manual stimulation. As we saw in Chapter 9, this is normal and not a dysfunction.

CAUSES Why do women have difficulties with orgasm? All women need effective stimulation. When a difficulty occurs, it may be because a woman is not getting the *kind* of stimulation she happens to need. As we saw in Chapter 9, what works for one woman may not work at all for another. A certain amount of experimentation and inventiveness may be needed for a woman to learn what "effective stimulation" means for her.

In other cases, especially in those where a woman has never had an orgasm from any kind of stimulation, the reason may be embarrassment and self-consciousness, especially about the genitals. Some women are ignorant about their sexual anatomy and are unaware of the erotic importance of the clitoris. Women who have never masturbated, especially, may lack awareness of their own potential for sexual response (Wakefield, 1988). Some women, like many men with erection problems, feel guilty about sex or have difficulty expressing their likes and dislikes to a partner. Cultural conditioning may lead a woman to view the movements and sounds of sex as unladylike. Like the woman quoted earlier who worried about her "jiggling butt," a woman may become a spectator at her own performance and be unable to let go. Occasionally a woman who has an orgasm problem with a male partner is trying to suppress a primarily homosexual orientation.

TREATMENT   Many therapists encourage a woman who has never experienced orgasm through any means to learn to have them through masturbation. Masturbation is an easier route to orgasm than coitus for most women. It fosters self-acceptance and responsibility for one's own sexual functioning, and it relieves the woman of any pressure to please a partner while she is learning about her own responses. Masturbation therapy was originally proposed by Joseph LoPiccolo and W. Charles Lobitz (1972) and has since been embellished and expanded by others. Two books, *For Yourself: The Fulfillment of Female Sexuality* (Barbach, 1975) and *Becoming Orgasmic: A Program of Sexual Growth of Women* (Heiman, LoPiccolo, & LoPiccolo, 1976), outline the basic steps.

A typical masturbation therapy program for women who have never had orgasms begins with body awareness exercises. The woman is instructed to examine her body visually, then touch it and explore it—first to feel more comfortable with it, and then for pleasure. She may then be given some suggestions on how to relax and may be encouraged to use fantasy and erotic literature to boost her level of arousal. Then she learns to masturbate, either manually, or if that does not seem to work, with a vibrator. She can proceed as gradually as she likes and has complete control over the type and level of stimulation. Once she is orgasmic in masturbation, she can then describe her needs to a partner. She may be encouraged to masturbate in front of the

Becoming orgasmic: self-stimulation

partner. This allows the partner to see directly what gives the woman pleasure (a picture is worth a thousand words, and the real thing is worth ten
thousand). It also increases emotional intimacy and helps a couple learn
about each other's needs. Manual techniques can be incorporated directly
into sex with the partner, or a couple can experiment with different coital
positions to find out which provides stimulation most like that available from
masturbation. However, masturbation exercises, although quite effective in
helping women learn to have masturbatory orgasms, often do not lead to
orgasms during intercourse (Payn & Wakefield, 1982; Wakefield, 1987).
(This does not necessarily mean the exercises have "failed" however; it all
depends on what you define as success.)

Some therapists believe that women can increase their sexual responsiveness and the probability of being orgasmic in intercourse by strengthen-
ing the muscles surrounding the lower third of the vagina. They assign **Kegel
exercises,** which were originally designed in the 1950s for women who experienced urinary "leakage" when they sneezed, coughed, or engaged in stren-
uous activities. A woman identifies the muscles in question by sitting on the
toilet and deliberately stopping the flow of urine. She may be instructed to
insert a finger into the vagina and contract the same muscles, so that she can
feel them squeezing the finger. After that she contracts the muscles several
times a day, gradually increasing the number of contractions. Kegel exercises
can be done anywhere, and any place, without anyone knowing about it.
Some therapists also believe they can be useful for men (see Zilbergeld,
1978). However, when we did a literature search on Kegel exercises, we discovered a total of only *eight* reports on their effects. One found positive
effects (Graber, Kline-Graber & Golden, 1981). In another, the exercises
enhanced subjective and physiological arousal, but only during the first week
of practice (Messe & Geer, 1985). In all the other studies, there were *no
effects* on arousal or orgasm (e.g., Chambless & DeMarco, 1985; Freese &
Levitt, 1984; Roughan & Kunst, 1981; Trudel & Saint-Laurent, 1983).
There is not even much evidence that orgasmic response is normally related
to genital muscle tone (Hoon, 1984). Assigning Kegel exercises seems to be
one of those ideas that people have latched onto without asking whether
there is empirical support for it.

Masters and Johnson's approach to the treatment of female orgasmic
problems in heterosexual intercourse is similar in many respects to the one
used for treating erection problems in men. Again, therapy begins with sensate-focus exercises. When the couple moves on to genital stimulation, the
woman's partner is told to sit with his back against pillows propped against
the headboard of the bed. He may recline slightly if he wishes. He then separates his legs, and the woman sits between them, facing in the same direction. She leans back a little with her back against his chest and her head
resting on his shoulder. Then she separates her legs and extends them across
the partner's. Masters and Johnson believe that this position makes the
woman feel secure and allows the partner maximum freedom to explore cre-

Becoming orgasmic: stimulation in the back-to-back position

atively the woman's entire body. The woman is told to place her hand lightly on her partner's and gently guide his hand to show him what kind of stimulation she wants. This is easier than putting a request into words or providing a detailed explanation. The man is encouraged to take a "light, teasing, nondemanding approach to touch and manipulation" and to avoid a direct attack on the clitoral glans unless the woman indicates that that is what she wants. When a couple feels completely comfortable with genital stimulation, they are asked to try intercourse with the woman on top. She is instructed to control pelvic thrusting while exploring the sensation of having a penis in her vagina. The man is then allowed to thrust too, but in a nondemanding way and at a pace specified by the woman. The couple is encouraged to separate two or three times and simply lie in each other's arms.

In general, treatment of secondary orgasmic problems is more complicated than treatment of primary problems, perhaps because secondary problems often involve relationship difficulties (McGovern, Stuart & LoPiccolo, 1975). In the following case treatment consisted of teaching the woman to associate orgasms brought on by manual stimulation with arousing thoughts about intercourse and insertion of an object—and eventually the partner's penis—into the vagina.

Mr. and Mrs. B, both 27 years old, complained that Mrs. B was unable to experience orgasm during intercourse, though she did have orgasms through masturbation or manual stimulation by Mr. B. Assessment of their situation revealed that Mrs. B was quite happy with their marriage, but Mr. B was not. Both partners were unaccepting of Mrs. B's sexual pattern. Mrs. B often rejected her husband's sexual advances. He was slightly more accepting of and satisified with their sexual relationship than she was. Their sexual interactions were filled with tension and anxiety.

Therapy began with sensate-focusing exercises. The couple was also asked to spend more time discussing nonsexual matters in a supportive way. After four therapy sessions, the Bs reported less tension and more enjoyment during sex. The therapists then began a six-step program to help Mrs. B attain orgasm in intercourse. Step 1 required her to use a fantasy of intercourse just prior to her masturbatory orgasms. Step 2 would have normally required Mr. B to observe his wife's masturbating sessions, but it was not necessary because he had already done so. In Step 3 Mrs. B was asked to buy a dildo or similar object so that she could get used to having something in the vagina. She preferred using various vegetables as dildo substitutes. She was orgasmic with these substitutes almost immediately. Step 4 consisted of having the woman fantasize about intercourse while using the dildo, and Step 5 required that the man observe these sessions. These steps went very quickly. At this point in therapy Mrs. B stopped thinking of herself as sexually cold and inhibited and began to consider herself a sexually creative and uninhibited woman.

Step 6, the transition to intercourse, also went smoothly. Mr. B was able to provide Mrs. B with the kind of stimulation she found best during masturbation. After 15 therapy sessions over a five-month period, Mrs. B was multiply orgasmic more than half the time during intercourse. Both partners said they accepted the initiation of sex from the other with pleasure. Mrs. B was more satisfied with their sexual relationship than she had been previously, and Mr. B's marital satisfaction increased dramatically. (adapted and condensed from Zeiss, Rosen & Zeiss, 1978, pp. 223–24)

In this case, both partners wanted the wife to learn to have orgasms in intercourse without manual stimulation. It is worth noting again, however, that the same "problem" might be "solved" by acceptance of manual stimulation as a valid way to have orgasms.

Premature Ejaculation

Men with the most common type of ejaculation problem, **premature ejaculation,** ejaculate too quickly. What is too quickly? Masters and Johnson say that a man is premature if 50 percent of the time he is unable to delay ejaculation until his partner reaches orgasm in intercourse. However, this approach is arbitrary, it ties prematurity to intercourse (surely a man could be too fast when receiving oral or manual sex, too), and it raises the spectre of a man thrusting away hour after hour with a partner who does not have orgasms in intercourse—and being labeled "premature"! Most people would probably agree that a man who ejaculates immediately with only minimal sexual stimulation, or one who ejaculates just as intercourse is about to begin or immediately after it starts, is ejaculating prematurely. In other cases, though, the definition of "too fast" depends on the needs of the individual man and his partner.

Many therapists believe premature ejaculation to be the most common sexual complaint among men—though it may not always cause them to seek therapy. Most men probably have at least one sexual experience in which they climax more rapidly than they want to. This is especially likely to happen if a man has not had sex for some time.

CAUSES   Habitual premature ejaculation can occur for many reasons. Therapists have suggested the following possible causes:

1. A man may be conditioned to ejaculate rapidly by early experiences with masturbation. Young men usually rush through it to get a quick release from sexual tension, often worrying about getting caught. So even though therapists generally regard masturbation as an important and useful developmental step (see Chapter 12), it may have this one drawback, at least for males.

Stolen moments   *Hasty sexual experiences during adolescence may make "quick responses" habitual, and even contribute to premature ejaculation problems later on.*

2.   A man may also be conditioned to ejaculate rapidly during early experiences with intercourse if he has to "do it" in a place where there is the risk of discovery—the back seat of a car, a drive-in movie, a lovers' lane, or the home of his girlfriend's parents. If all of a young man's early encounters are in such contexts, he may never have an opportunity to become sensitive to various stages in the buildup of sexual arousal and may not learn to pace himself effectively.

3.   Some teenagers engage in a practice in which the male, fully or partially clothed, rubs against the female's body until friction brings on an orgasm. This preserves the female's virginity and prevents pregnancy, but it also allows the male to relieve his sexual tension without giving any thought to his partner's needs (see Masters & Johnson, 1970).

4.   In older men, premature ejaculation sometimes appears to be related to early experiences with a prostitute who rushed the man along and perhaps praised his speediness in order to minimize the time she had to spend with him and maximize her profits.

5.   In some cases the causes may reflect personal and relationship problems. For example, a man who is angry at his partner may express his hostility by ejaculating too soon.

6.   Some men may ejaculate quickly because of a hypersensitivity to physical sexual stimulation. That is, they may simply have a lower physical threshold for orgasm than others (Strassberg et al., 1987).

TREATMENT   Whatever the precise origins of the problem, a man who ejaculates too quickly often becomes nervous in sexual encounters. He worries about his performance and about being criticized by a disappointed partner. His anxiety stimulates his nervous system, making it even harder for him to determine how aroused he is. Treatment typically does not focus on the anxiety, however, but on teaching the man to recognize the sensations he feels immediately before orgasm. The therapist encourages the man to deal with his problem in a sexual setting that is relaxed and sensual. He is *not* told to avoid sexual pleasure (as some men with a prematurity problem try to do) by mentally balancing his checkbook, biting his tongue, or watching the second hand on the clock. After all, what advantage is there in lasting ten or twenty minutes if you get nothing out of the experience erotically?

Two techniques are commonly used to teach ejaculatory control. The **stop-start method** was devised by James Semans (1956). A partner stimulates the man's penis manually until ejaculation is imminent, then stops until arousal subsides and the erection diminishes. Then the partner again stimulates the penis. This procedure is repeated several times so that the man can get used to receiving a great deal of stimulation without ejaculating. With repeated practice, he needs fewer and shorter pauses to sustain arousal and delay ejaculation until finally he is able to receive stimulation without any pauses at all. The **squeeze method,** used less often, is Master & Johnson's modification of the Semans procedure. The partner stimulates the man's penis manually until it is erect, but instead of pausing, squeezes firmly, with the thumb on the frenulum and the first and second fingers on the opposite side of the coronal ridge. Pressure is applied for three or four seconds. This does not hurt (women often have a hard time believing that), but it does immediately eliminate the urge to ejaculate. Typically the erection will also start to subside. The partner waits fifteen to thirty seconds, then resumes manual stimulation until a full erection again occurs, and repeats the entire procedure several times.

Both the stop-start and the squeeze techniques teach a man to "play with" his arousal level instead of allowing it to control him. Both procedures encourage communication between the partners. Some therapists recommend that a man first practice these techniques on himself during masturbation (LoPiccolo, 1978). This allows a man to gain confidence and reduce anxiety without feeling pressured to please a partner. Next, he and his partner can try the stop-start or squeeze technique during manual or oral stimulation. Then, if they wish, they can go on to insertion of the man's penis without thrusting, introduce slow thrusting, and eventually allow themselves to enjoy more abandoned movements. Another solution for some couples may be for the man to work on developing a capacity for multiple orgasms (see Chapter 5).

Ejaculatory Inhibition

Ejaculatory inhibition (which sometimes goes by the unfortunate name "retarded ejaculation") is the opposite of premature ejaculation. The man can maintain an erection for a long time—even indefinitely—but he has trouble ejaculating despite sexual excitement. An inability to ejaculate is analogous to an orgasmic problem in a woman; but, whereas orgasm problems in women seem to be relatively common, an inability to ejaculate is thought to be relatively rare, accounting for only 1 to 2 percent of all patients seen in therapy (Apfelbaum, 1980). (Mild versions of the problem, though, in which the difficulty occurs only occasionally, may be far more common than these numbers would indicate; see Kaplan, 1974.)

Some men cannot ejaculate under any circumstances. In most cases, though, a man has a problem only in coitus. In a few cases the penis actually feels numb in the presence of a partner, and erections are not accompanied by the usual erotic feelings but are merely reflexive. Apfelbaum (1980) characterizes men with retarded ejaculation as the "workhorses of sexual relationships"—people who can give sexually to others but feel uncomfortable about receiving erotic pleasure. Masters and Johnson (1970) have noted such presumably causative factors as severe religious orthodoxy, a specific traumatic experience, strong dislike for and rejection of the partner, and fear of pregnancy. Diseases and drugs that affect the nervous system may also interfere with the ejaculatory response. Still other possible causes include lack of interest in sex, unwillingness to ask for needed sexual stimulation, and relationship problems. Some men may delay ejaculation because they think good lovers always prolong intercourse, then be too tired to have an orgasm when they want to.

One common method of treatment is to have the partner manipulate the man's penis until he is close to ejaculating, then rapidly insert the penis into her vagina. If the timing is right, chances are that he will ejaculate. Kaplan (1974) calls this the "bridge maneuver." After repeated sessions, ejaculation should become easier. Apfelbaum (1980) uses a different strategy, which he calls "counterbypassing." During sex the man verbally expresses how worried he is and how pressured he feels. Venting his negative feelings may allow him to let go physically and ejaculate. Other techniques focus on increasing arousal.

EVALUATING SEX THERAPY: DOES IT WORK?

During the 1970s, sex therapy enjoyed a reputation for effectiveness that few other therapies could claim. This reputation rested heavily on results reported by Masters and Johnson in 1970. Masters and Johnson were reluctant to provide statistics on success, presumably because it was too hard to define. But they did report "failure rates," apparently based on cases clearly identifiable as failures. Most professionals interpreted the nonfailures as successes, though it was unclear just what sorts of outcomes the "nonfailure" group included.

All of Masters and Johnson's failure rates were low—some astoundingly low. For example, they reported a failure rate of only 2.2 percent for premature ejaculation, a condition, they wrote, that "should and can be brought fully under control in our culture during the next decade" (Masters and Johnson, 1970). Their overall failure rate was less than 20 percent. Later they reported similar results in the treatment of problems of homosexuals (Masters and Johnson, 1979). What's more, their results seemed to hold up quite well in a five-year follow up study.

Then doubts set in. Today, the extreme optimism of the early days has vanished, replaced by a more realistic view of what sex therapy can and cannot do. This change has been brought about by three related developments: criticism of Masters and Johnson, growing awareness of difficulties in evaluating therapy, and success rates lower than those first reported.

Criticism of Masters and Johnson

For years, Masters and Johnson's 1970 book, *Human Sexual Inadequacy*, was the bible of sex therapy. Few therapists questioned or even closely scrutinized their findings, perhaps in part because they had done so much to make sex therapy a respectable profession. It took a decade for misgivings to surface. The most direct attack appeared in an article by Bernie Zilbergeld and Michael Evans, ironically titled "The Inadequacy of Masters and Johnson" (1980).

Inviting proposition
Sexual problems do not have to be permanent. Many people have overcome their sexual difficulties and achieved a more gratifying sex life.

Zilbergeld and Evans did *not* say that Masters and Johnson's techniques were poor. What they did say is that evaluating Masters and Johnson's results was impossible because of sloppy and vague reporting of both results and treatment procedures. Specifically, they faulted Masters and Johnson for: (1) failing to report, or reporting in a confused way, the criteria used to assess success and failure; (2) reporting only global failure rates without distinguishing different degrees of improvement; (3) neglecting to provide important data about the characteristics of patients; (4) failing to explain that many patients were screened out of the program or were asked to leave therapy because of deep relationship problems or resistance to treatment; (5) glossing over the fact that only 29 percent of the original sample was available for the five-year follow-up; (6) being vague about how the follow-up study was done; and (7) failing to provide information about continuing contacts with patients by telephone. Zilbergeld and Evans also criticized Masters and Johnson's report on sex therapy with homosexuals.

Growing Awareness of Evaluation Problems

As sex therapy has become a more mature field, therapists have become increasingly sophisticated about the problems inherent in evaluating the outcome of their work. Evaluation problems are not unique to sex therapy. All mental health professionals must grapple with the difficulties of defining success, determining who should evaluate improvement, and identifying appropriate control groups. The first of these problems, defining success, is particularly thorny. Does success consist of removing a specific "symptom"? Does it mean increased satisfaction with sex? A better relationship between the partners?

Suppose a woman comes in for therapy because she has never had an orgasm. Should the therapist consider her "cured" or improved if, after therapy, she still fails to have orgasms but feels less guilty about sex, or enjoys it more? If she can have an orgasm with masturbation but not intercourse? If she has coital orgasms with manual stimulation but does not have "no-hands orgasms"? If she has orgasms in intercourse only 10 percent of the time, or 20, or 30? If she always has orgasms but hates sex? If she has orgasms and likes sex but despises her partner? Some writers have suggested that high success rates in the past may have been due in part to extreme flexibility in defining success. Definitional problems can probably never be completely solved, but careful reporting of evaluation methods will at least make it easier to interpret just what success rates really mean.

Falling Success Rates

Evaluation studies and clinical experience indicate that over the years high success rates have become harder and harder to obtain. "Where have all the easy cases gone?" sex therapists wonder. Not only is success harder to achieve, but "relapse rates" seem higher than they used to be. Patients get better, but after a few months or years they have the same old problem (De Amicus et al., 1985; Kilmann et al., 1986).

One possible explanation is that the goals of sex therapy have changed. During the early seventies, most therapists concentrated on specific dysfunctions, but gradually this narrow focus gave way to an emphasis on the enjoyment and satisfaction of both partners in a relationship—the last "stage" in the sexual response cycle (Ellison, 1987). This result was far more difficult to achieve. Thus in one study, 10 out of 16 men with erection problems were "cured" when improvement was defined as fewer erection failures, but only *one* could be classified as "cured" when success was defined as complete elimination of sexual problems in both husband and wife (Levine & Agle, 1978). In another study, all the women in a program for preorgasmic women learned to have orgasms. But only a few were able to integrate this change into their marriages or love affairs (Payn, 1980).

Other explanations of falling success rates are also possible. For example, early therapy programs may have dealt with highly selected groups of patients. These patients may have been better educated than most people, and extremely motivated. Remember, sex therapy initially was not as well accepted as it is today. You had to be highly motivated to try it. Now, however, a more diverse group of people may be seeking therapy. This group is bound to include some who are less motivated, less educated, and more difficult to treat than the original patients.

Another possibility is that the culture itself may have "cured" certain mild kinds of problems that used to be seen in therapy, by providing information through the media and promoting a more open and accepting attitude toward sex. This would leave only the more serious cases to be seen by therapists—for instance, cases in which severe relationship difficulties underlie specific sexual complaints.

None of the above remarks should be taken to mean that sex therapy is ineffective. On the contrary, it does work for many people. Assigning homework exercises may be too simplistic an approach in cases where serious psychological and relationship difficulties exist. And sex therapy probably cannot live up to expectations raised by the first glowing reports. But many troubled couples can testify that they have been helped by sex therapy, and therapists are starting to understand better exactly which factors are important for success (see Table 11–2).

Two of the most useful functions of the sex therapist are to provide accurate information about sex and to give permission to enjoy it. In a more perfect world, society itself would assume these functions, and people would not need assurance that it was fine to have a full and gratifying sexual relationship. But the world is not perfect, so sex therapists fill a need. They will have succeeded in their work when they are no longer necessary.

. . . .

TABLE 11–2
Influences on the outcome of sex therapy   Here are some factors believed to affect the success or failure of therapy. Their order of presentation does not reflect any assumptions about their relative importance.

Factor	Influence
Age	Older people, particularly men, tend to show less complete improvement.
Duration of sexual problem	Problems of longer duration are usually more difficult to treat, particularly in men.
Sexual history	Physically and emotionally rewarding sexual experiences in the past bode well for a positive response to therapy, especially for men.
Characteristics of the problem	Problems due to specific stresses are easier to treat than those that develop gradually. Intermittent problems are easier than continuous ones. Secondary problems are easier than primary ones, especially in men.
Psychological adjustment	Emotional problems can interfere with treatment gains.
Relationship between partners	Positive feelings toward a relationship are related to success, especially for women.
Willingness to work	Willingness to do "homework" and spend time and effort even after therapy ends enhances chances of success.
Therapist	Skill in assessing and treating sexual problems improves chances of success.

Source: Based on Cooper, 1981 and Kilmann & Mills, 1983.

. . . .

PERSONAL PERSPECTIVE

TAKING THE STRESS OUT OF SEX

Sex is like a garden; it must be tended. In a busy world, though, this may not be easy. The demands of school, work, and family distract and tire us, and sexual desire may wither.

If you are in an intimate relationship, you and your partner can use the following checklist (adapted from Wade, 1985) to explore the extent to which stress is putting a damper on your sex life. We suggest making a copy of the list and answering independently. Then you can use the results to initiate a discussion. But keep in mind that this is not a test! Our intention is not to turn sex itself into a source of stress: the items are only intended to increase sensitivity to warning signals that mean stress is finding its way into the bedroom.

Check those statements that are *usually* or *increasingly* true for each of you.

1. Making love seems more trouble than it's worth.

2. I'd like to have sex more often, but chores and responsibilities make that difficult.

3. While making love I find myself thinking about school, work, or personal problems.

4. I feel impatient when my partner takes a long time to become aroused or to have an orgasm.

5. We make love when I am mentally or physically tired.

6. I depend on alcohol or other drugs to relax me before sex.

7. During sex I feel guilty about taking time out from my other duties.

8. My partner and I start having sex without spending time together nonsexually.

9. "Fooling around" without having intercourse seems pointless.

10. When my partner takes the initiative, I feel he or she is making demands on my time or energy.

11. Right after orgasm I feel an urge to jump up and get on with some other activity.

12. My partner and I do not set any special time aside to be together.

13. Sex is fine, but I get anxious if it goes into "overtime."

14. Despite my interest, I have trouble switching from a nonerotic to an erotic mood.

15. My partner and I usually make love late at night or after every-thing else has been taken care of.

16. Children, phone calls, or visitors keep interfering with our privacy.

17. I am completely content with my sex life. (*If both of you check this item, you can probably ignore your responses to all the others.*)

If, after using this checklist, you think that stress is interfering with your sexual relationship, here are some suggestions for change.

1. *Create some transition time.* It can take time to move from one activity, such as studying, to another, such as sex. Try giving yourself a transition between activities to unwind and disengage from what you have been doing. As sex therapist Bernie Zilbergeld says, "A few minutes of peace and quiet can be worth four hours of foreplay" (quoted in Wade, 1985).

2. *Review priorities.* How important is sex in your life? If it is not too important, the solution to a stress problem may be to allow sex to take a back seat to other activities. If it is important, you may decide to deliberately put other activities aside when you are in an erotic mood.

3. *Schedule time for eroticism.* Many busy couples find it useful to "make dates" instead of leaving romance to chance. This may not sound very spontaneous, but making appointments with a spouse or lover can be a way of reserving time for spontaneity. According to sex therapist Carol Rinkleib Ellison, "If you light the pilot early, the furnace can warm up all day" (quoted in Wade, 1985).

4. *Create the right setting.* When stress threatens to distract you, you can focus your attention and emotions by taking extra care with the context: provide yourself with the right music, lighting, and so forth.

5. *Reassess the function of sex.* Sometimes people with high-stress lives start to see sex as a drain on their time and energy. But it is also possible to view sex as a way of recharging your batteries. Sex, after all, is a way for adults to relax and play. It releases tension and connects us to another person. It gives us a break and helps us regain perspective. When stress is sabotaging your enjoyment of life, you can choose to regard sex as part of the problem—or you can make it part of the solution.

IN BRIEF

1. Sex therapists believe that sexual functioning is healthy when physiology, behavior, attitudes, and feelings are in harmony. When one or more of these components of sexuality is out of phase with the others, a problem exists. However, definitions of specific sexual problems are influenced by cultural values and by implicit models of how sex ought to be performed.

2. Sexual problems may be primary (lifelong) or secondary (acquired); global or situational; and total or partial. No one knows for sure how

common sexual problems are; estimates depend on how narrowly or broadly problems are defined.

3. *Organic factors* that play a role in sexual problems include neurological, vascular, hormonal, and genital disorders, and the side effects of drugs. *Psychological factors* include a person's attitudes, feelings, personality traits, and outlook on life. *Relationship factors* include hostility between partners, boredom, conflicting sexual expectations, and poor communication. *Cultural factors* include negative cultural attitudes about sex, restrictive religious beliefs, and narrow gender roles. The causes of sexual problems interact, and in specific cases cause and effect can be hard to establish.

4. The basic goals of sex therapy are education, facilitation of open and honest communication, a reduction in anxiety about sexual feelings and performance, and promotion of behaviors that enhance sexual functioning. Sex therapy became an independent specialty after Masters and Johnson reported on their treatment program in 1970. The central feature of the Masters and Johnson approach is the assignment of sexual "homework" exercises, including *sensate focus* exercises, non-goal-oriented genital stimulation, and specific activities tailored to the particular problem being treated. Today most therapists use this basic approach, with variations. Many combine homework exercises with more traditional methods of psychotherapy and marriage counseling, and some use a systems approach to examine the hidden functions that a sexual problem may serve in a relationship.

5. *Inhibited sexual desire (ISD)* is characterized by a lack of interest in sexual contact. Some therapists consider low desire to be a problem only when there is a *sexual desire discrepancy* in a relationship. ISD and discrepancy problems are probably the most common of all sexual complaints, and the most difficult to treat, especially when relationship difficulties are the source. *Sexual aversion* is more extreme that ISD; it involves feelings of anxiety and even panic in sexual situations. Treatment usually focuses on working through feelings about prior negative experiences and reducing current anxiety.

6. Arousal problems include lack of lubrication in women and *erectile inhibition* in men. Occasional erection problems are common and are usually short-lived. Physiological factors contribute to a substantial proportion of persistent problems, although exactly how many is uncertain. In cases where the problem is mainly physical, a possible solution is a penile implant, but many sex therapists think they are prescribed too often. There are many possible psychological causes of erectile inhibition. Therapy focuses on improving communication and reducing performance pressure.

7. *Dyspareunia* is painful intercourse. When there are physical causes, dyspareunia may be eliminated by surgery, medication, or use of a lubricant. When there are psychological or relationship factors involved, therapy usually focuses on increasing a person's sense of control, decreasing fear and guilt, and improving trust and communication. *Vaginismus* causes pain before intercourse can even begin. Muscles around the lower third of the vagina contract spasmodically and involuntarily. Treatment often incorporates gradual dilation of the vagina.

8. The incidence of *anorgasmia* in women is uncertain, because of different ways of defining it. Research has tended to focus solely on coital orgasms, but an inability to have coital orgasms without additional manual stimulation is common and need not be perceived as a problem. Difficulties with orgasm may be due to inadequate stimulation, lack of knowledge about sexual anatomy, or psychological and cultural factors. Treatment often includes sensate focus exercises and nondemanding genital stimulation. Masturbation exercises are helpful in learning to have orgasms, although they do not necessarily lead to orgasms during intercourse. Kegel exercises are also commonly prescribed, but there is little empirical evidence that they enhance either arousal or orgasm.

9. *Premature ejaculation* is the most common type of ejaculation problem. There are many causes, including early conditioning of rapid ejaculation during masturbation and partner sex, relationship problems, and a lower than average physical threshold for orgasm. Treatment is aimed at helping the man recognize the sensations preceding orgasm so he can control the ejaculatory reflex. The most common technique is the *start-stop* technique.

10. *Ejaculatory inhibition* in men is analogous to anorgasmia in women, but appears to be much less common. Usually the man has a problem only in ejaculating during sexual intercourse. The causes vary, and include physiological factors, lack of interest in sex, unwillingness to ask for needed stimulation, and relationship problems. One common treatment technique is the "bridge maneuver."

11. Early optimism about the effectiveness of sex therapy has been tempered by criticisms of Masters and Johnson's reporting procedures, growing awareness of evaluation problems, and a decline in success rates. However, many troubled individuals and couples have been helped by sex therapy, and further research may clarify how positive results can be increased.

Key Terms

sexual problem *(384)*

primary vs. secondary
sexual problems *(384)*

global vs. situational
sexual problems *(384)*

spectatoring *(388)*

sensate focus *(398)*

sexual surrogate *(399)*

inhibited sexual desire (ISD) *(402)*

sexual desire discrepancy *(402)*

sexual aversion *(404)*

erectile inhibition *(405)*

nocturnal penile tumescence *(407)*

penile implant *(408)*

dyspareunia *(409)*

vaginismus *(410)*

anorgasmia *(411)*

Kegel exercises *(414)*

premature ejaculation *(416)*

stop-start technique *(418)*

squeeze technique *(419)*

ejaculatory inhibition *(419)*

The Origins and Development of Sexuality

CHAPTER TWELVE

C H A P T E R   T W E L V E

■

Sexual Development I: Childhood

●

Everyone has sex before marriage. We're born with it and express it in our relationships from infancy on.

Richard F. Hettlinger

Most sexologists assume that people have a capacity to be sexual long before they are physically mature. But what is the nature of this capacity? Are we born with a raging sexual instinct, or do we learn to have sexual feelings and needs? If we learn to be sexual, when do the most important lessons take place: during early childhood, late childhood, puberty, or adolescence? Is a child's sexuality anything like an older person's? Are children being sexual when they play doctor, or are they simply. . .playing doctor? And how does gender affect our sexuality? Right from the start, humans come in two sexual varieties, female and male. But when do we develop a psychological identity to go along with our physical one? And how do the lessons we learn about being boys and girls affect our sexual feelings and behavior as men and women?

Our culture does not expect children to fall madly in love or have passionate sex. Childhood is supposed to be a time of naiveté and innocence. Yet, as we will see, sexuality is far from dormant during childhood, though it may be quieter, less insistent, and less relationship-oriented than it is later on. Many children have experiences that in an older person would be labeled sexual. Children are also sexually curious, and by adolescence they have learned much about human bodies, along with assorted facts and myths about sex. A child's mind does not make the same connections as an adult's, imagine the same outcomes, or understand the erotic and social significance of sexual acts. But the experiences and feelings of childhood do set the stage for later sexual dramas.

In this chapter, we will consider first the formation of gender, which affects human sexuality in profound ways. We will then describe the range of sexual expression in childhood. Finally, we will look at some theories of how biology and culture interact to produce a sexual human being.

THE EMERGENCE OF GENDER

The term **gender** is used by different writers in different ways, but in its broadest sense it refers simply to the state of being male or female. Gender distinctions affect almost every aspect of our lives. They even influence people's behavior in situations where gender would seem to be irrelevant— for example, when grade school teachers make boys and girls line up separately to enter the classroom, or when newspapers dwell on how a female politician was dressed (Bem, 1981). Many jobs, sports, and domestic chores are no longer as "gender-linked" as they once were, but people's daily lives are still affected in thousands of ways by their identity as male or female. Jan Morris, a writer who was born male but underwent a sex-change operation in her mid-forties, was able to view the effects from both sides of the gender gulf. She wrote:

> We are told that the social gap between the sexes is narrowing, but I can only report that having, in the second half of the twentieth century, experienced life in both roles, there seems to me no aspect of existence, no moment of the day, no contact, no arrangement, no response, which is not different for men and for women. (1974, p. 148)

The process of becoming biologically, socially, and psychologically male or female is a complicated one that begins with conception and continues for many years after birth. To understand this process, we must distinguish among certain related but different aspects of psychosexual development. Here are some definitions to guide you in your reading:

1. **Biological sex** encompasses all the physical traits that combine to differentiate females from males, including genes and chromosomes, sex hormone levels, reproductive structures, external genitals, and the bodily distribution of hair and fat. Some of these traits are present before birth; others appear only at puberty. As we will see, occasionally a person has certain physical characteristics of a male or female while lacking others.

2. **Gender role** (or **sex role**) refers to the set of rules or norms governing behaviors and attitudes that a culture considers appropriate for a male or a female. Gender roles influence not only ambitions and aspirations, but how people speak and walk, cross their legs, and respond to the requests and demands of others. The rules governing such diverse behav-

iors are often subtle but powerful, and violations may bring derision and criticism. Gender roles are acquired through a process called **sex typing.** As we will see, this process begins literally at birth. Thus in our society, tiny tykes who have only just learned to talk can tell you who wears dresses and who wears ties, who plays with baby dolls and who plays with toy soldiers, who is expected to grow up to be a nurse and who a surgeon. But gender roles are not the same from culture to culture. In some societies, women wear skirts, cook the meals, or go marketing, while in others, men do these things.

3. **Gender identity** refers to one's subjective sense of oneself as male or female. A child who knows its gender and realizes that it will always be male or female is said to have a stable gender identity. Normally, gender identity is congruent with a person's sexual anatomy. However, for some people, known as *transsexuals*, gender identity and sexual anatomy are at odds.

4. **Sexual orientation** refers to a person's orientation to sexual partners of either the same or the other sex. One's sexual orientation may be homosexual, heterosexual, or bisexual. Sexual orientation should not be confused with gender identity: both homosexuals and heterosexuals almost always have a gender identity that is congruent with their biological sex.

Prenatal Gender Development

To locate the origins of gender, we must start at the beginning of human development—the very beginning, the moment of conception. The human ovum and the human sperm each contain twenty-three **chromosomes,** rod-shaped structures at the center of every body cell. Chromosomes are strands of DNA composed of genetic units known as **genes.** Genes carry coded instructions that determine an organism's inherited characteristics. When ovum and sperm merge to form a fertilized egg cell, the resulting forty-six chromosomes make twenty-three pairs. One of these pairs is responsible for the embryo's sex: it consists of a chromosome, known as an X, from the ovum and either an X or Y chromosome from the sperm. The father's contribution is the determining one: if he contributes an X, the child will have two Xs and be genetically female (XX); if he contributes a Y, the child will have an X and a Y and be genetically male (XY).

As we saw in Chapter 4, until about the sixth week of development, male and female embryos look the same. After that, previously undifferentiated tissue begins to develop into male or female genitals and reproductive organs. (You may want to review Figures 4–8 and 4–9 to refresh your memory on this process.) Scientists believe that if the embryo is genetically male

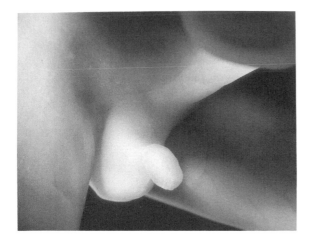 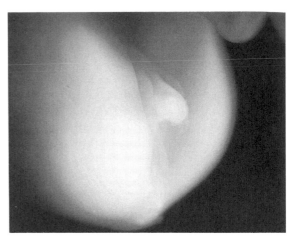

Look-alikes   *The clitoris and the penis develop from the same embryonic tissue and are difficult to distinguish during the early stages of fetal development. The right-hand photo shows a clitoris three months after conception; the left-hand photo shows a penis during the fourth month.*

(XY), a single gene on the Y chromosome, called the **testis determining factor (TDF)**, initiates the development of male anatomy. It appears to accomplish this by triggering production of a protein that in turn tells other genes to start the development of the male gonads, or testes. If the embryo does not have the TDF gene, at about nine weeks it develops a pair of female gonads, or ovaries. It is the presence or absence of the TDF gene, rather than the presence or absence of the Y chromosome per se, that is crucial. How do we know this? Occasionally a normal looking boy will be born with two X chromosomes or a normal looking girl will be born with an X and a Y. In the XX boys, one X chromosome always has a tiny bit of TDF-bearing Y chromosome attached, while in the XY girls, the Y chromosome always lack this bit. At present, the precise identity of the gene remains uncertain, but a newly-discovered gene called SRY (Sex-determining Region of the Y Chromosome) is a strong candidate (Sinclair et al., 1990).

Once the testis determining factor has had its effect, the direct influence of genes on prenatal gender development appears to be over. From that point on, it is the presence or absence of testicular tissue that is important. In normal male development, this tissue secretes three hormones. One, testosterone, stimulates a set of structures called the *Wolffian ducts* to develop into the vas deferens, the epididymis, and the seminal vesicles. A second substance, **Müllerian inhibiting substance (MIS),** inhibits the development of female organs from the *Müllerian ducts*, which eventually shrink. Finally, a derivative of testosterone, **dihydrotestosterone (DHT),** stimulates development of the scrotum and penis.

In normal female development, the ovaries begin to synthesize estrogens, the embryonic Wolffian ducts wither away, the Müllerian ducts are transformed into a uterus, Fallopian tubes, and the inner two-thirds of the vagina, and external female genitals develop. But remarkably enough, the latter three changes apparently can occur even without the presence of ovaries or estrogens. All that is necessary is the *absence* of significant quantities of male hormones.

In short, Nature's basic blueprint is for a female fetus. Only if certain "extras" are added—a TDF gene, Müllerian inhibiting substance, testosterone, and DHT—will the embryo develop into a male. For male organs to form properly, the hormones in question must be present in certain amounts during a critical period, probably from the eighth to the fourteenth week of fetal development.

Gender Assignment and Gender Identity

Along with a few other vital statistics, gender is customarily announced at birth and recorded on the baby's birth certificate. This labeling, or *gender assignment*, is ordinarily determined by the child's possession of male or female genitals.

Research shows that gender assignment affects the way parents perceive their little bundle of joy even before they cart the bundle home from the hospital. In one study, parents of newborn girls described their babies as softer, smaller, more finely featured, and more inattentive than did the parents of boys. Fathers, in particular, were influenced by a child's gender. They saw their sons as firmer, larger-featured, better coordinated, more alert, stronger, and hardier than mothers did. Men also saw their daughters as more inattentive, weak, and delicate than the women did. Actually, there were *no* objective differences between the boys and the girls in color, muscle tone, irritability, size, or other neurological and physical traits (Rubin, Provenzano & Luria, 1974). When it comes to gender, parental perceptions often have little to do with reality.

Generic baby *Is this a girl or a boy? The answer is likely to affect how you perceive and respond to the infant.*

No sooner are boys and girls perceived as different than they are treated differently. Almost all parents sex-type their children to some extent—with the toys they buy for them, the clothes they dress them in, the activities they encourage. Later, teachers and other adults do the same. Adults convey sex stereotypes and different expectations for the sexes even by the way they write and speak. Women use certain adjectives, such as *adorable* or *lovely*, and certain euphemisms, such as *powder room*, that are off limits, in most contexts, for men. Men give orders more directly than women ("Shut the door"), while women often soften their commands and requests by disguising them as questions ("Would you mind shutting the door?"). Moreover, the use of *men* or *mankind* to refer to humanity, and the use of *he* to refer to any person, sex unspecified, subtly tells children that *male* is synonymous with *human* while females are somehow extraneous, outsiders. Children understand the "gender neutral" use of *he* as masculine, and this usage affects their sex stereotyping of jobs (Hyde, 1984). (For a more complete description of sex-typing by parents, teachers, and the media, see Tavris & Wade, 1984.)

By age 3 or 4, most children prefer the activities and games that are culturally defined as "right" for their gender. They have observed who wears fingernail polish and skirts, who drives the car on family outings, who cleans the house, who is supposed to be tough and who can be soft and gentle. In short, they have determined the social rules that govern masculine and feminine activities in their culture.

However, not everyone emerges from childhood equally sex-typed (Bem, 1974; Tavris & Wade, 1984). Some people are cross sex-typed; a majority of their traits are ones traditionally associated with the other sex, rather than their own. And many people are psychologically **androgynous.** That is, they have both traditionally masculine and traditionally feminine qualities, in roughly equal proportions, and can flexibly adapt their behavior to suit the particular occasion. Today many parents are making a conscious effort to rear children who are not confined by narrow sex roles. (For an excellent guide on how to do this, see Letty Cottin Pogrebin's book, *Growing Up Free: Raising Your Kids in the 80's* [McGraw-Hill, 1980], which is still relevant in the 90s.)

Beyond gender roles
These children feel free to express their individuality rather than conforming to social expectations about the "appropriate" activities for boys and girls.

No matter what the degree of sex typing, by age five or six most children have a firm gender identity. They understand that they are biologically male or female and that they cannot change gender the way they can switch clothes or hairstyles. Gender identity is a stable and enduring aspect of personality; once formed, it is rarely questioned or debated. You may be heterosexual, homosexual, bisexual, asexual, or confused about your sexual orientation, but you are not likely to be confused about whether you are male or female. Notions of what it means to be "masculine" or "feminine" can and do change, not only during childhood but across the life span, as a result of both personal experiences and changing cultural expectations. But unless you are a transsexual (see Box 12–1), your fundamental biological and psychological identity as male or female will be with you always.

Boys and girls, however, are not always equally satisfied with their gender identities, or the roles that usually go along with them. When 2,000 schoolchildren in grades three through twelve were asked how their lives would change if they were a member of the other sex, girls said they would expect to be more assertive and self-reliant, freer, less concerned with appearance, and relieved of the burden of being treated as a sex object. Boys, in contrast, said they would expect to be less active, more restricted, more worried about appearance, more worried about violence against themselves, and more likely to be treated disparagingly as a sex object. Girls generally thought they'd be better off as males, but boys, especially grammar-school boys, tended to view girlhood as a fate worse than death. One third-grader put it succinctly: "If I were a girl, everybody would be better than me, because boys are better than girls" (Baumgartner, 1983).

THE EMERGENCE OF SEXUAL BEHAVIOR

Gender development is a relatively easy topic to research. The development of sexuality is not. Because our culture tends to regard sexual feelings and behavior in childhood as unnatural or harmful, Masters-and-Johnson-type studies of children are not ethically feasible. A researcher who wants to find out about children's masturbation cannot ask them to do it, and would also hesitate to ask them about it. Even Kinsey, who was always ready to break new ground in sex research, was cautious about studying children. He did interview 432 children between the ages of 4 and 14, but the results were not published in any detail until long after his death, and then in a rather obscure journal (Elias & Gebhard, 1969).

Because of these limitations, much of our information about childhood sexuality comes from adults. This is hardly ideal. We can ask adults about their childhood experiences, but memory is often a fallible guide to the past. We can ask parents to observe and report the behavior of their children, but parental observations are often unsystematic and biased. Yet despite these obstacles, we know from the available evidence that at least some—and probably all—children are physically capable of what appear to be sexual

BOX 12–1

The Mystery of Transsexualism

For many years, James Morris was a distinguished journalist and father of five. Today, Jan Morris is a widely published female writer. James and Jan are the same person—a transsexual.

In **transsexuals,** sexual anatomy and gender identity collide. Transsexuals feel that nature has played a cruel joke on them, trapping them in the wrong body. Often this feeling goes back as far as the person can remember. As one male transsexual recalled, ". . .[as a preschooler] I was so disappointed because every morning I'd reach down there and there it was. . . ." (quoted in Green, 1974, p. 47). In adulthood, the discrepancy between body and mind leads to confusion, dismay, and despair. Many transsexuals seek sex-change surgery to reconcile their bodies with their gender identities. Some, denied surgery, have mutilated themselves in an attempt to remove or change the offending organs.

Transsexualism has probably always existed. The Greeks believed in a goddess named Venus Catina who was sympathetic to feminine souls imprisoned in male bodies. During the seventeenth century the Abbe de Choisy disguised himself in order to pass as a woman. "Everyone was deceived," he wrote. ". . .I thought myself really and truly a woman" (quoted in Green, 1974). Transsexualism has been reported among preliterate as well as literate people. According to rough estimates, there are between 10,000 and 20,000 individuals in the United States who claim to be transsexuals (Restak, 1979). Perhaps one in every 100,000 biological males and one in every 400,000 biological females is transsexual (Pauly, 1985).

The first American to receive publicity as a transsexual was Christine (formerly George) Jorgensen, who went to Denmark in 1952 for a sex-change operation because the surgery was unavailable in the United States. In 1966, Johns Hopkins Hospital began to perform sex-reassignment operations. Since then, several thousand people have been operated on in the United States and some of these cases have captured public attention. Among sexologists and mental health professionals, the operation remains somewhat controversial; differences of opinion exist about its long-term psychological value. However, most transsexuals express satisfaction with the outcome of surgery and say they would make the same choice again (Blanchard, Steiner & Clemmensen, 1985; Lundstrom, Pauly & Walinder, 1984). Adjustment after the operation is best when the person is young, has support from friends and relatives, gets good results aesthetically, has no history of serious psychological disturbance, can "pass" easily as the desired sex, and has ongoing access to counseling (Lundstrom, Pauly & Walinder, 1984; McCauley & Ehrhardt, 1984; Ross & Need, 1989).

When a person applies for a sex-change operation, an extensive psychiatric evaluation is usually done to determine if the applicant is truly a transsexual and if the person has realistic expectations about the operation. Reputable clinics (not all are reputable) require the person to live as a member of the desired sex for one or two years prior to surgery to be sure that he or she can adapt to the drastic life changes required. During this time the person usually receives hormone treatments that alter appearance and make it easier to "pass" at work and in social situations. When a male takes estrogen, the contours of the body become more feminine, prostate secretions are reduced, and erections become less frequent. When a female takes androgen, a beard may develop, the clitoris enlarges, and fat deposits become less femalelike. (Other characteristics, such as pelvic structure and size of the Adam's apple, remain the same.) Surgery, then, completes a process that is already well underway.

Male-to-female surgery involves amputation of the penis and testes and creation of an artificial vagina. Artificial breasts are often implanted. The degree of erotic pleasure experienced after the operation depends on how the skin of the penis and scrotum was used and the extent to which nerves from the original genitals remain intact. Female-to-male conversions are more complicated and generally less successful from an aesthetic point of view. First the breasts, uterus, and ovaries are removed. Some individuals stop there. If the person does choose genital surgery, a scrotum is usually formed by fusing the labial tissue. This new scrotum may be filled with silicone testicles. Then a penis is constructed by taking a skin graft from the abdominal wall and fashioning it into a hollow tube. The resulting organ is not terribly realistic looking and cannot become erect unless a special implant is used (see Chapter 11). Its skin is insensitive, but arousal and often orgasm are possible because the clitoris is retained and embedded into the base of the tube.

The adult sex hormones of transsexuals do not seem to differ from anyone else's. Then how does transsexualism develop? Do prenatal hormones play a role? Does the person for some reason fail to identify with the same-sex parent? Do most parents of transsexuals tolerate or even encourage cross-sex behaviors and cross-dressing by their child? In some individuals, is transsexualism the response of a sensitive child to gender-based restrictions on dress, interests, and ambitions? Research has not yet answered these questions. Probably many factors, interacting in some complex way, are needed to explain how transsexuals manage to fend off the social pressures that usually turn babies with vulvas and vaginas psychologically into girls and babies with penises and scrotums psychologically into boys.

Transsexual parents
After the adults in this photograph first met, they learned that each felt trapped in the body of the wrong sex. They decided to marry, have a child, and then change their sexual identities by undergoing sex-change operations.

responses even in their earliest years. Let us look at these responses, and what they might mean socially and psychologically to a child.

Childhood Masturbation

Babies are born with all the anatomical structures required for sexual responding, and seem to have the necessary neurological "wiring" as well. Newborn baby girls lubricate vaginally. Ultrasound photographs show that males are capable of having erections in the womb. After birth, baby boys have erections regularly, both when asleep and when awake.

During the first two or three years of life most infants probably explore and fondle their own genitals. This activity, however, has to have a very different meaning for the child than it would for an adult, because the child does not yet have the capacity for the kind of erotic fantasy that usually accompanies adult masturbation. Typically infants play with their genitals in the same casual way that they play with their ears, noses, fingers, and toes. Through self-exploration they become acquainted with the parts of their bodies and the sensations produced when the different parts are rubbed, squeezed, and (if accessible) nibbled.

In the course of such exploratory play, at least some children deliberately masturbate to orgasm, or at least what looks like orgasm. Kinsey had some of his adult subjects observe and report the masturbatory activities of their own offspring. All told, parents reported orgasm in seven girls and twenty-seven boys under the age of four. (Kinsey did not say whether this was a tiny fraction or a large proportion of the children observed.) The youngest girl was only four months old, the youngest boy only five months. One eleven-month-old boy appeared to have fourteen orgasms within the space of about half an hour (Kinsey, Pomeroy & Martin, 1948). A sharp-eyed mother of a three-year-old girl gave the following detailed account:

> Lying face down on the bed, with her knees drawn up, she started rhythmic pelvic thrusts, about one second or less apart. . . .There were 44 thrusts in unbroken rhythm, a slight momentary pause, 87 thrusts followed by a slight momentary pause, then 10 thrusts, and then a cessation of all movement. There was marked concentration and intense breathing with abrupt jerks as orgasm approached. She was completely oblivious to everything during these later stages of the activity. Her eyes were glassy and fixed in a vacant stare. There was noticeable relief and relaxation after orgasm. A second series of reactions began two minutes later with series of 48, 18, and 57 thrusts. . . . (quoted in Kinsey et al., 1953, pp. 104–105)

A more recent survey of over 200 parents from around the country found that most had observed their children engaging in various forms of sexual self-stimulation (The Study Group of New York, 1983). Not only did the children use their hands, but many stimulated themselves by rubbing against objects and rocking back and forth. The parents reported that the children's behavior appeared to be purposeful, pleasurable, and comforting. One parent of a six-year-old said, "Oh, yes, he masturbates. He walks around with his little hand on his penis for hours. It started when he was a baby, I would say every night, going to sleep holding his penis. And almost any time he was uncomfortable, sleepy, upset, he would go and hold his penis. . . ." A parent of a girl recalled, "At approximately a year and a half of age, my daughter discovered her vagina and discovered it was fun and so on. . . .Then she discovered that rolling around on her bottle felt very good. She'd roll and push her bottle against her vagina and clitoris and have a great old time. This is at a very young age, probably two . . ."

As a child grows older, masturbation to orgasm becomes more and more likely. The percentage of children who masturbate in a deliberate way before adolescence is not known, however. Most psychoanalysts believe that childhood masturbation is nearly universal. On the other hand, in Kinsey's adult sample only 12 percent of females and 21 percent of males said they had masturbated by the age of twelve. But Kinsey's adults may have forgotten or repressed some of their childhood experiences with masturbation. In Kinsey's sample of children, 56 percent of the boys and 30 percent of the girls said they had already masturbated (Elias & Gebhard, 1969), and since some of these children were quite young, a certain proportion were destined to discover masturbation after their participation in the study.

It seems, then, that many, and perhaps most, children have the biological capacity to derive pleasure from self-stimulation. Indeed, in societies that are permissive about childhood sexuality, most children do masturbate by the age of six or eight (Ford & Beach, 1951). Kinsey speculated that in an uninhibited society at least half of all boys could climax by the age of three or four, and nearly all could do so within three to five years before the start of adolescence. Although he made no estimates for females, his observational reports on infants suggest that the orgasmic potential of girls is also high.

Sexual Play: Experiences with the Other Sex

For the first two or so years of life, children have little sexual or, for that matter, other social contact with one another. During their first years, tots are quite egocentric. That is, they are limited in their ability to imagine the world from the perspective of another person, so they are neither interested in nor capable of much social give-and-take. Typically two children

Fascinating discovery
It is normal for young children to explore their own bodies, both visually and through touch.

Look at that! *As children grow older, they become aware of, and curious about, anatomical differences between males and females.*

placed together at this age will be preoccupied with their separate activities and will notice each other only when they both want the same toy.

By the age of three or four, however, children become more sociable and a child may be ready for his or her first "romance." Boys and girls may hug and kiss and say they plan to marry when they grow up (Martinson, 1973), although what this really means to them is not clear. Preschoolers are aware of genital differences and may be fascinated by the fact that males stand up to urinate and females do not. They may observe each other with their pants down. By the time a child enters school, play becomes more organized. Children often rehearse the socially prescribed sex roles by playing house. During this period they may show one another their genitals and play doctor. Sometimes games like doctor produce a definite physiological response:

> The girl and I were age six. I suggested playing doctor. We took off our clothes and then she lay down on her stomach so I could give her a "shot." The closest thing to a shot was a pinch so I did that a few times lightly. . . .It was my turn to be the patient so I lay on my stomach while she examined me. Then I turned onto my back and let her gaze at me awhile. She messed around a little bit until I began to get what was for me my first memorable erection. . . .She started giggling; I couldn't help giggling either so we laughed heartily for a few minutes until she said, almost screaming "What is that?" I blurted out, "I don't know!" (quoted in Martinson, 1973, p. 31)

But by the time children in our culture begin grade school, most have begun to develop a sense of privacy about their bodies. Many insist on dressing and undressing themselves. By age nine a child's sense of personal privacy is usually very strong (The Study Group of New York, 1983). Show-and-touch games motivated by curiosity about the body become less frequent.

In the middle years of elementary school, overt interest in the other sex is generally either nonexistent or negative. Sometimes there is teasing and roughhousing, but boys and girls often profess to hate each other. Then, in the upper grades of elementary school, as puberty draws near, a more positive interest in the other sex begins to emerge. Some boys and girls may pair off and "go steady" for a week or two. Preadolescents typically express their interest in sex by telling dirty jokes, writing or whispering naughty words, or talking about sex with same-sex friends. By junior high, many begin attending mixed-sex parties, playing kissing games, dancing, and "making out" (Martinson, 1973).

In Kinsey's adult sample, about 30 percent of the women and 40 percent of the men recalled some heterosexual play before adolescence. (In his sample of children, 37 percent of the girls and 34 percent of the boys reported heterosexual experiences.) Much of this activity was limited to a single episode or a few unrelated incidents of exhibition and manual touching. Kinsey and his colleagues (1953) concluded that genital explorations in childhood "often amount to nothing more than comparisons of anatomy, in much the same way that children compare their hands, their noses or mouths, their hair, their clothing, or any of their other possessions." They also suggested that genital play may appeal to children because the genitals are mysterious (or made so by adults). Doing things that are forbidden by adults, and that are therefore socially dangerous, is fun.

However, some heterosexual experiences during childhood do go beyond mere "show and tell." Of those adults in Kinsey's sample who recalled any preadolescent heterosexual experiences, 17 percent of the females and 55 percent of the males reported some sort of coitus or attempt at coitus, although full penetration may or may not have been achieved. A sizable number of people also remembered sexual encounters with adults. (The sexual abuse of children is discussed in Chapter 15.)

Sexual Play: Same-Sex Experiences

Sexual contacts between children of the same sex are somewhat more common than other-sex contacts. This may be due largely to opportunity; in our society boys tend to play with boys and girls with girls, as you can easily observe for yourself by visiting any elementary school playground. Here is an example of a same-sex experience involving three girls:

I (a girl) encountered a sexual experience that was confusing at kindergarten age. . . . Some afternoons we would meet and lock ourselves in a bedroom and take our pants off. We took turns lying on the bed and put pennies, marbles, etc. between our labia. The other two liked to pretend they were boys and used a pencil for a penis. As the ritual became old hat, it passed out of existence. I enjoyed the sexual manipulation, for it was stimulating. Yet, I never wanted to pretend that I had a penis. (quoted in Martinson, 1973, pp. 38–39)

In Kinsey's adult sample, 33 percent of the women and 48 percent of the men recalled some kind of overtly homosexual play by the onset of adolescence. (The figures from children were 35 percent and 52 percent, respectively.) In a majority of cases, contact was limited to exhibition and manual manipulation of the genitals. About 3 percent of the females and 16 percent of the males had experienced oral-genital activity. In addition, 18 percent of the females had experienced insertion of something into the vagina, while 17 percent of the males had experienced anal intercourse, though not necessarily with full penetration.

Sexual Thoughts and Fantasies

Most studies of childhood sexuality have focused on overt behavior, but as we noted in Chapter 9, thinking about sex can be considered sexual behavior, too. And adults do not have a monopoly on sexual thoughts—or what appear to be sexual thoughts. In a study of children's fantasy narratives, Brian Sutton-Smith and David M. Abrams (1977) asked 150 children between the ages of five and ten to tell two or more stories of their own choosing; 24 of the children told tales about romantic, sexual, or tabooed behavior. This seems like a rather high percentage, when you consider that the researchers left it entirely up to the children to determine the stories' themes.

Two other interesting findings emerged in the Sutton-Smith and Abrams study. First, only boys (nine of them) told sexually explicit stories, but when it came to romantic stories, girls outnumbered boys seven to four. Second, older children tended to tell "dirtier" stories than younger ones. Children aged seven and younger talked about "spitting, shitting, pants down, naked girls, pee fights, . . .pinching asses and fucking." Children eight and older told stories about "having a boner, farting, tits, being horny, . . .eating shit, leaping on girls, whores, vaginas, and incest."

This study does not tell us how common such themes are in the fantasies of children. As the researchers themselves admitted, the results are best regarded as "a potentially instructive case study." Still, from the mouths of at least some babes may come thoughts that few adults suspect they have. This does not mean children *understand* everything they are saying when they tell sexual stories and jokes. Sometimes they are just trying to shock adults or impress their friends. Also, children filter sexual information gleaned from friends, adults, and television through their own childish ways of thinking. At a young age, for example, children tend to define sexual (and other) concepts in purely concrete, physical terms. If asked "How can any-one know if a newborn baby is a boy or a girl?" young children will often name irrelevant features ("He can tell by the eyebrows") or vague physical differences ("Girls have an exit and boys have a little willie") (Goldman & Goldman, 1982). We will return to children's understanding of sexual concepts again later in this chapter.

DEVELOPMENTAL INFLUENCES ON GENDER AND SEXUALITY

We have seen that maleness and femaleness begin to develop at conception and continue to develop in childhood, and that sexuality is expressed in thought and action throughout childhood. We now turn to the complex interplay of forces that combine to shape our emerging sexuality. Theorists have emphasized four kinds of influences: 1) hormones; 2) identification with the same-sex parent; 3) learning experiences; and 4) self-perceptions.

The Role of Hormones: Is Biology Destiny?

As we have seen, the direct role of genes in sex and gender seems limited to determining which set of gonads the fetus will have. Then, once the gonads are male or female, the prenatal hormones they secrete initiate the development of other sexual and reproductive organs. But this is not the only effect of prenatal hormones. Animal studies find that during a second critical period of development, after anatomical gender has been determined, the presence of testosterone influences development of nerve clusters in the brain, especially the hypothalamus (which, as we saw in Chapter 4, regulates adult sex hormone production). As a result, these nerve cell clusters differ in size in males and females. Sex hormones also affect specific hormone receptor sites in animal brains (see Weintraub, 1981). Although there is little direct evidence, many researchers assume that similar effects occur in human beings.

The $64,000 question is: Do these hormone-induced brain changes affect later sexual or gender-related behavior? Is the brain psychologically masculine or feminine right from the start? Let's examine the evidence.

RESEARCH WITH ANIMALS   The most direct evidence comes from research with animals, whose sex hormones can be manipulated in the laboratory. If testosterone is administered to genetically female rats during the second critical period (which for rats is during the first few days after birth), their brains will always be sensitive to male hormones and insensitive to female ones. Conversely, if male rats are deprived of testosterone during this period, their brains will later be sensitive to female hormones. The type of sensitivity the brain develops makes a big difference to the rat. Rats with testosterone-sensitized brains will respond to later injections of male hormones with male sexual behavior (such as mounting and thrusting), even if they are genetically female. Male rats castrated at birth will not respond this way, but they will behave sexually like females if they get later injections of female hormones (Young, Goy & Phoenix, 1964; Levine, 1966).

Rhesus monkeys also show distinct changes in behavior when scientists tamper with their hormones. Genetically female monkeys subjected to testosterone during a critical prenatal period are not only changed anatomically (they have penises and empty scrotums instead of clitorises and vaginal openings), but they also behave differently from other females. They threaten other monkeys more often, initiate more rough-and-tumble play, and are less likely to withdraw when another monkey approaches them. Their sexual play seems more masculine than feminine: like males, they frequently mount other animals (Goy, 1968; Phoenix, Goy & Resko, 1968; Young, Goy & Phoenix, 1964). By varying the timing of prenatal hormone injections, researchers can also produce monkeys that are anatomically female but behave like males (Weintraub, 1981).

Such studies strongly suggest (although they do not prove) that normal male and female animals are sexually and behaviorally different in part because they produce different prenatal hormones. But we cannot automatically assume that this conclusion applies also to human beings. For evidence on human beings, we must turn to a different kind of study.

RESEARCH WITH HUMAN BEINGS Obviously we cannot explore the effects of prenatal hormones on human behavior by intentionally manipulating fetal hormones. However, sometimes certain "experiments of nature" allow scientists to study such effects. Something goes awry in the hormone system of a developing fetus. As a result, the child is born with both male and female tissue and is therefore either a hermaphrodite or a pseudohermaphrodite. In true **hermaphroditism,** the child has both ovarian and testicular tissue, and usually ambiguous or mixed genitals (for example, a penis but also some sort of vaginal opening). This condition is extremely rare; fewer than a hundred cases have been recorded in this century. In **pseudohermaphroditism,** which is more common, the gonads and sex chromosomes match, but the external genitals are either inconsistent with the person's genetic sex or are ambiguous.

Female pseudohermaphroditism occurs when a genetically female fetus is exposed to excess androgens or androgen-like substances. Exposure before the twelfth week of gestation can lead to completely masculine external genitals, while exposure after this period causes only enlargement of the clitoris. One possible source of excess androgens is the mother. During pregnancy, she may have taken masculinizing hormones for medical reasons (this occurred in the 1950s, before the consequences were known), or she may have had an adrenal or ovarian tumor that secreted androgens. Another possible source is the fetus itself. In a condition known as the **adrenogenital syndrome (AGS),** a genetic defect causes the fetus's adrenal glands to produce

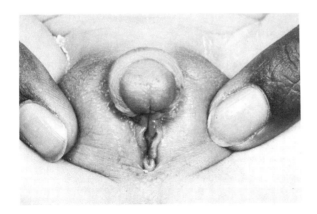

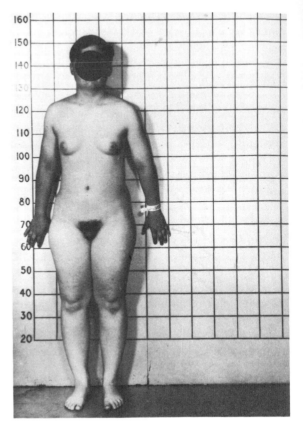

The adrenogenital syndrome (AGS)   *In this type of pseudohermaphroditism, a genetic defect may cause a female to be born with external genitals that are ambiguous in appearance. The full-body photograph shows a late-treated girl who underwent surgical feminization of her genitals after the photo was taken. The close-up shows clitoral enlargement in a female infant with AGS.*

abnormally high levels of androgens. Plastic surgery is usually performed to correct the external genitals of a female pseudohermaphrodite, and if the cause is AGS, hormones are given to prevent further exposure to high levels of androgens. From then on, female physical development proceeds as it normally would.

Male pseudohermaphroditism sometimes occurs because of abnormally low prenatal androgen levels, but the most common cause is insensitivity or resistance to androgens, due to a defect in the androgen receptors on the target cells. In an inherited disorder known as the **androgen insensitivity syndrome (AIS),** testosterone and other androgens, although present in normal amounts, have no effect at all on body tissues. The fetus has testes (which stay tucked up in the abdomen), but also develops a clitoris, labia, and a shortened vagina. No normal internal reproductive organs develop, because the Müllerian inhibiting substance causes the female set to shrink and the body's insensitivity to androgens prevents the development of the male set. A child born with the androgen insensitivity syndrome usually looks like, and is reared as, a normal girl. At puberty she develops breasts and other features of a woman's body in response to estrogen production in the undescended testes, but she does not menstruate because she has no uterus. The lack of menstruation may be the first sign that something is amiss; androgen insensitivity syndrome is the third leading cause of the failure to menstruate at puberty (Crapo, 1985). Once the condition is discovered, the testes, which are vulnerable to cancer because they did not descend, are usually removed, and a program of estrogen administration is started.

Male pseudohermaphroditism also occasionally occurs in fetuses that are able to produce and use testosterone. In these cases, an enzyme deficiency prevents the prenatal conversion of testosterone into dihydrotestosterone (DHT), which is necessary for the normal formation of the penis and scrotum. The child is born with normal male internal organs (except for the prostate), but with ambiguous genitals or an enlarged clitoris.

In the varieties of pseudohermaphroditism that we have described, biology starts the child out on one path, either genetically or hormonally, but in many cases socialization puts the child on another. Naturally, scientists want to know the outcome. Which influence ultimately wins out?

Until the mid-1970s, the answer seemed pretty clear: socialization. Several studies of pseudohermaphrodites in the United States found that whatever their genetic sex or prenatal hormone history, children reared as males usually became psychologically male, and children reared as female usually became psychologically female—even when surgical correction of the genitals did not take place (Money & Ehrhardt, 1972; Money, Hampson & Hampson, 1955). In two studies, androgenized (AGS) girls reared as females were found to be more "tomboyish" than girls in a matched control group (at least by their own accounts), and they also seemed less interested in the traditional female role (Ehrhardt, Epstein & Money, 1968; Ehrhardt & Baker, 1974). But other research found no such differences (McGuire, Ryan & Omenn, 1975). Some research suggested an increased probability of bisexual or homosexual interests in AGS girls during adolescence and adulthood, and AGS girls also tended to be "late bloomers" with respect to dating and romance (Money & Dalery, 1976; Money & Schwartz, 1977). But it was hard to know what effect genital surgery and lifelong hormone treatments might have had on these girls. Young women whose exposure to prenatal androgens was due to medications taken by their mothers during pregnancy, rather than to their own malfunctioning adrenal glands, reported exclusively heterosexual imagery and experience (Money & Mathews, 1982). Overall, there was little evidence that gender-related behavior or sexuality was determined by prenatal hormones.[1]

---

[1]In many studies on the sexual interests of pseudohermaphrodites, the subjects have been young, samples have been small, and control groups have been inadequate or nonexistent, making conclusions difficult to draw. However, during the 1980s, some research reports of pseudohermaphrodites again suggested a possible link between prenatal hormones and sexual orientation (Money & Lewis, 1982, 1987; Money, Schwartz & Lewis, 1984). We discuss the question of hormonal effects on sexual orientation more fully in Chapter 14, and focus here primarily on gender identity and gender-linked behaviors.

Then new reports challenged this conclusion. Julianne Imperato-McGinley and her colleagues at Cornell University described nineteen genetically male pseudohermaphrodites raised in two isolated villages in the Dominican Republic (Imperato-McGinley et al., 1974; Imperato-McGinley et al., 1979). These individuals all had the enzyme deficiency that prevents conversion of testosterone to DHT. Because prenatally they had produced normal amounts of testosterone and Müllerian inhibiting substance, they were born with male internal structures. But they also had a clitorislike sex organ, undescended testes, a closed vaginal cavity, and a labialike scrotum.

All of these male pseudohermaphrodites were initially reared as girls. But between the ages of seven and twelve they began to realize that they were different from other females. They failed to develop breasts, and they found tissue masses (actually, their testes) in the groin or scrotum. At puberty, something even stranger happened. Their bodies responded dramatically to the spurt of testosterone characteristic of males at that age, and the children began to change anatomically into boys! Their voices deepened, their undescended testes descended, and their enlarged clitorislike organs turned into penises. They even became capable of ejaculating sperm, although the urethral opening was located on the perineum and not on the penis, as in normal males.

How did these males-reared-as-females react to the amazing transformation of their bodies? One decided that he was male but continued to dress as a woman. Another maintained a female gender identity and gender role, married, and expressed a desire for a sex-change operation so that she could be physically as well as psychologically female. But all the remaining subjects adopted male roles. Not only did they go off to work as farmers, miners, and woodsmen, but they found female sexual partners and became sexually active as males. The researchers concluded from these cases that biology exerts a strong effect on both gender identity and sexual behavior, even in the face of conflicting socialization. Prenatal hormones, they suggested, set up the machinery for maleness by "masculinizing" the brain; pubertal hormones then activate that machinery.

Other scientists, however, were not so sure. Critics were quick to point out that at the time this study was done, all the subjects had already grown to the adulthood; some had even died. It was hard to be sure, after the fact, how consistent their upbringing as girls had been, or how clear a female gender identity they had developed before puberty. Villagers had referred to these children as *guevote*, a slang term equivalent to "balls at twelve," or *machihembra*, "first woman, then man." In the United States, children with DHT deficiency syndrome have remained female even after sprouting a penis at puberty (Rubin, Reinisch & Haskett, 1981). Perhaps the Dominican children had come under social pressure to change to a male identity.

A recent study of fourteen individuals with the same syndrome, in the Sambian society of Papua, New Guinea, supports this argument (Herdt & Davidson, 1988). In this study, the researchers had access to detailed anthropological data on the culture in question, and were able to conduct in-depth interviews with five of the living subjects. Nine of the subjects had been labeled males, but their upbringing was in many ways ambiguous. The other five were reared as females. These five did eventually switch gender roles, but they did not assume the status of normal men, either in their own eyes or in the eyes of others. Instead they became "turnim men," a stigmatized category. Moreover, they switched only under great external public pressure and psychological trauma (one of them after she married and was rejected by her husband). The researchers concluded that cultural expectations and environmental conditions are what govern a person's adult identity.

Where does this leave us? Perhaps the wisest course right now is to avoid either-or thinking. It is exceedingly difficult, in any study of human beings, to separate the possible effects of hormones from those of the social environment. Also, researchers often disagree on how to interpret the results of specific studies. It is clear, though, from studies of North American pseudohermaphrodites, that upbringing *can* often override any effects of prenatal hormones, especially if surgery brings the body into conformity with the gender assigned to a child by its parents and society.

We might compare the development of gender and sexuality to the construction of a house. Genes provide an initial blueprint. Prenatal hormones may provide a foundation. But one cannot predict the style of a house—Cape Cod, modern, or colonial—solely from the shape of its foundation. In the same way, prenatal hormones may influence sexuality and gender but do not preordain them. Experience determines the eventual sexual "style" that each of us develops.

The three remaining approaches to be discussed all explore the nature of that experience. Each is derived from a broader theory of human behavior and personality.

Identification: Freud's Hopeless Love Triangle

We have already touched on Sigmund Freud's psychoanalytic theory of human development in earlier chapters. Here we will focus more explicitly on his attempts to explain gender and sexual development.

Freud believed that we are all sexual from birth and that our sexual expression, from infancy on, unfolds in a series of predictable *psychosexual stages.* During the first year or so of life, a child is in the *oral stage;* the main erogenous zone is the mouth, and sexual impulses are expressed through activities like sucking. This stage is followed a year or so later by the *anal stage,* in which pleasure is centered in the anus and obtained through defecation. Between the ages of three and five the child enters the *phallic stage.* In boys, erotic pleasure is centered mainly in the penis. In girls, it is centered in the clitoris. Until this point, in both sexes, development can potentially go in either a masculine or feminine direction.

Envy, curiosity, or relief?
*These children are
learning about anatomical
sex differences firsthand.
An orthodox Freudian
might predict that the
little boy will respond
with "castration anxiety"
and the little girl with
"penis envy." But are
those the only possible
reactions? What thoughts
and feelings do you think
the children will
experience?*

The phallic stage, in Freud's view, is critical for the development of gender identity, sexual orientation, and the adoption of gender roles. For the first time, the child seeks a sexual object outside himself or herself. That object is the parent of the other sex. The result, according to Freud, is that the child comes to perceive the same-sexed parent as a rival, and so a sort of love triangle develops within the family. Freud, who had a flair for literary analogies, called the child's incestuous desire for the parent of the other sex the *Oedipus conflict*, after the Greek myth of Oedipus Rex, King of Thebes. According to the legend, Oedipus was abandoned at birth by his parents and grew up to marry his mother and murder his father, unaware of their true identities. When the truth came out, Oedipus, in remorse, blinded himself and went into exile.

According to Freud, the Oedipus conflict follows one course in boys and another in girls. Let's take boys first. A boy is sexually drawn to his mother, his primary and most nurturant caretaker, and wants to displace his father in her affections. At this age, the boy's sexual gratification comes from masturbating, and he feels proud of possessing a penis. But he notices that girls and women do not have penises, and this observation takes on an ominous meaning, for the boy concludes that females are people who have been castrated. (Medically, castration means removal of the testes, but Freud used the term to mean removal of the penis.)

The boy starts to worry about losing his penis; if it could happen to others, it could happen to him. At the same time he feels growing anxiety about his father, who is his competitor for his mother and therefore has a good reason for carrying out the dreaded deed. The panic of *castration anxiety* forces the boy to repress his desire for his mother—that is, to push it into the unconscious. Whereas the legendary Oedipus physically blinded himself, the boy with an Oedipus conflict mentally blinds himself to the fact that he has been sexually competing for his mother and has lost. The boy transforms his feelings of rivalry into a positive identification with his father and incorporates the father's authority and standards into his own emerging personality: "If you can't beat him, join him." In this way, the boy regains confidence in his ability to keep his penis and puts himself on the road to a masculine identity.

In girls, according to Freud, the Oedipus conflict takes a different and more complex form. Whereas in boys the Oedipus conflict is *resolved* because of castration anxiety, in girls the feeling of having been castrated *leads* to the Oedipus conflict. For girls there is no threat: they *have* been castrated. This assumption has immediate meaning. Once she learns about the penis, a girl "makes her judgment and her decision in a flash. She has seen it and knows that she is without it and wants to have it" (Freud, 1924).

And whom does the girl blame for the catastrophe that has befallen her? Why, her mother, who has "sent her into the world so insufficiently equipped." The girl therefore rejects her mother and seeks to displace her in her father's eyes. She becomes Daddy's darling. Driven by "penis envy," she turns to her father in the hope that he will give her a penis. But eventually she realizes that her wish cannot be granted. So she represses her desire for her father. By identifying with her mother and finding compensation in the fact that she will eventually be able to have a child, she takes the first steps toward a feminine identity. Nonetheless, she is apt to continue to feel inferior to men, because of lingering "penis envy," and if she is neurotic, she may try to resolve penis envy by being like men, perhaps by having a career.

After the resolution of the Oedipal conflict, and until the onset of puberty, said Freud, a child concentrates on making friends, learning sports, and wrestling with the mysteries of long division; sexual interest is minimal. Puberty marks the end of this "latency" period and the beginning of the final stage of development, the *genital stage*. In males, pleasure is once again obtained from stimulation of the penis, but in females sensitivity transfers from the clitoris to the more "feminine" vagina. (As we noted in Chapter 5, modern research does not support this claim.) In Freud's view, if the individual has passed successfully through all the previous stages, he or she will be ready for a stable—and heterosexual—relationship with another person.

Note that the central idea in Freud's theory of gender identity is *identification*. By identifying with the parent of the same sex, the child chooses not only to imitate the parent's behavior but to incorporate the parent's values, attitudes, and goals into his or her own personality, including those associated with the parent's gender. Any disruption of the usual identification process, according to Freudians, causes a disruption in the development of gender identity, sex roles, and sexual orientation.

Most psychologists and psychiatrists (including psychoanalysts) reject several premises of Freud's theory. Freud drew what he claimed were universal principles of childhood from the reports of people (mainly adult) living in a specific class (middle), culture (Viennese) and time (turn of the century). The patients had troubles that brought them to psychotherapy and did not necessarily represent everyone. Sexual tensions in families are rather common, but scientists have not demonstrated that Oedipal conflicts are universal or inevitable, or that all children respond to sex differences in anatomy in the same way.

Another criticism of Freud is that he oversexualized children. Many of Freud's patients said they had been sexually molested in childhood by their fathers, uncles or male friends of the family. Unable to believe these reports, Freud decided that his patients must be reporting fantasies, and this conclusion eventually led him to the notion of the Oedipal conflict. Modern research, however, suggests that Freud's patients were usually telling the truth about their experiences of sexual abuse (Masson, 1984; Rush, 1980; Sulloway, 1979). If so, then it was probably the inappropriate sexual motives of adults that caused the emotional problems of Freud's patients, rather than any repressed childhood desires of their own. A major assumption of Freud's theory, that children lust after their parents, appears to be grounded in Freud's own denial of reality.

Freud's observations are susceptible to many alternative interpretations. If women feel inferior to men, is it because of "penis envy" or the conditions of their lives? If a little girl appears to be fascinated by her brother's penis, is it because she considers it erotically superior to her own organ or because she envies his urinary ability to hit a moving target at three feet? Are little girls embarrassed by the clitoris, or simply unaware they have one? Psychologist Harriet Goldhor Lerner (1988, 1990) notes that in Freud's time the only word in *Webster's Dictionary* for the female genitals was *vagina;* absent were *clitoris, vulva,* and *labia.* Even today, parents, when talking to their children, often mistakenly use *vagina* to refer to everything "down there," avoiding the words *vulva* and *clitoris* (if they even know them) as if they were four-letter words. Lerner suggests that this conspiracy of silence is due in part to adults' fear that a discussion of the clitoris will bring up the topics of sexual pleasure and masturbation. The result is a "psychic genital mutilation": a little girl may feel ashamed and cheated—not because her external organ is smaller than a boy's, but because no one will acknowledge that she even has one.

These and other criticisms have forced many modifications in psychoanalytic theory. But even Freud's critics often accept certain parts of his theory. Many acknowledge the lasting effects that early childhood experiences can have on personality, and the unconscious roots of adult guilt, shame, and anxiety. Many also accept the concept of identification—but without assuming that its origins are sexual in nature.

Learning: The Social Environment

Learning theories attribute a child's gender and sexual development not to internal, unconscious wishes, but to the external environment. In this view, children do not spontaneously or naturally acquire a sexual sense of themselves; they have to be carefully taught. Their teachers are the people and events in their environment.

Learning approaches grew out of the behaviorist tradition in psychology, which holds that all voluntary behavior can be explained by a basic set of rules. The most important of these rules is that behavior is controlled by its consequences. If an act is followed by a reward, or reinforcer, it tends to recur; if it is followed by punishment, or is unrewarded, it tends to cease. If you want to know why a little girl becomes feminine or a little boy becomes masculine (or the reverse), find out what behaviors their parents, teachers, and friends have rewarded and punished.

But reinforcement and punishment are not the whole story. *Social-learning theorists*, who apply learning principles to human social behavior, point out that the social roles we learn as children encompass thousands of behaviors. If each behavior—and each component of each behavior—had to be separately reinforced, parents would be busy twenty-four hours a day rewarding and punishing. Another concept is necessary to explain how children acquire the subtleties of social behavior, and that concept is *observational learning*. In observational learning, a child acquires new responses by observing the behavior of a *model* rather than through direct experience. Children seem to have a general predisposition to imitate models even when the particular behavior being imitated is not immediately reinforced. Children tend to copy adults who are friendly, warm, and attentive (Bandura & Huston, 1961) or who hold power over them (Bandura, Ross & Ross, 1963; Mischel & Grusec, 1966). Since parents are usually both nurturant and powerful, they tend to make effective models.

A child does not actually have to perform a behavior to learn it; often, simply watching the behavior is enough. Whether the behavior is performed depends to a large extent on social rules of conduct and associated rewards and punishments (Bandura & Walters, 1963; Mischel, 1970). For example, a little boy may observe his father shaving and his mother applying lipstick and thus learn (become capable of) both behaviors. But by the time he reaches adolescence he will perform only the first behavior, having learned that a male who uses lipstick is likely to be ridiculed, or worse.

Human beings learn new behaviors quickly, in part because they have the advantage of language. Parents can simply tell a son that they disapprove of hitting girls or that they approve of aggressive performance on the soccer

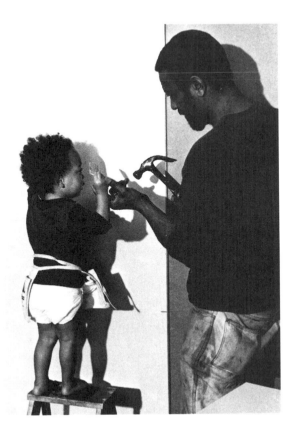 

Role models *Children often learn about their culture's gender-role expectations by observing and emulating their parents, but as the photograph on the right and the one on page 459 suggest, many parents today are transcending the traditional boundaries and are modeling more flexible behavior as well.*

field. Since their disapproval has been associated in the past with punishment, and their approval with reward, the parents' verbal comments are sufficient to control the child's behavior. Moreover, anticipated rewards and punishments can affect behavior as dramatically as real ones do. As psychologist Walter Mischel (1966) observes, "A man does not have to be arrested for wearing dresses in public to learn about the consequences of such behavior."

Social-learning theorists have pointed out that other-sex parents have as much to teach us about sex and gender as same-sex parents do. Fathers often encourage their daughters to be feminine and mothers often encourage their sons to be masculine, either by rewarding gender role behaviors directly or by playing a contrasting role themselves (Mussen & Rutherford, 1963). Other models are also important. Indeed, children have an entire smorgasbord of models, including parents, teachers, friends, media personalities, and brothers and sisters, and sometimes it is impossible to please all these models at once. Each of us, according to social-learning theory, is a unique blend of many influences.

As you might have inferred from our examples, most social-learning theorists have had more to say about gender than about sexual behavior.

Two exceptions are John Gagnon and William Simon, who have proposed a theory of sexual development that gives a central place to the influence of sexual "scripts" (see Chapter 5). Sexual scripts embody a culture's norms about what is erotic and the circumstances in which sex is appropriate. Scripts tell us not only what we should and should not do, but also how we ought to interpret our own feelings and desires. And these scripts must be learned (Simon & Gagnon, 1969; Gagnon & Simon, 1973).

Gagnon and Simon question the Freudian claim that psychosexual development is driven by an innate and powerful sex drive. If human beings did have such a drive, they say, they would not find it so easy to reduce their sexual activity or become totally celibate, as many men and women do. At the very least, the urgency of the drive has been overestimated. Moreover, say Gagnon and Simon, Freud erred in assuming that children understand as an adult would the nature of their feelings and behavior. Since children lack sexual scripts, they cannot assign the same meanings (e.g., lust, romantic love) to their behavior that an adult might. Without such meanings, genital stimulation may be pleasurable or comfortable for children without being erotic. As one adult recalled, "I can remember there was physical pleasure to be derived from fondling my genitals. Such fondling had no heterosexual overtones; the mere physical satisfaction was enough to develop this practice into a habit" (quoted in Martinson, 1973).

Gagnon and Simon, then, reject the Freudian claim that "the child is father to the man" (or the mother to the woman, as the case may be). Childhood sexual experiences may help children identify behaviors that bring bodily pleasure, but these experiences do not necessarily cause or lead directly to later sexual acts. Emotionally and mentally, such experiences may remain "unassimilated." What is most important about childhood for later sexual development is that this is the time when we pick up certain values related to sexuality: that sex is either "dirty" and shameful, or a normal expression of adult affection.

Self-Perceptions: A Cognitive Developmental Viewpoint

Learning theories describe how external events shape a child's behavior and personality, but say less about what the child contributes to the process. *Cognitive developmental theories* hold that a child's ability to imitate a model's behavior, or even to notice it, depends on the child's cognitive (mental) maturity and information-processing abilities. A two-year-old and a seven-year-old will respond quite differently to exactly the same events.

Decades ago, Swiss psychologist Jean Piaget demonstrated that changes in a child's ability to reason and understand events are due not to experience alone, nor to simple maturation of the nervous system, but to an interaction between the two. If a child lacks the proper mental structures to understand a particular concept, the child will not learn the concept, no matter how heroic the efforts of parents and teachers to teach it. But concepts do not spring forth, full-blown, in the child's mind; rather, they are acquired in an active process that involves assimilating information from the environment into existing mental structures and accommodating mental structures to new information from the environment. This process leads a child through an invariant sequence of cognitive stages, each characterized by a different set of rules for processing information and making connections between events.

Although Piaget himself did not investigate children's sexual thinking, others have found that his ideas help explain how children come to understand the "facts of life." For example, when Anne C. Bernstein (1976) interviewed children aged three to twelve about where babies come from, she found six separate stages in the development of their ideas about sex and reproduction. These stages made sense in terms of the children's changing cognitive abilities:

1. *Geography* At age three or four, children cannot understand cause and effect, or imagine a world without themselves and

Where *do* babies come from?   *The children who drew these pictures have the general idea, but have reworked the facts in accordance with their level of cognitive development. The drawing at the bottom was done by five-year-old Fumio, after he learned that Elfie, his cat, was going to have kittens. Explained Fumio: "Elfie found a mouse and ate it and then the kittens could grow in her stomach."*

everyone they know. They assume a baby that exists now must always have existed. The only question is: Where did the baby come from? A child may say babies come from tummies, or from "God's place," or that to get a baby parents must go to a baby store and buy one. One little girl thought that before her baby brother was in her mother's tummy, he must have been in someone else's.

2. *Manufacturing* At this stage, children believe people manu-facture babies the way they do refrigerators, TV sets, or auto-mobiles ("You put some eyes on it. . . .You make it with head stuff you find in the store. . . ." These children have never seen a baby factory or a rack of infants at the local supermarket. But because they are, in Piaget's term, "egocentric," they must interpret the world in terms of familiar processes, like shopping and making things.

3. *Transitional* At this stage, children incorporate some physiol-ogy into their explanations of reproduction, but have trouble combining social relationships, sexual intercourse, and the union of sperm and egg into one account. One seven-year-old said, "The sperm goes into the mommy to each egg and. . .makes the egg safe. So if something bump comes along, it won't crack the egg. The sperm comes from the daddy. It swims into the penis, and I think it makes a little hole and then swims into the vagina. It has a little mouth and it bites a hole."

4. *Concrete physiology* By this stage, children can think logically and can understand cause and effect, and past and future. But their understanding of how sperm and egg get together is still hazy: "They [the mother and father] have to come together or else the baby won't really get hatched very well. The seed makes the egg grow. It's just like plants. If you plant a seed, a flower will grow."

5. *Preformation* Children at this stage always mention sexual intercourse, or fertilization, though often with embarrass-ment. But they do not understand the details, and they think the baby emerges, preformed, from either the sperm or the egg. (Their ideas are not all that different from those of sci-entists of a few centuries ago.) One twelve-year-old boy said, "I guess the egg just has sort of an undeveloped embryo and when the sperm enters it, it makes it come to life. It gives it energy and things like that."

6. *Physical causality* By age twelve, children are usually able to bring together the physical and social factors in reproduction. They may still not have the story quite right, but their accounts are fairly sophisticated: "The sperm encounter one ovum and one sperm breaks into the ovum. . .and the cell separates and divides. . . .and the ovum goes through a tube and embeds itself in the wall of the, I think it's the fetus [the child means uterus] of the woman."

The cognitive developmental approach has also been used to explain how children acquire a sense of gender identity and learn gender roles. Psychologist Lawrence Kohlberg (1966, 1969) argued that the foundation of gender identity is established early in life, long before the child supposedly experiences an Oedipal conflict. Even two-year-olds, he noted, can apply the labels "boy" and "girl" correctly to themselves and others. This categorization "is basically a cognitive reality judgment rather than a product of social rewards, parental justifications, or sexual fantasies." That is, children learn the concepts "boy" and "girl" simply by observing the world and noting that gender is a category into which one can sort oneself and others.

Preschoolers, however, have a concept of gender that is much more concrete than an adult's. They rely on physical cues, like body size, dress, and hair style, to decide who belongs in which category. Girls are people with long hair; boys are people who never wear dresses. Many children at this stage think they can change their own gender at will, simply by getting a new haircut or outfit. They may even announce an intention to switch genders when they grow up. Attempts to teach a child a more sophisticated concept of gender at this stage are doomed, because the child lacks the mental machinery to understand that certain aspects of an object or person remain the same despite superficial transformations. It is not until age five or six that children can fully understand the permanence of gender. The precise point when this occurs depends more on the cognitive development of the child than on anything the parents or other adults may do.

Between the ages of four and eight, children actively set out to discover what it means to be male or female and to bring their own actions into line with the appropriate label. They do this, according to Kohlberg, because of an intrinsic desire to find consistency in the world and in themselves, and because being a "proper" girl or boy makes them feel competent. But despite the formation of a clear gender identity, they still tend to link psychological attributes of males and females to physical attributes. Since children perceive males as bigger, stronger, and more active, they also perceive them as more aggressive, smarter, and more dominant (Kohlberg & Ullian, 1974). They have an oversimplified notion of gender roles: boys cannot be nurses or flight attendants (and wouldn't want to be); girls cannot be soldiers or pilots (and wouldn't want to be). Consider a conversation Jason had at age six with his friend Nick and his mother (one of the authors), who overheard the boys saying that it was better to be a boy than a girl because of all the terrific things boys can do:

> *Mother:* What could you do if you were girls that you can't do because you're boys? Can you think of anything?
> *Jason:* Have a vagina.
> *Mother:* What else?
> *Jason:* Be a mother.
> *Mother:* What can boys do that girls can't?
> *Jason:* Be a father.
> *Nick:* Be a doctor.
> *Mother:* But women can be doctors, too.

Nick (patiently, as if explaining something to a slow child): No, those are called nurses.

As they grow older, children gain the cognitive maturity to define gender in terms of social conventions rather than physical attributes. A fifth-grader believes that people should act like men or "ladies" because "that's the way things are." Gradually, however, the child comes to recognize the need for some choice and flexibility. By the time they reach college age, Kohlberg argued, most people are ready to go beyond customary sex-role stereotypes.

Kohlberg's theory has been generally well-received, although it is often difficult to choose between it and the learning approach to explain particular findings. Critics, however, have noted that the theory does not explain why girls, despite their presumed need to become "proper" females, often value male activities and qualities more than female ones. Also, Kohlberg's theory implies a certain inevitability about gender stereotypes and distinctions. Sandra Bem (1985) has argued that gender is not an equally powerful organizing category in all societies. Bem believes that the human mind is set up to perceive and organize information according to networks of associations called *schemas*, but the culture determines which schemas are important and what sorts of associations they contain. In some societies, race, class, or caste are more powerful schemes than gender.

AS THE TWIG IS BENT

The perspectives we have discussed make different assumptions about children, development, and human nature. For example, they each assign the child a different role in his or her own development. Biological approaches stress prenatal events over which the child has no control whatever. Psychoanalytic theory focuses on the child's emotional reactions to anatomical differences; this is what Freud meant by his famous dictum "Anatomy is destiny." But Freud's child is acting in a drama that is not of his or her own choosing. Identification is forced on the child by the hopelessness of the child's incestuous wishes and the need to reduce anxiety. In contrast, social-learning theorists view the child from the outside, giving center stage to society's messages to the child rather than the inner mental life of the child. And cognitive developmental theories emphasize the active, intentional quality of the child's search for the meaning of sex and gender. The child takes the initiative in his or her own development by formulating hypotheses that change as the child's cognitive capabilities develop.

Perhaps someday the best feature of all these approaches will be combined into a single unified theory. Such a theory would take into account children's biological characteristics, their imitation of others, the rewards and punishments in the environment, and their self-perceptions. The theory would tell us how adults encourage or discourage specific biological predispositions, and how the child incorporates what he or she learns into a gender "schema" and a self-concept.

In the meantime, we can speculate about the significance of the developmental process for later sexual relationships. Consider, first, the possible consequences of acquiring a traditional gender role. If children learn that boys are supposed to be active (climb trees, play football) while girls are supposed to be sedate (sit on the bench, play jacks), this knowledge—remote as it may seem from sexual experience—may later translate into a belief that during sex men should do most of the moving and women should be more "ladylike." If children learn that men are supposed to be the initiators in life, later they may expect men to initiate sexual encounters and choreograph sexual acts. If males are supposed to be strong and silent and able to solve personal problems without asking for help, while females are allowed to be more expressive, heterosexual partners may develop different ways of communicating (or not communicating) about their sexual needs and feelings. If children learn that male ambitions and priorities are more important than female ones, later on they may assume that the woman should be the "servicer" in sex, or that the man's sexual response is the critical measure of the "success" of a sexual encounter. And if children learn to accept dominance and submission as right and normal in male-female interactions, later they may expect the same in the bedroom. Images of male dominance and female submission

No boys allowed
Sex-segregated play groups may teach boys and girls different strategies for dealing with others. Later on, these lessons may affect how the sexes get along in intimate relationships.

or passivity may pervade their erotic fantasies, and other models of sexual relationships may seem downright unsexy.

According to developmental psychologist Eleanor Maccoby (1988, 1990), another influence on intimate relationships is the self-segregation of boys and girls during childhood. From the age of three or four, boys and girls prefer to play with children of the same sex, even when they are under no pressure from grownups to do so. Maccoby believes this self-segregation occurs in part because girls are wary of how boys play. Boys tend to engage in more rough-and-tumble play than girls. On the average, they are more concerned with competition and dominance, and make more direct demands on others. In contrast, girls tend to try to influence each other with polite suggestions, a strategy that doesn't work too well with boys. Since it's no fun to play with someone who is hard to influence, the girls soon learn to avoid boys. And boys also avoid girls, for reasons that are less clear.

Maccoby argues that sex-segregated play groups are powerful socialization environments, in which boys and girls acquire different ways of interacting. Girls form close relationships with one or two other girls with whom they share confidences. Boys form friendships based more on mutual interests and activities. Girls practice using "enabling" styles of influence, such as acknowledging another person's comments or expressing agreement in order to keep an interaction going. Boys practice using "constricting" or "restrictive" styles, such as threatening, contradicting, boasting, or interrupting. In adolescence and adulthood, the two "cultures" finally come together, and both men and women must adapt. This adjustment may be difficult, especially for women, who are less likely to get from men the agreement and the opportunites to talk that they have always enjoyed with other females. In deep and enduring relationships, male and female interaction patterns tend to become less distinct, because most couples have shared goals and want to avoid conflict. But echoes of the past reverberate in the way men and women behave toward one another, with men more likely to use direct styles of influence and women more likely to use indirect ones (see Chapter 8), and with women making greater efforts to maintain harmony (Huston & Ashmore, 1986).

Gender, however, is not the only influence on sexual relationships. William Fisher and his colleagues (1988) propose that, beginning in earliest childhood, individuals acquire a basic disposition toward sexuality. This disposition can be measured along a continuum, with "erotophobia," or fear of sex, at one end and "erotophilia," or love of sex, at the other. The natural human tendency is in the direction of erotophilia, but repeated associations between sex and negative emotions in childhood can push a person toward erotophobia. In one study, erotophobia in college students was significantly correlated with the students' reports of parental strictness about sex, conservative attitudes, and avoidance of masturbation in childhood (Fisher et al., 1988). Erotophobia is something that can pass from one generation to the next. Erotophobic parents are less accepting of their own children's sexuality than are erotophilic parents. They provide less sexual information to their children and are less likely to answer sexual questions frankly (Lemery, 1983; Yarber & Whitehill, 1981). (The last chapter of this book offers some suggestions on how you can rear sexually healthy children, and avoid the unintentional transmission of erotophobia.)

During childhood, we participate in what are probably the most significant relationships of our lives, those with our caretakers. These and other early relationships set the stage for future intimacy, by teaching us (or failing to teach us) how to communicate our needs and wishes, express our emotions, respond to the needs of others, cooperate and compete, give and receive affection, and walk the scary tightrope between openness and self-protection. But if the stage is set in childhood, it is at puberty, with its dramatic physical and emotional changes, that the curtain finally rises. In the next chapter, we turn to the sexual scenarios of adolescence and adulthood.

· ·

INTIMATE MOMENTS IN FAMILY LIFE

PERSONAL PERSPECTIVE

Long before you learned to talk, you began learning how to be intimate and how to demonstrate affection. Your earliest teachers were your parents or caretakers, and perhaps other members of your household. You learned something every time you were held or cuddled. You learned every time you watched other family members kiss and hug. These exchanges themselves were not sexual, but they served to build a foundation for your future sexual life as an adult. This exercise gives you the opportunity to look back to your childhood and discover that foundation.

Not all children have healthy intimate and sexual experiences while growing up. You yourself may have grown up in a family in which sexual boundaries between adults and children were violated. There may have been inappropriate touching, fondling, or other disturbed sexual expressions that you, as a child, could not understand or prevent. We will discuss the distressingly widespread phenomenon of child sexual abuse in Chapter 15. Here, however, our focus is on the wide variations that exist in *healthy* intimate expression within families.

Every family has certain customs that guide its members' interactions with one another. Carrying the power of unwritten rules, these customs differ from culture to culture, and even from household to household within the same community. Some families are reserved or subdued; others are open and demonstrative.

Think about your childhood and your family's customs regarding intimacy and affection. How comfortable were the various members of your family with its unwritten rules? How comfortable were you? What happened when one of the rules was broken? How powerfully do the rules from your childhood guide your life today? Have you adopted your family's customs unquestioningly, or have you modified them or replaced them with different standards? What were the lessons to be learned in your family about:

1. *Nudity.* When and where was partial or total nudity allowed? Were there some rooms or settings where nudity was permitted, and others where it was not? Did the season of the year make any difference? Who could go about undressed and who could not? In some families, children may go without clothing, but adolescents and adults may not. In some, parents are comfortable in the nude with children of their own sex (e.g., mothers with daughters) but not with children of the other sex. Some parents take violations of the rules in stride, but others respond with anger or anxiety.

2. *Privacy.* In some families the door is always closed when anyone changes clothes or takes a bath, while in others the door is always open. What was the custom in your family? Do you recall feeling a need for more privacy during childhood? If so, how did your family respond to this need? (One eight-year-old we know protected her privacy with a hand-drawn sign on her door that said, "DANGER! KEEP OUT! BEWARE! BE SURE YOU HAVE INSURANCE. EIGHT PEOPLE CAME IN AND NONE CAME OUT." The warning was accompanied by a drawing of a cloud and the word "Poof," to portray the dire consequences of violating the child's boundaries.) How did you respond to the need of others (your parents, for example) for privacy?

3. *Kissing, hugging, and holding.* How was affection expressed in your family? Did members of your family kiss on the lips? Was everyone kissed in the same way? Were people comfortable giving or receiving hugs? Back rubs? Squeezes? Did your mother and father differ in how they showed affection for family members? As a young child, were you forced to kiss or hug relatives when you didn't want to? As you grew older, how did the expression of affection between you and others change? Did there eventually come a time when you or your parents no longer seemed comfortable kissing?

4. *Your body.* What messages did you get from your family, either subtle or direct, about your body? Were they accepting of your body, or critical? Did family members compare their physical proportions to those of others or to some standard of perfection? Which parts or aspects of your body did family members accept as they were, and which, if any, did they consider unsatisfactory?

Now that you are an adult, are you still responding to messages from childhood about your body?

IN BRIEF

1. The biological, social, and psychological development of *gender* affects human sexuality in many profound ways. This development begins with conception and continues for many years after birth.

2. Nature's basic blueprint is for a female fetus. For normal development of a male to occur, a TDF gene, Müllerian regression hormone, testosterone, and dihydrotestosterone must all be present, with the latter three active during a critical period of fetal development.

3. A newborn's gender assignment affects how parents respond to the child. Most parents and other adults *sex-type* their children to some extent. However, some people grow up to become cross sex-typed and many become psychologically *androgynous,* having both traditionally masculine and traditionally feminine qualities in roughly equal proportions. Whatever the degree of sex typing, by age five or six most children have a firm and stable *gender identity.* Girls in this culture tend to be less satisfied with their gender identity than boys, perceiving that they would have more privileges if they were male. *Transsexuals* are persons who have a gender identity at odds with their anatomy. Many transsexuals seek sex-change surgery. Transsexualism presents a challenge to theories of gender development.

4. The development of sexuality is more difficult to research than the development of gender, and much of our information comes from adults. However, it is clear that at least some, and probably all, children are physically capable of what appear to be sexual responses even in their earliest years. Newborn baby girls lubricate vaginally and newborn baby boys have erections regularly. During the first two or three years of life most infants probably explore and fondle their own genitals in a casual way, and some deliberately masturbate to orgasm. As children grow older, masturbation becomes more and more likely.

5. Sexual play with other children is common in childhood; children often kiss, touch, and play doctor. Usually they are limited to exhibition and manual touching, but some go farther. Experiences with the same sex are somewhat more common than experiences with the other sex, probably in part because of the segregation of the sexes during play activities. Children also seem to have what appear to be sexual thoughts, although it is not clear how common sexual themes are in children's fantasies or what meaning they have for the child.

6. Some theorists believe that the presence or absence of testosterone or other hormones during a critical period of fetal development, after anatomical gender has been determined, affects the brain and consequently later sexual or gender-related behaviors. Much of the evidence comes from studies of nonhuman animals, but some also comes from research on human *pseudohermaphrodites*. Studies have been done on people with the *adrenogenital syndrome (AGS)*, with the *androgen insensitivity syndrome (AIS)*, and with a prenatal enzyme deficiency that prevents the conversion of testosterone into dihydrotestosterone (DHT). Often biology starts these children out on one path, genetically or hormonally, but socialization puts them on another. Unfortunately, even in these cases, it is difficult to separate the possible effects of prenatal hormones from those of the social environment. Various studies have reported differing results, and have been interpreted in differing ways. Probably the safest conclusion is that prenatal hormones may have some influence on sexuality and psychological gender but do not preordain them. In many studies of pseudohermaphrodites, subjects have adopted an identity and role consistent with the gender assigned them, even when the gender assignment is at odds with sexual anatomy.

7. *Psychoanalytic theory* holds that gender and sexuality emerge from emotional conflicts early in life, particularly the Oedipal conflict. In the Freudian view, boys are motivated to identify with the father in order to relieve castration anxiety, and girls are motivated to identify with the mother because they come to realize that their wish for a penis cannot be granted. Freud's ideas are subject to many criticisms, including that he oversexualized children's motivations and misinterpreted their behavior. However, many psychologists and psychiatrists accept the importance of *identification*, although without necessarily assuming that its origins are sexual in nature.

8. *Learning theories* of gender and sexual development grew out of the behaviorist tradition in psychology. *Social-learning theorists* emphasize reinforcement, punishment, observational learning, and behavioral models. Gagnon and Simon note that without sexual "scripts," children's sexual behaviors may remain emotionally and mentally unassimilated, with different meanings than they would have for adults.

9. *Cognitive developmental theories* emphasize how children's mental abilities affect their understanding of sexual and gender-related concepts. Children's misunderstandings about "the facts of life" make sense in terms of changes in these abilities. Kohlberg argued that gender identity begins early, when children first recognize that they are boys or girls, but that children tend to have an oversimplified notion of gender roles.

10. The various perspectives on gender and sexual development make different assumptions about children, development, and human nature. A

unified theory would take into account children's biological characteristics, their imitation of others, the rewards and punishments in the environment, and children's self-perceptions.

11. Gender development may affect behavior, communication, and motivation in later sexual relationships. Cultural images of male dominance and female submission acquired early in life may pervade later erotic fantasies. The self-segregation of boys and girls during childhood may encourage different ways of interacting with and trying to influence others. During childhood, we may also acquire a basic erotophobic or erotophilic disposition toward sexuality. Finally, our early relationships with others affect later intimate relationships by teaching us how to communicate needs and wishes, express emotions, respond to the needs of others, give and receive affection, and walk the tightrope between openness and self-protection.

Key Terms

gender *(434)*

biological sex *(434)*

gender role *(434)*

sex typing *(435)*

gender identity *(435)*

transsexualism *(435)*

sexual orientation *(435)*

chromosomes *(435)*

genes *(435)*

testis determining factor (TDF) *(436)*

dihydrotestosterone *(436)*

androgynous *(438)*

hermaphroditism and pseudohermaphroditism *(449)*

adrenogenital syndrome (AGS) *(449)*

androgen insensitivity syndrome (AIS) *(450)*

psychoanalytic theory *(453)*

psychosexual stages *(453)*

Oedipus conflict *(454)*

castration anxiety *(455)*

identification *(455)*

social-learning theory *(457)*

observational learning *(457)*

model *(457)*

sexual scripts *(459)*

cognitive developmental theories *(460)*

schemas *(464)*

**CHAPTER
THIRTEEN**

CHAPTER THIRTEEN

■

Sexual Development II: Adolescence And Adulthood

●

*The power to animate
all of life's seasons is
a power that resides
within us.*

Gail Sheehy

hat kind of sex life do you think your parents have?

Several years ago, a group of researchers posed that question to students at a large midwestern university (Pocs et al., 1977). Over half thought their parents, who were mostly in their forties, had intercourse once a month or less. A fourth thought their parents abstained completely or had intercourse less than once a year. Only 4 percent estimated three to four times a week, and not a single student said more than four times a week.

Well, the students were wrong. Kinsey had found, years before, that married people in their forties had intercourse, on average, about seven times a month. The students also underestimated their parents' experiences with premarital and extramarital sex, especially their mothers'. Most could not imagine their parents having oral sex. Not only were many students unable to believe that their parents were sexually active, but some seemed not to *want* to believe it. Nearly one-fifth ignored questions about parental masturbation, and a few wrote in emotional responses, such as "This questionnaire stinks" and "What stupid-ass person made up these questions?"

Suppose the parents of those students had been asked about their children's sex lives. Do you think they would have been any more accurate? A few years ago, *People* magazine polled 1300 high school students and 500 parents of teens about teenage sex. The parents in this sample did, in fact, have fairly accurate perceptions of when young people start having intercourse: their average estimate was 16.1 years, compared to an average of 16.9 reported by the teenage sample. However, there were indications that the parents were less well informed about their *own* children. Eighty-one percent believed their sons and daughters were giving them honest answers about sexual feelings and experiences, but only 22 percent of the teenagers said they had been totally honest with their parents (Biema, 1987).

As you can see, parents and children sometimes view each other across a sexual generation gap. Measuring sex by the yardstick of their own experience, they may find it hard to imagine what sex is like for people born earlier or later than themselves. In this chapter we will explore some similarities that unite adolescents, adults, and the aged, as well as differences that distinguish them. The sexuality of a thirteen-year-old girl is not the same as that of a 33-year-old or a 73-year-old. Let's look first at some of the biological and psychological transformations that make adolescence such an unforgettable stage of life. (This chapter deals primarily with heterosexual behavior. Homosexuality and bisexuality in adolescence and adulthood are discussed in Chapter 14.)

PUBERTY

Puberty (from the Latin for "hair") is the period of life when a person's reproductive organs become mature. The process is a gradual one, not a sudden metamorphosis. For reasons not yet fully understood, the brain signals the pituitary gland to produce chemicals that stimulate the production of sex hormones by the gonads (see Chapter 4), and both internal and external sex organs grow in size. At the same time, growth hormone levels increase and, like Alice in Wonderland, pubescent boys and girls find themselves suddenly shooting up in height. The growth spurt usually begins about two years earlier in girls than in boys, a fact that sixth- and seventh-graders are often all too aware of. By sixteen or so, most girls have done all the growing they are going to do, but boys may continue to gain height throughout adolescence and even into their twenties (Marshall & Tanner, 1969, 1970). In both sexes, while the body is growing taller, it is also changing in shape and form, as **secondary sex characteristics,** nonreproductive physical features indicating maturity, begin to develop (for example, breasts in girls and facial hair in boys).

Physical Changes in Girls

In pubescent girls, an increase in follicle-stimulating hormone (FSH) from the pituitary gland causes the follicles surrounding egg cells in the ovaries to produce estrogen. Estrogen is responsible for most of the physical changes that accompany puberty in girls. Sometime later, luteinizing hormone (LH) stimulates ovulation, but for the first year or two of reproductive maturity, ovulation is often irregular.

For the girl herself, the most noticeable changes are not those occurring inside the ovaries, but the external ones that turn her child's body into that of a woman. The first such change is usually the appearance of breast buds, sometime between eight and thirteen years of age, typically at ten or eleven. Girls are often proud of this development and run right out to buy a "training" bra, although it is not clear just what it is supposed to train. Physical signs of adulthood are valued by young adolescents and bring them social status, which may explain why the onset of breast development in girls is associated with good adjustment, positive relationships with peers, and a positive body image (at least in white girls, the only ones on whom there are data) (Brooks-Gunn & Warren, 1988).

Judy Blume, who writes fiction for young people, captured the excitement and anxiety of breast development in her hilarious and poignant novel about preadolescence, *Are You There God? It's Me, Margaret* (1970). The heroine, eleven-year-old Margaret Simon, worries that she is not keeping up with her girlfriends, breast-wise. She confides her fears to the Almighty: *"I hate to remind you God...I mean, I know you're busy. But it's already December and I'm not growing. At least I don't see any real difference. Isn't it time God? Don't you think I've waited patiently? Please help me."* Finally Margaret decides that God helps those who help themselves and takes matters into her own hands, as have generations of real-life girls: she stuffs cotton padding into her bra.

Pubic hair usually appears shortly after breast development begins, although it may appear earlier. Underarm hair appears about two years after the first pubic growth. Pubic and underarm hair seem to grow primarily under the control of adrenal androgens in both females and males. Adrenal androgens are evidently also responsible for an increase in the production of oil and sweat glands, and thus for that dreaded sign of puberty, acne.

The most dramatic and symbolic event of female puberty is **menarche** [me-NAR-kee], the onset of menstruation. Menarche occurs on the average at twelve and a half years of age in North American girls but can occur normally at any time between ten and sixteen. The average age is believed to have dropped a few years over the past century and a half, possibly because of earlier maturity brought on by improved health and nutrition (Tanner, 1962). After menarche, bleeding occurs about every 28 days if the ovum released from the ovary at mid-cycle is not fertilized by a sperm (see Chapter 6).

Many societies recognize menarche with formal initiation rites. A widespread practice in tribal societies is to seclude the newly menstruating girl from the rest of the community and label her taboo. Natives of New Ireland, an island in the southwestern Pacific, used to keep postmenarche girls at home in cages for three or four years, until they got fat and pale, which was considered beautiful. The Kolosh Indians of Alaska locked pubescent girls up for a year in a tiny hut where the only ventilation was one small air hole (Delaney, Lupton & Toth, 1988). Theories abound to explain such practices. Some psychoanalysts believe that menstrual bleeding arouses castration anxiety or unconscious fears of mutilation. But other theorists regard menstrual rituals as an expression of a general contempt for women, or as a means of confining women to their reproductive roles. Some anthropologists have suggested that the seclusion of menstruating women is related to the methods of hygiene available to them: the greater women's access to running water, disposable absorbent pads, and other hygienic aids, the less likely they will be isolated during their periods (Wood, 1979). So far, however, this is just a hypothesis.

In our society, far from ritualizing menarche, we are likely to ignore it or refer to it only indirectly. Our discomfort is reflected in the fact that English appears to have more euphemisms for menstruation ("the curse," "that time of the month") than does any other European language (Farb, 1974). A national survey conducted for the Tampax corporation (Tampax, Inc., 1981) found that two-thirds of all Americans objected to discussion of menstruation in the office or in social situations, and one-quarter felt it was an unacceptable topic even at home. Many people objected when menstruation was first mentioned on television (in a 1973 episode of the situation comedy "All in the Family"). Today, print and television advertisements for feminine hygiene products are commonplace, but they often emphasize the need for a woman to deodorize herself and hide the "unhygienic" (and by implication, embarrassing) fact of menstruation from the world.

Many girls are happy to start menstruating; it's a sign of being grown up. But some girls get their period without ever having been told what to expect, and blood on their underpants comes as a shock. In the Tampax survey, over two-fifths of all women reported a negative reaction to their first period—fear, confusion, panic, or illness. More recent studies also find negative feelings to be common, especially among black adolescents, who are more likely than whites to report having been unprepared for the event (Scott et al., 1989).

Even girls who know what to expect may feel ambivalent about menstruation. It does involve some fuss and bother, and during the first few years, periods may be irregular and heavy. There is always the worry that it may come in the middle of Mr. Smith's math class, with no way to get to the bathroom. But social factors probably account for most of the embarrassment girls feel about what is, after all, a perfectly natural physiological process. Compounding this embarrassment is the common belief that menstruation is an emotional and mental handicap. As we will see in Chapter 18, there is no good evidence for this belief, but young girls (and boys) often accept the stereotypes (Parlee, 1974; Ruble & Brooks, 1977).

Physical Changes in Boys

As in girls, two pituitary hormones become active in boys at puberty. An increase in FSH initiates sperm production, although it is often some time before the sperm are mature and capable of merging with an ovum. Interstitial-cell-stimulating hormone (ICSH) initiates production of testosterone by the testes. Testosterone is responsible for most of the physical changes that accompany puberty in boys.

The first outward sign of these changes is usually growth of the testes and scrotum, at about ten to thirteen years of age. At about the same time, or

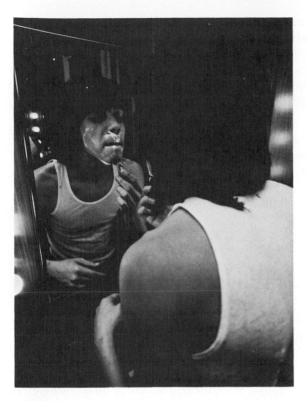

First shave *Western societies have few formal ceremonies to celebrate the onset of puberty, but there are some informal rites of passage. For example, many families view the removal of a boy's first fuzzy facial hair as a milestone marking the beginning of the end of childhood.*

perhaps a bit later, pubic hair begins to appear. This is followed by an increase in the size of the penis and the start of the spurt in body height. Meanwhile, the seminal vesicles and the prostate gland enlarge, and about a year after penile growth begins, ejaculation becomes possible. About two years after the first growth of pubic hair, a boy notices hair under his arms and on his face. Facial hair usually grows first at the corner of the upper lip, then above the lips, and finally on the cheeks. While the boy's face becomes hairier, his hairline above the forehead recedes—a development that continues into adulthood. Finally, by about age fourteen or fifteen, a boy's voice usually deepens because testosterone causes the larynx (voice box) to grow.

In many societies male puberty signals that the time is at hand to initiate a boy into adulthood, an event calling for much celebration. But in our society male puberty has received even less attention than female puberty (except in the Jewish rite of bar mitzvah). For the most part, boys must experience the trials and tribulations of this period in private. Many—perhaps most—boys experience a temporary enlargement of the breasts, which is probably caused by the small amount of estrogen produced in the testes. Naturally, this can be worrisome. And just as a girl may wonder if she will ever have breasts, a boy may wonder if he will ever find hair on his chin. The popularity of boys in junior high school and high school seems to be linked to physical development, and the boy whose development is a little slower than that of his friends may feel left out and embarrassed.

Perhaps the most exasperating aspect of puberty for a boy is the sudden unruliness of his penis, which may become erect for no discernible reason, in nearly any circumstance. In his essay "Being a Boy," Julius Lester (1976), a teacher of African-American studies, recalled with perhaps just a hint of hyperbole the hidden dangers lurking at a high school party, when he found himself dancing with a girl:

> ...I took her in my arms, careful not to hold her so far away that she would think I didn't like her, but equally careful not to hold her so close that she could feel the catastrophe which had befallen me the instant I touched her hand. My penis, totally disobeying the lecture I'd given it before we left home, was as rigid as [Alabama] Governor Wallace's jaw would be if I asked for his daughter's hand in marriage.
>
> God, how I envied girls at that moment. Wherever *it* was on them, it didn't dangle between their legs like an elephant's trunk. No wonder boys talked about nothing but sex. That thing was always there. Every time we went to the john, there *it* was, twitching around like a fat little worm on a fishing hook. When we took baths, it floated in the water like a lazy fish and God forbid we should touch it! It sprang to life like lightning leaping from a cloud. I wished I could cut it off, or at least keep it tucked between my legs, as if it were a tail that had mistakenly attached to the wrong end. But I was helpless. It was there, with a life and mind of its own, having no other function than to embarrass me. (p. 273)

The first ejaculation, which is probably the closest male analogue to menstruation in females, can, like menstruation, be either exciting or surprising. Many boys first learn about ejaculation not from friends or parents, but from "adult" magazines or their own experience (Gaddis & Brooks-Gunn, 1985). If a boy has never ejaculated through masturbation, the first ejaculation may occur when he is asleep, during a **nocturnal emission,** or "wet dream." Usually the first ejaculation is a positive experience, but if the boy does not know what to expect, he may be confused or think there is something wrong with him. Even a masturbatory ejaculation may be puzzling. Sex therapist Bernie Zilbergeld (1978) cites the recollection of one man who, as a thirteen-year-old at summer camp, tried to mimic the masturbatory mastery of his roommates:

> At first my investigations were a flop. I did just about everything I could think of to my penis—squeezing it, petting it, rubbing it between my hands, pushing it against my thigh, waving it around like a flag—and nothing happened. It hadn't occurred to me that it would help if I had an erection. Then, one day as I was absentmindedly stroking my penis and thinking that I would have to retire from such pursuits unless more rewarding results were forthcoming, I became aware of some pleasurable sensations. I kept stroking, my penis got hard, and the sensations felt better and better. Then I was overcome with feelings I had never before felt and, God help me, white stuff came spurting out the end of my

cock. I wasn't sure if I had sprung a leak or what. I was afraid but calmed down when I thought that since it was white it couldn't be blood. I kept on stroking and it hurt. I didn't know if the hurt was connected with the white stuff (had I really injured myself?) or if the event was over and my penis needed a rest. But I decided to stop for a moment. Of course I returned the next day and did it again. . . . (p. 14)

TEENAGE SEXUAL BEHAVIOR

Many adolescents regard the changes in their lives with a bewildering array of conflicting emotions: delight and anxiety, wonder and worry, confidence and confusion. And no wonder: sometime between their twelfth and twentieth birthdays, young people must adjust to the changes in their bodies, establish a sense of independence from their parents, decide about the future, take some financial responsibility for themselves, and choose which of their family's values to accept or reject. As if all this were not enough, they also come of age sexually and many have intercourse. Even those who engage in little or no sexual activity begin to be perceived by others as sexual beings. Sex and sexual attractiveness assume new meanings and importance, as adolescents discover new capacities for erotic love, for reproduction, for sexual response.

Masturbation

Despite our culture's traditional abhorrence of autoeroticism, masturbation provides most people with their first experience of orgasm. In the Kinsey study, 68 percent of all males ejaculated for the first time during masturbation (compared to 13 percent during a nocturnal emission, about 12 percent during coitus, and about 4 percent during a homosexual contact). Similarly, 40 percent of all females experienced first orgasm during masturbation (versus 27 percent during coitus, 24 percent during petting, 5 percent during an erotic dream, and 3 percent during a homosexual contact) (Kinsey, Pomeroy & Martin, 1948; Kinsey et al., 1953).

It is difficult to know how many teenagers masturbate by a particular age. We do have the recollections of adults. For example, in Kinsey's study, almost all the men recalled masturbating by age 20, with most having done so by age 14. Only about a third of the women in Kinsey's sample said they had masturbated by age 20, but in a more recent study, the figure was much higher, three-fourths (Masters, Johnson & Kolodny, 1986). But adults who are asked about their early behavior may misremember. Another approach is to ask teenagers directly. Using this method, Robert Coles and Geoffrey Stokes (1985) found that at age 18 only about 60 percent of boys and a quarter of girls had masturbated. But these figures may be too low, because some teenagers may be unwilling to acknowledge their masturbation to an adult.

Adolescent fantasy
Masturbation by teenage boys often occurs while they are viewing erotic materials, and the images and ideas in these materials may be incorporated into private sexual fantasies. What do you think the effect might be on later sexuality? (For more on erotica and pornography, see Chapter 16.)

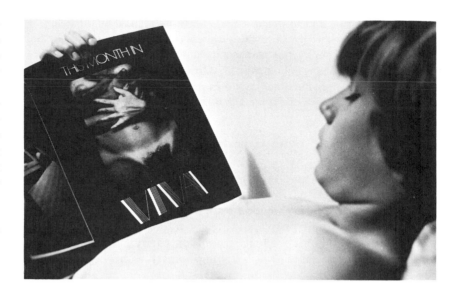

In the Coles and Stokes study, boys and girls said they knew there was nothing wrong or dangerous in masturbating, yet they clearly felt uncomfortable talking about it. Perhaps they were ashamed of masturbating because they did not regard it as "real" sex.

Whatever the exact figures, it is clear that adolescent boys and girls differ not only in the onset of masturbation, but in its frequency. In Kinsey's sample, the average [median] frequency for males up to the age of 15 was about 1.8 times a week, with 17 percent of all boys averaging between 4 and 7 times a week or more. For females of the same age the median frequency was only .5 times per week. Thus, by the end of adolescence the average male has far more experience with orgasm than the average female.

Why do these differences exist? Sociologists John Gagnon and William Simon (1973; Simon & Gagnon, 1969) have argued that biology provides part of the answer. The sudden rise in testosterone at puberty causes boys to experience something girls cannot, spontaneous erections. Although these erections may not always be sexually motivated, they do make a boy exceedingly conscious of his penis and increase the likelihood that he will discover its erotic potential. It is hard to ignore an erect penis.

Once a boy starts masturbating, the physical aspects of sex get strongly reinforced. Then psychology and culture take over. Many boys feel guilty and anxious about masturbating and about the forbidden erotic fantasies they may have while doing it. But paradoxically, these feelings may make the experience even more intense than it would otherwise be. Girls, on the other hand, often fail to discover masturbation, even though they possess all the physical equipment necessary for genital sex. Besides lacking the hormonal impetus, girls in our culture are discouraged from expressing physical sexuality. Most have little support from their peers for sexual exploration. Even though masturbation must be kept secret from disapproving adults, young boys often talk about it with each other, and may even stage contests ("circle jerks") to see who can shoot the farthest and fastest. When teenage girls masturbate they usually discover it on their own and do not talk to other girls about it. Instead, encouraged by the culture, they talk about dating, the emotional aspects of relationships, and how to make themselves sexually attractive.

You may be thinking that the sex difference in masturbation gives boys a sexual advantage. In some ways it probably does. Many sex therapists and sexologists believe that girls who do not masturbate miss a golden opportunity to learn how their bodies respond to erotic stimulation (Barbach, 1974; Wakefield, 1988). Indeed, Kinsey found that females who masturbate before marriage are more likely than others to have coital orgasms early in marriage. But, say Gagnon and Simon, male masturbation also has its negative side. Learning about one's sexuality in a context that is goal-oriented and even competitive can lead to detachment and an overly narrow genital focus in sexual activity.

After heterosexual intercourse begins, according to Gagnon and Simon, cultural "scripts" continue to reinforce male concern with genital sexuality and female concern with the social and emotional aspects of sex. In young adulthood, each sex must try to train the other in its particular area of expertise. But the course of this exchange does not always run smoothly. Well into adulthood, men and women may be reading their lines from somewhat different sexual scripts.

What do you think of this theory? Does it apply today as well as it did two decades ago? As we've seen, more women may now be discovering masturbation during adolescence (although a sex difference remains). The cultural scripts for men and women have also changed somewhat since Gagnon and Simon first proposed their theory. Yet as we will see, in certain ways young men and women are still on different planets as far as their sexual expectations are concerned. In times of cultural transition, some things change and some things stay the same.

Partnered Sex

American boys and girls have always been permitted a certain amount of sexual contact. At various times it has been called bundling, spooning, mugging, smooching, larking, sparking, necking, and petting. In Kinsey's sample even women born before 1900 had some premarital experience with petting. Most men and women experienced petting by the age of eighteen, and nearly everyone did before marriage. The most common "technique" was simple kissing, followed by deep kissing, stimulation of the female's breasts by the male, manual stimulation of the partner's genitals, and (much more rarely) oral-genital contact. Petting went on in the girl's home, in

Prom night *Important changes have taken place in teenage sexual and dating behavior during the past decades, but not everything has changed. As they have for generations, teenagers are still pairing off and dressing up for school-sponsored dances.*

parked cars, on porches, at social gatherings, in movie theaters, in buses and trains, and at "blanket parties."

In the 1950s, teenagers talked about getting to first, second, or third base—home plate being coitus. A "nice" girl was supposed to let a boy get no further than first base. In reality, though, many couples went on to second and even third. A girl might permit all sorts of sexual intimacies as long as she remained a "technical" virgin. When people today speak about a sexual revolution among the young, they are not referring to a revolution in petting, but in intercourse.

Actually, as we saw in Chapter 2, the United States and other Western countries have gone through not one sexual revolution, but two. The first occurred during the "Roaring Twenties." Kinsey found that although most women born before 1900 were virgins when they married, by the 1940s and 1950s virginity was honored more in word than in deed. Nearly half of all married women had had premarital intercourse, some as adolescents and some later. As for the men in Kinsey's sample, almost all of those with a grade school education had experienced premarital intercourse, as had 85 percent of high school graduates and 68 percent of those with some college education. "Promiscuity" was the exception rather than the rule: more than half of the women who had sex before marriage had only one partner (usually the fiancé), and only 13 percent had more than five partners. But Americans were certainly not as naive when they walked down the aisle as many preferred to believe.

The second sexual revolution began in the 1960s, a decade that saw enormous social upheaval: protests against U.S. military involvement in Southeast Asia, violent racial confrontations, political assassinations, the growth of social activism, the start of the hippie movement, and widespread use of illicit drugs. Sexual mores changed too, becoming much more permissive. One result was a striking increase in "premarital sex" among adolescents, an increase that reached a peak in the 1970s. The rise was especially dramatic for females. In the 1940s and 1950s, only about a fifth of 19-year-old single women reported having had intercourse (Kinsey et al., 1953). By the mid-1970s, the figure had climbed to about one-half (Zelnik & Kantner, 1977), and by the early 1980s, it stood at between two-thirds and three-fourths[1] (Hofferth, Kahn & Baldwin, 1987; Mott & Haurin, 1988). Not only were many more girls having intercourse during adolescence, but a substantial minority were having it early in their teens. There was an increase in the incidence of intercourse among boys, too. In Kinsey's sample, about 45 percent of white males had had intercourse by age 19. By the early 1980s the figure was about 78 percent and today it is about 85 percent (Mott & Haurin, 1988; Sonnenstein, Pleck & Ku, 1989). But the greater increase for girls meant that during the 1970s the gap between the sexes narrowed considerably, and it is now quite small.

Recent research suggests that the rise in premarital sex may have leveled off during the 1980s (Gerrard, 1987; Hofferth, Kahn & Baldwin, 1987; Mott & Haurin, 1988). Perhaps the figures on premarital intercourse simply

---

[1]During the 1970s, the percentages on premarital intercourse were much higher for young black women than for whites, but the figures for black women leveled off during the decade while white rates continue to climb. Black rates today are around 80 percent.

Making out   *To many pre-teens and young teenagers, this seems like a terrific way to end a party, but others would feel uncomfortable. One young person may experience kissing as erotic while at the same age another may be merely playacting or responding to peer pressure.*

reached a natural "ceiling"; that is, once most teenagers were having inter-course by the end of adolescence, the figures could not continue to climb much higher.

A dramatic change has also occurred during the past few decades in teenagers' experiences with oral-genital sex. Many teenagers today try cunnilingus or fellatio before they have had their first experience with inter-course. This is a reversal of the pattern that used to hold (Gagnon & Simon, 1987; Newcomer & Udry, 1985). Teenagers often see oral and other non-coital forms of sex as having certain advantages: there is no need to worry about birth control, and they can enjoy sexual pleasure, sexual experimentation, and sexual intimacy while technically still remaining virgins.

Behavioral scientists do not fully understand the factors that influence teenagers to have—or not have—sex. They do know, however, that sexual expression in *early* adolescence tends to be associated with early physical maturity (especially in boys), peer pressure to be sexually active, poor family communication, poor academic performance, low educational aspirations, and living in a single-parent household (Brooks-Gunn & Furstenberg, 1989).

Feelings About Sex

Margaret Mead once noted that "the language of tables and variables . . . has replaced Latin as the acceptable language for the discussion of sex" (quoted in Peplau, Rubin, & Hill, 1977). But what do all the numbers on adolescent sex mean? How do young people *feel* about sex?

Early in the sexual revolution, three sexual standards prevailed among adolescents: a conventional view that abstinence was best, a traditional view that premarital sex was acceptable for males but wrong for females (the double standard), and a more liberal view that premarital sex was acceptable as an expression of love and affection between two people (Reiss, 1969; R.R. Bell, 1966). Since that time, the liberal view has become the most widely endorsed among young people. Most studies find that teenagers generally consider intercourse perfectly acceptable if a couple is in love. Some also endorse sex without love if both partners want it, but the ideal for most boys and girls is sex in a caring relationship. Young women are more willing now to have sex without waiting for a long-term commitment (DeLamater and MacCorquodale, 1979). At the same time, fewer young men are now having their first intercourse with a prostitute or casual acquaintance; they are choosing instead to wait for a more serious relationship (McCabe, 1987).

However, the increased acceptance of the liberal standard among young people does not mean that the double standard is dead, or that sex means exactly the same thing to boys and girls. Consider:

- Most people now regard premarital sex favorably if a couple is in love, but when disapproval surfaces, it is more likely to be directed at females than males. For example, Coles & Stokes (1985) found that parents were less tolerant of sexual activities by daughters than by sons.

- Sexually active college women increasingly accept their own sexuality. They tend to be independent and assertive and feel good about themselves (Scanzoni & Fox, 1980). But a younger teenage girl who has many partners still risks her "reputation" more than a boy would (McCormick & Jesser, 1983).

- People of both sexes generally have their first experience with a boyfriend or girlfriend. But boys are still somewhat more likely than girls to have that first experience with a friend or stranger (Jessor et al., 1983; Coles & Stokes, 1985).

- In Hunt's (1974) interviews with young people, only a fifth of the males, but over half the females rated their first experience with intercourse as neutral or unpleasant. And in the Coles and Stokes study (1985) girls were more likely than boys to feel sadness, ambivalence, or dissatisfaction after "the first time." Some still valued virginity. Others were disappointed with the experience itself. One said, "...people *enjoy* this?"

- Males and females alike say that ideally sex should occur with someone you love. But "love" can mean something different to a teenage boy than to a teenage girl. In the Coles and Stokes study, more than half the sexually active 15-year-old girls said they expected to marry their most recent sexual partner. (The realities of teenage love mean, of course, that most were indulging in wishful thinking.) In contrast, 82 percent of the sexually active 15-year-old boys said they did *not* plan to marry their most recent partner.

- Young people are trying sexual activities that their parents thought taboo at the same age, but there is some evidence that teenage boys and girls differ in their liking for some of these practices. Coles and Stokes found that more 17- and 18-year-old girls than boys had performed oral sex, but girls were less enthusiastic about both cunnilingus and fellatio. "It appears," wrote the authors of the study, "that many of the teenage girls who do give oral sex do so less for their own pleasure than for their partners'."

- In bars, young women flirt as much as young men do, and often they make the first subtle move, using eye contact or a change in voice (Perper & Fox, 1980). But in general, boys and young men are still expected to ask for dates, initiate sex, and pay the bills, while girls and young women get to accept or decline (Green & Sandos, 1983; Allgeier, 1981; Zellman & Goodchilds, 1983; McCormick & Jesser, 1983).

Many of these findings can be understood as the result of American dating customs, which encourage both sexes to regard female sexuality as a valuable "medium of exchange" in a relationship, a sort of bargaining chip, rather than something to be enjoyed by the girl for its own sake. The boy's part of the bargain is usually to pay for dates. Young women in our classes tell us they often feel guilty, or at least uncomfortable, when they refuse to have sex after a young man has financed a certain number of dates. Young men, for their part, may feel misled or cheated.

What happens when a young women who views sex as a resource to be used with restraint goes ahead and has intercourse early in a relationship? Most likely she will need to justify her behavior to herself. She may rationalize that she was "swept away" by the candlelight and the sweet nothings that Herman whispered in her ear. Or she may convince herself that Herman loves her, despite evidence to the contrary. Sex educator Carol Cassell (1984) notes that this sort of self-deception can be a way for a girl to deny her

"He said if I didn't do it, he wouldn't love me anymore."

"AND YOU KNOW WHAT? I GOT angry. It was such a trashy thing to say. Like I was so desperate for him I'd jump off a cliff or something.

We didn't have any birth control. I started out saying it was just the wrong time.

Then I started thinking it was the wrong guy.

After he said that, he put on this big act about it. If he really cared, he'd have let it drop. He'd have given me time.

I mean, you don't have to be the brain of the world to know you don't have sex without protection.

And you sure don't make a baby with a guy who thinks he can threaten you."

Nobody should pressure anybody to have sex. Especially if you feel you're not ready. Or prepared. It's a fact of life that if you have sex without safe, effective birth control, you're going to get pregnant. Who should be responsible for birth control? It can be you, it can be him, even better when it's both. If you need information or just someone to talk to, call your nearest Planned Parenthood. We can help. That's what we're here for.

 Planned Parenthood®
Federation of America

810 Seventh Avenue
New York, NY 10019

Bad bargain *Posters like this one address not only the problem of teenage pregnancy but also the psychological context in which adolescents make their sexual decisions.*

true sexual desires or the nature of the sexual bargain. It can also be a way to cope with a loss of power that comes from cashing in her "chips."

Teenage Pregnancies

During the past two decades, over one million U.S. teenagers have become pregnant each year—equivalent to about two new pregnancies a minute. In a typical year, more than one of every ten women under age twenty becomes pregnant (Hayes, 1987). Most of these pregnancies are unintended. About 40 percent end in abortion, another 10 percent in miscarriage, and the rest in birth (Trussell, 1988).

The good news is that birth control use rose among teenagers in recent years due mainly to the use of condoms. The number of teenage boys saying they used condoms the last time they had intercourse rose from only 21 percent in 1979 to 57 percent in 1988 (Sonenstein, Pleck & Ku, 1988). The bad news is that many teenagers, especially young ones, still do not use birth control, or use it only sporadically. And only a minority use effective methods when they first become sexually active (Moore et al., 1987).

The rate of *births* to teenagers actually dropped between the 1960s and the mid-1980s. What increased was the number of legal abortions and the number of babies born to *unmarried* teens (Hayes, 1987; Moore, 1989). A generation ago, most pregnant teenagers were already married or they got married quickly under parental pressure. Today, those who do not have abortions are likely to become single mothers. Young fathers usually disappear from the picture, unprepared for or unwilling to assume the responsibilities of parenthood. Over 90 percent of unmarried teenage mothers choose to keep their babies and most raise them alone (Moore et al., 1987).

Neither a teenage mother nor her baby is likely to have an easy time in life. The mother is more likely than other girls to leave high school without graduating, go on welfare, and live below the poverty line. The baby is more likely than other children to be sick (or even die), to be physically or emotionally abused, and, as it grows up, to have educational and emotional problems. Most disturbing, the children of teenage mothers are at high risk of becoming high school dropouts and teenage parents themselves. In one study, over 80 percent of girls who gave birth before age 15 were themselves daughters of teenage mothers (Wallis, 1985). Many committed and hardworking teenage mothers manage well, but for all too many American adolescents, pregnancy triggers a downward spiral, educationally and financially, for both themselves and their children (Furstenberg, Brooks-Gunn & Chase-Lansdale, 1989; Hayes, 1987; Teti & Lamb, 1989).

Why do so many American teenagers get pregnant without wanting to? Part of the answer has to do with misconceptions about conception. Many young people still mistakenly believe that pregnancy can't occur the first time or first few times one has intercourse. In actuality, about a fifth of all first-time teen pregnancies occur within one month of the first intercourse, and about half within six months (Hofferth, 1987).

Another part of the answer lies in adolescent psychology. Teenagers are especially susceptible to illusions of invulnerability and uniqueness; they think *they* will escape the laws of probability that affect everyone else. This belief may be reinforced if they have sex and a pregnancy does not immediately result. They may tell themselves, "You see, it didn't happen last time. I'll take my chances." In addition, adolescents typically have sex sporadi-

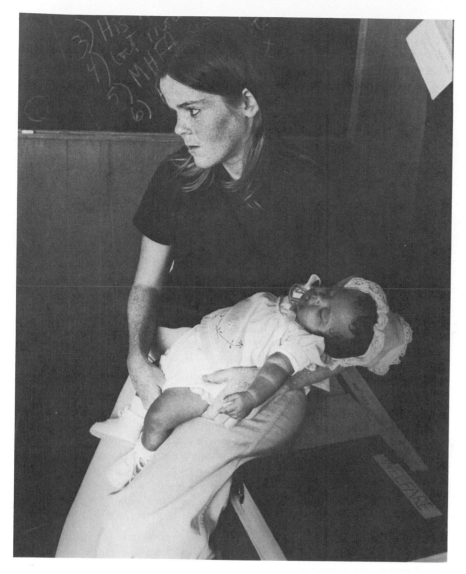

Children having children
The educational and financial prospects for most unmarried teenage mothers are bleak. Some, however, do manage well. This young mother's future will depend in part on whether she graduates from high school and emerges from adolescence without having another child. Some schools now have support programs for pregnant adolescents and teenage parents.

cally; they do not know when or even if sex will take place. Taking a pill every day or carrying a pack of condoms with you is difficult when you are not sure that such precautions will be necessary—and you are worried that your parents might find out. Because of taboos against adolescent and pre-marital sex, a young person may also resist acknowledging his or her own sexuality. The double standard compounds this problem for girls. A girl who has had sexual intercourse several times knows, of course, that she is having sex, but she may not incorporate sexuality into her self-concept. She may not think of herself as a "sexually active" person. Girls, and boys too, often fail to make a conscious decision to become sexually active. It "just happens."

People of any age can find it embarrassing to discuss contraception with a sexual partner, especially in the early stages of a relationship. Adolescents, who are less experienced than older people in sexual matters, are especially likely to find the subject awkward. And factors unrelated to sex may also be involved in the failure to use contraceptives. Many teenagers have trouble setting goals; a child of one's own may provide an instant identity and give life a sense of purpose it seems to lack. An unmarried teenager with a troubled family life may hope that a child will give her the love she cannot get from her parents, and bolster her sense of self-worth.

But there are other causes for teenage pregnancies that go beyond the personal and psychological. Many people do not realize that teen pregnancy rates are higher in the United States than in almost any other developed country—exceeded only by those of Iceland, Greece, Hungary, and Rumania. The U.S. rate is two to five times higher than Western Europe's and almost twenty times higher than Japan's (Westoff, Calot & Foster, 1983). A study by The Alan Guttmacher Institute (Jones et al., 1985) suggests why. Teenagers in the United States are not more sexually active than their counterparts in other developed countries. The critical difference is that they use birth control less consistently and effectively and are not able to obtain it as easily and cheaply.

Consider five countries with far lower teenage pregnancy rates than in the U.S.: England/Wales, Canada, France, the Netherlands, and Sweden. These countries have established birth control clinics to serve the specific needs of young people. (The clinics are not perceived as places where only poor people go.) Adolescents also get up-to-date information about sexuality and contraception in school and in the media. Governments in these countries are more concerned with adolescent pregnancy than with adolescent sex. In contrast, Americans concerned about teenage pregnancy are divided into two camps, those who want to encourage birth control and those who want only to reduce sexual activity. American teenagers have inherited the worst of all possible worlds as far as the risk of pregnancy is concerned. All about them are messages that sex is romantic, exciting, and fun—which, of course, it can be. And all about them are unmarried people (including, often, their own divorced parents) enjoying sex. Yet few adults offer young people good reasons for delaying sex ("Just say no"), and birth control is sometimes difficult to get. In the last chapter of this book we will explore how improved sex education might address some of these issues.

ADULT SEXUALITY

Social scientists interested in human development used to concentrate almost entirely on childhood and adolescence. Like most people, they assumed that toward the end of the teenage years the once pliable clay of personality became rigid and set. Children grew; grownups adapted. Children went through distinct stages, each with a unique set of problems and challenges; the postadolescent terrain was uniform, lacking significant peaks or valleys. But all that has changed. Today developmental psychology is life-span psychology. Scientists are busily reexamining all sorts of assumptions about adulthood, including sexual ones.

At the same time, changes have occurred in the ways adults live their lives. In days gone by, most lives followed a predictable course: dating, early marriage, parenthood, grandparenthood, retirement with one's spouse. This pattern is still common, but so are others. A person may remain single without being labeled a lonely bachelor or an old maid; delay marriage; marry several times; cohabit without getting married; or marry but forgo children. Marriage has hardly gone out of style; but for many people today, marriage is like a party where people arrive late and leave early. Many couples are postponing children, and many children live with a single parent, usually the mother. There are more married couples without children under eighteen than with children. So many Americans have adopted so many different lifestyles that only 15 percent live in a traditional family with a working father, a homemaker mother and dependent children (U.S. Bureau of the Census, 1986).

Along with changes in the lives of individuals have come changes in social norms about the way adults should behave. We can trace some of these social changes by comparing media depictions of adults over the past few decades. In the 1950s, family television programs like "Father Knows Best" and "Leave It to Beaver" portrayed parents as staid and conservative. Anyone over thirty-five was clearly middle-aged, and anyone over fifty was old. Fathers were patient and wise. Mothers were proper matrons who wore dresses and high-heels even while preparing dinner. In contrast, many of today's media parents are close to their offspring in both behavior and interests—and they are not always perfect role models (for example, on "Married . . . with Children" or "The Simpsons").

Sex Without Marriage

If you are a single adult, you have lots of company. During the 1950s, nearly everyone married early (women before they reached 21 and men before 23); staying single was not considered "respectable." People often marched to the altar because it was the thing to do, whether or not marriage—or their partner—actually suited them. Today there is still social pressue to marry, but people are not in such a rush to tie the knot. Young people are taking longer to leave the nest—and some keep coming back. In their early twenties, most men (78 percent) and women (61 percent) are still single. As for people in their late twenties or early thirties, the majority are married, but the proportion of people at those ages who have never married has more than doubled since 1970 (U.S. Bureau of the Census, 1988). According to one estimate, about 13 percent of women and 10 percent of men remain permanently single (Bloom & Bennett, 1986).

The ranks of the single have no doubt swelled in part because of changes in sexual mores. It is no longer necessary to marry in order to have

The traditional family
During the 1950s the word "family" usually meant a breadwinner father, a stay-at-home mother, and their children.

access to regular sex. Society is far more tolerant of sexual activity among single adults than it once was, and the vast majority of single adults are sexually active. In addition, a traditional female motive for marrying, financial security, has faded, because most women now work outside the home. People of both sexes today often postpone marriage in order to concentrate on educational and career goals.

SINGLE LIFESTYLES   According to old stereotypes, single adults are promiscuous, or unappealing, or lonely (or, if they are none of these, then they must be lesbian or gay). But none of these characteristics describes a typical single person these days. In fact, there is no typical single person, nor is there a typical single lifestyle. Some single adults are celibate, either by choice or because they do not have a sex partner. Others have recreational sex in casual relationships with successive partners or have more than one partner at a time. Some singles are in exclusive, long-term relationships. Others prefer "serial monogamy," having successive serious relationships but no permanent or long-term one. Some single people live alone, with relatives, or with roommates. Others share quarters with a sexual partner.

Although some people are forced to remain single because their psychological problems or low social status make them seem unattractive to others, they are not typical. In one study of 482 single adults in Canada, about half viewed their single status as a matter of deliberate choice rather than the result of chance or uncontrollable circumstances (Austrom & Hanel, 1985). Most did not see themselves as wary of commitment or marriage; they had high standards and had simply not met the right person yet. Fewer than half the respondents expressed dissatisfaction with being single; a quarter were

Changing families *In the 1990s the word "family" can mean many things: a family with a breadwinner and homemaker, working parents with or without children, single parents and their children, step-families, and even people who live together in an intimate relationship without marriage.*

satisfied and the rest were neutral. The more friends and social support people had, the more likely they were to be satisfied.

In another study, too, the level of contentment with singlehood was high: 55 percent of the women and 50 percent of the men said being single had been either "wonderful" or "basically fine" (Simenauer & Carroll, 1982). (Of course, it is possible that some of those claiming satisfaction were rationalizing or lying, but the same could be said of married people who claim satisfaction.) The most frequently mentioned advantages of the single life were mobility and freedom, time to pursue personal interests, the single social life, and privacy. However, the respondents admitted that being single also presented "plenty of problems." The most frequently mentioned ones were loneliness, the "dating grind," a restricted social and sexual life (mentioned by 10 percent of the women and 12 percent of the men), and a tendency to become rigid, self-centered, and selfish.

A concern of many unpartnered single adults is how to find other people for social and romantic relationships. Some single people meet others at single bars and in single apartment complexes. Respondents in the Canadian survey gave high marks to parties, introductions by mutual friends, contacts in the workplace, and group hobbies or sports activities. They gave low marks to dating services and personal ads, although in the late 1980s the popularity of both increased.

The availability of partners depends, in large part, on demographics. For several decades, women have outnumbered men in all decades of life (although this is reversing for people under 30). Since women often "marry up" and men often "marry down" (see Chapter 8), highly educated women have been particularly "disadvantaged" in terms of the number of "eligible men" available. But the size of the disadvantage is a matter of controversy. Some experts believe it is quite large (Bennet, Bloom & Craig, 1989) while others think it is disappearing (Moorman, 1987).

COHABITATION   Prior to the 1970s, few researchers paid much attention to **cohabitation,** the state of living with a sexual partner without being married. Then, in the short space of a decade, the estimated number of cohabiting couples tripled. In 1980, the federal government for the first time took an official head count of heterosexual cohabitors (dubbed "POSSLQs," an acronym for "Persons of the Opposite Sex Sharing Living Quarters"), and by 1988, the official tally stood at over 2.6 million couples, four times the estimated number in 1970 (U.S. Bureau of the Census, 1988). Forty-four percent of people who married for the first time during the early 1980s had cohabited prior to marriage, as had 58 percent of divorced people. Nearly sixty percent of all Americans in their thirties have lived at some time with someone of the other sex (Bumpass & Sweet, 1989).

People choose to cohabit, just as they choose to marry, for a variety of reasons. Cohabitation can be a way of preparing for marriage, an alternative to marriage, or simply a very steady form of "going steady." One couple may move in together to see if they are compatible before taking "the big step" and another because two can live more cheaply than one. Some people may choose cohabitation because they are disillusioned with marriage. Others may prefer cohabitation to marriage because they want their relationship to be based solely on freely given love and not on a legal document. And some prefer cohabitation because they see it as easier to get out of than marriage (although the emotional pain of a breakup may be just as great).

Research finds that most cohabiting couples eventually marry or break up; cohabitation does not usually become a permanent substitute for marriage (Tanfer, 1987). In their study of American couples, Philip Blumstein and Pepper Schwartz (1983) had trouble finding unmarried couples who had lived together for as long as ten years. As Blumstein and Schwartz point out, cohabitation is a situation, whereas marriage is an institution. When people are bound to each other legally as well as emotionally, they may be more motivated to keep a relationship going despite some bad times. However, the apparent scarcity of long-term cohabitors may be due in part to the fact that widespread cohabitation is relatively new. Also, our knowledge of cohabitation is based mostly on studies of young never-married couples. Older cohabitors may have more stable relationships.

In the Blumstein and Schwartz study, cohabiting couples fell into three groups. One consisted of those who were trying out living together before making it official. A second group consisted of couples who did not at first intend to marry, but gradually found their commitment deepening. Believing that marriage was no longer something to be avoided, they eventually wed. A third group seemed dedicated to cohabitation as a way of life and were not planning on either marrying or separating.

One benefit of cohabiting is regular sex. Blumstein & Schwartz found that cohabiting couples in their sample had more frequent sex than married couples of the same age. Cohabiting can also meet people's needs for companionship and emotional security. Cohabiting partners are apt to socialize as a couple, and for many, living together is a welcome escape from the "dating game." For some, living together provides a better context than marriage for creating an egalitarian heterosexual relationship, because marriage tends to bring along with it many gender-role expectations and obligations (Kotkin, 1983).

However, cohabitation also has certain drawbacks. Despite its growing popularity, social criticism of cohabitation is still widespread. Parents and other family members may express their disapproval in no uncertain terms. The lack of social support for cohabiting is reflected in the absence of standard terms for referring to cohabiting partners. Couples must fall back on such inexact labels as "friend," "partner," "girlfriend," "boyfriend," "mate," "lover," "significant other," and "spousal equivalent." Legally, cohabiting couples live in a sort of limbo. They are not protected by the property laws governing marriage. Unless there is a written contract specifying which belongings are separate and which are jointly owned, the ending of a relationship can lead to a protracted tug-of-war over possessions. Yet couples who decided to forego marriage in order to maintain their financial independence may find that their arrangement carries obligations very like those of a marriage, because in some states courts will award "palimony" to one of the partners, based on the same considerations underlying alimony in a divorce. And in some states, cohabitation becomes "common-law marriage" after a certain number of years, with all the legal rights and obligations of marriage.

During the 1970s, many social scientists speculated that cohabiting before marriage would increase the chances of subsequent marital success, because when the partners did finally wed, they would have few illusions about one another. But these predictions have not been borne out. Although there is still not much research on this question, married couples who lived together before marriage do not seem any more satisfied or adjusted than other married couples, and may even be less so (Booth & Johnson, 1988; DeMaris & Leslie, 1984; Watson & DeMeo, 1987). Indeed premarital cohabitation appears to be associated with an increased probability of divorce (Bennett, Blanc & Bloom, 1988; Riche, 1988). This latter finding does not necessarily mean, however, that cohabitation spoils marriage. Couples who have cohabited may simply be less committed than other people to marriage and more willing to leave a marriage that is unsatisfying.

Sex in Marriage

Marriage has sometimes been attacked as growth-inhibiting or boring. Yet most people seem to feel that marriage holds the best promise of fulfilling their needs for belonging, security, and closeness. Marriage brings social recognition of a couple's relationship and provides (ideally, at least) the emotional and economic stability desirable for the rearing of children. About nine out of every ten adults in the United States will marry at least once.

TYPES OF MARRIAGES   Expectations about marriage have changed over the past hundred years. In the nineteenth century, marriage was often an arrangement between an owner (the husband) and his property (the wife). When a disagreement arose, the husband's will prevailed. Sex was an obligation for both spouses, but neither worried too much about its quality or the emotional bond between the partners. In contrast, modern marriages are expected to provide friendship and companionship. Sex is not supposed to be a marital duty or procreational chore but an expression of love and affection and a source of mutual pleasure. According to sociologists Letha and John Scanzoni (1976), modern marriages usually take one of three forms. In the *head-complement* marriage, husband and wife play traditional roles but the husband regards his wife as someone who "completes" him, his "other half," and feels responsible for giving her love and affection. In the *senior-partner/ junior-partner* marriage, the wife gains a certain degree of power because she works for pay outside the home and contributes to the family finances. However, the husband's job or career has priority over the wife's and the wife is still expected to do most of the household chores. In the *equal-partner* marriage, husband and wife share power. They are equally committed to their careers, and they share domestic chores flexibly.

At present, the most common American marital arrangement is the senior-partner/junior-partner marriage. Philip Blumstein and Pepper Schwartz (1983) point out that this type of marriage is efficient (decision-making takes less time when one person has the final say) and may be the easiest for most people to maintain, given the fact that marital expectations have long been based on male-female inequality. Many of the couples in Blumstein and Schwartz's study who were striving to create equal-partner marriages in the early 1980s felt they were fighting an uphill battle. Yet when spouses do manage to achieve a roughly equal balance of power in decision making, marital satisfaction is high (Gray-Little & Burks, 1983).

Whatever their form, modern marriages often have heavy burdens placed on them. Over the last century, extended families have become rare, and in many places, people barely know their neighbors. As a result, the nuclear family must handle alone (or with paid help) responsibilities that were once carried out with the help of others, including childcare, caring for ill family members, the creation of a social life, and the providing of emotional intimacy. When dissatisfaction exists in a marriage, it may be due not to the inadequacies or selfishness of the partners, but to the size and weight of the demands they must meet.

SEXUAL SATISFACTION   Is marital sex as satisfying as most people hope it will be? That depends on what you mean by satisfaction. We already saw that in adolescents, behavior and feelings are sometimes at odds. The same is sometimes true of their elders.

It is clear that over the past half century, sexual behavior within marriage has changed, and most people would say for the better. Married people appear to be having sex more frequently than they once did, although not all studies agree on this point. As we saw in Chapter 9, sexual activity also lasts longer than it used to, with the largest changes having occurred among working-class couples. The Playboy survey (Hunt, 1974) found that married people were having sex more "imaginatively" and "voluptuously" than in previous decades: they used a greater variety of positions and techniques, and were much more likely to have oral-genital sex. A large majority of the respondents said that sex was "mostly" to "very" pleasurable.

We might conclude, as did Morton Hunt in the Playboy study, that sexual liberation has "had its greatest effect, at least in numerical terms, within the safe confines of the ancient and established institution of monogamous marriage."

Tying the knot *In every culture there are rituals and ceremonies to formally mark the beginning of marriage. Shown here are a Cambodian wedding (upper-left), a civil marriage at New York City Hall (upper-right), a Hindu wedding (lower-left), and a Moroccan wedding (lower-right).*

There is only one problem: if the marriage bed is as happy a place as Hunt said it is, sex therapists would be going hungry; in actuality their business is brisk. To understand this paradox, we must once again move beyond behavioral statistics to the exploration of motives, emotions, and attributions of meanings.

One of the few in-depth studies to explore married people's feelings about sex was done by sociologist Lillian Rubin during the mid-1970s (L. Rubin, 1976). She interviewed 50 working-class and 25 professional middle-class couples. Her findings stand in stark contrast to those of the Playboy survey: every single couple reported problems in sexual adjustment.

To be sure, these married people were less inhibited than their parents had been. Most of the men wanted their wives to be sexually free and open-minded. But at the same time the working-class men expected a certain naivete. Their wives seemed to sense this ambivalence, for they often mentioned that their husbands had taught them everything they knew about sex—even in cases where the wife had been previously married. Working-class women seemed reluctant to relax their restraints for fear of appearing cheap, and these fears were not entirely without foundation. Although their husbands urged them to take the initiative sometimes, when the women did so they risked being accused of aggressiveness and lack of femininity. Thus working-class women found themselves in an impossible double bind. (Middle-class husbands were less likely to send such mixed messages to their wives.)

Most of the working-class men in this study expressed concern if their wives did not experience orgasm. But this concern, according to Rubin, seemed to spring from the men's need for confirmation of their competence as lovers rather than from sensitivity to their wives' needs. As a result, many of the women experienced what men have known all too well: performance pressure. They viewed the requirement to have an orgasm as just one more demand to fulfill, for someone else's sake.

According to Rubin, many of these couples' problems reflected a failure to communicate about sex. But some husbands and wives had trouble understanding one another even when they did talk, because they attributed different purposes to sex. One wife could not understand how her husband could be ready for sex at bedtime when they had hardly spoken for several days or had just had a fight. The husband felt that his request for sex was an expression of love and he was angry when his wife was unresponsive. The wife complained that although her husband spoke of making love, it didn't feel like love to her. Rubin believes that the husband's desire for sex was not simply an urge for sexual release, but was the result of a socialization process that discourages male expression of emotion in all areas but sex. In contrast, according to Rubin, the woman's plea for love independent of sex seemed to stem from a socialization process that encourages female emotional expression in all areas *except* sexual expression. (You might say that Rubin's couples were Gagnon and Simon's adolescents, grown up.)

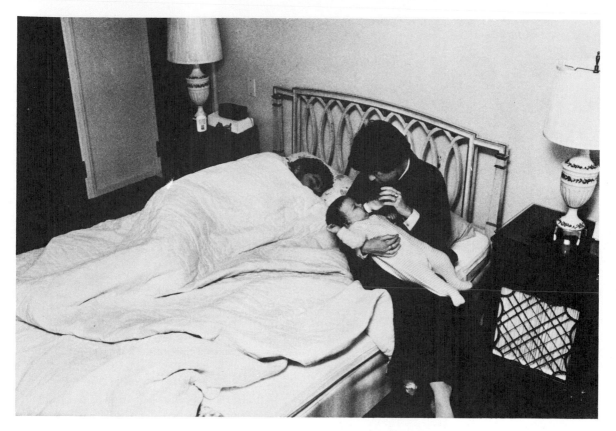

Two decades later, it is possible that men and women are better able to transcend the narrow gender roles Rubin described, increasing their chances for mutual understanding and thus for sexual satisfaction. But sexual satisfaction is a complicated thing. Happily married couples usually say they have a good sex life; no doubt a good relationship enhances sex, and good sex enhances a relationship. Yet good sex does not *guarantee* marital bliss; couples who are not emotionally close sometimes say their sex life is fine. Nor does a happy marriage guarantee great sex; in many successful unions, some of the zing goes out of sex with the passage of time (see Box 13–1). Married life can be satisfying with little or no sex, and miserable with lots of it, depending on the people and the circumstances. The feelings of a couple about sex, and their agreement on its place in their lives, are what count. Long-married couples are usually content with their sex lives, but few name sex as a major reason for their happiness in the relationship. Most see sex as just one aspect of a successful marriage, along with understanding, friendship, and respect (Lauer & Lauer, 1986).

And baby makes three
The arrival of a child inevitably changes a couple's relationship. For example, sex is likely to become less spontaneous when children are around. The ultimate effect of children on a relationship will depend on how well the couple adapts to change and whether they are able to make time for one another.

Extramarital Sex

People seem to find extramarital sex tantalizing even as they publicly condemn it. In novels like Leo Tolstoy's *Anna Karenina* or Gustave

BOX 13–1

Monogamy and Monotony

A problem that can crop up in marriage, or in any long-term sexual relationship, is sexual boredom. Sexologists have not yet done much research on this problem, but if popular magazines are any indication, boredom in the bedroom is fairly common. Magazine covers are always promising to help readers pep up their sex lives. Our own students often want to know what to do about a sexual relationship that is getting dull.

One probable cause of boredom is predictability. Any activity that always occurs at the same time, in the same place, in the same way, can become stale after a while. Once the challenge of conquest is over and people feel secure about a partner's affection and loyalty, they may get lazy about the courtship aspects of love and sex. The maneuvers and preparations that were once a kind of psychological foreplay to sex may become a thing of the past.

But predictability is not the whole story. Long-term relationships by their very nature lack the kinds of challenges, frustrations, and obstacles that can add zest to a new relationship (see Chapter 8). And sexual boredom may also be part of a more general boredom with life or with one's partner. Part of the exhilaration of a new relationship comes from finding out about the other person, peeling back the layers of his or her personality until you discover the hidden parts that others are not privileged to see. But suppose that after a few years of marriage or cohabitation two people have settled into the proverbial rut, seeing the same friends, watching the same TV shows, doing the same work at their jobs. A partner who complains that "there is no mystery anymore" may be telling the simple truth.

Some people try to cure sexual boredom by finding a new partner. This strategy may produce the desired results in the short run, but it is dangerous. As the text points out, if a couple has an agreement to

Flaubert's *Madame Bovary*, the reader is torn between sympathy for the adulterous heroine and recognition that her act is destined to bring misery to all concerned, including herself. (Anna ultimately throws herself in front of a train; Madame Bovary dies an excruciating death after drinking poison.) Even in Victorian times, when monogamy was the unquestioned standard, stories about straying husbands and wives were staples of popular culture—and a look at contemporary television soap operas indicates that they still are.

The insistence on monogamy in our society is not typical of all cultures. In their survey of preliterate societies, Ford and Beach (1951) found that fewer than one-sixth of the 185 societies studied had an absolute restriction on monogamy. The rest permitted some form of polygamy (multiple

remain monogamous, a secret fling may pose a serious threat to their relationship. Also, recent findings challenge the assumption that "the more the merrier" when it comes to sex partners, at least for women. A comparison of women who had had one lifetime sex partner with women who had had a few partners (2 to 5) or many (6 or more) failed to find any differences in reported levels of physiological or psychological sexual satisfaction (Davidson & Darling, 1988).

Then what is the solution to sexual monotony? The answer no doubt depends on the cause. If people are bored because they are too inhibited to enjoy a varied sex life, then they might want to work on overcoming those inhibitions, with or without professional help (see Chapter 11). If sex always occurs every Saturday at nine o'clock, a couple might consider trying out different places and times. If sexual monotony is a symptom of boredom with life, the answer might be to stop worrying about sex and instead expand one's personal horizons, by getting a new hobby, taking an adult education course, or making a commitment to a political or social cause. When people grow intellectually and emotionally, they become more stimulating for others to be with, and more interesting to themselves as well. In other words, if you want to avoid boredom, don't be boring!

Monotony in monogamy is not inevitable. Several decades ago humanist psychologist Abraham Maslow (1954) noted that self-actualizing individuals, people who are creative and who are doing what they want to do in life, commonly say their sex lives are improving all the time. Their sensual and physical satisfactions increase as they become more familiar with a partner and more emotionally attached. Sexual happiness, as Maslow observed, need not depend on novelty. It is inextricably bound up with the way a person responds to what life has to offer: with apathy or enthusiasm, detachment or delight.

spouses), although the majority of people did not necessarily take advantage of this opportunity. Between two- and three-fifths of the societies allowed some freedom to engage in extramarital liaisons, although typically there were strict rules about when and with whom one could have such liaisons. In some cultures extramarital sex was formalized in some way and recognized more or less openly, while in others there was tacit approval as long as the participants were discreet.

Americans' attitudes about extramarital sex depend on who is involved. They are tolerant (not to mention curious) about the sexual affairs of music and movie stars, but they may not abide adultery in a religious leader or politician. In the late 1980s, the indiscretions of Democratic presidential

Charismatic cad
Americans have ambivalent feelings about extramarital sex. The character of J. R. on Dallas—*the personification of the middle-aged playboy—arouses in viewers a mixture of feelings, including disapproval, fascination, and perhaps a little envy.*

candidate Gary Hart cost him the nomination, and those of evangelist Jimmy Bakker cost him his ministry. Sex surveys consistently find that Americans are fairly tolerant of extramarital sex in the abstract, but not for their own spouses. This is as true for young people as for older ones.

Extramarital sex provides us with another example of the belief-behavior gap (see Chapter 1). Although most married Americans do not endorse adultery, many of them stray at least once. Kinsey, who felt that his subjects were not altogether open about their extramarital sex, estimated that about half the husbands and a quarter of the wives in his studies had had intercourse with someone other than their spouses by the age of forty. Since then, the incidence of extramarital sex appears to have increased, especially among women (although most studies have been on limited samples). Gail Wyatt, Stefanie Peters, and Donald Guthrie (1988), studying a group of women aged 18 to 36, found that 37 percent had had extramarital sex compared to the 15 percent Kinsey found among women in this age bracket. The increase was particularly evident among women with a high school education or less. A decline in the double standard, increased contact between men and women in the workplace, and the availability of effective birth control may all have contributed to a general increase in extramarital sex among women, and women may soon "catch up" to men, if they have not already done so.

But statistics can only tell us so much about extramarital sex. What motivates married people to seek another lover? One possibility is sexual boredom and the desire for sexual variety, as we discussed in Box 13–1. But as Hunt (1974) pointed out, some of the gratifications of an affair may not be strictly sexual. An individual may want to experience the excitement of doing something forbidden, prove sexual desirability, recover a lost capacity for romantic love, or get even with a spouse. Comparing monogamous with non-monogamous couples, Blumstein and Schwartz (1983) found no evidence that non-monogamous spouses have less marital sex, are less happy with their sex lives, or are even less happy with their marriages. But they do seem less certain that their relationships will last. Blumstein and Schwartz conclude that bad feelings about a marital relationship will not necessarily propel people into extramarital affairs; the critical factor is a lack of commitment to a future with one's spouse.

Extramarital sex often means something different to women than men. Blumstein and Schwartz (1983) found that a woman was more likely than a man to be emotionally as well as sexually involved. Men searched for variety more often than women did and had more extramarital partners, while women tended to want a special relationship. According to Blumstein and Schwartz, "Men are conditioned to find outside sex more appealing, yet their ability to seal off such experiences emotionally means these encounters are of diminished significance."

CONSENSUAL EXTRAMARITAL SEX A small minority of married couples in the United States have agreed to set aside the conventional rules of sexual fidelity. Some have an **open marriage,** in which the spouses agree that both are free to have close or intimate relationships with other partners. As originally described by Nena and George O'Neill in their 1972 book, *Open Marriage,* such an arrangement is based on honesty, trust, and lack of possessiveness, and may or may not include sexual activity with other partners, depending on the agreement between the spouses. When sexual freedom is part of the arrangement, some partners agree to tell one another (sometimes in great detail) about their outside involvements. Others say, in effect, "Go ahead and do it, but I don't want to know about it."

Another type of consensual extramarital sex is **swinging,** in with both partners participate together. Swinging includes mate swapping, sex between a couple and another man or woman, and group sex, in which several people interact sexually. Swingers find each other in several ways: through advertisements in magazines and swingers' publications, introductions at bars and parties, and personal references from other swingers (Bartell, 1970). Open marriages are probably more common than swinging marriages. In their sample of over 3,500 couples, Blumstein & Schwartz (1983) found that in fifteen percent both partners had "an understanding that allows non-monogamy under some circumstances." But in Hunt's 1974 sample only about two percent had ever participated in mate swapping, and many of them had only one such experience. Group sex was as rare, or rarer.

No matter what the particular provisions for consensual extramarital sex, Blumstein & Schwartz (1983) found that couples always had limits that made outside sex predictable and allayed fears and insecurities that might threaten the marriage. Some rules were aimed at preventing the outside affair from affecting the welfare of the other partner (not spending money on someone else, not bringing home a sexually transmitted disease). Other rules had to do with discretion (keeping the affair from the neighbors or children) or, most important, safeguarding the emotional primacy of the marital relationship (never having sex in the couple's bed, never seeing the same person twice, never having sex with a mutual friend.) Yet only a few of the married couples in this study who had open relationships or engaged in swinging did so without running into complications.

IS IT WORTH IT? To enjoy the benefits of monogamy, people must deliberately choose to forgo certain sexual opportunities (see Chapter 8). Those who have extramarital sex decide not to make these sacrifices. What is the result of this decision?

Philip Blumstein and Pepper Schwartz (1983) found that most couples' lives are dramatically altered when one or both partners decide to venture outside of the relationship, particularly when the couple has previously agreed to remain monogamous. The impact depends to some extent on whether this decision results in an isolated episode or an ongoing series of encounters, a full-blown affair or a simple sexual adventure, a furtive and secret relationship or one known and acknowledged by the spouse. Whatever its form, however, infidelity is usually seen as a breach of the marriage contract and therefore tends to be experienced as a betrayal—as cheating. The person having the affair is likely to feel guilty, and the other spouse is likely to feel pain and hurt if the affair is discovered.

Those who favor extramarital sex argue that it can be a source of personal growth and increased self-esteem, and, in some cases, can even strengthen a marriage. A spouse who feels sexually, emotionally, or intellectually deprived in his or her marriage may blossom as the result of an affair. And a marriage that can encompass outside sex without breaking apart may emerge stronger for the experience. Some of our students have reported sexually open relationships that work for both partners. But Blumstein & Schwartz (1983) found that husbands and wives who had had extramarital sex were more likely than other couples to break up, no matter when the affair occurred. And another study, comparing 34 sexually open couples and 39 sexually exclusive couples, found that after five years, only about two-thirds of the open couples (as compared to 82 percent of the exclusive couples) were still together (Adams and Rubin, 1984.) Of course, it is hard to prove cause and effect. It is possible that spouses who engage in extramarital sex are simply less committed to their marriages in the first place. But it also seems likely that extramarital affairs contribute to marital breakups.

Sex After and Between Marriages

Currently there is one divorce in the U.S. for every two marriages, and the median length of marriage is only 6.8 years. Millions of adults have made a major life transition involving social and financial adjustments and changed living arrangements, because of divorce.

Divorce is not only a release from an unworkable marriage; it can be an opportunity to develop personal autonomy and strength. However, unless it has been particularly friendly, a divorce can also take a toll on a person's self-esteem. There is likely to be a period of grief and mourning, even if the end of the marriage was welcomed. Anger, guilt, feelings of relief, and the pain of rejection may all occur, sometimes simultaneously. And no matter what other feelings surface, there is almost always sadness over the dissolution of what was supposed to be "forever."

Divorced people who reenter the "sexual marketplace" have a special set of sexual problems and concerns. After years of easy access to sex, an individual who wishes to be sexually active must relearn the dating game and try to meet potential partners. As Sally Wendkos Olds (1985) points out:

> The changes in mores that took place while these people were out of the sexual search present a dizzying array of questions for people who were brought up to expect sex to exist only as part of a relationship. What is a "relationship"? The product of two dates or twenty? Does a relationship imply exclusivity? Can a man say no without losing his self-respect and the respect of the women he turns down? Can a person be a good parent and a seeker of sex at the same time? How does age affect one's desirability as a sex partner? (pp. 166–167)

The transition from marriage to dating may bring a newfound sense of sexual freedom. But it is also likely to activate ambivalence about intimacy, or anger and hurt remaining from the trauma of divorce. In an attempt to cope with these feelings, some people decide to take a vacation, at least temporarily, from intimate relationships. Others engage in superficial sexual relationships. A 35-year-old salesman forced himself to have sexual relations with women even when he had no genuine desire to do so:

Drawing by Opie © 1980 The New Yorker Magazine, Inc.

"Dearly beloved, we are gathered here yet again . . ."

It took me three years to get it through my head that I didn't have to screw every woman I took out. I used to make an all-out try with every one of them—and let me tell you, if I didn't find the gal appealing, it could be a rough trip, and afterwards I'd be furious with myself. But somehow I had to. I felt that if I didn't come on like the superstud of all time, they'd think I was a fag, or hung-up or something. (quoted in Hunt, 1974, p. 251)

Despite such problems, most divorced people do reestablish a satisfying sex life after parting from their spouses. All of the divorced men and most of the women in the Playboy study had experienced intercourse during the past year. Like never-married older adults, divorced people in the Playboy study tended to be more experimental and casual about sex than younger single people and to have had more partners within the past year.

Most divorced people—about three-fourths of divorced women and five-sixths of divorced men—remarry, about half of them within three years after their divorce (Cherlin, 1981). But middle-aged and older divorced women are at a disadvantage when it comes to remarriage, because there is a tight supply of men their age among the unattached. The problem is exacerbated by a mating pattern called "dipping." Dippers are older men, primarily divorced ones, who "dip" far down into the age pool to marry women ten or twenty— or more—years younger than they are. This pattern is common among men who choose to start a new family after a divorce; overwhelmingly they do so with women younger than their first wives.

SEX AND AGING

What is the effect of aging on sexuality? The most prevalent notion in our culture is that sex is the prerogative of the young. Many people believe that once a person reaches fifty or sixty, the spirit may be willing but the flesh is too weak for "that sort of thing." In this view, sexual interests in older people are inappropriate. In fact, however, many adults remain healthy, vigorous, and physically and sexually active well into old age.

In *The Joy of Sex* (1972), Alex Comfort pointed out that when old people do stop having sex it is for basically the same reasons they give up bicycle riding: poor health, not having a bicycle (partner), and thinking it will look silly. The attitudes of others may also deny older people their human right to sexual expression. In many nursing homes men and women are rigidly segregated except for supervised social occasions. Attendants and staff members thoughtlessly barge into rooms without knocking, forgetting that old people, too, may wish to masturbate. The institutionalized elderly are forced to sneak sex on the sly, just as teenagers do.

An alternate view holds that sexuality can be a joy for most of a person's life. This view has emerged due to efforts of activist groups like the Gray Panthers to educate the public about social discrimination against the elderly. For the most part, sex educators welcome the increasing awareness that sexuality does not suddenly stop because a person has reached fifty, sixty, or seventy. But this view, too, can be carried too far if it denies that age has *any* effect on sexual functioning, as when one of our students wrote on an exam, "Most people can continue to perform sexually just as they always have until the day they die."

The truth lies somewhere between the two extremes. People can and do continue to need sexual love and physical intimacy in old age, and some

Never too old *Young people sometimes do not realize that older people can feel sexual passion and caring. The rewards of sex are similar throughout life: physical pleasure, emotional intimacy, and a sense of connection with another human being.*

remain sexually active even into their nineties. In a study of 200 healthy men and women aged 80 to 102 living in residential retirement facilities, four-fifths of the men and two-thirds of the women reported engaging in sexual touching and caressing. Almost two-thirds of the men and one-third of the women said they had sexual intercourse at least sometimes. Many people did not answer the question on masturbation, but of those who did, three-fourths of the men and two-fifths of the women said they masturbated at least some-times (Bretschneider & McCoy, 1988). In another study, of preferred sexual activity from young adulthood to old age, only half the sample of 102 men and women aged 60 to 85 reported a change. Most of those who changed had previously enjoyed intercourse but now preferred either another activity, for example petting or masturbation, or no activity. Among unmarried women, the availability of a male partner was central to whether a change in preference was reported. Overall, in both sexes, changes were primarily related to physical factors associated with aging (Turner & Adams, 1988). Physical changes are an inevitable component of the aging process but, as we shall see, their effect on sexual functioning is not always predictable.

The Physical Changes of Aging

In both sexes, as aging occurs, changes in the hormonal system affect the body in various ways. We will examine these changes separately for women and men.

PHYSICAL CHANGES IN WOMEN At about the age of forty a woman's ovaries begin to produce less estrogen than they did previously, and ovulation may become irregular. In the late forties—but sometimes sooner and sometimes later—menstruation ceases. The ovaries atrophy, and eventually, perhaps within five years or so, they cease to produce any estrogen or progesterone. The adrenal glands continue to produce estrogen, but the overall level of the hormone in the body falls to about a sixth of what it once was. Fertility usually ceases when bleeding stops, but sometimes it continues for a year or two afterwards. The cessation of menstruation is called **menopause,** while the entire period of declining reproductive capacity is called the **climacteric.**

Menopause is associated with some temporary physical symptoms. The most frequent one is the "hot flash" (or "hot flush"). Rapid dilation of blood vessels occurs and is experienced as a rush of warmth. The woman suddenly feels hot from the waist up and may perspire heavily. Then, when the flash is over, she may feel chilled. Hot flashes are related to declining estrogen levels, but other hormones may also be involved.

Other complaints sometimes reported include headache, nausea, fatigue, heart palpitations, and backache, all of which may or may not be linked to a reduction in estrogen. Contrary to common belief, however, menopause is *not* an emotional crisis for most women. Most women do *not* experience increased depression, anxiety, or irritability. Of course, middle age can be a challenging time for women; a woman may worry about her physical attractiveness, face decisions about reentering the job market or returning to school if she has been a homemaker, or decide to reevaluate her career or job goals. But menopause is, for most women, not a major trauma.

Then where did people get the idea that it was? For many years, the only information we had on women's responses to menopause came from women who were in therapy, or women who had experienced surgically-induced menopause because of removal of their ovaries. Many of these women were depressed. But studies of women undergoing natural menopause find that typically it is "no big deal." When Bernice Neugarten (1967) asked one hundred women what changes worried them the most, only four mentioned menopause. Widowhood, getting old, fear of cancer, and having children leave home were all of greater concern. Most of the older women in this study rated menopause as more unpleasant for *other* women than for themselves, and younger women expected it to be worse than older women reported it to be. In a more recent study of 8,000 randomly selected menopausal women, a team of epidemiologists found that the vast majority had no particular feelings about menopause or viewed it as positive and liberating (because they no longer had to worry about pregnancy or have monthly periods). Only three percent of the women regretted having reached menopause (McKinlay, McKinlay & Brambilla, 1987).

What about the effects of declining estrogen levels on sexual functioning? First, the good news: there is no reason to expect declining levels of estrogen to reduce a woman's desire for sexual relations. In fact, falling estrogen levels may lead to an increase in desire because worries about pregnancy are a thing of the past and because testosterone produced by the woman's adrenal glands (which probably does increase sexual arousal) is no longer opposed by estrogen (Kaplan, 1974).

Now, the not-so-good news: the reduction of estrogen causes gradual changes in the sex organs that can interfere with enjoyment during coitus. The skin of the vulva becomes thinner and less elastic, the subcutaneous fat beneath the major lips is reduced, the vagina shrinks, and the vaginal opening becomes less elastic. These changes may make penile insertion a bit more difficult than it once was. In addition, contractions of the uterus that occur during orgasm sometimes cause pain. Most important, the reduction of estrogen causes the lining of the vagina to become less elastic, thinner, and more susceptible to abrasion, inflammation, and infection. Sometimes this results in irritation of the membranes during coitus.

Not all these symptoms occur in all women, but when they do, they can be distressing. At present a woman can choose among a number of possible solutions. She may decide to forego penile-vaginal intercourse in favor of other sources of sexual gratification. She may also consider seeking **hormone replacement therapy (HRT),** daily doses of estrogen and progesterone to replace hormones the body no longer produces in quantity. Estrogen given alone has been linked with an increased risk of endometrial cancer, but the addition of progesterone almost eliminates this risk. (Since it does this by inducing the monthly shedding of the uterine lining, monthly bleeding continues.) HRT can counteract the effects of menopause on the vaginal tissues and maintain vaginal lubrication. In addition, it reduces hot flashes and protects against *osteoporosis* ("brittle bones"), a disease that can lead to life-threatening bone fractures (Ettinger, 1988). However, HRT is not without risks. One concern is a possible link to breast cancer (Adami et al., 1989; Doress, Siegal et al., 1987), at least when estrogen is taken alone (see Chapter 18). HRT can also aggravate certain medical conditions, such as high blood pressure. Critics remain wary of the routine prescribing of HRT, because over the past half century the administration of estrogen for nonmenopausal reasons (e.g., DES to prevent miscarriage) has had many unforeseen consequences and side effects (Tavris, forthcoming).

Women without a family history of osteoporosis who are experiencing temporary symptoms of menopause might consider using HRT on a short-term basis, then tapering off (under a doctor's supervision). Another alternative, for alleviating vaginal dryness and discomfort, is to apply a topical estrogen cream directly to the vagina. Topical administration does not alleviate other symptoms of menopause, but it also does not carry the possible risks of orally administered HRT. Some women may find that using a non-hormonal lubricant is sufficient for alleviating vaginal discomfort. As with all medical decisions, a woman should inform herself as fully as possible about her options, discuss them with her medical practitioner, consider her personal and family medical history, and then make her own choice.

Finally, age also brings certain changes in the sexual response cycle. For example, lubrication begins more slowly and is reduced in quantity and there are fewer contractions during orgasm. But such changes do not prevent a woman from enjoying sexual activity. According to Hite (1976), most women—including many in their sixties and seventies—who answered her questions about age felt that their sexual pleasure had actually increased with the years. Sexual activity itself, in fact, seems to slow many of the physical effects of aging in women. Changes such as loss of tissue elasticity and reduction in mucous membranes are less pronounced in women who are sexually active through intercourse or masturbation than in women who are sexually inactive (Leiblum et al., 1983). Although it's hard to be certain of cause and effect, the moral may be: "Use it or lose it."

PHYSICAL CHANGES IN MEN   Just as estrogen declines with age in women, testosterone declines in men. The fall of male testosterone levels probably occurs because of a reduction in the number of androgen-producing cells in the testes. But the slope of the decline is much less abrupt than it is for estrogen in females, and the experts disagree on when it begins. Some researchers believe that after the age of twenty or so it is all downhill for testosterone production, at least until age sixty, when the drop appears to level off. Others believe the decline does not begin until the thirties, forties, or even fifties. In any case, unlike women, men don't lose their fertility in middle age.

Middle age can be a difficult time for a man in a society that makes a fetish of youth. A man may suddenly realize that he is never going to fulfill the ambitions of earlier years. He may look at his spreading middle and his receding hairline and start to doubt his physical—and especially his sexual—attractiveness. He may discover that his children are about to move out just as he has decided to get to know them better. As he looks around him, he sees men of his own age having heart attacks and strokes, and he must face the spectre of his own mortality. The result can be an emotional crisis in which the man questions everything he has done, while having to come to terms with the limited possibilities for real change, given the reduced job opportunities available to older people in our society. (The importance of cultural factors is indicated by the fact that these problems appear to be nonexistent in societies that honor and reward old age: see Lear, 1973.) In addition to all this, a man may worry about his ability to function sexually. After all, testosterone is ebbing. Is there any truth in all those nasty jokes about dirty old men?

It is true that in men, just as in women, hormonal changes produce physical changes in the body. In some (but not all) men the testes become smaller. The scrotal skin becomes thinner and less elastic and does not get as congested during arousal as it once did. Seminal fluid may become thinner, and less of it may be produced. Sperm count may decline and sperm may become less lively (though there is debate about this). As men grow older the prostate gland tends to enlarge and may put pressure on the urethra, causing decreased urine flow. It is not uncommon for aging men to develop benign or malignant tumors of the prostate, and surgical and hormonal treatments for prostate cancer may cause some problems in sexual functioning (see Chapter 18). There are also some normal changes in the sexual response cycle. Erections occur more slowly, there are fewer contractions during orgasm, ejaculation is less forceful, and the refractory period lengthens.

Although there are many exceptions, in general, frequency of erection declines with age. Indeed, in most men it falls off gradually from about the age of twenty. Although most endocrinologists believe that the decline is related in some way to the fall of testosterone, a direct cause-and-effect relationship has never been proven. Do men whose frequency falls off most sharply also experience the steepest decline in hormone production? We do not know. Many nonhormonal factors could also cause sexual interest and ability to wane, including poor health, changes in the central nervous system, stress, fatigue, and preoccupation with other concerns. In any case, the physical effects of aging do not prevent men from enjoying sex, any more than they prevent women from doing so. Most surveys of married men indicate that most men over sixty-five can and do continue to have intercourse regularly.

According to Masters and Johnson (1966), a man's sexual history, like a woman's, affects his level of sexual activity in later years. "The most important factor in the maintenance of effective sexuality for the aging male," they write, "is consistency of active sexual expression." In the Kinsey study (1948) the younger a man began sexual activity, the more likely he was to be active at age fifty. Again, proving cause and effect is difficult. But at the very least, it is clear that people do not have to worry about conserving their sexual energy the way nations need to save fossil fuels.

Young at heart   *As the number of middle-aged divorced people increases and the population ages, our ideas about sexuality across the life span are changing. These middle-aged singles are enjoying themselves at a singles dance sponsored by a suburban Connecticut church.*

Probably the one thing an aging man does have to fear is fear itself. Some older men say that although it takes longer for them to get an erection, they have better control over ejaculation—a distinct advantage both for them and for their partners. But many men perceive the penis as a sexual barometer—the faster it rises, the better the forecast. If erection takes a little longer, they say "This is it. I'm old, I'm going downhill, I might as well give up." In short order, their negative expectations may interfere with performance and result in a self-fulfilling prophecy.

Cultural Barriers to Sexuality in Old Age

American culture glorifies youth; no wonder people sometimes expect old age and even middle age to be sexless. Countless media messages tell us daily that youth and beauty equal sexiness, and people with wrinkles, gray hair, or age spots need not apply. The bias against age is especially hard on women, whose physical qualities have been an important attribute in the sexual bargaining that has taken place historically. Of course, there are older

Quest for perfection
Role models like Jane Fonda have inspired millions of people to improve their physical fitness, which everyone agrees is beneficial. But images of sexy, youthful-looking older people can also be intimidating, because most of us cannot hope to look like Jane Fonda (or Robert Redford). At what point does the equation of sex appeal with perpetual youth become an exercise in frustration?

women who are admired for their looks—Joan Collins, Jane Fonda, Lena Horne, Raquel Welch and many others. However, these older women are seen as attractive precisely because they do not "look old"; they appear to be much younger than their age.

The "marriage squeeze" becomes particularly acute for women in old age, not only because they are "losing their looks" but because men tend to die earlier than women do. For every ten women over 65 there are fewer than seven men. For every 50 widows there are only about 13 widowers.

Another barrier to sexual expression for both sexes in middle and old age is the opposition of their grown children. Grown children frequently oppose remarriage of a parent, thinking it ridiculous. It is a curious irony that the same parents who may have refused to acknowledge their children's sexuality may find the tables turned in their old age.

But old age need not be a sexual wasteland. Sexual response may slow down a bit, but in the immortal words of Abigail Van Buren, "Dear Abby," "Just because you can no longer Charleston all night doesn't mean you can't waltz for an hour." As in all stages of life, individual preferences exist. Some older people happily continue to enjoy a lusty sex life for as long as they live. Some welcome age as an excuse for withdrawing from sexual activity, though not necessarily from affection. And some gradually settle into a slower, gentler sexual pace or replace intercourse with other sexual activities (Turner & Adams, 1988). Poet Robert Browning passionately voiced the possibilities of old age when he wrote,

Grow old along with me!
The best is yet to be,
The last of life, for which the first was made.

· ·

THE FIRST TIME

Whether the first experience with intercourse is profound or awkward, it is an event very few of us will forget. But it is only one of many milestones that mark sexual development in adolescence and adulthood. Dozens of biological, psychological, and social events divide our sex lives into "before" and "after." Sometimes we are keenly aware of having crossed some boundary forever; for instance, there is no returning to virginity. In other cases we do not realize until later that our lives have taken a different direction or that we have been changed by the experience.

Our "first times" can fill us with excitement, apprehension, confusion, fear, ecstasy, or a jumble of different emotions. This exercise asks you to step back and take stock of the sexual milestones in your life and your reactions to them. First you will focus on where you have been, then on where you might be going. Putting your sex life in a developmental perspective—seeing sex as a lifelong venture—may allay sexual anxieties. It may also help you appreciate the truth of the old saying, "Practice makes perfect."

Part A. *Up until now...*

With the discussion in this chapter as a guide, begin by recalling events and relationships from your youth, adolescence, and adulthood that you consider personal sexual milestones. Group your memories into

- *biological events* (for example, the first time you menstruated, had an erection or ejaculation, or had an orgasm)

- *behaviors* (for example the first time you kissed, made love, masturbated, or used birth control)

- *people and relationships* (for example, the first person you kissed, had oral sex with, or fell in love with)

Part B. *From now on...*

Now, recalling the discussion of adulthood and aging from this chapter, think about events and perhaps relationships that you anticipate will mark your future sexual development. Include

- *biological events* (for example, menopause, changes in health, or signs of aging)

- *behaviors* (for example, sexual activities you have not tried, periods of celibacy, or changes in birth control practices)

- *people and relationships* (for example, marriage or remarriage, divorce, or new partners and relationships)

In Part A, how did past milestones affect your emotional or sexual development? Which ones still seem important, and which ones have faded in significance? In considering the past, you may uncover some painful experiences, some funny ones (although they may not have been so funny at the time), some embarrassing moments, some poignant recollections. How were you affected by these experiences at the time they occurred, and how do you feel about them now? Feelings, both good and bad, are a part of life. Ask yourself whether you have accepted that what happened, happened . . . and cannot be changed.

In Part B, what do your expectations of the future tell you about your attitudes toward middle and old age? Do you feel gloomy or optimistic about the future? Can you see yourself as a sexual person in old age? (If not, where and when do you think your sexuality will diminish or disappear?) Can you imagine yourself feeing sexual passion with an older partner? Most important, how might the way you are presently living your life affect your sexual future?

IN BRIEF

1. *Puberty* is the period of life when a person's reproductive organs mature. Girls experience breast growth, the appearance of pubic and underarm hair, and the onset of menstruation (*menarche*). Boys experience growth of the penis and testes, the appearance of pubic, underarm, and facial hair, deepening of the voice, and the first ejaculation. Usually menarche and first ejaculation are positive events, but if a young person is unprepared for these experiences they may be upsetting, worrisome, or confusing.

2. Masturbation provides most people with their first experience of orgasm, but boys are more likely to masturbate during adolescence than girls are, for reasons that may be both physical and cultural. Gagnon and Simon argue that this sex difference and cultural "scripts" foster a concern with genital sexuality in males and the social and emotional aspects of sex in females.

3. American adolescents have always been permitted a certain amount of sexual contact, but beginning in the 1960s, the incidence of intercourse increased dramatically, especially among girls. By the early 1980s, a majority of both sexes were having intercourse by age 19, with only a small gender gap remaining. A large change also occurred in teenagers' experience with oral-genital sex.

4. The view that premarital sex is acceptable if it is an expression of love or affection is widely accepted among American adolescents. However,

increased acceptance of intercourse by both sexes does not mean that the double standard is dead. Sex differences remain in sexual feelings, attitudes, and motives, and most teenagers continue to play traditional roles in dating and in the initiation of sex.

5. The use of birth control among teenagers has increased in recent years, but many adolescents, especially younger ones, do not use effective contraception or use it only sporadically, and teenage pregnancy rates continue to be high. Most unmarried teenage mothers who do not have an abortion choose to keep their babies, and most raise them alone. For many of these mothers, pregnancy triggers a downward spiral, educationally and financially, for both themselves and their children.

6. American teenagers get pregnant without wanting to for a variety of reasons, including ignorance about conception, feelings of invulnerability, the sporadic nature of their sex lives, difficulty in acknowledging their own sexuality, embarrassment about discussing contraception with a partner, difficulty in setting goals, and a desire for a child as an answer to personal problems. However, the causes go beyond the personal and psycholgical. Teenage pregnancy rates are higher in the U.S. than in almost any other developed country, despite similar rates of sexual activity, in part because other countries have policies that permit teenagers easier access to contraception.

7. The average age of marriage is higher than it was a few decades ago, and today most people in their early twenties are still single. There is no typical single person or single lifestyle. Most unmarried people feel they are single as a matter of choice rather than because of chance or uncontrollable circumstances. Satisfaction with singlehood is common, but singles also mention certain problems, such as loneliness and the "dating grind."

8. Cohabitation has increased dramatically in the U.S. since 1970. Some cohabiting couples want to try out living together before "tying the knot," some move in together without any intention of marrying but then change their minds, and some are dedicated to remaining unmarried. Research finds that most cohabiting couples eventually marry or break up, but much of this research has focused only on younger couples. Cohabiting can meet people's needs for sex, companionship, and emotional security, but it also has certain social and legal drawbacks. There is no evidence that cohabiting before marriage either increases or decreases the chances of subsequent marital happiness.

9. Most adults marry at least once. Modern marriages usually take one of three forms: *head-complement, senior-partner/junior-partner, and equal-partner,* with the second type currently most common. Sexual behavior in marriage has become more frequent and varied than it was in

Kinsey's time, and most married couples say sex is pleasurable. However, research done in the 1970s suggests that feelings do not always match behavior, at least among working-class couples. Husbands and wives sometimes attach different meanings to sex, as Gagnon and Simon's theory of sexual development might predict.

10. Extramarital sex provides a good example of the "belief-behavior gap." Although most married Americans do not endorse extramarital sex, many of them have experienced it at least once. Kinsey found that half of all husbands and a quarter of all wives had an extramarital affair before age 40, and since then the incidence appears to have increased, especially among women. People seek an outside lover for many reasons, not all of them sexual. Women seem more likely than men to become emotionally as well as sexually involved with an extramarital partner. A small minority of couples have agreed to engage in consensual extramarital sex. But extramarital sex tends to be seen as a betrayal, and it is associated with an increased probability of a breakup.

11. Millions of Americans have experienced divorce. Divorced people have a special set of sexual problems and concerns when they reenter the sexual "marketplace." Dating may bring a newfound sense of sexual freedom, but may also activate ambivalence about intimacy, or negative feelings remaining from the trauma of divorce. Nonetheless, most divorced people reestablish a satisfying sex life within a relatively short period of time, and most remarry.

12. During menopause, estrogen levels in women decline and fertility ceases. Certain uncomfortable physical symptoms may occur, most notably "hot flashes." But contrary to common belief, menopause is not an emotional crisis for most women. After menopause, sexual arousal does not usually decrease, but thinning of the vaginal walls and other changes may cause some discomfort during intercourse. Many women seek hormone replacement therapy at or after menopause but HRT has some risks and a woman should inform herself fully before making a decision.

13. Male testosterone levels fall off with age, but men, unlike women, do not suddenly lose their fertility. Aging in men is associated with changes in the testes and scrotum, a thinning of the seminal fluid, and an increased risk of prostate problems. Erections tend to occur more slowly, ejaculation is less forceful, the refractory period tends to lengthen, and the frequency of erections may decline. However, none of these changes need prevent a man from continuing to enjoy sexual activity.

14. The glorification of youth, and the associating of sexuality with youth, can discourage sexual activity in older people. Age can be particularly hard on women, who often have trouble finding partners. But old age need not be a sexual wasteland; sexual love, expressed in a variety of ways, can be a source of joy at all stages of adult life.

Key Terms

puberty *(474)*

secondary sex characteristics *(474)*

breast buds *(475)*

menarche *(475)*

nocturnal emissions *(478)*

teenage pregnancy *(487)*

cohabitation *(494)*

head-complement marriage *(496)*

senior-partner/junior-partner marriage *(496)*

equal-partner marriage *(496)*

open marriage *(503)*

swinging *(504)*

menopause *(509)*

climacteric *(509)*

hormone replacement therapy (HRT) *(510)*

CHAPTER FOURTEEN

■

Sexual Orientation

•

The Great Society can only be as great as its people, and the people can only be great [if] they know, appreciate, love, understand and express their diversity....

**Del Martin and
Phyllis Lyon**

I f you are a heterosexual, try imagining what life would be like in a culture that condemned sexual love between men and women. In such a culture, you might work hard to keep your lover's identity hidden from your parents and friends. When out with your partner, you might worry about running into someone who was not supposed to know about your relationship. At work or at home, you might hesitate to display a picture of your partner. You might pretend to be romantically interested in the same sex and deny any interest in the other one. You might keep quiet when your friends gossiped about their romantic involvements instead of boasting, seeking advice, or praising the object of your affections, like everyone else.

Heterosexism, prejudice and discrimination against homosexuals, is pervasive in our culture and colors the thinking of many, if not most, people—liberals as well as conservatives, social scientists as well as lay people, and sometimes even homosexual people themselves. Although open hatred toward lesbians and gays is no longer as socially acceptable as it once was, feelings of suspicion, discomfort, and contempt remain. Movies still make fun of homosexuality; people still refer to homosexuals disparagingly as "queers," "faggots," or "dykes." Even heterosexuals who consider themselves free of prejudice often have a bias to see the world in solely heterosexual terms; for example, they may assume that everyone they meet is "straight."

To be sure, gay men and lesbians have made great strides during the past few years in their quest for civil and human rights. The Federal government no longer denies employment to job applicants solely because of sexual orientation, as it once did. Many national and international corporations now have policies forbidding discrimination against homosexuals in hiring or promotion. More lesbians and gays than ever are refusing to stay "in the closet" about their sexual orientation; fear of homosexuality, they point out, is a heterosexual problem, not a homosexual one. Congress now has two openly gay members (as of 1990), and gays and lesbians serve in many state and local political offices. In the 1980s, in Bunceton, Missouri (population 419), Mayor Gene Ulrich won reelection with an 88 to 6 victory. His 11-year relationship with his male lover was accepted so matter-of-factly that the two were given a married couple's discount when they joined the chamber of commerce (Shilts, 1984).

Yet true acceptance seems far off. Many people, including military personnel, still lose their jobs solely because of their sexual orientation. In many places, landlords can legally refuse to rent to gay and lesbian tenants. Homosexual parents often lose custody of their children, despite extensive evidence that they are as good at parenting as anyone else. Although some religious denominations welcome homosexual members, ordain lesbians and gays as ministers, and endorse lesbian and gay rights, others harshly con-

A gay war hero   *In 1975 Leonard Matlovich, a highly decorated Air Force sergeant and Viet Nam veteran, publicly acknowledged his homosexuality and was promptly discharged. He is shown here standing next to his own tombstone, for which he wrote this inscription: "When I was in the military they gave me a medal for killing two men and a discharge for loving one." Matlovich died in 1988 of AIDS.*

demn homosexuality. Pope John Paul II has said that when laws are passed protecting "behavior to which no one has a conceivable right," people should not be surprised when "irrational and violent reactions increase." In 1989, delegates representing 14.7 million Southern Baptists declared homosexuality to be a "perversion of divine standards and a violation of nature and of natural affections."

Prevailing attitudes often find expression in legal codes. Twenty-four states and the District of Columbia have "sodomy" laws on the books prohibiting "crimes against nature" (Press et al., 1986). Although the wording of these laws is often vague, they are usually interpreted as encompassing oral-genital and anal sex and they are usually enforced only against homosexuals. Penalities range up to 20 years in prison (in Georgia and Rhode Island). In a 1986 case involving a Georgia statute (*Hardwick v. Bowers*), the U.S. Supreme Court ruled 5 to 4 that states may outlaw sexual acts between homosexuals, even when those acts are practiced by consenting adults in their own homes. One of the justices writing for the majority specifically stated that constitutional protections of privacy enjoyed by heterosexuals do not necessarily extend to homosexuals, even when the acts involved are the same. The court cited the "ancient roots" of prohibitions against homosexuality—an argument, critics were quick to point out, that could also be used to justify slavery or animal sacrifice.

Because gay and lesbian couples cannot legally marry, they miss out on inheritance rights, alimony rights, tax benefits, insurance benefits, and other "next of kin" privileges. Consider what happened when a drunk driver crashed into Sharon Kowalski's car in 1983, leaving her brain damaged, without speech, and able to move only her right hand. After the accident, Sharon's partner, Karen Thompson, drew on her professional skills as a professor of physical education to help Sharon learn to sip from a glass, comb her hair, and communicate with a typewriter. But when Karen revealed that she and Sharon had been lovers for many years, Sharon's father petitioned for and won full guardianship of his daughter, then refused to let the two women see each other. Only after years of costly legal battles did Karen finally regain the right to visit her life partner.

Clearly **sexual orientation,** one's orientation towards partners of the same or the other sex, affects more than simply sexual behavior. In this chapter, we will focus primarily on the impact of homosexuality, simply because most research on sexual orientation has been on this topic. Keep in mind, however, that most questions about homosexuality can also be asked of heterosexuality: Why does it occur? How does it develop? How does it affect self-concept and a person's sense of identity? How is it expressed in love and sex? As you read, take a look at your own assumptions and see if you can identify any mistaken impressions or unsupported notions about sexual orientation that might be lurking around in the back of your mind. Ask yourself: How does you own sexual orientation influence who you are in the world?

Tragic case   *This photo shows Karen Thompson (on the left) and her life partner Sharon Kowalski, before Sharon was severely disabled in a car accident. After the accident Karen had to fight for the right to see her companion. Lesbians and gay men are often denied rights heterosexuals take for granted.*

THE VOCABULARY OF SEXUAL ORIENTATION: WHAT'S IN A NAME?

At the outset, a few words on terminology are in order. According to the dictionary, the term **heterosexual** describes anyone who is sexually attracted primarily to people of the other sex, whereas **homosexual** describes anyone who is attracted primarily to same-sex partners. In actual usage, *homosexual* is sometimes used only for males, possibly because of the widespread but erroneous belief that the prefix *homo* comes from the Latin for "man" (as in *homo sapiens*), when in fact it derives from the Greek for "the same" (as in *homogeneous* and *homonym*). In this chapter, we follow common usage in scientific writing and use both *heterosexual* and *homosexual* for both men and women.

Gay is widely used as a synonym for homosexual, with *straight* the corresponding synonym for heterosexual. The term *gay* has been around for decades, but its origins are obscure. To many politically active people, *gay* seems more positive than *homosexual*, in the same way that *black* or *African-American* is more positive than Negro and *woman* is more positive than *lady*. "*Gay*," writes psychologist Stephen F. Morin (1977), "is proud, angry, open, visible, political, healthy, and all the positive things that *homosexual* is not."

In practice, *gay*, like homosexual, is often understood to refer specifically to men. Indeed, the current practice among many homosexual people is to reserve *gay* for men and to use **lesbian** for women. Using a single term for both sexes, they note, may falsely imply that homosexual men and women are alike simply by virtue of their sexual orientation. Also, the ambiguous use of *gay* to refer either to all homosexual people or only to men tends to make lesbians invisible, just as the use of "he" to refer either to a male or to a person whose gender has been unspecified tends to make women in general invisible. Accordingly, in this chapter we use *gay* specifically for men and *lesbian* for women. (*Lesbian* derives from Lesbos, a Greek island where in ancient times the female poet Sappho ran a sort of finishing school for girls. Although Sappho was married and had a child, her few surviving poems suggest that her greatest passion was for women.)

Bisexual is a term used to describe a person who is attracted to both sexes. Some people use the word only for people who are about equally attracted to men and women; others use it for anyone who does not have an exclusive attraction to one sex or the other. As we will see, by this second, broader definition, many people are bisexual. Researchers have often classified as gay or lesbian people who might better be called bisexual.

Like all socially-defining labels, the various terms associated with sexual orientation—homosexual, gay, lesbian, bisexual, heterosexual, straight—tend to distort our perceptions of individuals by implying a uniformity that does not exist. Homosexuals make up one of the most diverse minorities in American society, one that cuts across socioeconomic, racial, political, and professional lines. And for homosexuals, as for heterosexuals, sexuality is only one part of life. As Evelyn Hooker, a pioneering researcher on homosexuality, once put it in an interview:

> We like things in nice neat packages, so we stereotype all groups. But the world isn't that simple. Chicanos, blacks and Jews have the same range of characteristics and concerns that other people have. So do homosexuals. They aren't *just* homosexuals...they also read books, paint, go to the movies, miss the bus, work, have fights, vote, and pay taxes. (quoted in Chance, 1975, p. 52)

Labels make it easy to forget that people of all sexual orientations are also cab drivers, cashiers, farm workers, salespeople, students, and parents.

THE STATISTICS OF SEXUAL ORIENTATION

The easiest questions about sexual orientation might seem to be statistical ones: What proportion of the population is heterosexual? homosexual? bisexual? But these questions are harder to answer than you might think.

Suppose Rona has sexual relations only with other women, has never had sexual relations with men, fantasizes only about female lovers, calls herself a lesbian, and affiliates socially and politically with lesbian groups. It is pretty clear that Rona is lesbian. But such consistency is the exception, not the rule. Surveys find that at least half of all men who identify themselves as gay have had intercourse with a woman, and about three-fourths have been sexually aroused by a woman (Bell & Weinberg, 1978; Saghir & Robins, 1973; Weinberg & Williams, 1974). And heterosexual experience is even more common among women who identify themselves as lesbians (Bell & Weinberg, 1978; Saghir & Robins, 1973).

Similarly, many people who regard themselves as heterosexual have had homosexual experiences. These experiences often occur in early adolescence and are not repeated later on. In some cases, they take place in special situations, such as single-sex boarding schools or prisons, where the other sex is not available or where sexual activity is a convenient way to express domination over others. But many same-sex experiences are simply occasional departures from heterosexuality. A study of sex between men in public rest rooms found that 54 percent of the participants were married and living with their wives and children (Humphreys, 1970). Using Kinsey's percentages and the 1974 census figures on married men and women, Morton Hunt (1977) estimated that at least one million wives and two or three million husbands have homosexual experiences outside of marriage while continuing to think of themselves as completely or primarily heterosexual.

Homoerotic love   *Many famous figures have experienced an erotic attachment to persons of the same sex. Poet Walt Whitman (on the left) was in love with Peter Doyle, a trolley car conductor. Although biographers disagree on whether he ever acted on his homosexual feelings, those feelings are apparent in some of his poetry ("I am indifferent to my / own songs—I will go / with him I love").*

TABLE 14–1

Kinsey's sexual orientation rating scale.   Kinsey and his colleagues devised this scale because they felt that the usual division of people into only two sexual orientations, heterosexual and homosexual, was inadequate.

0	1	2	3	4	5	6
Exclusively heterosexual	Predominantly heterosexual, only incidentally homosexual	Predominantly heterosexual, but more than incidentally homosexual	Equally heterosexual and homosexual	Predominantly homosexual, but more than incidentally heterosexual	Predominantly homosexual, but incidentally heterosexual	Exclusively homosexual

Source: Based on Kinsey, Pomeroy, & Martin, 1948.

Because many people have had both homosexual and heterosexual experiences, Alfred Kinsey and his colleagues (1948) argued that there is no such thing as a homosexual person—only homosexual acts. "The world," they wrote, using a rather unfortunate metaphor, "is not to be divided into sheep and goats....The living world is a continuum in each and every one of its aspects. The sooner we learn this concerning human sexual behavior the sooner we shall reach a sound understanding of the realities of sex." To capture the diversity of sexual experience, Kinsey devised a seven-point scale, with exclusive homosexuality and exclusive heterosexuality at the two ends and various mixtures in between, depending on the ratio of homosexual to heterosexual experience and arousal (see Table 14–1). A person might fall between the two poles for any number of reasons. One individual might enjoy sex with a partner of the other sex but prefer same-sex love relationships. Another might be exclusively homosexual for a period of time but then become predominantly heterosexual, or vice versa. Yet another might fantasize about a same-sex partner but never act out the fantasies.

Kinsey's point—that it's impossible to classify people into rigid categories—found quick acceptance among researchers and in the homosexual community. But his attempt to do away with labels for people was a flop. The reason: Kinsey ignored the important issue of *identity*. Sexual behavior may be fluid and complex, but at any given moment in time, people tend to *want* to label themselves. As sociologist John Gagnon (1990) notes, people rarely experience themselves, for example, as "a jar filled with 50% heterosexual and 50% homosexual acts." Therefore, instead of interpreting the seven points on Kinsey's scale as arbitrary locations on a continuum, people transformed them into descriptive labels: they began to refer to themselves or others as a "Kinsey 6" or a "Kinsey 3."

BOX 14–1 **Bisexuality And Sexual Flexibility**

Like death and taxes, race and anatomical sex are certainties of life, inevitable and unchanging. (Well, almost: a few people do manage to cheat on their taxes or change their sex.) But sexual orientation may be a different matter, according to psychologist Carla Golden (1987).

As a teacher for six years at a northeastern women's college, Golden was unofficial counselor to many young women exploring their sexual and personal identities. She discovered that some lesbian women felt their sexual orientation was beyond their control, but others felt it was self-consciously chosen. Some experienced their lesbianism as a central, enduring part of themselves; others saw it as more fluid and dynamic. Moreover, some women who called themselves bisexual were engaged in exclusively homosexual or exclusively heterosexual activity, while some who called themselves heterosexual were engaged in exclusively lesbian activity. In a group of 95 students, almost two-thirds identified themselves as heterosexual, 26 percent as bisexual, and 9 percent as lesbian. But when asked what their actual practices were, 72 percent said heterosexual, 20 percent bisexual, and only 4 percent lesbian.

Golden noticed that although far more women said they were bisexual than lesbian, bisexual issues and concerns were rarely discussed on campus and in classrooms. There seemed to be an unspoken expectation for women to declare themselves as either lesbian or straight, and therefore many hesitated to acknowledge their bisexual feelings. Pressure came from both lesbian and straight women. Many lesbians who assumed that straight women could have sexual feelings for other women rejected the idea that a lesbian could ever have sexual feelings for men. If a lesbian was unwilling to state that she was entirely uninterested in men sexually, other lesbians concluded that she was confused, was having difficulty coming out, was fighting the acceptance of

Today researchers recognize that behavior and identity are not always linked. A man may marry in order to pass as heterosexual but continue to feel intense emotional and erotic attraction only to men and to think of himself as gay. An individual who has had only heterosexual or homosexual experiences might nonetheless adopt the label *bisexual* (see Box 14–1). To capture such complexity, psychologists have devised a variety of tests that assess various aspects of a person's sexual orientation. One, the Klein Sexual Orientation Grid (Klein, 1980; Klein, Sepekoff & Wolf, 1985) uses a seven-point scale to measure seven separate facets of orientation, including sexual attraction,

a stigmatized identity, or was going through a "bisexual phase."

As Golden points out, psychologists usually assume that human beings strive for congruence between their feelings, activities, and identities. But for some people, she says, that assumption may be wrong. If freed from social pressure to declare themselves, some of us might be perfectly willing to have our sexuality remain fluid and flexible, whatever label we used for ourselves. Sociologist John Gagnon (1988) observes that this willingness may be subject not only to personal proclivities but also to cultural circumstances. During historical periods when homosexuality must be kept secret and homosexual communities are homogeneous and highly sexualized, people seem to feel that they need to settle on a single, fixed identity for themselves. But when homosexual culture is diverse, and when options other than marriage or celibacy exist, changes in sexual fantasy and conduct may occur over the life span.

The view that people label, interpret, and explain their sexual identities in varying ways is part of a more general view of human behavior known as *social constructionism* (Greenberg, 1989; Kitzinger, 1988; Tiefer, 1989). Social constructionists argue that the meanings assigned to any human experience will depend on the culture, the era, and the individual; no one meaning is the "real" or "essential" one. Thus the way one person experiences his or her sexual orientation may be quite different from the way another person experiences the "same" orientation.

Is sexual orientation as flexible as Golden's results seemed to indicate? Why do some people regard their sexual orientation as a fixed and stable part of themselves, while others view it as a matter of chance or choice? How does the culture that people live in affect the way they interpret their experiences as lesbians, gay men, straight women, and straight men? As you can see, many questions about sexual orientation remain to be answered.

sexual behavior, sexual fantasies, emotional preference, social preference, self-identification, and hetero/homosexual lifestyle (see Table 14–2).

Once you recognize how complicated sexual orientation is, the question "How many people are homosexual (or straight, or bisexual)?" loses much of its meaning. Still, we can get a rough idea of the incidence of homosexual versus heterosexual experience in the general population from surveys. And that incidence is clearly higher than many people think. In his 1948 book, Kinsey announced to a startled world that 37 percent of all men had at least one sexual experience with another man leading to orgasm, and

. . . .

TABLE 14–2
The Klein Sexual Orientation Grid

To complete this grid, you rank yourself on a seven-point scale (1 being exclusively homosexual, 7 exclusively heterosexual) for each of the seven facets of sexual orientation listed—for the present, for the past, and to describe your ideal self. The resulting 21 scores provide a far richer view of a person's sexual orientation than do the simplistic labels that most of us rely on.

	Past	Present	Ideal
Sexual attraction			
Sexual behavior			
Sexual fantasies			
Emotional preference			
Social preference			
Self-identification			
Hetero/homosexual lifestyle			

half reported experiencing some kind of erotic response to another man on at least one occasion. Women's responsiveness to women was considerably lower, but by no means negligible: the corresponding figures were 13 percent and 20 percent. Kinsey himself was astonished. Taken as a whole, his data suggested that the ability to experience homosexual arousal is common.

Over the years there have been many criticisms of Kinsey's estimates. Some people think they are too low; many think they are inflated (Fay et al., 1989; Hunt, 1974). What is absolutely clear, however, is that many people have at least some firsthand experience with homosexual behavior. This is remarkable when you consider the strong taboo against homosexuality in our culture and the very real penalties for it. Kinsey's percentages for lifelong exclusive homosexuality may seem small (4 percent for men, about 2 percent for women), but they represent millions of people. If we add to these numbers the many men and women who are primarily homosexual but who have had some cross-sex experience, we see that self-identified homosexuals constitute a sizable minority group in our society. If you are heterosexual you probably know at least one gay, lesbian, or bisexual person and probably many—whether you realize it or not.

PSYCHOLOGICAL VIEWPOINTS

For many years, most psychologists and other social scientists regarded homosexuality as a "condition" to be identified, treated, and, if possible, prevented. Researchers focused on finding the causes of this condition and on "diagnosing" it. The guiding assumption was that heterosexuality was normal and right, homosexuality abnormal and wrong. Many ostensibly objective research reports were full of pejorative terms, like "perversion," "degenerate," "psychopathology," and "disturbed" (Smith, 1979.)

During the 1950s, Evelyn Hooker (1957) became the first social scientist to put the assumption of abnormality to the test. A heterosexual herself, Hooker was persuaded to switch from the study of neurotic rats to the study of male homosexuals by some gay friends. They felt that someone ought to study "people like them"—gays who functioned well, led stable lives, and did not need psychiatric help. Hooker could not study a random sample of gay men (nor can researchers today; to draw a random sample, you need to know exactly who belongs to the population in question, and we don't know this for homosexual people). Instead, she did the next best thing, by matching gay and straight men for age, IQ, and amount of schooling. Then she gave all the men personality tests and asked experienced clinicians to examine the results and rate each man on a scale of adjustment, from superior to disturbed. The results: the clinicians did no better at identifying who was homosexual than if they had flipped a coin. Moreover, they did not judge the two groups as different in terms of psychological adjustment.

Other researchers, using a variety of methods, have confirmed these findings (Kurdek, 1987; Wilson, 1984), and some have even found gay and lesbian people to be psychologically healthier in certain respects than straight people (Freedman, 1975; Oberstone & Sukoneck, 1976). Mark Freedman (1975) has noted that the quest for identity forced upon homosexual people by a hostile society requires them to discover and live by their own values. In doing so, he argues, they develop a well-defined sense of purpose and a genuine self-acceptance. According to Freedman, homosexuals also find it easier than heterosexuals to transcend the narrow, restrictive gender roles that so often limit emotional expression.

In early 1974 the American Psychiatric Association voted to remove homosexuality from its official list of mental disorders. In 1975 the American Psychological Association passed a similar resolution on the non-pathological status of homosexuality. Homosexuality in and of itself would no longer be considered an illness, although a person could be diagnosed as having a sexual disorder if he or she experienced severe distress because of homosexuality and wished to change orientations. (It wasn't until 1987 that this category was also eliminated.)

In recent years, there has been a huge increase in research on homosexuality, much of it published in a scientific journal specifically devoted to the topic (the *Journal of Homosexuality*). Indeed, the American Psychological Association now has an entire organizational division devoted specifically to the study of gay and lesbian issues. Because of changing attitudes, the emphasis in psychological research has also changed. In articles published between 1967 and 1974, the most frequent topics were causes, psychological adjustment, and techniques of diagnosis (Morin, 1977). Missing were studies on the dynamics of lesbian and gay relationships, the development of a positive lesbian or gay identity, and the unique problems of lesbian and gay children, adolescents, and elderly people. But between 1979 and 1983, more than half of all studies published were on such "special topics" as aspects of the gay or lesbian experience and homosexual relationships. The number devoted to causes had fallen by half, and there were hardly any studies on assessment and diagnosis (Walters, 1986).

Along with changes in research, the attitudes of psychotherapists toward homosexuality have undergone a transformation. Although some individual therapists (particularly psychoanalysts) still consider homosexuality a disorder, most therapists with up-to-date training do not. This is a more dramatic shift than you might realize. When the age-old view of homosexuality as a sin gave way in the late nineteenth century to the view that it was an illness, people began to look for ways of changing homosexuals into heterosexuals. Illnesses, after all, cry out for cures. Over the years, homosexuals have been subjected to hypnosis, intensive psychoanalysis, prefrontal lobotomy, electroconvulsive shock treatments, and chemical castration. Behavioral therapists have tried to "cure" people of homosexuality by injecting them with nausea-producing drugs that cause vomiting and then exposing them to photographs or slides of same-sex nudes, the idea being to associate anxiety and fear with images of same-sex partners (McConaghy, 1970; McConaghy, Proctor & Barr, 1972).

Behavioral therapist Gerald Davison (1976) was one of the first psychotherapists to take a strong stand against the "conversion" of homosexuals. Davison argued that although guilt and shame produced by public hostility might drive some homosexuals to seek a conversion, cooperating with such a request simply supports a social system that views homosexuality as a sickness. Instead of trying to change homosexuals, said Davison, therapists ought to try to change social attitudes.

Critics like Davison view conversion as analogous to trying to change black people into white people by bleaching their skin. Not only is conversion unethical, they argue, but it is also doomed. In the past, some therapists reported fairly high "success" rates (for example, Masters & Johnson, 1979), but these results only occurred when patients were carefully screened beforehand and had already had a great deal of heterosexual experience. Many were probably incorrectly labeled as homosexual when in fact they were bisexual. Critics of conversion also point out that behavior is easier to change than fantasies, thoughts, and preferences. A "cured" homosexual may simply give up intense and passionate homosexual relationships for ho-hum heterosexual ones in which there is little emotional involvement. Moreover, the "conversion" may not last. Most important, conversion locates the "problem" in the victim, rather than in the perpetrators of prejudice against gay and lesbian people.

In recent years, conversion has become pretty much a dead issue among most therapists. Most agree that exclusive homosexuality, like exclusive heterosexuality, is difficult or impossible to change. However that doesn't mean that conscious or unconscious biases among therapists have disappeared. To counteract such biases, some therapists who are themselves gay or lesbian now specialize in serving a gay or lesbian clientele. They help their clients to understand how the burdens and pressures that heterosexual society places on homosexuals can sometimes cause feelings of anxiety or insecurity, and they provide supportive models of homosexual life (Ross, 1988). They also help clients deal with problems that seem especially prevalent in lesbian or gay relationships. For example, according to some therapists, lesbians are especially sensitive to power imbalances in relationships, and may fear dependency as they struggle for a new identity as a woman while rejecting the traditional view of femininity (Burch, 1987). And because gay men in a relationship often permit one another outside sexual partners, they may be more likely than other couples to search for specific ways of reducing feelings of jealousy (McWhirter & Mattison, 1984). Finally, gay therapists have tried to help their fellow gays deal with the loss of friends or lovers to AIDS, as well as the feelings of helplessness and fear that can occur in the face of life-threatening illness.

SOME ASPECTS OF HOMOSEXUAL EXPERIENCE

By now, it should come as no surprise to you that there is no typical homosexual person, just as there is no typical heterosexual. The life of a gay man who builds his social life around gay bars bears little resemblance to the life of a gay insurance executive who lives a quiet life with his partner of fifteen years. Occupation, social class, ethnicity, place of residence, and gender all influence how we experience our sexuality, whether we are gay, lesbian, straight, or bisexual. Still, some common patterns do characterize the life experiences of many gay and lesbian people. In Chapter 13, we discussed some aspects of heterosexual life, such as heterosexual dating, marriage, and divorce. As we discuss some aspects of gay and lesbian life, keep in mind that none is universal in lesbian and gay communities.

Discovering One's Homosexuality and Coming Out

How old were you when you first became aware of your sexual orientation? Three? Six? Twelve? Perhaps the realization came when you and a friend crept into a closet with a flashlight to explore the tantalizing mysteries of anatomy. Perhaps it was later, when you started to fantasize about touching another person's body or developed a crush on some sexy celebrity. Perhaps it was not until you started to date and discovered that a strange but sweet tension existed between you and members of the other sex—or that it *didn't* exist, although all the books said it should. Probably, though, you cannot pinpoint the exact year when you first knew your sexual orientation. For

Parental support

Homosexuals may fear rejection by family members, but not all parents are unsupportive of their gay or lesbian children.

most of us, such awareness evolves gradually, from an unlabeled and nebulous feeling to a definite and clearly articulated sense of identity.

For heterosexuals, the emergence of a sexual identity is supported by cultural norms and customs. But for those who are not heterosexual, becoming aware of one's sexual orientation means bucking the tide. At first, this may be so threatening that the person tries to deny his or her homosexual feelings. As one lesbian recalled:

> I was in my mid-teens when I first noticed that I found it more exciting to look at women's bodies in magazines, or on the beach, than at men's. I would see some well-built girl in a bathing suit, and stare at her, and imagine myself kissing her and fondling her all over, and I'd feel very sexually excited, much more so than I had ever been with any boy. When I was eighteen and in college, I became very close to my roommate. We were really very warm and together. She'd walk about the room in the nude, and I would practically faint, I wanted so badly to hold and kiss her. And I would look away, and tell myself that I wasn't gay, I *wasn't!* (quoted in Hunt, 1977, pp. 99–100)

Young lesbian and gay people may go to great lengths to pretend to be heterosexual. They may put themselves in situations where they are likely to be seduced by a person of the same sex, then disclaim any responsibility since they were not the initiator ("It happened because I was drinking"). They may tell themselves that since they do not fit the stereotype of the effeminate male or masculine female, they are not really homosexual. A young woman may assure herself that although she loves a particular woman, her feelings do not make her a lesbian. A young man is more likely to tell himself that because he is *not* emotionally involved with his partners he is not really gay (de Monteflores & Schultz, 1978).

Some young lesbian and gay people are aware of their true feelings but lack the vocabulary to describe them, even to themselves. For years they may think they are alone in having such feelings. This sense of uniqueness is especially likely if they live in places where lesbian and gay organizations and meeting places are hard to find. When researcher Barry Dank (1971) asked gay men how they would have answered the question "Are you a homosexual?" just before high school graduation, some said they didn't really know at that time what one was.

Because gay and lesbian adults often fear being exposed (if they are still closeted), and because they fear being accused of "enticing" young people into homosexuality, they may hesitate to get involved in helping homosexual teenagers deal with their fears and concerns (Malyon, 1985). As a result, a homosexual teenager may have few role models with which to identify. And heterosexual friends are usually not available as confidants, either; adolescents are known for their intolerance of differences, especially sexual ones. It is not hard to understand why many young lesbian and gay people feel emotionally and socially isolated, and why some enter adulthood demoralized and depressed (Hetrick & Martin, 1987). Recently some special programs have been established to extend social support to these teenagers, give them a place to be with other gays or lesbians, and help them resolve their feelings of alienation.

Acknowledging one's homosexual identity—**coming out** to oneself and others—is an important milestone in a lesbian or gay person's life. One man, who came out at the age of twenty-three after several years of homosexual activity, went to a gay bar, looked at the "normal-looking and acting" men there, and said to himself, "Wow, I'm home" (Dank, 1971). Self-identification is sometimes difficult. Because all homosexual people grow up in a culture that condemns homosexuality, many must deal with internalized anti-homosexual attitudes. But coming out also often brings a great sense of relief. There may be a conscious rejection of previously accepted negative stereotypes and a new sense of self-acceptance, especially if the person identifies with a community of gay or lesbian people.

Once a person has accepted his or her homosexuality, a decision must be made about whether to come out to family members, friends, employers, and others. The interval between a person's first awareness of attraction to the same sex and the first disclosure to a heterosexual sometimes extends over a decade or more (McDonald, 1982). Coming out to others does not necessarily mean wearing a button proclaiming "I am a homosexual." But it does require that the person honestly answer questions about his or her sexuality and refuse to pretend to be something that he or she is not. This kind of self-disclosure can be a risky proposition, since the reactions of others are not predictable. But the alternative, living a double life, is in many ways more stressful, because it prevents a person from achieving congruence between the public and private self (de Monteflores & Schultz, 1978). In one study of gay men (Weinberg & Williams, 1974), attempts to "pass" in straight society were associated with depression, social awkwardness, and guilt or shame, primarily because of worry about exposure or its consequences. Men who were highly involved with other gay people had fewer psychological problems than those who were less involved, probably because of the support they received and its positive impact on their self-image and self-esteem.

Relationships

In 1970, psychologist Alan Bell and sociologist Martin Weinberg, of Indiana University and the Kinsey Institute, interviewed nearly a thousand male and female homosexuals living in the San Francisco Bay Area. After several years of analyzing their data, Bell and Weinberg published their findings in a book called *Homosexualities* (1978). The plural form of the title was no accident; Bell and Weinberg found that like gay and lesbian people, gay and lesbian relationships are diverse.

Intimate moment
Like heterosexual relationships, homosexual relationships range from the casual to the deeply committed and entail a range of pleasures and problems.

Almost three-fourths of the men and women in Bell and Weinberg's sample fit into one of five distinct relationship categories.

1. *Close-coupled* individuals lived with a special partner to whom they were sexually faithful. Their lives were quiet, monogamous, and stable, and their relationships resembled heterosexual marriages. They scored high on self-acceptance and general happiness. Here is an interviewer's brief description of one close couple:

   She and her roommate were obviously very much in love. Like most people who have a good, stable, five-year relationship, they seemed comfortable together, sort of part of one another, able to joke, obviously fulfilled in their relationship. They work together, have the same times off from work, do most of their leisure activities together....They sent me home with a plate of cookies, a good symbolic gesture of the kind of welcome and warmth I felt in their home. (p. 220)

2. *Open-coupled* individuals lived with a special sexual partner but were less happy than close-coupled people with their situation and sought or wished for sexual satisfaction outside the primary relationship:

   He tries to give the appearance of happiness with his roommate but cruises [looks for sexual partners] continually, feels grave guilt about this, and says that it contributes to his domestic travail. He stopped me from introducing myself to his roommate, as if I were a pickup he wanted to keep secret.

   As she talked I discovered that her lover is very jealous and that she (the respondent) would like to date men and explore her own sexual orientation further, but that her lover was demanding a long-term commitment and she was not free to try out other relationships. (p. 222)

3. *Functional* individuals led single, sexually active lives and were roughly comparable to heterosexual "swinging singles." They seemed happy and had few, if any, sexual problems, although they did not score as well as close-coupled persons in these respects. They were "energetic and self-reliant, cheerful and optimistic, and comfortable with their highly emphasized sexuality." An example:

   He was a very energetic and open kid, looking much younger than twenty-seven. He seemed to be feeling very happy, likes his job in the Merchant Marine, and enjoys being back for just short stays. Although this militates against long-term relationships, he really enjoys his feeling of independence. (p. 224)

4. *Dysfunctional* homosexuals were single and sexually active, but troubled and unhappy. Often they regretted their homosexuality. They were apt to worry about their sexual adequacy and to consider themselves unappealing:

> I see his admission to being a "chicken queen" [a gay man who prefers very young partners] as a way for him to relive or act out his lost youth. He drives to the Tenderloin "meat rack," picks up young hustlers, drives them to Redwood City, and then pays them for sex. (pp. 225–226)

5. *Asexuals* were single individuals who had few partners, engaged in little sexual activity, and had narrow sexual repertoires. They tended to spend their leisure time alone and to have little contact with friends. They did not seem too interested in finding a special partner. However, their homosexuality had not caused them any special difficulties. Bell and Weinberg argued that the quiet, withdrawn lives of asexuals were the result of "an underlying apathy toward the panoply of human experience" rather than their sexual orientation:

> He seemed like a totally ineffectual, frightened, withdrawn sort of person. He was desperately shy and seemed very afraid of me for the first part of the interview.

> She was a bit cool and businesslike. Her difficulties with interpersonal relations were hinted at when she said she tends to be suspicious of people who are "too nice." When the interview was over she was pleasant, but it felt superficial. (p. 227)

Critics of the Bell and Weinberg study have argued that their sample was not necessarily representative of all homosexuals, and that, in any case, people probably shift categories depending on life circumstances. As John Gagnon (1979) noted, "An uncoupled person could change from functional to dysfunctional. A coupled, faithful person could become unfaithful. The data are therefore more likely to reflect current living arrangements than homosexualities...." But of course, the same could be said of data on *heterosexual* relationships. Perhaps the thing to notice about Bell and Weinberg's categories are that they are just those you might expect to find for any large group of people, whatever their sexual orientation.

Another study, by sociologists Philip Blumstein and Pepper Schwartz (1983) took a different tack. Blumstein and Schwartz interviewed gay, lesbian, and straight couples about issues of money, work, and sex:

- *Money.* Money was a central issue for many couples, because it raised problems of trust, commitment, and security. Lesbians and straight people living together without marriage were the most likely to emphasize financial independence and self-sufficiency for both partners. This kept them equal, but eliminated an opportunity to develop trust and stability. Married couples, in contrast, tended to function as a financial team. They became more interdependent, but they also fought some pitched battles over money, battles that could sometimes slide over into abuse. Gay men seemed to have the hardest time of all about money. Like other men in this society, they tended to see earning power as necessary for self-esteem. If one man's earning power was greater than the other's, he gained an advantage over his partner, who then felt inadequate. Financial inequality also occurred in married couples, but gay men felt more uncomfortable about it.

■ *Work.* For all couples in which both partners worked, there were formidable challenges: dealing with competition, dividing up housework, finding time to be together. Men in relationships, whether gay or straight, tended to match their own success against their partner's, while lesbians did not. Heterosexual men might take pleasure in a woman's success, but only as long as it did not challenge their own. They did not accept women as full partners, and they expected the woman to do most of the housework, even if she held a full-time job. Same-sex couples, in general, tended to share more off-hours activities and interests than straight ones.

■ *Sex.* As we will see in a later section, sexual attitudes and behavior are often related more closely to people's gender than to their sexual orientation. In the Blumstein and Schwartz study, gender differences often interfered with empathy and understanding in heterosexual couples. Because men were expected to initiate more, women often felt a lack of control over their own sexual experience, and men felt pressed to perform. If a woman took most of the initiative, both frequency and satisfaction tended to suffer. But gender roles also affected same-sex couples. In lesbian couples, sometimes neither partner was comfortable with being sexually "aggressive," and sexual activity declined. In contrast, in male couples, sometimes each man wanted to be the initiator, which caused competition and dissension. But in general, a shared outlook helped same-sex couples. In male couples, each partner could understand the other's need for sexual variety (although this understanding did not necessarily erase feelings of jealousy). In female couples, partners tended to share an awareness of the dangers of nonmonogamy.

Other studies have found that sexual satisfaction in homosexual relationships tends to be high. Lesbians and gay men have the advantage of knowing, on the basis of their own responses, what is likely to please a partner. As you may recall from Chapter 9, Masters and Johnson (1979) found that committed lesbian and gay couples spent more time at and got more involved in sensuous activities than did married heterosexuals. In another study, bisexual and lesbian women reported more orgasms per week (8.8 and 6.2, respectively) than did heterosexuals (4.7). Bisexuals and lesbians were also far more likely to describe their orgasms as strong (86 percent and 80 percent, respectively) than were heterosexual women (48 percent). Undesired behavior was experienced more with male partners than with female partners, regardless of the female partner's sexual orientation (Bressler & Lavender, 1986).

Lesbian, gay, and straight couples, then, often face somewhat different issues. Perhaps the largest difference of all is that married straight couples have the support and blessing of society, while lesbian and gay couples usually do not, and may even have to face the opposition of their own relatives. We want to point out, however, that in most respects, homosexual and heterosexual relationships present people with similar joys and challenges. Overall, same-sex couples and straight couples are equally satisfied—or miserable (Howard, Blumstein & Schwartz, 1986, 1987; Kurdek & Schmitt, 1986). Whatever their sexual orientation, couples tend to feel happiest when both partners are equally involved, power is shared, and attitudes and backgrounds are similar (Peplau, Padesky, & Hamilton, 1982).

Roles and Styles

In the popular mind, a gay man speaks with a lisp, lets his hand droop limply from his wrist, wears an earring in one ear, and walks with a mincing gait; he is a man who is a caricature of a female. Similarly, lesbians are thought to wear their hair like men, dress in oxfords and leather jackets, and walk like the stereotypical truck driver.

Like most oversimplified images, these images of homosexuality contain a kernel of truth—but just a kernel. Some gay men do have an effeminate style (an exaggeration of feminine mannerisms—not typical of most women, we should note). Similarly, some lesbians do adopt a "butch" style, especially when they are first coming out and feel they must make a definite statement about their identity (Lyon & Martin, 1970). On the other hand, the other extremes also occur. For example, some gay men glorify traditional masculine styles by wearing leather and other "masculine" garb, and some despise effeminate gays for reflecting society's notion of homosexuality instead of forging their own image.

Because extreme mannerisms capture our attention, it is easy to overestimate their prevalence among homosexuals. But most researchers who know the gay community well believe that those who adopt exaggerated styles of dress and demeanor are a minority—perhaps 5 to 20 percent of all gay people. Even rarer are homosexuals who actually cross-dress. (Cross-

Gay blades *Many of the public's ideas about homosexuality have come from negative images in the media, but in recent years more sympathetic portrayals have begun to appear. In the comedy film Victor/Victoria, Robert Preston played a gay man and Julie Andrews played a female female impersonator—a woman pretending to be a man earning a living by playing the on-stage role of a woman. The plot was complicated but the message simple: the qualities that make people appealing and fun are not related to sexual orientation.*

dressing is sometimes a way to be outrageous and shock the straight world.) Homosexuality seems as common among those paragons of American masculinity, male college athletes, as in the general population (Garner & Smith, 1977).

In one study of personal mannerisms (Berger et al., 1987), homosexual and straight men and women watched videotaped interviews of six gay men, six lesbians, six straight men, and six straight women. The interviews consisted of a series of innocuous questions, such as "What is your favorite movie?" The subjects' task was to guess the sexual orientation of the people in the tapes. Gay men did better than the other subjects, mainly because they were good at recognizing other gay men. But the main finding was that four-fifths of the subjects could do no better than chance at guessing other people's orientation. Although this study has many weaknesses (for example, the people in the tapes were not necessarily representative of their respective sexual orientations), it does suggest that observers usually cannot identify a person's sexual orientation by looks and mannerisms alone.

Heterosexuals often have misconceptions about the roles gay men and lesbians play in relationships. In earlier decades, some homosexual couples assumed the traditional roles of "husband" (breadwinner, decision-maker, door-opener) and "wife" (cook, social secretary, home decorator). Today, however, most do not. As one gay man put it, "We are just a couple of happily married husbands" (quoted in Saghir & Robbins, 1973). Lesbians are especially concerned with establishing equality in decision making and financial responsibilities (Lynch & Reilly, 1985/1986). Lesbians are also more likely than other people to reject stereotypes in their perceptions of themselves, the "ideal woman" and the "ideal man" (Hellwege, Perry & Dobson, 1988).

Occasionally homosexual people do have a preference for a particular "role" in lovemaking. As we noted in Chapter 9, sex for homosexuals includes the same acts as it does for straight people, with the exception of vaginal/penile intercourse. Among gay men, the most common practices are manual stimulation, fellatio, and anal intercourse; among lesbians, they are manual stimulation and cunnilingus. Some individuals prefer to be either the receiver or the performer in anal or oral sex. But nearly every study finds that most are willing to and do act out both parts, even in casual relationships. In their laboratory observations of committed couples, Masters and Johnson (1979) saw rigid adherence to roles during sexual activity in only one out of twenty homosexual couples.

Gay and Lesbian Culture

Being homosexual or straight can affect a person's social activities, friendships, values, and even place of residence. This is what gay and lesbian people mean when they talk about having their own "life style." Outside large cities the differences between gay, lesbian, and straight life styles may be subtle. But in places like New York, Boston, Chicago, Houston, Los Angeles, and San Francisco, many gay men, and to a lesser extent lesbians, identify with a subculture that has its own unique institutions and customs, analogous to those of ethnic subcultures. Many gay men locate their homes and even their businesses in gay "ghettos," where most of the gathering spots cater to a gay clientele and homosexuality is generally accepted (Levine, 1979). In some cities, certain streets are populated almost exclusively by homosexuals. There are lesbian and gay newspapers, book stores, travel agencies, housing cooperatives, and churches.

In some places, the urban gay and lesbian subcultures are distinguished not only by their meeting places but by styles of dress and speech patterns. (Several homosexual expressions have found their way into the vocabularies of heterosexuals; heterosexuals now say they are going out to "cruise," or refer to themselves as "closet" Republicans or "closet" radicals.) The urban homosexual subculture has long had its own brand of humor, known as *camp*. Camp involves a love of the extravagant and the exaggerated and seeks to convert the serious into the frivolous, or vice versa. (Camp is more common among gay men than lesbians.)

Despite many differences in how same-sex attraction is expressed cross-culturally, at least some contemporary lesbian and gay customs and terms appear to have ancient origins. The color purple appears in mythology, history, and the arts as a gay symbol. The name of a great Celtic lesbian warrior, Queen Boudica (pronounced Bow-dyka) may have provided the origin for the term "bulldike" (Grahn, 1984).

Solidarity   *Gay men and lesbians have effectively organized to increase public understanding of homosexuality, lobby for their rights, and provide services in gay and lesbian communities.*

Having a sense of community has been a great help to gay men and lesbians during the AIDS crisis, and the crisis, in turn, has strengthened gay people's sense of community. (There are almost no cases of sexually-transmitted AIDS among lesbians, but lesbians have been active in AIDS education, and many have social and political ties to gay men.) However, not all homosexual people, or even a majority, identify with a lesbian or gay subculture. The extent to which a person participates in such a subculture probably depends on personal tastes, social class, geography, degree of acceptance by the heterosexual society, political activism, and the risk that coming out poses to a person's job and community standing. In recent years, some gay "ghettos," such as the Castro district in San Francisco, have become more integrated, and many homosexual urban-dwellers have left the cities for the suburbs.

Parenthood

For some people, being lesbian or gay means foregoing parenthood. As one lesbian recalled:

> One of my mother's big disappointments was the fact that there would be no grandchildren. I love both of my parents a great deal, and I would do almost anything for their happiness, but I couldn't do that. I think I was saddened, too, when...I knew that I wasn't ever going to have children. And I would like to have some...for myself (quoted in Simon & Gagnon, 1967, p. 279)

Many homosexual people, however, do have children. In most cases, the children were born during previous marriages to heterosexuals. But increasingly, lesbians and gay men are opting for other ways of becoming parents. Lesbians are taking advantage of artificial insemination, using

Gay fathers *Being homosexual doesn't mean you can't be a parent; many lesbians and gay men are successfully raising children.*

sperm from a sperm bank, a private anonymous donor, or a male friend. Artificial insemination requires only semen and an ordinary syringe, and many lesbians accomplish it without going through a doctor. Some lesbians and gay men have cooperated in artificial insemination or have had intercourse together for the express purpose of having a child that both could parent. And some homosexual people have adopted children. (In most states such adoptions are handled as a single-parent adoption; if the adoptive parent has a partner, that person has no legal rights of parenthood. Some couples have drawn up private contracts dealing with parental rights and obligations [Pollack & Vaughn, 1987], but such contracts have not yet been tested in the courts.) During the late 1980s, there was something of a "baby boom" in the lesbian community.

Straight people sometimes wonder whether the children of lesbian and gay parents can become well-adjusted adults. It is certainly true that homosexual parents may have to help their children cope with the discrimination and hostility of others, just as African-American, Hispanic, and other minority parents do. If a homosexual parent or the parent's partner is still closeted, homosexuality may become a family secret, and the child may worry about unwittingly divulging it. If the parent is "out," the child may have to deal with the teasing and taunts of other kids. But there is no evidence that the children of lesbian and gay parents grow up with more psychological problems than other children do. Studies of children with lesbian mothers find that they do not differ from other children in terms of gender identity, gender role, or general adjustment (Hoeffer, 1981; Kirkpatrick, Smith & Roy, 1981; Green et al., 1986). In an interview study of 23 homosexual and 16 straight single parents, most of the participants reported positive relationships with their children (Harris & Turner, 1985/1986).

Male-Female Differences

As we have mentioned, gay men and lesbians often have different outlooks on love and sex, just as straight men and women do (see Chapters 8 and 13). In many respects, the way people express their sexuality, and the meanings they attach to it, have less to do with being homosexual or heterosexual than they do with being a man or a woman.

According to most research, at any given point in time, lesbians are more likely than gay men to be in a long-term, committed relationship. For example, in the Bell and Weinberg study (1978), about half the men, versus three-quarters of the women, were currently involved in a relatively stable relationship. Lesbians also seem to place more value on emotional expressiveness in their close relationships (Peplau & Gordon, 1983). Gay men and lesbians alike usually value romance and look for warmth, love, and companionship, and most have had at least one long-term relationship. But at the same time, gay men seem less willing to give up their freedom and independence to preserve a long-term affair. In a study that explored the costs and benefits of relationships, women—lesbian and straight—reported investing more in relationships and being more committed to maintaining their relationships than did men (Duffy & Rusbult, 1985/1986).

A recent study asked people their reasons for having sex (Leigh, 1989). For people in stable relationships, regardless of sex or sexual orientation, pleasure was the best predictor of the frequency of sex. But in general, men gave more importance than women did to sexual pleasure, conquest, and the relief of tension as reasons for having sex, and women gave greater importance than men did to emotional closeness. These sex differences occurred for both heterosexuals and homosexuals (although they tended to be larger for the heterosexuals). Similarly, women, regardless of sexual orientation, were more likely than men to say that lack of interest and enjoyment were important reasons for *not* having sex.

Sex differences in the motives and meanings attached to sex are reflected in statistics on the number of partners gay men and lesbians have.

Close couple *Studies find that gay men are less likely than lesbians to stay in a long-term relationship, but many gay men do make a long-term commitment to one cherished partner.*

Kinsey found that 22 percent of the gay men in his sample, but only 4 percent of the lesbians, had had 11 or more partners. In Bell and Weinberg's (pre-AIDS) study, which surveyed people from an area known for its relatively laissez-faire attitudes toward homosexuality and its abundant opportunities for cruising, the differences were even more dramatic. Most lesbians reported having had fewer than 10 sexual partners, and most of their partners were women they cared about. Almost half said that they had never had a one-night stand, and few were interested in "cruising." In contrast, the average gay man in the sample reported *hundreds* of sexual partners, and over a quarter reported a *thousand* or more. Only a quarter said they felt some affection for most of their partners. Almost all the men cruised at least occasionally, and one-night stands were common. Even if these findings were not representative of lesbian and gay people nationally, or if some of the men were exaggerating their sexual exploits, the sex differences are remarkable.

Since the AIDS epidemic began, many gay men have significantly reduced the number of sexual partners they have, including anonymous partners (Feldman, 1986). (In addition, the use of safer sex practices by gay men, particularly in certain urban areas, has increased, as we will discuss in Chapter 17.) However, casual sex among gay men has hardly disappeared. In one study in New York City, 80 percent of gay men reported a decrease in the number of sexual partners over a period of six months, yet few of the men had entirely given up having multiple anonymous partners; in fact, having such partners remained the most common sexual pattern (Siegel et al., 1988).

What accounts for male-female differences in number of partners among homosexual people? One possibility is that closeted lesbians find it easier to maintain a stable relationship without arousing suspicion and hostility. In our culture women can kiss one another and show other signs of affection in public without being labeled gay. Males cannot, and so they may be tempted to limit their relationships to the purely—and fleetingly—sexual. Another possibility is that there is some fundamental difference in the nature of male and female sexuality, rooted in biology and our evolutionary history. A third explanation is that in the course of growing up, males are more likely than females to learn a competitive type of sexuality that emphasizes genital satisfaction and devalues fidelity, while females are more likely than males to learn a romantic type of sexuality that emphasizes love and values commitment (see Chapter 13). Gay men may simply be living out a male "sexual script" and lesbians a female one. Would straight men also have hundreds of partners if women were as available to them as male partners are to gay men?

THE ORIGINS OF SEXUAL ORIENTATION

Early sexual development is still poorly understood, as we discussed in Chapter 12. Our ignorance is especially great when it comes to why some children grow up to be straight and others gay or lesbian. Most psychological theories emphasize either the environment or biology. We will review some of these theories, and then examine the difficulties that beset all of them. Notice, as you read this section, that most of the theories take heterosexuality as a given, and try to explain why some people depart from it.

Genetic Explanations

Many people believe that genetics must contribute to homosexuality, but evidence for this belief is sparse. In one frequently cited study, Irving Kallman (1952) reported on 85 pairs of twins, in which at least one twin was homosexual. He found perfect *concordance* in the 40 identical twin pairs—that is, whenever one twin was homosexual, so was the other. In contrast, the degree of concordance for the 45 fraternal twin pairs (twins who developed from separate eggs and, like other siblings, shared only half their genes) was not significant.

But Kallman's work was flawed. We would expect *some* concordance among the fraternal twins to exist, since, after all, they did share half their genes. In other words, Kallman's findings seem too "good" to be true—and in fact, various other researchers have failed to replicate them. Also, since the twins were reared together, it was impossible to separate genetic from environmental influences. In a more recent study, researchers attempted to overcome this last drawback by studying identical twins who had been reared apart since birth (Eckert et al., 1986). Out of 55 pairs of twins, five pairs (two male, three female) had at least one homosexual member, and a sixth pair (female) had a bisexual member. All the female pairs had only one lesbian member. In one male pair, both twins were gay, and in the remaining pair it was not clear whether both were gay. Unfortunately, the small number of homosexual twins in the study does not permit strong conclusions.

In a different kind of study, Bernard Zuger (1989) determined the sexual orientations of people who were close relations of effeminate boys. Most of the boys eventually became homosexual, but the incidence of homosexuality among their parents, siblings, uncles, and aunts was about the same as estimated for the general population. These results cast doubt on a simple genetic explanation of sexual orientation.

Hormonal Explanations

Another possibility is that sex hormones influence the development of sexual orientation. A number of researchers believe such effects occur before birth, during a critical period between the middle of the second and the end of the fifth month of fetal development. The general idea is that high prenatal androgen levels predispose an individual to be sexually attracted to females, whereas low androgen levels predispose an individual to be attracted to males, regardless of the individual's genetic sex. That is, high androgen levels are linked to heterosexuality in males and homosexuality in females, whereas low androgen levels are linked to homosexuality in males and heterosexuality in females (Dörner, 1976; Ellis & Ames, 1987). (As we saw in Chapter 12, a similar theory has been proposed to explain the development of gender identity, one's sense of oneself as male or female, as well as various gender-related behaviors. The evidence, you may recall, was conflicting and subject to different interpretations.)

The notion that prenatal hormones affect sexual orientation is based partly on animal research. As was discussed in Chapter 12, if a rat or guinea pig gets a dose of testosterone during a critical period (which for these animals is shortly after birth), the animal's brain will always be sensitive to male hormones and insensitive to female ones. If the animal does not get testosterone during the critical period, later its brain will be sensitive to female hormones. The effects on the animal's sexual behavior are striking. For example, an adult female rat treated with testosterone during the critical period will not arch her back and elevate her pelvis to show sexual interest, as a normal female rat would, even if she is injected with female hormones. Moreover, if you give her enough male hormones at maturity, she will go through the entire male sexual ritual of mounting another rat and making thrusting motions, undeterred by the fact that she has no penis (Levine, 1966). Similarly, male rats that have had their testes removed at birth, so that they cannot produce testosterone, later respond to injections of female hormones by trying to behave sexually like females (Young, Goy & Phoenix, 1965; Levine, 1966). Specific brain areas affected by the presence or absence of testosterone during the critical period seem to control specific male and female sexual behaviors (Arnold & Gorski, 1984).

But we should be wary of generalizing from these results to human beings. A human being's sexual orientation encompasses not only behavior, but also fantasy, thoughts, plans, and a self-concept. Moreover, human beings, unlike laboratory animals, are flexible in their sexual behavior, and neither human males nor females are confined to stereotyped gender-linked behaviors during lovemaking. Of course, only men can insert a penis into an orifice, but people of *both* sexes kiss, caress, use a variety of sexual positions, and give and receive oral-genital stimulation.

To test the hormonal hypotheses, then, it is necessary to get information on human beings. One way to do this is to study *pseudohermaphrodites*, people born with ambiguous genitals or with genitals that do not match their genetic or gonadal sex. Generally speaking, pseudohermaphroditism occurs when a genetically female fetus is overexposed to androgens or a genetically male fetus is underexposed to androgens. Surgery is usually performed to bring the genitals in line with the sex of assignment. (Chapter 12 gives a more complete description.) By studying pseudohermaphrodites, researchers have an opportunity to see what, if anything, happens to sexual orientation when there is too much or too little androgen before birth.

Unfortunately, the results of this research, like the results on gender identity and gender-role behaviors, are inconclusive. Most pseudohermaphrodites seem to acquire a heterosexual orientation relative to the gender in which they were reared, regardless of genetic sex or their prenatal hormonal status (Ehrhardt & Meyer-Balhberg, 1981). However, an attraction to the same sex may be more common among pseudohermaphrodites than in the general population. The best evidence comes from a study of 30 genetically female adult pseudohermaphrodites whose condition was caused by an overproduction of fetal androgens before birth. All of these individuals had had their genitals corrected surgically and all had been reared as girls. At the time of the study, 40 percent were heterosexual, 20 percent bisexual, 17 homosexual, and 23 percent noncommittal (Money, Schwartz & Lewis, 1984).

Another way to look for hormonal effects on sexual orientation is to study adult hormone levels, which may be affected by prenatal levels. Although heterosexuals and homosexuals do not seem to differ in their levels of testosterone or estrogen, some studies have reported a more subtle kind of difference in men (Dörner et al., 1976; Gladue, Green & Hellman, 1984). In these studies, gay and straight men were given an injection of estrogen. Women usually react to such an injection with a slight drop in luteinizing hormone (LH), one of the important reproductive brain hormones (see Chapter 6). This drop is followed, over the next few days, by a sharp surge in LH. The researchers found that heterosexual men rarely showed such a pattern, but gay men did, although the increase in LH was not as steep as in women. These results produced quite a stir among researchers studying sexual orientation. But unfortunately for the hormonal hypothesis, a more recent study has failed to replicate them. Instead, both gay and straight men experienced a drop in LH, followed by a moderate increase (Hendricks, Graber & Rodriguez-Sierra, 1989).

At this point, you may be feeling rather confused. Does biology affect sexual orientation or not? The answer, we feel, is a resounding "maybe." So far, the evidence is not strong. One reason is that studying the possible effects of hormones on sexual orientation is frustratingly difficult. Researchers cannot simply measure the hormone levels of fetuses and then follow them for two decades or so after birth to see how they develop; taking the measurements would pose a threat to the fetuses. As we've seen, researchers *can* study pseudohermaphrodites, but then they cannot be sure the findings will apply to anatomically normal individuals. They can also study adults, but stress, sexual activity, disease, drug use, and other physical and emotional factors can all affect adult hormone levels and thus the results of research.

Psychoanalytic Explanations

The traditional psychoanalytic position on sexual orientation is that homosexuality is a pathological condition resulting primarily from disturbed family relationships during early childhood; biology may play a role, but it is only a secondary one. Unfortunately, the psychoanalytic approach tends to confuse sexual orientation with gender identity, the sense of being male or female.

According to Freud, we are all born psychologically bisexual. That is, we are not naturally attracted to any particular type of "love object"; rather, we are capable of feeling attracted to either a male or female, and we retain this capacity throughout life. The partner we actually select depends primarily on early childhood experiences.

As we saw in Chapter 12, Freud believed that the critical experience in psychosexual development is the Oedipal conflict, which occurs between the ages of about three and six. In the normal course of events, a young child falls in love with the parent of the other sex and comes to view the same-sex parent as a sexual rival. Eventually, however, the child is forced to accept the fact that these incestuous wishes are hopeless. If all goes well, the child represses these wishes, identifies with the parent of the same sex, resolves to find a mate like the opposite-sex parent, and acquires an "appropriate" sense of masculinity.

In the development of the homosexual-to-be, according to traditional psychoanalysts, this sequence goes awry for a variety of reasons. The child may be *fixated*, or arrested, at an earlier stage of development, when the primary sexual object was the self. This fixation supposedly produces an abnormal *narcissism* (love of self), that prevents a sexual attachment to the parent of the other sex. In adulthood the person looks for a partner who will mirror the person him- or herself. In other cases, the absence of the same-sex parent may short-circuit the usual process of same-sex identification. In still other cases, the child may fail, for one reason or another, to repress an incestuous desire for the parent of the other sex; therefore any attachment to that parent will arouse intense anxiety and may later generalize to other members of the opposite sex. One psychoanalyst who was influential in the 1960s, Irving Bieber, argued that the combination of a seductive and overprotective mother and a father who fails to act as a role model drives the male child into homosexuality as a "pathologic alternative" (Bieber et al., 1962).

Freud seems to have been rather ambivalent about homosexuality. Although he considered it abnormal, he did not consider it an illness and did not think therapists should try to "cure" it. For Freud, the essential difference between heterosexuals and homosexuals was that the latter act out a tendency inherent in all of us and develop it as a preference. In the early 1930s, forty years before the American Psychiatric Association decided that homosexuality was not a disorder, Freud wrote to the mother of a gay son, "Homosexuality is assuredly no advantage but it is nothing to be ashamed of, no vice, no degradation...we consider it to be a variation of the sexual function...Many highly respectable individuals of ancient and modern times have been homosexuals, several of the greatest men among them...." (Freud, 1961). Many of Freud's successors, however, have been far less tolerant. Because of their obvious bias against homosexuality, their theories have fallen from favor in recent years. Critics point out that psychoanalysts have based their conclusions almost entirely on the retrospective accounts of patients in therapy, and on their own subjective "clinical impressions," rather than hard data.

Most damaging to the psychoanalytic approach, controlled studies fail to support the "smother mother" theory, or any other explanation based on early family relationships. Alan Bell, Martin Weinberg, and Sue Kiefer Hammersmith (1981), under the auspices of the Kinsey Institute, used a sophisticated statistical technique called path analysis to analyze the retrospective self-reports of 979 homosexuals and 477 heterosexuals living in the San Francisco Bay Area. They found that boys who grew up with dominant or seductive mothers and weak or inadequate fathers were no more likely to become homosexual than anyone else. Lesbians were more likely than other women to have rejecting mothers and detached or hostile fathers, but daughter-parent relationships had only a weak connection to a woman's eventual sexual preference. The authors concluded that the role of parents in a child's sexual orientation has been "grossly exaggerated," and that there is little evidence to support psychoanalytic explanations of homosexuality.

Learning Explanations

According to the behavioral school of psychology, most human actions are governed by their consequences. Any act that is rewarded is strengthened and becomes more likely to reoccur, and any act that leads to pain or discomfort is weakened and becomes less likely to reoccur. This rather simple principle has been demonstrated in hundreds of experiments with animals and human beings. *Social-learning theories*, which are an extension of behavioral principles, also emphasize the cultural knowledge people acquire through observation of other people (models) and exposure to cultural messages during socialization.

Learning approaches suggest that a person's sexual orientation is learned the way any other set of behaviors and attitudes is learned. For example, if a person's first fantasies or experiences with manual or oral sex happen to occur in the course of youthful sexual exploration with a person of the same sex, then the pleasure that occurs may make another homosexual act more likely, and the accumulation of rewarding experiences may eventually lead to a definite preference. If early masturbation is accompanied by images of the same sex, those images may become highly erotic to the person through a process known as *classical conditioning*. Or if a child has a very unpleasant experience with a person of the other sex, he or she may lean toward homosexuality. Similar arguments can be made about the acquisition of heterosexuality.

One interesting theory, which combines learning factors with biological ones, suggests that homosexuality is most likely to develop in people whose "sex drive" matures early in adolescence, when they are still associating mostly with same-sex friends and feeling their greatest emotional attachment to such friends. In this view, heterosexuality is more likely to develop in those whose sex drive matures later, because by then the culture is encouraging dating (Storms, 1981). More research is needed on this theory.

Learning approaches may help explain the wide cultural differences that exist in attitudes about, and experiences with, homosexuality (Baldwin & Baldwin, 1989). In Western societies, early same-sex experiences are a private matter. But among the Sambia, a tribe of Papua New Guinea, young males are *required* to spend 10 or more years before marriage in exclusively homosexual relations. In the years just before puberty, they must ingest semen while participating in fellatio with older boys, a practice that is considered essential for growing into manhood (Herdt, 1984). Often the boys must at first be forced into performing fellatio, under threat of punishment; they are usually frightened, and there is little pleasure involved. For them, homosexual behavior is a means to an end, a necessary step on the road to heterosexuality. As boys grow older, and assume the role of recipient of fellatio, they come to enjoy their homosexual activities more, but at the same time, they undergo intense initiation rituals that emphasize females as objects of erotic interest. Moreover, all adult role models are heterosexual. Under these conditions, homosexual acts do not appear to lead to the kind of enduring and positive homosexual orientation that characterizes exclusively gay men in the West. After marriage, same-sex contacts may continue, but after the birth of the first child they usually cease. (For more on cross-cultural differences in attitudes toward homosexuality, see Chapter 1.)

Unfortunately for learning explanations, there is little evidence that early experiences have anything to do with sexual orientation in our own society. Bell, Weinberg, and Hammersmith (1981) found that people who were exclusively homosexual as adults had not had fewer heterosexual dating experiences (indicating, by the way, that gay and lesbian people are not less adept than others at attracting the other sex). Nor were they more likely to have been traumatized by an early heterosexual experience. They were less likely than heterosexuals to have enjoyed their youthful heterosexual encounters, but that might have been a *result*, not a cause, of their sexual orientation.

Another study, headed by psychiatrist Richard Green (1987), followed 44 effeminate boys for a period of 15 years. These boys preferred dolls to "boys' toys," avoided playing with other boys, and liked to dress up as girls. Three-fourths of them grew up to be either homosexual or bisexual. In comparison, in a control group of 35 masculine boys, only one boy became bisexual and none became predominantly homosexual. Did the effeminate boys *learn* to be effeminate—and to be homosexual? The parents of some of the boys did seem more tolerant of early feminine behavior than other parents; for example, some kept photographs of their sons dressed as girls. But in general, parental characteristics and behavior were *not* associated with later sexual orientation.[1]

Learning approaches must contend not only with this negative evidence, but also with the fact that rewards overwhelmingly favor heterosexuality in most cultures, yet many people become homosexual or bisexual. In our own society, young people are bombarded by media images extolling heterosexual love. Even before they know what the words "fag" or "queer" mean, children hurl them at one another as ultimate insults. The pressures, then, are all in the direction of heterosexuality. As sociologist Frederick L. Whitam (1977) observed, "one of the most amazing aspects of homosexuality is that it emerges without a script. Children seem to be sexual beings who invest others and situations with their own childish eroticism."

Concerns about Causes

So what *does* cause homosexuality, or any other sexual orientation? The only answer possible, at least at present, is "who knows?" Even gay and lesbian people, who have given a lot of thought to this question, have not reached a consensus. Many say that because they felt "different" from earliest childhood, there must be some genetic or hormonal explanation. However, their memories could be colored by a need to view their orientation,

---

[1] Other researchers have also reported a link between "gender nonconformity" in boyhood and later homosexuality. We should point out, however, that although many "effeminate" boys do become gay, this does *not* necessarily mean that most gay men were effeminate as children. As for women, Bell and his colleagues (1981) found that four-fifths of lesbian women said they were not highly feminine as children—but so did two-thirds of the heterosexual women. Thus gender nonconformity seems to be a better predictor of homosexuality in men than in women.

which is so widely denounced, as inevitable. And not all homosexual people have such memories; many do not recall feeling gay or lesbian until well into adolescence or even adulthood.

Some lesbian writers have observed that the reasons women report becoming lesbian vary widely:

> Some of us choose to be lesbians because we found that in our relationships with women the spiritual qualities and psychological or emotional connections give us great satisfaction and empower us in our own potentials. Some of us choose to be lesbians for more strictly political reasons, in order to counter heterosexual privilege and to develop nonaggressive and nonhierarchical structures for interpersonal relationships....Others of us feel that our connections and attractions have always been exclusively to women and that a lesbian identity has led us to discover who we are despite the lack of models available to us. Others feel we were born lesbians. Some of us recognize our ability to relate intimately, sexually, and emotionally to both men and women" (Boston Lesbian Psychologies Collective, 1987).

Many social scientists believe that genetic, hormonal, family, and learning factors must all interact in some complex way to produce a person's sexual orientation. Others believe that there are several different ways to arrive at a sexual orientation, with biology perhaps most influential in some people and learning in others, and that therefore two people with the "same" sexual orientation may experience it quite differently. Multiple causation, after all, is the rule in human development. Consider school performance. Joan, John, and Jennifer may all be straight A students, but for different reasons. Joan may be highly intelligent, in part because of her genetic makeup (most research indicates that heredity plays some role in intelligence) and in part because she grew up in an intellectually stimulating family. John may do well because he works hard to win the approval of his father, who is aloof and hard to please. Jennifer may excel because in the fourth grade she had an inspiring teacher who praised her and told her that she had the capacity to do anything she wanted to do. Why should we expect sexual preference to be any easier to explain than school performance?

A few scientists, however, take a more radical position: that the search for "causes" should be abandoned, because of its political implications. Sociologist John Gagnon (1987) argues that most of the work on causes "has derived not from its scientific interest, but from social and political struggles over the moral value of 'homosexuality.' " In Gagnon's view, even unbiased research on causes fuels a popular belief in the defective origins of the "homosexual." Biological explanations, which many gay and lesbian people now favor, will not decrease fear of homosexuality, he says, but instead could lead eventually to a search for biological interventions to prevent it. Lesbian and gay people, according to Gagnon, ought to recognize that even friendly research about origins asks people to account for themselves and explain why they are "different" (Gagnon & Michaels, 1989). Perhaps that is why no one has asked whether heterosexuals have deficiencies in certain hormones; whether straight men unconsciously fear castration by other males; whether such "traumatic" experiences as smelling bad body orders in sweaty gyms or public toilets cause heterosexuals to develop an aversion to the bodies of people of their own sex; or whether children and teenagers become heterosexual because they are seduced by a member of the other sex (Smith, 1979).

Do you think lesbian and gay people should stop cooperating with researchers investigating the causes of sexual orientation? What are the political and social implications of the various "explanations" of homosexuality? How can we study the origins of heterosexuality, along with those of homosexuality—or can we?

ATTITUDES TOWARD HOMOSEXUALITY: FROM HOMOPHOBIA TO ACCEPTANCE

Three decades ago homosexuality was rarely mentioned in public, or in private for that matter. Today it is the topic of newspaper and magazine articles, public demonstrations, television talk shows, sitcoms, and dramas. The greater visibility of lesbians and gays in American society is probably due partly to a general liberalization of sexual attitudes, partly to the increased political consciousness and activism of lesbian and gay people, and partly to the advent of AIDS. The homosexual community now supports many organizations and institutions dedicated to affirming lesbian and gay pride and the rights of lesbian and gay people.

Along with increased visibility, there has been some increase in acceptance by the general population. But anti-homosexual sentiment is still very much alive, as we saw at the start of this chapter. In a public opinion poll conducted during the 1960s, respondents rated homosexuals as the third most dangerous group in the United States—after communists and atheists (Aguero, Bloch & Byrne, 1984). During the seventies, support for at least some legal rights for homosexuals increased, but a majority of people continued to view homosexuality as obscene and vulgar, and said they preferred not to associate with homosexuals (Levitt & Klassen, 1974). Between 1982 and 1987, support for legalizing homosexual relations dropped from 45 percent to only 33 percent, perhaps because the AIDS epidemic, which first hit the gay community, aroused anti-gay feelings. Two years later almost half the population again supported legalization, but a third were definitely opposed (Gallup Poll, 1989). Young people do not seem to be any more tolerant than older ones. A statewide survey of almost 3,000 junior and senior high school students in New York found greater hostility toward lesbian and gay people than toward racial or ethnic minorities (Governor's Task Force,

1988). Surveys of college students in recent years have found that most students hold negative attitudes toward homosexuality (Kurdek, 1988).

Researchers and gay and lesbian activists often use the term **homophobia** to refer to antigay feelings. A phobia is a persistent and irrational fear; by analogy, homophobia is the persistent and irrational fear of homosexuality. However, homophobia is in many ways more like a prejudice than a phobia, because along with fear, it includes hatred and anger (Hancock, 1986). In recent years, homophobia may have increased. Reports of violence against gays, including murder, rape, and assault, have jumped dramatically. So have reports of verbal abuse. Although some of these changes may be due to improved reporting, survey results suggest that they are real. As many as 92 percent of gay people say they have been the victims of verbal abuse or intimidation, and as many as a quarter report being physically attacked because of their sexual orientation (Herek, 1989). A report to the National Institute of Justice concluded that gay people are probably the most frequent victims of hate violence (Finn & McNeil, 1987).

Many observers believe that the AIDS epidemic has fueled the flames of homophobia and has led to the increase in antigay acts (National Gay & Lesbian Task Force, 1988). This is not quite the same, however, as saying that AIDS has *caused* antigay feeling. As psychologist Gregory Herek (1989) points out, homophobia existed long before the AIDS crisis. What AIDS may have done is provided a convenient rationalization for abuse and discrimination.

Even those who publicly profess tolerance towards gays may consciously or unconsciously be "heterosexist." In one study of these deeper emotional responses (Morin, Taylor, & Kielman, 1975), researchers observed the behavior of men who were being interviewed about their attitudes toward homosexuality and other sexual issues. In some cases, the interviewer wore a Gay and Proud button and was introduced as a member of the Association of Gay Psychologists. In other cases, the interviewer wore no button and was introduced as a graduate student. Participants who thought their interviewer was gay professed more positive attitudes toward homosexuals than the other subjects did. But they also positioned their chairs at a greater distance from the interviewer! Body language, it seems, speaks louder than words.

Social scientists have proposed several possible reasons why some people become homophobic (Hancock, 1986; Herek, 1984; Weinberg, 1972):

1. *Lack of contact.* Some people lack experience and contact with openly self-identified gay men and lesbians. Therefore, the everyday behavior of gay or lesbian couples, such as holding hands, may seem strange and shocking to them.

2. *Religious and social values.* Some people believe that gay and lesbian relationships threaten the family as it has tradition-

ally been defined, although it is not always clear exactly what this means. (Families consisting of mothers, fathers, and children are not going out of style.) Other people oppose homosexuality on religious grounds. Male homosexuality is explicitly prohibited in the book of Leviticus, and in the writings of St. Paul—along with all other forms of nonprocreative sex.

3. *Gender-role socialization.* Some homophobic people wrongly believe that all lesbians act like men and all gay men act like women. If a person has been brought up to feel insecure about any departure from traditional masculinity and femininity, such perceptions may be threatening and confusing.

4. *Sexuality.* A person who expresses hatred of homosexuals perhaps "doth protest too much." As we have seen, many heterosexuals have at least occasional sexual fantasies involving the

They're obviously not American *German Chancellor Helmut Kohl and French President François Mitterrand hold hands at a memorial ceremony for soldiers killed in World War I. In the U.S., touching by men is often interpreted as sexual, and in part because of widespread homophobia, most American men would not feel comfortable expressing friendship in this way.*

same sex, and many—perhaps most—have the potential to experience same-sex attraction. Such thoughts and feelings may be extremely threatening to some people. Their homophobia may be a form of denial, a way of reassuring themselves and others that they are indeed purely heterosexual.

In general, people with negative attitudes toward homosexuality are more likely than others to:

- lack personal contact with lesbians and gay men
- have colleagues and peers who also hold negative attitudes
- live during adolescence in rural areas or small towns
- be males who are older and less well educated than the general population
- be religious, attend church frequently, and subscribe to a conservative religious ideology
- hold traditional, restrictive attitudes about gender roles
- be sexually restrictive and experience sexual guilt
- have an authoritarian personality (perceive the world in a rigid, inflexible fashion) (Herek, 1984).

These characteristics are similar to those of people who are prejudiced against racial or ethnic minorities. Indeed, racism, sexism, and "erotophobia" (sexual fearfulness) are all correlated with homophobia (Ficarrotto, 1985).

Most studies find that homophobic harassment of homosexuals, especially violence, is directed more toward gay men than toward lesbians, although both groups suffer from it. Several reasons are possible. Some straight men consider lesbian sex erotic—witness the abundance of lesbian scenes in pornographic movies and magazines aimed at a heterosexual audience. Heterosexuals generally do not feel this way about gay male sex. Also, gay men are more numerous than lesbians and affiliate more often with a visible subculture, and may therefore make easier targets. Some people have difficulty believing that sex without insertion of a penis is real sex, and they may see sex between two women as merely "fooling around." Finally, since the male role has traditionally been more highly valued by society than the female role, a gay man's behavior may seem like a greater transgression ("You can't blame women for wanting to be like men, but why would anyone want to be like a woman?").

Most studies have also found heterosexual men to be more homophobic than heterosexual women, especially toward gay men (Kite, 1984). For example, in the Morin, Taylor, and Kielman study cited earlier, men placed themselves about three times as far away from a purportedly gay male interviewer than women did from a purportedly lesbian interviewer. Men's greater homophobia may be due in part to anxiety about their own masculinity. In our society, in which fathers spend less time with children than mothers do and most elementary school teachers are women, little boys may have trouble figuring out what it means to be male. All they know for sure is what males must *not* do: behave like females. For ideas about maleness, they may turn to media images, which are highly exaggerated. And they may never be sure they have "achieved" what has never been clearly defined. Their insecurity, then, may be aroused by gay men, whom they regard (on the whole, incorrectly) as unmasculine. Since they have learned to regard sexual success with women as a badge of masculinity, they may also find men who don't care about such success to be puzzling and odd. In one writer's words, "After years of struggle to achieve a precarious masculine identity, many heterosexual men feel threatened by the sight of homosexuals, who appear to them to be disdainful of the basic requirements of manhood" (Weinberg, 1972).

We might close this chapter by asking what kinds of characteristics are related to *positive* attitudes toward homosexuality. Although this question has rarely been raised, there is evidence that people with positive attitudes hold flexible ideas about male and female behavior. They seem also to have attained a high level of moral reasoning. When presented with moral dilemmas, they are able to apply principles of conduct based on individual conscience and universal human rights instead of relying on conventional rules and regulations (Kurdek, 1988).

Although the most obvious victims of homophobia are gay men and lesbians, homophobia exacts a price from all of us. In a world without homophobia, straight men might feel more comfortable about showing affection and support to each other and might have closer relationships with each other. Fathers might allow themselves to kiss and hug their sons more often. Men and women alike might feel more comfortable about rejecting narrow and confining rules of dress and gesture. Lovers might worry less about who is the "assertive" one during lovemaking. Most important, in a world without homophobia, all of us might be better able to appreciate the special qualities that each individual, of whatever sexual orientation, can bring to the world.

• •

ARE YOU HOMOPHOBIC?

PERSONAL PERSPECTIVE

If you regard yourself as heterosexual, you can use this exercise to examine your attitudes and feelings toward other sexual orientations. For each of the following situations, ask yourself what you would do and feel. (If you regard yourself as gay or bisexual, consider the implications of each situation for yourself and others.) Notice not only your thoughts ("This is wrong," "That's fine, she'd still be the same person") but also any gut-level emotional responses (anger, disgust, discomfort, surprise, cheerfulness, enthusiasm....). Are your thoughts and emotions consistent?

Where do you think your attitudes about sexual orientation, positive or negative, came from?

1. Your best friend, a male, tells you that he is homosexual. What do you say to him? How do you feel about the future of your friendship? Are you willing to double date with your friend and his partner? Are you tempted to try to "talk him out of" being gay? Suppose your best friend is female; does that change any of your answers? What if it's not your best friend, but your brother or sister?

2. You are an apartment manager. Two women apply for an apartment in your building. As you are showing them around, you notice one of them putting her arm around the other. Do you find yourself wondering about their sexual orientation? Are you tempted to ask them questions about their personal life? If their references check out, will you rent them the apartment? What if they are two men?

3. You are the parent of a female college student. One day your daughter tells you she has something important to talk to you about. She wants you to know that she is a lesbian and she is in love with a wonderful woman. What is your first reaction? Do you tell her that her sexual orientation is fine with you? Do you cry? Do you holler? Do you suggest she invite her partner over so you can meet her? Do you propose psychotherapy? What if your child is a son rather than a daughter?

4. You are planning a small party for some friends. One of the friends is homosexual and the rest are straight. Do you hesitate to invite your homosexual friend? Do you feel obliged to inform your other friends of the person's sexual orientation? Do you have any concerns about what your friends will think? About what your parents will think (if you are living with them)? Do you encourage your homosexual friend to bring a date? How will you feel if your friend and his/her date dance together, or hold hands?

5. You are working at a part-time job, waiting on tables in a restaurant. You have been getting to know one of your co-workers, whom you like very much. One day, this person tells you that she or he is bisexual. How do you respond to this disclosure? Are you worried that the person might "come on" to you? You had been planning to invite your co-worker over to listen to some music; do you still want to extend the invitation? Are your reactions affected by whether the person is male or female?

IN BRIEF

1. All sexual orientations are not treated equally. *Heterosexism* is common in our culture. Although gays and lesbians have made great strides in recent years in their quest for civil and human rights, discrimination against them occurs in hiring, housing, custody cases, and many other areas.

2. It is hard to estimate the prevalence of homosexuality in the population because not everyone falls neatly into either the heterosexual or homosexual category. Moreover, identity, feelings, and behavior are not always completely consistent; many people who identify themselves as homosexual have had heterosexual experiences and vice versa. It is clear, however, that self-identified homosexuals and bisexuals constitute sizable minorities in our society.

3. Homosexuality was once listed in the manual of mental disorders used by psychiatrists and psychologists, but this is no longer so. Research has shown that as a group, homosexuals are no more disturbed than heterosexuals and in certain respects may even be psychologically healthier. Most therapists are no longer interested in trying to "cure" homosexuality.

4. *Coming out* is an important process for gays, lesbians, and bisexuals. Some young gay and lesbian people may go to great lengths to pretend to themselves or others that they are heterosexual, and often they feel socially and emotionally isolated. Acknowledging one's homosexuality can be risky, but living a double life is in many ways more stressful.

5. Homosexual relationships are diverse. Lesbians and gays may live monogamously with a partner; live with a special partner but not monogamously; be happy leading a single, sexually active life; be troubled and unhappy leading a sexually active life; or show little interest in sexual activity. These "life styles" may not differ much from those of heterosexuals, although heterosexual, lesbian, and gay couples do sometimes face somewhat different problems regarding money, work, and sex. Overall, same-sex and straight couples seem to be equally satisfied with their relationships.

6. Most lesbians and gays do not conform to popular stereotypes about homosexuality. Most are not identifiable by dress or demeanor, most do not assume the traditional husband and wife roles in relationships, and most do not play a particular role during lovemaking.

7. In certain cities, many gay men, and to a lesser extent lesbians, identify with a subculture that has its own unique institutions and customs, analogous to those of ethnic subcultures. In some places such subcultures are distinguished by styles of dress and even speech patterns.

8. Many homosexual people have children. In some cases, the children were born during marriages to heterosexuals. But increasingly, lesbians and gay men are taking advantage of other ways of becoming parents, such as artificial insemination or adoption. There is no evidence that the children of homosexual parents are any less well-adjusted than those of heterosexual parents.

9. Homosexual women and men often have different outlooks on love and sex, just as straight women and men do. Although both gay men and lesbians usually value romance and look for warmth, love, and companionship in their relationships, gay men seem less willing to give up their freedom and independence to preserve a long-term affair. Lesbians have fewer partners than gay men do and are less interested in impersonal or casual encounters. Both biological and learning explanations have been offered to explain such differences.

10. The origins of sexual orientation are poorly understood. Genetic, hormonal, psychoanalytic, and learning explanations have all been proposed, but the evidence is conflicting and inconclusive. Many social scientists believe that several factors must interact in some complex way to produce a person's orientation, or that different people may arrive at a given orientation by different routes. Some social scientists take a more radical position: they believe that the search for causes should be dropped because it supports the popular belief that homosexuality is a deficiency to be explained. They note that few people search for the causes of heterosexuality.

11. *Homophobia* may have increased in recent years, fueled in part by reactions to the AIDS epidemic, which hit the gay community first. Possible causes of homophobia include a lack of contact with gays and lesbians, religious and social values, rigid gender roles, and fear of one's own homosexual fantasies or feelings. Racism, sexism, and "erotophobia" are all correlated with homophobia. Most studies find homophobic harassment of homosexuals to be directed more often toward gay men than lesbians, although both groups suffer from it. Most studies also find heterosexual men to be more homophobic than heterosexual women, especially toward gay men.

12. Positive attitudes toward homosexuality are associated with flexible ideas about male and female behavior and a high level of moral reasoning. Although the most obvious victims of homophobia are gay men and lesbians, homophobia exacts a price from all of us.

Key Terms

heterosexism *(521)*   heterosexual *(524)*   lesbian *(525)*

sexual
orientation *(523)*   homosexual *(524)*   gay *(524)*

bisexual *(525)*

social constructionism *(529)*

coming out *(535)*

close-coupled homosexuals *(537)*

open-coupled homosexuals *(537)*

functional homosexuals *(537)*

dysfunctional homosexuals *(538)*

asexual homosexuals *(538)*

gay and lesbian culture *(542)*

homophobia *(556)*

Social and Health Issues

CHAPTER FIFTEEN

C H A P T E R F I F T E E N

■

Sexual Abuse And Exploitation

•

If anything is sacred, the human body is sacred.

Walt Whitman

exual acts, when freely chosen, can be friendly or funny, playful or passionate, romantic or routine. But unfortunately, many sexual encounters are *not* freely chosen. They occur, instead, because one person threatens, coerces, or uses force against another. Such experiences have nothing to do with "love-making." For the unwilling participant, they are humiliating, exploitive, harrowing, and sometimes even fatal. For the perpetrator, sex may be the means, but it is not always the end; often the motives are control, power, or the need to humble and degrade another human being.

Sexual exploitation includes sexual harassment, various forms of rape and sexual aggression, and the sexual abuse of children, including incest. In all these cases, the perpetrator takes advantage of a situation in which he or (more rarely) she can dominate or manipulate the victim. The victim has no choice, or consents only under duress, or is unable to exercise free choice because of age, mental state, or physical condition. The perpetrator may rationalize the exploitive actions in various ways, but in reality is concerned only with selfish goals, ignoring the harm being done to the other person, or oblivious to it. The survivor of sexual exploitation usually suffers serious short-term harm, both mental and physical, and often suffers long-term harm as well.

Why do some people use sex to abuse and hurt others or selfishly gratify themselves? Why do they find sexual exploitation to be sexually exciting? Most people look for the answers in the personal pathology of the offender, or irrationally blame the victim. But the shocking prevalence of sexual exploitation in our society, and differences in its occurrence from one society to another, lead to a different conclusion. In this chapter, we will see that sexual exploitation has as much to do with prevailing cultural attitudes as it does with the personal characteristics of individual offenders. The very ordinariness of sexual exploitation makes it a problem for all of us, both male and female.

RAPE

In Western law, the traditional definition of **rape** is "unlawful carnal knowledge of a woman by force and without her consent." But in the United States, states vary somewhat in their definitions. In some states, rape is said to occur only if a male's penis has penetrated a female's vagina. Others have broadened their definitions to include other sexual acts, such as forced oral-genital contact, anal penetration, or penetration of the victim's vagina by objects, recognizing that forced noncoital sex can be just as traumatic as the "classic" coital rape. Most states mention physical force or the threat of force when defining rape, but several also include situations in which the perpetrator overcomes the victim by getting her drunk, drugging her, or using deception of some sort. Some states provide for different degrees of rape, depending on the extent to which force or violence is used. Other states avoid the word *rape* altogether, since it tends to arouse certain prejudices, usually directed against the victim. Instead they refer to sexual assault, sexual battery, or criminal sexual conduct.

Incidence and Prevalence

It is hard to determine the exact incidence of rape (the number of rapes that occur in a given time period) or its prevalence (the number of people who have ever been raped). According to federal figures, about 91,000 rapes were reported in the United States in 1987 (U.S. Bureau of the Census, 1988). But these figures are misleading, because rape is one of the most underreported of all crimes. Many survivors are embarrassed to reveal publicly that they were raped. Others decide not to bring charges because they feel their chances of getting justice are slim or they fear retaliation by the rapist. In many cases police have discounted reports and refused to pursue them (Russell, 1982).

In an attempt to overcome these problems, government researchers have conducted *community surveys*, calling or visiting households selected at random to ask about the occupants' experiences. Questions on rape have usually been embedded in a more general survey. One such study, by the U.S. Department of Justice (1985), estimated that 1.66 of every thousand females over 12 years of age was a victim of rape or attempted rape in 1983.

It could happen anywhere   *This scene, from the movie* The Accused, *shows people joking and flirting much as they might at any bar or gathering place in the United States. But in the film (based on a true case), the men, along with several other patrons of the bar, subsequently rape the woman on top of the pinball machine as a crowd cheers them on. The film raises disturbing issues: What accounts for the high incidence of rape in our society and the existence of callous attitudes toward rape victims?*

But this figure, too, is almost certainly far too low, because the study relied on a narrow definition of rape and used survey techniques that were not well-designed for eliciting reports of traumatic or embarrassing experiences.

Two other studies reveal a much different picture. In one, conducted in 1978, sociologist Diana Russell (1982, 1984) had specially trained female researchers interview 930 women aged 18 or older, selected randomly from households in San Francisco. (Federal statistics on reported rapes suggest that San Francisco's rape rate is not unusual for an urban area.) In Russell's sample, 19 percent of the women reported at least one experience that met the legal definition of rape in most states at that time, and 31 percent reported at least one attempted rape. Altogether, 41 percent of the women had experienced at least one completed or attempted rape, and half these women had experienced more than one attack. (Group rape was counted as a single attack.) When rape by husbands was included, the figures were even higher. Only about 1 in ten of these incidents was ever reported to the police. For just the 12 months prior to her study, Russell estimates, there were 35 rapes for every 1,000 women over the age of 17 in San Francisco, *13 times* as many as the official figures for females of all ages in that city.

In other research, psychologist Mary Koss and her colleagues (1987) surveyed nearly 6,200 college students on 32 campuses across the country. About 15 percent of the women reported at least one experience that met legal definitions of forcible rape, and 12 percent reported at least one attempted rape. Altogether, 28 percent had experienced rape or attempted rape since the age of 14. Only 5 percent of the incidents were ever reported to the police. Other studies have reported similar figures (DiVasto et al., 1984; Mims & Chang, 1984; Parrot & Allen, 1984).

The key question is: What are a woman's lifetime chances of being raped? Taking into account that a woman's vulnerability depends partly on her age, Russell estimates that a woman living in the United States has about a one in four chance of being the victim of at least one *completed* rape at some time in her life, and almost a one in two chance of being the victim of a completed or attempted rape (Russell & Howell, 1983). If you consider that over one-fourth of Koss's college women had *already* experienced a completed or attempted rape, and that most of these women were still quite young, Russell's estimates seem realistic. These figures tell us that a woman in the United States is more likely to confront a rapist at some time in her life than she is to get cancer, and almost as likely to confront a rapist as she is to get divorced.

Some women are at greater risk of being raped than others. Almost all studies show that women in their late teens and early twenties tend to run the highest risk. And single women are at greater risk than married ones (perhaps in part because they also tend to be younger). Other "risk factors," however, are less clear. Some studies, most of them based on reported cases, find that poor women are more vulnerable than more affluent ones. However, Diana Russell found no such correlation; in fact, her findings were in the opposite direction (see also Ageton, 1983). Similarly, the federal government finds African-American women to be more vulnerable than others, but Russell found Native American and white women to be slightly more vulnerable than African-Americans.

Statistics aside, it is clear that females of all ages, races, and life styles are potential rape victims—babies and grandmothers, rich women and poor. When nurse Ann Wolberg Burgess and sociologist Lynda Lytle Holmstrom (1974) studied all adult rape victims in the emergency ward of Boston City Hospital during a one-year period, they found that the group included women of all races and ethnic groups; professional women, blue collar workers, homemakers, students, and women on welfare; women aged 17 to 73; single, married, divorced, separated, cohabiting, and widowed women; women with zero to ten children; pregnant women (one in her eighth month) and women who had recently given birth; attractive women and plain women. The only thing all the victims had in common is that they were female and they were raped.

Men, too, are sometimes raped, usually by other men. These incidents, which typically involve anal penetration, do not usually show up in official statistics because they tend to be unreported or are prosecuted under different charges. In large cities, youth gangs sometimes use rape to humiliate rival gang members. Rape in prison is epidemic (Cotton & Groth, 1982; Davis, 1968; Sagarin, 1976). A study of sexual assaults in the Philadelphia prison system found that nearly every slightly-built young man was approached sexually within his first day or two as an inmate. Many of these men were raped by gangs of convicts; others sought protection by "voluntarily" agreeing to a sexual relationship with one particular aggressor.

The typical prison rapist did not view himself as a homosexual, or commit rape simply to reduce sexual tension. Rather, like many men who rape women, prison rapists used assault to conquer and degrade their victims, telling them, "We're going to take your manhood," or "We're gonna make a girl out of you" (Davis, 1968).

When women are charged with rape it is usually because they have served as accessories to the crime (for example, by holding a weapon on the victim). This does not mean that men are never sexually coerced by women or pressured to have sex on a date. In one study of almost a thousand college students, almost *everyone*, male and female, had engaged in unwanted sexual activity of some sort, and men were actually *more* likely than women to report having had unwanted intercourse (Muehlenhard & Cook, 1988). However, the nature of the pressure tends to differ for men and women. Although there is overlap in the reasons given for unwanted sex, women are more likely than men to report being physically threatened or harmed, and men are more likely than women to mention peer pressure, intoxication, gender-role concerns, a desire to be popular, and a desire to be "experienced" (Muehlenhard & Cook, 1988; Sorenson et al., 1987).

Types of Rape

What sort of mental image do you have of rape? Do you conjure up a stranger surprising a lone woman in a dark alley? Do you imagine violence—a weapon, or a beating? Does the victim struggle, or does she submit quietly out of fear for her life? Whatever your image of rape, you are probably right, for at least some rapes.

Researchers have distinguished four different types of rape, according to the circumstances in which they occur.

ACQUAINTANCE RAPE   Official government statistics say that most rapes are committed by strangers, and this is also the common stereotype. In truth, **acquaintance rapes,** committed by someone known to the victim, are far more frequent. In Russell's study, a woman was *eight times* more likely to be attacked by someone she knew than by a stranger. In Koss's college sample, *89 percent* of all rapes were committed by men the women knew, and more than half occurred on dates (Koss et al., 1988). Other studies, too, find that the typical rapist is known to his victim (Muehlenhard & Linton, 1987; Mynatt & Allgeier, 1990). Far from being a deranged stranger, the rapist may be a neighbor, boss, fellow employee, fellow student, or even a boyfriend.

Do you find yourself resisting these findings? If so, you are not alone; their implications are, indeed, unsettling. Even victims often avoid facing the reality of acquaintance rape. In Koss's study, almost three-fourths of the women who had been forced into sex avoided using the word *rape* to label their experience. In another study, 16 percent of the women reported being forced by an acquaintance or date to have intercourse against their will, yet only 2 percent said they had been raped (Parrot & Allen, 1984). The harsh truth about the prevalence of acquaintance rape forces us to confront a fact that most of us would rather avoid: that rape is more likely to intrude on our lives than we might think. It also raises disturbing questions about male-female relations, which we return to in a later section.

Much of the recent research on acquaintance rape has focused on **date rape.** In studies of college students, about half of all rapes reported by women have been on dates. These incidents often involve lying, drugs, extortion, fraud, or verbal intimidation rather than weapons or fists (Kanin, 1985), although physical violence can and does occur. Psychologist R. Lance Shotland (1989) suggests that there are three distinct types of date rape, each with its own characteristics and dynamics:

1. In *beginning rape*, the rape occurs on the first date. The rapist is likely to be an antisocial person who is insensitive to the suffering of others. He may make a date with the woman with the explicit intention of raping her. Later he may justify his behavior by telling himself he was "led on."

2. In *early date rape*, the rape occurs after a few dates, as the couple gets to know each other and establishes the rules of their relationship. The man may be a sexually aggressive person who has difficulty coping with frustration and controlling his own impulses. He may assume his date has similar (but disguised) desires, misperceiving her as extremely interested in sex when in fact she is merely mildly interested or is just being friendly. This man is likely to hold beliefs that excuse or trivialize rape.

3. In *relational date rape*, the couple has dated regularly and misunderstanding about sexual intentions is not a factor. Instead, the man may feel that since he has paid for the dates, he is justified in forcing the woman into sex. He may also feel that if he doesn't have intercourse with her, that means the relationship is not "going anywhere." He may compare himself with other men who he assumes are having sex with their partners, or with the women's previous partners, and conclude that he is coming off second best—so he forces intercourse.

Shotland and others note that American dating rituals actually promote the kind of miscommunication that can lead to "early" date rape. In our culture, as in many others, young people seldom learn how to discuss their sexual intentions openly and honestly with each other. Instead, they rely on subtle, ambiguous signals and on assumptions about when sex is "supposed" to occur. To make things worse, dating "scripts" often assign roles to men and women that are adversarial from the start (Warshaw, 1988). According to these scripts, men are supposed to show their masculinity by making the first move. Young men are often encouraged by friends to press a date for sexual favors and see how "far" they can get. Women, on the other hand, sometimes feel they must offer some protest even when they are interested in sex, so as not to appear "loose." In one study, 39 percent of women undergraduates said they had engaged in token resistance to sex at least once, saying "no" when they actually had an intention of engaging in sexual intercourse (Muehlenhard & Hollabaugh, 1988). In addition, if a woman has been trained to be "polite," or is anxious about being accepted, she may not know how to assertively and clearly signal her disinterest in sex. Thus women who are serious when they say no may not be taken seriously.

However, miscommunication cannot be the sole cause of date rape. By its very nature, date rape implies a devaluing of women. Men who have lied, made false promises, or used other strategies to get a woman to have sex against her will are more likely than other men to condone physical as well as verbal coercion (Craig, Kalichman & Follingstad, 1989). During many date rapes, the woman screams, cries, and begs not to be raped, yet the rape occurs anyway. In such cases, the man is not confused; he is hostile. In some college fraternities, slang expressions reflect dehumanizing attitudes toward women. The term *ledging,* for instance, refers to a situation in which one fraternity member invites others to eavesdrop on his "conquest" of a naive woman so that they can taunt her about it afterwards. The term derives from the idea that the rape and subsequent harassment could drive the woman to suicide (jumping off a ledge) (Warshaw, 1988).

Most victims of date rape do not commit suicide, but they may lose faith in their own judgment, their trust in others (especially men), and their willingness to love:

> When I started college a year ago I was still a virgin, and a real romantic. . . . After only a few weeks, this senior asked me out. The first date was fun, but on the second date he asked me to his room for a beer, and within a few minutes he was holding me down on the bed. He put his hand over my mouth so no one could hear me screaming, and forced himself on me. Afterwards, he was obviously afraid of being caught. But I was just in shock. I kept denying what had happened, even though I was upset and depressed. Recently I went to a counselor and was able to face the fact that I had been raped. But at present, I still feel hurt and betrayed, and I still have a lot of fear about sex. (Authors' files.)

MARITAL RAPE **Marital rape** is actually one variety of "acquaintance" rape, perhaps the most frequent type. In Russell's San Francisco sample, one out of seven married women had experienced marital rape and two-thirds of these women had been assaulted more than once. One-fifth were still married to the man who had raped them (Russell, 1990).

Against her will   *In this classic scene from* Gone With the Wind, *marital rape is endorsed and romanticized; Clark Gable carries a struggling Vivian Leigh to bed, and the next morning she awakes with a smile on her face and love in her heart. Eroticized images of sexual conquest and submission give a false picture of what real-life forced sex is like.*

Until recently, a husband who forced his wife to have sex was exempt from prosecution. This exemption dates from the seventeenth century, when English jurist Sir Matthew Hale asserted that in signing the marriage contract, a wife agreed to provide sexual services to her husband and could not retract her consent. By law, a wife was the property of her husband and so he could do whatever he wanted to her (Brownmiller, 1975). Rape was not a crime against a woman, but a violation of male property rights—a father's property rights if the victim was unmarried, a husband's if his wife was raped by another man.

Few people questioned the marital rape exemption until the 1970s, when some states finally eliminated it. Since then, most other states have partially or completely removed the exemption, and many have successfully prosecuted men for marital rape. But only sixteen states and the District of Columbia treat marital rape in the same way they would any other sexual assault, and in nine states, husbands still cannot be prosecuted unless a couple is living apart or is legally separated or has filed for divorce (Russell, 1990). As recently as 1980, the American Law Institute described spousal rape as part of "the ongoing process of adjustment in the marital relationship."

As in date rape, victims of marital rape often do not realize that their ordeal can be labeled rape. This is true despite the fact that marital rape is often associated with great brutality and physical abuse (Finkelhor & Yllo, 1985). Accounts of these rapes make painful reading. One woman recalled,

"He would put a pillow over my head when he wanted to have sex and I didn't. He didn't want others to hear me scream" (in Russell, 1990).

STRANGER RAPE   Stranger rapes are the type most likely to be reported and investigated. Most of these rapes are not spur-of-the-moment acts committed by a man who is suddenly carried away by overwhelming sexual urges and who exploits an opportune moment; they are premeditated. In one study of rapists incarcerated at a California mental hospital (Chappell & James, 1976), almost two-thirds of the men reported at least some planning, and planning was apparent even in the reports of those who claimed there was none. Planning typically meant selecting a place to contact the victim that would minimize the chances of detection, but some planning also took place after the rapist spotted a potential victim:

> As we drove past the corner to make a turn to go by the laundromat, I looked over there. There was this woman in cutoffs—young and wore glasses and was pretty. There was nobody else there so I decided I was going to make my attempt. The man dropped me off at home and I hurried into the house to change my clothes. Grabbed a butcher knife from the kitchen...and went to the back door, because there were neighbors in the front....I went to the laundromat. She was still there. I sneaked up on her so she wouldn't see me approaching and I went in and messed around....she had her back turned on me and I grabbed her from behind and told her to take it easy and if she did what I wanted, everything would be okay. I said, "Let's go to the restroom." (in Chappell & James, 1976, p. 12)

A rapist who does not know his victim is concerned with finding a place where he can get away with the assault. The circumstances are likely to be more important to him than any particular characteristics of the victim. (Is she alone? Does she live in an easily entered home or apartment?) However, some researchers believe that certain traits traditionally associated with femininity—politeness, helpfulness, submissiveness—can make a woman especially vulnerable to a certain type of rapist, the type who initially tests an intended victim's reactions. A study in Denver found that one-fourth of the women attacked by a stranger during a two-year period were responding to the rapist's request for help. The rapist might ask his victim for a match or for directions, or might request entrance to her home to make an emergency phone call. After the rapist identified a potential victim, he would test her to see how easily intimidated she was. For instance, he might ask an intimate question, make a suggestive remark, or touch her (Selkin, 1975).

The potential for violence and even murder exists during any rape, but the threat is greatest in stranger rape. Most of these attacks involve physical force of some kind: holding, pushing, slapping, beating, or choking. Many involve a weapon. Violence is especially likely during group (or "gang") rapes, which account for between one-fourth and two-fifths of all stranger rapes. Most victims of physical attacks during rape suffer bodily injuries. These injuries may be associated with the sexual act itself, but many are not. They include scratches, cuts, bruises, black eyes, unconsciousness, internal injuries, knocked out teeth, broken bones, and knife or gunshot wounds. In one study (McDermott, 1979), almost ten percent of the cases involved broken bones, internal injuries, or wounds from a weapon, most often a knife. Sometimes a sharp object is thrust into the woman's vagina. Obviously rape is nothing like seduction. Victims often say they were as terrified of being killed or seriously hurt as they were of being sexually violated.

STATUTORY RAPE   **Statutory rape** (also called unlawful intercourse) is a sexual offense that departs from the general definition of rape given earlier in this chapter. It refers to intercourse with a person who is below a certain age of consent, with or without the person's agreement; force or deception are not at issue. The laws of many states prohibit intercourse with males and females who are below some specified age, but others protect only females. In practice, it is almost always males who are prosecuted.

Statutory rape laws are based in part on the assumption that the state has an interest in protecting young girls from pregnancy. They also reflect general agreement that until a certain age, young people cannot understand the risks of sexual activity (e.g., pregnancy, emotional dependency, and sexually transmitted diseases) and are therefore vulnerable to exploitation. Controversy exists, however, about what that certain age is. Nearly everyone believes that preadolescent children of both sexes should be protected from adults who try to take advantage of them. Too-early sex can interrupt the normal progression of psychosexual development and traumatize a child, as we will see later in this chapter. But what about teenagers? Is a girl of 13 or 14 always unable to decide whether or not to have intercourse? What about a girl of 16? Or eighteen, the age of consent in most states? The average age of first intercourse for girls in the United States is now about 16 (see Chapter 13). Should a 16-year-old girl's sexual partner be subject to criminal prosecution? Does his age make a difference?

There has been little public discussion of these questions, nor have courts given them much attention. One exception: In 1981, the U.S. Supreme Court ruled against a young California man who protested his statutory rape arrest on the grounds that the state law, which outlawed intercourse with girls under age 18 but not boys, discriminated against males and was based on sexual stereotypes. At the time of his arrest the young man was 17 and his sexual partner was 16. In its decision, the court held that the state had a legitimate right to use the law to try to prevent teenage pregnancy.

You can see that statutory rape laws raise many difficult issues, different from the ones raised by forcible rape. In the remainder of this chapter, we will be concerned only with sexual acts involving an unwilling or incapacitated person.

Motives for Rape

We have seen that rape can occur in various circumstances. It can also involve various motives. It has become a cliché that rape is not a sexual crime, but a crime of violence and power. The truth, however, is a little more complicated. In many, and probably most, acquaintance rapes, sexual gratification does seem to be a primary goal. As noted previously, date rapes may occur without much planning, and may result in part from miscommunication or from the man's belief that he "deserves" to get sex from the woman and has the right to take it, no matter what the woman's feelings. Stranger rapes, too, are sometimes motivated primarily by sexual impulses. A man happens to meet a woman he perceives as "loose" or a woman whose ability to resist is impaired (for example, because she is inebriated), and he takes advantage of the situation by forcing sex on her.

Other rapes clearly involve nonsexual motives. According to one proposal, based on work with over a thousand rapists in clinical settings, these motives include anger, power, and sadism (Groth & Hobson, 1983):

- In *anger rape*, the assault is unplanned and savage, prompted not by a need for sexual release but by rage and contempt for women. The rapist may see his attack as revenge for the humiliation and rejection he feels he has suffered at the hands of women. Although his victim is likely to be unknown to him, he vents his resentment and fury by brutalizing or degrading her (for example, by forcing her to perform fellatio or anilingus on him).

- In *power rape*, sexual gratification may be involved, but the main motive is the need to exert control and power over another person. The rapist typically lacks real power in his life; he feels like a failure, deals poorly with stress, and is insecure in his masculinity. Usually he uses just enough force to get his victim to submit. The rape is likely to be planned, and the rapist may rape habitually.

- In *sadistic rape*, the attack is planned, ritualistic, and extremely brutal, often involving bondage and torture. To the rapist, aggression and sexuality are the same thing. Power, anger, or both become eroticized; the rapist gets sexual pleasure by tying, biting, burning, or beating.

Although researchers find it helpful to categorize types of rapes and the motives for them, keep in mind that such categories are not mutually exclusive. In any particular instance of rape, the perpetrator may have a mixture of motives, including the venting of anger, the expression of power, contempt for women, and a desire for sexual release.

Who Rapes?

Just as there are many popular images of rape, there are many images of the rapist. In films and books, including romance novels written for women, rapists are sometimes portrayed as handsome, dashing, James Bond types who only have to use a *little* force, since women inevitably melt in their strong arms. Or they are depicted as psychotic, sadistic killers, unfeeling sociopaths, or leering sex-starved boors who can't control their lust.

Until recently, much of what we knew about real rapists came from studies of convicted offenders, men who had, by and large, committed stranger rapes (Baxter et al., 1984; Groth & Burgess, 1977; Levin & Stava, 1987). These studies have found that most convicted rapists are not James Bonds, nor are they psychotic. Many do have personality problems, such as low self-esteem, resentment, an inability to cope with stress, or a tendency to express anger through aggression. Some are also socially isolated and socially inept, worried about their masculinity, and unable to sustain a mature sexual relationship. And many have a history of antisocial behavior for which they feel no remorse. Yet surprisingly, most convicted rapists are not so disturbed that they would stand out in a crowd. Nor are they sexually deprived. In one study of 133 offenders, most of the rapists had some sort of sexual relationship with a consenting partner or at least had access to consenting partners. At least a third were married and having regular intercourse with their wives (Groth & Burgess, 1977).

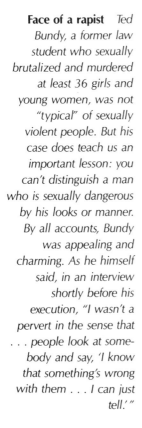

Face of a rapist *Ted Bundy, a former law student who sexually brutalized and murdered at least 36 girls and young women, was not "typical" of sexually violent people. But his case does teach us an important lesson: you can't distinguish a man who is sexually dangerous by his looks or manner. By all accounts, Bundy was appealing and charming. As he himself said, in an interview shortly before his execution, "I wasn't a pervert in the sense that . . . people look at somebody and say, 'I know that something's wrong with them . . . I can just tell.'"*

In the past few years, as the widespread prevalence of date and marital rape have become known, the "ordinariness" of most rapists has become even more apparent. Indeed, men who have forced sex on a woman are often difficult to distinguish from the man next door. As we have seen, some *are* the man next door (or a classmate, a co-worker, a friend's brother, or a brother's friend). In one study of college men, 28 percent reported using coercion to obtain sex and 15 percent reported forcing a woman to have intercourse (Rapaport & Burkhart, 1984). In another study, two-fifths of college men admitted using verbal coercion to get a woman to have sex and a third said they had threatened or used actual physical force (Mosher & Anderson, 1986).

On the average, men who rape tend to be in their late teens or early twenties and are sometimes even younger. According to the FBI, the number of arrests for rape committed by boys 18 years of age or younger rose by 14 percent between 1983 and 1987. But rapists, like their victims, are a varied group, and come from all adult age groups, all races, and all socioeconomic groups.

What, then, sets men who rape apart from the majority of men? Studies find that young men who have forced sex on a woman are more likely than other men to hold calloused views of women and to accept beliefs that condone rape. They are also more likely than other young men to have family problems, to be involved with delinquent friends, to have friends who approve of coercing "provocative" women, and to feel pressured by friends to "prove their masculinity" by "scoring" (Ageton, 1983; Kanin, 1985). They are less responsible and less well socialized than other men, more likely to consider women untrustworthy and manipulative, and more likely to regard men and women as adversaries (Rapaport & Burkhart, 1984).

Perhaps the most alarming fact about rape, however, is that many young men who have *not* raped say they can picture themselves doing it. In studies by psychologist Neil Malamuth (1981, 1984), about a third of American and Canadian college men have admitted that there is "some likelihood" they would force a woman to have sex against her will if she rejected them and if they knew they could get away with it. According to Malamuth, "There are a substantial number of men in the general population who show similar response patterns and attitudes as convicted rapists" (in Turkington, 1987). These findings indicate that rape cannot be explained solely in terms of psychological disorder. Clearly something else is going on, when so many apparently "normal" young men can imagine themselves committing a damaging act against a woman under the "right" circumstances. We will return to this matter later, when we look more closely at the causes of rape.

Surviving Rape

Depictions of rape in films and on television often fail to show what happens to the survivor, her friends, and her relatives after the attack. What happens to a woman when she has suffered the most extreme invasion possible of her physical and psychological integrity?

In their study of rape survivors, Burgess and Holmstrom (1974) discovered that most women go through a predictable sequence of emotional reactions, which the researchers labeled the **rape trauma syndrome:**

- In the *acute phase* of the syndrome, which lasts from a few days to several weeks, a woman experiences severe disorganization. Some women express fear, anger, and anxiety by crying, smiling, or becoming tense and restless; others hide their feelings behind a calm and composed exterior. During this period victims suffer the effects of physical trauma, such as soreness, bruising, vaginal infection, genital irritation, and rectal bleeding or pain. Many complain of headaches, fatigue, sleep problems, loss of appetite, and stomach pains. Some suffer unwarranted but powerful feelings of shame, self-blame and guilt.

- In the *reorganization* phase, which lasts from a few months to several years, a rape survivor may have problems functioning at work, home, or school. Some women quit their jobs. In the Burgess and Holmstrom sample, which consisted primarily of victims of stranger rape, almost half of the women changed residences and some moved several times, apparently because they feared a repeat attack by the rapist. Many women had disturbing dreams. Some developed irrational fears of the indoors or outdoors or of being alone or in crowds. Some became afraid of sex. Women with previous physical, psychiatric, or social problems had especially severe symptoms, including depression, psychotic behavior, psychosomatic disorders, suicidal behavior, and problems with alcohol and drugs.

Subsequent studies have verified the reactions originally described by Burgess and Holmstrom (e.g., Atkeson et al., 1982; Becker et al., 1982; Kilpatrick, Veronen & Best, 1985). Many of these symptoms are typical of *post-traumatic stress syndrome*, an emotional disorder often found in people traumatized by war, torture, and natural disasters. In this syndrome, there may also be recurrent thoughts or "flashbacks" about the experience, "psychic numbing" (detachment from others and loss of the ability to feel happiness, intimacy, and sexual desire), extreme alertness, and difficulty concentrating. Rape, however, has certain unique consequences not usually part of the post traumatic stress syndrome—for example, difficulties in relating to men, feelings of degradation, and self-blame. (Self-blame is especially likely when the victim knew her attacker beforehand [Mynatt & Allgeier, 1990].)

The emotional repercussions of rape can continue for many years (Kilpatrick et al., 1985; Esper & Runge, 1988). A woman may never again feel

The trauma of rape   *A physician comforts a woman who has been emotionally devastated by a sexual assault. Survivors of rape often benefit from talking at length to a sympathetic listener about their ordeal. The survivor's family and close friends may also benefit from talking to a professional about their feelings of fear and anger.*

safe walking or living alone. Physical problems, too, may linger. In one study, women who had been raped at least two years prior to the study reported worse overall health, more visits to doctors, more symptoms of illness, and more problems with reproductive physiology than did other women (Phelps, Wallace & Waigandt, 1989).

In recent years, police departments and hospitals have become increasingly sensitive about the rape victim's ordeal, and have taken steps to minimize it as much as possible. In some cities, a counselor is assigned to the woman from the time she makes her initial report. But a review of research found that biases against the victim still exist in some places (Aubrey, 1988). Police officers are sometimes less likely to believe a rape victim if she is a lesbian, if she is obese, or if she did not physically resist her attacker. Juries, too, are sometimes influenced by characteristics of the victim that have nothing at all to do with the facts of the case, such as her attractiveness, her socioeconomic status, her experience with drugs or alcohol, and whether she has been raped before. In 1989, a jury acquitted a Georgia drifter of raping a 22-year-old woman because she had been wearing a white lace miniskirt, a tank top, and no underwear when she was kidnapped at knifepoint from a restaurant parking lot. The jury foreman explained, "We all feel she asked for it for the way she was dressed" (*Time*, October 16, 1989, p. 37). Law professor Susan Estrich (1987) notes that legal definitions of "reasonable" resistance against rape do not take into account the paralyzing effects of fear. The legal system expects a woman to fight back like a "real man" despite her social conditioning and the unequal power relationships between women and men. It ignores the fact that even an implied threat of violence can be terrifying, whether or not the victim knows her assailant and whether or not the assailant uses a weapon. It focuses on the response of the victim rather than the ability of any "reasonable" man to know the difference between a sexual invitation and forced sex. As many writers have pointed out, such biases do not exist in the prosecution of other crimes. The legal system does not ask whether the victim of a robbery or mugging offered "reasonable" resistance.

Unfortunately, many people still think that a woman who is raped is somehow responsible for the assault. Therefore, even if a rape survivor does not blame herself, friends and relatives may do so either consciously or unconsciously. If you know a woman who has been raped and she confides in you, keep in mind that what she needs most is support and reassurance, so that she can regain a sense of safety and control over her life. When listening to her describe her ordeal, don't focus on your pain about what happened, question her actions prior to the rape ("Why didn't you get away while you could?") or try to make decisions for her. Simply listen, even if she repeats her account over and over. And keep in mind that rape survivors often need to talk not only to a friend or lover about their pain, but also to a professional counselor or therapist.

Why Does Rape Occur?

After all the distressing findings you have just read, you might be wondering why rape is so common. Why are acts associated by most of us with love and intimacy sometimes used to terrorize or humiliate?

One answer emphasizes the pathological rage or callousness of the rapist and traces the causes of his psychopathology to an early distressing sexual experience, the experience of growing up in an abusive family, or a disturbed relationship with his mother. Such explanations, however, are based mostly on clinical studies of dangerous offenders incarcerated in psychiatric facilities and prisons. What about other rapists? During wartime, perfectly normal, average, and unexceptional young men commit rape, simply to get even with or humiliate the enemy. United States history is marred by the rapes of thousands of African-American and Native American women by white men who were respected members of their communities (Brownmiller, 1975). Most rapes, as we have seen, are committed by men who cannot be classified as seriously disordered.

These facts have led many writers to conclude that social and cultural influences must be a more important underlying cause of rape than is individual psychopathology. In this view, sexual coercion is the predictable consequence of socially prescribed gender roles. The typical rapist is not deranged or insane; he is merely an extremist (Metzger, 1976). The culture itself, after all, links aggressiveness with stereotypes of male sexuality: A man's penis becomes his "weapon" (as in the old military ditty, "This is my rifle, this is my gun; one is for fighting, the other for fun"). Music, films, books, and advertisements broadcast the message that subjugation of a female by a male is at the heart of erotic heterosexuality. Many rock lyrics even celebrate rape and physical abuse of women during sex. It is therefore no accident that anger and the need to dominate find expression in a *sexual* act; a mugging alone will not suffice.

Research finds that cultural tolerance of rape is widespread, among the young as well as among adults. When Los Angeles teenagers aged 14 to 18 were asked whether it is ever permissible for "a guy to hold a girl down and force her to have sexual intercourse," 82 percent of both males and females replied "Never." But when these teenagers were asked if forced sex was all right in specific situations—for instance, when a girl got a boy sexually excited or when the boy was very aroused—many were more lenient. Overall, only 44 percent of the girls and 24 percent of the boys rejected forced sex in all the situations presented (Giarrusso et al., 1979).

In a similar survey of 1,700 junior high school students, two-thirds of the boys and almost half the girls thought a man had a right to have intercourse with a woman without her consent if a couple had been dating for at least six months. A fourth of the boys and a sixth of the girls said a man had a right to have intercourse with a woman without her consent if he spent money on her. Half the boys and two-fifths of the girls said a man had a right to kiss a woman if he spent a lot of money on her—which 12-year-olds

Rape fantasies for sale
Pornography linking sex and aggression eroticizes and legitimizes rape (see Chapter 16). The small print on this adult theater marquee reads: "He was taught to kill. Rape was his own idea."

defined as *ten to fifteen dollars* (Kikuchi, 1988). In still another study, only 18 percent of college students strongly condemned forced sex under all nine hypothetical situations presented. A fifth of the men thought forcible rape on dates could conceivably be acceptable (Fischer, 1986).

Feminist writers have argued that rape is not only a cultural phenomenon but also a political one. By this they mean that rape functions to keep women in a subordinate position, much as the lynching of black men once functioned to keep all blacks fearful and oppressed (Brownmiller, 1975). Even traditional male protection of women may contribute to the exploitation of women. In a now-classic article entitled "Rape: The All-American Crime," Susan Griffin (1971) argued that chivalry perpetuates a sexual double standard that punishes those women who dare to step out of line by depriving them of male protection. Unless a woman is "above reproach" (sexually inexperienced), she is blamed for her own victimization.

Preventing Rape

The picture seems bleak, doesn't it? How can the appallingly high incidence of rape in our society be reduced? The answer will depend in part on what we think its causes are.

PUNISHMENT   One simple answer is to increase the punishment for rape. This approach keeps some rapists off the streets and may deter others. However, there is no evidence so far that punishment has had a major impact on rape rates. Severe penalties can even backfire; in some cases juries have refused to convict the rapist because they did not want to see a life sentence or the death penalty imposed. In any event, since most rapes go unreported, punishment does not affect the majority of rapists.

Every once in a while someone suggests using either surgical or chemical (hormonal) castration as an alternative form of punishment. The reasoning is that castration will eliminate an offender's motivation for committing more crimes. But there are many problems with this approach. As we saw in Chapter 5, castration does not always affect sexual arousal or response. Even when it does, a man is still able to commit violent crimes, including rape with objects. Chemical castration often has negative side effects. And the effects of surgical castration can be reversed if the rapist seeks androgen injections once he is free of the legal system.

TREATMENT OF OFFENDERS   Another strategy that focuses on the individual offender is treatment and rehabilitation. In one approach, called relapse prevention, offenders learn to deal with their fantasies and impulses, cope with the intense anger, depression, or anxiety that often precede a relapse, and resist the rationalizations that habitual rapists typically use to deny responsibility for their actions (Nelson et al., 1988; Miner et al., 1989). This type of program and similar ones have reported promising results.

Fighting back   *These women are learning physical strategies for defending themselves against sexual assault. Employing a combination of strategies, both physical and nonphysical, is likely to be more effective than relying on only one.*

Like punishment, however, treatment alone is unlikely to solve our society's rape problem. Rapists differ in their personalities and motives, and it is not clear which treatment approach should be used for which offenders. More important, treatment, like punishment, only reaches convicted and incarcerated offenders, who comprise only a tiny proportion of all those who commit rape.

SELF-DEFENSE AGAINST RAPE   A third strategy focuses on the potential victim. Police departments sometimes advise women to cooperate or to rely on verbal resistance alone, on the grounds that death is a fate worse than rape. A strong, determined rapist can pin a woman down and force her legs apart, or simply hold a knife to her throat to force compliance. A woman's active cooperation is not required: men have raped unconscious women, and even dead women. But women's groups and feminist writers argue that submission is too often confused with consent, leading to the myth that women want to be raped and reducing the chances of a successful prosecution. They argue that women can and should learn effective methods of self-defense to protect themselves. Although self-defense tactics do not guarantee avoidance of rape, women who actively resist are more likely to escape than those who don't (Medea & Thompson, 1974; Bart & O'Brien, 1985; Caignon & Groves, 1987).

Most women do, in fact, resist an assailant. Strategies include reasoning, trying to get help, crying, "causing a scene," screaming, running, fighting, or throwing something at the rapist. Unfortunately, no one method works in all situations. Some rapists become more violent if the victim resists either verbally or physically; others are put off by refusal or resistance but become excited if the woman seems weak, distressed, or passive (Brodsky, 1976). In choosing which strategies to use, a woman must judge not only what her assailant is like, but also the situation (How feasible is escape? Are there other people within hearing range? Does the assailant have a weapon?). In interviews with 94 women, sociologist Pauline Bart (1981) found that those who successfully resisted rape were more likely to have used several strategies in combination whereas women who were unsuccessful tended to rely primarily on talking. And women who screamed and physically struggled were more likely to escape being raped than those who used talking or pleading. But each situation is unique; we have known women who successfully talked their way out of a rape situation.

Men against rape *Both sexes can do their part to educate people about rape. This poster of* The Rape of the Sabine Women *was distributed by a fraternity and has been displayed in fraternity houses around the country. Small print at the bottom of the poster reads, "Against her will is against the law."*

We advise our own women students to be prepared to protect themselves if attacked or threatened sexually. Self-defense courses can provide some techniques and give women the confidence to use them. We also advise women to communicate clearly and assertively with dates about their interest or lack of interest in sex; to be careful not to let alcohol or drugs reduce their ability to defend themselves; to refuse dates with men who seem hostile or aggressive; and to trust their instincts about a potentially dangerous situation.

But why should rape prevention be only a woman's responsibility? If you are a man, here are some steps *you* can take:

- Educate other men about rape myths and realities.

- When you want to become sexually intimate with a date or girlfriend, ask her how she feels about it instead of trying to interpret nonverbal signals.

- If a man seems to be canvassing a neighborhood in a suspicious manner, question him or report his presence to police.

- Write letters of protest about the romanticization of rape in films and television programs.

- Object when other men tell rape jokes or make disparaging remarks about women.

CHANGING ATTITUDES   A fourth approach to preventing rape is a cultural one. Not all cultures are "rape-prone." For example, in West Sumatra, rape is almost unknown. Anthropologist Peggy Reeves Sanday (1986) finds that societies with low rape rates tend to value nurturance and nonaggression and allow men and women to share power. Societies with high rates tolerate or glorify violence, equate masculinity with toughness and aggression, give men more economic and political power than women, and encourage men to conceal feelings of dependency and vulnerability.

According to the cultural approach, eliminating rape therefore requires changes in prevailing cultural attitudes about sexuality and gender. People will need to learn that men can and should control their own sexuality and that women have a right to say "no" at any time, including when they have previously said "yes." People will also have to become conscious about the sexual exchange that occurs as part of ordinary dating rituals, and the unspoken assumption in our culture that female sexuality is a commodity. Relationships between men and women will have to become more egalitarian, and images of male conquest and female submission will have to lose their strong erotic appeal. (In the next chapter, we will examine how certain types of pornography reinforce and perpetuate such images and increase the acceptance of rape myths.)

Cultural change, of course, is not easy; the caveman image of sexuality runs deep. But we all pay a terrible price for rape. No woman, no matter what her position in life, can consider herself free as long as she must live by what one of our colleagues calls a "rape schedule" (Is it too late to go out alone? Do I dare work an evening shift? Is it safe to walk to the parking lot without a male escort?). The elaborate precautions that women must take to avoid sexual violence, and the restrictions they must accept on their freedom of movement, are a constant reminder to them of their vulnerability (Caignon & Groves, 1987). Men, too, are touched by rape, and not only because their mothers, lovers, wives, and daughters may become victims. As long as women must fear some men, they may not fully trust any man. The widespread occurrence of forced sex poisons the relationship between men and women with distrust and suspicion.

SEXUAL HARASSMENT

Rape deprives a woman of her privacy, her dignity, and control over her own body. But the same ends can be accomplished in other ways; rape is simply one end of a continuum that includes many kinds of **sexual harassment.** Sexual harassment includes the promise of rewards for sexual cooperation, the threat of punishment for noncooperation, and such offensive behaviors as crude or sexist remarks, staring, and leering. At work, in school, in all sorts of situations, many people are the recipients of unwanted sexual remarks and advances, some of them crossing the line between harassment and outright sexual coercion.

ON THE JOB Under federal law, sexual harassment in the workplace is illegal. Individuals can be held liable, and so can companies, if they do not take immediate action to stop the harassment. Legally, harassment is defined as unwelcome sexual advances, requests for sexual favors, or other verbal or physical conduct of a sexual nature when:

- submission to such conduct is made explicitly or implicitly a condition of a person's employment;

- submission to or rejection of such conduct is used as the basis for employment decisions affecting the individual; or

- such conduct has the purpose or effect of unreasonably interfering with an individual's work performance or creating an intimidating, hostile, or offensive working environment.

Men are sometimes sexually harassed on the job; 15 percent reported harassment in one study (Tangri et al., 1982). But women are far more commonly the victims. In various surveys, between 40 and 90 percent of all employed women report having been harassed at work (Gutek, 1985; Tangri et al., 1982; U. S. Merit Systems Protection Board, 1981; Loy & Stewart, 1984). In one study of women in a variety of occupations (Gold, 1987), the most frequent types of harassment were "gender harassment" (for example, antiwoman jokes and sexist remarks) and seductive behavior (for example,

The power dynamics of touch   *In our society, touch implies privileged access to another person. By his touch and body language, her boss establishes his own higher status and imposes physical intimacy in an inappropriate setting and without her consent.*

unwanted sexual attention). But over ten percent of the women reported experiencing subtle bribery to cooperate sexually and 7 percent reported direct bribes. Slightly over 8 percent reported subtle or actual negative consequences for being uncooperative. Over a fifth had experienced unwanted attempts by men to touch or fondle them, over 17 percent had experienced forceful attempts, nearly 3 percent had experienced attempted rape, and 1.5 percent had been raped. Unmarried women and women of color are more likely to be harassed than are married women or white women (Fain & Anderton, 1987). And blue collar women, such as carpenters, truck drivers, plumbers, and other tradeswomen, appear to be more vulnerable than white collar workers (attorneys, accountants, businesswomen) or pink collar workers (primarily secretaries) (Gold, 1987). But sexual harassment is a potential problem for all women.

The punishment for resisting a boss's or supervisor's harassment may be a poor performance rating, demotion, a reduction in pay, or getting fired. Workers who quit—not an easy step to take when other jobs are scarce—may find themselves ineligible for unemployment compensation, because sexual harassment is not always considered a sufficient reason for leaving one's job. Even if the worker does get compensation, it may be only a fraction of his or her previous earnings. In addition to the financial threat that harassment poses, there are also emotional consequences. Many victims of workplace harassment feel humiliated, angry, nervous, ashamed, or helpless (Hamilton et al., 1987; Loy & Stewart, 1984).

ON CAMPUS   Faculty-student sex is hardly new, but only in recent years has its full extent been recognized. Many faculty-student liaisons occur because of subtle, or not so subtle, coercion by the instructor. The instructor may imply or announce that unless a student "puts out," the instructor will lower the student's grade in a course or write a poor letter of recommendation. As one instructor told his student, "You know I want to sleep with you. You know I can do a lot for you; I have a great deal of influence. Now, of course I don't want to force you into anything but I'm sure you're going to be sensible about this" (in Dziech & Weiner, 1984, p. 10). Even when there is no pressure, the ethics of professor-student sex are questionable, especially when the student is taking a class from the professor or may do so in the future. The professor has power over the student's grades and sometimes the student's career, so the student is not really as free to refuse as it might seem.

In various studies, 20 to 40 percent of female college students, and a smaller number of males, have reported some form of sexual harassment by instructors. Harassment may include not only sexual "invitations" and threats but also crude or inappropriate comments. Some students have been humiliated in front of an entire class. To cope with harassment, students may try to ignore the overtures, talk about their boyfriends (or girlfriends), stop coming to office hours and classes, drop out of their majors, or even leave school (Dziech & Weiner, 1984). Like many rape victims, they may erroneously blame themselves. Because of fears of reprisal, few file formal complaints.

DURING PSYCHOTHERAPY   Every major association of mental health professionals holds sex with a patient or client to be unethical. A psychotherapist who violates this code can lose membership in the organization as well as his or her state license to practice. Yet many therapists do so anyway. For example, in a survey of psychologists belonging to the psychotherapy division of the American Psychological Association, 12 percent of male psychologists and 3 percent of female psychologists reported having sexual contact with their clients (Pope, Levenson, & Schover, 1979).

In therapist-client sexual relationships, clients are at a distinct disadvantage. Often they are in therapy because of loneliness, difficulties in relationships, or low self-esteem, and so are unusually susceptible to the attentions of a powerful authority figure. No matter how the affair ends, the patient almost always suffers negative effects. If the patient breaks off the affair or accuses the therapist of exerting pressure, the therapist may retaliate by labeling the patient psychotic or paranoid. If the therapist ends the affair, the emotional distress may be intense. Some rejected patients try to kill themselves, or become so disordered that they must be committed to a men-

Unwanted attention
Some people think women should be flattered by whistles and catcalls from strangers, but this woman is upset, not flattered. How would you interpret these men's intentions? What message does their behavior send?

tal facility (Pope & Bouhoutsos, 1986). Even if there is no obvious emotional damage, the client cannot get appropriate therapy from a therapist who is also a lover; therapists need to maintain professional detachment in order to be objective in planning treatment.

IN THE STREET   On a national television talk show, the audience was asked how it felt about catcalls, whistles, and the teasing of women on the street or in other public places. Most people thought such acts were harmless, and a few women said they appreciated having their sexual charms noticed. These responses overlooked the fact that sometimes there is an element of violence beneath the apparently good-natured hassling. When a woman ignores a man's unwelcome attentions, he may follow her or block her path. Catcalls can become obscene and hostile. Shouting or whistling can reduce the woman to an object. In the words of one woman, "We are never secure. There's some old goon yodeling over there—some idiot making kissing noises from a passing car. It's an assault on your dignity, a constant interruption of your thought, your mood, your privacy" (in Sanderson, 1980).

The difference between harmless flirting and sexual harassment depends on the initiator's intentions, the recipient's reaction, the setting, and the extent to which the two people already know each other. Most people enjoy good-natured flirting but do not want to be harassed. Where would *you* draw the line? Does the gender of the initiator or the recipient make a difference? Which situations are appropriate for flirting and which are not?

Dealing with Sexual Harassment

There are several steps a person can take if she or he is harassed. The following suggestions apply to on-the-job harassment but can be adapted to other situations as well:

1. At the first sign of harassment, document all incidents with dates, places, times, names, and exactly what was said, and record the names of any witnesses. Include your physical and emotional reactions.

2. Confide in trustworthy co-workers (some of them may also have been victimized), and ask witnesses to write statements on your behalf. Be sure to state the facts accurately, in order to avoid a charge of slander.

3. Talk to the harasser, firmly asserting that you are not interested in sexual offers or remarks and that the inappropriate behavior must stop immediately or you will take further action. If you cannot talk directly to the harasser, write a letter and hand it to the person in the presence of a witness. (Keep a copy.)

4. If the harassment continues, talk to the offender's supervisor. If the supervisor does not act, complain to the next level of management.

5. If all else fails, file a complaint with your city or state human rights commission or fair employment practices agency, ask the local office of the Equal Employment Opportunity Commission to investigate, or pursue legal action.

Most universities and colleges have a formal grievance procedure for students who feel they have been harassed. Psychotherapy patients who are harassed can inquire about filing ethics charges by calling the local chapter of the appropriate professional association (for example, the county psychological or psychiatric association) or contacting the state agency in charge of licensure.

Even if you are not a victim of sexual harassment yourself, you can take steps to discourage it, by insisting on a professional atmosphere at work and school, and by helping others to see that although love and sex are grand, some settings are entirely inappropriate for sexual interactions.

CHILD SEXUAL ABUSE

Probably no form of sexual exploitation has elicited as much concern in recent years as the one we turn to next. In **child sexual abuse,** the victim is legally a minor and the offender is an adult or older child or adolescent. In *intrafamilial* abuse, or *incest;* the offender is a relative. In *extrafamilial* abuse, the offender is unrelated to the victim. Acts of child sexual abuse range from genital exhibition to vaginal, anal, or oral penetration.

In a few cultures, such as Mangaia in the South Pacific, pubescent children are reportedly initiated into coitus by adults as a matter of course (see Chapter 1). Most cultures, however, including our own, fiercely condemn adult-child sexual contact. Yet despite this condemnation, such contact is astonishingly common in the U.S. As with rape and sexual harassment, reported cases are only the tip of the iceberg. According to estimates, nearly one in four children today is a victim (Crewdson, 1988). Various studies, differing in the methods and definitions used, report figures somewhat higher or lower than these (see Russell, 1983; Wyatt, 1985; Finkelhor, 1984), but whatever the precise incidence, it is clear that *millions* of children are victimized annually.

Although many people believe that incest is the most common type of child sexual abuse, this is probably not true. In Diana Russell's study of women in San Francisco, 71 percent of the women who were abused in

Child molester   *Many parents rightly warn their children to beware of strangers who offer them candy or try to entice them into a car. However, children also need to learn that inappropriate touching is not always done by strangers. Indeed, research finds that most sexual abuse of children is committed by someone the child knows and trusts.*

childhood were abused by a nonrelative. In her sample as a whole, 16 percent reported abuse by a relative before age 18, and 12 percent before age 14. In contrast, almost one-third of the women reported at least one experience of abuse by a nonrelative before 18, and 20 percent before 14 (Russell, 1986). Most extrafamilial abusers are known to the child: a friend of the family, a teacher, or a neighbor. In Russell's study, only 15 percent of women abused by a nonrelative were abused by a stranger.

Most offenders in child sexual abuse cases are men. Both boys and girls are abused, but a majority of victims (particularly of incest) are girls. Some child sexual abuse involves extreme force, injury, and even murder. In most cases, however, extreme force is not used. It is unnecessary. Young children typically do not understand the sexual significance of what is happening. (For example, they may report that the offender was urinating on them when in fact he was ejaculating.) A child who knows the offender may believe him at first when he says he is only playing a game, or the child may initially think the sexual contact is just another form of affection. Some children may be deceived by the adult's explanation that sexual activity is a necessary part of "sex education." A child may also feel intimidated by the adult, or may be confused about the difference between affection and abuse, especially when the offender is a friend or trusted authority figure. Children are used to taking orders from adults, and may feel they have no choice but to obey.

Older children are more likely to recognize the sexual nature of the adult's behavior, but are often afraid to reveal what is happening. The adult may reinforce this fear with physical abuse and threats of retaliation if the victim "tells." In some cases, especially in father-daughter incest, the child may keep silent because she loves the adult and does not want to be disloyal or see the family break up.

Extrafamilial Sexual Abuse

Researchers and clinicians sometimes refer to extrafamilial abusers as **pedophiles** (from the Greek for "lover of children"). A pedophile, or in more common parlance, a child molester, is a person, usually a man, who prefers children as sex partners, sometimes exclusively (see Chapter 10). One researcher, Nicholas Groth (1979) distinguishes the "fixated" pedophile, who believes himself to be in love with children, from the "regressed" pedophile, whose sexual involvement with children begins during a period of unusual stress in his life. A regressed pedophile may have led an apparently normal married life for many years before he began abusing.

Because studies of child sexual abuse often lump extrafamilial abuse and incest together, or are based only on convicted offenders, it is hard to put together a psychological portrait of extrafamilial abusers. Various studies have described them as passive, inadequate, dependent, antisocial, impulsive, insecure, immature, socially inept, isolated, moralistic, guilt-ridden, and generally maladjusted. Some child molesters have criminal records. Yet others are respected citizens (until they're caught)—for example, teachers, scout leaders, or others who have frequent contact with young children. Some abusers are violent and mentally disturbed; most are not. (The more severe the sexual offense, the more likely the offender is to be seriously disturbed [Underwager et al., 1986]). Many abusers were themselves abused during childhood (Groth, 1979; Gaffney et al., 1984), but just how many is uncertain.

In Russell's study, over half of the extrafamilial abuse cases were classified as "very severe" (actual or attempted intercourse, fellatio, cunnilingus, anilingus, or anal intercourse). Over a quarter were classified as "severe" (actual or attempted genital contact, unclothed, including manual touching or penetration, breast contact, or simulated intercourse). The rest were classified as "least severe" (sexual kissing, sexual touching of buttocks, thigh, leg, or clothed breasts or genitals). In contrast, 23 percent of incest cases were "very severe," 41 percent were "severe," and 36 percent were "least severe." Sexual attacks that involve serious injury or murder are almost entirely extrafamilial.

Incest

Incest is sexual contact between two persons who are related but not married to each other. Incest taboos are nearly universal (see Box 15–1). In the United States, incest laws require that the relationship be close enough to make marriage between the two people illegal. But most states interpret the law broadly and include abuse by a step-relative or person related to the victim by adoption. And sometimes, charges are brought against an unrelated person acting in a role of authority within the family (for example, a mother's permanent live-in boyfriend). Some laws specify that intercourse must occur, but social scientists generally use "incest" to include both noncoital and coital contact.

In the past, incest was thought to be extremely rare. Often when women disclosed incestuous experiences to their therapists, they were not believed. Early in his career, Sigmund Freud, the father of psychoanalysis, did consider such reports valid and concluded that his patients' experiences accounted for their later unhappiness. But then he changed his mind, deciding that his patients were merely reporting fantasies, not real incidents. Their emotional problems, Freud decided, were not due to actual abuse, but to unconscious guilt about the incestuous desires they had felt as children and had since repressed. Freud's notion that it is children, not adults, who are sexually seductive became the cornerstone of his theory of psychosexual development, and influenced an entire generation of social scientists (see Chapter 12). Today we know it is likely that many, if not most, of Freud's patients were reporting real events (Sulloway, 1979; Masson, 1984).

BOX 15–1

The Almost-Universal Taboo

Contrary to popular belief, the taboo against incest within the nuclear family is not universal. During the reign of the Ptolemies in ancient Egypt, it was the rule for royal brothers and sisters to wed, presumably to protect the purity of the bloodline. The ancient Persian nobility is said to have tolerated marriages not only between siblings but also between parents and children. Brother-sister incest was accepted in the ruling families of both the ancient Hawaiians and the Peruvian Incas. Even the Bible describes some incidents of incest that went unpunished: Moses is said to have been the son of his nephew and aunt, Abraham married his half-sister, and Cain and Abel married their twin sisters, although in their cases there were extenuating circumstances; there was no one else around.

But these are only exceptions to a rule that is *almost* universal. A study of 250 preliterate societies found that all of them banned nuclear family incest and extended the taboo to some or all relatives outside the nuclear family (Murdock, 1949). No society allows incest without restriction. In nearly all cultures, violations of incest taboos are met with disgust and condemnation.

How did incest taboos originate, and why are they so pervasive? One frequently cited hypothesis, the *natural aversion hypothesis*, holds that close kin who grow up together feel a natural sexual aversion to one another that is reflected in the taboo. But the evidence is not strong. On Israeli communal farms (kibbutzim), unrelated boys and girls reared together in small living groups rarely marry as adults, nor do they seem to feel sexually attracted to one another. On the other hand, Eskimo children who are betrothed early in life and then reared together under one roof show no particular aversion to one another as adults. More important, if a natural aversion to incest existed, a taboo against it would be unnecessary.

Another view, the *genetic hypothesis*, is that incest taboos evolved so that the human species could avoid the negative genetic effects of inbreeding. Inbred animals are sometimes less hardy and less resistant to diseases than hybrids, because recessive genes for defects and diseases exist in the species' "gene pool." Inherited disorders are also sometimes more common than would normally be expected in inbred human populations. But it is unclear whether human inbreeding *generally* leads to increased physical or mental problems, or, if so, whether such problems are severe enough to explain the strength of incest taboos. Brother-sister incest did not seem to have a noticeable effect on the health of the Ptolemies. Cleopatra, for example, who was known for both beauty and brains, was the product of generations of incest; her husband was both her brother and her uncle (Justice & Justice,

1979). Also, the genetic hypothesis does not explain why parent-child incest usually evokes greater loathing than brother-sister incest, although the presumed genetic risks are the same. Nor does it explain taboos involving distant relatives or persons related only by marriage or adoption.

Three other hypotheses are based not on biology but on social considerations:

- *The role strain hypothesis* holds that incest taboos permit the establishment of well-defined roles within the family. Without such roles, parental authority and family obligations would be confused and parents would be less effective in socializing their children. Indeed, role confusion does seem to characterize many incestuous families. However, although the role-strain hypothesis offers a reasonable explanation for taboos against parent-child incest, it works less well for incest with siblings or more distant relatives.

- *The family cohesiveness hypothesis* suggests that the incest taboo supports the smooth functioning of the family by reducing the chances of sexual jealousy among the members. However, societies do exist in which sisters may share a husband, or brothers a wife, and in such societies jealousy seems under control (Lester, 1972).

- *The social alliance hypothesis* holds that incest taboos exist to ensure that people will marry nonrelatives, and thus form new social and political alliances. This promotes social harmony, and permits the peaceful exchange of goods. Small groups cannot be self-sufficient; trade with others is necessary if a group is to survive, increase its wealth, and improve its standard of living. According to anthropologist Yehudi Cohen (1978) the social alliance hypothesis helps explain why small societies often extend the incest taboo to distant relatives and even nonrelatives. As for industrial societies, fewer people are involved directly in trade, but the emotional and cultural health of the society continues to depend on a diversity of ideas and life styles. This fact may explain why the taboo survives, although it may narrow to include only close relatives. However, it does not seem to account for the emotional intensity with which the taboo is enforced (Meiselman, 1978).

Perhaps no one explanation can account for all variations of the incest taboo. But if social factors explain such taboos, as seems likely, then as long as we are a social species and as long as the family is the basic unit for rearing children, such taboos will probably always exist.

Until two decades ago, references to incest in the pyschological litera-ture consisted mostly of isolated case histories; there were no systematic studies. Then, during the late 1970s, apathy suddenly changed to interest. The reasons were political as much as scientific. Feminists, who had worked to raise the public's consciousness about rape, turned their attention to sex-ual exploitation within the family. Increasing frankness about sexually taboo topics probably also contributed to the sudden "discovery" of incest. Books and articles began to appear.

Since then, estimates of incest's prevalence have steadily risen. Alfred Kinsey (who did not ask directly about incest) thought that perhaps 4 or 5 percent of adult females in his sample had been approached sexually during childhood by a male relative. But in Diana Russell's San Francisco sample, 16 percent of the women reported at least one such experience before the age of 18, and 12 percent before age 14 (Russell, 1986). Another carefully conducted survey of households in Los Angeles obtained even higher figures (Wyatt, 1985). (Lest you think that there's something unusual about Califor-nia, the Los Angeles study found that women who grew up in that state were somewhat *less* likely than other women to have experienced incest.)

Yearly cases of incest, then, number not in the hundreds but in the tens or hundreds of thousands. Of those people now alive in the United States, many millions will at some point in their lives be involved, in some way, in incest. Although cases in poorer neighborhoods are especially likely to come to the attention of social workers, incest occurs at every socioeco-nomic level and in every ethnic group.

In law enforcement and social welfare agency statistics, the most com-mon type of incest is father-daughter, but other types may be at least as com-mon. For example, in Russell's survey, 24 percent of the cases involved a father (biological, step, foster, or adoptive), but 25 percent involved an uncle. In another study, of college students (Finkelhor, 1979), brothers were reported as the most frequent perpetrators. Estimates of mother-son and father-son incest require further studies. (Some experts believe that boys are victimized more often than current statistics indicate.) Cases of sister-sister and mother-daughter incest also occur, but appear to be relatively rare.

Clinicians and researchers would like to know what sorts of traits set perpetrators of incest apart from other people. They would also like to know if families in which incest occurs differ in predictable ways from other families. To answer such questions, one must compare families in which incest occurs with other families that are similar in size, income, and other characteristics. To date, few such studies have been done.

Most of what we do know comes from clinical studies of father-daugh-ter incest. These studies find that although some incestuous fathers are seri-ously disturbed and lacking in conscience, unable to care about anyone but themselves, most incestuous fathers do not fit this description. Nor are most of these fathers dangerous to people outside their own families. But incestu-ous fathers do often have personality problems. Sometimes they come from a background of emotional deprivation that leaves them hungry for love and affection but unable to express their needs nonsexually. Sometimes they are arrogant, domineering, and abusive, yet extremely dependent on their wives and children, limiting their social lives to their families. Psychologists Blair and Rita Justice (1979) call this personality type *symbiotic*. They believe that the "basic issue in incest is not sex but the need for closeness, nurturing, and stimulation."

Many clinicians feel that unhealthy family dynamics also contribute to father-daughter incest. For example, the family may encourage a kind of role reversal between mother and daughter, pushing the daughter to become a "little mother" and cater to the needs of other family members (Justice & Justice, 1979). Moreover, because of her own problems, the mother may be unable to stop her husband from abusing and controlling her and the children. But disturbed family relationships cannot be directly blamed for father-daughter incest. Many families are "dysfunctional," yet in only some of them does the father choose to sexually abuse his daughter.

Father-daughter incest often continues for several years. Sometimes it comes to an end when the daughter confesses to her mother or someone else. Disclosure is likely to throw the family into a crisis. Many mothers are supportive of their daughters, but some refuse to believe them or to come to their aid, out of loyalty to the husband, jealousy of the daughter, or fear of losing financial support. An unsupportive mother may try to ignore the truth, or may turn on the daughter and punish her. Other adults may also blame the victim instead of the perpetrator. Father-daughter incest usually does not end up in the hands of authorities. Most often the daughter reaches late adolescence and leaves home.

At the present time, information on other kinds of incest is too meager and too conflicting to allow any conclusions about the dynamics involved. For example, authorities are divided about the general consequences of brother-sister incest. Past studies have found that as adults, participants sometimes look back on such experiences as positive, and a recent study found no relationship, either positive or negative, between brother-sister incest and later sexual behavior or adjustment (Greenwald & Leitenberg, 1989). But clinicians often see cases of brother-sister incest that involve great emotional suffering for the person who was not the initiator. Often one sibling has threatened, humiliated, and degraded another. One study found that even when the incest was supposedly consensual, women who had had sexual contact with their brothers had lower self-esteem than other women (Sorrenti-Little et al., 1984). As we saw in Chapter 12, young children sometimes explore each other's bodies out of mutual and innocent curiosity, but cases of brother-sister sex can involve sexual exploitation, and not just curiosity.

The Emotional Consequences of Child Sexual Abuse

During the 1970s, a few sex researchers suggested that some adult-child sexual contacts could be harmless, or even beneficial. The term "positive incest" began to appear in papers and lectures. Today, with better data, we know that adult-child sex is likely to be traumatic for victims and leave lasting psychological wounds.

What exactly is it, however, that is harmful about such sex? If the child is physically traumatized or injured, the answer is easy. But often no force is used, and sometimes the child actually finds the physical sensations pleasurable. In such cases, the dangers are more subtle, although no less devastating. According to researchers David Finkelhor and Angela Browne (1985), the dangers fall into four general categories:

- *Traumatic sexualization* The abuse may distrupt normal sexual development and lead to distorted sexual norms.
- *Betrayal* The child may feel betrayed because a trusted adult has harmed the child or failed to provide protection.
- *Powerlessness* If the abuse is repeated and the child feels unable to stop it, the child may feel helpless to control events.
- *Stigmatization* If adults blame the child or don't believe the child the results may be shame, a negative self-image, and low self-esteem.

Specific short- and long-term effects of childhood sexual abuse include fear, anxiety, panic attacks, "flashbacks," depression, anger, low self-esteem, isolation, impulsiveness, nightmares, self-destructiveness, and inappropriate sexual behavior (Browne & Finkelhor, 1986; Courtois, 1988; Alter-Reid et al., 1986). Some victims dissociate themselves from bodily awareness, becoming numb and oblivious to pain. Some develop amnesia for some or all of the traumatic experiences. In general, boys and girls seem to experience similar symptoms, but boys are especially likely to become aggressive and angry, girls to feel depressed and guilty (Bruckner & Johnson, 1987).

Teenagers who have been abused are more likely than other adolescents to see life as meaningless, feel a loss of control over their lives, feel isolated, and distrust others (Boisso, Lutz, & Gray, 1989). Sexual abuse is frequently found in the backgrounds of substance abusers, runaways, and prostitutes, as well as persons with multiple personality disorders, eating disorders, and other psychological dysfunctions.

As in rape, many of the effects of sexual abuse are similar to the symptoms of the post traumatic stress syndrome. Having listed some of these outcomes, however, we should note that not all victims are equally damaged. To assume that the lives of *all* survivors are permanently ruined, or that any apparently healthy survivor must be "in denial," is to ignore the astonishing resilience of the human spirit. Such assumptions may actually make survivors of abuse feel more hopeless than they would otherwise. The effects of sexual abuse depend in part on how severe the abuse was, how frequently it occurred, how long it lasted, who the perpetrator was (parent-child incest is especially damaging because of the betrayal involved and the child's dependence on the abuser), and how supportive adults were once the abuse was disclosed. Also critical is the survivor's interpretation or explanation of the experience. In a study of men and women who had been abused before age 18, those with poor psychological adjustment tended to attribute their experiences to stable, or unchanging causes, as in "I was molested because children are always exploited by adults in this world." Survivors who attributed their experiences to unstable causes, as in "I was molested because I was unlucky enough to be in the wrong place at the wrong time," did significantly better (Seidner, Calhoun, & Kilpatrick, 1985).

Legal Responses to Child Sexual Abuse

The sexual abuse of children raises many legal problems, most beyond the scope of this chapter. We think you should be aware, however, of a predicament that can occur in prosecuting child molestation or incest cases.

The legal system has often been callous about the needs and rights of those victimized by child sexual abuse. Sometimes, prosecutors, judges, and juries have mistaken lack of resistance with "seductiveness" and blamed the victim. Many victims have been ignored or automatically accused of lying. Children's testimony has not been trusted, and their reports have been dismissed as fantasies, even though studies find that false reports of child sexual abuse are actually quite rare (Jones & McGraw, 1987).

In recent years, however, different sorts of problems have come to light. In some places, police officers, prosecutors, and mental health professionals, in their eagerness to see perpetrators convicted, have been careless in their procedures. In one notorious case involving many accusers and many defendants, young children were interviewed together instead of separately and were questioned until they were mentally and emotionally exhausted. Over time, their accounts became contradictory and some became increasingly bizarre; as a result, it was impossible to determine which of the allegations were valid, and most of the charges were eventually dropped.

Interviewing children requires special expertise. Most children will not deliberately lie about sexual abuse, but like anyone else, they may misremember, become confused, feel pressured to comply with expectations, or misinterpret what happened. Recent research has increased our understanding of just what the strengths and weaknesses of children's testimony are (see Goodman & Helgeson, 1988, for a review). Children's errors tend to be errors of omission rather than commission. That is, children often recall less than adults do, but what they do remember tends to be quite accurate, especially when they are recalling an event that affected their well-being or safety. However, children do often depend more than adults on memory cues; they are likely to say nothing at all if an adult simply asks, "What happened?" As a result, interviewers must often probe and even ask leading questions ("He took off your clothes, didn't he?"). In general, children who have not been abused will resist such questions; that is, they will not say that

Teaching about sexual abuse *This is from a "Spiderman" comic book that has been used to educate children about inappropriate touching and to encourage disclosure of such touching.*

Spider-Man and Power Pack TM: & © 1990 Marvel Entertainment Group, Inc. All rights reserved.

something happened when it didn't. But children younger than four are sometimes suggestible (although there is little evidence that they can be led to fabricate an entire event). And in rare cases, a child may give obviously false responses.

These facts raise a dilemma: Because a terrified child may be holding back the truth about an assault, a questioner may need to persist despite the child's initial denials. Yet care must be taken that this persistence does not pressure the child to say things that are inaccurate. Mistakes made in a sexual abuse investigation can have profound consequences. Innocent people may be wrongly accused; abusers may escape punishment and be free to abuse again; and abused children may experience a sense of betrayal when the legal system lets them down. For all these reasons, efforts are now being made to improve procedures for questioning children and for assessing evidence in child abuse cases.

Preventing Child Sexual Abuse

What can be done to prevent child sexual abuse? One approach is to educate children about "good" and "bad" touching. Many schools have implemented programs to do just that. However, some psychologists and educators are beginning to call for better monitoring of these programs because of potential dangers. For example, if teachers do not tell children that "bad" touches can feel good, a child may be unable to label abuse correctly when it occurs. Young children do not understand abstract descriptions of abuse; explanations must be presented in concrete terms, using words children understand (Gilbert et al., 1988). Also, it is important not to make youngsters anxious about all physical touching, or to discourage parents and teachers from affectionately touching and cuddling young children.

Other prevention efforts include treating abusers, working for better reporting laws, and improving child protective agencies. However, once again, we suggest that in thinking about sexual exploitation we need to consider not only the individual offender but also the culture in which the offender lives. Our culture often eroticizes children, in ads for cosmetics, jeans, and other products, and in countless media images of older men pining away for teenage girls (Crewdson, 1988). What sort of impact might these images have on susceptible individuals? Consider, too, that although our society professes great love for its children, in many ways it seems to devalue them. We scrimp on child welfare services, exclude children from adults-only communities, and pay low wages to adults who work with children, to name just a few examples. Our culture also has a long history of regarding children as parental property. Emotional abuse, physical abuse (in the guise of discipline), and neglect of children are all commonplace. Many people enter parenthood with no special training for it and little awareness of the conflicts and negative emotions that are bound to arise.

In future years, social scientists and clinicians will learn more about the psychological and social origins of the sexually exploitive acts discussed in this chapter. Hopefully their research will increase our understanding of how to prevent these acts. In the meantime, we urge you to consider what *you* can do to prevent sex, which ought to be an expression of caring and intimacy and a special source of pleasure, from becoming, instead, a violation and a betrayal.

. . . .

SEDUCTION OR RAPE?

PERSONAL PERSPECTIVE

In date rape, miscommunication, insensitivity, and poor judgment may all play a role. What might have begun as an act of seduction turns gradually, or suddenly, into an act of exploitation. This exercise invites you to explore your own perceptions of date rape by considering the following scenario, as related by the two participants (Hughes & Sandler, 1987):

Patty's Account
"I knew Bobby from my statistics class. He's cute and we are both good at statistics, so when a tough midterm was scheduled, I was glad that he suggested we study together. It never occurred to me that it was anything except a study date. That night everything went fine at first. We got a lot of studying done in a short amount of time so when he suggested we take a break I thought we deserved it. Well, all of a sudden he started acting really

romantic and started kissing me. I liked the kissing but then he started touching me below the waist. I pulled away and tried to stop him but he didn't listen. After a while I stopped struggling; he was hurting me and I was scared. He was so much bigger and stronger than me. I couldn't believe it was happening to me. I didn't know what to do. He actually forced me to have sex with him. I guess looking back on it I should have screamed or done something besides trying to reason with him but it was so unexpected. I couldn't believe it was happening. I still can't believe it."

Bob's Account

"Patty and I were in the same statistics class together. She usually sat near me and was always very friendly. I liked her and thought maybe she liked me, too. Last Thursday I decided to find out. After class I suggested that she come to my place to study for midterms together. She agreed immediately, which was a good sign. That night everything seemed to go perfectly. We studied for a while and then took a break. I could tell that she liked me, and I was attracted to her. I was getting excited. I started kissing her. I could tell that she really liked it. We started touching each other and it felt really good. All of a sudden she pulled away and said 'Stop.' I figured she didn't want me to think that she was 'easy' or 'loose.' A lot of girls think they have to say 'no' at first. I knew once I showed her what a good time she could have, and that I would respect her in the morning, it would be OK. I just ignored her protests and eventually she stopped struggling. I think she liked it, but afterward she acted bummed out and cold. Who knows what her problem was."

What Patty recalls as forced sex, Bob justifies as seduction. How did this situation come about, and how could it have been prevented? In reflecting on these issues, ask yourself these questions:

- What unwarranted assumptions about each other did Patty and Bob make?

- What verbal and nonverbal messages did they send, intentionally or not?

- What psychological needs and pressures might have influenced their actions?

- What false beliefs about sexuality, dating, or the other sex contributed to the incident?

- How did gender roles affect what happened?

- Why are Patty's and Bob's perceptions so far apart?

- What might each person have done differently?

Reflecting on these questions may give you insights into how the roles we play and the scripts we follow can contribute to sexual exploitation. Understanding such influences, however, does not mean we must *excuse* what happened. Nothing a woman does can ever justify a man's raping her.

IN BRIEF

1. *Rape* has traditionally been defined as "unlawful carnal knowledge of a woman by force and without her consent." Some states include acts other than coitus, and several include situations in which a woman is deceived or incapacitated. It is difficult to know the exact incidence of rape, because it is greatly underreported. But research indicates that a woman living in the U.S. may have a one in four chance of being the victim of at least one completed rape and almost a one in two chance of being the victim of a completed or attempted rape. Some women are at greater risk than others, but all women are potential rape victims, whatever their age, race, or life style. Men, too, are sometimes raped, usually by other men. The rape of males is epidemic in prisons.

2. Like college women, most college men report having engaged in unwanted sexual activity. But the reasons for having unwanted sex tend to differ for men and women, with men more likely than women to mention peer pressure and a desire to be popular, and women more likely than men to report threatened or actual physical force.

3. *Acquaintance rapes* are far more frequent than stranger rapes. American dating rituals often cast women and men in adversarial roles and promote the kind of miscommunication that can lead to *date rape*. However, miscommunication is not the entire explanation for date rape, since by its very nature, date rape also implies a devaluing of women.

4. *Marital rape* may be the most frequent type of acquaintance rape. Until recently, husbands who forced sex on their wives were exempt from prosecution. Victims of marital rape often do not realize their ordeal can be labeled rape, even though marital rape is often associated with great brutality.

5. *Stranger rapes* are the type of rape most likely to be reported and investigated. Most stranger rapes are premeditated. Certain traditionally feminine behaviors, such as politeness and helpfulness, may encourage a rapist who is unknown to the victim to make a rape attempt, but circumstances seem to play a greater role than do characteristics of the victim. Stranger rapes have the greatest potential for violence and serious physical injury to the victim.

6. *Statutory rape* is intercourse with a person who is below a certain age of consent, with or without the person's agreement. Statutory rape laws raise certain difficult issues that differ from those raised by forcible rape. Controversy exists over what the age of consent should be.

7. Motives for rape include a desire for sexual release (especially in acquaintance rapes), the venting of anger against women, the need to feel powerful, and sadistic impulses. In any particular instance, the perpetrator may have a mixture of motives.

8. Studies of convicted rapists, most of whom have committed stranger rapes, find such men to have certain characteristic personality problems. However, it has become clear that psychological disturbance cannot explain the majority of rapes. In general, men who rape hold more calloused views of women than other men and are more likely to accept beliefs condoning rape. They are also more likely to have family problems and to have friends who pressure them to "score" and who approve of coercing women. But a large minority of college men say they have used coercion or force to get sex, and many young men who have not raped say they can picture themselves doing it. Thus something besides psychological disturbance must be involved in rape.

9. Rape is one of the most extreme invasions possible of a person's physical and psychological integrity. Consequently, survivors often experience a sequence of negative emotional reactions called the *rape trauma syndrome*. The emotional and physical repercussions of rape can continue for many years. In recent years, police departments and hospitals have become increasingly sensitive about the rape victim's ordeal, but in some places the legal system is still biased against the victim.

10. Psychological explanations of rape emphasize the pathological rage or callousness of the individual rapist. But because most rapists cannot be classified as seriously disordered, social and cultural factors, including attitudes toward women and sexuality, must also be important. Cultural tolerance of rape is widespread, among adolescents as well as adults.

11. Approaches to preventing rape include increased punishment of offenders, better treatment programs for offenders, the use of self-defense by women, and the elimination of cultural attitudes that foster rape.

12. *Sexual harassment* occurs in the workplace, on college campuses, during psychotherapy, and in public places in the form of catcalls and "teasing." Victims of harassment may suffer financially (if it occurs on the job) and emotionally. There are steps victims can take to discourage and protect themselves from harassment.

13. *Child sexual abuse* affects millions of children annually. *Extrafamilial abuse* usually involves someone the child knows. *Pedophiles*, people who

prefer children as sex partners, have been described in various studies as maladjusted and immature, but some child molesters are (until they're caught) respected members of the community. Extrafamilial abuse is often severe; that is, it often involves actual or attempted intercourse, and oral and anal sex acts.

14. In the past, *incest* was thought to be extremely rare, but we now know that it affects hundreds of thousands of children each year. In official statistics, the most common type of incest is father-daughter, but there is controversy about which type is actually most common. Most of what we know about incest comes from clinical studies of father-daughter incest. These studies find incestuous fathers to have certain characteristic personality problems, such as extreme dependence on their families and an inability to express their needs nonsexually. Many clinicians feel that unhealthy family dynamics also contribute to father-daughter incest.

15. The emotional consequences of child sexual abuse include traumatic sexualization, feelings of being betrayed, powerlessness, and stigmatization. The severity of the effects depends on how severe the abuse was, how frequently it occurred, how long it lasted, who the perpetrator was, how supportive adults are once the abuse is disclosed, and how the survivor interprets and explains her or his experience. Prevention has focused on educational programs for children, the treatment of abusers, and attempts to improve the legal and child protective systems. However, as with rape, cultural attitudes also need to be addressed.

Key Terms

sexual exploitation *(567)*

rape *(568)*

acquaintance rape *(571)*

date rape *(572)*

marital rape *(573)*

stranger rape *(575)*

statutory rape *(576)*

anger, power and sadistic rapes *(577)*

rape trauma syndrome *(580)*

posttraumatic stress syndrome *(580)*

sexual harassment *(588)*

child sexual abuse *(593)*

extrafamilial sexual abuse *(593)*

pedophile *(594)*

incest *(595)*

incest taboos *(596)*

**CHAPTER
SIXTEEN**

CHAPTER SIXTEEN

■

Sex as a Commodity

●

Do we desire what is forbidden?. . .What is the connection between the erotic and danger, the erotic and comfort?

Amber Hollibaugh

F or most of us, sex is one of the most personal and private of human activities. Yet it is also a marketable commodity, on sale directly through prostitution and symbolically through pornography. Prostitution may not really be the world's "oldest profession" (spear-making and witch-doctoring may have come first), but it does have a long past. And books and pictures designed to arouse sexual desire were around long before the invention of the printing press. Today the commercial cornucopia of sexual products and services extends to magazines, live sex shows, mail-order films, audio- and videotapes, party records, photographic services, dial-a-porn messages, and even computer graphics. Sexually explicit materials, once the monopoly of the literate few, are now available to everyone. Their easy availability has helped to blur the once-clear line between private and public behavior (Kindrick, 1987).

Until a few years ago, controversy over commercial sex focused almost entirely on moral and legal issues. Those who opposed restrictions saw their opponents as repressive reactionaries, lacking in respect for the Bill of Rights and its guarantee of freedom of expression. Those who favored restrictions saw their opponents as immoral libertines, willfully ignoring the effects of "smut" and prostitution on individual virtue and social order. It was pretty easy to predict people's views on pornography or prostitution on the basis of their religious or political convictions. But today things are more complicated. Some "conservatives" now accept previously unthinkable sexual references and innuendoes on television and in films. Some "liberals" now oppose at least some forms of commercial sex. Antipornography rallies may attract both right-wingers and radical feminists.

What has not changed in the debate about pornography and prostitution is a fundamental conflict: the conflict between the right of the individual to be free of interference ("Don't tread on me") and the duty of government to protect citizens from harm ("There oughta be a law"). In this chapter we will examine the history of pornography and prostitution, consider arguments for and against regulating these two ancient forms of commerce, and see what modern social science research can teach us about their causes and effects. As you read, try to imagine yourself in the role of an expert who has been asked to testify before a legislative committee that is considering the revision of antipornography or antiprostitution laws. Ask yourself what position *you* would take.

PORNOGRAPHY

One hallmark of being human is the ability to represent experience symbolically. Virtually every kind of human behavior has found its way into words or images, and sex is no exception. Our prehistoric ancestors had hardly climbed down from the trees when they began to scratch depictions of human genitals and sexual acts on the walls of their caves. As the species grew more sophisticated, so did its art, progressing from cave drawings to erotic clay figures, phallic statues, bas-relief sculptures, and elaborate poetic descriptions.

Sexually explicit materials produced for profit first found a mass audience in the West during the seventeenth century. This development coincided with an increase in the number of people who could read and who could afford to buy the books and pamphlets made possible by the invention of the printing press. Even in supposedly puritanical America there was a market for erotic literature. Before the Revolution a colonist named Isaiah Thomas secretly imported sheets of John Cleland's bawdy novel, *Fanny Hill, or Memories of a Woman of Pleasure*, binding them and selling them under the counter to his customers. *Fanny Hill* became the first book ever prosecuted as obscene in the United States (in 1921), and it was still the object of censorship as late as 1966.

By the second half of the nineteenth century, during the Victorian era, pornography was being sold in unprecedented quantities both in America and in Europe. In an ambitious study of this period, Steven Marcus (1966) described the cultural split personality that resulted:

> For every warning against masturbation issued by the official voice of
> culture, another work of pornography was published; for every caution-

ary statement against the harmful effects of sexual excess uttered by medical men, pornography represented. . .endless orgies, infinite daisy chains of inexhaustibility; for every assertion about the delicacy and frigidity of respectable women made by the official culture, pornography represented legions of maidens, universes of palpitating females; for every effort made by the official culture to minimize the importance of sexuality, pornography cried out—or whispered—that it was the only thing in the world of any importance at all. (pp. 283–84)

As the pornography market grew, so did individual and organized opposition to it. Some zealots tried to ban any reference to sex or sexual anatomy, no matter how innocent. In 1818 an Englishman named Thomas Bowdler published a ten-volume expurgated version of Shakespeare's works that was popular for decades on both sides of the Atlantic. Bowdler arrogantly disregarded both the spirit and the structure of the great master's writings, removing, for example, the drunken porter scene from *Macbeth* and completely altering the ribald character of Falstaff. (Today the word *bowdlerized* means expurgated in a prudish and insensitive manner.) Even the Bible did not escape the blue pencils of self-appointed guardians of public purity. In 1833, Noah Webster, whom we remember today for his famous dictionary, published an edition of the King James Version of the Bible "with amendments."

In the United States, legislative censorship of pornography dates from 1842, when Congress prohibited the importation of indecent and obscene prints and paintings. In 1865, in response to reports of widespread circulation of pornography among Civil War troops, Congress prohibited the mailing of obscene books and pictures. In 1872 it passed the more comprehensive Comstock laws, banning the distribution, mailing, or importation not only of sexual materials but also of birth control and abortion information. The Comstock laws launched a forty-year antiobscenity crusade by the legislation's chief promoter, Anthony Comstock. At the end of his career, in 1913, Comstock boasted that he had personally destroyed some 160 tons of obscene literature (Rugoff, 1971).

Today, efforts are still being made to censor material almost no one but extremists consider obscene. In recent decades, local, state, and national organizations have pressured schools and libraries to ban or restrict the circulation of such books as John Steinbeck's *The Grapes of Wrath*, Ken Kesey's *One Flew Over the Cuckoo's Nest*, J.D. Salinger's *Catcher in the Rye*, and even *The Diary of Anne Frank*. In 1986, a town in Texas tried to ban all depictions of nudity below the navel. Local marshals promptly warned retailers that they had better remove an issue of *Cosmopolitan* magazine from the shelves because it contained an article showing a "tummy tucking" operation (*Time*, July 21, 1986). (At the last moment, the local District Attorney stepped in to say that the law did not apply in this case.)

Yet despite a slew of local, state, and federal regulations governing the sale and distribution of obscene materials, most people, including teenagers,

Playmates *Many children gain access to erotic materials at an early age. Some people think that such exposure is unhealthy; others contend that it's usually harmless and can even be educational. Should young children be protected from publications like* Playboy? *Can they be? What do you think?*

say they have seen sexually explicit X-rated materials of one sort or another. In one telephone survey, 84 percent of high school students reported such exposure, a figure higher than for adults. The average age of first exposure was 16 years, 11 months. The average age at which males saw their first issue of *Playboy* or a similar soft-core magazine was only 11 years (Bryant, 1985).

What is Pornographic?

We have been using *pornography*, *erotica*, and *obscenity* rather loosely, but to most people these words have somewhat different meanings. **Erotica** (from the Greek for "of, or caused by, love") is a general term for literature or art dealing with sexual themes. **Pornography** (from the Greek for "writing of or about prostitutes") is often used in the same way, but according to the dictionary it applies specifically to literature, art, or photography that is sexually obscene—that is, lewd, disgusting, repulsive, and offensive to modesty or decency. **Obscenity** is the term used in legal rulings to refer to sexually explicit material that is not constitutionally protected. The word *erotica*, then, tends to be morally neutral, while *pornography* sometimes has negative implications, and *obscenity* usually does. The problem is: How does one draw clear lines between these categories?

THE MORAL STANDARD   The traditional approach has been to rely on moral distinctions to establish what is offensive to decency and what is not. Courts in the United States set the precedent over half a century ago in a case involving James Joyce's celebrated novel *Ulysses,* which is now generally considered one of the literary masterpieces of the twentieth century. Here is one of the then-controversial passages from the book; it invites the reader to eavesdrop on the stream-of-consciousness musings of a woman about her lover, or, more specifically, about his phallic proportions:

> yes because he must have come three or four times with that tremendous big red brute of a thing he has I thought the vein or whatever the dickens they call it was going to burst through his nose. . .like iron or some kind of a thick crowbar standing all the time he must have eaten oysters I think a few dozen. . .no I never in all my life felt anyone had one the size of that to make you feel full up he must have eaten a whole sheep after whats the idea making us like that with a big hole in the middle of us like a stallion driving it up into you because thats all they want out of you with that determined vicious look in his eye I had to half shut my eyes still he hasn't such a tremendous amount of spunk in him when I made him pull it out and do it on me considering how big it is so much the better in case any of it wasn't washed out properly the last time I let him finish in me nice invention they made for women for him to get all the pleasure. . . . (p. 727)

By today's standards this passage is not legally obscene. It contains no "dirty" words and nothing more explicit than "that tremendous big red brute of a thing." But it *is* potentially arousing, it *is* about a penis, and it was one of the passages that kept the book from being imported to the United States for some years. Then in 1933 a federal judge ruled that *Ulysses,* taken as a whole, had literary merit and was not written with the intention of depraving public morals, so it was not obscene after all, and could be imported and sold.

That is more or less where matters stood until a landmark Supreme Court decision in 1957 *(Roth v. United States).* For the first time, the Supreme Court tackled the constitutional issues inherent in censorship. Obscenity, said the Court, is not covered by the First Amendment, which protects freedom of speech and freedom of the press, and, by extension, free expression in books, films, and other media. The Court defined obscenity as material whose dominant theme would seem "to the average person, applying contemporary community standards," to appeal "to prurient interest." But the Court did not clarify whether "prurient interest" meant an interest in "perverted" forms of lust or merely an interest in sexual desire.

Since then, the Court has struggled several times to elaborate on what it means by obscenity. The current standard is from a 1973 case involving a

Art or obscenity?   *Police officers blocked the entrance to Cincinnati's Contemporary Arts Center after the museum and its director were charged with obscenity for exhibiting sexually explicit photographs by Robert Mapplethorpe. The officers emptied the museum of visitors and seized evidence. Of 175 photographs, seven were at issue: five of sadomasochistic homosexual acts and two of children with their genitals exposed. The case touched off a furor over the First Amendment rights of artists and art exhibitors. The exhibit wound up drawing a record crowd of 81,000 people. In late 1990, after deliberating only two hours, a jury acquitted the defendants.*

pornography distributor who sent unsolicited advertisements through the mail *(Miller v. California).* In a 5–4 decision, the Court offered a three-part definition. A work was to be considered obscene if (1) it depicted or described sexual conduct in a patently offensive way; (2) the work, taken as a whole, lacked "serious literary, artistic, political, or scientific value"; and (3) an average person, applying contemporary community standards, would find that the work, taken as a whole, appealed to prurient interest. This decision specifically gave states the right to decide what was obscene. Subsequent decisions the next year extended that right to every town and hamlet in America.

Since the 1973 ruling, cities and counties have been free to prosecute and convict movie and video producers, actors, magazine writers, and publishers who have never set foot in their jurisdictions. Yet ironically, after the Miller ruling, there was a *drop* in the number of prosecutions for obscenity. Confusion remained, and still remains, about just what should count as legally obscene. There are still no specific guidelines for determining whether a work is "offensive," or whether it has any "serious" scientific, literary, artistic, or political value (how serious is "serious," and what does "any" mean?). It also remains unclear how the "average person" (whoever that is) is supposed to know what a community's standards are. Is the "community" the state, city, neighborhood, or block? The Supreme Court itself has recognized these problems. Only a year after the *Miller* decision, it overturned a unanimous jury verdict that the film *Carnal Knowledge* was obscene, noting that juries do not have "unbridled discretion" to judge local standards when the material involved is not "hardcore."

Well then, we might ask, what is hardcore? Supreme Court Justice Potter Stewart once declared that although he could not define hardcore pornography, "I know it when I see it." But if obscenity cannot be spelled out legally, then a person involved in the production or distribution of sexually explicit materials has no way of knowing until arrested whether he or she is breaking the law—a situation that violates the basic American principle of due process. So far, no one advocating censorship on traditional grounds has found a clear way out of this dilemma.

THE DISCRIMINATION STANDARD   A more recent approach to regulating sexually explicit materials focuses not on morality but rather on the harm and discrimination that women suffer as a result of pornographic themes and images. Sexually explicit materials do not always depict simple lovemaking. Many contemporary books, magazines, and films feature sexual sadism, usually directed against women. Sometimes female characters are "merely" humiliated verbally, subordinated, or used as objects. Sometimes they are whipped, beaten, tortured, raped, mutilated, or murdered. Often they are portrayed as willing, even enthusiastically willing, victims of abuse.

The pervasiveness of such portrayals depends on the particular type of pornography. For example, violence in at least one "soft core" magazine, *Playboy*, appears to have declined since 1977 and is now fairly rare (Scott & Cuvelier, 1987). In contrast, a recent examination of 45 widely available X-rated video cassettes found that over half of the explicitly sexual scenes were primarily concerned with domination and exploitation, typically by men of women. Almost a quarter of the explicit scenes showed at least one act of physical violence (whipping, pinching, slapping, hair-pulling, bondage, or kicking), with the recipient in apparent pain or discomfort. Fourteen percent of the scenes reinforced the myth that women liked to be raped (Cowan et al., 1988).

Many critics of pornography, especially feminist critics, feel that these themes are the real issue in the pornography debate. In a landmark article, writer Gloria Steinem (1978) noted that feminists have no objection to erotic materials that focus on sensuality and warmth and that portray people who choose freely, as equals, to enjoy sex together. What many feminists do find obscene are images of domination, degradation, humiliation, and coercion. They argue that violent or demeaning pornography is more than simply "offensive"; by promoting contempt for women, it deprives them of equal opportunities for participation in society. It also encourages potential rapists to feel that they are merely giving in to a normal urge. In the words of writer Robin Morgan (1978), "Pornography is the theory and rape is the practice." (Later in this chapter, we will examine social science research on this issue.)

Feminist critics have also cited other dangers in violent or demeaning pornography. Child abusers have sometimes used materials involving children to try to convince their victims that sex between adults and children is perfectly normal. Both these victims and the children used in the so-called "kiddie-porn" suffer great emotional harm. Some women who have participated in pornographic films and tapes have been forced to do so to avoid being beaten or even murdered. One famous pornography star, "Linda Lovelace," has described being forced to take part in the hit pornographic film of the 1970s, *Deep Throat* (Lovelace & McGrady, 1980, 1986).

Law professor Catherine MacKinnon (1984, 1985) and writer Andrea Dworkin (1985) contend that traditional obscenity laws are futile and misguided. They have, instead, championed a different approach to curbing pornography, one that emphasizes discrimination against women and the violation of their civil rights. As of this writing, however, there have been only two attempts to translate this approach into law. In 1983, the Minneapolis city council enacted an ordinance that defined pornography as "the sexually explicit subordination of women, graphically depicted whether in pictures or in words, in which women are represented in one or more of the following ways: dehumanized as sexual objects, things, or commodities; as sexual objects who enjoy pain or humiliation; as sexual objects who experience sexual pleasure in being raped; as sexual objects tied up, cut up, mutilated, bruised, or physically hurt; in postures of sexual submission or sexual servility, including by inviting penetration; as beings reduced solely to their body parts, including but not limited to vaginas, breasts, and buttocks; as whores by nature; being penetrated by objects or animals; in scenarios of degradation, injury, or torture, shown as filthy or inferior, bleeding, bruised, or hurt in a context that makes these conditions sexual." Instead of treating pornography as a criminal matter, the ordinance allowed individual women to bring a civil suit against anyone who forced them to take part in the production of pornography; anyone who forced pornography on them (for example, in the workplace); and anyone who assaulted or attacked them in a manner caused by a specific example of pornography. A woman could also bring a class action suit on behalf of all women, against anyone who trafficked in pornography.

The Minneapolis ordinance was passed but was then vetoed by the mayor, who was afraid the city would be mired in legal battles. A short time later, a coalition of feminists and conservative Republicans succeeded in getting Indianapolis to pass a similar law, which was signed by the mayor. Critics of the law argued that because it banned depictions of women as "sexual objects for domination, conquest, violence, exploitation, or use," and did not take into account the literary or artistic merits of a work, it could conceivably be used against anyone who "trafficked" in such works as the *Iliad*, or *Lady Chatterly's Lover*, or paintings such as *The Rape of the Sabine Women*. The courts quickly struck down the law as vague, overly broad, and an unconstitutional restriction of free speech.

The MacKinnon-Dworkin approach to pornography has split the feminist community. Many feminists consider it a brilliant and necessary strategy in the fight against rape and the exploitation of women. Others oppose it because of concerns about First Amendment rights or because they do not think pornography should be singled out as the primary culprit in violence against women. Such writers worry that ultimately censorship will do women more harm than good, as moralists take advantage of it to ban or discourage any materials that threaten the status quo, including feminist writings (Burstyn, 1985). As you can see, the political and legal issues surrounding the MacKinnon-Dworkin approach are difficult ones.

A Tale of Two Commissions

If pornography leads directly, or even indirectly, to antisocial behavior, then some sort of governmental intervention in its distribution may be justified. If it does not, then First Amendment protections should apply. Which is the case? Until the late 1960s, almost nothing was known about the actual effects of pornography, although plenty of people were ready to offer strong opinions on the subject. Then, in 1967, Congress authorized the Presidential Commission on Obscenity and Pornography to study the matter and recommend regulations for controlling the flow of obscene materials. The 18-member Commission (which we will call the "1970 Commission" for short) included social scientists, psychiatrists, members of the clergy, attorneys, and others with some expertise on the topic. The commissioners surveyed existing research and funded scores of new studies. In two years they spent over two million dollars and in 1970 they published eight volumes of data and a lengthy report.

The results, however, were not at all what Congress had expected. Instead of recommending new legal restrictions, the majority of the Commission members actually recommended *repeal* of all laws prohibiting the access of adults to pornography. The Commission's most controversial finding was that no link had been demonstrated between pornography and aggressive or antisocial behavior.

The Senate promptly rejected the report by a vote of sixty to five. President Richard Nixon called the Commission "morally bankrupt" and said he would ignore its findings. These reactions were based on moral and political considerations. However, there were, in fact, some serious weaknesses in the Commission's work. Much of the research it sponsored was flawed. Most of the studies relied on surveys and interviews rather than experimental techniques, which are preferable if you want to reach conclusions about cause and effect (see Chapter 3). Also, there was hardly any research done on violent pornography, perhaps because it was not in widespread circulation during the 1960s. Research conducted since the Commission's report, much of it experimental in nature, calls several of the Commission's findings into question, as we will see.

In 1985, the Reagan administration created a second pornography commission, the Attorney General's Commission on Pornography, which became known as the Meese Commission after then-Attorney General Edwin Meese. The Meese Commission had far less money to spend than the 1970 Commission, only $400,000. Its 11 members did not conduct or sponsor any original research. Instead they took testimony from experts (although few social scientists were called) and from individuals who considered themselves to be victims of pornography. They also made three well-publicized field trips to pornography shops. In 1986, they issued a 1,940-page report. Unlike the 1970 Commission, the Meese Commission concluded that there *is* a causal link between violent pornography and both (a) acceptance of rape myths, and (b) aggression toward women. The Commission also concluded that there is "some causal relationship" between nonviolent but degrading

The Commission concludes. . . *In 1986, then-Attorney General Edwin Meese received the final report of a specially appointed Commission on Pornography. People immediately pointed out the irony of his accepting the report in front of the semi-nude statue "Spirit of Justice."*

material and the level of sexual violence in American society. As for erotica that is neither violent nor degrading, the Commission acknowledged that there was no evidence to suggest a link with violence, but added that "none of us think the material in this category. . .is in every instance harmless." The Commission went on to recommend a broad range of steps to curb pornography, including ways for citizens to monitor the lyrics of rock music and bring pressure on sellers of explicit material, whether the material was legally obscene or not.

Civil libertarians were quick to charge that the Meese Commission had been biased from the start. Six of its eleven members, including the chair, had publicly called for government action against pornography before hearings ever began. While the Commission was still taking testimony, it issued a letter to more than 10,000 stores, including the 7-Eleven chain, suggesting that they remove *Playboy* and *Penthouse* from their shelves or risk being cited for distributing pornography. (Many, including the 7-Eleven stores, complied.) After the report came out, several experts complained that the Commission's recommendations had gone beyond the existing data. Two members of the Commission itself, including the only social scientist, issued a minority view: "Efforts to tease the current data into proof of a causal link" between exposure to pornography and the commission of sexual crimes, they wrote, "cannot be accepted" (U.S. Department of Justice, Attorney General's Commission on Pornography, 1986, p. 129). Critics also argued that whereas the 1970 Commission had reported only on the tamer types of erotica, the Meese Commission focused too much on the violent and degrading varieties. Several writers noted that the commissioners, who had been immersed in pornography for a year, did not seem worried about its possible harmful effects on *them*.

Which governmental group was closer to the truth, the 1970 Commission or the Meese Commission? Let's take a look at what existing research has to say about the effects of pornography on sexual arousal, conventional sexual behavior, and antisocial attitudes and acts.

Effects on Sexual Arousal

It probably won't come as any surprise that sexually explicit materials tend to be sexually arousing, although perhaps not as arousing as private sexual fantasies (Byrne & Lamberth, 1971). Like fantasies, erotic materials can be used as "mental aphrodisiacs." Some people like to read erotic stories aloud or browse through pictures or photographs with a lover.

It is commonly assumed that men are more aroused by erotica than women are. Kinsey's findings supported this view. In his sample, about half the men, versus only twelve percent of the women, said they had been aroused by erotic photographs, drawings, and paintings. The results were similar for erotic stories (Kinsey et al., 1953). But subsequent studies have questioned Kinsey's conclusion that men are more aroused by explicit sex.

When people are exposed in the laboratory to depictions of consensual sex and then asked immediately afterward to describe their physiological reactions, a majority of both sexes report signs of arousal and sex differences are not large (Schmidt & Sigusch, 1973). And when researchers actually measure and record responses to erotic materials as they are occurring, again, sex differences are not dramatic. Either women in Kinsey's sample were unaware of or reluctant to report their own arousal, or women's responses to erotica have changed since Kinsey's time.

In one study, psychologist Julia Heiman (1975) had men wear a thin, flexible, mercury-filled tube called a strain gauge around the base of the penis. This device measures blood volume and pressure pulse, recording the slightest indication of an erection. Female subjects wore a small acrylic cylinder, a photoplethysmograph, just inside the vagina; it contains a photocell and light source, and registers changes in blood volume and pressure pulse, early signs of arousal in females. The subjects listened to four kinds of stories: erotic ones containing explicit sex, romantic versions of the same stories, and stories that were neither romantic nor erotic. In general, women were as likely as men to be aroused by the erotic stories. Both sexes were more aroused by straight, unadorned sex than by romance alone. There was no evidence that the women preferred romantic-erotic stories to those that were just erotic. In fact, when asked to rate the stories, women gave higher arousability ratings to the erotic stories than men did (see also Steinman et al., 1981). Of course, such findings cannot tell us whether women's responses are as intense or enjoyable as men's; they simply establish that as many, or nearly as many, women show some physiological signs of arousal.

For most people, the most stimulating depictions of sexual acts involve heterosexual intercourse, genital caresses, fondling of the female breasts, and oral sex. The least stimulating involve sadism, nude males, and fellatio and anal sex between men (Byrne, 1977). However, a substantial proportion of college men are sexually aroused by sexual violence. In fact, over half of college men are sexually aroused to some degree by rape depictions in which the victim is portrayed as eventually enjoying the assault; 20 to 30 percent are substantially aroused by rape depictions in which the victim shows only horror and suffering; and about ten percent are sexually aroused by depictions of violence with little sexual content (Malamuth, cited in Russell, 1988). Men who endorse male domination over women, and men who say they might rape a woman who had rejected them if they knew they could get away with it, are more likely than other men to be sexually aroused by depictions of rape (Malamuth & Check, 1983a; Malamuth, Check & Briere, 1986). So are actual rapists (Quinsey, Chaplin & Upfold, 1984).

Women, too, are sometimes aroused by eroticized depictions of rape. When psychologist Wendy Stock (1983) presented college women with a rape myth audiotape, in which a rape victim was portrayed as sexually enjoying an assault, the subjects showed as much genital and subjective arousal as when they heard a tape of consensual intercourse. However, *all* of the

Sex for sale *Stores selling adult books, videos, and other kinds of sexually explicit items can be found in the downtown areas of cities all over the world.*

women in the study responded with low levels of genital and subjective arousal to a realistic portrayal of rape, in which the victim experienced only fear and pain.

To fully understand people's responses to erotica and pornography, we must look beyond their physiological responses and their reports of arousal or nonarousal. As you may recall from Chapter 5, sexual arousal has a cognitive, or mental, component. Two people who become physiologically aroused by some depiction will not necessarily attach the same *meaning* to their responses. Thus, although both sexes often experience physiological arousal to explicit materials, men generally say they enjoy pornography more than women do. When pornographic materials are degrading to women (whether violent or not), women, despite their physiological responses to the materials, may feel angry or ashamed. Nondegrading erotica tends to affect a women's moods positively, but both violent and nonviolent degrading images have a negative effect (Senn & Radtke, 1986).

Studies done for the 1970 Commission also show that whatever their gender, people who feel shy or guilty about sex, or who hold extremely

Take it off *For years it was assumed that women wouldn't attend, much less enjoy, strip shows. But since the 1970s, some nightclubs have featured "ladies' nights" with entertainment by male "bumpers and grinders." It is not clear, however, whether most women attending such shows respond sexually to them, or whether they simply enjoy the opportunity to flout convention.*

moralistic views about pornography, are less likely than others to give positive ratings to erotic material that they admit they find arousing. In one study, people classified as sexual liberals or sexual conservatives rated 60 erotic slides on their offensiveness, sexual arousal value, entertainment value, and acceptability. For the conservatives, but not the liberals, the more arousing the pictures were, the *more offensive* and *less entertaining* they were perceived to be (Wallace & Wehmer, 1972).

Many sex therapists recommend nonviolent erotica to people who are inhibited about sex or who have specific sexual dysfunctions. A therapist may recommend explicit slides, movies, books, or photographs, both as a way of imparting information and as a way of encouraging clients to feel comfortable with common sexual practices. But such recommendations must be made with care. They may backfire if the client is repulsed or disgusted by the materials. Also, depictions of highly attractive and "well-endowed" men and women performing highly athletic sexual acts may cause some people to become less satisfied with their own partner's physical appearance or sexual performance (Zillman & Bryant, 1988). Of course, advertisements and ordinary R-rated movies showing gorgeous people and enthusiastic sex might have the same result.

Effects on Attitudes Toward Women

As we have seen, many feminists believe that pornography increases male callousness toward women. Research tends to bear them out *for certain kinds of depictions.* Portrayals of *mutually consenting* sexual activity do not seem to have any negative effects on male attitudes. However, materials that are demeaning or debasing to women *may* have such effects, and materials that combine sex and violence, especially those that show women as willing victims of violence, almost certainly *do* have such effects.

Let us consider, first, the nonviolent but demeaning materials. In one series of studies, Dorf Zillman and Jennings Bryant (1982, 1984) had unmarried men and women watch six "stag films" a week for six weeks. The films showed women as responsive to just about any kind of sexual stimulation and ready to accommodate any and every sexual request. Compared to people who saw fewer films, or no films at all, these viewers became less supportive of sexual equality, more accepting of male dominance in intimate relationships, and more lenient toward a rapist whose crime was described in a newspaper article. The men also became more sexually calloused toward women, as reflected in their increased acceptance of such statements as "A man should find them, feel them, fuck them, and forget them," and "If they are old enough to bleed, they are old enough to butcher."

Similarly, Canadian psychologist James Check (1985) found that men exposed to dehumanizing film clips were more likely than men exposed to simple erotica (or to no explicit sex at all) to say they might commit a rape if no one would ever find out about it. However, other studies, using feature-length films, have failed to find negative changes in attitudes toward women or in self-reported likelihood of rape (Linz et al., 1988; Malamuth & Ceniti, 1986). Perhaps demeaning materials have such negative effects only when the demeaning images are "concentrated" (Donnerstein, Linz, & Penrod, 1987).

What about pornography that is actually violent? Here the evidence is clearer: In laboratory studies, depictions of sexual force and aggression against women usually produce calloused attitudes toward women (Briere, Malamuth, & Check, 1985; Malamuth, 1984; Malamuth & Check, 1980, 1985). After exposure to such material, men are more likely to trivialize the trauma that a woman suffers from being raped and to think the victim enjoyed it. They are also more apt to endorse various rape myths—for example, that any healthy woman can successfully resist a rapist if she wants to, or that a woman who "lets things get out of hand" is responsible if she is raped.

Such effects are strongest when pornographic materials portray women as enjoying being sexually victimized (Malamuth, 1984). And these portrayals have a particularly strong effect on men who have previously rated themselves as quite likely to rape if they knew they could get away with it (Malamuth & Check, 1985). (As we saw in Chapter 15, the proportion of Canadian and American college-aged men who rate themselves this way is high, about one-third.) Recent research has found that men who give them-selves high "rape-proclivity" ratings are also more likely than other men to *use* sexually violent pornography in their own lives (Demare, Briere & Lips, 1988).

Effects on Aggression Against Women

Negative attitudes are disturbing enough; do some kinds of pornogra-phy also increase actual aggression against women? The 1970 Commission, you will recall, said no. They based this conclusion largely on interview stud-ies with imprisoned sex offenders and other criminals, who reported not more, but less exposure to pornography than other men. But these studies had many shortcomings. For example, they relied on the honesty of impris-oned offenders—not necessarily the most trustworthy of subjects. Also, they failed to address the possibility that rapists are more heavily influenced than other men by pornography, even if they are not exposed to more of it. As we saw earlier, there is indeed evidence that rapists are more sexually aroused than other men by descriptions of rape (Quinsey, Chaplin, & Upfold, 1984).

Research conducted since the 1970 Commission report has taken a dif-ferent tack, using experimental techniques rather than surveys and inter-views, and ordinary men (usually college students) as subjects. In a typical study, a female confederate of the experimenter, posing as a fellow subject, "primes" a man to act aggressively by provoking him—for example, by insulting him. Then the subject is exposed to sexually explicit pictures, films, or written passages, or, if he is in a control group, to neutral materials. Finally, as part of a second, presumably unrelated study, the subject is given an opportunity to hurt the confederate—for example, by shocking her as part of a "learning" experiment. (The shocks are never real, but the subject doesn't know that.) The question is, will an angry man aggress more against a woman if he has just been exposed to sexually explicit materials?

The answer, once again, depends on the *kind* of materials, with the results paralleling those found in studies on attitudes. For ordinary nonvio-lent erotica, the answer is "probably not." For nonviolent but degrading materials, the results of research are conflicting. But for violent materials, the answer, from many studies, is a definite "yes"; exposure does seem to increase the disposition to aggress (Malamuth, 1978; Donnerstein, 1980; Donnerstein & Berkowitz, 1981).

Now we come to a critical point: *The antisocial effects of violent pornogra-phy are due to their violence, not their sexual explicitness.* R-rated films shown in neighborhood theaters and on television can also increase male acceptance of rape myths (Malamuth & Check, 1981) as well as actual aggressiveness, if these films depict sexual aggression in a positive light. Consider the results of one important study by Edward Donnerstein, Leonard Berkowitz, and Daniel Linz (1986). The researchers showed men a film with aggression

against women but no sex; one with sex but no aggression; or one with neither sex nor aggression. The aggression-only film produced more aggression
than the sex-only film, which in fact produced no more aggression than the
neutral film. In a follow-up, the researchers then doctored one film so that it
showed either sexual aggression, or only the aggression, or only the sex. Men
who saw only the aggression expressed the most callous rape attitudes. *Half*
these men said they might rape a woman if they knew they could not get
caught, as compared to 25 percent of the men who saw sexual violence, and
11 percent of the men who saw only sex.

As Donnerstein, Berkowitz, and Linz (1987) point out, far more people
are exposed to violence in sexually nonexplicit materials than in hard-core
pornography. And the nonexplicit materials have plenty of sexual violence.
In fact, a Canadian study found that videos that would be R-rated in the
United States actually contained more aggressive and sexually aggressive
content than did videos that would be X-rated. And the violence in the R-
rated videos was more severe (Palys, 1986).

"Slasher" films that are popular with teenagers (such as "Halloween"
and the "Friday the 13th" series) often pair mild erotic scenes with sudden
and gory violence. The slasher is usually male; the victims are both male and
female, but sexiness and sexual activity are most often associated with
female victims who get killed—only "pure" women survive (Cowen, 1989).
These films are especially likely to desensitize viewers to the brutality of violence and the degradation of women, even though they do not usually depict
common rape myths. In the laboratory, prolonged exposure to such films
produces more calloused attitudes toward rape victims among both men
(Linz, Donnerstein & Penrod, 1988) and women (Krafka, 1985). And outside the laboratory, a recent study finds, the frequency of watching slasher
films correlates with acceptance of rape myths among both college men and
college women (Cowan et al., 1989).

Ironically, note Donnerstein, Linz, and Penrod (1987), by banning
nonviolent X-rated films but permitting violent R-rated films, society may
be telling young people that sexual violence is fine but nonviolent sexual
relations are not. "We find it curious," they write, "that under the present
system, the whole genre of slasher films, which graphically depict mutilation
of women and which may be desensitizing viewers, fall into the same rating
category as films that may contain no sex or violence but that have two or
more instances of the 'harsher sexually derived words.'"

Implications for the Real World

The research we have just reviewed supports many feminist assertions
about pornography. It suggests that sexually violent pornography, and perhaps nonviolent but degrading pornography as well, encourages men to associate sexuality with violence, believe that women want to be raped, and
underrate the injuries of rape victims. These changes in attitude may make

rape and other forms of sexual violence against women more likely. As sociologist Diana Russell (1988) notes, by making forced sex seem acceptable, dehumanizing women as mere objects, and promoting the myth that women enjoy rape, pornography may undermine some men's internal and social inhibitions against acting on aggressive desires.

Not everyone agrees, however, that the results of laboratory studies are generalizable to the real world. In real life, do men exposed to a lot of violent pornography subsequently commit more sexual crimes or antisocial acts than other men? Few studies have addressed this question directly, but some researchers have tried to answer it by examining relationships between crime rates and the general availability of pornography.

Over two decades of research have focused on Denmark, which legalized the sale of printed pornography in 1967 and other forms of pornography in 1969. According to researcher Berl Kutchinsky (1985), sexual offenses, including rape, child molestation, and voyeurism, actually decreased by 30 percent in 1969. The decline continued in the years following (except for rape, which increased somewhat, perhaps because of better reporting). Many opponents of censorship feel the Danish experience proves that pornography does not automatically lead to sexual crimes and social disorder. But critics are unconvinced. The decrease in sexual crimes in Denmark, they say, may be partly due to the decriminalization of various sexual offenses (Court, 1984). Moreover, what is true for Denmark, a small, homogeneous country with a relatively affluent population and a low crime rate, may not apply to other countries.

In the United States, there is some evidence that rape rates in the 50 states are related to the number of adult magazines sold in each state (Baron & Straus, 1986; Scott & Schwalm, 1988). States like Alaska and Nevada, which have high rape rates, tend to have high sales of such magazines. States like Maine and West Virginia, with low rape rates, tend to have low sales. But correlations like these can be tricky to interpret. Perhaps in places with high rape rates, men who are *already* disposed to rape are buying a lot of adult magazines. Perhaps preexisting attitudes toward women affect both magazine sales and rape statistics. Or a general "macho ethic" may explain both high magazine sales and high rape statistics. Some support for this third interpretation comes from the fact that sales of outdoor magazines, such as *Field and Stream* and *American Rifleman*, are also related to the incidence of reported rapes (Scott, 1985).

Let us assume, however, that the laboratory results do generalize to the real world, and that some forms of pornography, under some conditions, encourage anti-female attitudes and violent sexual acts in at least some people. What, then, is the solution? As we have seen, for many people the answer is either government restrictions or civil suits against pornographers. Others, however, including some of the researchers whose studies we have discussed, remain leery of both these approaches. Donnerstein, Linz, and

Penrod (1987), for example, point out that because sexually violent depictions tend to promote aggression against women even when they are not sexually explicit, legal suppression of such depictions would have to extend into every form of communication. Another problem is that in our legal system, it is not enough to show that certain depictions or descriptions have a general tendency to do harm; you must prove that a *specific* depiction or description has led directly to a *specific* instance of harm, which is exceedingly difficult to do.

For these reasons, Donnerstein, Linz, and Penrod call, instead, for public education programs about the effects of various kinds of pornography so that people can make informed choices about the materials to which they expose themselves. In making your own informed choices, we urge you to keep in mind what research has confirmed: that not all sexually explicit material is alike. We have focused in this chapter largely on violent and demeaning pornography, because it is clearly problematic. But explicit materials may also be playful, funny, raunchy, romantic, passionate, sensuous, or deliciously decadent. Moreover, not all explicit depictions are antiwoman; indeed, women are now writing their own erotica (for example, in Barbach, 1984) and producing their own explicit videos (Leo, 1987).

Studies on the effects of pornography are bound to continue, because we still do not have all the answers. Social science research alone cannot resolve the controversies surrounding pornography; the issues are not just psychological, but also legal, political, and philosophical. However, the results of research can contribute to critical thinking about pornography and help each of us to reach a well-considered judgment.

PROSTITUTION

A **prostitute** is a person who engages in sexual acts with various partners in exchange for money or other forms of payment. Historically, prostitution has taken many forms. In some cultures, certain prostitutes had religious as well as sexual duties. Throughout ancient Greece, high-class prostitutes called *hetaerae* wielded considerable influence with generals, statesmen, men of letters, and other social leaders. The hetaerae, who were the best educated of all Greek women, underwent special training for their work and charged extremely high prices. They were praised for their wit as well as their beauty, and their admirers sometimes set up statues of them in temples and other public buildings (Bullough, 1964). But the ordinary prostitute has never lived such a glamorous life. In ancient Rome, the typical brothel was a sordid, smelly place where women solicited customers by sitting or standing outside tiny cubicles. During the Middle Ages, European prostitutes were forced to live in special quarters and wear distinctive clothing or arm bands to set themselves apart from respectable women. Today the ordinary prostitute is still usually treated as a social outcast, a situation that activists in the profession are trying to change.

Despite widespread condemnation of the prostitute herself, over the centuries her work has often been considered necessary for the protection of "good" women's chastity. Men, it was assumed, needed some outlet for their natural lust. The ancient Hebrews, despite their harsh attitudes toward nonmarital sex, seem to have accepted prostitution as a fact of life (Bullough, 1964). (Those who know the Bible may recall that a prostitute named Rahab aided Joshua's spies in Jericho and continued practicing her profession after the walls of the city came tumbling down.) Even the Christian Fathers were rather tolerant of prostitution. St. Augustine worried that without it the world would quickly become polluted with lust. St. Thomas Aquinas compared prostitution to a sewer in a palace: if the sewer were removed, the palace would fill with pollution. Although prostitutes were excluded from church membership unless they gave up their wanton ways, they were also recognized as a necessary evil.

Serious efforts to rid Europe of prostitution date from about the sixteenth century. During the Protestant Reformation, church leaders attacked prostitution vehemently. At the same time, a growing fear of venereal disease led people to demand severe punishments for prostitutes. During the eighteenth and nineteenth centuries, some countries licensed brothels, required medical inspections of prostitutes, and cracked down on street solicitations. None of these efforts to control prostitution had much success.

In colonial America, prostitution was much less common than in Europe. In New England, Puritanism kept it to a minimum. In the South, the availability of slaves and indentured servants, who were vulnerable to the sexual demands of their masters (which often took the form of rape), reduced the demand for prostitutes. But in the second half of the nineteenth century, the picture changed. Mass immigration and the Industrial Revolution converged to produce enormous cities full of poor people living in squalid conditions. Many young women turned to prostitution as a way to escape a miserable home life or unbearable factory jobs. Some followed men to the West, where a shortage of women increased the demand for prostitutes' services.

As prostitution flourished, opposition to it grew. The first anti-prostitution law was passed by Illinois in 1908. Other states quickly followed suit. Today prostitution is illegal throughout the United States, except in a few counties of rural Nevada where brothels (but not streetwalking) are permitted. In Canada, only *solicitation* (offering sexual services in a public place) is illegal. But public attitudes of North Americans are ambivalent: books and films sometimes portray the prostitute as a greedy and immoral predator, but just as often she is presented as a victim of forces beyond her control, or a "whore with a heart of gold." Laws against prostitution are often honored only in the breach; "escort services" that are actually prostitution services routinely advertise in the Yellow Pages and accept credit cards.

Types of Prostitution

No one really knows how many full-time and part-time female prostitutes there are, but in the United States estimates have ranged from a quarter- to a half-million. An unknown number of men also work as prostitutes, usually catering to male clients (see Box 16–1). Most of the research on prostitution has been on the female side of the industry.

Prostitutes (also called *hookers* or *hustlers* by the public and *working women* or *sex workers* by themselves) live many different kinds of lives, depending on their social class, income, and type of business. That fact probably explains why different studies have often led to opposite conclusions about what being a prostitute is like. One study of New York street prostitutes found them to be the embodiment of sexual freedom (Carmen & Moody, 1985). In contrast, a study of street prostitutes in the San Francisco Bay area concluded that there are no "happy hookers," and that prostitutes are exploited and abused both physically and emotionally (Silbert & Pines, 1982).

In general, prostitutes fall into four categories:

1. *Call Girls*   earn more than other prostitutes and tend to live comfortably. Many come from middle-class backgrounds. They make most of their contacts by personal referral and by telephone, often through an answering or "escort" service or a madam working from a "call house." Therefore they are not usually visible to the public, at least not while they are working. Low visibility means that the call girl is rarely arrested or subjected to police harassment. Because a call girl is highly paid, she is expected to give more "personalized" service than other prostitutes. For example, she is expected to be pleasant, to know her customers by name, and to be aware of a client's special preferences. Occasionally she may be called upon to serve as a social companion, for example by attending parties or other social functions with the customer. Most call girls are self-employed.

2. *In-House Prostitutes* work in **brothels,** special houses presided over by a **madam,** or business manager. The madam is typically a prostitute or former prostitute who has business and managerial skills. At one time brothels were common in large cities. They reached their peak in the late 1930s and then began to decline because of public and police opposition. Today's brothels are usually inconspicuous houses or apartments, and many are open only during the day, when vice squads are less active. The madam may meet clients elsewhere and transport them to the house or use cooperative taxicab drivers to do so. When the "house" is a "massage parlor," the arrangement for sexual services is

BOX 16–1

Male Prostitution: The World Of The Boy Hustler

Women do not hold a monopoly on prostitution; males also sell sex for money and favors. Some, known as *gigolos,* usually sell their services to women who are older than themselves and may also function as companions and escorts. The majority of male prostitutes, however, serve a male clientele. A few are highly paid companions of the wealthy, but most are street hustlers and are very young. Some eventually drift into other criminal activities.

A classic study of boy prostitutes by Albert Reiss, Jr. (1961) found that teenage hustlers who catered to adult males typically did not think of themselves either as homosexuals or as prostitutes. Reiss's subjects were members of gangs that encouraged hustling and taught members how to do it. The boys viewed hustling as an easy way to make money, one that was considerably less risky than robbery or other criminal activities. Most eventually gave it up to get a legitimate job or to become involved in more serious crimes.

In the mid-1970s, writer Robin Lloyd (1976) interviewed both young hustlers and their customers. In his book *For Love or Money: Boy Prostitution in America,* Lloyd reported that the boys he spoke to were not gang members but loners, often runaways. They were recruited by pimps and other hustlers who offered them a place to stay, spending money, and a feeling of belonging. Typically the boys came from deprived, unhappy homes and were emotionally and financially vulnerable to the promises of recruiters. The customers came from all socio-economic groups and walks of life. Although they had homosexual interests, they were not usually members of the openly gay community. Many were married and had families.

According to Lloyd, an encounter between a male hustler and his client is different from one between a female hustler and her client. A female prostitute need not have orgasms on the job. Her customer,

made after the customer is inside a private massage room. The prostitute usually provides manual stimulation of the customer's penis (a hand job") or oral sex.

3. *Streetwalkers,* as their name implies, solicit customers on the street, usually by smiling and starting a conversation or going up to the customer's car. If the man is responsive, the prostitute takes him to her room or a nearby hotel or motel with which she may have some sort of business arrangement. Streetwalkers charge lower rates than other sex workers, and

however, does usually have an orgasm; after all, that is what he is paying for. But in a transaction between males, the roles are often reversed: the boy plays a passive role (for example, in fellatio) and has an orgasm, while the customer may content himself with arousal, body contact, and perhaps masturbation. For the boys Lloyd talked to, such an arrangement was important, because they typically believed themselves to be heterosexual and therefore needed to conceal or deny any feelings of attraction toward the customer. (The motives of the customer are less clear.)

Unfortunately, there has been little research on male prostitution during the past decade. However, the research that does exist suggests that young boys, like young girls, often leave home and start hustling out of a desire for autonomy and a need for belonging (Lowman, 1987). Like female prostitutes, male prostitutes have a status hierarchy, with street hustlers at the bottom, bar hustlers in the middle, and call boys and escort prostitutes at the top. Advancement through the ranks appears to be relatively easy (Luckenbill, 1986). In recent years, more male prostitutes seem to be identifying themselves as homosexuals (Earls & David, 1989).

Most people denounce boy prostitution, and feel repugnance toward sexual relations between children and adults. But criminal laws are not likely to be any more effective against boy prostitution than against its female counterpart. In his book, Lloyd suggested that boy prostitution exists because of many factors, including drugs, a failing public school system, the apathy and abusiveness of many parents, inadequate sex education, a repressive juvenile correctional system, and materialism, which teaches children that the goal of life is to make money. If he is right, then boy prostitution will diminish only when attitudes toward children in trouble change and society makes a commitment to their welfare.

they often limit contact to a specified time period. Many streetwalkers hang out in twos and threes as protection against muggers, and in order to look more legitimate. Streetwalkers tend to get arrested more frequently than do other sex workers and are more likely to be harassed by the police. As one former prostitute recalled, "Before they would put us in the police car, they would take our purses, dump them on the ground, and make us pick the things out of the gutter" (Lockett, 1987). Women of color are disproportionately represented among street prostitutes.

4. *B-Girls* or *Bar-Girls* use a bar as a base of operation and then take their clients to their room or to the client's own hotel room. In exchange for the bar owner's cooperation, bar-girls often encourage their customers to order plenty of drinks (sometimes at inflated prices) and they may also pay the bar owner a percentage of their profits.

Streetwalkers and bar-girls are more likely than other prostitutes to have a **pimp,** a man who offers protection from criminals; raises bail; hires lawyers; buys the prostitute clothes, jewelry, and drugs; provides living quarters; and sometimes finds customers (in which case he is also a *procurer*). In exchange for these services, the pimp lives off the prostitute, taking a sizable chunk of her earnings. Pimps are often domineering and abusive to "their" prostitutes. Like battered wives, a prostitute may put up with abuse for many reasons, including feelings of powerlessness, loyalty, and fear of retribution if she leaves.

Many sex workers, especially those who entered the work voluntarily because of the money and those who are not dependent on a pimp, resent being thought of as passive or exploited victims (Bell, 1987). They argue that prostitution is simply a service industry, and that the prostitute has a right to use her body as she wishes. Historically, efforts to portray prostitutes as innocent and passive victims have often worked against the prostitute herself, because any woman who failed to behave like a victim and "repent" gave up her claim to sympathy (Hobson, 1987).

However, the reality is that many prostitutes do suffer from economic, social, and sexual powerlessness. In various Asian and Latin American countries, women and children are forced into prostitution. They may be bought, sold, and shipped like so much merchandise from one country to another. In India, girls as young as eight have been sold to temples by their impoverished parents. In exchange for a large contribution, the temple gives the girl to a "patron." When he is through with her he sends her to a large city to work as a *devadasi*, or common prostitute (Barry, Bunch, & Castley, 1984). In the United States, almost a third of all prostitutes are thought to be under the age of 18, and the average age of entry into the profession is only 14 (U.S. Department of Health, Education, and Welfare, 1978).

Whatever their age, streetwalkers are in constant danger of being assaulted or raped by customers ("johns") or abused by pimps. The biggest beneficiaries of prostitutes' work are not the women themselves, but the owners of hotels, convention centers, gambling houses, and other tourist attractions that depend on prostitution to bring in business. These people are often respectable citizens who maintain a discreet distance from prostitution and disclaim any knowledge of it (Sheehy, 1973).

Feminist writers are divided on the issue of prostitution, just as they are divided on pornography (Hobson, 1987). Some see prostitution as a legitimate way for women to control their sexuality and gain economic independence. Others see it as sexual slavery that institutionalizes female depen-

dence on men and reinforces the image of women as sexual commodities. As historian Barbara Meil Hobson (1987) observes, "For many feminists sexual liberation [has meant] eliminating the power dynamics in sexual relations. But prostitutes in their trade must implicitly accept them and use them to advantage; this is the essence of 'turning a trick.'"

Why Women Become Prostitutes

There are no doubt many reasons for choosing to become a prostitute, but explanations of voluntary prostitution generally fall into two broad categories: psychological and economic.

PSYCHOLOGICAL MOTIVES   Psychoanalysts have argued that women choose to be prostitutes because of personality and emotional problems—an unconscious hostility toward men, a need to debase themselves in order to "get even" with a rejecting mother, or unresolved Oedipal issues. Indeed, a recent study of adolescent prostitutes did find them to be less psychologically healthy than either nonprostitute delinquents or nondelinquent girls.

Under arrest   *Being arrested is a routine part of a streetwalker's life. A great deal of time and public resources are spent rounding up prostitutes, holding them in jail, trying them, and supervising their probation.*

The young prostitutes also held more negative attitudes toward men and were more cynical and alienated (Gibson-Ainyette et al., 1988). However, it is hard to know whether these characteristics caused the girls to become prostitutes or were the results of being a prostitute.

Another psychological factor may be a history of sexual abuse. In a number of studies, a high percentage of current or former prostitutes have reported such abuse (for example, Bagley & Young, 1987; McMullen, 1986; Silbert & Pines, 1983). However, since all current studies are of small, special samples, it is hard to know for certain the percentage of prostitutes sexually abused as children. Certainly not all prostitutes were sexually abused children, and most sexually abused children do not grow up to be prostitutes. Many prostitutes deny that sexual abuse was a factor in their choice of work (Bell, 1987).

What about sexual problems in adulthood? Little is known about the adult sexual adjustment or satisfaction of prostitutes. In one exploratory study of streetwalkers, most of the women said they enjoyed intercourse and oral sex at least some of the time with customers and most or all of the time with their own lovers. Two-thirds of the women said they usually or always had orgasms with customers, and all of them said they usually or always had orgasms with their lovers. Only one woman reported all contacts with customers and lovers to be nonerotic. Most of the women had private sex lives and most claimed prostitution had a beneficial impact on their sexual satisfaction with their own lovers (Savitz & Rosen, 1988). But one wonders whether these women were being completely honest. Streetwalkers often have many clients a night, with sexual encounters quite brief and male orgasm the only goal. It is hard to imagine these women "usually or always" having orgasms with their clients. Indeed, in one collection of writings by prostitutes, the women said their work was *not* sexy, and that they were simply acting a role (Bell, 1987).

A further psychological factor is a need to establish some sense of independence and autonomy. In interviews with streetwalkers, Nanette Davis (1978) found that most of the women had been labeled troublemakers by parents, neighbors, and teachers before becoming prostitutes. Prostitution seemed to provide a way out of a troubled home life. But the women did not simply decide one day to become hookers. Rather, they drifted from casual sex into paid sex, attracted by the prospect of glamour and excitement, encouraged by friends, or recruited by a pimp who offered them affection and security. They did not label themselves as prostitutes until they were arrested or until a pimp started to demand that they work harder. Eventually, however, a sense of identity and belonging developed, which made it difficult for them to leave "the life" despite its hazards and inconveniences.

ECONOMIC MOTIVES   The second type of explanation for why women voluntarily enter prostitution emphasizes its financial inducements (Bell, 1987). Streetwalkers typically come from poor backgrounds and have little education. To a young woman whose skills limit her to a minimum-wage job, prostitution can seem like a golden opportunity. Even a middle-class woman may be tempted by the financial rewards. A woman does not have to be emotionally disturbed to make such a choice. Indeed, one study of a group of 95 prostitutes (including call girls, in-house prostitutes, and streetwalkers) found no more pathology among them than among control subjects matched for age, marital status, and education (contradicting the findings for adolescents mentioned earlier). The only exceptions were suburban housewives working as prostitutes and streetwalkers who were drug addicts. Call girls and in-house prostitutes were indistinguishable from teachers, lawyers, social workers, nurses, and saleswomen—except for their incomes, which were much higher (Exner et al., 1977).

Some writers, emphasizing the financial motives in prostitution, observe that sexism and discrimination encourage or force women to use whatever resources they possess in order to survive (e.g., James et al., 1975). These writers point out that prostitutes are not the only women willing to exchange sexual services for money or other favors. As we saw in Chapter 13, in the traditional dating situation, the woman often feels under some obligation to repay her date for his expenses by dispensing sexual favors. Traditionally, marriage has also involved the exchange of sexual and other services for material goods and financial security. Many cultures encourage men to regard female sexuality as a commodity and women to view themselves as sexual prizes.

Why Men Use Prostitutes

A man's motives for visiting a prostitute may seem obvious: he has a sexual need and a prostitute is a convenient way to satisfy it. But in many cases, the client's motives go beyond simple sexual desire. Researcher Martha Stein (1974, 1977) observed sexual transactions between 64 New York City call girls and 1,242 upper-middle-class white customers. She eavesdropped through peepholes, one-way mirrors, and doors left ajar, and even hid on occasion in a bedroom closet. She also spoke with prostitutes in bars, brothels, massage parlors, and on the street. Stein found that customers patronized prostitutes for five basic reasons: 1) to obtain sexual release without courtship or commitment; 2) to seek sexual variety (learn new techniques or act out socially taboo desires); 3) to enjoy social entertainment (especially when visiting prostitutes along with other men); 4) to enhance their status (by sending friends or business clients to the prostitute); and 5) to have a relationship. The last category applied to the largest group of men, almost half the sample. A "relationship" could mean romance, having someone to tell one's problems to, acting out sexual fantasies of submission to a woman, acting as a paternalistic protector to a young woman, or seeking "maternal comfort." Over half the men who sought a relationship used the call girl as a sort of therapist; they asked for help with personal problems, requested reassurance, and even sought sexual counseling. Stein concluded that call girls function as an underground sexual health service for upper-middle-class men.

Men also visit prostitutes for other reasons. Since prostitution involves little socializing unless the man wants it and pays for it, and little risk of rejection, it may appeal to men who are lacking in social skills. Also, prostitutes make sex available to men who, because of physical or mental disabilities, may have difficulty finding a sexual partner. Don't assume, though, that only social or sexual "rejects" seek out prostitutes. Most studies find the typical customer of call girls to be an average, middle-class, middle-aged man. In Stein's sample, 58 percent of the customers were married and most were businessmen or professionals. Newspapers frequently run stories about well-known public figures who have been caught patronizing female or male prostitutes.

Prostitution and the Law

Street prostitutes comprise a large proportion of women arrested each year in the United States. Although most are merely fined, prostitutes make up about 30 percent of the population in most women's jails, and they serve longer sentences than others who commit misdemeanors (James & Withers, 1975). In recent years some legislatures have passed new laws that jail HIV-positive or AIDS-infected prostitutes if they continue to work at their trade (although at present there is little evidence that prostitutes, who are avid users of condoms, have played a significant role in spreading the disease [Shilts, 1989]). Yet history teaches us that making prostitution a crime does not eliminate it—at least, not in democratic countries with a tradition of due process.

Some people have argued that if anybody should be arrested, it is the customers. After all, customer demand is the ultimate reason for prostitution's existence—it takes two to tango. Most laws do not penalize the customer at all, or, if they do, they are unenforced. Many people condemn the prostitute but sympathize with, or at least are neutral about, the customer, perhaps because male customers are not violating their gender role (men are supposed to be lustful) while female prostitutes *are* violating theirs (women are supposed to be respectable). But penalizing customers could backfire. When action has been taken against them—even such mild action as sending citations to their homes—there have been immediate protests, and the practice has been dropped (Hobson, 1987).

Many civil libertarians and prostitutes' groups believe that as consenting adults, the prostitute and her customer should be free to make any sort of sexual arrangement they wish to. They argue that if prostitution were *decriminalized*, then the police could use their time more effectively to fight crimes that have identifiable victims: murder, rape, assault, and robbery. With decriminalization, prostitutes would be entitled to health insurance, workers' compensation, and social security benefits. And, of course, they would be more likely, if their work were decriminalized, to pay taxes.

Others argue for *legalization with regulation*. Under this system the government would license brothels, require medical inspections, and collect taxes. As we saw earlier, this is not a new idea; it was tried in eighteenth- and nineteenth-century Europe. Legalized prostitution seems to work fairly well today in some European cities, especially Amsterdam, which has an official red-light district. Recently, however, an increase in the number of juvenile prostitutes, increased violence, and the spread of heroin in prostitute centers has decreased European tolerance for such districts (Hobson, 1987). In any case, this approach may not be appropriate in the United States, where ordinary street crime is higher. A few years ago, Boston tried to restrict prostitution to a special "combat zone," along with strip joints and peep shows. Within a short period, criminals flocked to the area, crime skyrocketed, businesses complained, and authorities once again began to arrest prostitutes.

In the rural Nevada counties that have legalized and regulated brothels, residents tend to view the prostitutes (though not the owners or madams) as pariahs. The civil liberties of the prostitutes are actually more restricted in certain ways than they would be otherwise. Prostitutes are often confined to certain sections of town and are allowed to leave the brothel only at certain times of the day. One town limits when prostitutes

Prostitutes united
Prostitutes have organized to improve their public image and their working conditions. Margo St. James, founder of Coyote (Cast Off Your Old Tired Ethics), is shown at a Washington, D.C. rally for decriminalization of prostitution.

can shop and what establishments they can enter (Symanski, 1984; Hobson, 1987). Regulation, like criminalization, focuses attention on the prostitute as "the problem," and not on her customers or the conditions that promote the profession.

THE FUTURE OF COMMERCIAL SEX

Ultimately, time and social changes may solve some of the problems raised by the selling of sex. Both pornography and prostitution seem to thrive in societies that have a sexual double standard, disparage women, and view sex as dirty and embarrassing. Prostitution is also associated with limited roles and employment opportunities for women. If society becomes more relaxed about consensual sex, rejects the double standard, and achieves true equality between men and women, then perhaps the appeal of prostitution and pornography will decline.

In Denmark, where sexual attitudes are more tolerant and relaxed than in the United States, pornographers reportedly must depend on tourists for sales. In contrast, in the U.S., hardcore pornography is still a multimillion-dollar business. Even "legitimate" materials, such as rock lyrics, often feature graphic sexual descriptions (frequently involving the subordination of women). But some kinds of pornography have fallen off in popularity. During the late 1980s, adult magazine circulation dropped, adult movie houses and bookstores closed all over the country, and there was reportedly a decline in the X-rated video business.

The use of prostitutes in the United States has also declined. At the time of Kinsey's study (1948), 69 percent of white males had visited a prostitute by age forty-five, but younger men went only one-half to two-thirds as frequently as older men. Two decades later, Morton Hunt (1974) estimated that the use of prostitutes by single young men was only half as common as it had been in the 1940s. Younger men with some college education were unlikely to have experienced sex with a prostitute. And younger men in general were much less likely than older ones to say their first experience with sexual intercourse was in a house of prostitution. Hunt attributed these findings to the fact that "as dating partners have become sexual partners, prostitutes have been unnecessary and undesirable." But we should keep in mind that many variables affect the demand for prostitutes. In Sweden, sex-for-hire has not disappeared as sexual liberation has increased; in fact, the prostitution business may have grown more widespread (Hobson, 1987).

In this chapter we have emphasized the importance of thinking critically about the sale of sex and sexual images. The causes and effects of buying and selling sex are complex. Not all prostitution is the same; the life of a successful call girl is different from that of the average streetwalker. Similarly, not all sexually explicit images are the same. Images of consensual sex are probably harmless mental aphrodisiacs. But the evidence indicates that eroticized images of female subjugation both reflect and contribute to anti-women attitudes, and are likely to promote sexual aggression against women as well. No doubt our society will be struggling for many years to find ways of reducing the negative effects of pornography and prostitution without eroding our cherished rights of free speech and privacy.

. . . .

PORNOGRAPHY: WHERE DO *YOU* DRAW THE LINE?

Just about everyone considers certain kinds of materials to be pornographic: for example, videotapes of adults having sex with children. But in other cases, pornography is in the eye of the beholder. Book shop owner Jake Zeitlin once told of exhibiting some works by well-known photographer Edward Weston, when an elderly woman came in and said, "I am going to get the police to arrest you for showing obscene pictures." The woman then pointed to a photograph of two eggs and a cross-section of an artichoke. "Madam," said Zeitlin, "permit me to compliment you on your active imagination."

As we saw in this chapter, distinctions can be made among various kinds of sexually explicit depictions. Many writers distinguish erotica (inoffensive materials) from pornography, which they define as offensive or demeaning. Others use *pornography* more broadly, and distinguish three types: nonviolent, nonviolent but demeaning, and violent. Which sorts of distinctions strike you as most useful? And where do *you* draw the lines? Consider the following three passages. Which, if any, in your opinion, are erotic? Which are pornographic? Are you comfortable with any of them? Would you share any with a friend or lover? What are your criteria for making your judgments?

1.   "It's in the afternoon, and you're in a room with a woman, Nancy, and you're going to screw her. You tell her she might as well give in. She's saying she doesn't want to, that she wants to leave. And you are just taking out the knife. You tell her to take her clothes off. You see her blond hair. She's big. You are telling her to go on and take her clothes off. She's slipping off her panties, and now she's slipping off her bra. You can see her tits there. You tell her to lie back and she's reluctant to, and you just slap her a little, slap her a little as she's lying down now. You've got a nice big erection. You're getting right on top of Nancy. She's got big thighs and you stick your dick into her there, all the way, deep into her. And she's fighting you. You slap her a little and tell her to be quiet. She's starting to scream now and cry. You're holding her down, forcing yourself on her and you can tell that she likes it. She is telling you to stop, to please stop. You can tell that she is really getting excited now. She is really aroused."

2.   "He lay her back against the pillows, and gently sculpted her body with one finger, drawing it close to her center, and then moving it away, drifting around her breasts and all the way down her belly, and then

up again, touching her with his tongue and his heart and his fingers, but with nothing else, and after hours of it, she was writhing and begging him for something more, but he wouldn't do it. Instead, he let her feel him, and touched her gently with his throbbing organ. He ran it over her like a satin hand, and she bent down and began to kiss it, and touch him gently until he was writhing as she was, and then first with his lips, and then with his fingers, he touched her and felt her grow frightened and rigid.

" 'It's all right, Hil. . .it's all right. . .I won't hurt you. . .I. . .please baby. . .please let me. . .please. . .Oh, God, you're so beautiful. . .' "

3.   [The following passage describes an interlude involving three people: the narrator (a woman), and two brothers, Bela and Paul.]

"Without words, Bela's hands showed me how beautiful, how long, strong and praiseworthy Paul was. He added kisses to his stroking, and after a moment I followed, safely above the waist at first, then to the small of the back, which made the spine arch and sink in, to the side where the sensitive flesh shivered and shrank away. The skin on Paul's ass was smooth under my lips. Bela's head bumped mine and he grinned at me, a little sheepishly. I saw that his cock was stretching and thickening as we worked on Paul. . .

[Bela] knelt up and urged me to sit on his lap, lean back against his muscular body. His hands cupped my buttocks a moment then slid under to my thighs. With his effortless strength he lifted me, doubling me back on myself, opening me. I could feel myself parting like the sections of an orange. Paul knelt, too. His cock was hardening and lifting, darkening to that evening-rose color that throbs like the deepest organ note. I heard it with my ears, my teeth, my bones. The vibration shook all of us, stronger deeper, as he found his place. The same note filled the hollowness, a bone-shaking drone that never altered as he pushed in and in. Above and behind him the leaves were willowgreen, amber, translucent jade, sounds open and lonely as flutes and oboes. A bird sang and the notes fell down like flakes of fire."

You might be interested in where these passages come from. Passage #1 is a slightly abbreviated version of one that has been used in research on violent pornography (Malamuth & Check, 1980). It eroticizes rape and promotes the myth that women enjoy being assaulted. Passage #2 is from best-selling author Danielle Steel's novel, *Kaleidoscope* (N.Y.: Dellacorte Press, 1987, pp. 194–195). Passage #3 is from a true, first-person account by Syn Ferguson, in *Pleasures: Women write erotica*, edited by psychologist Lonnie Barbach (N.Y.: Perennial/Harper & Row, 1984, pp. 244 and 247).

Did the quality of the writing in these passages affect your judgments in any way? Does knowing where these selections are from, and why they were written, matter?

IN BRIEF

1.   Sex becomes a marketable commodity when it is sold directly through prostitution or symbolically through pornography. These activities raise a fundamental conflict between the right of the individual to be free of interference and the duty of government to protect citizens from harm.

2.   In the United States, legislative censorship of pornography dates back a century and a half. The traditional approach has relied on moral distinctions to establish what is obscene and what is not. The Supreme Court has ruled that a work is obscene if it depicts or describes sexual conduct in a patently offensive way; if the work, taken as a whole, lacks serious literary, artistic, political, or scientific value; and if an average person, applying contemporary community standards, would find that the work, taken as a whole, appeals to prurient interest. But these criteria are subjective and ambiguous, and therefore difficult to apply in practice.

3.   A more recent approach to regulating sexually explicit materials holds that materials depicting the humiliation, subordination, rape, or torture of women promote rape and violate women's civil rights. So far, however, efforts to translate this approach into law have not been successful.

4.   Two federal commissions have examined the impact of pornography on antisocial behavior. The first, in 1970, found no causal link, but the second, reporting in 1986, concluded that there is a link between violent pornography and both the acceptance of rape myths and aggression toward women. The work of both commissions has been attacked by critics.

5.   For most people, the most sexually stimulating types of erotica involve heterosexual intercourse, genital caresses, fondling of the female breasts, and oral sex. However, a substantial proportion of men and some women are sexually aroused by eroticized depictions of sexual violence.

6.   Portrayals of mutually consenting sexual activity do not seem to promote negative attitudes toward women, but research finds that materials that are demeaning or debasing to women may have such effects. Materials that combine sex and violence, especially those that show women as willing victims of violence, almost certainly do have such effects.

7.   Similarly, portrayals of mutually consenting sexual activity do not seem to increase the probability of aggression toward women; results are conflicting on the effects of nonviolent but degrading materials; and exposure to sexually violent materials does seem to increase aggression.

8. Studies have found that the antisocial effects of violent pornography are due to their violence, not their sexual explicitness. However, controversy exists about both the generalizability of these results to the real world, and the appropriate steps to take if they do generalize. Psychological research can help an individual arrive at an informed opinion on these matters, but the issues surrounding pornography are also legal, political, and philosophical.

9. Prostitution has a long history, as do efforts to eradicate it. Currently prostitution is illegal throughout the United States except in a few counties of rural Nevada, where brothels are permitted. In Canada, only solicitation is illegal. Public attitudes toward prostitution are ambivalent.

10. An unknown number of males work as prostitutes. Most have a male clientele, but they do not always regard themselves as homosexual. Like female prostitutes, male prostitutes often get into the business when they leave home as adolescents, and they have a status hierarchy, with street hustling at the bottom.

11. *Call girls, in-house prostitutes, streetwalkers* and *B-girls* differ in social class, income, and mode of operation. For example, call girls are highly paid, are often self-employed, and are usually not visible to the public, whereas streetwalkers and bar-girls are less well-paid, often have pimps, and are visible and therefore vulnerable to abuse and arrest. Prostitutes often resent being thought of as passive or exploited victims, but many do suffer from economic, social and sexual powerlessness.

12. Some explanations of why women become prostitutes emphasize psychological factors, such as personality and emotional problems, a history of sexual abuse, and a need for independence and autonomy. Other explanations emphasize financial inducements and reject the assumption that prostitutes are generally more disturbed than other women.

13. Men use the services of prostitutes for many reasons: to obtain sexual release, seek sexual variety, enjoy social entertainment with other men, enhance their status among acquaintances, or establish some sort of relationship with a call girl. Prostitution may appeal to men who are lacking in social skills or have difficulty finding a sexual partner, but most studies find the typical customer of call girls to be an average, middle-class, middle-aged man, and many customers are businessmen or professionals.

14. Many civil libertarians and prostitutes' groups support the decriminalization of prostitution, citing various advantages both to society and to prostitutes themselves. Others argue for legalization with regulation,

although so far this approach has not worked well when it has been tried in the U.S.

15. Both pornography and prostitution seem to thrive in societies that have a sexual double standard, disparage women, and view sex as dirty and embarrassing. As these conditions change, pornography and prostitution may lose some of their appeal. But our society will no doubt continue to struggle for some time with the complex issues these activities raise.

Key Terms

erotica *(612)*

pornography *(612)*

obscenity *(612)*

moral standard for pornography *(613)*

discrimination standard for pornography *(615)*

prostitute *(627)*

solicitation *(628)*

call girls *(629)*

in-house prostitutes *(629)*

brothels *(629)*

madam *(629)*

streetwalkers *(630)*

B-girls *(632)*

pimp *(632)*

procurer *(632)*

decriminalization *(636)*

legalization with regulation *(637)*

**CHAPTER
SEVENTEEN**

CHAPTER SEVENTEEN

■

Sexually Transmitted Diseases

•

We can protect ourselves only by protecting others and sharing what we know.

Mary Catherine Bateson & Richard Goldsby

Imagine that you are a tiny, finicky bug destined to spend your life in exclusive association with human beings. You enjoy warm, close, dark environments; you cannot tolerate light or fresh air. But you like to travel and so you depend on people getting very close together and bring their warm, moist body parts into contact. As a result, you love it when people have sex. As long as people keep changing their sex partners, you can journey for free all around the world, moving from one host to the next.

That is the way it is for most of the bacteria, viruses, parasites, and other microorganisms responsible for sexually transmitted diseases. Their existence depends on human sexual activity. The more partners people have, the greater travel opportunities the "bugs" have, and the larger their populations. Although there are effective cures for most sexually transmitted diseases, human sex practices keep these diseases alive and well.

Until the late 1970s, sexually transmitted disease was commonly called **venereal disease** or **VD.** The word *venereal* means "pertaining to Venus," Venus being, paradoxically enough, the ancient Roman goddess of love and beauty. Traditionally, VD referred to only five diseases: gonorrhea, syphilis, and three others that are rare in the United States (chancroid, lymphogranuloma venereum, and granuloma inguinale). Nowadays, the terms **sexually** transmitted disease and **STD** are preferred and these terms refer to a range of infections and infestations commonly spread by sexual contact. Some STDs are spread *only* sexually; others can be transmitted from person to person in nonsexual ways, but sex is their primary route.

Sexual activity does not *cause* STDs; germs and parasites do. But sex sets up conditions that are ideal for the transmission of these bugs: close, prolonged, skin-to-skin contact. The agents of most other human disease can thrive outside our bodies, in our water or food, in the bodies of animals or insects, or even in the air. We can protect ourselves from them by mounting public sanitation campaigns (Boil that water! Kill those mosquitoes!). The agents of sexually transmitted diseases, for the most part, thrive only inside the human body. To protect ourselves, we must directly prevent their transmission from one person to another.

Many of the organisms causing STDs are quite fragile. For example, neither the AIDS virus nor the gonorrhea bacterium can survive long outside the human body and both are easily killed with a mild solution of household bleach. Why, then, do these delicate microbes plague us? The answer is that sexually transmitted diseases are well adapted to human sexual habits. In order to be free of STDs we need to change those habits and this is easier said than done. Also, moral issues tend to get mixed up with medical ones. Fear, embarrassment, and judgmental attitudes about sex often get in the way of effective education and prevention. We will discuss the problems of prevention in the last section of this chapter. But first let's look at the most common sexually transmitted diseases. (One word of caution: Because new findings are coming in almost daily on some of these diseases, it is impossible for a textbook to be entirely up-to-date in this area. We urge you to take responsibility for your own health by seeking the most current information. The National STD Information Hotline phone number is 1-800-227-8922. The hours are 8 a.m. to 11 p.m. EST. The 24-hour AIDS Hotline number is 1-800-342-2437.)

BACTERIAL INFECTIONS OF THE CERVIX AND MALE URETHRA

Bacteria are microscopic one-celled organisms, many of which produce diseases. Several different bacteria can cause infections of the cervix *(cervicitis)* in women and inflammation of the urethra *(urethritis)* in men. If not treated, these infections are likely to spread up through the reproductive organs. Men with untreated urethritis may develop *epididymitis*, an inflammation of the epididymis, the coiled tube that sits atop each testis. If both epididymal structures are affected, scarring may lead to infertility. Women may develop a severe infection of the pelvic organs called **pelvic inflammatory disease** (PID) (see Chapter 6). PID is not only painful but it may cause scar tissue to develop in the Fallopian tubes. If the scarring blocks the passageway completely, the woman will be infertile. Scarring may also narrow the tubes just enough so that an egg cannot pass through. In that case a fertilized egg may embed itself in the Fallopian tube. As we saw in Chapter 6, this condition, known as a *tubal* pregnancy, is potentially life-threatening.

The two major causes of cervicitis and urethritis are gonorrhea, which has been studied for more than a century, and chlamydia, a relative newcomer on the research scene.

Gonorrhea

Gonorrhea [gon-ur-REE-uh] has probably been with us for thousands of years, if not longer. The Old Testament (Leviticus, 15:2) tells us that when a man has an "issue"—usually interpreted to mean a urethral discharge due to gonorrhea—he is "unclean." The Greeks also knew gonorrhea but thought the discharge was due to the flow of semen; the word *gonorrhea* comes from *gonos*, Greek for "seed," and *rhoia*, Greek for "flow." About seven hundred years ago the French named gonorrhea *clap*, perhaps deriving the term from the Old French word for brothel, *clapier*. The word *clap* is now part of American slang, along with *drip* and *a dose*. The French also coined the name *la chaude pisse*, which in polite terms means hot urine and refers to a common symptom of the disease in men (Stiller, 1974.)

While gonorrhea is responsible primarily for female cervical and male urethral infections, the throat and rectum can also be sites of infection. The microbe involved, the gonococcus bacterium, enters the body by way of warm, moist tissues called mucous membranes. Transmission can occur during penile-vaginal intercourse, during anal intercourse, and when the penis comes in contact with the upper throat. (The mouth itself does not provide

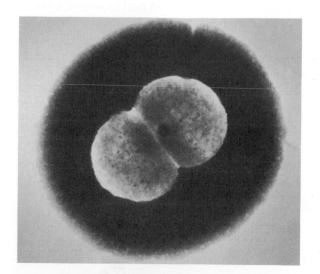

Neisseria gonorrhoeae
These one-celled organisms, named after Albert Neisser, the German dermatologist who discovered them in 1879, are the cause of gonorrhea. As this electron microscope photograph shows, the bacteria appear in pairs. Close relatives of these microbes exist harmlessly in the mouth and throat.

the right environment for the bacterium.) Gonorrhea is not usually transmitted from the vagina to the throat during cunnilingus because gonococcus bacteria are rarely present in vaginal tissue. A man's chance of catching gonorrhea after one exposure to the infection is estimated to be around 20 percent; a woman's chance is approximately 50 percent. The risks increase substantially with repeated exposures. In 1989, approximately 733,000 new cases of gonorrhea were reported in the United States. But gonorrhea often goes unreported, and its actual incidence has been estimated at about two million new cases annually (Hatcher et al., 1988).

Gonorrhea cannot pass from a pregnant woman to a fetus in the womb, but bacteria in the vaginal canal can infect a baby during birth. Newborns infected with gonorrhea are susceptible to several complications, including pneumonia and blindness. In 1884 a German obstetrician discovered that drops of 1 percent solution of silver nitrate in the eyes of newborns killed any existing infection. Today newborns' eyes are routinely treated with silver nitrate or antibiotics.

SYMPTOMS   Symptoms of gonorrhea may show up within two to five days after exposure but can take up to 30 days to appear. An infected man may experience an urge to urinate frequently and urination may be painful. The urine may contain thick pus, or there may be a cloudy penile discharge. In women, the major symptom is a greenish or yellow-green vaginal discharge. Gonorrhea in women sometimes also causes *cystitis*, a urinary tract infection characterized by an urge to urinate and a burning sensation during urination (see Chapter 18). In both sexes, gonorrhea contracted by the "receiving" partner during anal intercourse may cause a discharge from the rectum, and contraction by the "active" partner during fellatio may cause a sore throat and swollen glands.

These are symptoms that *can* occur. However, an estimated 20 to 40 percent of infected men and as many as 80 percent of infected women notice *no* symptoms at all. And even when they do occur, symptoms in both males and females may go away by themselves, and the person may again appear to be healthy. But until the disease is treated, the person remains infectious and can give it to others. If gonorrhea is not treated, the bacteria may eventually make it into the bloodstream. Then infection can also damage various other parts of the body, including the joints and the lining of the heart, although this is not common.

DIAGNOSIS   In men who have a discharge, a medical practitioner can tentatively diagnose gonorrhea in a matter of minutes, by examining a drop of pus on a slide under a microscope. But although bacteria are usually visible, they may be difficult to identify. The best way to be sure, and usually the only way in women, is to swab the tissues that may be infected—including the cervix, anal canal, and throat—and prepare a *culture* (grow the bacteria for a day or two under special laboratory conditions). As the germs multiply they become easier to identify. If there are definite symptoms, or a high probability of infection exists, many medical practitioners will treat a person for gonorrhea even before getting laboratory results.

TREATMENT   Until the 1930s, there was no effective treatment for gonorrhea. If the disease caused blockage of a man's urethra, a device resembling a pipe cleaner was passed up the urethra to widen it and make urination easier, but this did not cure the disease (Stiller, 1974). Then doctors discovered that sulfa drugs could kill gonococci. Everyone broke out the champagne to celebrate. What they did not count on was the adaptability of the hardy little gonorrhea bugs, which developed a resistance to the drugs, eventually making treatment with sulfa useless.

The matter of resistance is often misunderstood. When germs become resistant, they do not individually get stronger, nor do they get "used to" a treatment. Whan happens is this: in any population of microbes, some will be a little more resistant to a drug than others. The drug kills off most of the bugs, but a few hardy ones may live to see another day, reproduce themselves, and infect another human being. At the same time, genetic mutations—spontaneous changes in the genes of some microbes—may produce new strains that are especially resistant to the drug. As the drug is used more and more, killing off weak bugs, the resistant bugs become a larger and larger percentage of the total population, until they are a majority. Then the drug no longer works, or a larger dosage must be used. It is the evolutionary principle of "survival of the fittest," applied to microbes.

In the 1940s, researchers discovered that penicillin given by injection could also kill gonococci. The timing couldn't have been better. World War II was on, and STDs tend to be one of the victors in any war. Penicillin was so effective that, once again, everyone assumed the gonococcus was doomed. And after the war gonorrhea rates did plunge. But by the late 1950s, gonococci were showing resistance to penicillin, just as they had to sulfa, and the rates began to rise again. As a result, the dosage has had to be increased considerably. Since the 1940s, the curative dose has doubled five times, from 150,000 to 4.8 million units (Hubbard, 1977; Hatcher et al., 1988).

During the Vietnam war, prostitutes in Southeast Asia kept themselves looking healthy by routinely taking low doses of penicillin. This practice helped create penicillin-resistant strains of gonorrhea that were brought back to the United States by American servicemen. These strains have continued to multiply. Between 1984 and 1987 alone the incidence of penicillin-resistant gonorrhea increased fourfold in the United States (*Morbidity and Mortality Weekly Report*, Centers for Disease Control, March 6, 1987). Today, penicillin remains the cheapest and most effective treatment for most cases of gonorrhea, but other antibiotics are also being used. Unfortunately, recent reports from around the world indicate that some gonorrhea strains are now also resistant to two backup drugs, tetracycline and spectinomycin. Gonorrhea can still be cured; however, the cure may be more expensive and take longer than it used to.

Crime and punishment
Before the discovery of effective treatments for diseases like gonorrhea and syphilis, the military relied heavily on scare tactics and threats. But messages such as the one on this pre-World War I poster probably discouraged people from seeking treatment and thus increased the spread of disease. Negative attitudes about sex still interfere with the eradication of sexually transmitted diseases.

Which Side Will You Choose?

THE NATION'S WARD

THE GOVERNMENT provides for men disabled by disease or injury when contracted in line of duty.

THE NATION'S OUTCAST

VENEREAL DISEASES do not originate in line of duty. When a sailor contracts venereal disease his pay is stopped and he is not allowed liberty.

After treatment, a person should return for a test to make sure the disease is really gone. To ensure recovery, the patient should wait for an "all clear" report before engaging in sexual activity. Gonorrhea does not give any immunity: you can get it again as soon as you are cured. Researchers have been trying for several years to develop a vaccine against gonorrhea, but so far they have not succeeded.

Chlamydia

Chlamydia (kluh-MID-ee-uh) is the most common of all STDs. An estimated four million new cases were expected to occur in the U.S. in 1990 (Centers for Disease Control, personal communication). The disease takes its name from the tiny and elusive bacterium that causes it, *Chlamydia trachomatis.* Chlamydia has probably always been with us, but it could not be isolated and studied in the laboratory until 1965, and it wasn't until 1984 that an easy, accurate diagnostic test became available. The transmission of chlamydia is similar to that of gonorrhea, and the symptoms are also quite similar. The two infections often coexist; probably 25 percent of men and 40 percent of women with gonorrhea also have chlamydia (Hatcher et al., 1988). In addition, probably half of men with a condition known as **nongonococcal** or **nonspecific urethritis (NGU or NSU)** are infected with chlamydia. (When male urethritis is not caused by either gonorrhea or chlamydia it is most often due to a microorganism called *Ureaplasma urealyticum.*) The labels NGU and NSU reflect past diagnostic procedures. When a man's symptoms looked like gonorrhea but the tests for gonorrhea turned up negative, he was diagnosed as having NGU or NSU.

If untreated, chlamydia, like gonorrhea, can spread and cause epididymitis, PID, sterility, and tubal pregnancy. Between 1970 and 1985 the rate of tubal pregnancies quadrupled, and chlamydia is thought to be the major culprit (Chow et al., 1990). Chlamydia is also associated with cystitis.

Besides being sexually transmitted, chlamydia can be transmitted to a baby during birth. The baby may develop a serious eye infection or pneumonia. Chlamydial infections in pregnant women are linked to an increased risk for spontaneous abortions, stillbirths, and premature delivery.

SYMPTOMS   About 70 percent of women and 10 percent of men with chlamydial infections have no symptoms and may not know they are infected. In women, the signs (when present) include a slight vaginal discharge, painful urination and a frequent need to urinate (indications of cystitis), and pelvic pain (an indication of PID). Men usually have a watery or milky discharge from the urethra and a painful, burning sensation when urinating. Symptoms appear from one to three weeks after exposure; thus chlamydia usually has a longer incubation period (time between transmission and the first symptoms) than does gonorrhea.

DIAGNOSIS   Until recently, chlamydia was diagnosed in men simply by ruling out gonorrhea. In women, who are usually asymptomatic, it typically

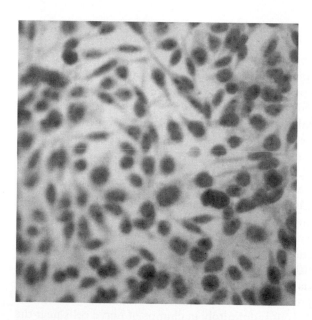

Chlamydia trachomatis
This tiny bacterium causes chlamydia, the most common of all sexually transmitted diseases. It enters the body through the vagina, urethra, rectum, or mouth.

went undiagnosed and untreated. Now, however, there are laboratory tests that can diagnose chlamydia in both men and women from samples of genital secretions (Hammerschlag, 1989). These tests are not always done routinely, so a sexually active person may need to request them.

TREATMENT One major difficulty in treating chlamydia is that, like gonorrhea, it is so often "silent," or asymptomatic. A second stumbling block is that even though chlamydia looks like gonorrhea, penicillin treatments are completely ineffective for chlamydia. The recommended drugs for chlamydia are tetracycline, doxycyline, or erythromycin. Because chlamydia so often coexists with gonorrhea, it is currently recommended that people being treated for one disease should routinely be treated for the other at the same time. The person must take the full dose of all prescribed medications to be completely cured and to prevent the development of more persistent strains of the bacteria. Until completely cured, a person should not engage in sexual activity. Erythromycin treatment for a pregnant woman with chlamydia not only cures her but significantly reduces the chance of her baby being born infected.

VIRAL INFECTIONS

Viruses are submicroscopic infectious agents that replicate themselves inside living cells. They do not respond to antibiotics so they are often difficult or impossible to eliminate. Several different viruses are sexually transmitted, including those causing herpes, genital warts, hepatitis B, AIDS and cytomegalovirus.

Genital Herpes

The word *herpes* comes from a Greek word that means "creeping." Varying forms of the herpes virus are responsible for chickenpox, mononucleosis, shingles, "cold sores," and genital herpes. The latter, technically known as **herpes genitalis,** is caused by two clinically indistinguishable types of the *herpes simplex virus (HSV)*. Type 1 used to appear primarily on the mouth (oral herpes) and Type 2 on the genitals, but this distinction is no longer clear-cut: both types are now found in both locations, perhaps because of the prevalence of oral-genital sex. It is estimated that 200,000–500,000 new cases of genital herpes occur annually in the United States and between 10 and 25 million Americans are estimated to be infected (Centers for Disease Control, personal communication; Johnson et al., 1989). Efforts to develop a herpes vaccine are underway (Hatcher et al., 1988).

At the point where the HSV enters the body, an infection, in the form of one or more small sores, appears. Then, after a time, the infection disappears. The virus is still present, however. It travels into the body along sensory nerve fibers and hides out indefinitely in clumps of nerve cells near the

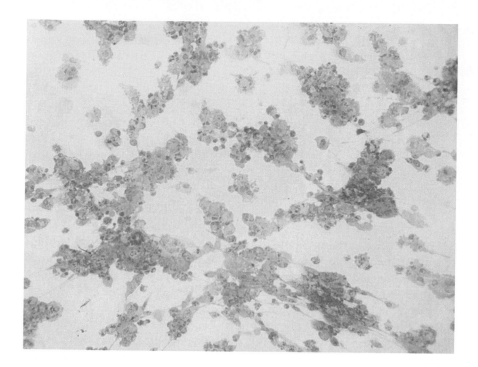

Herpes simplex virus (HSV) *These organisms belong to a large family of viruses that cause a variety of diseases. Direct contact with herpes simplex viruses can lead to a genital or oral herpes infection.*

brain (in oral herpes) or in the lower spinal cord (in genital herpes). In most people the virus will occasionally travel back down the nerve and cause recurrent infections.

Herpes is spread by direct contact with HSV. If enough active viruses come in contact with an area where the skin is thin (the genitals, around the mouth, or the eyes) or where skin is broken, the virus enters to begin a new infection. Almost everyone has been exposed to HSV (typically by contact with cold sores), but individuals seem to differ in their resistance to it. Modes of sexual transmission include genital, anal, and oral sex. In the case of oral herpes, the virus can also be spread by kissing. Because the virus can live for several hours in tap and distilled water and on plastic and other surfaces, it is possible to contract herpes nonsexually (for example, by sharing a drinking glass). Finally, the disease can be contracted by touching a sore and then immediately touching a susceptible location. Herpes is self-inoculating; that is, a person can start a new infection on his or her own body by touching a susceptible body part with a hand on which there are viruses.

Women with genital herpes have an increased risk of cancer of the cervix and are advised to have regular Pap tests (see Chapter 18). Pregnant women who contract herpes run a higher than average risk of miscarriage. A baby whose mother has an active herpes outbreak at the time of birth runs a risk of catching the disease during a vaginal delivery. Herpes in a newborn can cause blindness, brain damage, and even death. To protect the baby, a Caesarean section should be performed.

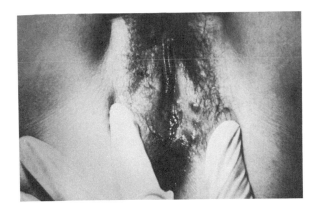 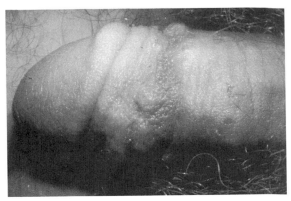

Genital herpes blisters

Small, fluid-filled blisters on or near the genitals are the primary symptom of active genital herpes. The blisters are typically itchy and painful. Eventually they rupture and form a crust before healing.

SYMPTOMS   At the point of contact, one or more small, fluid-filled blisters occur. During the first episode, the sores usually appear within 2 to 20 days after contact. The first episode lasts an average of two to three weeks; recurrent episodes average five to ten days. Shortly before the sores appear, there may be a tingling or itching sensation in the area. Once formed, the sores can be very painful. They rupture, "weep," develop scabs, heal, and finally disappear. (Sores on the cervix often do not hurt and may therefore go unnoticed.) Sometimes the person also has headaches, a fever, or pelvic pain. Active viruses can be present on the skin from the first tingling until the sores are completely gone; the individual is likely to be highly contagious for this entire period.

Until recently, it was thought that herpes could not be transmitted when a person with the virus was asymptomatic. Recent evidence, however, indicates that this is not so (Mertz et al., 1988). Often a person who is unaware of any symptoms actually does have sores. And in women, at least, viruses may occasionally be "shed" even when there are no sores (Brock et al., 1990). What is not clear, however, is the risk of transmission when there are no sores present. Currently many experts estimate the risk to be quite low, but others disagree. Further research is needed on this question.

No one knows why, but different people have different recurrence patterns. Some people have frequent attacks (once a month or so), others (probably most) have only occasional ones, and some lucky souls (about 25 percent) have only one attack and then never have another one. Flareups appear to be triggered by stress, injury, illness, fever, surgery, sun exposure, menstruation, some foods and medications, and depression.

DIAGNOSIS AND TREATMENT   Trained medical persons can usually diagnose genital herpes by looking at the blisters. Pap smears and culture tests will also reveal the disease. Unfortunately, as of this writing there is no cure for herpes. The antiviral drug *acyclovir* (trade name Zovirax), taken orally, is helpful in reducing the symptoms and shortening episodes. Acyclovir ointment is also available but is most useful for the initial outbreak. A person with herpes should refrain from intimate contact from the first warning symptoms until the sores completely disappear.

The popular press has featured sensationalistic accounts of herpes that seem to imply that a person with herpes cannot lead a normal sex life. For most people, this is untrue. During latent periods a person probably is not highly contagious. Precautions against intimate contact during an active outbreak and the use of condoms at other times can prevent transmission. Certainly, herpes is nothing to take lightly. The discomfort associated with herpes is not only physical but emotional because the victim never knows when the virus will reactivate. Some people have frequent, bothersome episodes. Herpes can be dangerous if it gets in a person's eyes or infects a newborn. But for most people, most of the time, herpes is just an unfortunate nuisance.

Genital Warts

Genital warts, or *Condylomata acuminata*, are epidemic in the United States: there are now an estimated 500,000 to 1 million new cases a year. The disease is caused by a small, slow-growing virus called *human papillomavirus (HPV)*. Genital warts have been associated with early sexual activity, multiple sex partners, and irregular use of contraception (Hatcher et al., 1988). Transmission is by direct contact. HPV is thought to have an average incubation period of two to three months, but in some people the warts appear earlier and in others they may not appear until several years after exposure (Centers for Disease Control, personal communication).

Like the herpesvirus, the human papillomavirus is statistically associated with cervical cancer and precancerous conditions in the cervix. It is important for women who have been exposed to these viruses to have regular, yearly Pap tests. Genital warts are often aggravated during pregnancy, sometimes making a vaginal delivery impossible. Babies delivered vaginally to a mother with genital warts are quite susceptible to infection and are not easily cured.

Genital warts vary considerably in appearance. They may occur singly or in bunches as soft, pink cauliflower-like, or flat gray growths on and around the genitals. Sometimes they are impossible to miss, but when they are small they may go unnoticed. Conventional treatment is to burn or cut the warts off. Chemical burning, laser surgery, liquid nitrogen freezing, or electrosurgery may be used. Genital warts can be difficult to cure.

Cytomegalovirus (CMV)

The **cytomegalovirus (CMV)** is an extremely common virus that can be sexually transmitted. It is found in the saliva, cervical secretions, urine, semen, breast milk, feces, or blood of many healthy people. In adults it usually causes no specific symptoms, but it is sometimes implicated in fevers, lung infections, hepatitis, mononucleosis, or a combination of these. Diagnostic tests are complex, the infection is difficult to diagnose, and there is no specific treatment. Fortunately, any illness it causes usually clears up.

Babies, though, are not so lucky. CMV can cross the placental barrier from a pregnant woman to the fetus, resulting in severe deformities, including an abnormally small head and brain, and hearing loss. Congenital CMV is a little-appreciated but major consequence of unprotected sexual activity (Hatcher et al., 1988). Approximately 50,000 infants a year in the United States are born with congenital CMV.

Hepatitis B

Hepatitis B (also known as serum hepatitis) is a viral liver disease spread by sexual contact and by contaminated needles. It can also be transmitted by infected mothers to their infants at birth. An estimated 5 to 20 percent of the general population in the United States has at one time or another been infected. Cases of hepatitis B in the United States increased almost 70 percent between 1978 and 1984; an estimated 300,000 new cases are now diagnosed each year (Kane et al., 1989). Although gay men are at especially high risk for hepatitis B, reported cases among gay men have decreased, probably because of behavioral changes in response to the AIDS crisis (for example, increased use of condoms). Hepatitis B is transmitted by the exchange of bodily fluids during sex and the sharing of contaminated needles. It is often associated with anal sex practices.

In some cases, the disease goes unrecognized. However, it may produce fever, fatigue, diarrhea, depression, loss of appetite, and sometimes severe abdominal pain. The urine may darken, and jaundice (yellowing of the skin and eyes) may develop. No treatment exists for hepatitis B. Usually victims recover after a period of weeks or months. On rare occasions, however, they die from resulting cirrhosis of the liver or liver cancer.

In 1981 the FDA approved a vaccine that protects against hepatitis B. Immunization is urged for members of high-risk groups, such as health-care workers, IV drug users, and homosexual men. Research to perfect a second vaccine is underway.

AIDS and ARC

When this book was first published, hardly anyone in the United States had seen or heard of the disease we know as **acquired immune deficiency syndrome** or **AIDS.** Now, only a few years later, we are threatened with a worldwide AIDS epidemic.

AIDS first came to the attention of the medical community in the United States in 1981, when the Centers for Disease Control reported five cases of *Pneumocystis pneumonia*, a rare pneumonia, in young, previously healthy homosexual men. Less than a month later, reports appeared of a rare

Tribute *The AIDS Memorial Quilt, a project of the privately-funded Names Project, consists of thousands of handmade 3-by-6-foot panels, each one honoring an individual who died from the effects of AIDS. Sections of the quilt have been displayed around the world.*

skin cancer, *Kaposi's sarcoma*, again in young gay men. Previously this disease had occurred almost exclusively in elderly men of Southern or Eastern European descent. Within a year, researchers had identified the source of both diseases, a new illness initially called GRID (for Gay-Related Immune Deficiency) but renamed Acquired Immune Deficiency Syndrome. The disorder impaired the immune system to such an extent that the body could not ward off diseases that would ordinarily be no threat. At that time, in 1982, there were 413 documented cases.

In April 1984, American and French researchers independently announced the discovery of the AIDS virus. The number of cases in the United States had grown to 4,087.

Within a year, the federal government licensed a test which identified antibodies to the AIDS virus in blood. Once this antibody test became available, in March 1985, blood banks immediately began using it to test blood products. By then, the total number of AIDS cases had climbed to 8,797.

In October 1986, the U.S. Surgeon General, Dr. C. Everett Koop, and the National Academy of Sciences, began a major public education campaign about AIDS. For their protection, said Dr. Koop, children should begin learning about AIDS as early as the third grade. By then there were 26,875 cases.

Less than four years later, in 1990, over 136,000 cases of AIDS had been reported in the United States and 83,000 people had died of the disease. World-wide, an estimated 700,000 people had AIDS, and the number was expected to increase ten-fold in the next decade if no cure was found.

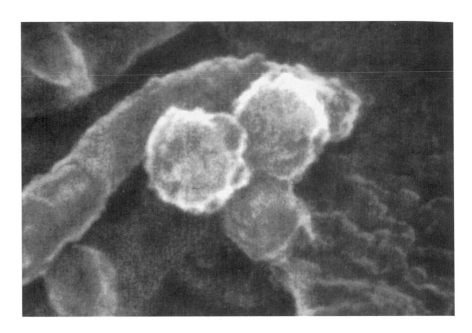

Human immunodeficiency viruses (HIV)   *This photo shows a cluster of the viruses that cause AIDS, magnified 200,000 times. The bumps on the surface of each virus are critical to its ability to infect the body, because these bumps contain sites that bind to receptors on human cells. Once a virus enters a cell, it sheds its outer coat and inserts its genetic material into the cell, forcing the cell to become a virus factory.*

AIDS is caused by a virus known as **human immunodeficiency virus** or **HIV.** HIV is a *retrovirus*, an infectious agent capable of entering cells and taking over their normal genetic processes. HIV invades several types of host cells, among them a specific type of white blood cell in the immune system, the helper T-cell. At first, the immune system responds to HIV, as it does to all invading cells, by forming antibodies to fight off this foreign microorganism. In most other infections, antibodies will destroy the invading microorganisms and the person will get well. But certain unique properties of HIV effectively outwit the body's natural defense system. HIV can hide out inside a person's T-cells for many years, unrecognized by the immune system and, therefore, unchallenged. At some point, perhaps when the person's immune system is stressed by another infection, HIV explodes into activity. It preempts the genetic processes of its host cell, turning the cell into an HIV "factory" that allows HIV to reproduce thousands of times faster than any ordinary virus would. In the course of this rampant replication, HIV demolishes the host cell. Eventually, the person's T-cells are entirely destroyed and his or her immune system is permanently disabled. Without a functional immune system, a person is defenseless against ever-present microorganisms that would otherwise be harmless. These "opportunistic diseases" prove to be fatal for people who die of AIDS. HIV viruses also have the ability to invade the central nervous system, causing damage to the brain and spinal cord.

SYMPTOMS   People infected with HIV fall into three different groups:

1.   *Infected-but-healthy.* At the time of this writing, it is estimated that there are over one million infected-but-healthy people

in the United States. Sometimes, shortly after infection, people infected with HIV experience symptoms resembling those of mononucleosis (lymph node enlargement, fatigue, and a rundown feeling) and then appear to become healthy again. Although asymptomatic, HIV carriers are, nevertheless, contagious.

2. *ARC patients.* Some people infected with HIV develop **AIDS related complex (ARC).** ARC indicates that the person's immune system is becoming disabled. Some people with ARC may be only mildly ill. However, others suffer persistent fevers, rapid weight loss, swollen lymph glands, and chronic fatigue. Though many ARC victims die as the result of HIV infection, they are not officially counted in AIDS mortality figures.

3. *Full-blown AIDS.* AIDS is diagnosed when a person's immune system is disabled (as indicated by a T-cell blood count) and the person suffers from one or more characteristic diseases. These include severe *Candida* yeast infections of the mouth and throat, pneumonia caused by a protozoan called *Pneumocystis carinii*, hepatitis B, herpes infections (and infections caused by other viruses in the herpes family, such as Epstein-Barr and cytomegalovirus), various bacterial infections, including tuberculosis and *Salmonella*, and certain cancers (B-cell lymphomas and *Kaposi's sarcoma*, a skin cancer that first shows as purplish-violet skin spots and often spreads to the lymph nodes and spleen). The effects of AIDS on the brain and nervous system include encephalitis (an inflammation of brain cells), dementia (intellectual and emotional deterioration), progressive weakness, and paralysis or impairment of coordination. AIDS patients typically suffer severe symptoms from a combination of several afflictions as their immune systems gradually fail (see Box 17–1).

Over the past few years, estimates of the maximum incubation period for AIDS have continually increased. Currently we know that the time between initial infection and the onset of AIDS can be as short as a few weeks and as long as 11 or 12 years. But it is possible that some infected people can remain healthy for a much longer time before developing the disease. Because we don't know yet what the maximum incubation period is, we also do not know how many healthy people with HIV, and how many ARC patients, will eventually go on to develop full-blown AIDS.

TRANSMISSION   All current evidence indicates that HIV CANNOT be transmitted by insect bites or casual contact; you do not get it by shaking hands, hugging, living with, or working with an infected person. HIV is not

BOX 17–1

An AIDS Sufferer Speaks

At an AIDS conference, a person with AIDS spoke about their experience with the disease. Here are some excerpts:

I got AIDS in a sexually promiscuous time, in the late '70s in New York, when we didn't know what was out there. People like myself, who've grown up in a technological society, believed that there would be a pill or a drug or an antibiotic that would cure any sexually transmitted disease I had. And this worked for many years. So I caught AIDS, so to speak, out of ignorance. And I caught it at a time when no one else knew about it. It galls me when I hear one of these reporters mention that the babies who contract AIDS through their mother are the *innocent* victims of AIDS, as though the rest of us are somehow *guilty* victims. There's no such thing as an innocent or guilty victim of AIDS. Either you have AIDS or you don't have AIDS. It doesn't make any difference how it was contracted. To have it is to have a disease that will end your life.

That *anyone* has AIDS is a tragedy. But we live in a society that very much wanted to believe that this was a gay disease. And somehow if it's a gay disease, and gay people are just going to kill themselves off, it won't affect the rest of us, or what *The New York Times* would call "the general population." It hurts me very deeply to read that I'm not part of the general population. It hurts me very deeply to read that it's not important that I have AIDS because it's not affecting most people. . . .[E]very human life is of value. The statistics about AIDS are irrelevant. Whether it's 30,000 here, or 600 in England, or one in Japan, it's all irrelevant. Whether a person who has AIDS is an i.v.-drug user, or contracted it in the womb, or is a mother who contracted it from a husband, or is a gay man, doesn't matter. That we make this matter tells us something about ourselves, not about the person suffering from AIDS. And we will I hope be mindful of the kind of compassion that's needed for anyone who is suffering.

The issues are such simple issues, once you have AIDS, and once you experience blood transfusions on a regular basis, and chemotherapy, and oxygen tanks in the bedroom in case you can't breathe. Monday morning, I got up and I couldn't walk for two hours. The pain in my bones was so great that I just couldn't be on my feet.
. . .I have AIDS, and AIDS is not my problem any longer. AIDS is *your* problem, and I hope you'll do something about it.

Source: *Newsweek*, August 10, 1987, pp. 38–39.

The tragedy of AIDS
This terrible disease has killed hundreds of thousands of people worldwide, most of them in the prime of life.

passed from one person to the other through the air, in food, or in water, nor can it penetrate intact skin. If casual contact or insect bites did spread HIV, AIDS and ARC would be much more prevalent.

HIV has been isolated from the blood, semen, vaginal secretions, urine, saliva, tears, and breast milk of infected individuals. All the documented modes of transmission involve introduction of a bodily fluid containing HIV directly into a person's (or fetus's) bloodstream in one of the following ways:

1. *Sexual contact in which HIV viruses have access to the bloodstream.* Both anal intercourse and coitus have been documented as modes of transmission. During anal intercourse, the surface membranes and blood vessels of the anus and rectum are vulnerable to small tears. Such tears permit the virus carried in semen to enter the bloodstream of the receiving partner. In coitus, HIV may be transmitted through tiny, invisible lesions in the genitals. Transmission through oral-genital sex is thought to be less likely, but cannot be ruled out at this time.

2. *The sharing of contaminated hypodermic needles and syringes.* Drug users often share paraphernalia; from two to as many as fifty people may use a single needle. Contaminated blood clinging to a needle is passed from user to user. The risk is increased by addicts' practice of drawing blood back into the syringe in order to flush out any remaining drug. Intravenous drug use has contributed greatly to the spread of AIDS.

3. *Prenatal infection.* An infected mother can pass HIV to her baby during pregnancy or at delivery. At this writing, over 2,200 children in the United States have full-blown AIDS and the number is increasing steadily. Almost all were born to mothers who are IV drug users.

4. *Transfusions of contaminated blood.* Before blood screening was possible, some recipients of transfusions or blood products contracted AIDs. Now, however, blood donated in the United States is tested and any HIV-infected units are discarded. The chances of receiving HIV from a transfusion are currently remote.

In the United States, AIDS is concentrated in certain high-risk groups, primarily homosexual and bisexual men and intravenous drug users. But in some third-world countries, AIDS is primarily a heterosexual disease. The major factors in sexual transmission are probably similar: anal intercourse and multiple partners. In addition, untreated genital lesions may increase the chances of HIV getting into the bloodstream. In this country, heterosexual transmission accounts for only 4 or 5 percent of all cases, but this is up from 1 percent less than a decade ago. Infection rates are increasing especially rapidly among women, African-Americans, and Hispanics.

DIAGNOSIS Currently two tests are used to identify people infected with HIV, ELISA (for enzyme-linked immunoassay) and the Western blot, a more complicated and expensive test. Both tests, which are highly reliable (98 to 99 percent), detect the presence of specific HIV antibodies in a blood sample. Because ELISA can give "false positive" results, a positive result is followed up by a Western blot test. Negative results may or may not mean the person is uninfected. Why? There are at least two varieties of HIV; the tests are only sensitive to one specific variety and will give negative results to a carrier of any other variety. Furthermore, since the tests only reveal the presence of HIV antibodies, they are useless during the period between infection (i.e., the moment when HIV enters one's bloodstream) and the development of antibodies. The process of developing HIV antibodies, called *seroconversion,* usually takes between six weeks and six months—but, it may be a few days or many months, and some people with AIDS apparently do not ever seroconvert (Bateson & Goldsby, 1988). A second, and even third, test six months to a year after the first (during which time the person refrains from all high-risk activities) is recommended.

Medical and social realities create certain dilemmas for individuals who seek testing. Usually a medical diagnosis is the first step in curing a person's ailment. Not so with an HIV-positive test; there is currently no cure for a ravaged immune system. A positive test, however, makes it possible for a person to get appropriate counseling and begin early treatments to forestall some of the effects of the infection. As we will see, currently available treatments can prolong and increase the quality of life. A confirmed positive HIV test warns a woman that, should she become pregnant, her child will be at risk. Confirmed negative results are a relief. (Remember, however, that after confirmed negative results, a person remains vulnerable to contracting the disease through high-risk behaviors.)

Because there are few legal safeguards against losing one's job, housing, and medical insurance as a result of a positive test, many people believe that HIV testing should be entirely voluntary and anonymous.

TREATMENT   As of this writing, AIDS is an incurable and fatal disease. An anti-viral drug called AZT (zidovudine) has prolonged the lives of many AIDS sufferers, but the long-term effects and results of this powerful (and expensive) medication are currently unknown. Another drug, pentamidine, has proved to be effective against the effects of pneumocystis carinii pneumonia. Several other drugs have been approved by the U.S. Food and Drug Administration as treatments for the many opportunistic infections associated with AIDS and many more are currently being tested. However, as yet, no vaccine is available to protect against, and no treatment can prevent, HIV's destruction of the immune system.

Much remains to be discovered about the nature of HIV, its effects, its spread, and its treatment. Progress is being made, and researchers are optimistic that a vaccine will eventually be found; at least 30 possible vaccines are being tested around the world. The mysteries of AIDS will be unraveled but, unfortunately, not before many, and perhaps most, of us have lost someone we know or love to this terrible disease.

SYPHILIS

Apparent references to the symptoms of **syphilis** can be found in documents going back to the earliest stages of recorded history (see Box 17–2). In the Bible descriptions of "leprosy" often sound more like syphilis. On the wall of a brothel in the ruins of Pompeii (destroyed A.D. 79), there is the following bit of graffiti: "The most beautiful woman of that establishment had the disease capable of producing eating ulcers."

Syphilis may have evolved from an ancient bacterium that lived on human skin in tropical climates. According to one theory, around 3000 B.C. people began to migrate to cooler, drier climates and to wear more clothes, and this left fewer moist body surfaces for the bacteria to survive on. In fact, only those strains that could live in the genital and anal regions survived. At that point, syphilis became a sexually transmitted disease (Hackett, 1963). Then, in about 1494, a mutation apparently changed syphilis into a more virulent form that people wrongly assumed to be a brand new disease. The sixteenth century was an era of social turmoil—war, expulsions of entire populations, relative sexual freedom, and increased travel. Conditions were ripe for the spread of STDs and syphilis became epidemic throughout Europe.

BOX 17–2

The Many Aliases Of Syphilis

Nations have always been quick to stake out competing claims for new inventions and discoveries, but no one, understandably enough, has wanted to take credit for syphilis. Instead they have pointed the finger of blame at others and have named the disease accordingly. The Biblical Hebrews apparently called syphilis the Botch of Egypt (Stiller, 1974). The Italians, Germans, and English called it the French disease or French Pox. The French, in turn, called it the Neapolitan or Italian disease. The Flemish and Dutch called it the Spanish disease; the Portuguese called it the Castilian disease; the East Indians and Japanese called it the Portuguese disease; the Persians called it the Turkish disease; the Polish called it the German disease; and the Russians called it the Polish disease. A contemporary French soldier, however, rose above such chauvinism when he described syphilis as "the disease of him who has it."

Syphilis was also called the great pox, which distinguished it from smallpox, a completely unrelated disease that we now know is caused by a virus. In his poem *Don Juan* (1818), Byron was referring to syphilis when he wrote: ". . .the small pox has gone out of late;/Perhaps it may be follow'd by the great." An eighteenth-century physician gave the disease a more obscure, Latin name, *lues veneris* (*lues* means disease or sickness), and doctors today still sometimes call syphilis *lues*.

The name *syphilis* originated in 1530, when the Italian poet-physician Girolamo Fracastoro—who was probably the first person to describe the process of infection—published a long poem entitled *Syphilis sive Morbus Gallicus* (Syphilis or the French Disease). In the poem, Syphilus, a shepherd in Hispaniola, the West Indies island that is now divided between Haiti and the Dominican Republic, is disrespectful to the sun god. As punishment, the god strikes Syphilus down with a new and horrible disease that is henceforth to bear his name, though with slightly altered spelling. However, Fracastoro did not live to see syphilis become a household word. In fact, the name did not really catch on until the middle of the nineteenth century. Unfortunately, the disease got along fine without it.

During the eighteenth century, people thought that gonorrhea and syphilis were different manifestations of the same disease. John Hunter, a brilliant English physician, made himself into a human guinea pig to prove it. Hunter inoculated his own penis with pus from another man's gonorrheal discharge and waited to see what would happen. A short time later he developed the symptoms of both gonorrhea and syphilis. Unlike most STD sufferers, Hunter was delighted with his symptoms, because he thought he had

Syphilis?   *The sores on this pre-Columbian clay figure suggest that syphilis may have been present in the New World before Christopher Columbus arrived. Tradition has it that Columbus's sailors contracted the disease in America and brought it back to Europe with them. But many historians believe that syphilis was already present in the Old World, as well as the new, by the time Columbus set sail.*

proved his hypothesis. But an experiment is only as good as the control the experimenter has over the situation and the subjects. What Hunter did not know was that his donor happened to have both gonorrhea and a latent case of syphilis. Hunter had given himself both diseases at once! His syphilis may have contributed to the heart disease that killed him years later, making him a martyr in the cause of science. A few decades after his death, other scientists demonstrated that gonorrhea and syphilis are alike only in their association with sexual activity.

Syphilis is caused by a bacterium called *Treponema pallidum*. It is nearly always spread through sexual contact, including penile-vaginal, penile-anal, oral-genital, and mouth-mouth. However, the syphilis bug can also pass directly through broken skin. Doctors and dentists have been known to get syphilis on a fingertip after touching a patient's sore with an ungloved hand.

In 1989, about 111,000 new cases of syphilis were reported in the United States (Centers for Disease Control, personal communication). The incidence of syphilis rose dramatically in the late 1980s, reversing an earlier trend of decreasing incidence. Between 1987 and 1989, the number of reported cases tripled. For every reported case there are no doubt many unreported ones.

SYMPTOMS   Syphilis develops relatively slowly. The average incubation period is about three weeks, but the time varies from ten to ninety days, depending on how many bugs are present during transmission. The bacteria make straight for the person's blood stream, and by the time the case is full-blown, billions may be in circulation.

Treponema pallidum *This corkscrew-shaped bacterium, the villain in syphilis, was discovered in 1905 by two German physicians. The first part of its name comes from the Greek words for "to turn" and "thread" and the second part from the Latin word for "pale." The microbe belongs to a family of bacteria known as spirochetes (spy-ruh-keets) and has close cousins living harmlessly in the mouth.*

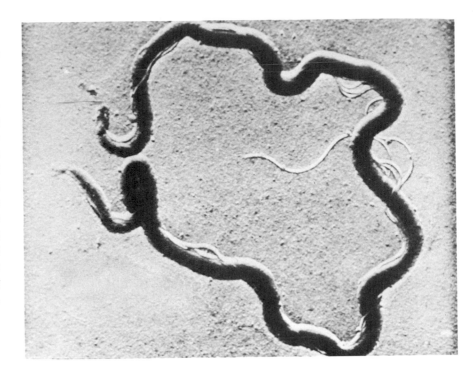

Syphilis occurs in four stages:

1. *Primary syphilis.* The main primary-stage symptom is a single, painless sore called a **chancre** (pronounced SHAN-ker), located at the place where the syphilis germs entered the body. The chancre has a ring of rubbery tissue around its base and tends to break down on top to form an open sore. The chancre teems with bacteria, making the disease extremely contagious. Bacteria also may get into the lymph nodes in the groin and make them swell. However, about 90 percent of infected women and 40 to 60 percent of infected men show no symptoms, misinterpret their symptoms, or fail to notice them. (A small chancre can be hidden by folds of skin; one on the cervix is out of view.) In any case, symptoms disappear in a few weeks even without treatment. However, the disease remains highly contagious.

2. *Secondary syphilis.* During this stage, which occurs from a week to several months later and usually lasts a few months, the disease spreads to other parts of the body. The main symptom is a rash, which may be all over the body or anywhere on it, including the palms of the hands, soles of the feet, and even inside the mouth. This rash is usually painless

and goes away without treatment. Other secondary symptoms include a sore throat, bone and joint aches, a mild fever, headache, and loss of hair. The symptoms are easily confused with those of other conditions. During this stage the infection is still highly contagious.

3. *Latency-stage syphilis*. No symptoms are apparent during this stage. The disease is "silent" and after a year or so is not contagious. Nevertheless, for five, ten or even twenty years, the bacteria may be at work attacking various organs of the person's body. Some people with syphilis—a minority—seem to recover spontaneously. Some probably die of other causes before the disease gives them any serious trouble. But others are not so lucky.

4. *Late-stage syphilis*. During this stage the harm to body organs become obvious. The most serious conditions involve damage to the heart, blood vessels, eyes (causing blindness), spinal cord, and brain (causing mental disorders). Syphilis can kill; an estimated *100 million* people have died from it, worldwide, since the turn of the century (Chiappa & Forish, 1976). However, in the U.S. late-stage syphilis is no longer common.

Unlike most bacteria, syphilis bacteria can pass through the placenta in pregnancy and infect the fetus. This can happen even after the woman is no longer infectious to others. The danger is greatest from the second trimester of pregnancy on. If the baby does not die, it is born with secondary or even late syphilis. There are several signs of the disease, including a caved-in bridge of the nose, blindness, deafness, bodily deformities, and, later, notched, peculiarly shaped teeth.

DIAGNOSIS During the primary stage, a medical practitioner may be able to diagnose syphilis by observing bacteria taken from the chancre or lymph nodes under a special microscope. Within a few weeks enough organisms are in the blood stream to make a blood test feasible. The test detects antibodies to the bacterium and can be used even during latency and late syphilis. But no test is foolproof, and the medical practitioner needs to take into account the person's symptoms and sexual history in making a diagnosis.

TREATMENT For hundreds of years, doctors searched desperately for a way to cure syphilis. They locked their patients in stuffy rooms and made them sweat. They gave them a drug made from the bark of a tree from the West Indies. They starved them, or put them on special diets. They had them inhale mercury fumes, swallow mercury, or smear their bodies with mercury ointments. Mercury treatments might actually have done something for the symptoms, but they also caused bone damage, loose teeth, and even death. The treatment, in other words, could be worse than the disease.

Harsh treatment for syphilis *A seventeenth-century French woodcut ridicules "the Spaniard afflicted with the Neapolitan disease." In those days, one supposed cure for syphilis was to isolate the hapless victims in barrels and subject them to mercury fumes. Not only was this remedy of little use, but it was dangerous and sometimes even fatal.*

L'ESPAIGNOL AFFLIGÉ DV MAL DE NAPLES.

In 1919, Dr. Paul Ehrlich discovered that an arsenic compound could clear up syphilis. But the treatment was lengthy, was not always effective, and produced side effects. Many patients decided they would rather die of their syphilis than continue the treatment (Chiappa & Forish, 1976).

That is where things stood until World War II, when penicillin proved to be a real cure-all, as far as syphilis was concerned. Today syphilis is easily treated. As a result, it is rare to see a case that has progressed beyond the secondary stage. Penicillin is usually given in one large or several smaller doses, in a slower-acting, longer-lasting form than that used for gonorrhea. (Substitutes are available for those allergic to penicillin.) The drug cures the disease at any stage, although it cannot reverse organ damage that has already occurred. The earlier the treatment, the faster the cure. However, it is proving difficult to treat some patients who have syphilis with AIDS and some doctors believe the impaired immune system of such patients allows syphilis to progress more rapidly than normal (Johns, Tierney & Felsenstein, 1987).

PARASITIC INFESTATIONS

Parasites are organisms that live in or on other organisms, returning nothing of value to their hosts. Two kinds of parasites are often (although not exclusively) transmitted by sexual contact. Each of the bugs described below can also be caught without being sexually close to a carrier.

Pubic Lice

Pubic lice (known formally as *pediculosis pubis* and informally as *crabs*) are tiny yellowish-gray animals that love genital hair but sometimes also make their home in underarm hair, eyelashes, eyebrows, and beards. They burrow into the skin to suck their host's blood, just like ticks on the family pet. The tiny organisms can also live for about twenty-four hours on surfaces other than the human body, and their eggs (nits) can survive on other surfaces for several days. Thus you *can* get them by touching the bedding, clothes, or furniture of an already-infested person.

Usually a person feels pubic lice before seeing them because lice ordinarily itch unbearably. To the naked eye they look like little dots, but under a powerful microscope they resemble crablike monsters out of a grade B movie. Soap and water can't get rid of them because they stubbornly attach themselves with their pincers to the base of the hairs. Their eggs attach to the hairs too, so new lice must be killed as they hatch. Certain medicated creams, lotions, and shampoos, some sold over the counter, will do this. (One popular product is called Kwell; it requires a prescription.) Clothing and linen should be disinfested by washing them in hot water.

Scabies

Scabies is caused by a little mite barely visible without a microscope. Female mites burrow beneath the outermost layer of the skin to lay their eggs. Scabies mites like to live in armpits, groins, penises, and buttocks, but they are not at all choosy. They are sometimes visible on fingers and wrists and have been known to attack infants on the face and feet (Hubbard, 1977). Like pubic lice, they can be transmitted by contact with bedding and other objects. Not only do they itch, but they cause blistering of the skin. Sometimes men who have scabies think they have syphilis. Kwell is a good treatment for scabies.

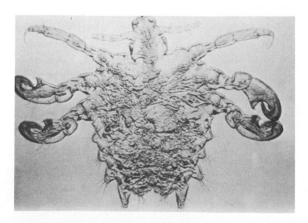

A pubic louse   *Aptly nicknamed the crab louse, this little monster, much magnified in this photograph, usually causes extreme itching. It is related to lice that live on the head and body. Fortunately, several products will kill pubic lice.*

VAGINITIS

Vaginitis is a general term for an inflammation of the vagina. Nearly all women experience some form of vaginitis during their lifetime. There are three main types of vaginitis.

Trichomoniasis, called "trich" for short, is an infection caused by *trichomonas vaginalis*, a one-celled protozoan that lives in the genital and urinary tracts of men and women. Trichomoniasis is often transmitted sexually, but it can also be picked up by contact with moist objects like towels and toilet seats. In women, it usually causes a thin, frothy, bad-smelling white or yellowish vaginal discharge. There is often pain and itching of the vulva. In men, it occasionally causes nongonoccocal urethritis (Hubbard, 1977). Men with trich may experience a feeling of irritation deep in the urethra, especially during urination or ejaculation, but usually they have no symptoms. Trich is treated with an oral medication called Flagyl. When taking Flagyl, a patient must abstain from all alcoholic beverages. Pregnant women should never take this drug.

Monilia (or **candidiasis**) occurs in women when *candida albicans*, a yeastlike fungus normally found in the vagina, overmultiplies. In women, monilia causes itching, burning, and a thick, white discharge that may smell yeasty and resembles cottage cheese. Some women seem especially susceptible to monilia. Also, diabetes, pregnancy, treatment with certain antibiotics, and oral contraceptives all seem to produce favorable conditions for this fungus. The majority of monilia cases in females do not involve sexual transmission (Hatcher et al., 1988). But men can get monilia from their female partners, and may experience such symptoms as irritation of the glans and foreskin of the penis, irritation of the urethra, and a urethral discharge. Prescription suppositories can clear up women's monilia; ointments work for both sexes.

Bacterial vaginosis is commonly caused by the overgrowth of a bacterium called *gardnerella vaginalis*, although other organisms can also be involved. It is characterized by a vaginal discharge that smells like ammonia or has a "fishy" odor. Occasionally there is a burning sensation during urination. Men can also harbor gardnerella vaginalis, but they usually have no symptoms. The primary mode of transmission for both sexes is heterosexual intercourse. To avoid passing the infection back and forth, a woman's partner or partners should be treated when she is; the treatment is Flagyl or ampicillin.

Women who get vaginitis frequently should try to keep the vulva dry. In persistent cases, some doctors may recommend special douches to maintain the proper balance of acidity and alkalinity in the vagina. Feminine hygiene sprays may increase the chances of getting vaginitis by irritating the skin of the vulva. A reliable source for additional information on vaginitis is *Our Bodies, Ourselves* (1984) by the Boston Women's Health Book Collective.

OTHER STDS

We conclude our directory of STDs with brief descriptions of some of the less common ones.

Enteric infections are most often seen in homosexual males. They are caused by a variety of sexually transmissible bacteria, viruses, protozoa, and other organisms commonly carried in the gastrointestinal tract, and they are spread primarily by oral-anal contact. Symptoms include mild to severe abdominal pain and cramping, diarrhea, nausea, and vomiting. Treatment is based on the particular organism causing the trouble.

Several sexually transmitted diseases are relative strangers in the United States.

1. *Chancroid* is caused by a bacillus called *Hemophilis ducreyi*. Women with chancroid usually do not have any symptoms. Men usually develop a painful ulcer on the penis often accompanied by a *bubo* (a swollen, inflamed lymph gland in the groin). Chancroid is treated with erythromycin.

2. *Lymphogranuloma venereum* is caused by a variety of chlamydia trachomatis. Common in Asia and Africa, this disease is becoming more prevalent in some areas of the southern United States. The primary symptom is a painless ulcer that often goes unnoticed. Stiffness, aching and swelling in the groin follow. This disease is treated with tetracycline and other antibiotics.

3. *Granuloma inguinale* is very rare in the United States. It causes painless but destructive ulcers on the genitals and is treated with tetracycline or other antibiotics.

WHY WE AREN'T RID OF STDS

If you ask people why they think STDs are so common, many will give a one-word answer: promiscuity. Books aimed at teenagers often suggest that there is no way to lick STDs except for everyone to swear off sex before marriage and to stick to one partner afterward.

It is certainly true that since most transmission occurs during sexual activity, the more activity, the less likely that STD bugs will suffer from a housing shortage. It is also true that people with STDs who have many partners do more than their share to spread STDs to others. That is why prostitution and "cruising"—casual sex with strangers—has traditionally been associated with sexually transmitted disease. Increased sexual activity, however, does not entirely explain the problem. As we have seen, most STDs are easily cured diseases. If smallpox can be treated almost out of existence, why can't most STDs be brought under control? The reasons are partly medical, partly psychological, and partly societal.

Medical Obstacles

Most sexually transmitted diseases have inherent characteristics that make them difficult to eradicate. For example, STDs provide little or no natural immunity. You can get chicken pox or the German measles only once, but you can get gonorrhea, syphilis, and chlamydia again and again. If Chris gets treatment for an STD but Chris's partner, Pat, does not, Chris may get a new case from Pat soon after treatment. By the time Pat does go in for treatment, Chris may already have a new case and be ready to reinfect Pat—and you have what STD specialists call the "ping-pong effect."

Because people with STDs often have no obvious symptoms, they can infect others without knowing it. As we have seen, HIV infection can be "silent" for years, and many people with gonorrhea and chlamydia *never* have symptoms. Syphilis symptoms disappear, but the person remains highly contagious for about a year. Herpes viruses can "shed" when there are no obvious symptoms. Moreover, carriers of one disease are often carriers of others (a discovery unwittingly made long ago, you will recall, by John Hunter). Treatment may be difficult when a person has more than one infection. And the more prominent infection may mask the less obvious one so that necessary treatment may be overlooked.

Laboratory researchers face many technical obstacles in their fight against STDs. An AIDS vaccine, for example, has been difficult to develop. Vaccines operate by stimulating the production of antibodies, the immune system "soldiers"; but HIV is able to elude antibodies because it can change the structure of its surface antigens. Antigens stimulate the production of antibodies that are tailor-made to find and fight off the invading virus. But by the time the immune system has produced an antibody that recognizes a particular HIV antigen, the antigen may have changed beyond recognition. Cures for STDs have also proven to be elusive, and as we have seen, even when there is a cure, the microbes may become "resistant."

Psychological Obstacles

Despite the medical obstacles, treatment is available for almost every STD. Yet people do not always seek this treatment when they need it. Admitting sexual activity to others, especially strangers, can be embarrassing for young, single people, especially if they feel guilty about their sexual activity. People of all ages may deny having STDs because they believe, falsely, that only "promiscuous" people can get them, and the label STD does not fit their self-image. Many of us harbor an irrational belief that people with STDs are dirty, that normal, decent people don't get these diseases. It can be psychologically more comfortable to deny an STD than to seek help. Sometimes treatment is delayed, too, out of fear of pain, or anger at the inconvenience. Most STD clinics are very good, but they are public places and people don't always feel comfortable going to them. Private physicians

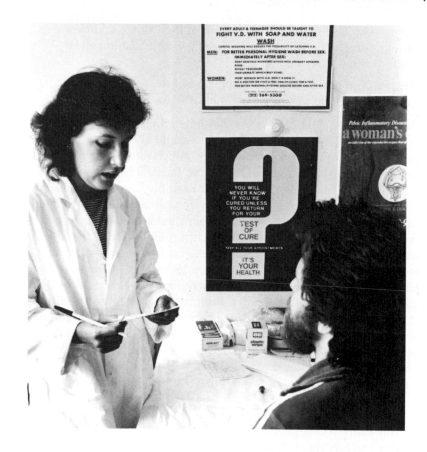

Getting treated for an STD *At this clinic run by the New York City Department of Health, doctors and technicians are helpful and nonjudgmental. When people avoid getting treatment for an STD, they endanger their own health and that of their partners.*

are expensive, they tend to be less experienced than clinic doctors in dealing with STDs, and some may have negative feelings of their own about STDs.

Psychological obstacles also contribute to difficulties in communicating with partners about STDs. Many people are afraid of offending a potential sex partner by bringing up the topic. It is easier to assume a sex partner to be disease-free than to ask. And asking does not guarantee an honest answer; given an opportunity for sex, some people will lie. In a recent study, over 400 sexually experienced college students were asked how honest they would be in a variety of situations, if honesty threatened their chances of having sex or dating the other person (Cochran, 1988; Cochran & Mays, 1990). The results:

- 20 percent of the men and 4 percent of the women said they would claim to have tested negative on the AIDS test when they hadn't actually taken the test.

- 47 percent of the men and 42 percent of the women said they would report fewer previous sexual partners than they really had had.

- 23 percent of the men and 10 percent of the women said they would never tell a new partner that they were also involved with someone else.

- Over a third of the men and 10 percent of the women admitted to having told a lie in order to have sex with someone.

Before herpes and AIDS became widespread, there was a tendency to think that STDs were not so bad; after all, they could always be cured. We are now much more aware of the devastating effects of certain STDs on future fertility and, in the case of AIDS, on life itself. This awareness has produced some modifications in behavior. For example, a review of studies on high-risk behavior among white, urban gay and bisexual men concluded that "dramatic changes have occurred, the amount and kinds of which probably exceed anything documented to date in the public health literature" (Stall, Coates, and Hoff, 1988). As a result, the overall rate of new HIV infections among this population declined in the late 1980s. But the same review also found that in certain cities the level of risk for HIV infection remains high, because many gay men still practice unprotected anal sex with multiple partners. Experts are concerned that certain specific high-risk groups, including intravenous drug users and minority gay and bisexual men, are not being reached by public education campaigns and have not made significant changes in behavior (Peterson & Marín, 1988). Experts also believe that some gay and bisexual men who previously practiced "safe sex" are no longer doing so.

In Chapter 13, we saw that the use of condoms has increased among teenagers. But many young people still do not use condoms, because they are embarrassed to buy them, find it hard to discuss them, or believe they interfere with sexual pleasure, and so their risk of STD infection remains high. In a recent study of 5,500 Canadian college students, many reported having multiple sexual partners and participating in anal intercourse, yet only a quarter of the men and about a sixth of the women said they always used condoms—and the more partners the students reported, the *less* likely they were to use condoms. As the researchers noted, "While the majority of these students know which sexual activities increase the risk of HIV transmission and also know about safe sexual practices, many still engage in risky behavior. . . . Knowledge per se was not typically translated into safer behavior" (MacDonald et al., 1990).

Societal Obstacles

Still other barriers on the road to solving the STD problem are societal ones. As a society, we never have been completely committed to eliminating STDs. In the 1960s more money was apparently spent on eliminating athlete's foot than syphilis (Rosebury, 1971). In the mid-1970s, when *each* B-1 bomber cost $84 million, we spent only about $52 million a year on STD control (Boston Women's Health Book Collective, 1976). In 1980, for every $3,500 spent by the National Institutes of Health, only $7.50 was devoted to research on all STDs combined (versus $250 for diabetes research) (Johnston, 1980).

Lack of commitment to fight STDs is due, in part, to a belief that STDs are a just punishment for sin: as ye sow, so shall ye reap. Until World War II, the United States Army considered venereal disease a crime. Soldiers with syphilis or gonorrhea got no pay and sometimes were sent to jail. An officer with an STD could lose his commission (Stiller, 1974). Although the army no longer punishes STD victims, some people still seem to think that an STD itself is some sort of divine punishment instead of a human disease. Negative attitudes not only about STDs but also about homosexuals, drug addicts, and racial minorities have caused some people to be insensitive to the suffering of AIDS victims.

Fear and misunderstanding of AIDS have prompted calls for mandatory testing and quarantine (social exile) of entire groups of people. Opponents have questioned the cost and effectiveness of such measures, as well as the invasion of privacy they would require. Mandatory premarital testing for syphilis has been successful in curbing that disease because the test is inexpensive and because there is a cure. People who test positive are not denied insurance or fired from their jobs. None of this holds true for currently available HIV antibody testing.

WHAT YOU CAN DO

As tenacious as sexually transmitted diseases are, they are also preventable. But, prevention is not as simple as keeping our fingers crossed or as easy as getting a shot. Prevention begins with an informed knowledge of STDs. Knowledge enables us to be rational when fear leads us toward apathy, at one extreme, or terror at the other. Prevention also requires an understanding that, although sex is a powerful urge, it is under our control. We *can* refrain from infection-spreading activities when we are infectious. We can adopt a careful sexual life style—literally, one full of care for our partners and for ourselves.

Safe sexual behavior is the key to protecting yourself and to eradicating STDs. The microbes responsible for sexually transmitted diseases can't get around without our help. They are not at all picky about whom they live with—to a microbe, people who are rich, poor, atheistic, religiously devout, homosexual, heterosexual, moral, immoral, beautiful, plain, and ugly are all the same. Here are some important behavioral guidelines.

1. The safest behavior is, of course, *sexual abstinence*. (Remember, however, that a few STDs can be acquired in nonsexual ways.) For most people, though, abstinence is not a practical long-term solution.

Be prepared *The condom has made a definite comeback in the United States. Before the 1980s, condoms were often hidden behind the cash register, and were rarely advertised. But all that has changed. Today, public health agencies, manufacturers, and public interest groups promote condom use with attention-getting slogans, such as "Don't go out without your rubbers" and "What can we get from using a condom?" Nothing . . . but pleasure and protection."*

© *PPSI PO Box 1336, Sausalito, CA 94966*

2. *A long-term monogamous relationship* is another alternative. Monogamy has taken on a renewed appeal for many people, with the spread of herpes and AIDS. Monogamous sex is safe sex, provided both partners are unaffected to begin with.

3. *Use a latex condom* for penile sexual contact with anyone other than a long-term, exclusive partner. As we noted in Chapter 7, latex condoms provide significant protection against penile transmission of all STDs, including HIV and genital herpes. The use of condoms is as important for women as for men because STDs threaten not only a woman's health and future fertility but also, if she is pregnant, her fetus. Refer back to pages 237–38 for instructions on the proper use of a condom.

4. Along with condoms, the *use of spermicides* containing nonoxynol-9 is also recommended. Nonoxynol-9 kills many sexually transmitted organisms.

5. Syphilis and herpes can be spread by touching the sores. If you are around someone with any type of active herpes, *take extra care with hygiene;* for example, wash your hands frequently. If you have herpes or feel an episode coming on, avoid touching the area.

6. *Do not engage in penile-anal contact except with an uninfected, long-term monogamous partner.* During sex play, if a finger or an object is inserted into the anus, the finger or object should be washed with soap and water before there is any further oral or genital contact with it. Oral-anal contact is only a "safe sex practice" with an uninfected, long-term monogamous partner, and even then it can result in enteric infections.

7. Keep in mind that the more people you have sex with, the greater your risk of getting an STD. It is also extremely risky to have sex with a stranger, with a person who has had numerous partners, with a person who is an intravenous drug user, or with a person who has had sex with an intravenous drug user.

8. If you have reason to think you might have an STD (because you have been exposed or because you have some symptoms), *seek diagnosis and treatment* right away. Do not wait in hopes that the problem will go away by itself. If you have contracted a disease, follow the recommended treatment procedures exactly. Do not resume sexual activity until you are cured.

9. *Periodic health examinations* and lab tests will uncover asymptomatic STDs. They are recommended for everyone who is sexually active and is not in a long-term monogamous relationship.

Finally, you can protect yourself and your sexual friends by taking care of yourself and your sexuality. The better your general health and fitness, the less risk you run of catching many of the common STDs. Taking care of yourself involves more than getting good nutrition, plenty of sleep, and exercise. It also involves caring enough for yourself to set limits so that you do not get pressured into having sex against your better judgment. It means saying no to an opportunity for unprotected sex—even when sex appears to be what you want most in all the world. It means overcoming feelings of fear, shame, guilt, and embarrassment enough so that you can talk about sexual health with every one of your sex partners. You cannot count on anyone else taking care of you when it comes to your sexual health. You cannot assume, no matter how bright, honest, beautiful, or charming a new partner is, that he or she will necessarily act in your best interests when it comes to sex.

In order to stop the spread of STDs, we must be considerate of our sexual partners, too. This means never deceiving a prospective partner if you have a disease or suspect you could be infected. Being honest may mean setting aside pride, shame, and sexual desire. Treating other people as we would like to be treated ourselves results in loving and responsible sex. Even if STDs were miraculously eliminated tomorrow, this would still be an excellent guideline for good sexual relationships.

**PERSONAL
PERSPECTIVE**

. . . .

"WHO, ME?": YOUR REACTIONS TO STDS

This exercise presents you with several different situations and asks you to imagine what you would say, do, and feel in each. Its purpose is to help you clarify your attitudes about sexually transmitted diseases. We hope that in the process, you will recognize not only the difficulty but also the importance of communicating honestly about STDs.

Situation 1: You are single and have been dating several people for the past few months. During this time you have had sex with two of them. Last week you noticed an unusual discharge and went to the Health Service for a checkup. Today you learned that you tested positive for gonorrhea. The Health Service has told you that your sexual contacts must be informed. You can let the Health Service handle this, or you can do it yourself. You decide that you want to tell both people yourself. You know that one of your partners passed the disease to you, but you don't know which. You also know that you may have passed it on to the other partner. How do you think you would feel in this situation? What conflicts or fears might it arouse? What, exactly, would you say to each person? What would you want your partners to know, and what might you suggest they do?

Situation 2: You are not sexually involved right now and haven't been for almost a year. While reading this chapter you noticed increased itching in your genital area. At first you assumed that this was simply the result of the power of suggestion and reading about itchy diseases. But now, taking a good look, you notice some tiny grayish specks at the base of your pubic hairs. What has happened and what should you do? How do you feel?

Situation 3: You have genital herpes and experience an outbreak two or three times a year. About two months ago you met a warm, intelligent, sexually attractive person. The two of you hit it off and are spending more and more time together. It has come to the point of sexual intimacy but—there is no doubt about it—you feel an outbreak of herpes coming on. You know you may be contagious, but at the same time you strongly want to share a sexual experience with your desirable new friend. What are your options? What are your worries or fears? What, precisely, will you say to this person? Is there a chance that you would not say anything?

Situation 4: You have finally decided to marry the person of your dreams. The two of you have known each other for over a year and have been sexually intimate for a couple of months. The wedding is approaching and, as part of getting a marriage license, you both are required to have a blood test for syphilis. Your test is negative, but the test for your spouse-to-be is positive. How do you feel? What questions go through your mind? What do you think you might say or do?

Situation 5: You are in your mid-thirties. You have decided that now is the perfect time for you to become a parent. However you have just been told that a previous STD, which went undetected and untreated, has damaged your reproductive system. Therefore, the likelihood of your having biological offspring is less than 2 percent. How do you feel? Suppose you could have anticipated this problem earlier, when you were in your twenties? How might that knowledge have affected your sexual behavior then?

IN BRIEF

1. A number of bacteria, viruses, parasites, and other microorganisms are transmitted exclusively or primarily during sexual activity. Formerly called *venereal diseases (VD)*, these infections and infestations are now known as *sexually transmitted diseases*.

2. Two bacterial diseases, *gonorrhea* and *chlamydia*, are common causes of *cervicitis* in women and *urethritis* in men. If not treated, these diseases can lead to serious infections of the internal reproductive organs (*pelvic inflammatory disease* and *epididymitis*). These infections may threaten fertility in both sexes and result in tubal pregnancies; they also threaten the health of newborns if transmitted during delivery.

3. In men, the main symptoms of gonorrhea are a penile discharge and painful urination. Women sometimes have a vaginal discharge. But most women and many men show no initial symptoms. The standard treatment for gonorrhea is penicillin or other antibiotics.

4. *Chlamydia*, a bacterial infection with symptoms similar to those of gonorrhea, is probably the most common STD in the United States. Chlamydia is thought to be responsible for half of all cases of *nongonococcal* or *nonspecific urethritis* (*NGU* or *NSU*). Most women with chlamydia do not show any initial symptoms. Several antibiotics (but not penicillin) are effective treatments for chlamydia.

5. Viral STDs include *genital herpes, genital warts, cytomegalovirus, hepatitis B*, and *AIDS*. In herpes, herpesviruses (*HSV*) enter the body and invade specific nerve fibers. One or several painful sores appear at the point of entry; after a time, these sores heal without treatment but the disease can reappear at any time, especially with physical and emotional stress. Herpes is contagious while the sores are developing and when they are present; the risk of infection when the virus is dormant is uncertain, but thought to be low. Pregnant women with active herpes can pass the infection on during childbirth, with serious consequences for the newborn. At this time there is no cure for herpes.

6. The most common viral STD in the United States is *genital warts*, which are caused by the human papillomavirus (HPV). This disease is statistically linked with cervical cancer in women and can be transmitted to a baby during delivery. Several methods of curing warts are used with varying degrees of success.

7. *Cytomegalovirus (CMV)* is an extremely common virus that usually causes no problems, but which can produce a number of symptoms. CMV is difficult to diagnose and cure. It is associated with serious prenatal defects.

8. *Hepatitis B* is a liver disease spread by sexual contact, infected needles, and by infected mothers to babies during birth. Symptoms often go unrecognized. There is currently no cure for hepatitis B, but a vaccine is available and it is recommended for high-risk groups.

9. *Acquired immune deficiency syndrome (AIDS)* and *AIDS related complex (ARC)* are caused by the *human immunodeficiency virus (HIV)*. The primary modes of transmission are sexual contact (coitus and anal intercourse), the sharing of contaminated hypodermic needles and syringes, and prenatal infection. HIV screening of blood supplies has all but eliminated transfusions as a source of infection in the United States. HIV infection is NOT spread by casual contact; HIV must enter a person's blood stream in order to cause infection. The virus invades the immune system; AIDS occurs when the immune system becomes disabled and the person becomes susceptible to a number of opportunistic infections. People who are HIV-positive may be healthy, may have ARC, or may have AIDS; all are contagious. At the present time AIDS is considered a fatal disease. Many questions about AIDS remain unanswered.

10. The incidence of *syphilis*, a bacterial STD, has risen dramatically in recent years. In primary-stage syphilis, the main symptom is a small chancre at the point where bacteria entered the body. In secondary-stage syphillis, the main symptom is a rash. In the latent stage, there are no symptoms, and after about a year, the victim is no longer contagious. However, the bacteria may be doing damage to body organs, damage not obvious until the final stage (the late stage). Within a few weeks after syphilis is contracted, it can be diagnosed by a blood test. Penicillin is an effective cure at all stages. Syphilis can cross the placental barrier and infect a fetus; congenital syphilis may result in death or a number of deformities.

11. The major *parasitic* STDs are *pubic lice* and *scabies*. They can be picked up from infested clothes and other objects or be sexually transmitted. Pubic lice attach themselves to pubic hairs. Scabies is caused by a microscopic mite that burrows into the skin. Although annoying, neither scabies nor pubic lice is dangerous and they can both be cured.

12. *Vaginitis,* an inflammation of the vagina, sometimes, but not always, is transmitted sexually. The common vaginal infections are *trichomoniasis,* caused by a sexually transmitted parasite; *monilia* (also known as *candidiasis* or a yeast infection), caused by overproduction of a yeast fungus that normally lives in the vagina; and *bacterial vaginosis,* commonly caused by gardnerella bacteria. These infections are characterized by vaginal discharges and itchiness. They can be treated and cured.

13. The epidemic of STDs in the United States is due to complex factors. Medical obstacles to STD control include the absence of symptoms in many people, the fact that sexually transmitted diseases provide no natural immunity, and difficulties in the development of effective vaccines. Psychological obstacles, including guilt and embarrassment, prevent many individuals from seeking treatment. Psychological barriers also impede honest communication between sexual partners about STDs. Societal obstacles include punitive attitudes and the inadequate commitment of resources for eradicating STDs.

14. The best ways to prevent STDs and to protect yourself are to stay informed, engage in only the safer sexual practices, and care for yourself and your partners.

Key Terms

sexually transmitted disease (STD) *(645)*

gonorrhea *(647)*

chlamydia *(650)*

cervicitis *(646)*

urethritis *(646)*

pelvic inflammatory disease (PID) *(646)*

epididymitis *(646)*

nongonococcal urethritis (NGU)/ nonspecific urethritis (NSU) *(650)*

herpes genitalis *(652)*

herpes virus (HSV) *(652)*

genital warts *(655)*

human papillomavirus (HPV) *(655)*

cytomegalovirus (CMV) *(655)*

hepatitis B *(656)*

acquired immune deficiency syndrome (AIDS) *(656)*

AIDS related complex (ARC) *(659)*

human immuno- deficiency virus (HIV) *(658)*

syphilis *(663)*

chancre *(666)*

pubic lice *(669)*

scabies *(669)*

vaginitis *(670)*

trichomoniasis *(670)*

monilia (candidiasis) *(670)*

bacterial vaginosis *(670)*

enteric infection *(671)*

■

Psychosexual Well-Being

●

Sex is a part of total health. . . . it belongs to you, *the person, and it's part of . . . your total personality structure.*

Mary Calderone

No text on human sexuality would be complete without a discussion of sexual health. After all, human sexuality is not just "academic." Whether we are researchers, clinicians, teachers, or students, most of us who study sexuality hope to use our knowledge to improve our own sexual health, the sexual health of our children, and perhaps even the sexual health and well-being of our society.

But what, exactly, *is* "sexual health"?

Clearly, it includes the avoidance of physical problems associated with the sexual and reproductive organs, such as cancers, infections, and other illnesses. In this chapter we will recommend some ways for you to take care of your sexual and reproductive organs, reduce the chances of disease, and detect early warning signs so that if you do get ill you can get prompt treatment. (We have covered sexually transmitted diseases separately in Chapter 17.) Sexual health also includes adaptation to any unavoidable disabilities. Therefore, we will also discuss some ways of dealing with disabilities.

Sexual health is also psychological, which is why we have called this chapter "*Psycho* sexual Well-Being." We have already addressed certain psychological aspects of sexual health in previous chapters: for example, the ability to communicate effectively about sex (in Chapter 11). In this chapter, we will suggest some guidelines for rearing sexually healthy children and propose some issues for you to ponder as you construct your own definition of sexual well-being.

THE SEXUAL BODY
IN SICKNESS AND IN HEALTH

It's a sad fact, but true, that the human body is a vulnerable contraption, prone to all sorts of ailments and afflictions. The sexual and reproductive organs of the body are no exception. We begin, therefore, with a brief review of some diseases of these organs. In our discussion, the term *risk factor* will refer to any factor statistically associated with a higher-than-average chance of developing a disease, whether or not the factor is causally related to the disease. Space does not permit us to cover every major illness affecting the sexual and reproductive organs. For further information, you might consult your medical practitioner, your student health service, the American Cancer Society, or the National Cancer Institute Cancer Information Service (telephone: 1-800-CANCER).

The Prostate Gland

The prostate, as you will recall from Chapter 4, is a chestnut-shaped gland located just below the bladder and about two inches above the rectum. Within this gland, the ejaculatory ducts meet and open into the urethra. The prostate is tiny in young boys but begins to grow at puberty and continues to increase in size with age, especially after the mid-forties. Several medical problems can beset this organ, but by far the most serious is prostate cancer, which strikes about 100,000 men a year and in 1989 killed 28,500. One of every 11 men will develop this disease at some time during his lifetime. Prostate cancer is the third most common cancer in men (next to skin cancer and lung cancer) and the third leading cause of cancer deaths in men. Although the disease is rare in Africa, for some unknown reason African-American men have the highest incidence rate in the world.

The risk of prostate cancer increases with age, with four-fifths of all cases diagnosed in men over 65. A suspected risk factor is the high consumption of dietary fat. Certain cancer-causing substances in the workplace may also play a part. Warning signs of prostate cancer include problems with urination (frequent urination, difficulty in starting or holding back urination, an inability to urinate, painful or burning urination, or a weak or interrupted flow of urine); blood in the urine; painful ejaculation; and continuing pain in the lower back, pelvis, or upper thighs. (Several of these signs also occur with other kinds of prostate problems, as discussed below.) But in the earliest stages of prostate cancer, there are often no symptoms.

Most prostate cancers begin in the part of the organ that can be felt by rectal examination (see Figure 18–1). An alternative technique, using ultrasound to detect small cancers, is also being investigated. The National Cancer Institute and the American Cancer Society recommend that all men over 40 have a rectal exam annually. If the physician detects a hard area or lump, various tests are done, including a *biopsy* (removal of a small tissue sample for

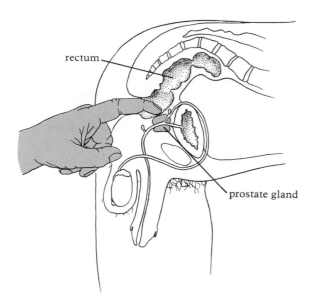

rectum

prostate gland

FIGURE 18–1
Prostate examination
Part of the prostate gland can be felt when a finger is inserted into the rectum. A medical practitioner can usually detect any irregular or unusually firm area. Because the prostate is relatively vulnerable to disease, this procedure is an important part of routine physical examinations for men over the age of forty.

analysis under a microscope). If the cancer is small and slow-growing, as most prostate cancers are, the doctor may recommend using hormones or anti-cancer drugs to shrink it, and radiation or surgery. If the cancer has spread or is fast-growing, the usual treatment is surgical removal of the prostate (a **prostatectomy**), either alone or in combination with other treatments. In a radical prostatectomy, the seminal vesicles are removed as well. During the last two decades overall survival rates for men with prostate cancer have climbed from 48 percent to 71 percent, and the survival rate for patients whose cancers are diagnosed early is now 84 percent.

A prostatectomy can interfere with a man's ability to have erections, because the small nerves controlling blood flow to the penis are located near the prostate and removal of the gland can sever those nerves. However, some surgeons now use a technique devised in the early 1980s that seems to leave the nerves intact and increase the likelihood of retaining full erections. Some men lose their ability to have erections but then regain it after a few months. We still do now know why some men recover full erections and others do not, although age is one factor; younger men are more likely to recover their erections (Schover, 1988b). Whether erections recur or not, a radical prostatectomy causes infertility because the prostate gland and seminal vesicles are no longer available to produce seminal fluid. At the moment of orgasm, little or no semen will come out. Sperm cells manufactured in the testes are reabsorbed into the body. Some men say a "dry" orgasm feels entirely normal; others say it is weaker or shorter than a "wet" one (Schover, 1988b).

Another prostate problem, which can occur in younger men as well as older ones, is **prostatitis**, an inflammation due to bacterial infection, infection by other microorganisms, or unknown causes (in which case it may be called "prostatosis"). The symptoms of prostatitis include fever; pain in the penis, lower abdomen, lower back, or perineum (the area between the scrotum and the anus); and problems with urination. Prostate infections are treated with antibiotics.

In older men, the prostate may become enlarged, usually because of a benign tumor (**benign prostatic hypertrophy**). The enlarged gland presses on the urethra, obstructing the flow of urine and producing a frequent urge to urinate and other urinary problems. Over half the men in the United States over age fifty have this condition to some extent. If symptoms are mild, no treatment may be necessary. If they are more severe, a urologist (a physician specializing in male reproductive disorders) can remove the excess tissue using a procedure called *transurethral resection of the prostate*, or *TURP*. Transurethral resection, which is major surgery, involves inserting an instrument into the urethra and using electrocautery to pare away the overgrowth and widen the urethral path. Most men who have had TURP experience retrograde ejaculation (backup of the ejaculate into the bladder during orgasm) because during surgery the sphincter muscle between the urethra and the bladder is cut. The result is "dry" orgasms and infertility. However, the sensations of orgasm are often unaffected. Most partners of men who have had TURP do not care about the lack of expelled semen, and erection problems are *not* a commonly reported side effect. But of course, if a man *thinks* his functioning will be impaired, his anxiety and fear could produce a self-fulfilling prophecy.

Medical researchers are currently investigating several possible alternatives to TURP. These include, among others, various drug treatments; the use of ultrasound to pulverize the enlarged tissue so that it can be sucked out with an aspirator; use of microwaves to shrink the excess tissue; and a procedure in which doctors run a tiny balloon through a catheter to the prostate and then inflate the balloon at high pressure to open up the urethral passage.

The Testes

The testes are vulnerable to a relatively rare form of cancer, one that accounts for about 1 percent of all cancers in males, or about 5,600 new cases a year. Testicular cancer is most likely to strike between the ages of 20 and 35—and in fact is one of the most common types of cancer in men aged 15 to 34 (Algood, Newell & Johnson, 1988). It occurs more often in white men than black men. Men who have an undescended testicle or who had a testicle descend into the scrotum several years after birth have a higher than normal risk. (Normally the testes descend from the lower abdomen into the scrotum about two months before birth.) For this reason, undescended testes should be corrected surgically by the age of two or three. Other risk factors

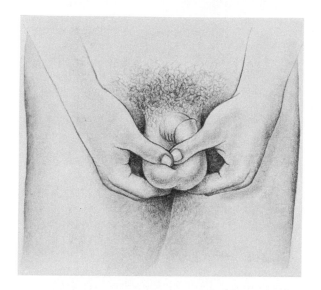

FIGURE 18–2

How to examine your testes   *The best time for a testicular self-examination is after a hot bath or shower, when the scrotal skin is most relaxed. Standing in front of a mirror, look for any swelling on the scrotum. Then examine each testis by placing your index and middle fingers on its underside and your thumb on top. Gently roll the testis between the thumb and fingers, feeling for small lumps or a general enlargement. Do not confuse the epididymis, located on the top and back of the testis, with an abnormality; the epididymis usually feels spongier than a tumor would. It's normal for one testis to be slightly larger than the other.*

include having a case of mumps after puberty that caused the testes to swell and having a biological mother who had abdominal or pelvic X-rays during pregnancy. There is also some evidence that men whose mothers took diethylstilbestrol (DES) during pregnancy for the prevention of miscarriage may have an increased risk. Testicular cancer can *not* be caused by injury of the testes, sexually transmitted diseases, masturbation, or frequent sex.

Symptoms of testicular cancer include an enlarged testicle, a feeling of heaviness in a testicle, or a small hard lump on a testicle. Sometimes there is a dull ache in the lower abdomen or the groin, but pain does not usually occur until the later stages. Unlike most prostatic tumors, testicular tumors often grow rapidly and the cancer quickly spreads to other parts of the body, so early detection is critical. All men should get into the habit of examining their testes, preferably every month. The procedure is simple (see Figure 18–2). All men should also have a regular checkup that includes a testicular exam.

Many changes in the testicular area turn out to be caused by harmless cysts, or by an infection of the epididymis, which can be cleared up with antibiotics. But you should bring all changes to the attention of a physician immediately. Only a few years ago, the prognosis for testicular cancer patients was bleak, but today survival rates are excellent, and almost all cases that are detected and treated early can be cured. Treatment typically consists of surgical removal of the affected testicle followed by drug treatments and in some cases radiation therapy. Because cancer rarely affects both testes, fertility and sexual functioning are usually not affected. If a man wishes, he can have an artifical testicle placed in the scrotum with the weight and feel of a normal testicle.

Another reason to stay fit *Recent evidence suggests that women who stay active and exercise regularly are at lower risk for breast cancer than those who are sedentary.*

The Breasts

For reasons not yet understood, the United States has an extremely high rate of breast cancer, and it has been rising for the past two decades. About one in ten American women eventually develops the disease, making it the most common cancer in women and the second leading cause of cancer deaths in women (after lung cancer). Men, too, can get breast cancer, but it affects them far less often, probably because they have less breast tissue than women. Men also have lower levels of estrogen, and estrogen contributes to the growth of certain kinds of breast tumors.

Although breast cancer can and does occur at all ages, women over 50 are more likely to get it than younger women. Other risk factors include having a close female relative who had the disease (especially before menopause), starting to menstruate early or reaching menopause late, obesity, never being pregnant, and having one's first child after age 30. Recent research suggests that women with an unusually high percentage of dense breast tissue—connective and epithelial (lining) tissue as opposed to fatty tissue—may also face an increased risk, because breast cancer occurs most often in these cells (Saftlas et al., 1989). There is also some evidence that women who are inactive are more susceptible to breast cancer (and uterine cancer) than are women who have been athletic since youth (Frisch et al., 1987). It's possible that exercise prevents the development of estrogen-dependent tumors by reducing estrogen levels or by causing the body to produce a less potent form of the hormone.

In recent years, several studies have suggested a link between breast cancer and two dietary factors: fat intake and alcohol consumption (Longnecker et al., 1988; Toniolo et al., 1989; Brisson et al., 1989). Both a high-fat diet and moderate consumption of alcohol may increase the risk of cancer by increasing the production of estrogen. Dietary fat may also increase the body's supply of "free radicals," molecules that make cells more accessible to certain fat-soluble cancer-causing substances. However, not all studies support a connection between cancer and diet. And even if dietary factors are important, they may operate in complex ways. For example, the effects of dietary fat may depend on what other kinds of foods a woman eats and whether she had a specific type of benign breast disease before developing cancer (Hislop et al., 1990). At this writing we cannot draw any firm conclusions about the impact of fat intake or alcohol consumption on breast cancer. Still, there are many good reasons for eating a low-fat diet and cutting back on alcohol consumption, and if you have certain risk factors for breast cancer, these steps certainly can't hurt.

In Chapter 13, we noted that estrogen and progestin are often used to treat certain symptoms of menopause and help prevent osteoporosis (brittle bones) in postmenopausal women. Some researchers are concerned that the use of such hormone replacement therapy (HRT) during and after menopause may be another risk factor for breast cancer (Adami et al., 1989; Mack & Ross, 1989; Mills et al., 1989). If they are correct, the increase is probably modest, but because so many women get the disease, the absolute number of women affected could be large. However, like the diet-breast cancer link, the connection between HRT and breast cancer is controversial. Some researchers think there is no link, and some think HRT actually *protects* against breast cancer (Bengtsson, 1989; Gambrell, 1990). Hopefully, research during the next few years will resolve this critical issue.

Early warning signs of breast cancer include an unfamiliar lump in the breast, swelling under the arm, dimpling or pulling of the skin on the breast, a persistent rash or skin irritation on the breast, flaking or scaliness of the nipple, inversion of a previously noninverted nipple or vice versa, discharge from the nipple, or pain and tenderness in the breast. These signs do not necessarily mean you have cancer, but they do mean you should see a health practitioner immediately. If breast cancer is detected and treated early, while it is still localized in one small area, the survival rate is excellent; in such cases, 85 to 90 percent of patients are still alive after five years. But once the cancer grows or spreads to lymph nodes in surrounding areas, the odds for survival drop considerably.

Having a mammogram
This procedure looks awkward, but most women find that it involves little or no discomfort. Large-scale studies find that women over fifty who have regular mammograms have a 30 percent lower risk of dying from breast cancer than other women.

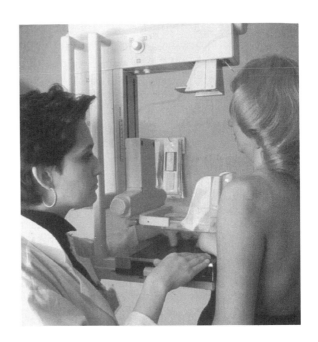

For many years, the standard treatment for breast cancer has been an operation called a **mastectomy.** A *partial mastectomy* removes part of the breast, a *modified radical mastectomy* removes the whole breast, and a *radical mastectomy* removes the breast, surrounding lymph nodes, and underlying muscles. But in recent years researchers have reported good results with other forms of therapy, including **lumpectomy** (removal of only the tumor and immediately surrounding tissues), radiation therapy, chemotherapy, and hormone therapy. Indeed, a lumpectomy combined with radiation treatment is as effective as removal of the breast (Fisher et al., 1989). In 1990, a federal advisory panel convened by the National Institutes of Health concluded that lumpectomy, followed by radiation, is preferable to mastectomy in a majority of cases (Smigel, 1990). Most U.S. patients still undergo a mastectomy, but the use of lumpectomy is now likely to increase. This is great news for women, for the trauma of mastectomy does not end with the surgery. Not only is there a long, painful recovery period, but sexual problems often occur after the operation (Schover, 1988a). First, there is the loss of an organ that provides erotic sensation. Second, there may be chronic pain in the chest and shoulder, which interferes with erotic pleasure. Third, and most important, in a culture that regards the female breast as a major erotic asset and even a symbol of femininity, the loss of one or both breasts is often emotionally devastating. A woman may become understandably self-conscious with her sexual partner or reluctant to become intimate with a new partner. A previously shaky relationship may be strained to the breaking point. Support groups and reconstructive surgery can help a woman through the experience, but breast reconstruction also has some risks.

Early detection of breast cancer not only increases the chances of survival but also reduces the necessity for drastic surgery. There are three things an individual can do to increase the odds of early detection. First, all women should have a clinical breast exam by a medical practitioner as part of a regular health checkup. Second, all women and men should become experts at examining their own breasts. Many women normally have lumpy breasts. Therefore each woman needs to learn what is normal *for her*, so that she can detect changes. The best time for premenopausal women to do an exam is right after menstruation, when the breasts are least likely to be swollen and tender. Women who are pregnant, who are past menopause, or who have had a hysterectomy should try to do the exam at about the same time each month. Box 18–1 describes the recommended procedure.

The third step women should take, beginning in the mid-thirties, is to have a **mammogram,** which is a special low-radiation X-ray. Although not infallible, mammography can often detect a lump when it is still tiny, long before it can be felt manually by either the woman or her health practitioner. The American Cancer Society currently recommends that a baseline mammogram be done between the ages of 35 and 40 and that routine mammograms be done at one- or two-year intervals in women in their forties and annually in women aged 50 and older.

Unfortunately, most women are still not getting regular mammograms. Some fear that the radiation itself will cause tumors, although the low doses now widely used minimize this risk. (The machinery used should deliver less than one "rad" of absorbed radiation per breast; the most up-to-date machines deliver much less.) Another barrier is cost; mammograms obtained through private clinics and laboratories can be fairly expensive, and at present Medicare and many private insurers will not pay for them. On the positive side, some medical centers and clinics now sponsor low-cost screenings. Your local American Cancer Society chapter may be able to give you a list of such services in your community.

If you do find a lump, or lumps, in your breast, do not panic. Between a fifth and a third of all women have lumps because of a noncancerous condition known as **fibrocystic condition.** These benign (noncancerous) lumps are caused by the formation of fluid-filled sacs (cysts) or an overgrowth of fibrous tissue. Most such lumps do not increase the risk of breast cancer. With regular self-examinations women can usually learn to distinguish pre-existing fibrocystic lumps from any new lumps that may appear. The causes of fibrocystic condition are not yet known, but hormones may play a role. At one time it was thought that a substance in caffeine also contributed to the condition, but controlled studies have cast doubt on such a connection (Heyden & Fodor, 1986; Levinson & Dunn, 1986).

BOX 18–1

How to Examine Your Breasts

The American Cancer Society recently revised its instructions for doing a breast self-examination. First, observe your breasts in a mirror with your arms relaxed at your side; with your hands on your hips; with your arms raised above your head; and with your arms hanging down as you bend slightly forward. Look for changes in contour, shape, and skin and nipple color and texture, and for evidence of discharge from the nipples. Then lie down and use your left hand to examine the right breast, holding your right arm at a right angle to the rib cage with the elbow bent. To use the side-lying position, lie on your left side, rotating the right shoulder to the flat surface, as in drawing A. This position is the best one for examining the outer half of the breast, especially if the breast is large. To use the flat position, lie flat on your back with a pillow or folded towel under the right shoulder (B). A woman with small breasts may need only this position. To examine the left breast, reverse the procedure, using the right hand, and lie on the right side or flat with the pillow or towel under the left shoulder. Use the pads of three or four fingers to examine every inch of your breast tissue. Move your fingers in circles about the size of a dime and don't lift them between palpations. You can use powder or lotion to help your fingers glide easily. Vary the pressure from light to deep for each palpation to examine the full thickness of the tissue. Use one of three "search" patterns. For the vertical strip pattern, start in the armpit, proceed down to the underside of the breast, move a finger's width toward the middle of the body and continue upward to the collarbone, then repeat until you have covered all the breast tissue (C). For the wedge pattern, imagine your breast divided like the spokes of a wheel and examine each segment, moving from the outside toward the nipple and then back to the outside, then moving over a finger's width and repeating until you have covered all the breast tissue (D). For the circle pattern, imagine your breast as the face of a clock. Start at 12 o'clock and palpate along the boundary of each circle until you return to your starting point. Then move down a finger's width and continue in ever smaller circles until you reach the nipple (E). Finally, you should examine the tissue beneath your armpit while your arm is relaxed at your side, and squeeze your nipples gently to check for any unusual discharge.

Source: Adapted from Breast Self-Examination: A New Approach, *a brochure published by the American Cancer Society.*

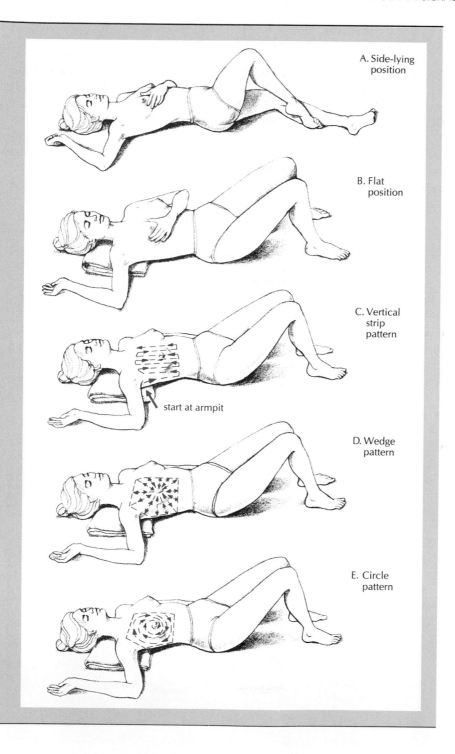

A. Side-lying
position

B. Flat
position

C. Vertical
strip
pattern

start at armpit

D. Wedge
pattern

E. Circle
pattern

The Cervix and Uterus

The cervix and the uterus are common sites of cancer in women. According to the American Cancer Society, cervical cancer struck about 13,000 women in 1989 and killed about 6,000; uterine (endometrial) cancer struck 34,000 and killed 4,000. Cervical cancer is more common in black women than white women, but for endometrial cancer the reverse is true. Death rates for both cervical and uterine cancer have been declining dramatically for the past few decades because of earlier detection. When detection occurs early, survival rates are 80 to 90 percent. For both cervical and uterine cancer, the most important warning sign is an unusual discharge or unusual vaginal bleeding.

Risk factors for cancer of the uterine lining include a history of infertility, failure to ovulate, obesity, and prolonged estrogen therapy. Uterine cancer is most common in older women. Risk factors for cervical cancer include having first intercourse at an early age, having multiple sex partners, and having genital herpes. If a woman's male *partner* has had many lovers, her odds of getting cervical cancer are also greatly increased (Slattery et al., 1989a; Zunzunegui et al., 1986). On the other hand, celibate women hardly ever get cervical cancer. And women who use barrier methods of contraception (the diaphragm or condoms) are less likely than other women to get the disease (Kjaer et al., 1989; Slattery et al., 1989a). All these facts suggest that cervical cancer may be caused by a microorganism that can be transmitted

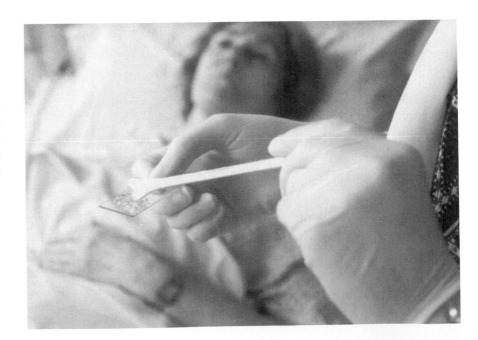

Pap test *A medical practitioner smears cervical cells on a slide so they can be examined under a microscope for signs of cancer or other abnormalities. Most women find the procedure of having the cells removed to be painless.*

sexually. Researchers currently believe that the most likely culprits are variants of the human papillomavirus (HPV), which in other forms causes genital warts (see Chapter 17).

Recent studies suggest another, nonsexual risk factor in cervical cancer: cigarette smoking may increase the odds of getting the disease by more than threefold (Slattery et al., 1989b). The mechanism is unclear, but perhaps cancer-causing components of smoke can travel through the blood stream into cervical tissues and somehow activate the HPV virus or make the cervix more vulnerable to the virus.

Cervical and uterine cancer are nearly always curable when caught early. A medical practitioner can check the health of the cervix by doing a **Pap test.** (*Pap* is an abbreviation of Papanicolaou, the name of the physician who developed the test.) A medical practitioner simply uses a small spatula, brush, or swab to remove some cells from the cervix for examination under a microscope. The cells are then smeared on a slide and sent to a laboratory where they are stained and inspected to see if any of them are abnormal. The major cancer organizations now advise yearly Pap tests starting at age eighteen or when a woman becomes sexually active. After three consecutive negative results, a woman might have less frequent tests "at the discretion of her doctor." Women who have had genital herpes or other sexually transmitted diseases, who had early sexual activity or have had frequent sex with many partners, or who smoke, should continue to have the test annually. Medical opinion is divided about whether annual tests are necessary for other women.

Abnormal cells in the cervix do not necessarily indicate a malignancy. Positive Pap results often occur because of a condition called *dysplasia*, which is noncancerous (although it can be a precursor of cancer). In that case the abnormal cells can be destroyed by cryotherapy (extreme cold), electrocoagulation (intense heat delivered by electric current), or localized surgery. When cancer is diagnosed the treatment is usually a **hysterectomy,** surgical removal of the entire uterus, and/or radiation. Hysterectomies are also done for other reasons—too often, as we discuss in Box 18–2.

The Pap test is also used to check for uterine cancer but is less effective than for cervical cancer. Women who are at high risk of developing uterine cancer are advised to have a biopsy of the endometrial tissue at menopause. Precancerous changes in the uterine lining may be treated with the hormone progesterone. Cancer is usually treated by a hysterectomy and/or radiation. Note, however, that not all uterine tumors are cancerous. Up to a third of all women develop benign tumors in the uterine wall, called **fibroid tumors,** or simply *fibroids*. These growths may cause pain and bleeding between periods, but often they produce no symptoms at all.

You should know that false negatives—reports of "no cancer" when cancer actually exists—are a serious problem with Pap smears. Reading a Pap test is a tedious job that takes time and concentration. Unfortunately, in some laboratories technicians are underpaid and overworked, and worse, are paid on a per slide basis, which rewards them for rushing (Bogdanich, 1987).

BOX 18–2

Too Many Hysterectomies?

In 1946, in a medical paper titled "Hysterectomy: Therapeutic necessity or surgical racket?," a gynecologist reported that of 246 hysterectomy patients he studied, almost half had shown no symptoms or had no pathology of the uterus. The physician warned his colleagues that unnecessary hysterectomies were becoming alarmingly common (in Tavris, forth coming). But that physician's warnings went unheeded. Today, nearly half a century later, over 650,000 hysterectomies are performed annually, making the operation the second most common major surgery for women in the United States (after Caesarean sections). More hysterectomies are done in the U.S. than in any other western country. Yet the necessity for the procedure is often highly questionable. In fact, according to one Stanford physician, between *50 and 90 percent* of all hysterectomies are either avoidable or unnecessary (Robin, 1986).

Everyone agrees that a hysterectomy can be lifesaving in cases of uterine or advanced cervical cancer or serious pelvic infections that have not responded to drugs. The operation can also bring relief from debilitating pain in cases of severe endometriosis and certain other conditions. Most hysterectomies, however, are *not* done for these reasons. Among the most frequent patients are women with *fibroid tumors*, benign (usually harmless) tumors of the uterus, which as we noted in the text sometimes cause pain or bleeding but usually cause no serious symptoms. To critics of hysterectomy, removing a healthy organ when symptoms are mild or nonexistent is entirely unwarranted.

Sometimes hysterectomies are done because of painful menstrual bleeding, irregular-looking cells in the cervix, uterine prolapse (slippage), or because a woman is past menopause and "doesn't need her uterus anymore." In the latter case, the reasoning is that since uterine cancer *may* occur someday, the organ might as well be removed. But consider: prostatic cancer occurs in 1 of every 11 men (see text), yet no one suggests that men have healthy prostate glands removed "just in case." Hysterectomies are almost twice as common as prostatectomies, even though prostate cancer is over twice as common as uterine and cervical cancer combined!

Like any major surgery, hysterectomy carries significant risks. Most patients suffer at least some complications (Hufnagel, 1988). About six

As an informed consumer, you have a right to ask whether the lab analyzing your test has been licensed or accredited by a professional organization and how its technicians are paid. Cut-rate mail order laboratories tend to be less reliable than others, so if your doctor sends specimens out of the local area, you might ask why.

in 1000 have significant complications that require rehospitalization and may lead to chronic disability; about 3 of every 1,000 patients die (Robin, 1986). Often the patient's ovaries are also removed, in a procedure called an *oophorectomy*. As a result, the body's level of estrogen, which protects against osteoporosis and possibly heart disease, falls off abruptly. (During normal menopause, the decline is more gradual.) Although the patient can take hormone replacement therapy (HRT) to make up for the lost estrogen, as we've seen HRT also poses some possible dangers.

The effects of hysterectomy on sexual functioning are controversial. Many authorities feel the operation has no effect on sexual pleasure or orgasm (Shover, 1988a). When we have asked friends who have had hysterectomies about this issue, they have told us that indeed, for them there were no sexual problems. Some women even find that their sex lives improve because of relief from pain or bleeding. But other women do report a loss of sexual desire, arousal, or sensation. Possible physical causes include hormonal changes, scar tissue, damage to nerves during surgery, loss of sensation from uterine vasocongestion and elevation, and the elimination of uterine contractions during orgasm. Possible psychological causes include depression and grief after the operation.

For many conditions now treated by hysterectomies, less drastic approaches exist. For example, fibroids can be monitored with ultrasound for any sudden changes and simply left alone if they are not causing severe problems. (Fibroids tend to shrink on their own after menopause.) If the tumors do cause problems or begin to grow rapidly, a less extensive operation called a *myomectomy* can be done to remove them without taking out the entire uterus. Treatments that are safer or simpler than a hysterectomy are also available for irregular or heavy bleeding, menstrual pain, and precancerous conditions of the cervix or uterine lining (Greenwood, 1989).

A woman whose doctor suggests a hysterectomy for a non-life-threatening condition should consider getting at least one other opinion from a physician who is not professionally associated with the first doctor. Information on the risks and complications of the operation is available from Hysterectomy Educational Resources and Services (HERS), 422 Bryn Mawr Avenue, Bala Cynwyd, PA 19004 (telephone: 215-667-7757).

The Ovaries

Ovarian cancer struck about 20,000 women in 1989, killing about three-fifths of them. Although it affects only about one and a half percent of all women, ovarian cancer causes more deaths than any other cancer of the

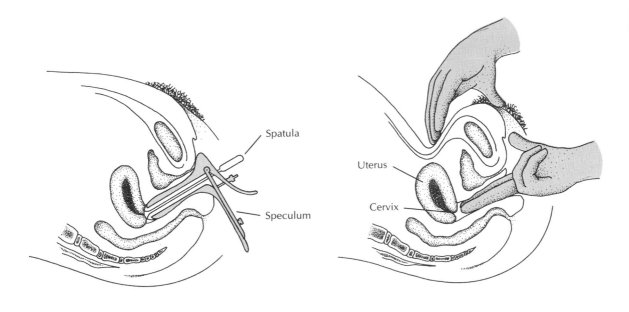

Spatula

Speculum

Uterus

Cervix

FIGURE 18–3

Pelvic examination In a pelvic examination, a medical practitioner first inserts a plastic or metal speculum *into the vagina to hold the walls apart, then inspects the vagina and cervix for lesions and other signs of infection. A spatula is used to take cells for a Pap test. Then comes a bimanual exam. The practitioner places two fingers into the vagina and presses with the other hand on the lower abdomen to check the position of the internal organs and for unusual growths or tenderness.*

female reproductive system, except for breast cancer. It can occur in young women and even children, but the risk increases with age and is highest after age 65. Other risk factors include a family history of ovarian cancer, obesity, never having borne children, and a personal history of breast or endometrial cancer. Rates are higher than normal for nuns, Jewish women, and women who have never married.

Unfortunately, ovarian cancer is a fast-spreading disease that usually causes no obvious symptoms until late in its development. Sometimes, however, an accumulation of fluid causes an enlargement of the abdomen, and occasionally there is abnormal vaginal bleeding, abdominal pain, or a feeling of indigestion. Early detection is critical; survival rates are excellent *if* the cancer is treated early (Young et al., 1990). Therefore, all women should have an annual pelvic examination to look for ovarian abnormalities. (Figure 18–3 shows how a pelvic examination is done.)

A cyst or tumor on the ovary does not necessarily mean cancer; most such growths are benign and disappear by themselves. However, if cancer is suspected surgery may be necessary to obtain a biopsy and other tests may be needed. If cancer is diagnosed, options include surgery (removal of the uterus, the ovaries, and the Fallopian tubes), drug therapy, or radiation. Researchers are currently working to develop more effective treatments.

The Bladder

Many women at some time suffer from **cystitis,** a urinary tract infection (UTI) affecting the bladder. The microbes causing infection reach the bladder by way of the urethra. Men don't usually get serious UTIs until old age, when prostate problems may trigger them, because the urethra is much longer in men than in women and so bacteria are less likely to make it to the bladder.

Cystitis can be caused by various types of bacteria, including those that cause gonorrhea and chlamydia (see Chapter 17), but the blame usually goes to a bacterium that lives happily in the intestines of healthy people, *E. Coli*. It's possible that *E. Coli* can enter the urethra through the urethral opening if a woman wipes herself from the anus toward the vulva after a bowel movement. Frequent or vigorous heterosexual intercourse also seems to create conditions ripe for cystitis ("honeymoon cystitis"), perhaps by irritating the urethral opening or pushing bacteria into it. One study found that college students being treated for urinary tract disorders were significantly more likely to have had recent sexual intercourse than students being treated for other problems (Strom et al., 1987). Use of the diaphragm has also been linked to UTIs (Foxman & Frerichs, 1985; Remis et al., 1987; Strom et al., 1987).

The symptoms of cystitis include a frequent desire to urinate, a feeling that you can't quite empty your bladder, and burning sensations during urination. The infection can usually be cleared up by antibiotics, although some cases are stubborn. Effective treatment is important, because if the infection gets to the kidneys those organs may be damaged.

Another bladder problem, which has a similar name although it is a separate disorder, is **interstitial cystitis** (IC). IC is a chronic inflammation of the bladder wall that causes bleeding, scar tissue formation, and pain. Scarring may prevent the bladder from expanding normally and the person may have to urinate frequently, sometimes dozens of times a day. The pain may be excruciating. Unfortunately, the causes are presently unknown, diagnosis is difficult, and there is no cure, although an anti-inflammatory drug may help reduce symptoms.

A number of folk remedies exist for urinary tract infections (see Boston Women's Health Collective, 1984). One of the most popular is drinking cranberry juice. Some researchers agree that cranberry juice might actually help treat or prevent UTIs, perhaps by acidifying the urine or preventing bacteria from adhering to the lining of the bladder (Sobata, 1984). But others think the juice only makes an infection worse, or at best is an unreliable treatment. Two other steps that may help are drinking lots of water (which flushes out the urinary tract) and urinating immediately after intercourse (which does the same). Women with persistent severe infections might ask a physician about the pros and cons of taking "suppressive" antibiotics—single doses of antibiotics used after intercourse.

Toxic Shock Syndrome

Toxic shock syndrome (TSS) is a systemic infection thought to be caused by toxins produced by bacteria that normally live harmlessly on the skin, in the nose, or in the vagina. These bacteria seem to multiply rapidly in the presence of certain kinds of absorbent tampons, which explains why women are the most frequent victims. However, TSS is also associated with skin lesions, insect bites, shingles, and other conditions, so men and children can also get the disease. Symptoms include high fever, severe nausea, vomiting and diarrhea, dizziness or fainting, and a sunburn-like rash. The illness can quickly lead to delirium, shock, and even death.

After the tampon-TSS link was recognized a decade ago, the tampons that appeared to be responsible were taken off the market. The number of reported cases of TSS began to decline. As of 1986, the incidence rate was .5 per 100,000 people (about 1200 cases a year), down from a rate of 10 per 100,000 people in 1980 (Gaventa et al., 1989). Deaths from TSS are now rare—about 75 a year. However, because about half of all TSS cases still involve menstruating women, women are advised to use the least absorbent tampons needed, to change tampons every few hours, and to alternate if possible between pads and tampons. If TSS symptoms appear during menstruation, remove a tampon if one is being worn, and get to a doctor quickly.

The PMS Controversy

Since the mid-1980s, the popular press has been full of stories about "premenstrual syndrome (PMS)." Women having his syndrome are said to become depressed, irritable, anxious, and tense for several days—and sometimes up to two weeks—before the onset of their periods. Some books have referred to "millions" of PMS sufferers, and clinics have sprung up across the country to treat the victims. In 1987, the American Psychiatric Association included PMS in an appendix to its diagnostic manual, giving it the impressive name "late luteal phase dysphoric disorder" and calling for further study. What is the actual evidence for this "syndrome"?

The first thing to know about "PMS" is that there is no medical agreement about its definitions, its causes, or its treatment. Published definitions include as many as 150 different symptoms, ranging from lethargy to restlessness (two states that would seem to be mutually exclusive). Almost any physical or psychological state, be it asthma, blurred vision, depression or sleeplessness, can qualify as part of the "illness." Proposed causes include progesterone deficiency, an estrogen/progesterone imbalance, low magnesium, high sodium, a prostaglandin deficiency, steroid fluctuations, and a fall in the level of endorphins, the brain's natural opiates. Yet there is no convincing evidence that any of these conditions are actually involved. Treatments range from vitamins to hormone injections, with little evidence that any particular treatment works better than a placebo.

Certain physical discomforts, such as uterine cramps, breast tenderness, and water retention clearly occur in many women before and at the beginning of menstruation. These normal changes have physical causes, and if they are severe they can be alleviated medically. However, controversy exists about the prevalence of psychological symptoms associated with menstruation, such as moodiness, irritability, and depression. Certainly many women say they have such symptoms. However it is easy for a woman to notice mood changes when they occur premenstrually and forget about those times when the symptoms did *not* occur premenstrually. Also, it is easy for a woman to blame a mood change on her impending period when she is premenstrual even though she might attribute the exact same "symptom" at other times to such factors as a bad day at work, a tough exam at school, or problems in a relationship.

How would you study the symptoms of "PMS" to find out if their association with menstruation were real? For many years, researchers simply surveyed women, overlooking such problems as faulty memories and self-fulfilling prophecies. The subjects were typically women undergoing psychotherapy, who as a group might be expected to report more symptoms than women not in therapy. During the past decade, researchers have improved on such approaches by polling women (and sometimes men) who are not in therapy about their physical and psychological well-being, *without revealing the true purpose of the study*. One method is to ask people to report symptoms for a single day, then find out *later* which women were premenstrual on that day. Another method is to have people keep daily symptom and mood diaries for two months. In either case, *when women do not know menstruation is being studied*, the relationship between symptoms and menstruation weakens or even disappears. Moreover, when women do not know the purpose of the study, they do not report more emotional symptoms or mood swings than men do (Alagna & Hamilton, 1986; Burke, Burnett & Levenstein, 1978; Englander-Golden, Whitmore & Dienstbier, 1978; McFarlane, Martin & Williams, 1988; Slade, 1984; Vila & Beech, 1980).

The power of expectations can be seen clearly in one study, in which Mary Brown Parlee (1982) asked seven women to fill out mood and activity questionnaires every day for 90 days, without telling them why. At the end of this period, after learning the reason for the study, the women all said they had been more anxious, irritable, and depressed around menstruation. In fact, however, their daily diaries showed just the *opposite* pattern: depression, fatigue, sleepiness, confusion, and hostility were actually lower premenstrually and menstrually than at ovulation. Parlee wryly observed that her findings seemed to support a "premenstrual elation syndrome."

Other research has looked for links between menstruation and performance, and has not found them. For example, studies show that premenstrual women do no worse on tests of intellectual ability than those who are between periods, nor is their ability to work, study, or take college exams impaired in any way (Golub, 1976).

Based on the psychological literature, the best conclusion is that only a small percentage of women have severe physical or emotional distress associated with menstruation—true "PMS." A somewhat larger number suffer from clinical depression or anxiety throughout the month and then get worse (or notice their symptoms more) before their periods. But in the general population, the psychological symptoms associated with "PMS" are not widespread. And for most women, bodily changes due to menstruation are fairly subtle. How those changes get interpreted will depend on a woman's attitudes, personality, activities, and concerns. One person might construe such changes as nervousness or moodiness, another might interpret them as creative energy or vitality, and still another might simply ignore them.

DEALING WITH DISABILITY

Chronic and permanent disabilities can affect sexual functioning in people who are otherwise healthy. Millions of adults have some type of disability. Some suffer from serious illnesses or have had strokes; some suffer from congenital diseases and defects; some have been injured in accidents or military battles. Here are some obstacles to sexual functioning that many disabled people face:

- *Negative body image.* Because of narrow cultural definitions of sexual attractiveness, even able-bodied people often worry about their physical appearance. Disabled people may feel especially uncomfortable with their bodies, and as a result they sometimes lack confidence in social situations or feel unlovable and inadequate (Schover & Jensen, 1988).

- *Lack of information.* Parents, teachers, and caretakers of disabled children often view them as asexual and therefore give them no sex education. When sex education is available, it often fails to address the special concerns of young people with serious physical or mental limitations.

- *Opposition by caretakers.* Parents of disabled young people often discourage them from expressing their sexuality and institutions for disabled people may not give them the privacy they need for masturbation or sex with a partner. In one home for disabled youths, boys found masturbating were forced to do it in public to shame them and keep them from doing it again (Gordon & Snyder, 1989).

- *Pain.* Many illnesses and disabilities involve pain, either from the condition itself or from treatments for it. Severe pain is not usually compatible with erotic feeling; it distracts one's attention, causes fatigue, interferes with pleasant sensations, and in some cases limits mobility.

- *Lack of social acceptance.* Many able-bodied people feel awkward around disabled people, either ignoring them or asking inappropriate questions. Or they think that because a disabled

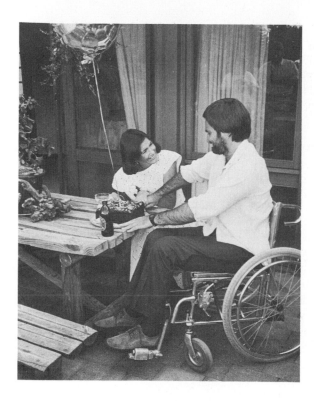

Bride and groom *This photo captures a moment of affection between newlyweds, after their informal wedding ceremony. The groom is a paraplegic. Unfortunately, able-bodied people sometimes see just the wheelchair, and not the person.*

person is dependent on others for physical help, the person must be spoken to and treated like a child. Pity may cause an able-bodied person to be unintentionally patronizing or to stare at disabled people, yet avoid direct eye contact with them. Little wonder that disabled individuals often worry about being rejected socially.

■ *Anxiety or depression.* If a medical condition causes progressive deterioration or is life-threatening, anxiety or depression can drive out thoughts of sexual activity, as the person focuses attention on the struggle to survive. In chronic but non-life-threatening conditions, the biases and misconceptions of able-bodied people can make disabled people feel shut out and discouraged.

■ *Physical limitations.* Depending on the condition, a disability may interfere with muscular coordination, voluntary movement, genital reflexes, bodily sensation, or bowel and bladder functions. These problems can all affect sexual functioning. In addition, speech or hearing difficulties make it difficult to communicate words of passion or intimacy, and blindness prevents sexual eye contact.

TABLE 18–1 Disabilities and Chronic Illnesses: Sexual Effects and Adjustments	Problem and Effects on Sexuality	Possible Adjustments
	Arthritis: Painful joints, reduced mobility and fatigue may interfere with sexual expression.	Medications and applications of moist heat help ease pain. Certain sexual positions can ease pressure on joints.
	Blindness and deafness: Sexual functioning is unaffected but important visual or auditory aspects of sexual communication are limited.	Physical contact becomes a significant mode of communication. Special compensatory education may be necessary to make up for gaps in sexual knowledge and social interaction skills.
	Cerebral Palsy (CP): Lack of voluntary muscle control, spastic movements, and rigidity may make sexual activities and sexual communication awkward or impossible without assistance. Spasms may occur during arousal. Erotic genital sensation is not impaired, but pain may interfere with pleasure.	Assistance may be required to position the body for masturbation or mutual sexual activities. Pillows to support limbs may ease spasms. Experimentation with positions may help alleviate spasms and pain.
	Diabetes: This disease is a major cause of erectile difficulties in men. More research on women is necessary, but evidence indicates that some diabetic women experience sexual desire, arousal, and orgasmic difficulties.	Noncoital sexual expression is an option for men who cannot attain erections. Acceptance of the disease is associated with a better sexual adjustment.

Yet despite such obstacles, many seriously disabled persons are vitally interested in love and sex and are able to establish satisfying sexual relationships. Even a terminally ill person may appreciate the special joys and comforts of sexual expression. It is beyond the scope of this book to cover physical disabilities in detail, but Table 18–1 provides a brief summary of how certain common medical conditions may affect sexual functioning and some adjustments that disabled persons and their partners can make.

Fortunately, many organizations now exist to educate the able-bodied about disability and provide social support and recreational opportunities for disabled people. The media have also helped some. For example, the 1989

Problem and Effects on Sexuality	Possible Adjustments
Heart Disease: Anxiety and fear of heart attack may curtail sexual functioning. Cardiovascular impairment may make strenuous sexual activity inadvisable.	Anyone with heart disease should obtain clear instructions from a physician regarding advisable limits for sexual expression. When sex is resumed, minimize stress.
Mental Disabilities: Children with below-average mental abilities often have a developmental lag in psychosexual interests but physical development and capacity are usually normal. Mentally retarded adults suffer primarily from a lack of sex education and an affirmation of their sexual rights.	Mentally retarded children can learn that masturbation is normal and acceptable in private. In adolescence they should be taught sexual responsibility (for sexual hygiene, contraception, and prevention of STDs) and social skills.
Multiple Sclerosis (MS): This progressive neurological disease affects mobility, vision, and sensory functioning. Symptoms vary, often fluctuating in severity. It is not uncommon for MS patients to experience sexual problems ranging from loss of interest and sensation to incontinence.	Medications help with pain and spasms. Sexual positions that minimize exertion are suggested. Artificial lubricants relieve dryness.
Stroke (Cerebrovascular Accident): Paralysis and impaired motor coordination may interfere with sexual activities and sensitivity.	Noncoital sexual activities and various different positions can be used.

film *My Left Foot* realistically depicted the life of Irish artist and writer Christy Brown, who was born with cerebral palsy. The film movingly conveyed Brown's sexual frustrations as a young man, frustrations that ended with his marriage to an able-bodied woman. Disabled people can help all of us gain a greater appreciation of the physical and psychological adaptability of human beings, and the right of all human beings to know love and sexual closeness.

Spinal cord injuries (SCIs), which have been the subject of much research, provide a good example of how even severe disability need not destroy a person's sexuality. An injury to the spinal cord disrupts the neural pathways between the brain and the rest of the body. Injuries to the lower half of the cord may paralyze the lower half of the body (paraplegia). Higher level injuries may paralyze all four limbs (quadriplegia). Sensation may also be impaired. If the injury is partial—that is, if the cord is not completely severed—motor and sensory abilities often improve with time. But if the cord is completely severed, the effects are irreversible.

Since erection is a spinal reflex, it can be affected by spinal cord injury. In general, the degree of impairment depends on the site of the injury. If it is above the erection center (above the sacral area of the spinal cord), a man can usually continue to have reflexive erections, though he will not be able to feel them occurring. In various studies, from 48 to 92 percent of men with spinal cord injuries have retained the ability to have an erection (Higgins, 1979). Interestingly, however, this ability is not completely predictable on the basis of the type of injury (Narum & Rodolfa, 1984). Some men with complete high-level lesions report having erections in response to erotic thoughts. A few men even report having psychologically caused erections but not reflexive ones, although this ought to be anatomically impossible! Ejaculation is more likely than erection to be disrupted by a spinal cord injury; most men with SCIs do not ejaculate or experience an orgasm (Cornelius, 1982).

Unfortunately, less research has been done on the sexual responses of women than men with SCIs. We do know that women with spinal cord injuries are apt to lose sensation in the vulval area (Berard, 1989). According to the Task Force on Concerns of Physically Disabled Women, when a lesion occurs above a certain point in the cord (probably the sacral area) a woman may continue to respond to genital stimulation with clitoral erection, vaginal lubrication, and labial swelling; otherwise she does not. Women with spinal cord injuries can usually experience a normal pregnancy and delivery.

Some men who cannot have erections because of a spinal cord injury choose to have a penile implant inserted (see Chapter 11). However, many couples decide instead to expand their definition of sexual behavior and shift the focus from penile-vaginal intercourse (in the case of heterosexual couples) or other activities requiring an erect penis. Some people with SCIs say that body parts controlled by areas of the cord above the injury become unusually sensitive to erotic stimulation, bearing out what we saw in Chapter 4: that any area of the body can become erogenous, depending on a person's history and physiology. An acquaintance of ours, herself disabled, told us of a male quadriplegic who was erotically aroused by stimulation of the tip of his right thumb. When a friend saw him at a party rubbing the thumb on the rim of a champagne glass, the friend jokingly accused him of masturbating! Some people have even reported experiencing orgasms in a nongenital part of the body, as in the case of this paraplegic woman:

> I have erratic, vague sensation in my vagina and clitoris. When I have an orgasm, I feel most of the pleasure in my knees—it's a nerve transfer thing, I guess. I'm probably the only woman in the world whose knees come. . . . (quoted in Shaul et al., 1978, p. 21)

THE SEXUALLY HEALTHY CHILD

You could be completely free of disease and sound of body yet not be sexually healthy. As we pointed out at the start of this chapter, sexual health has a psychological as well as a physical side. The psychological qualities that contribute to sexual health evolve over a lifetime, along with wisdom, sensitivity, and self-acceptance.

The foundations of psychosexual well-being (or the lack of it) are laid down in childhood. But unfortunately, in our society, children usually struggle along with their psychosexual development without much help from adults. Most children and teenagers *want* to get sound information about sexuality from their mothers and fathers (Bennett, 1984). And most parents say they are willing to answer their children's questions. Yet the fact is that parents are rarely a child's primary source of information about sex. Research involving thousands of college students has found that only about 15 percent of students are satisfied with the sexual information and values that were conveyed to them by their parents (Gordon & Snyder, 1989).

Then what *is* the primary source of sexual information for children and teenagers in the United States? You can probably guess. Since Kinsey's time, sex surveys have shown that children depend mainly on their friends (Gebhard, 1977; Hunt, 1974; Papini et al., 1988; Sorenson, 1973; Thornburg & Aras, 1986). Parents play little role in their children's sex education even when family communication on other matters is good (Fisher, 1987). Those parents who do attempt to talk about sexuality tend to stick to anatomical sex differences and the basics of pregnancy and birth and ignore everything else. In one study of 1,400 Cleveland parents, picked to represent a cross section of parents across the country, fewer than half of parents of 11-year-olds had so much as mentioned intercourse to their children, and even fewer had talked about contraception. Only about 60 percent of those with prepubescent daughters had told them about menstruation, and almost none of the parents had told their sons about nocturnal emissions (Roberts & Gagnon, 1978).

Also missing from parental sex education is much discussion of feelings. As John Gagnon and William Simon (1973) pointed out two decades ago, adults often unwittingly dehumanize sex by omitting feelings. "The most typical imagery," wrote Gagnon and Simon, "is that of the noble sperm heroically swimming upstream to fulfill its destiny by meeting and fertilizing the egg. The sexual act is described in ways that either misrepresent or totally obscure the source of pleasure and meaning in the act." Gagnon and Simon related the experience of a mother of two who diligently explained how babies are made, giving what she thought was a pretty good description. Her child listened and said, "Then you've done it twice."

School programs often do no better. Although most Americans support such programs, and most children in major cities now get at least some sex education in the classroom, teachers often limit discussion to the stark facts of reproduction—the "plumbing" of sex rather than its emotional and social

Sex ed   *The widespread ignorance of American children about sexuality and reproduction has prompted a growing number of school districts to offer improved sex education, beginning in the early grades.*

aspects. And even this kind of sex education is often not available until adolescence (Kirby, 1984). Many college students (unless they have taken a course in human sexuality) have never seen a condom; some think fertility peaks right before a woman's period and some don't know a clitoris from a carburetor.

The extent of children's sexual illiteracy was revealed a few years ago in a study by Ronald and Juliette Goldman (1982). The Goldmans interviewed Australian, North American, British, and Swedish children aged 5, 7, 9, 11, 13 and 15. They asked the children about sexual concepts, not about the children's own behavior. In general, the North American children were the least well informed. For example, only 23 percent of the North American nine-year-olds could describe genital differences between newborn baby boys and girls, versus 60 percent of the Australian children, 35 percent of the British, and 40 percent of the Swedish. The Swedish children were the only ones who were aware of sexual pleasure (60 percent of them). The Swedish children also knew the most about pregnancy and contraception. (Sweden has had compulsory sex education in the schools since 1957.) A more recent study found a similar lack of knowledge in a sample of almost 2,000 teenagers. Despite the fact that over 60 percent reported some previous sex education, on the average these teenagers correctly answered less than half of the 50 items on a test of sexual and contraceptive knowledge (Eisen & Zellman, 1988).

Even when there is good sex education at school, a child's spontaneous questions are likely to occur at home, and parents need to be able to respond. Most sex educators suggest guidelines like the ones below (see Gordon, 1976, 1986):

1. Parents should first realize that sex education does not begin when a child reaches puberty, starts school, or asks the first question about sex. It begins in earliest infancy, when parents unconsciously transmit attitudes about the human body while holding, diapering, or toilet training the child. Young children also learn a great deal from the general emotional climate in the home. If parents never display affection to each other, the child may infer that touching is wrong.

2. Explicit, verbal sex education needs to begin early, to establish that the parent is "askable." Waiting until you think the child is "old enough" may decrease your credibility and make communication difficult and awkward. "Silence," say Gordon and Snyder (1989), "teaches no less eloquently than speech," but it teaches the wrong lessons. Sex education does not consist of a single "heart to heart" talk; it is an ongoing process.

3. Adults should try to adapt their explanations to the child's level of cognitive development. As we saw in Chapter 12, a child's ability to assimilate sexual concepts changes with age and experience. There is no sense in trying to describe the seminiferous tubules of the testes to a 4-year-old. However, parents should use the proper terms for the major sexual body parts, such as the vagina, penis, vulva, and clitoris, in order to convey that sexual organs are as natural (and mentionable) as noses and toes. If small children can learn to say "teenage mutant Ninja turtles" they can learn to pronounce a few short Latinate terms.

4. Parents should not react to a child's early genital play by scolding or punishing the child, or by trying to provide a distraction. A child *needs* to explore his or her body. Some parents have trouble maintaining their composure when they find a child masturbating. They should keep in mind that they don't have to say or do *anything*, at least until they have calmed down. However, many sex educators believe the best response is a brief acknowledgement that what the child is doing feels good. This does not mean the child gets to masturbate in the parlor when Grandma and Grandpa are over. Children older than two or three are capable of understanding that some acts are supposed to be done in private.

5. Many (but not all) sex educators believe that nudity in the bath and bedroom provides a natural opportunity to introduce some anatomical facts of life. But both adults and children also have a right to demand privacy—for example, by closing the door—when they want it. Most children become modest at some point, and their modesty should be respected.

6. Honesty is the best policy. If parents feel uneasy about discussing some aspect of sexuality, they can begin by acknowledging their discomfort. Sol Gordon suggests they say something like, "It's not always easy for me to talk about sex, but there's no reason to be ashamed of sexual feelings or thoughts—everybody has them. I may have been brought up with different ideas about it, but it will still be good if we could talk together."

7. Parents should always answer a child's question immediately instead of postponing a reply. It helps to be prepared; one should think about how one will respond to various questions *before* they're asked. If a child is shy and asks no questions, the parent should take the initiative. For example, a parent might start a conversation about sex by pointing out a pregnant woman; most children will be interested in knowing how she got that way. Reading a children's book on sexuality together is another strategy for starting a discussion.

These are the general guidelines. Often, however, even the best-intentioned adults leave out some important topics. Here are a few of them (from Wade, 1988):

- *What sexual acts are.* Some adults try to avoid describing the actual mechanics of sex, fearing that if they tell their children the "how" of sex, the kids will want to give it a try. Research, however, finds no consistent association between sex education and age of first intercourse (Eisen & Zellman, 1987; Kirby, 1984). Just as children know about cars but don't normally try to drive one, those who know about sex don't rush right out to sample some. Besides, clear descriptions of sexual acts are necessary if children are to understand contraception and how STDs are transmitted. As former Surgeon General C. Everett Koop has observed, "You can't talk of the dangers of snake poisoning and not mention snakes."

- *Sexual pleasure.* As we mentioned, keeping the focus solely on making babies, without mentioning sexual pleasure, misleads a child about the true motives for having sex. But children eventually discover, from television, pornography, teen novels, and their friends, that most acts of sex have nothing to do with babies and some have nothing to do with love. They will realize they have been deceived and may conclude that adults are hypocrites. Of course, if a parent feels sex should only occur when there is love and commitment, the parent should say so. But at the same time, a parent can introduce the idea of sexual pleasure to a young child by casually noting that when two people have sex it's usually because it makes them both feel good. An older child might be told that as sexual activity continues both partners enjoy it more and more, until they experience a peak of intense pleasure called an "orgasm."

"Forget 'the birds and the bees.' Let's discuss how you stand on abortion and gay rights.

- *Good reasons for waiting.* Most adults agree that young people can get into trouble if they have sex before they comprehend its consequences and before they are able to make sound decisions. Often, however, a parent's discussion with a teenager boils down to one message: Don't. The same is true in schools; one federally financed chastity workbook for junior high school students contains such slogans as "Don't be a louse, wait for your spouse." Historically, adult moralizing never stopped young people from becoming sexually active, or lowered teenage pregnancy rates (L. Gordon, 1990). A better approach might be to give teenagers *positive* reasons for holding off on sex. For example, a parent might tell a teenager in a caring way that the parent wants the child to have a good first experience, and that this kind of experience is most likely to occur in a safe, secure, adult relationship. Parents can also discuss some of the emotional hazards of sexual intimacy, such as increased vulnerability and dependency.

- *Sexual ethics.* All children need to learn about honesty and respect for other people's needs and wishes—qualities that will determine the kinds of intimate relationships they will have when they grow up. Teenagers also need to appreciate the ethical implications of having sex with someone to boost one's own self-confidence, to get attention, to satisfy curiosity, or to impress friends. And they should understand the importance of full consent of both parties. As we saw in Chapter 15, many teenagers consider forced sex to be acceptable under some circumstances, and date rape is a growing problem on high school and college campuses.

- *Homosexuality.* Most heterosexual parents are not well-prepared for discussing homosexuality because of their own uneasiness about it. One thing they can do is try to learn more about homosexuality themselves. They can also teach their children to respect the sexual dignity of others and to refuse to join in when other children verbally attack each other with taunts of "fag" or "lez."

When explaining the "facts of life" to young children, parents of adopted children will need to explain both the facts of adoption and the facts of conception. A possible approach (based on the personal experience of one of the authors) is to explain that there are two ways for grownups to get a child. One is to "make" the child by having intercourse. The other is to go to an agency or person that finds parents for children who do not already have them. You might explain further, depending on the child's age, that it is not always possible for a man and a woman who make a baby to keep the child. Sometimes they cannot afford to raise a child and sometimes they are not really ready to be parents, which is a big job. You can point out that both ways of "getting" a child, making it or adopting it, make parents feel very lucky. It may be easier for very young children to understand adoption if the adoptive parents reserve the words *mother*, *father*, and *parents* for themselves and refer to the biological parents as *birth parents* or as "the man and woman who made you." Nowadays, of course, there are actually more than two ways of "getting" a child. Children whose birth involved a surrogate mother, sperm-donor father, *in vitro* fertilization, or one of the other technologies discussed in Chapter 6 will need to be told about their origins, too.

Finally, just as parents can say too little about sex to their children, they can also say more than a child wants or needs to know at the moment. The child will let you know if you go on too long, by getting bored or changing the subject. For young children, learning about sex is merely part of

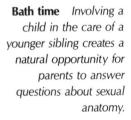

Bath time *Involving a child in the care of a younger sibling creates a natural opportunity for parents to answer questions about sexual anatomy.*

learning about the world in general, without the special significance adults attach to it. Sex educators like to make this point by telling stories like the one about the child who asked how babies were made. After the child's mother explained, she nervously inquired, "Is there anything else you'd like to know?" "Yes," replied the child. "How do birds fly?"

THE SEXUALLY HEALTHY ADULT

What would be the outcome of a sexually healthy upbringing? A sexually healthy adult, of course. But what does *that* mean? We began this book by pointing out that definitions of sexual health vary from generation to generation and culture to culture; what one era or society considers "sick" another may consider desirable. Even within a society, people often disagree strongly about what constitutes psychosexual well-being. Yet despite the difficulties in defining psychosexual health, we would like to offer the following brief "checklist" of attributes that sexologists believe contribute to sexual happiness and satisfaction. This list is not meant to be exhaustive; we know we have overlooked some important attributes, simply because there are so many possibilities. We urge you to use this list as a springboard for your own thinking. What would you add to it? Is there anything you would modify or delete?

1. *Self-esteem.* Low self-esteem or a lack of self-respect probably accounts for many of the sexual mistakes people make: doing things they don't really want to, having sex when they'd rather not, clinging smotheringly to a partner, allowing themselves to be exploited or abused, abusing and exploiting others. People with low self-esteem may send out nonverbal signals that say, in essence, "I'm nobody; don't bother with me." Or they may become bullies as a way of heading off rejection. They may also "try too hard" in social situations, making those around them feel obligated and uncomfortable. Sexually healthy people can accept their own small foibles and flaws and work realistically on more serious ones. They feel good enough about themselves to establish standards for what they want and deserve in sexual relationships. They don't have to prove themselves superior to others in order to feel "okay."

2. *A good body image.* Are you a little heavier or lighter than you'd like? Do you wish your chest were flatter or fuller, that you had more or less hair in certain places, that you had skinnier or fuller legs, or smoother skin? Join the crowd! All of us see physical imperfections in ourselves when we measure ourselves against prevailing cultural standards. But the

sexually healthy person has learned to accept these imperfections and concentrate on positive features. Such a person does not feel a need to apologize for his or her body to a sexual partner.

3. *The ability to make self-affirming choices.* Sexually healthy people are willing and able to make informed, positive choices about birth control, pregnancy, protection against disease, sexual partners, and sexual acts. They do not act impulsively, allow themselves to be "swept away" by the situation or pressure from others, or turn decision-making over to a partner. Gordon and Snyder (1989) relate how one woman exercised her right to make positive choices:

> One young woman at a university in Ohio told us of her meeting an invitingly handsome man at a party one night. They spent the evening dancing and talking, and discovered that they had a broad range of shared interests, including hiking and gourmet foods. When the party was dwindling and he asked her back to his room, she hesitated. She didn't have a single compelling reason for not wanting to have sex with him. She just didn't feel like it and felt uneasy about what might be a one-night stand. And besides, she was feeling horny, which only added to her ambivalence. Her decision, after mulling it over, was not to go home with him. If the relationship couldn't survive that, she reasoned, it wasn't worth pursuing. Her wisdom in this area was summed up with these words: My simple feeling of "I don't want to" was reason enough not to. Why did I need a fancy reason to say no to sex? (p. 88)

Of course, making choices includes not only nay-saying but yea-saying: knowing not only what you don't want to do, but want you *do* want.

Being human, sometimes we make poor choices. A sexually healthy person takes responsibility for the consequences. Sometimes the consequences are dramatic and life-altering, such as a pregnancy. Sometimes they are more subtle, such as feeling uneasy about getting into a situation you didn't really want to be in, or hurting someone emotionally. Taking responsibility begins with acknowledging what happened.

4. *Acceptance of others.* Most of us have had the experience of falling head over heels for someone and thinking that the object of our affection is "just perfect." Then, on closer inspection, the beloved turns out to be not quite so perfect after all. He has pimples on his back; she has cellulite on her thighs. He eats too fast; she snores. If we require a sex-

ual partner to be perfect, we are destined to be disillusioned, again and again. Of course, this does not mean one
must find *everyone* sexually appealing. We all have certain
priorities and requirements in intimate relationships regarding both physical and psychological traits (see the *Personal
Perspective* at the end of this chapter). However, people who
have a fairly wide "window of acceptance" will be less
likely than others to let a partner's minor flaws get in the
way of passion and desire.

5. *Sexual energy.* "Sexual energy" is our admittedly vague term
   for sexual interest and appetite, similar to what Freud
   called "libido." It is what the romantic among us might call
   sexual passion and the less romantic might call lust. We suspect that most people who find sexual satisfaction in a relationship have active sexual feelings—sexual energy, if you
   will—with or without the relationship. We are not saying
   that one ought to act on every (or any) "surge" of sexual
   energy one feels, but simply that sensuality and sexual
   enthusiasm are qualities of the individual that exist apart
   from any particular relationship.

6. *Flexibility.* We believe that sexually healthy people have a
   certain open-mindedness about sexual experience. They
   are willing to consider and perhaps try a new experience
   (say, oral sex, if they have never tried it), *if* it does not violate their integrity and does not harm or exploit others. This
   sort of flexibility gives the person's partner the freedom to
   reveal himself or herself fully, to be honest about what he or
   she would like, and to be natural and spontaneous. As one
   young man put it:

   What makes our sex life good is that I know she won't laugh at me
   for my little quirks and preferences. I can even masturbate in front
   of her and she won't criticize or be turned off. It seems to me that
   a relationship built on "can'ts" and "no-nos" is going to be frustrating for one partner or both. (authors' files)

7. *Communication skills.* Sexual health includes the ability to
   communicate clearly but tactfully your sexual needs, preferences, and intentions—what you expect or do not expect
   from an intimate relationship. Good communication means
   not saying yes when you mean no and not saying no when
   you mean yes. We discussed some guidelines for effective
   sexual communication in Chapter 11. However, sexual
   communication is more than a skill to be acquired by following some steps in a book. It is also mutual caring, openness to intimacy, and honesty.

8. *Trust.* Since so much is revealed in sexual relationships, sexually healthy people need the ability to trust. Trust, however, is a gift that we must learn to give wisely, to those who will respect and cherish it. Some people deserve our trust, but others will abuse it. We can't know which category a person falls in when we first meet the person; such a discrimination takes time and familiarity. Trust is typically "achieved" when our expectations about another person's behavior are met (Has he been there when I needed him? Has she kept her word?). For most (but not all) people in our culture, an important expectation in a committed relationship is sexual exclusiveness and fidelity.

9. *Empathy.* Empathy is the ability to identify with the feelings, thoughts, and attitudes of another person. One can probably be "good in bed," in terms of technique, without having any genuine concern for one's partner. But technique is not everything. Sexually healthy people are genuinely sensitive to the needs of others. They are concerned with their own gratification but also with their partner's. They are able to distinguish what they themselves are feeling from what the partner is feeling. They do not exploit others—for example, by blackmailing a partner into having sex as "proof" of love or commitment.

A person with all these attributes will put sex in perspective, and value sex without exaggerating its importance or becoming obsessed with it. Such a person will have constructive ways of coping with stress, pain, and loss (all inevitable in life) and will not use sex to "numb out." Sexual health is apt to take some time to achieve. As Gordon and Snyder (1989) observe, most people have some insecurities and doubts about themselves. Most people have also had sexual experiences they regret or feel angry or guilty about. Sexual growth consists in part of coming to terms with past traumas so that they do not rules our lives, and learning from the mistakes we have made.

THE SEXUALLY HEALTHY SOCIETY

We do not come into the world with ready-made ideas about sexuality; we *construct* our ideas, and our constructions are influenced by the assumptions and practices of the culture we live in. It follows that sexual "health" is not solely a personal issue, but a cultural one as well. If we make a few assumptions consistent with a democratic tradition—that the exploitation of others is wrong, that human beings have a right to seek happiness so long as they don't hurt others, and that the dignity of the individual deserves respect—then it is clear that societies as well as individuals can be sexually healthy or unhealthy. In these closing words, we encourage you to envision what a sexually healthy *society* might look like. Here are some possibilities for you to agree or argue with:

- Sex would be seen as a positive, meaningful, joyful aspect of human life—still private and personal, perhaps, but not shameful.

- Males and females would be valued and respected equally and would have equal rights and responsibilities in sexual matters.

- The right to say no to the sexual overtures of another person would be regarded by all as inalienable, with *no* exceptions, and neither adults nor children would be sexually exploited.

- The media would not glamorize and eroticize sexual exploitation and callousness, and they would portray a variety of body types and shapes as erotically appealing.

- Heterosexual, bisexual, and homosexual orientations would be respected equally. Individuals would be judged by their character and behavior toward others and not by the identity of their sexual partners. People would not only tolerate sexual differences but would honor and defend them.

- There would be respect for individual differences in sexual values and choices; people would not feel socially pressured either to be sexually active or to deny their sexuality.

- Parents and schools would take responsibility for providing comprehensive, candid sex education for children and teenagers and would prepare young people for the biological, social, and psychological changes of adolescence and adulthood.

- Birth control would be affordable and readily available to all who needed it, so that no child would be born unwanted. Government funding for safer, more effective methods of contraception would be generous.

- Society would fully commit itself to eradicating sexually transmitted diseases through research, education, and treatment.

- Private, consensual sexual acts between adults would not be criminalized.

That's what *we* think. We invite you, as you finish this book, to define your *own* ideals for a sexually healthy society and for your personal sexual well-being.

Human sexuality—a universal source of connection and intimacy

. . . .

YOUR CONDITIONS FOR SEX

One of the chief benefits of a course in human sexuality is the opportunity to clarify what you need and want in your own sexual life. As sex therapist Bernie Zilbergeld observes in his book *Male Sexuality* (1978), just as a car has certain requirements that must be met if it is to function at its best, so human beings have certain requirements for optimal sexual functioning. These "conditions" for good sex include any circumstances that enhance one's sexual experiences:

> A condition is anything that makes you more relaxed, more comfortable, more confident, more sexual, more open to your experience in a sexual situation. Another way of looking at conditions is that they are the factors that clear your nervous system of unnecessary clutter, leaving it open to receive and transmit sexual messages in ways that will result in satisfying sex for you. (Zilbergeld, 1978, p. 83)

What conditions make sex good for you? Take some time now to focus your thoughts and write down your requirements. Writing will help you be specific and thorough. In doing this exercise, try not to censure yourself; include conditions that may at first seem odd or unusual. Zilbergeld advises that except for conditions involving pain or harm to you or your partner, your goal should be self-acceptance. He suggests that a good way to discover your conditions is to compare the best sexual experiences you have had with some that did not turn out so well. However, if your memory is fuzzy, if you are relatively inexperienced, or if none of your experiences has been satisfying, you can simply use your imagination.

Here are some areas to consider: your physical health; feelings about yourself, including your body; the use of alcohol and other drugs; preoccupation with other matters in your life; fears about performance; concerns about pregnancy or sexually transmitted diseases; physical characteristics of your partner; personality traits of your partner; sexual responsiveness of your partner; degree of emotional intimacy with your partner; feelings about your partner; sexual acts, positions, rhythms, and techniques; sexual fantasies; degree of novelty or familiarity in the situation; degree of privacy; activities before and after sex; and conformity to your own ethical standards (for example, regarding sexual fidelity). As you make the list, be as precise as possible and feel free to consider other kinds of issues.

Now look over your list. Which of your conditions depend entirely on you and which have more to do with your partner or require the partner's cooperation? Which conditions have the highest priority and which are merely optional? How might knowing your conditions help you make wise decisions and choices about sexual relationships?

Your conditions for sex may change, as you yourself do. Defining one's sexuality is an ongoing, dynamic process, a part of life's great adventure.

IN BRIEF

1. The sexual and reproductive organs are subject to a number of physical disorders. In men, *prostate cancer* is the most common. *Prostatectomy*, anticancer drugs, and radiation are the usual treatments; prostatectomy can interfere with the ability to have erections. *Prostatitis*, an infection of the prostate, may occur at all ages. In older men a benign tumor often causes prostate enlargement *(benign prostatic hypertrophy)*.

2. Although *testicular cancer* is generally rare, it is one of the most common types of cancer in young men. All men should examine their testes for signs of this disease. Most cases detected early can be cured.

3. *Breast cancer* is the most common cancer in women. A number of risk factors for breast cancer have been identified, and research is being done on possible connections with fat and alcohol consumption and hormone replacement therapy. Early detection is critical; women should do a breast self-exam once a month. Middle-aged and older women should have yearly *mammograms* to screen for breast cancer. Treatments include *mastectomy, lumpectomy*, radiation, and chemotherapy. Sexual problems after mastectomy are common. Many lumps in women's breasts are due to a *fibrocystic condition*, which is noncancerous.

4. Death rates from *cervical* and *uterine cancer* have decreased in the past few decades due to early detection. The *Pap test* is instrumental in finding these cancers, and women should have this test done regularly. Cervical cancer is thought to be caused by a virus that can be sexually transmitted. *Hysterectomy* and radiation are the usual treatments for cervical and uterine cancer. Hysterectomy is also done for other problems, but the operation is not always justified. For example, *fibroid tumors* that are not growing can usually be treated in other ways or left alone.

5. *Ovarian cancer* is less common than other cancers affecting women, but it is more deadly. It is fast-spreading and usually causes few symptoms. Most ovarian cysts are not cancerous.

6. *Cystitis* is a urinary tract infection (UTI) that is far more common in women than men. It is caused by bacteria that travel through the urethra to the bladder and it is usually easily treated with antibiotics. *Interstitial cystitis* is a chronic, painful, and untreatable inflammation of the bladder.

7. *Toxic shock syndrome (TSS)*, a serious illness that is often related to the use of highly absorbent tampons, has become less prevalent since certain tampons were removed from the market. However, women who use tampons are cautioned to seek immediate treatment if they have TSS symptoms.

8. Despite widespread interest in the "premenstrual syndrome (PMS)" there is no medical agreement about its definition, causes, treatment,

or incidence. Many women experience cramps and other physical symptoms before and at the start of their menstrual periods, but careful psychological research finds that severe emotional symptoms related to menstruation are not common in the general population. A number of factors determine how women interpret the normal bodily changes of the menstrual cycle.

9. People with chronic and permanent disabilities often face special obstacles to sexual functioning, such as physical pain and lack of social acceptance by able-bodied people. Nonetheless, many disabled people are vitally interested in love and sex and are able to establish satisfying sexual relationships.

10. Sexual health has a psychological as well as a physical side. The foundations of psychosexual well-being are laid down in childhood, but most North American children do not get adequate information about sex from adults. Sex educators advise parents to be aware of how sexual attitudes are transmitted nonverbally, to recognize genital exploration is normal, to adapt explanations to the child's level of development, to acknowledge discomfort about sexual issues honestly, and to answer a question when it is asked. Parents should explain what sex acts are, discuss sexual pleasure, give teenagers good reasons for postponing sex, discuss sexual ethics, and teach respect for the sexual dignity of others.

11. Attributes of the sexually healthy adult include self-esteem, a good body image, the ability to make self-affirming choices, acceptance of others, "sexual energy," flexibility, communication skills, trust, and empathy. Sexual health is apt to take some time to achieve.

12. Sexual health is not solely a personal issue, but a cultural one as well. Societies, as well as individuals, can be sexually healthy or unhealthy.

Key Terms

risk factor *(684)*

prostate gland *(684)*

biopsy *(684)*

prostatectomy *(685)*

prostatitis *(686)*

benign prostatic hypertrophy *(686)*

transurethral resection of the prostate (TURP) *(686)*

mastectomy (partial, modified radical, and radical) *(690)*

lumpectomy *(690)*

mammogram *(691)*

fibrocystic condition *(691)*

Pap test *(695)*

dysplasia *(695)*

hysterectomy *(695)*

fibroid tumors *(695)*

urinary tract infections (UTIs) *(698)*

cystitis *(698)*

interstitial cystitis *(699)*

toxic shock syndrome (TSS) *(699)*

"premenstrual syndrome (PMS)" *(700)*

Glossary

●

abortion   The emptying of the uterus during pregnancy, which terminates the pregnancy; it may be spontaneous or induced.

acquaintance rape   Rape in which the perpetrator is someone the assaulted person knows; a common type is date rape.

acquired immune deficiency syndrome (AIDS)   A life-threatening, blood-borne disease spread through semen or blood that has been infected with the human immunodeficiency virus (HIV). AIDS weakens the immune system and increases susceptibility to opportunistic infections that can cause death.

activating effects   In sexology, the effects of adult sex hormones on sexual behaviors.

adrenal cortex   The outer part of the adrenal gland; a source of androgens, estrogens, and progesterone in both sexes.

adrenal glands   Two endocrine glands, located above the kidneys, that secrete adrenalin and other hormones, including sex hormones.

adrenogenital syndrome (AGS)   A condition in which a genetic defect causes the adrenal glands of a genetically female fetus to produce abnormally high levels of androgens, resulting in masculinized external genitals.

afterbirth   The placenta and other membranes expelled from the uterus after childbirth.

agape [ah-GA-pay]   Unselfish or altruistic love; it does not depend on erotic attraction.

AIDS   *See* acquired immune deficiency syndrome

AIDS-related complex (ARC)   A condition caused by HIV infection in which the particular opportunistic diseases characteristic of AIDS are not present but the immune system is weakened; it is characterized by various symptoms, such as fever and swollen glands, and is often a precursor of AIDS.

amniocentesis   A diagnostic procedure in which amniotic fluid is withdrawn from the uterus of a pregnant woman and analyzed to determine if certain genetic or other abnormalities exist in the fetus.

amniotic fluid   The fluid in the amniotic sac; it maintains a constant temperature and provides a comfortable, protective, weightless environment for the developing embryo or fetus.

amniotic sac   The innermost membranes surrounding the embryo or fetus; it is filled with amniotic fluid. Also called the *amnion*.

anaphrodisiacs   Substances that depress sexual functioning or desire.

androgen insensitivity syndrome (AIS)   An inherited condition in which a genetically male fetus produces normal amounts of androgen but the cells of the body do not respond to these hormones, so that the external genitals develop as female.

androgenous   Having both traditionally masculine and traditionally feminine qualities in roughly equal proportions.

androgens [AN-droh-jens]   Masculinizing hormones produced principally in the testes but also in the ovaries and the adrenal cortices of both sexes.

anilingus   Oral stimulation of the anus.

anorgasmia   In women, an inability to have, or difficulty in having, orgasms; sometimes called inhibited female orgasm.

anus [AY-nus]   The termination or outlet of the rectum.

aphrodisiacs   Substances reputed to arouse sexual passion or enhance sexual performance; their actual existence has been difficult to establish.

areola [uh-REE-uh-luh]   The ring of dark skin surrounding the nipple of the breast.

artificial insemination (AI)   The injection of semen into a woman's vagina or uterus by means of a syringe or other device for the purpose of initiating pregnancy.

ascetic   Self-denying; renouncing a life of physical comfort in favor of austere self-discipline, especially as an act of religious devotion.

autoerotic asphyxia   The practice of cutting off one's own oxygen while masturbating in an attempt to heighten sexual feelings; it can be fatal.

autonomic nervous system (ANS)   The part of the nervous system that controls involuntary bodily functions, such as heart beat and salivation.

bacterial vaginosis   A vaginal infection caused by a variety of bacteria.

basal body temperature (BBT) method   A fertility awareness method of birth control that relies on the slight shift of body temperature at ovulation for the determination of "unsafe" days when a woman can get pregnant. Also called the *temperature method*.

Bartholin's glands   Two small glands of the vulva, located on the inner surfaces of the minor lips; their function is uncertain.

bestiality   *See* zoophilia

biological sex   A term encompassing all the physical traits that, in combination, differentiate females from males, including genes and chromosomes, sex hormone levels, reproductive structures, external genitals, and the bodily distribution of hair and fat.

biopsy   A procedure in which a tissue sample is obtained and examined under a microscope.

birth control   Voluntary limitation or prevention of childbirth by means of contraception or abortion.

bisexual Having a sexual orientation both toward partners of the same sex as oneself and partners of the other sex.

blastocyst An embryo at an early stage of development, when it consists of a round, hollow cluster of about a hundred cells.

brothel A house of prostitution.

bulbourethral glands *See* Cowper's glands

candidiasis *See* monilia

case study A detailed examination and description of a selected individual.

castrate To surgically remove the testes or ovaries.

cavernous bodies (corpora cavernosa) Two cylinders of spongy tissue in the penis.

celibacy Intentional abstinence from sexual relations or renunciation of marriage.

cervical cap A thimble-shaped contraceptive device that covers the cervix and stays in place by suction.

cervical mucus method A fertility awareness method of birth control in which a woman examines her cervical mucus to determine the "unsafe" days when she can get pregnant. Also called the *ovulation* or *Billings method*.

cervix [SIR-viks] The lower part, or neck, of the uterus; it extends into the vagina.

chancre [SHAN-ker] A painless sore; an early symptom of syphilis.

child molester An adult who approaches or has sexual contact with children for the purpose of sexual arousal and gratification.

child sexual abuse Sexual exploitation of a minor.

chlamydia [kluh-MID-ee-uh] A sexually transmitted disease caused by the *chlamydia trachomatis* bacterium; it is thought to be the most prevalent of all STDs.

chorionic villi sampling (CVS) A diagnostic procedure in which tissue on the outermost membrane surrounding a fetus is removed for examination; it is useful for detecting birth defects early in pregnancy.

chromosomes Rod-shaped structures, within the nucleus of a cell, containing genetic material.

circumcision The surgical removal of the foreskin of the penis.

climacteric [cli-MAK-tur-ik] The period of decreasing reproductive capacity in women, culminating in menopause.

clinical evaluation study A study that measures the success or failure of treatment or therapy techniques; also called *outcome study*.

clitoral glans The tip of the clitoris; it is usually the only part of the clitoris that is externally visible.

clitoral shaft A part of the clitoral body, not usually externally visible, containing two tunnels of spongy tissue that fill with blood during sexual arousal.

clitoridectomy The surgical removal of the clitoral body (glans and shaft).

clitoris [CLI-ter-us or cli-TOR-us] A small, cylindrical organ located above the urethral opening, just below the mons area; consists of a glans (tip), a shaft, and two extensions (crura) that connect to the pelvic bone.

closed field settings Settings in which people have little choice about interacting.

cohabitation Living together in a sexually intimate relationship without being married.

coitus [CO-i-tus] Vaginal-penile intercourse.

coitus interruptus *See* withdrawal

combination pills Oral contraceptives containing both synthetic estrogen and progestin.

coming out The process of acknowledging one's homosexual or bisexual orientation to oneself and others.

commitment The avowed or inferred intent of a person to maintain a relationship.

companionate love A stable type of love characterized by affection, trust, and loyalty, and based on familiarity with the loved one.

complementarity The ability to complete or make whole; in close relationships, the provision by each partner of qualities and talents the other lacks.

conception The inception of pregnancy.

conceptus A developing organism in the womb; an embryo or fetus.

condom A thin sheath of latex or animal membrane, worn over the penis, that keeps sperm from getting into the vagina during coitus and helps prevent the transmission of sexually transmitted diseases.

congenital diseases Diseases existing at birth.

contraception Prevention of conception.

contraceptive sponge A pillow-shaped polyurethane contraceptive device containing spermicide; it is placed deep in the vagina, up against the cervix.

coprophilia Sexual interest in and arousal to excrement.

corona A sensitive ridge of tissue on the penile glans that slightly overhangs the shaft.

corpora cavernosa *See* cavernous bodies

corpus luteum A structure that forms in the ovary from a ruptured follicle; it secretes progesterone.

corpus spongiosum *See* spongy body

correlation A measure of how strongly two or more variables are related to each other; it does not imply a cause-and-effect relationship between the variables.

Cowper's glands Two small male glands, located on either side of the urethra, that secrete a clear, sticky fluid during sexual arousal, before ejaculation. Also called *bulbourethral* [bul-bow-you-REE-thral] *glands.*

crura (of the clitoris) Two extensions of the clitoral shaft that connect to the pelvic bone.

crura (of the penis)   Two extensions of the penile shaft that connect to the pelvic bone. Singular: *crus*.

colpotomy   A method of tubal sterilization in which the Fallopian tubes are reached through the vagina.

cunnilingus [cun-i-LIN-gus]   Oral stimulation of a female's genitals.

cystitis   A urinary tract infection affecting the bladder; it is caused by various types of bacteria.

date rape   Rape that occurs during the course of a date.

DES (diethylstilbestrol)   A synthetic estrogen, derived from coal tar, that has been used as postcoital ("morning after") contraception.

diaphragm   A soft, dome-shaped, rubber contraceptive device that fits over the cervix; it holds spermicide and acts as a barrier to sperm during intercourse.

dihydrotestosterone (DHT)   A derivative of testosterone; it stimulates prenatal development of the scrotum and penis in a genetically male fetus.

dilation and evacuation (D and E)   An abortion technique, usually used between the thirteenth and twentieth week, in which the cervix is dilated and the fetal material is removed by curretage, suction, and forceps.

donor insemination (DI)   Artificial insemination in which the sperm comes from a volunteer or paid donor rather than the woman's partner.

double standard   The granting of greater opportunity or liberty to one individual or group than another, especially the granting of greater sexual privileges to men than to women.

douching   Washing out the vagina with water or a special solution.

dualism   The philosophical belief that soul and body are separate and antagonistic entities.

dysmenorrhea [dis-men-oh-REE-uh]   Painful menstruation.

dyspareunia [dis-puh-ROO-nee-uh]   Genital pain or discomfort during or just after sexual intercourse.

ectopic pregnancy   The development of a fertilized ovum outside the uterus; it can be life-threatening. *See also* tubal pregnancy

ejaculate [ee-JACK-yah-lut]   *See* semen

ejaculation   The discharge of seminal fluid from the penis.

ejaculatory duct   The terminal portion of the vas deferens; it is embedded in the prostate gland and opens into the urethra.

ejaculatory inhibition   A condition in which a man has trouble ejaculating despite sexual excitement; it is usually restricted to difficulty ejaculating in the vagina. Also called *inhibited male orgasm*.

embryo   An organism in the early stages of prenatal development—in human beings, the first eight weeks of gestation.

embryo transfer   A procedure in which a fertilized, developing egg (embryo) is removed from the uterus of one woman and placed in the uterus of another woman for gestation.

emission   The first stage of ejaculation, when internal structures contract, forcing seminal fluid into the urethral bulb.

endocrine [EN-doe-krin] glands   Organs that produce hormones and release them into the bloodstream.

endometriosis [en-doh-MEE-tree-OH-sis]   An often painful condition in which endometrial tissue grows in abdominal locations outside the uterus.

endometrium [en-dow-MEE-tree-um]   The mucous membrane lining of the uterus.

epididymis [eh-pi-DID-i-mus]   A tightly coiled C-shaped tube that perches atop the testis and in which sperm mature.

equity   Fairness; it exists in a relationship when each partner's benefits from the relationship are roughly proportional to what he or she contributes to it.

erectile inhibition   The formal term for persistent difficulty in attaining or maintaining an erection in response to sexual stimulation.

erection   The process in which the penis becomes rigid and increases in size because of vasocongestion; the term is sometimes used to refer to clitoral swelling as well.

erogenous zone   Any area of the body that is erotically sensitive.

eros   A Greek term sometimes used to denote romantic, passionate, highly eroticized love.

erotica   Literature, art, or photography dealing with sexual themes.

estradiol [ES-truh-DIE-ul]   An important estrogen.

estrogen replacement therapy   *See* hormone replacement therapy

estrogens [ES-trow-jens]   Feminizing hormones produced principally in the ovaries but also in the testes and in the adrenal cortices of both sexes.

ethnographic study   A study of an entire subculture or society.

eunuch   A male who has been castrated, i.e., has had his testes removed; also refers to a male whose testes have not developed.

excitement phase   The first stage in Masters and Johnson's model of the sexual response cycle, during which the penis becomes erect and vaginal lubrication begins.

exhibitionism   Exposure of one's genitals to an unsuspecting person as a way of experiencing sexual arousal.

experiment   A research method in which some factor of interest is systematically manipulated or varied in order to study its effects on behavior.

expulsion   The second stage of ejaculation, when contractions along the length of the penile urethra and around the base of the penis force seminal fluid out of the penis.

Fallopian tubes   Ducts attached to each side of the uterus that transport ova from the ovaries to the uterus; the site of fertilization.

fellatio [fel-AY-shee-oh]   Oral stimulation of a male's genitals.

fertility awareness methods   Birth control methods that rely on prediction of the fertile and infertile phases of a woman's menstrual cycle. During the fertile period a couple can abstain from sexual activity, use a barrier method of birth control, or use only noncoital sexual techniques.

fertilization   The union of an ovum and a sperm, resulting in conception.

fetishism   Sexual arousal in response to an inanimate object or body part.

fetus   An unborn organism after the earliest stages of prenatal development—in human beings, after the eighth week.

fibrocystic condition   A noncancerous condition characterized by breast lumps caused by cysts or the overgrowth of fibrous tissue.

fibroid tumors   Tumors, usually noncancerous, in the uterine wall; also called *fibroids*.

field of eligibles   The set of people whom the culture considers appropriate for an individual to date or marry.

follicle   A hollow, pod-like cluster of ovarian cells within which an ovum matures; follicles also secrete estrogen.

follicle-stimulating hormone (FSH)   A gonadotropin; in females it stimulates ovarian follicle development and the secretion of estrogen by the developing follicle; in men it stimulates sperm production.

foreplay   Manual or oral stimulation of erogenous areas of the body, such as the breasts, the inside of the thighs, and the genitals; the term is misleading, as such stimulation can occur during, after, or without intercourse, as well as before it.

foreskin   A fold of skin that extends from the shaft of the penis and covers or partially covers the glans. Also called the *prepuce* [PREP-us].

frenulum   A thin strip of sensitive skin connecting the glans of the penis to the shaft. Also called the *frenum*.

frottage [froh-TAZH]   The practice of touching or rubbing against a nonconsenting person for purposes of sexual arousal or gratification. Also called *frotteurism*.

gamete intrafallopian transfer (GIFT)   A procedure in which both sperm and ova are placed directly into a woman's Fallopian tubes for fertilization.

gay   In general use, a synonym for homosexual; however, many homosexuals prefer the term *lesbian* for homosexual women and use *gay* only in reference to homosexual men.

gender   The state of being male or female; sometimes used more narrowly to refer to the social and psychological characteristics associated with being male or female, as opposed to physical characteristics.

gender identity   One's subjective sense of oneself as male or female.

gender role   The set of rules or norms governing attitudes and behaviors that a culture considers appropriate for a male or a female. Also called *sex role*.

genes   The chromosomal units that determine inherited characteristics. Genes on the X and Y chromosomes determine genetic sex.

genital tubercle   In an embryo, a rounded projection of tissue that develops into either male or female external genitals.

genital warts   A sexually transmitted viral infection of the genitals, caused by the human papillomavirus (HPV).

genitals   Technically, the internal and external sexual and reproductive organs; in actual use, the term usually refers only to the external organs.

gestation [jeh-STAY-shun]   The period from conception to delivery, which in human beings lasts nine and a half lunar months.

glans   *See* clitoral glans; penile glans

gonadotropins   Hormones released by the pituitary gland that travel through the bloodstream to the ovaries or testes; gonad-stimulating hormones.

gonads [GOH-nads]   Reproductive glands that produce sex hormones and cells that are able to unite with other cells to start a new organism; ovaries or testes.

gonorrhea [gon-uh-REE-uh]   A sexually transmitted disease of mucous membranes caused by the gonococcus bacterium.

Grafenberg spot (G spot)   A small area in or behind the front (anterior) wall of the lower vagina reported by some researchers to be sexually sensitive in some women; its prevalence and even its existence are controversial.

hedonism   The pursuit of or devotion to pleasure; also, the doctrine that only that which is pleasant is good.

hepatitis B   A viral liver disease spread primarily, but not exclusively, by sexual contact.

hermaphroditism   A rare condition in which an organism has both ovarian and testicular tissue. *See also* pseudohermaphroditism

herpes   A sexually transmitted disease occurring on or near the genitals or the cervix or around the mouth; it is caused by the herpes simplex virus and characterized by small blisters.

heterosexism   Prejudiced attitudes or discriminatory behavior toward homosexuals by heterosexuals; also, the tendency to see the world solely in heterosexual terms, e.g., by thinking of all romantically-involved couples as consisting of a male and a female.

heterosexual   Having a sexual orientation toward partners of the other sex.

homologous organs   Male and female organs that develop from the same embryonic tissue.

homophobia   An irrational fear or loathing of homosexuality.

homosexual   Having a sexual orientation toward partners of the same sex as oneself.

hormone replacement therapy (HRT)   The administration of hormones that are no longer being produced by the body or are being produced only at low levels; the term usually refers to the administration of estrogen and progestin during or after menopause.

hormones   Chemical substances that are secreted by endocrine glands and that affect the functioning of other organs.

human chorionic gonadotropin (HCG)   A hormone secreted at the site where the ovum implants in the uterus; breakdown products of HCG in a woman's blood or urine are an indication of pregnancy.

human immunodeficiency virus (HIV)   The virus that causes AIDS and ARC.

human papillomavirus (HPV)   A virus that causes genital warts and that in certain forms is suspected of causing cervical cancer.

hymen   A membrane that partially covers the vaginal opening of most but not all females who have never had sexual intercourse.

hypersexuality   Sexual insatiability; a compulsive orientation to sex.

hypogonadism   A condition in which production of hormones by the testes or ovaries is abnormally low; it is caused by various diseases of the endocrine system.

hypothalamus [hi-po-THAL-uh-mus]   A part of the brain that regulates various bodily processes; it causes the pituitary gland to release gonad-stimulating hormones (gonadotropins).

hysterectomy   Surgical removal of the uterus.

in vitro fertilization (IVF)   A procedure in which fertilization occurs outside a woman's body, in a laboratory dish; the resulting embryo is then implanted in the woman's uterus for gestation.

incest   Sexual contact between persons who are closely related (other than spouses).

infertility   The inability to conceive after a year or more of having sexual intercourse without birth control, or an inability to maintain a pregnancy long enough for the fetus to survive outside the womb.

informed consent   A research subject's consent to participate in a study after receiving information about possible risks or discomfort.

inhibited female orgasm   *See* anorgasmia

inhibited male orgasm   *See* ejaculatory inhibition

inhibited sexual desire (ISD)   A low level or absence of sexual desire; a lack of interest in sexual fantasy and activity.

instillation procedure   An abortion technique used between the sixteenth and twenty-fourth week, in which uterine contractions are artificially stimulated so that the fetus and placenta will be expelled.

interdependence   The ability of two people to influence each other's thoughts, plans, actions, and emotions; it is a defining feature of close relationships.

interstitial (Leydig's) cells   Cells that produce the hormone testosterone in the testes; located in the tissue between the seminiferous tubules.

interstitial cystitis (IC)   A chronic, painful inflammation of the bladder wall.

interstitial-cell-stimulating hormone (ICSH)   A gonadotropin; in men it stimulates production of testosterone; in women it is called luteinizing hormone (LH) and brings on ovulation.

intrauterine device (IUD)   A birth control device, usually made of plastic, that is inserted into a woman's uterus and left there until the avoidance of pregnancy is no longer desired or another birth control method is chosen.

introitus [in-TROW-I-tus]   The external opening of the vagina, not visible unless the minor lips are spread apart.

intromission   Insertion of the penis into the vagina.

Kegel exercises   Exercises prescribed to strengthen pelvic muscles.

labia majora   *See* major lips

labia minora   *See* minor lips

laboratory observation   Observation of research subjects under controlled conditions in a laboratory.

laparoscopy   A method of tubal sterilization performed with a laparoscope; two incisions are required.

lesbian   A female with a homosexual orientation.

Leydig's cells   *See* interstitial cells

limbic system   A part of the brain involved in various emotional and behavioral processes, including sexual responsiveness.

lumpectomy   Surgical removal of a breast tumor and the immediately surrounding tissues.

luteinizing hormone (LH) [LOOT-in-eye-zing]   A gonadotropin; in women it brings on ovulation and causes ruptured follicles to secrete progesterone and some estrogen; in men it is called *interstitial-cell-stimulating hormone (ICSH)* and stimulates production of testosterone.

madam   A female business manager in a house of prostitution.

major lips (labia majora)   Two fatty folds of skin that extend downward from the mons and provide protection for the vaginal opening and other delicate parts of the vulva.

mammary glands   Milk-producing glands in a woman's breasts that become active after childbirth.

mammogram   A low-radiation X ray used to diagnose breast cancer and other breast abnormalities.

menarche [meh-NAR-kee]   The initial onset of menstruation; it typically occurs at about age twelve-and-a-half in North American girls.

marital rape   Rape in which the perpetrator is the victim's spouse.

masochism (sexual)   The need or desire to experience pain, suffering, or humiliation for the purpose of sexual excitement.

mastectomy   Surgical removal of some or all of the breast.

masturbation   Stimulation of one's own genitals for sexual gratification.

matching principle of attraction   The principle that people generally prefer as dating and marriage partners those who are similar to themselves in interests, personal characteristics, and background.

menopause   The cessation of menstruation; it usually occurs gradually, typically in a woman's late forties or early fifties.

menstruation   The periodic discharge from the uterus of sloughed off endometrial cells, blood, and mucus; it occurs about once a month if conception has not occurred and is followed by renewal of the uterine lining.

mini-pill   An oral contraceptive containing only progestin.

minilaparotomy   A method of tubal sterilization using one small abdominal incision.

minor lips (labia minora)   Two pinkish, hairless folds of skin in the vulva that are bordered by the major lips.

monilia   A vaginal infection caused by the overgrowth of a yeast-like fungus that lives normally in the vagina; it is also called *candidiasis* and is commonly referred to as a "yeast infection."

mons pubis [mons PEW-bis]   A mound of fatty tissue that lies about six inches below a woman's navel and is covered with pubic hair. Also called *mons veneris* or simply *mons*.

morning-after pill   A synthetic hormone taken after coitus to prevent pregnancy; it is believed to prevent implantation of the fertilized ovum.

Müllerian ducts   Embryonic structures that develop, in females, into the Fallopian tubes, uterus, and inner two-thirds of the vagina.

myotonia   Muscular tension; it increases during sexual arousal.

necrophilia   Sexual interest in corpses.

neuroendocrine system   The nervous system and the endocrine glands.

nipples   The tips of the breasts.

nocturnal emission   Ejaculation during sleep.

nocturnal penile tumescence (NPT)   Partial penile erection during rapid-eye-movement sleep; it occurs predictably in men who do not have physical impairment of erectile capacity.

nongonococcal urethritis (NGU)   A sexually transmitted disease of the male urethra caused by several microorganisms, but primarily *chlamydia trachomatis*. Also called *nonspecific urethritis (NSU)*.

nonspecific urethritis (NSU)   *See* nongonococcal urethritis

norms   Standards and rules that govern the way a society expects people to behave in everyday life.

obscene telephone calling   Shocking, embarrassing, or manipulating a stranger on the telephone in order to achieve sexual arousal.

obscenity   A term used in legal rulings for sexually explicit material that is not constitutionally protected. *See also* pornography

oocytes [OH-uh-sites]   Immature egg cells in the ovary.

open field settings   Settings in which opportunities to form relationships exist but the physical environment does not dictate interaction with any particular individual.

open marriage   A marriage in which the spouses agree that each is free to have close or intimate relationships with other partners; such relationships may or may not involve sexual behavior, depending on the agreement.

oral contraceptives (OCs)   Synthetic female hormones taken regularly by mouth for the purpose of preventing conception. Popularly called "the Pill" or "birth control pills."

orgasm   The intense, pleasurable sensation and release of sexual tension experienced at the culmination of sexual arousal; the third stage in Masters and Johnson's model of the sexual response cycle.

orgasmic platform   The swelled walls of the lower vagina during the plateau phase of the sexual response cycle; the swelling is due to vasocongestion.

ovaries   Two small organs that produce ova, estrogen, and progesterone; the female gonads. The ovaries lie on either side of the uterus and are connected to it by ligaments.

ovulation   The maturation and release of an egg from an ovary.

ovum [OH-vum]   An egg cell which, when fertilized by a sperm, develops into an embryo.

Pap test   A clinical test in which cells are removed from the cervix and/or vagina and examined under a microscope; it is used to screen for cervical cancer.

paraphilias   Unconventional and often bizarre sexual behaviors.

parasympathetic nervous system   A subdivision of the autonomic nervous system generally responsible for conserving energy and keeping bodily processes functioning at a steady rate.

participant-observer   A researcher who has joined the group or culture being studied.

passionate love   An unstable type of love characterized by a turmoil of intense emotions and based on lack of familiarity with the loved one.

pedophilia   A primary or exclusive interest in children as sexual objects. *See also* child molester

pelvic inflammatory disease (PID)   A condition characterized by inflammation of the female pelvic organs, usually as a result of bacterial infection.

penile glans   The smooth tip, or head, of the penis; it is usually more sensitive than the shaft.

penile implant   A device surgically implanted in the penis that permits mechanically produced erections in a man who cannot otherwise have erections.

penile shaft   The part of the penis located between the glans and the root.

penis   The most sexually sensitive part of the male genitals, located above the scrotum. It consists of a glans (tip), a shaft, and two extensions (crura) that connect to the pelvic bone. Both urine and semen are expelled from the body through the penis.

perineum [pair-uh-NEE-um]   A sexually sensitive area of tissue that separates the anus from the lower part of the vulva in women and from the scrotum in men.

phasic pills   Combination oral contraceptives that deliver a constant level of estrogen throughout the menstrual cycle but varying levels of progestin for different phases of the cycle.

pheromone   An airborne compound which, when produced and released by an organism, affects the physiology or behavior of other members of the same species.

philia   A Greek term sometimes used to denote friendship or affinity for another person.

physical attractiveness stereotype   The belief that good-looking people have desirable personality and character traits.

pimp   A man who offers prostitutes protection and performs various services for them in exchange for a sizable percentage of their earnings.

pituitary gland [pi-TOO-uh-tair-ee]   A small endocrine gland attached to the lower surface of the brain that releases many hormones and regulates other endocrine glands; one of its functions is to produce gonadotropins.

placenta   A network of tissues attached to the uterine wall and connected to an embryo or a fetus by the umbilical cord; it supplies oxygen and nutrients and provides for the elimination of waste products.

plateau phase   The second stage in Masters and Johnson's model of the sexual response cycle, during which the orgasmic platform forms, the clitoris retracts, and the testes increase in size, elevate, and rotate.

pornography   A term that is often used as a synonym for erotica, but that also refers more narrowly to sexually explicit literature, art, or photography that is considered lewd.

premature ejaculation (PE)   A condition in which ejaculation occurs rapidly with only minimal sexual stimulation, or occurs before, upon, or shortly after penetration and before the man wishes.

"premenstrual syndrome" (PMS)   A cluster of physical and psychological symptoms said to occur in some women just before menstruation. The prevalence of the psychological symptoms is controversial; controlled research indicates that severe or disabling "PMS" symptoms do not occur in most women.

prepuce   *See* foreskin

priapism   A disorder characterized by a persistent, usually painful, erection.

probability sample   A sample that matches the population from which it was drawn on important characteristics, such as age and sex.

progesterone [pro-JES-teh-rone]   A hormone produced primarily in the ovaries and essential for the maintenance of pregnancy; it is also produced in smaller quantities in the testes and in the adrenal cortices of both sexes.

progestin   A synthetic progesterone.

prostaglandins   Hormone-like substances that stimulate the muscles of the uterus to contract.

prostate   A male gland that produces part of the seminal fluid; it lies just below the urinary bladder, and surrounds the ejaculatory ducts and part of the urethra. Also called *prostate gland*.

prostatectomy   Surgical removal of the prostate gland.

prostatitis   Inflammation of the prostate gland.

prostitute   A person who engages in sexual acts with various partners in exchange for money or other forms of payment.

pseudohermaphroditism   A condition in which the external genitals are either inconsistent with genetic sex or are ambiguous.

puberty   The period of life, between childhood and adolescence, in which the reproductive organs mature.

pubic lice   Tiny parasites that attach themselves to pubic hairs and burrow into the host's skin; they are often, but not always, sexually transmitted.

pubococcygeus (PC) muscle [pew-boh-cok-si-GEE-us]   A ring of muscle tissue located behind the vaginal walls.

puritan ethic   Principles of conduct that emphasize moral rigor and the sinfulness of luxury and pleasure.

random sample   A sample in which any member of the population in question has the same probability as any other of being selected, and in which selection of one individual has no influence on the selection of another.

rape   Any sexual act that occurs without a person's consent because of threatened or actual force; the term is sometimes also used to include situations in which the perpetrator uses drugs or deception so that the victim cannot give free and informed consent.

rape trauma syndrome   A predictable sequence of emotional reactions experienced by the victim of a rape.

rectum   The lower part of the large intestine.

refractory period   A period after a man's orgasm during which he is unable to experience another orgasm.

resolution phase   The fourth stage in Masters and Johnson's model of the sexual response cycle, during which the body returns to an unaroused state.

retrograde ejaculation   A condition in which sphincters do not work properly and seminal fluid enters the bladder instead of being forced out of the body through the penis.

rhythm method   A fertility awareness method of birth control in which the length of a woman's menstrual cycle is used to calculate the "unsafe" days when she can get pregnant.

roles   Positions in society that are governed by norms.

sadism (sexual)   The infliction of pain or humiliation as a preferred or necessary element of sexual excitement.

sadomasochism (SM)   The combination of sadistic and masochistic motivations and behaviors. *See* sadism; masochism

sample   A subset of individuals from a population, used to estimate characteristics of the population.

scabies [SKAY-beez]   Almost microscopic mites that live between skin cells; they are often, but not always, sexually transmitted.

scrotum [SCROW-tum]   A muscular sac that hangs loosely behind the penis and that contains the testes.

secondary sexual characteristics   Nongenital characteristics specific to each sex, such as breasts in females, and facial hair and a deepened voice in males.

self-disclosure   The revelation of one's needs, values, emotions, and feelings to another person.

self-monitoring   The tendency to monitor one's behavior and modify it depending on the social situation in which one finds oneself.

semen [see-men]   A sticky, off-white substance consisting of sperm and seminal fluid; during ejaculation about a teaspoonful is expelled through the urethral opening on the penile glans. Also called *ejaculate*.

seminal fluid   The fluid ejaculated, along with sperm, when a man has an orgasm.

seminal vesicles   Two male glands that produce a sticky, alkaline secretion that nourishes sperm and makes them capable of movement.

seminiferous tubules   Thin, convoluted tubes in the testes where sperm production takes place.

sensate focus   The process of touching a partner's body (except for the genitals and a female partner's breasts) and communicating about likes and dislikes; when conducted in a non-goal-oriented manner, it can reduce performance pressure and increase sensual pleasure.

seroconversion   A change in status from one in which no antibodies to an infectious agent are evident to one in which such antibodies are evident; indicates exposure to the infectious agent.

sex   A term used to refer to sexual activities, sexual urges or motives, or genital or anatomical status as male or female.

sex chromosomes   The pair of chromosomes that determines the genetic sex of an embryo; females normally have two X chromosomes, whereas males normally have an X and a Y.

sex flush   A measles-like rash that may cover the upper abdomen and spread to the chest during sexual arousal.

sex role   *See* gender role

sex typing   The developmental process by which cultural gender roles are acquired.

sexology   The scientific study of human sexuality.

sexual aversion   Persistent or extreme aversion to and avoidance of sexual contact with a partner; it is marked by anxiety and even panic in sexual situations.

sexual desire discrepancy   A marked difference between sexual partners in sexual desire, leading to disagreement about how frequently sexual activity should take place.

sexual harassment   Unwanted sexual remarks or advances; it often involves sexual demands or threats by someone in a higher position of power than the person at whom the harassment is directed.

sexual orientation   One's orientation to sexual partners of either the same or the other sex; a person's sexual orientation may be homosexual, heterosexual, bisexual, or ambivalent.

sexual response cycle   The sequence of physiological reactions in human sexual arousal; some descriptions also include psychological reactions.

sexual scripts   Learned and culturally shared norms that define what kinds of stimuli are erotic and what situations are appropriate for sexual behavior.

sexual surrogate   In sex therapy, a person who serves as a temporary sexual partner when the client does not have a partner who can participate in the treatment; the use of sexual surrogates is controversial.

sexuality   A term encompassing the psychological, physical, and social qualities that contribute to the subjective sense of oneself as a sexual person.

sexually transmitted disease (STD)   Any infection or disease spread exclusively or primarily by sexual contact; the term includes but is not limited to conditions traditionally called *venereal diseases*.

shaft   *See* clitoral shaft; penile shaft

smegma   A pungent, waxy material secreted by small glands on the underside of the penile glans.

social exchange theory   The theory, in social psychology, that the decision to begin or continue a relationship depends on the same kinds of factors that operate in the economic marketplace, i.e., rewards, costs, expectations, and available or perceived alternatives.

sonogram   *See* ultrasound scan

spectatoring   Masters and Johnson's term for mentally monitoring and evaluating one's own behavior and responses during sexual activity.

sperm   The male reproductive cell; when mature, it can fertilize an ovum.

spermicides   Chemicals that destroy or immobilize sperm.

spermatic cord   A rubber-like tube that encases part of the vas deferens.

spermatogenesis [sper-ma-toh-GEN-i-sus]   Sperm production; it occurs in the seminiferous tubules of the testes.

spongy body   A chamber of spongy tissue in the penis; the urethral tube runs down its center. Also called *corpus spongiosum*.

squeeze technique   A treatment for premature ejaculation that involves stimulating the penis manually until ejaculation is imminent, then squeezing the penis in a particular manner to eliminate the man's urge to ejaculate.

statutory rape   Sexual relations with someone below the legal age of consent.

STD   *See* sexually transmitted disease

sterility   The complete and permanent absence of fertility; the inability to reproduce.

sterilization   Surgery performed to induce permanent infertility.

stop-start technique   A treatment for premature ejaculation that involves stimulating the penis manually until ejaculation is imminent, then discontinuing the stimulation until arousal subsides.

storge [stor-gay]   A Greek term denoting attachment or affectionate love.

surrogate mother   A woman who volunteers to carry to term and bear a child for someone else; conception is usually accomplished through artificial insemination or in vitro fertilization.

survey   A research method that uses questionnaires or interviews to ask people about their experiences, attitudes, or opinions.

swinging   Extramarital sex in which both partners participate; it may include mate swapping, group sex, or sex between a couple and another man or woman. The term is also used in a more general sense to mean sexually free and uninhibited.

sympathetic nervous system   A subdivision of the autonomic nervous system generally responsible for activating the organism and increasing energy output.

sympto-thermal method   A fertility awareness method of birth control that combines the cervical mucus and basal body temperature methods.

syphilis   A blood-borne sexually transmitted disease caused by the *Treponema pallidum* bacterium.

testes [TES-teez]   Two egg-shaped organs, located in the scrotum, that produce sperm and testosterone; the male gonads. The testes are also called *testicles*.

testicles   *See* testes

testosterone [tes-TOS-tur-own]   A principle "male" sex hormone (androgen), produced by the testes.

toxic shock syndrome (TSS)   A systemic infection thought to be caused by toxins produced by bacteria that live normally in the nose or vagina or on the skin; it occurs most often in menstruating women using highly absorbent tampons.

transsexual   A person who feels trapped in a body that is at odds with his or her true physiological gender.

transvestism   Dressing in the clothing of the other sex for the purpose of sexual arousal and gratification.

triangular theory of love   Robert Sternberg's theory that love consists of an emotional component (intimacy), a motivational component (passion), and a cognitive component (commitment).

trichomoniasis [trick-oh-mon-I-uh-sis]   A vaginal infection, usually sexually transmitted, that is caused by a one-celled protozoan called *Trichomonas vaginalis*.

trimester   A three-month period; the term is used to describe the phases of pregnancy.

tubal pregnancy   The development of a fertilized egg inside a Fallopian tube; it is the most common type of ectopic pregnancy.

tubal sterilization   A method of sterilization in which the Fallopian tubes are cut, cauterized, clamped, or tied off.

ultrasound scan   A diagnostic imaging technique that uses reflected high-frequency sound waves to examine internal body structures; one of its applications is the detection of fetal abnormalities. Also called a *sonogram*.

umbilical cord   The connecting structure between the placenta and an embryo or fetus.

urethra [you-REE-thruh]   The tube that carries urine from the bladder during urination, and, in males, semen during ejaculation.

urethral bulb   The part of the urethra in which seminal fluid is trapped during the emission stage of ejaculation.

urethral opening   The external opening of the urethra.

urethritis   An infection or inflammation of the urethra.

urophilia   Sexual interest in and arousal to urine.

uterus [YOU-ter-is]   The organ in which a fertilized egg develops during pregnancy; it is located behind the vagina, between the bladder and the rectum. Also called *womb*.

vacuum curettage   An early-abortion technique in which the embryonic or fetal material is suctioned out of the uterus.

vagina   A flexible, sheathlike canal that receives the penis during heterosexual intercourse, that serves as the passageway for the fetus during birth, and through which menstrual fluid is discharged.

vaginismus [vag-in-IZ-mus]   A condition in which muscles around the lower third of the vagina contract spasmodically and involuntarily; the spasms cause discomfort or pain and interfere with intercourse.

vaginitis   An inflammation of the vagina.

varicocele [VAR-i-koh-SEAL]   A varicose vein in the scrotum; it can cause infertility.

vas deferens [vaz DEF-ur-ens]   A duct that conveys sperm away from the epididymis. Plural: *vasa deferentia*.

vasectomy   A sterilization technique in which the vas deferens is cut, cauterized, clamped, or tied off.

vasocongestion   Engorgement of bodily organs and tissues with blood.

venereal disease (VD)   *See* sexually transmitted disease

vestibular bulbs   Erectile tissue located between the minor lips on each side of the vaginal opening.

volunteer bias   A bias in research findings due to the use of volunteers rather than a representative sample.

voyeurism   The act of covertly watching other persons who are nude, undressing, or engaged in sexual activity, for the purpose of sexual gratification.

vulva   The female external genitals.

withdrawal   An undependable contraceptive measure in which the penis is withdrawn before ejaculation. Also called *coitus interruptus*.

Wolffian ducts   Embryonic structures that develop, in males, into the vas deferens, epididymis, and seminal vesicles.

zoophilia [ZOH-uh-FIL-ee-uh]   Sexual interest in animals. Also called *bestiality*.

zygote   A fertilized egg cell.

References

●

Abramson, P. R. 1973. The relationship of the frequency of masturbation to several aspects of personality and behavior. *Journal of Sex Research* 9:132–42.

Adami, H. O., Persson, I., Hoover, R., Schairer, C., & Bergkvist, L. 1989. Risk of cancer in women receiving hormone replacement therapy. *International Journal of Cancer* 44:833–39.

Adams, G. R. 1981. The effects of physical attractiveness on the socialization process. *In:* G. W. Lucker, K. A. Ribbens, & A. McNamara, Jr. (Eds.), *Psychological aspects of facial form* (Craniofacial Growth Series). Ann Arbor: University of Michigan Press.

Adams, J., & Rubin, A. 1984. Outcomes of sexually open marriages: A five year follow-up. Paper presented at the Eastern Region meeting of the Society for the Scientific Study of Sex, Philadelphia.

Addiego, F., Belzer, E. G., Jr., Comolli, J., Moger, W., Perry, J. D., & Whipple, B. 1981. Female ejaculation: A case study. *Journal of Sex Research* 17:13–21.

Adler, J. D., & Boxley, R. L. 1985. The psychological reactions to infertility: Sex roles and coping styles. *Sex Roles* 12(3/4):271–86.

Adler, N. E., David, H. P., Major, B. N., Roth, S. H., Russo, N. F., & Wyatt, G. E. 1990. Psychological responses after abortion. *Science* 248:41–44.

Ageton, S. S. 1983. *Sexual assault among adolescents.* Lexington, MA: Heath.

Aguero, J. E., Bloch, L., & Byrne, D. 1984. The relationships among sexual beliefs, attitudes, experience, and homophobia. *Journal of Homosexuality* 11:95–107.

Akert, R. M. 1984. Terminating romantic relationships: The role of personal responsibility and gender. Paper presented at the annual meeting of the American Psychological Association, Toronto.

Alagna, S. W., & Hamilton, J. A. 1986. Science in the service of mythology: The psychopathologizing of menstruation. Paper presented at the annual meeting of the American Psychological Association, Washington, D.C.

Algood, C., Newell, G., & Johnson, D. 1988. Viral etiology of testicular tumors. *Journal of Urology* 139:308–10.

Allgeier, E. R. 1981. The influence of androgynous identification on heterosexual relations. *Sex Roles* 7:321–30.

Alter-Reid, K., Gibbs, M. S., Lachenmeyer, J. R., Sigal, J., & Massoth, N. A. 1986. Sexual abuse of children: A review of the empirical findings. *Clinical Psychology Review* 6:249–66.

Althof, S. E., Turner, L. A., Levine, S. B., & Risen, C. et al. 1987. Intracavernosal injection in the treatment of impotence: A prospective study of sexual, psychological, and marital functioning. *Journal of Sex & Marital Therapy* 13:155–67.

Altman, I. 1974. The communication of interpersonal attitudes: An ecological approach. *In* T. L. Huston (Ed.), *Foundations of interpersonal attraction.* New York: Academic Press.

Altman, I., & Taylor, D. A. 1973. *Social penetration: The development of interpersonal relationships.* New York: Holt, Rinehart and Winston.

Altrocchi, J. 1980. *Abnormal behavior.* New York: Harcourt Brace Jovanovich.

Alzate, H. 1985. Vaginal eroticism: A replication study. *Archives of Sexual Behavior* 14:529–37.

Alzate, H., & Londono, M. 1984. Vaginal erotic sensitivity. *Journal of Sex and Marital Therapy* 10:49–56.

Amberson, J. I., & Hoon, P. W. 1985. Hemodynamics of sequential orgasm. *Archives of Sexual Behavior* 14:351–60.

American Psychiatric Association. 1987. *Diagnostic and statistical manual of mental disorders.* 3rd ed., rev. Washington, D.C.: American Psychiatric Association.

Antill, J. K. 1983. Sex role complementarity versus similarity in married couples. *Journal of Personality and Social Psychology* 45:145–55.

Apfelbaum, B. 1980. The diagnosis and treatment of retarded ejaculation. *In* S. R. Leiblum & L. A. Pervin (Eds.), *Principles and practice of sex therapy*. New York: Guilford Press.

Archer, R. L. 1980. Self-disclosure. *In* D. M. Wegner & R. R. Vallacher (Eds.), *The self in social psychology*. New York: Oxford University Press.

Arnold, A. P., & Gorski, R. A. 1984. Gonadal steroid induction of structural sex differences in the central nervous system. *Annual Review of Neuroscience* 7:413–42.

Atkeson, B. M., Calhoun, K. S., Resick, P. A., & Ellis, E. M. 1982. Victims of rape: Repeat assessment of depressive symptoms. *Journal of Consulting and Clinical Psychology* 50:96–102.

Atwood, J. D., & Gagnon, J. 1987. Masturbatory behavior in college youth. *Journal of Sex Education & Therapy* 13:35–42.

Aubrey, M. 1988. Rape victims: Public beliefs, diminished credibility, and case processing decisions. Paper presented at the annual meeting of the American Psychological Association, Atlanta, GA.

Austrom, D., & Hanel, K. 1985. Psychological issues of single life in Canada: An exploratory study. *International Journal of Women's Studies* 8:12–23.

Bachrach, C. 1984. Contraceptive practice among American women, 1973–1982. *Family Planning Perspectives* 16:253–59.

Bagley, C., & Young, L. 1987. Juvenile prostitution and child sex abuse: A controlled study. *Canadian Journal of Community Mental Health* 6:5–26.

Baldwin, J., & Baldwin, J. I. 1989. The socialization of homosexuality and heterosexuality in a non-Western society. *Archives of Sexual Behavior* 18:13–29.

Bancroft, J. 1984. Hormones and human sexual behavior. *Journal of Sex and Marital Therapy* 10: 3–21.

Bandura, A., & Huston, A. C. 1961. Identification as a process of incidental learning. *Journal of Abnormal and Social Psychology* 63:311–18.

Bandura, A., Ross, D., & Ross, S. A. 1963. A comparative test of the status envy, social power, and secondary reinforcement theories of identificatory learning. *Journal of Abnormal and Social Psychology* 67:527–34.

Bandura, A., & Walters, R. H. 1963. *Social learning and personality development*. New York: Holt, Rinehart and Winston.

Barbach, L. G. 1974. Group treatment of preorgasmic women. *Journal of Sex and Marital Therapy* 1:139–45.

Barbach, L. G. 1975. *For yourself: The fulfillment of female sexuality*. Garden City, NY: Doubleday.

Barbach, L. (Ed.). 1984. *Pleasures: Women write erotica*. New York: Perennial/Harper & Row.

Barlow, J. G., Sakheim, D. K., & Beck, J. G. 1983. Anxiety increases sexual arousal. *Journal of Abnormal Psychology* 92:49–54.

Baron, L., & Straus, M. A. 1986. Four theories of rape: A macrosociological analysis. *Social Problems* 34(5):467–89.

Barry, C., Bunch, C., & Castley, S. (Eds.). 1984. *International feminism: Networking against female sexual slavery*. New York: United Nations International Women's Tribune.

Bart, P. B. 1981. A study of women who both were raped and avoided rape. *Journal of Social Issues* 37:123–37.

Bart, P. B., & O'Brien, P. H. 1985. *Stopping rape: Successful survival strategies*. Elmsford, NY: Pergamon Press.

Bartell, G. D. 1970. Group sex among the mid-Americans. *Journal of Sex Research* 6:113–30.

Bateson, M. C., & Goldsby, R. 1988. *Thinking AIDS: The social response to the biological threat*. Reading, MA: Addison-Wesley.

Baumgartner, A. 1983. "My daddy might have loved me": Student perceptions of differences between being male and being female. Paper published by the Institute for Equality in Education, Denver.

Baxter, D., Marshall, W., Barbaree, H., Davidson, P. P., & Malcolm, P. 1984. Deviant sexual behavior: Differentiating sex offenders by criminal and personal history, psychometric measures, and sexual response. *Criminal Justice and Behavior* 11:477–501.

Beach, F. A. 1977. Cross-species comparisons and the human heritage. *In* F. A. Beach (Ed.), *Human sexuality in four perspectives*. Baltimore: Johns Hopkins University Press.

Beck, J. G., Barlow, D. H., Sakheim, D. K., & Abrahamson, D. J. 1984. Sexual responding during anxiety: Clinical versus nonclinical patterns. Paper presented at the 18th annual meeting of the Association for the Advancement of Behavior Therapy, Philadelphia, PA.

Beckelman, L. 1986, August 3. Beyond the pill. *This World (San Francisco Examiner and Chronicle)*.

Becker, J., Skinner, L., Abel, G., Howell, J., & Bruce, K. 1982. The effects of sexual assault on rape and attempted rape victims. *Victimology: An International Journal* 7:106–13.

Beer, W. R. 1984. *Househusbands: Men and housework in American families*. South Hadley, MA: J. F. Bergin.

Beggs, V. E., Calhoun, K. S., & Wolchik, S. A. 1987. Sexual anxiety and female sexual arousal: A comparison of arousal during sexual anxiety stimuli and sexual pleasure stimuli. *Archives of Sexual Behavior* 16:311–19.

Bell, A. P., & Weinberg, M. S. 1978. *Homosexualities: A study of diversity among men and women*. New York: Simon and Schuster.

Bell, A. P., Weinberg, M. S., & Hammersmith, S. 1981. *Sexual preference: Its development in men and women*. Bloomington: Indiana University Press.

Bell, L. (Ed.). 1987. *Good girls/bad girls: Sex trade workers confront feminists*. Seattle, WA: The Seal Press.

Bell, R. R. 1966. *Premarital sex in a changing society*. Englewood Cliffs, NJ: Prentice-Hall.

Bem, S. L. 1974. The measurement of psychological androgyny. *Journal of Consulting and Clinical Psychology* 42:155–62.

Bem, S. L. 1981. Gender schema theory: A cognitive account of sex typing. *Psychological Review* 88:354–64.

Bem, S. L. 1985. Androgyny and gender schema theory: A conceptual and empirical integration. *In* T. B. Sonderegger (Ed.), *Nebraska symposium on motivation, Vol. 32. Psychology and gender*. Lincoln: University of Nebraska Press.

Bengtsson, C. 1989. Aspects of hormone replacement therapy in the post-menopause. *Maturitas* 11:35–41.

Benjamin, H. 1966. *The transsexual phenomenon*. New York: Warner.

Bennett, N. G., Blanc, A. K., & Bloom, D. E. 1988. Commitment and the modern union: Assessing the link between premarital cohabitation and subsequent marital stability. *American Sociological Review* 53:127–38.

Bennett, N. G., Bloom, D. E., & Craig, P. H. 1989. The divergence of black and white marriage patterns. *American Journal of Sociology* 95:692–722.

Bennett, S. M. 1984. Family environment for sexual learning as a function of fathers' involvement in family work and discipline. *Adolescence* 19:609–27.

Benton, C., Hernandez, A., Schmidt, A., Schmitz, M., Stone, A., & Weiner, B. 1983. Is hostility linked with affiliation among males and with achievement among females? A critique of Pollak and Gilligan. *Journal of Personality and Social Psychology* 45:1167–71.

Berard, E. J. 1989. The sexuality of spinal cord injured women: Physiology and pathophysiology. A review. *Paraplegia* 27:99–112.

Berger, G., Hank, L., Rauzi, T., & Simkins, L. 1987. Detection of sexual orientation by heterosexuals and homosexuals. *Journal of Homosexuality* 13:83–100.

Bergler, E., & Kroger, W. S. 1954. *Kinsey's myth of female sexuality*. New York: Grune & Stratton.

Bernstein, A. C. 1976, January. How children learn about sex and birth. *Psychology Today* 9(8):31–35, 66.

Berscheid, E. 1980. Commentary on "Love at first sight: A Myth" by B. I. Murstein. *Medical Aspects of Human Sexuality* 14(9):41.

Berscheid, E. 1981. An overview of the psychological effects of physical attractiveness and some comments upon the psychological effects of knowledge of the effects of physical attractiveness. *In* G. W. Lucker, K. Ribbins, & J. A. McNamara (Eds.), *Psychological aspects of facial form* (Craniofacial Growth Series). Ann Arbor: University of Michigan Press.

Berscheid, E. 1985. Interpersonal attraction. *In* G. Lindzey & E. Aronson (Eds.), *Handbook of social psychology, Vol. 2*. New York: Random House/Erlbaum.

Berscheid, E., & Campbell, B. 1981. The changing longevity of heterosexual close relationships: A commentary and forecast. *In* M. Lerner (Ed.), *The justice motive in times of scarcity and change*. New York: Plenum.

Berscheid, E., & Fei, J. 1977. Perceived dependency, insecurity, and love in heterosexual relationships: The eternal triangle. Mimeographed report.

Berscheid, E., & Walster, E. 1974. A little bit about love. *In* T. L. Huston (Ed.), *Foundations of interpersonal attraction*. New York: Academic Press.

Berscheid, E., & Walster, E. 1978. *Interpersonal attraction*. 2nd ed. Reading, MA: Addison-Wesley.

Bieber, I., Dain, H. J., Dince, P. R. et al. 1962. *Homosexuality: A psychoanalytic study of male homosexuals*. New York: Basic Books.

Biema, D. V. 1987, April 13. What's gone wrong with teen sex? *People:* 110–21.

Billings, E. L., Billings, J. J., & Catarinch, M. 1974. *Atlas of the ovulation method.* Collegeville, MN: Liturgical press.

Blanchard, R., Steiner, B. W., & Clemmensen, L. H. 1985. Gender dysphoria, gender reorientation, and the clinical management of transsexualism. *Journal of Consulting and Clinical Psychology* 53:295–304.

Blood, R. O. Jr., 1967. *Love match and arranged marriage.* New York: The Free Press.

Blood, R. O., Jr., & Wolfe, D. M. 1960. *Husbands and wives: The dynamics of married living.* New York: The Free Press.

Bloom, D. E., & Bennett, N. G. 1986. Childless couples. *American Demographics* 8:22–25.

Blume, J. 1970. *Are you there God? It's me, Margaret.* New York: Dell.

Blumstein, P., & Schwartz, P. 1983. *American Couples.* New York: Morrow.

Bogdanich, W. 1987, November 2. Lax laboratories: The Pap test misses much cervical cancer through labs' errors. *Wall Street Journal:* 1(W).

Bohlen, J. G., Held, J. P., & Sanderson, M. O. 1980. The male orgasm: Pelvic contractions measured by anal probe. *Archives of Sexual Behavior* 9:503–21.

Bohlen, J. S., Held, J. P., Sanderson, M. O., & Ahlgren, A. 1982. The female orgasm: Pelvic contractions. *Archives of Sexual Behavior* 11:367–86.

Boisso, C. V., Lutz, D. J., & Gray, S. A. 1989. Psychological characteristics of adolescent males who have been sexually abused. Paper presented at the annual meeting of the American Psychological Association, New Orleans, LA.

Booth, A., & Johnson, D. 1988. Premarital cohabitation and marital success. *Journal of Family Issues* 9:255–72.

Boston Lesbian Psychologies Collective. 1987. Introduction. *In* Boston Lesbian Psychologies Collective (Ed.), *Lesbian psychologies: Exploration and challenges.* Urbana and Chicago: University of Illinois Press.

Boston Women's Health Book Collective. 1976. *Our bodies, ourselves: A book by and for women.* 2nd ed. New York: Simon and Schuster.

Boston Women's Health Book Collective. 1984. *The new our bodies, ourselves.* New York: Simon and Schuster (Touchstone).

Botwin, C. 1985. *Is there sex after marriage?* Boston: Little, Brown.

Bouton, K. 1987, April. Fertility and family—How my obsession with pregnancy almost obscured my real goal. *Ms.:* 92ff.

Braiker, H. B., & Kelley, H. H. 1979. Conflict in the development of close relationships. *In* R. L. Burgess & T. L. Huston (Eds.), *Social exchange in developing relationships.* New York: Academic Press.

Brasch, R. 1973. *How did sex begin?* New York: David McKay.

Brecher, E. M. 1979. *The sex researchers.* Expanded ed. San Francisco: Specific Press.

Brehm, S. 1985. *Intimate relationships.* New York: Random House.

Bremer, J. 1959. *Asexualization: A follow-up study of 244 cases.* New York: Macmillan.

Bressler, L. C., & Lavender, A. D. 1986. Sexual fulfillment of heterosexual, bisexual, and homosexual women. *Journal of Homosexuality* 13:109–22.

Bretschneider, J. G., & McCoy, N. L. 1988. Sexual interest and behavior in healthy 80- to 102-year-olds. *Archives of Sexual Behavior* 17:109–29.

Briere, J., Malamuth, N. M., & Check, J. V. 1985. Sexuality and rape-supportive beliefs. *International Journal of Women's Studies* 8:398–403.

Bringle, R. G., Roach, S., Adler, C., & Evenbeck, S. 1977. Correlates of jealousy. Paper presented at the annual meeting of the Midwestern Psychological Association, Chicago, IL.

Brisson, J., Verreault, R., Morrison, A. S., Tennina, S., & Meyer, F. 1989. Diet, mammographic features of breast tissue, and breast cancer risk. *American Journal of Epidemiology* 130: 14–24.

Brock, B. V., Selke, S., Benedetti, J., Douglas, J. M., Jr., & Corey, L. 1990. Frequency of asymptomatic shedding of herpes simplex virus in women with genital herpes. *Journal of the American Medical Association* 263:418–20.

Brodsky, S. L. 1976. Prevention of rape: Deterrence by the potential victim. *In* M. J. Walker & S. L. Brodsky (Eds.), *Sexual assault.* Lexington, MA: Heath.

Brody, J. E. 1984, March 27. "Autoerotic death" of youths causes widening concern. *New York Times* 133:17(N), C1(L).

Brooks-Gunn, J., & Furstenberg, F. F. 1989. Adolescent sexual behavior. *American Psychologist* 44:249–57.

Brooks-Gunn, J., & Warren, M. P. 1988. The psychological significance of secondary sexual characteristics in nine- to eleven-year-old girls. *Child Development* 59:1061–69.

Broude, G. J., & Green, S. J. 1976. Cross cultural codes on twenty sexual attitudes and practices. *Ethology* 15:409–29.

Brown, L. 1983, April. Feminist sperm bank interest compounding daily. *Psychology of Women* (Newsletter of Division 35 of the American Psychological Association) 10(2):8–9.

Browne, A., & Finkelhor, D. 1986. Impact of child sexual abuse: A review of the literature. *Psychological Bulletin* 99:66–77.

Brownmiller, S. 1975. *Against our will: Men, women and rape.* New York: Simon and Schuster.

Bruckner, D. F., & Johnson, P. E. 1987. Treatment for adult male victims of childhood sexual abuse. *Social Casework* 68:81–87.

Bryant, J. 1985. Testimony to the Attorney General's Commission on Pornography Hearings, Houston, Texas. Unpublished transcript: pp. 128–57. [Cited in Russell, 1988.]

Bryson, J. B. 1977. Situational determinants of the expression of jealousy. Paper presented at the annual meeting of the American Psychological Association, San Francisco, CA.

Buchanan, J. 1985. Ecstasy in the emergency department. *Clinical Toxicology Update* 7(4):1–6.

Bullough, V. L. 1964. *The history of prostitution.* New Hyde Park, NY: University Books.

Bullough, V. L. 1976. *Sexual variance in society and history.* New York: John Wiley & Sons.

Bumpass, L., & Sweet, J. 1989. National estimates of cohabitation. *Demography* 26(4):615–25.

Burch, B. 1987. Barriers to intimacy: Conflicts over power, dependency, and nurturing in lesbian relationships. *In* Boston Lesbian Psychologies Collective (Ed.), *Lesbian psychologies: Explorations and challenges.* Urbana and Chicago: University of Illinois Press.

Burgess, A. W., & Holmstrom, L. L. 1974. Rape trauma syndrome. *American Journal of Psychiatry* 131:981–86.

Burgess, E. W., & Wallin, P. W. 1943. Homogamy in social characteristics. *American Journal of Sociology* 48:109–24.

Burke, D., Burnett, G., & Levenstein, P. 1978. Menstrual symptoms: New data from a double-blind study. Paper presented at the annual meeting of the Western Psychological Association, San Francisco, CA.

Burke, R. J., Weir, T., & Harrison, D. 1976. Disclosure of problems and tensions experienced by marital partners. *Psychological Reports* 38:531–42.

Burstyn, V. (Ed.). 1985. *Women against censorship.* Vancouver: Douglas McIntyre.

Buster, J. E., Bustillo, M., Thorneycroft, I. H. et al. 1983, July 23. Non-surgical transfer of in vivo fertilised donated ova to five infertile women: Report of two pregnancies [letter]. *Lancet* 2(8343):223–24.

Buunk, B., & Bringle, R. G. 1987. Jealousy in love relationships. *In* D. Perlman & S. Duck (Eds.), *Intimate relationships: Development, dynamics, and deterioration.* Newbury Park, CA: Sage Publications.

Byrne, D. 1977. The imagery of sex. *In* J. Money & H. Musaph (Eds.), *Handbook of sexology.* Amsterdam: Elsevier/North Holland.

Byrne, D., & Lamberth, J. 1971. The effect of erotic stimuli on sex arousal, evaluative responses, and subsequent behavior. *In Technical Report of the Commission on Obscenity and Pornography, Vol. 8.* Washington, D.C.: U.S. Government Printing Office.

Caignon, D., & Groves, G. 1987. *Her wits about her: Self-defense success stories by women.* New York: Harper & Row.

Calhoun, L., Selby, J., & King, H. E. 1981. The influence of pregnancy on sexuality: A review of the current literature. *Journal of Sex Research* 17:139–51.

Camarena, P., & Sarigiani, P. 1985. Gender influences on intimacy development in early adolescence. Paper presented at the annual meeting of the American Psychological Association, Los Angeles, CA.

Campbell, C. 1976, August. What happens when we get the manchild pill? *Psychology Today* 10(3):86–88, 90–91.

Carey, P., Howards, S., & Vance, M. 1988. Transdermal testosterone treatment of hypogonadal men. *Journal of Urology* 140:76–79.

Carmen, A., & Moody, H. *Working women: The subterranean world of street prostitution.* New York: Harper & Row.

Carnes, P. J. 1983. *The sexual addiction.* Minneapolis, MN: CompCare.

Carson, S. 1988. Sex selection: The ultimate in family planning. *Fertility and Sterility* 50:16–19.

Cassell, C. 1984. *Swept away: Why women fear their own sexuality.* New York: Simon and Schuster.

Castleman, M. 1985, March/April. Toxics and male infertility. *Sierra* 70:49–52.

Chamberlain, D. B. 1989. Babies remember pain. *Pre- & Peri-Natal Psychology Journal* 3:297–310.

Chambliss, D. L., & DeMarco, D. 1985. Pubococcygens, Kegel exercises, and female coital orgasm: Reply to Jaynes. *Journal of Consulting and Clinical Psychology* 53:271–72.

Chance, P. 1975. Facts that liberated the gay community [Interview with Evelyn Hooker]. *Psychology Today* 9(7):52, 54–55, 101.

Chappell, D., & James, J. 1976. Victim selection and apprehension from the rapist's perspective: A preliminary investigation. Paper presented at the Second International Symposium on Victimology, Boston, MA.

Check, J. V. 1985. *The Hostility Toward Women Scale.* (Unpublished doctoral dissertation). Winnipeg, Canada: University of Manitoba.

Cherlin, A. 1981. *Marriage, divorce, remarriage.* Cambridge, MA: Harvard University Press.

Chesser, E. 1971. *Human aspects of sexual deviation.* London: Jerrolds Publishing.

Chiappa, J. A., & Forish, J. J. 1976. *The VD book.* New York: Holt, Rinehart and Winston.

Chow, J. M., Yonekura, M. L., Richwald, G. A., Greenland, S., Sweet, R. L., & Schachter, J. 1990. The association between chlamydia trachomatis and ectopic pregnancy; A matched-pair case-control study. *Journal of the American Medical Association* 263:3164–67.

Cirese, S. 1985. *Quest: A search for self.* 2nd ed. New York: Holt, Rinehart and Winston.

Clark, M. S., & Reis, H. T. 1988. Interpersonal processes in close relationships. *Annual Review of Psychology* 39:609–72.

Cochran, S. D. 1988. Risky behavior and disclosure: Is it safe if you ask? Paper presented at the annual meeting of the American Psychological Association, Atlanta, GA.

Cochran, S. D., & Mays, V. M. 1990. Sex, lies, and HIV [letter]. *New England Journal of Medicine* 322:774–75.

Cocks, J. 1982, July 12. How long till equality? *Time:* 20–29.

Cocores, J., & Gold, M. 1989, February. Substance abuse and sexual dysfunction. *Medical Aspects of Human Sexuality:* 22–31.

Cohen, M. L., Seghorn, T., & Calmas, W. 1969. Sociometric study of sex offenders. *Journal of Abnormal Psychology* 74:249–55.

Cohen, S. 1981. *The substance abuse problems.* New York: Haworth Press.

Cohen, S. 1985. *The substance abuse problems: Vol. II. New issues for the 1980s.* New York: Haworth Press.

Cohen, Y. 1978, July. The disappearance of the incest taboo. *Human Nature* 1(7):72–78.

Coles, R., & Stokes, G. 1985. *Sex and the American teenager.* New York: Harper & Row.

Collins, J. A., Wrixon, W., Janes, L. B., & Wilson, E. H. 1983. Treatment-independent pregnancy among infertile couples. *New England Journal of Medicine* 309:1201–06.

Comfort, A. (Ed.). 1972. *The joy of sex: A cordon bleu guide to lovemaking.* New York: Crown.

Cooper, A. J. 1981. Short-term treatment in sexual dysfunction: A review. *Comprehensive Psychiatry* 22:206–17.

Cornelius, D. 1982. *Who cares? Handbook on sex education and counseling services for disabled people.* Baltimore: University Park Press.

Cotton, D., & Groth, A. N. 1982. Inmate rape: Prevention and intervention. *Journal of Prison and Jail Health* 2:45–57.

Court, J. H. 1984. Sex and violence: A ripple effect. *In* N. M. Malamuth & E. Donnerstein (Eds.), *Pornography and sexual aggression.* Orlando, FL: Academic Press.

Courtois, C. A. 1988. *Healing the incest wound: Adult survivors in therapy.* New York: Norton.

Cowan, G. 1984. The double standard in age-discrepant relationships. *Sex Roles* 11:17–23.

Cowan, G. 1989. The pairing of sex and violence in R-rated videocassettes. Paper presented at the annual meeting of the American Psychological Association, New Orleans, LA.

Cowan, G., Hayes, P., Anderson, B., & Kelley, D. 1989. Who watches slasher films? Paper presented at the annual meeting of the American Psychological Association, New Orleans, LA.

Cowan, G., Lee, C., Levy, D., & Snyder, D. 1988. Dominance and inequality in x-rated videocassettes. *Psychology of Women Quarterly* 12:299–311.

Cox, D. 1988. Incidence and nature of male genital exposure behavior as reported by college women. *Journal of Sex Research* 24:227–34.

Craig, M. E., Kalichman, S. C., & Follingstad, D. R. 1989. Verbal coercive sexual behavior among college students. *Archives of Sexual Behavior* 18:421–34.

Crapo, L. 1985, Winter. It's a girl, it's a boy. *Stanford Magazine:* 24–29.

Crenshaw, T., Goldberg, J., & Stern, W. 1987. Pharmacologic modification of psychosexual dysfunction. *Journal of Sex and Marital Therapy* 13:239–50.

Crewdson, J. 1988. *By silence betrayed: Sexual abuse of children in America*. Boston: Little, Brown & Co Inc.

Crosby, F. 1986. Work. *In* C. Tavris (Ed.), *EveryWoman's emotional well-being*. New York: Doubleday.

Croughan, J. L., Saghir, M., Cohen, R., & Robins, E. 1981. A comparison of treated and untreated male cross-dressers. *Archives of Sexual Behavior* 10:515–23.

Crouse, B. B., & Mehrabian, A. 1977. Affiliation of opposite-sexed strangers. *Journal of Research in Personality* 11:38–47.

Cutler, W. B., Preti, G. et al. 1986. Human axillary secretions influence women's menstrual cycles: The role of donor extract from men. *Hormones and Behavior* 20:463–73.

D'Augelli, J. F., & D'Augelli, A. R. 1979. Sexual involvement and relationship development: A cognitive approach. *In* R. W. Burgess & T. L. Huston (Eds.), *Social exchange in developing relationships*. New York: Academic Press.

D'Emilio, J., & Freedman, E. B. 1988. *Intimate matters: A history of sexuality in America*. New York: Harper & Row.

Danjou, P., Alexandre, L., Warot, D., Lacomblez, L., & Puech, A. J. 1988. Assessment of erectogenic properties of apomorphine and yohimbine in man. *British Journal of Clinical Pharmacology* 26:733–39.

Dank, B. M. 1971. Coming out in the gay world. *Psychiatry* 34:180–97.

Darling, C. A., Davidson, J. K., & Conway-Welch, C. 1990. Female ejaculation: Perceived origins, the Grafenberg spot/area, and sexual responsiveness. *Archives of Sexual Behavior* 19:29–47.

DATTA Panel. 1989. Diagnostic and therapeutic technology assessment. Intrauterine devices. *Journal of the American Medical Association* 261:2127–30.

Dauw, D. C. 1988. Evaluating the effectiveness of the SECS' surrogate-assisted sex therapy model. *Journal of Sex Research* 24:269–75.

Davenport, W. H. 1977. Sex in cross-cultural perspective. *In* F. A. Beach (Ed.), *Human sexuality in four perspectives*. Baltimore: Johns Hopkins University Press.

Davidson, J. K., & Darling, C. A. 1988. The sexually experienced woman: Multiple sex partners and sexual satisfaction. *Journal of Sex Research* 24:141–54.

Davies, N. 1984. *The rampant god: Eros throughout the world*. New York: William Morrow.

Davis, A. J. 1968, December. Sexual assaults in the Philadelphia prison system and sheriff's vans. *Trans-Action* 6(2): 8–16.

Davis, N. J. 1978. Prostitution: Identity, career, and legal-economic enterprise. *In* J. M. Henslin & E. Sagarin (Eds.), *The sociology of sex: An introductory reader*. New York: Schocken Books.

Davison, G. C. 1976. Homosexuality: The ethical challenge. *Journal of Consulting and Clinical Psychology* 44:157–62.

De Amicis, L. A., Goldberg, D. C., LoPiccolo, J., Friedman, J., & Davies, L. 1985. Clinical follow-up of couples treated for sexual dysfunction. *Archives of Sexual Behavior* 14:467–89.

de Monteflores, C., & Schultz, S. J. 1978. Coming out: Similarities and differences for lesbians and gay men. *Journal of Social Issues* 34(3):59–72.

de Waal, F. 1989. *Peacemaking among primates*. Cambridge, MA: Harvard University Press.

Deaux, K., & Hanna, R. 1984. Courtship in the personals column: The influence of gender and sexual orientation. *Sex Roles* 11:363–75.

Degler, C. N. 1974. What ought to be and what was: Women's sexuality in the nineteenth century. *American Historical Review* 79:1467–90.

DeLamater, J., & MacCorquodale, P. 1979. *Premarital sexuality: Attitudes, relationships, behavior*. Madison: University of Wisconsin Press.

Delaney, J., Lupton, M. J., & Toth, E. 1988. *The curse: A cultural history of menstruation*. Rev. ed. Urbana and Chicago: University of Illinois Press.

Demare, D., Briere, J., & Lips, H. M. 1988. Violent pornography and self-reported likelihood of sexual aggression. *Journal of Research in Personality* 22:140–53.

DeMaris, A., & Leslie, G. R. 1984. Cohabitation with the future spouse: Its influence upon marital satisfaction and communication. *Journal of Marriage and the Family* 46:77–84.

Demos, J. A. 1970. *A little commonwealth: Family life in Plymouth Colony*. New York: Oxford University Press.

Denny, N., Field, J., & Quadagno, D. 1984. Sex differences in sexual needs and desires. *Archives of Sexual Behavior* 13:233–45.

Dermer, M., & Thiel, D. J. 1975. When beauty may fail. *Journal of Personality and Social Psychology* 31:1168–76.

Dion, K. K. 1986. Stereotyping based on physical attractiveness: Issues and conceptual perspectives. *In* C. P. Herman, M. P. Zanna, & E. T. Higgens (Eds.), *Physical appearance, stigma, and social behavior: The Ontario symposium on personality and social psychology (Vol. 3).* Hillsdale, NJ: Erlbaum.

Dion, K. K., Berscheid, E., & Walster, E. 1972. What is beautiful is good. *Journal of Personality and Social Psychology* 24:285–90.

Dion, K. K., & Stein, S. 1978. Physical attractiveness and interpersonal influence. *Journal of Experimental Social Psychology* 14:97–108.

DiVasto, P., Kaufman, A., Rosner, L., Jackson, R., Christy, J., & Pearson, S. B. T. 1984. The prevalence of sexually stressful events among females in the general population. *Archives of Sexual Behavior* 13:59–67.

Donnerstein, E. 1980. Aggressive erotica and violence against women. *Journal of Personality and Social Psychology* 39:269–77.

Donnerstein, E., & Berkowitz, L. 1981. Victim reactions in aggressive erotic films as a factor in violence against women. *Journal of Personality and Social Psychology* 41:710–24.

Donnerstein, E., Berkowitz, L. & Linz, D. 1986. Role of aggressive and sexual images in violent pornography. [Unpublished manuscript, University of Wisconsin, Madison; cited in Donnerstein, Linz, & Penrod, 1987.]

Donnerstein, E., Linz, D., & Penrod, S. 1987. *The question of pornography: Research findings and policy implications.* New York: Free Press.

Doress, P. B., Siegal, D. L., & The Midlife and Older Women Book Project (in cooperation with the Boston Women's Health Book Collective). 1987. *Ourselves, growing older: Women aging with knowledge and power.* New York: Simon and Schuster (Touchstone).

Dörner, G. 1976. *Hormones and brain differentiation.* Amsterdam: Elsevier.

Dörner, G., Rohde, W., Seidel, K., Haas, W., & Schott, G. 1976. On the evocability of a positive oestrogen feedback action on LH secretion in transsexual men and women. *Endokrinologie* 67:20–25.

Doshi, M. 1986. Accuracy of consumer performed in-home tests for early pregnancy detection. *American Journal of Public Health* 76:512–14.

Driscoll, R., Davis, K. E., & Lipitz, M. E. 1972. Parental interference and romantic love: The Romeo and Juliet effect. *Journal of Personality and Social Psychology* 24:1–10.

Duffy, S. M., & Rusbult, C. E. 1985/1986. Satisfaction and commitment in homosexual and heterosexual relationships. *Journal of Homosexuality* 12(2):1–23.

Dunn, M. E., & Trost, J. E. 1989. Male multiple orgasms: A descriptive study. *Archives of Sexual Behavior* 18:377–87.

Dworkin, A. 1985. Against the male flood: Censorship, pornography and equality. *Harvard Women's Law Journal* 8:1–29.

Dziech, B. W., & Weiner, L. 1984. *The lecherous professor: Sexual harassment on campus.* Boston: Beacon Press.

Earls, C., & David, H. 1989. A psychosocial study of male prostitution. *Archives of Sexual Behavior* 18:401–19.

Eckert, E. D., Bouchard, T. J., Bohlen, J., & Heston, L. L. 1986. Homosexuality in monozygotic twins reared apart. *British Journal of Homosexuality* 148:421–25.

Ehrenreich, B., & English, D. 1973. *Complaints and disorders: The sexual politics of sickness.* Old Westbury, N. Y.: Feminist Press.

Ehrhardt, A. A., & Baker, S. W. 1974. Fetal androgens, human central nervous system differentiation, and behavioral sex differences. *In* R. C. Friedman, R. M. Richard, & R. L. Vande Wiele (Eds.), *Sex differences in behavior.* New York: Wiley.

Ehrhardt, A., Epstein, R., & Money, J. 1968. Fetal androgens and female gender identity in the early-treated adrenogenital syndrome. *Johns Hopkins Medical Journal* 122:160–67.

Ehrhardt, A. A., & Meyer-Bahlburg, H. F. L. 1981. Effects of prenatal hormones on gender-related behavior. *Science* 211:1312–18.

Eisen, M., & Zellman, G. 1987. Changes in incidence of sexual intercourse of unmarried teenagers following a community-based sex education program. *Journal of Sex Research* 23:527–44.

Eisen, M., & Zellman, G. 1988. Sexual contraceptive knowledge deficits teenagers bring to school-based clinics. Paper presented at the annual meeting of the American Psychological Association, Atlanta, GA.

Elias, J., & Gebhard, P. 1969. Sexuality and sexual learning in childhood. *Phi Delta Kappan* 50:401–05.

Ellis, L., & Ames, M. A. 1987. Neurohormonal functioning and sexual orientation: A theory of homosexuality-heterosexuality. *Psychological Bulletin* 101:233–58.

Ellison, C. R. 1987. Intimacy-based sex therapy. Paper presented at the 8th World Congress for Sexology, Heidelberg, West Germany.

Englander-Golden, P., Whitmore, M. R., & Dienstbier, R. A. 1978. Menstrual cycle as focus of study and self-reports of moods and behaviors. *Motivation and Emotion* 2:75–86.

Esper, J. A., & Runge, C. J. 1988. The long-term effects of rape on lifestyle and psychological functioning. Paper presented at the annual meeting of the American Psychological Association, Atlanta, GA.

Estrich, S. 1987. *Real rape: How the legal system victimizes women who say no*. Cambridge, MA: Harvard University Press.

Ettinger, B. 1988. Prevention of osteoporosis: Treatment of estradiol deficiency. *Obstetrics and Gynecology* 72:12S–17S.

Exner, J. F., Jr., Wylie, J., Leura, A., & Parrill, T. 1977. Some psychological characteristics of prostitutes. *Journal of Personality Assessment* 41:474–85.

Fahrner, E. 1987. Sexual dysfunction in male alcohol addicts: Prevalence and treatment. *Archives of Sexual Behavior* 16:247–57.

Faich, G., Pearson, K., Fleming, D. et al. 1986. Toxic shock syndrome and the vaginal contraceptive sponge. *Journal of the American Medical Association* 255:216–18.

Fain, T. C., & Anderton, D. L. 1987. Sexual harassment: Organizational context and diffuse status. *Sex Roles* 17:291–311.

Falbo, T., & Peplau, L. A. 1980. Power strategies in intimate relationships. *Journal of Personality and Social Psychology* 38:618–28.

Farb, P. 1974. *Word play: What happens when people talk*. New York: Knopf.

Farber, L. H. 1966. "I'm sorry, dear." *In* R. Brecher & E. Brecher (Eds.), *An analysis of Human Sexual Response*. New York: New American Library.

Farkas, G. M. 1977. Drugs and sexual response. Paper presented at the annual meeting of the American Psychological Association, San Francisco, CA.

Farkas, G. M., Sine, L. F., & Evans, I. M. 1978. Personality, sexuality, and demographic differences between volunteers and nonvolunteers for a laboratory study of male sexual behavior. *Archives of Sexual Behavior* 7:513–20.

Fay, R. E., Turner, C. F., Klassen, A. D., & Gagnon, J. H. 1989. Prevalence and patterns of same-gender sexual contact among men. *Science* 243:338–48.

Feder, H. H. 1984. Hormones and sexual behavior. *Annual Review of Psychology* 35:165–200.

Feldman, D. A. 1986. AIDS health promotion and clinically applied anthropology. *In* Feldman, D. A., & Johnson, T. M. (Eds.), *The social dimensions of AIDS: Method and theory*. New York: Praeger.

Feshbach, N. 1985. Chronic maternal stress and its assessment. *In* J. N. Butcher & C. D. Spielberger (Eds.), *Advances in personality assessment, Vol. 5*. Hillsdale, NJ: Erlbaum.

Ficarrotto, T. J. 1985. Racism, sexism, and erotophobia: Attitudes of heterosexuals toward homosexuals. Paper presented at the annual meeting of the American Psychological Association, Los Angeles, CA.

Findlay, J., Place, V., & Snyder, P. 1989. Treatment of primary hypogonadism in men by the transdermal administration of testosterone. *Journal of Clinical Endocrinology and Metabolism* 68:369–73.

Finkelhor, D. 1979. *Sexually victimized children*. New York: Free Press.

Finkelhor, D. 1984. *Child sexual abuse: New theory and research*. New York: Free Press.

Finkelhor, D., & Browne, A. 1985. The traumatic impact of child sexual abuse: A conceptualization. *American Journal of Orthopsychiatry* 55:530–41.

Finkelhor, D., & Yllo, K. 1985. *License to rape: Sexual abuse of wives*. New York: Holt, Rinehart and Winston.

Finn, P., & McNeil, T. 1987. *The response of the criminal justice system to bias crime: an exploratory review*. Contract Report submitted to the National Institute of Justice, U.S. Department of Justice. (Available from Abt Associates, Inc., 55 Wheeler St., Cambridge, MA 02138-1168.)

Fischer, G. J. 1986. College student attitudes toward forcible date rape: I. Cognitive predictors. *Archives of Sexual Behavior* 15:457–66.

Fisher, B., Redmond, C., Poisson, R., Margolese, R. et al. 1989. Eight-year results of a randomized clinical trial comparing total mastectomy and lumpectomy with or without irradiation in the treatment of breast cancer. *New England Journal of Medicine* 320:822–28.

Fisher, T. D. 1987. Family communication and the sexual behavior and attitudes of college students. *Journal of Youth and Adolescence* 16:481–95.

Fisher, W. A., Byrne, D., White, L. A., & Kelley, K. 1988. Erotophobia-erotophilia as a dimension of personality. *Journal of Sex Research* 25:123–51.

Fisher, W. A., & Gray, J. 1988. Erotophobia-erotophilia and sexual behavior during pregnancy and postpartum. *Journal of Sex Research* 25:379–96.

Fitz, D., & Gerstenzang, S. 1978. *Anger in everyday life: When, where and with whom?* (ERIC Document Reproductive Service No. ED 160–966). St. Louis: University of Missouri.

Fitzgerald, R., & Fuller, L. 1982. I hear you knocking but you can't come in: The effects of reluctant respondents and refusers on sample survey estimates. *Sociological Methods and Research* 11(1):3–32.

Ford, C. S., & Beach, F. A. 1951. *Patterns of sexual behavior.* New York: Harper & Row.

Fordney-Settlage, D. S., Motoshima, M., & Tredway, D. R. 1973. Sperm transport from the external cervical os to the Fallopian tubes in women: A time and quantitation study. *Fertility and Sterility* 24:655.

Forrest, J. D., & Henshaw, S. K. 1983. What U.S. women think and do about contraception. *Family Planning Perspectives* 15:157–66.

Foxman, B., & Frerichs, R. R. 1985. Epidemiology of urinary tract infection: I. Diaphragm use and sexual intercourse. *American Journal of Public Health* 75:1308–13.

Frank, E., Anderson, A., & Rubinstein, D. 1978. Frequency of sexual dysfunction in "normal" couples. *New England Journal of Medicine* 299:111–15.

Franklin, D. 1984, February 18. Routine fetal scans nixed. *Science News:* 102.

Franklin, D. 1989, November 12. The anti-sperm vaccine. *This World (San Francisco Examiner & Chronicle):* 20.

Freedman, M. 1975, March. Homosexuals may be healthier than straights. *Psychology Today* 8(10):28, 30–32.

Freeman, D. 1983. *Margaret Mead and Samoa: The making and unmaking of an anthropological myth.* Cambridge, MA: Harvard University Press.

Freese, A. L. 1972, March. Group therapy with exhibitionists and voyeurs. *Social Work:* 44–52.

Freese, M., & Levitt, E. E. 1984. Relationships among intravaginal pressure, orgasmic function, parity factors, and urinary leakage. *Archives of Sexual Behavior* 13:261–68.

Freud, S. 1905. Three essays on the theory of sexuality. *In* J. Strachey (Ed.), *The standard edition of the complete psychological works of Sigmund Freud, Vol. 8.* 1964 edition. London: Hogarth Press and The Institute of Psycho-Analysis.

Freud, S. 1924. Some psychical consequences of the anatomical distinction between the sexes. *In* J. Strachey (Ed.), *The standard edition of the complete psychological works of Sigmund Freud, Vol. 19.* 1964 edition. London: The Hogarth Press and the Institute of Psycho-Analysis.

Freud, S. 1960. *A general introduction to psychoanalysis* (trans. J. Riviere). New York: Washington Square Press.

Freud, S. 1961. *Letters of Sigmund Freud, 1873–1939* (E. L. Freud, Ed.). London: Hogarth Press.

Friedl, E. 1975. *Women and men: An anthropologist's view.* New York: Holt, Rinehart and Winston.

Frisch, R. E., Wyshak, G., Witschi, J., Albright, N. L., Albright, T., & Schiff, I. 1987. Lower lifetime occurrence of breast cancer and cancers of the reproductive system among former college athletes. *International Journal of Fertility* 32(3):217–25.

Fromm, E. 1956. *The art of loving.* New York: Harper & Row.

Furstenberg, F. F., Brooks-Gunn, J., & Chase-Lansdale, L. 1989. Teenaged pregnancy and childbearing. *American Psychologist* 44:313–20.

Gaddis, A., & Brooks-Gunn, J. 1985. The male experience of pubertal change. *Journal of Youth & Adolescence* 14:61–69.

Gaffney, G. R., Lurie, S. F., & Berlin, F. S. 1984. Is there familial transmission of pedophilia? *Journal of Nervous and Mental Disease* 172:546–48.

Gagnon, J. H. 1979, March. Review of *Homosexualities: A study of diversity among men and women,* by A. P. Bell & M. S. Weinberg. *Human Nature* 2(3): 20, 22–24.

Gagnon, J. H. 1987. Science and the politics of pathology. *Journal of Sex Research* 23:120–23.

Gagnon, J. H. 1988. Sex research and sexual conduct in the era of AIDS. *Journal of Acquired Immunodeficiency Syndromes* 1:593–601.

Gagnon, J. H. 1990. Gender preferences in erotic relations, the Kinsey scale and sexual scripts. *In* D. P. McWhirter, J. M. Reinisch, & S. A. Sanders (Eds.), *Homosexuality-heterosexuality: Concepts of sexual orientation*. New York: Oxford University Press.

Gagnon, J., & Michaels, S. 1989. Answer no questions: The theory and practice of resistance to deviant categorization. [Unpublished draft manuscript.]

Gagnon, J. H., & Simon, W. 1973. *Sexual conduct: The social sources of human sexuality*. Chicago: Aldine.

Gagnon, J. H., & Simon, W. 1987. The sexual scripting of oral genital contacts. *Archives of Sexual Behavior* 16(1):1–25.

Gallagher, W. 1986, February. The etiology of orgasm. *Discover* 7(2):51–59.

Gallup Organization [D. Colasanto]. 1989, October 25. Tolerance of homosexuality on rise among public. *Gallup Poll News Service* 54(24):1–3.

Gambrell, R. D., Jr. 1990. Estrogen-progestogen replacement and cancer risk. *Hospital Practice* 25:81–85, 88, 91.

Garner, B., & Smith, R. W. 1977. Are there really any gay male athletes? An empirical survey. *Journal of Sex Research* 13:22–34.

Gaventa, S., Reingold, A. L., Hightower, A. W., Broome, C. V., Schwartz, B. et al. 1989. Active surveillance for toxic shock syndrome in the United States, 1986. *Review of Infectious Disease* 11(Suppl. 1): S28–S34.

Gay, P. 1984. *The bourgeois experience: Victoria to Freud. Vol. I: Education of the senses*. London: Oxford Press.

Gebhard, P. H. 1966. Factors in marital orgasm. *Journal of Social Issues* 22(2):88–95.

Gebhard, P. H. 1969. Fetishism and sadomasochism. *In* J. H. Masserman (Ed.), *Dynamics of deviant sexuality*. New York: Gruen & Stratton.

Gebhard, P. H. 1977. The acquisition of basic sex information. *Journal of Sex Research* 13:148–69.

Gebhard, P. H., & Johnson, A. B. 1979. *The Kinsey data: Marginal tabulations of the 1938–1963 interviews conducted by the Institute for Sex Research*. Philadelphia: Saunders.

Georgakopoulos, P. A., Dodos, D., & Mechleris, D. 1984. Sexuality in pregnancy and premature labour. *British Journal of Obstetrics and Gynaecology* 91:891–93.

Gerrard, M. 1987. Sex, sex guilt, and contraceptive use revisited: The 1980s. *Journal of Personality and Social Psychology* 52:975–80.

Giarrusso, R., Johnson, P., Goodchilds, J., & Zellman, G. 1979. Adolescents' cues and signals: Sex and assault. Paper presented at the annual meeting of the Western Psychological Association, San Diego, CA.

Gibson-Ainyette, I., Templer, D. I., Brown, R., & Veaco, L. 1988. Adolescent female prostitutes. *Archives of Sexual Behavior* 17:431–38.

Gilbert, D. G., Hagen, R. L., & D'Agostino, J. A. 1986. The effects of cigarette smoking on human sexual potency. *Addictive Behaviors* 11:431–34.

Gilbert, N., Berrick, J. D., LeProhn, N., & Nyman, N. 1988. *Protecting young children from sexual abuse: Does preschool training work?* New York: Lexington Books.

Gilligan, C. 1982. *In a different voice*. Cambridge, MA: Harvard University Press.

Gladue, B. A., Green, R., & Hellman, R. E. 1984. Neuroendocrine response to estrogen and sexual orientation. *Science* 225:1469–99.

Glina, S., Reichelt, C., Leao, P., & Reis, J. 1988. Impact of cigarette smoking on papaverine-induced erection. *Journal of Urology* 140:523–24.

Goergen, D. 1975. *The sexual celibate*. New York: Seabury.

Gold, Y. 1987. The sexualization of the workplace: Sexual harassment of white, blue, and pink-collar women. Paper presented at the annual meeting of the American Psychological Association, New York, NY.

Goldberg, D., Whipple, B., Fishkin, R., Waxman, H., Fink, P., & Weisberg, M. 1983. The Grafenberg spot and female ejaculation: A review of initial hypotheses. *Journal of Sex and Marital Therapy* 9:27–37.

Golden, C. 1987. Diversity and variability in women's sexual identities. *In* Boston Lesbian Psychologies Collective (Ed.), *Lesbian psychologies: Explorations and challenges*. Urbana and Chicago: University of Illinois Press.

Goldman, R., & Goldman, J. 1982. *Children's sexual thinking*. Boston: Routledge & Kegan Paul.

Golub, S. 1976. The effect of premenstrual anxiety and depression on cognitive function. *Journal of Personality and Social Psychology* 34:99–104.

Goodall, J. 1986. *The chimpanzees of Gombe: Patterns of behavior*. Cambridge, MA: Belknap Press of Harvard University Press.

Goodman, G. S., & Helgeson, V. S. 1988. Children as witnesses: What do they remember? *In* L. Walker (Ed.), *Handbook on sexual abuse of children.* New York: Springer.

Gordis, R. 1978. *Love and sex: A modern Jewish perspective.* New York: Farrar, Straus & Giroux.

Gordon, L. 1990. *Woman's body, woman's right: Birth control in America.* Rev. ed. New York: Penguin.

Gordon, S. 1976. Freedom for sex education and sexual expression. *In* S. Gordon & R. W. Libby (Eds.), *Sexuality today and tomorrow: Contemporary issues in human sexuality.* North Scituate, MA: Duxbury Press.

Gordon, S., 1986, October. What kids need to know. *Psychology Today:* 22–26.

Gordon, S., & Snyder, C. W. 1989. *Personal issues in human sexuality: A guidebook for better sexual health.* 2nd ed. Boston: Allyn and Bacon.

Gosselin, C., & Wilson, G. 1980. *Sexual variations.* New York: Simon and Schuster.

Goulart, F. S. 1987, April 27. What's your sex IQ? *San Francisco Chronicle.*

Governor's Task Force on Bias-Related Violence. 1988. *Final report.* (Available from Division of Human Rights, 55 West 125th St., New York, NY 10027.)

Goy, R. W. 1968. Organizing effects of androgen on the behavior of rhesus monkeys. In R. P. Michael (Ed.), *Endocrinology and human behavior.* London: Oxford University Press.

Graber, B., Kline-Graber, G., & Golden, C. J. 1981. A circumvaginal muscle nomogram: A new diagnostic tool for evaluation of female sexual dysfunction. *Journal of Clinical Psychiatry* 42:157–61.

Grahn, J. 1984. *Another mother tongue: Gay words, gay worlds.* Boston: Beacon Press.

Gray-Little, B., & Burks, N. 1983. Power and satisfaction in marriage: A review and critique. *Psychological Bulletin* 93:513–38.

Green, S. K., & Sandos, P. 1983. Perceptions of male and female initiators of relationships. *Sex Roles* 9:849–52.

Green, R. 1974, February. Children's quest for sexual identity. *Psychology Today* 7:44–47, 50, 51.

Green, R. 1987. *The "sissy boy syndrome" and the development of homosexuality: A 15-year prospective study.* New Haven, CT: Yale University Press.

Green, R., Mandel, J. B., Hotvedt, M. E., Gray, J., & Smith, L. 1986. Lesbian mothers and their children: A comparison with solo parent heterosexual mothers and their children. *Archives of Sexual Behavior* 15:167–84.

Greenberg, D. G. 1989. *The construction of homosexuality.* Chicago: University of Chicago Press.

Greendlinger, V., & Bryne, D. 1987. Coercive sexual fantasies of college men as predictors of self-reported likelihood to rape and overt sexual aggression. *Journal of Sex Research* 23:1–11.

Greenwald, E., & Leitenberg, H. 1989. Long-term effects of sexual experiences with siblings and nonsiblings during childhood. *Archives of Sexual Behavior* 18:389–99.

Greenwood, S. 1989. *Menopause, naturally: Preparing for the second half of life.* Rev. ed. Volcano, CA: Volcano Press.

Gregersen, E. 1982. *Sexual practices: The story of human sexuality.* New York: Franklin Watts.

Griffin, S. 1971, September. Rape: The all-American crime. *Ramparts* 10:26–35.

Griffith, J. 1983. Emotional supports and psychological distress in Anglo and Mexican Americans. Paper presented at the annual meeting of the American Psychological Association, Anaheim, CA.

Grigg, F., Fletcher, G. J. O., & Fitness, J. 1989. Spontaneous attributions in happy and unhappy dating relationships. *Journal of Social and Personal Relationships* 6:61–68.

Groth, A. N. 1979. *Men who rape.* New York: Plenum.

Groth, A. N., & Burgess, A. W. 1977. Rape: A sexual deviation. *American Journal of Orthopsychiatry* 47:400–06.

Groth, A. N., & Hobson, W. 1983. The dynamics of sexual assault. *In* L. Schlesinger & E. Revitch (Ed.), *Sexual dynamics of anti-social behavior.* Springfield, IL: Thomas.

Guha, S. K. 1985. Contraception in male monkeys by intra-vas deferens injections of a pH lowering polymer. *Contraception* 32:109–18.

Gutek, B. 1985. *Sex and the workplace.* San Francisco: Jossey-Bass.

Hacker, H. M. 1981. Blabbermouths and clams: Sex differences in self-disclosure in same-sex and cross-sex friendship dyads. *Psychology of Women Quarterly* 5:385–401.

Hackett, C. J. 1963. On the origins of the human treponematoses. *Bulletin of the World Health Organization* 29:7–41.

Hagestad, G., & Smyer, M. 1982. Dissolving long-term relationships: Patterns of divorcing in middle age. *In* S. Duck (Ed.), *Personal relationships. 4: Dissolving relationships.* New York: Academic Press.

Hale, N. G., Jr. 1971. *Freud and the Americans: The beginnings of psychoanalysis in the United States, 1876–1917.* New York: Oxford University Press.

Hamilton, J., Alagna, S., King, L., & Lloyd, C. 1987. The emotional consequences of gender-based abuse in the workplace: New counseling programs for sex discrimination. *Women and Therapy* 6:155–82.

Hammerschlag, M. R. 1989. Chlamydial infections. *Journal of Pediatrics*, 114:727–34.

Hancock, K. A. 1986. Homophobia. Paper developed by the Committee on Lesbian and Gay Concerns, American Psychological Association, Washington, D.C.

Hansen, G. L. 1985. Dating jealousy among college students. *Sex Roles* 12:713–21.

Hardin, C. 1970. *Birth control.* Indianapolis: Bobbs-Merrill.

Hariton, E. B. 1973, November. The sexual fantasies of women. *Psychology Today* 6(10): 39–44.

Harris, M. B., & Turner, P. H. 1985/1986. Gay and lesbian parents. *Journal of Homosexuality* 12(2):101–13.

Hart, B. L. 1978. Reflexive mechanisms in copulatory behavior. *In* T. E. McGill, D. A. Dewsbury, & B. D. Sachs (Eds.), *Sex and behavior: Status and prospectus.* New York: Plenum.

Hatcher, R. A., Guest, F., Stewart, F., Steward, G. K., Trussell, J., Bowen, S. C., & Cates, W. 1988. *Contraceptive technology 1988–1989.* 14th rev. ed. New York: Irvington.

Hatfield, E. 1984. The dangers of intimacy. *In* V. J. Derlega (Ed.), *Communication, intimacy, and close relationships.* Orlando, FL: Academic Press.

Hatfield, E. 1988. Passionate and companionate love. *In* R. J. Sternberg & M. L. Barnes (Eds.), *The psychology of love.* New Haven, CT and London: Yale University Press.

Hatfield, E., & Sprecher, S. 1986. Measuring passionate love in intimate relationships. *Journal of Adolescence* 9:383–410.

Hawkins, R. A., & Oakey, R E. 1974. Estimation of oestrone sulphate, oestradiol-17β and oestrone in peripheral plasma: Concentrations during the menstrual cycle and in men. *Journal of Endocrinology* 60:3–17.

Hayes, C. D. 1987. Adolescent pregnancy and childbearing: An emerging research focus. *In* S. L. Hofferth & C. D. Hayes (Eds.), *Risking the future: Adolescent sexuality, pregnancy, and child-bearing, Vol. 2.* Washington, DC: National Academy Press.

Hayes, S. H., Brownell, K. D., & Barlow, D. H. 1978. The use of self-administered covert sensitization in the treatment of exhibitionism and sadism. *Behavior Therapy* 9:283–89.

Hazelwood, R. R., Deitz, P. E., & Burgess, A. W. 1983. *Autoerotic fatalities.* Lexington, MA: Lexington Books/E. C. Health.

Heiman, J. R. 1975, April. The physiology of erotica: Women's sexual arousal. *Psychology Today* 8(11):90–94.

Heiman, J. R., LoPiccolo, L., & Lo Piccolo, J. 1976. *Becoming orgasmic: A sexual growth program for women.* Englewood Cliffs, NJ: Prentice-Hall.

Helgeson, V. S., & Sharpsteen, D. J. 1987. Perceptions of danger in achievement and affiliation situations: An extension of the Pollak and Gilligan versus Benton et al. debate. *Journal of Personality and Social Psychology* 53:727–33.

Hellwege, D. R., Perry, K., & Dobson, J. 1988. Perceptual differences in gender ideals among heterosexual and homosexual males and females. *Sex Roles* 19:735–46.

Hendrick, C., & Hendrick, S. S. 1986. A theory and method of love. *Journal of Personality and Social Psychology* 50:392–402.

Hendrick, S. S. 1981. Self-disclosure and marital satisfaction. *Journal of Personality and Social Psychology* 40:1150–59.

Hendricks, S. E., Graber, B., & Rodriguez-Sierra, J. F. 1989. Neuroendocrine responses to exogenous estrogen: No differences between heterosexual and homosexual men. *Psychoneuroendocrinology* 14:177–85.

Henshaw, S. K. 1986. Trends in abortion, 1982–1986. *Family Planning Perspectives* 18:34.

Henshaw, S. K. 1987. Characteristics of U.S. women having abortions, 1982–1983. *Family Planning Perspectives* 19(1):5–9.

Henshaw, S. K., & Silverman, J. 1988. The characteristics and prior contraceptive use of U.S. abortion patients. *Family Planning Perspectives* 20(4):158–68.

Herdt, G. H. 1984. *The Sambia: Ritual and gender in New Guinea.* New York: Holt, Rinehart and Winston.

Herdt, G. H., & Davidson, J. 1988. The Sambia "turnim-man": Sociocultural and clinical aspects of gender formation in male pseudohermaphrodites with 5-alpha-reductase deficiency in Papua, New Guinea. *Archives of Sexual Behavior* 17:33–56.

Herek, G. 1984. Beyond "homophobia": A social psychological perspective on attitudes toward lesbians and gay men. *Journal of Homosexuality* 10:1–21.

Herek, G. 1989. Hate crimes against lesbians and gay men: Issues for research and policy. *American Psychologist* 44:948–55.

Hessellund, H. 1976. Masturbation and sexual fantasies in married couples. *Archives of Sexual Behavior* 5:133–47.

Hetrick, E. S., & Martin, A. D. 1987. Developmental issues and their resolution for gay and lesbian adolescents. *Journal of Homosexuality* 14:25–43.

Heyden, S., & Fodor, J. G. 1986. Coffee consumption and fibrocystic breasts: an unlikely association. *Canadian Journal of Surgery* 29:208–11.

Higgins, G. E., Jr. 1979. Sexual response in spinal cord injured adults: A review of the literature. *Archives of Sexual Behavior* 8:173–96.

Highwater, J. 1990. *Myth and sexuality*. New York: New American Library.

Hill, C. T., Rubin, Z., & Peplau, L. A. 1976. Breakups before marriage: The end of 103 affairs. *Journal of Social Issues* 32(1):147–68.

Hill, W. F. 1978. Effects of mere exposure on preferences in nonhuman mammals. *Psychological Bulletin* 85:1177–98.

Himes, N. E. 1970. *The medical history of contraception*. New York: Schocken Books.

Hislop, T. G., Band, P. R., Deschamps, M., Ng, V., Coldman, A. J., Worth, A. J., & Labo, T. 1990. Diet and histologic types of benign breast disease defined by subsequent risk of breast cancer. *American Journal of Epidemiology* 131:263–70.

Hite, S. 1976. *The Hite report: A nationwide study of female sexuality*. New York: Dell.

Hite, S. 1981. *The Hite report on male sexuality*. New York: Alfred A. Knopf.

Hobson, B. M. 1987. *Uneasy virtue: The politics of prostitution and the American reform tradition*. New York: Basic Books.

Hochschild, A. (with A. Machung). 1989. *The second shift: Working parents and the revolution at home*. New York: Viking.

Hoeffer, B. 1981. Children's acquisition of sex-role behavior in lesbian-mother families. *American Journal of Orthopsychiatry* 51:536–44.

Hofferth, S. L. 1987. Contraceptive decision-making among adolescents. *In* S. L. Hofferth & C. D. Hayes (Eds.), *Risking the future: Adolescent sexuality, pregnancy and childbearing (Vol. 2)*. Washington, DC: National Academy Press.

Hofferth, S. L., Kahn, J. R., & Baldwin, W. 1987. Premarital sexual activity among U. S. teenage women over the past three decades. *Family Planning Perspectives* 19:46–53.

Holmes, L. 1978, October. How fathers can cause the Down Syndrome. *Human Nature* 1(10): 70–72.

Holtzworth-Munroe, A., & Jacobson, N. S. 1985. Causal attributions of married couples: When do they search for causes? What do they conclude when they do? *Journal of Personality and Social Psychology* 48:1398–1412.

Homans, G. C. 1961. *Social behavior: Its elementary forms*. New York: Harcourt.

Hooker, E. 1957. The adjustment of the male overt homosexual. *Journal of Projective Techniques* 21:18–31.

Hoon, P. W. 1984. Physiologic assessment of sexual response in women: the unfulfilled promise. *Clinical Obstetrics and Gynecology* 27:767–80.

Howard, J. A., Blumstein, P., & Schwartz, P. 1986. Sex, power, and influence tactics in intimate relationships. *Journal of Personality and Social Psychology* 51:102–09.

Howard, J. A., Blumstein, P., & Schwartz, P. 1987. Social or evolutionary theories? Some observations on preferences in human mate selection. *Journal of Personality and Social Psychology* 53:194–200.

Hsu, F. L. K. 1981. *Americans and Chinese: Passage to difference*. 3rd ed. Honolulu: University Press of Hawaii.

Hubbard, C. W. 1977. *Family planning education*. 2nd ed. St. Louis: C. V. Mosby.

Hufnagel, V. 1988. Male and female sexual surgery: The conspiracy against the uterus. Paper presented at the annual meeting of the American Association of Sex Educators, Therapists and Counselors, San Francisco, CA.

Hughes, J. O., & Sandler, B. R. 1987. *"Friends" raping friends: Could it happen to you?* Washington, D.C.: Project on the Status and Education of Women, American Association of Colleges.

Humphreys, L. 1970. *Tearoom trade: Impersonal sex in public places*. Chicago: Aldine.

Hunt, M. 1967. *The natural history of love*. New York: Minerva Press.

Hunt, M. 1974. *Sexual behavior in the 1970s*. Chicago: Playboy Press.

Hunt, M. 1977. *Gay: What you should know about homosexuality*. New York: Pocket Books.

Hupka, R. B. 1981. Cultural determinants of jealousy. *Alternative Lifestyles* 4(3):310–56.

Huston, T. L., & Ashmore, R. D. 1986. Women and men in personal relationship. *In* R. D. Ashmore & R. K. Del Boca (Eds.), *The social psychology of female-male relations*. New York: Academic Press.

Hyde, J. S. 1984. Children's understanding of sexist language. *Developmental Psychology* 20: 697–706.

Imperato-McGinley, J., Guerrero, L., Gautier, T., & Peterson, R. E. 1974. Steroid 5α-reductase deficiency in man: An inherited form of male pseudohermaphroditism. *Science* 186: 1213–15.

Imperato-McGinley, J., Peterson, R. E., Gautier, T., & Sturla, E. 1979. Androgens and the evolution of male-gender identity among male pseudohermaphrodites with 5α-reductase deficiency. *New England Journal of Medicine* 300:1233–37.

James, J., & Withers, J. 1975. *In* J. James, J. Withers, M. Haft, & T. Theiss (Eds.), *The politics of prostitution*. Seattle, WA: Social Research Associations.

James, J., Withers, J., Haft, M., & Theiss, T. 1975. *The politics of prostitution*. Seattle, WA: Social Research Associations.

Jancin, B. 1989. Prenatal gender selection appears to be gaining acceptance. *Obstetrical and Gynecological News* 23:30.

Jarvik, M. E., & Brecher, E. M. 1977. Drugs and sex: Inhibition and enhancement effects. *In* J. Money, & H. Musaph (Eds.), *Handbook of sexology*. Amsterdam: Elsevier/North Holland.

Jensen, S. B. 1986. Sexual dysfunction in insulin-treated diabetics: A six-year follow-up study of 101 patients. *Archives of Sexual Behavior* 15:271–83.

Jessor, R., Costa, F., Jessor, L., & Donovan, J. E. 1983. Time of first intercourse: A prospective study. *Journal of Personality and Social Psychology* 44:608–26.

Jick, H., Walker, A. M., Rothman, K. J. et al. 1981. Vaginal spermicides and congenital disorders. *Journal of the American Medical Association* 245:1329–32.

Johns, D. R., Tierney, M. & Felsenstein, D. 1987. Alteration in the natural history of neurosyphilis by concurrent infection with the human immunodeficiency virus. *New England Journal of Medicine* 316:1569–72.

Johnson, R. D. 1972. *Aggression in man and animals*. Philadelphia: W. B. Saunders.

Johnson, R. E., Nahmias, A. J., Magder, L. S., Lee, F. K., Brooks, C. A., & Snowden, C. B. 1989. A seroepidemiologic survey of the prevalence of herpes simplex virus type 2 infection in the United States. *New England Journal of Medicine* 321:7–12.

Jones, D. P. H., & McGraw, J. M. 1987. Reliable and fictitious accounts of child sexual abuse. *Journal of Interpersonal Violence* 2:27–45.

Jones, E., Forrest, J., Goldman, N., Henshaw, S., Lincoln, R. et al. 1985. Teenage pregnancy in developed countries: Determinants and policy implications. *Family Planning Perspectives* 17:53–63.

Jong, E. 1974. *Fear of flying*. New York: Signet.

Joyce, J. 1940. *Ulysses*. New York: Modern Library.

Justice, B., & Justice, R. 1979. *The broken taboo: Sex in the family*. New York: Human Sciences Press.

Kallman, F. J. 1952. Comparative twin study on the genetic aspects of male homosexuality. *Journal of Nervous and Mental Disease* 115:283–98.

Kane, M. A., Alter, M. J., Hadler, S. C., & Margolis, H. S. 1989. Hepatitis B infection in the United States. Recent trends and future strategies for control. *American Journal of Medicine* 87(3A):11S–13S.

Kanin, E. 1985. Date rapists: Differential sexual socialization and relative deprivation. *Archives of Sexual Behavior* 14:219–31.

Kantner, J. F., & Zelnik, M. 1972. Sexual experience of young unmarried women in the United States. *Family Planning Perspectives* 4(4):9–18.

Kantner, J. F., & Zelnik, M. 1973. Contraception and pregnancy: Experiences of young unmarried women in the United States. *Family Planning Perspectives* 5(1):21–35.

Kaplan, H. S. 1974. *The new sex therapy*. New York: Brunner/Mazel.

Kaplan, H. S. 1977. Hypoactive sexual desire. *Journal of Sex and Marital Therapy* 3:3–9.

Kaplan, H. S. 1979. *Disorders of sexual desire*. New York: Brunner/Mazel.

Kay, C. R., & Hannaford, P. C. 1988. Breast cancer and the pill—a further report from the Royal College of General Practitioners' oral contraception study. *British Journal of Cancer* 58: 675–80.

Kegeles, S. M., Adler, N. E., & Irwin, C. E., Jr. 1989. Adolescents and condoms. Associations of beliefs with intentions to use. *American Journal of Diseases in Childhood* 143:911–15.

Kelley, H. H., Berscheid, E., Christensen, A., Harvey, J. H., Huston, T. L., Levinger, G., McClintock, E., Peplau, L. A., & Peterson, D. R. 1983. *Close relationships*. New York: W. H. Freeman.

Kelley, H. H., & Thibaut, J. W. 1978. *Interpersonal relations: A theory of interdependence*. New York: Wiley-Interscience.

Kelsey, M., & Kelsey, B. 1986. *Sacrament of sexuality*. Warwick, NY: Amity House.

Kendrick, W. 1987. *The secret museum: Pornography in modern culture*. New York: Viking Penguin.

Kephart, W. M. 1967. Some correlates of romantic love. *Journal of Marriage and the Family* 29: 470–74.

Kephart, W. M., & Jedlicka, D. 1987. *The family, society, and the individual*. 6th ed. New York: Harper & Row.

Kessler, J. 1988. When the diagnosis is vaginismus: Fighting misconceptions. *Women & Therapy* 7:175–86.

Kikuchi, J. J. 1988, Fall. Rhode Island develops successful intervention program for adolescents. *NCASA News:* 26–27.

Kilmann, P. R., Boland, P. R., Norton, S. P., Davidson, E., & Caid, C. 1986. Perspectives of sex therapy outcome: A survey of AASECT providers. *Journal of Sex and Marital Therapy* 12:116–38.

Kilmann, P. R., & Mills, K. H. 1983. *All about sex therapy*. New York: Plenum.

Kilpatrick, D. G., Best, C. L., Veronen, L. J., Ruff, M., Ruff, G. A., & Allison, J. C. 1985. The aftermath of rape: A 3-year longitudinal study. Paper presented at the annual meeting of the American Psychological Association, Los Angeles, CA.

Kilpatrick, D. G., Veronen, L. J., & Best, C. L. 1985. Factors predicting psychological distress among rape victims. *In* C. R. Figley (Ed.), *Trauma and its wake*. New York: Brunner/Mazel.

Kinsey, A. C., Pomeroy, W. B., & Martin, C. E. 1948. *Sexual behavior in the human male*. Philadelphia: W. B. Saunders.

Kinsey, A. C., Pomeroy, W. B., Martin, C. E., & Gebhard, P. H. 1951. *Sexual behavior in the human female*. Philadelphia: Saunders.

Kipnis, D., & Schmidt, S. 1985, April. The language of persuasion. *Psychology Today* 19(4):40–46.

Kirby, D. 1984. *Sexuality education: An evaluation of programs and their effects*. Santa Cruz, CA: Network Publications.

Kirkpatrick, M., Smith, K., & Roy, R. 1981. Lesbian mothers and their children: A comparative survey. *American Journal of Orthopsychiatry* 51:545–51.

Kite, M. E. 1984. Sex differences in attitudes toward homosexuals: A meta-analytic review. *Journal of Homosexuality* 10:69–82.

Kitzinger, C. 1988. *The social construction of lesbianism*. Newbury Park, CA: Sage.

Kjaer, S. K., Teisen, C., Haugaard, B. J., Lynge, E., Christensen, R. B. et al. 1989. Risk factors for cervical cancer in Greenland and Denmark: A population-based cross-sectional study. *International Journal of Cancer* 44:40–47.

Klein, F. 1980, December. Are you sure you're heterosexual? or homosexual? or even bisexual? *Forum:* 41–45.

Klein, F., Sepekoff, B., & Wolf, T. J. 1985. Sexual orientation: A multi-variate dynamic process. *Journal of Homosexuality* 11(1/2):35–49.

Klonoff-Cohen, H. S., Savitz, D. A., Cefalo, R. C., & McCann, M. F. 1989. An epidemiologic study of contraception and preeclampsia. *Journal of the American Medical Association* 262:3143–47.

Klüver, H., & Bucy, P. C. 1939. Preliminary analysis of functions of the temporal lobe in monkeys. *Archives of Neurology and Psychiatry* 42:979–1000.

Knafo, D., & Jaffe, Y. 1984. Sexual fantasizing in males and females. *Journal of Research in Personality* 19:451–62.

Knussmann, R., Christiansen, K., & Couwenbergs, C. 1986. Relations between sex hormone levels and sexual behavior in men. *Archives of Sexual Behavior* 15:429–45.

Kogan, B. A. 1980. *Health*. 3rd ed. New York: Harcourt Brace Jovanovich.

Kohlberg, L. 1966. A cognitive-developmental analysis of children's sex-role concepts and attitudes. *In* E. E. Maccoby (Ed.), *The development of sex differences*. Stanford: Stanford University Press.

Kohlberg, L. 1969. Stage and sequence: The cognitive-developmental approach to socialization. *In* D. A. Goslin (Ed.), *Handbook of socialization research and theory*. Chicago: Rand McNally.

Kohlberg, L., & Ullian, D. Z. 1974. Stages in the development of psychosexual concepts and attitudes. *In* R. C. Friedman, R. M. Richard, & R. L. Vande Wiele (Eds.), *Sex differences in behavior*. New York: John Wiley & Sons.

Koss, M. P., Dinero, T. E., Seibel, C. A., & Cox, S. L. 1988. Stranger and acquaintance rape: Are there differences in the victim's experience? *Psychology of Women Quarterly* 12:1–24.

Koss, M. P., Gidycz, C. A., & Wisniewski, N. 1987. The scope of rape: Incidence and prevalence of sexual aggression and victimization in a national sample of higher education students. *Journal of Consulting and Clinical Psychology* 55:162–70.

Kotkin, M. 1983. Sex roles among married and unmarried couples. *Sex Roles* 9:975–85.

Kowl, A. (Ed.). 1978. *High times encyclopedia of recreational drugs*. New York: Stonehill Publishing Company.

Krafka, C. L. 1985. Sexually explicit, sexually violent, and violent media: Effects of multiple naturalistic exposures and debriefing on female viewers. (Unpublished doctoral dissertation.) Madison, WI: University of Wisconsin.

Kurdek, L. A. 1987. Sex role self schema and psychological adjustment in coupled homosexual and heterosexual men and women. *Sex Roles* 17:549–62.

Kurdek, L. 1988. Correlates of negative attitudes toward homosexuals in heterosexual college students. *Sex Roles* 18:727–38.

Kurdek, L. A., & Schmitt, J. P. 1986. Relationship quality of partners in heterosexual married, heterosexual cohabiting, gay, and lesbian couples. *Journal of Personality and Social Psychology* 51:711–20.

Kutchinsky, B. 1985. Pornography and its effects in Denmark and the United States: A rejoinder and beyond. *Comparative Social Research: An Annual* 8:301–30.

Ladas, A. K., Whipple, B., & Perry, J. D. 1982. *The G spot and other recent discoveries about human sexuality*. New York: Holt, Rinehart and Winston.

Laschet, U. 1973. Antiandrogen in the treatment of sex offenders: Mode of action and therapeutic outcome. *In* J. Rubin & J. Money (Eds.), *Contemporary sexual behavior: Critical issues in the 1970s*. Baltimore: Johns Hopkins University Press.

Lauer, J., & Lauer, R. 1986. *Til death do us part: How couples stay together*. New York: Haworth Press.

Lear, M. W. 1973, January 28. Is there a male menopause? *New York Times Magazine*.

Lee, J. A. 1974, October. The styles of loving. *Psychology Today* 8(5):43–50.

Lee, J. A. 1988. Love-styles. *In* R. J. Sternberg & M. L. Barnes (Eds.), *The psychology of love*. New Haven, CT and London: Yale University Press.

Leiblum, S., Bachmann, G., Kemmann, E., Colburn, D., & Swartzman, L. 1983. Vaginal atrophy in the postmenopausal woman. The importance of sexual activity and hormones. *Journal of the American Medical Association* 249:2195–98.

Leiblum, S., & Rosen, R. (Eds.). 1988. *Sexual desire disorders*. New York: Guilford Press.

Leigh, B. C. 1989. Reasons for having and avoiding sex: Gender, sexual orientation, and relationship to sexual behavior. *Journal of Sex Research* 26:199–209.

Lemery, C. R. 1983. Children's sexual knowledge as a function of parent's affective orientation to sexuality and parent-child communication about sex: A causal analysis. (Unpublished master's thesis.) London, Ontario: University of Western Ontario.

Leo, J. 1987, March 30. Romantic porn in the boudoir; the VCR revolution produces X-rated films for women (and men). *Time* 129:63.

Lerner, H. G. 1988. *Women in therapy*. New York: Harper & Row.

Lerner, H. G. 1990, May/June. What's a vulva, mom? *New Directions for Women:* 10.

Lerner, R. M., & Karabenick, S. A. 1974. Physical attractiveness, body attitudes, and self-concept in late adolescents. *Journal of Youth and Adolescence* 3:307–16.

Lester, D. 1972. Incest. *Journal of Sex Research* 8:268–85.

Lester, J. 1976. Being a boy. *In* D. S. David & R. Brannon (Eds.), *The forty-nine percent majority: The male sex role*. Reading, MA: Addison-Wesley.

Levin, R. J., & Wagner, G. 1985. Orgasm in women in the laboratory—Quantitative studies on duration, intensity, latency, and vaginal blood flow. *Archives of Sexual Behavior* 11:367–86.

Levin, S. M., & Stava, L. 1987. Personality characteristics of sex offenders: A review. *Archives of Sexual Behavior* 16:57–79.

Levine, M. P. 1979. Gay ghetto. *In* M. P. Levine (Ed.), *Gay men: The sociology of male homosexuality.* New York: Harper & Row.

Levine, S. 1966, April. Sex differences in the brain. *Scientific American* 214:84–90.

Levine, S. B., & Agle, D. 1978. The effectiveness of sex therapy for chronic secondary psychological impotence. *Journal of Sex & Marital Therapy* 4:235–58.

Levine, S., Althof, S., Turner, L., Kursh, E., Bodner, D., Resnick, M., & Risen, C. 1989, April. Benefits and problems with intracavernosal injections for the treatment of impotence. *Medical Aspects of Human Sexuality:* 38–40.

Levinger, G. 1977. The embrace of lives: Changing and unchanging. *In* G. Levinger & H. L. Rausch (Eds.), *Close relationships: Perspectives on the meaning of intimacy.* Amherst: University of Massachusetts Press.

Levinson, W., & Dunn, P. M. 1986. Nonassociation of caffeine and fibrocystic breast disease. *Archives of Internal Medicine* 146:1773–75.

Levitt, E. E. 1983. Estimating the duration of sexual behavior: A laboratory analog study. *Archives of Sexual Behavior* 12:329–35.

Levitt, E. E., & Klassen, A. D., Jr. 1974. Public attitudes toward homosexuality. *Journal of Homosexuality* 1:29–43.

Lightfoot-Klein, H. 1989. *Prisoners of ritual: An odyssey into female genital circumcision in Africa.* Binghamton, N.Y.: Haworth Press.

Limentani, A. 1987. Perversions: Treatable and untreatable. *Contemporary Psychoanalysis* 23: 415–37.

Linz, D., Donnerstein, E., & Penrod, S. 1988. The effects of long-term exposure to violent and sexually degrading depictions of women. *Journal of Personality and Social Psychology* 55: 758–67.

Lips, H. 1991. *Women, men, and power.* Mountain View, CA: Mayfield.

Liskin, L., & Blackburn, R. 1987. Hormonal contraception: New long-acting methods. *Population Reports,* 15:K58–K87.

Little, R. E., & Sing, C. F. 1987. Father's drinking and infant birth weight: Report of an association. *Teratology* 36:59–65.

Lloyd, R. 1976. *For money or love: Boy prostitution in America.* New York: Vanguard Press.

Lockett, G. 1987. What happens when you get arrested. *In* F. Delacoste & P. Alexander (Eds.), *Sex work: Writings by women in the sex industry.* Pittsburgh, PA: Cleis Press.

Long, J. W. 1982. *The essential guide to prescription drugs.* 3rd ed. New York: Harper & Row.

Longnecker, M. P., Berlin, J. A., Orza, M. J., & Chalmers, T. C. 1988. A meta-analysis of alcohol consumption in relation to risk of breast cancer. *Journal of the American Medical Association* 260:652–56.

LoPiccolo, J. 1978. Direct treatment of sexual dysfunction. *In* J. LoPiccolo & L. LoPiccolo (Eds.), *Handbook of sex therapy.* New York: Plenum.

LoPiccolo, J., & Lobitz, W. C. 1972. The role of masturbation in the treatment of orgasmic dysfunction. *Archives of Sexual Behavior* 2:163–72.

LoPiccolo, J., & LoPiccolo, L. (Eds.). 1978. *Handbook of sex therapy.* New York: Plenum.

LoPiccolo, L. 1980. Low sexual desire. *In* S. R. Leiblum & L. A. Pervin (Eds.), *Principles and practice of sex therapy.* New York: Guilford Press.

Lovelace, L., & McGrady, M. 1980. *Ordeal.* Secaucus, NJ: Citadel Press.

Lovelace, L., & McGrady, M. 1986. *Out of bondage.* Secaucus, NJ: Citadel Press.

Lowman, J. 1987. Taking young prostitutes seriously. *Canadian Review of Sociology and Anthropology* 24:99–116.

Loy, P. H., & Stewart, L. P. 1984. The extent and effects of the sexual harassment of working women. *Sociological Focus* 17(1):31–43.

Luckenbill, D. F. 1986. Deviant career mobility: The case of male prostitutes. *Social Problems* 33:283–96.

Luker, K. 1975. *Taking chances: Abortion and the decision not to contracept.* Berkeley: University of California Press.

Lundstrom, B., Pauly, I. B., & Walinder, J. 1984. Outcome of sex reassignment surgery. *Acta Psychiatrica Scandinavica* 70:289–94.

Lutjen, P., Trounson, A., Leeton, J., Findlay, J., Wood, C., & Renou, P. 1984, January 12–18. *Nature* 307(5947):174–75.

Lynch, J. M., & Reilly, M. E. 1985/1986. Role relationships: Lesbian perspectives. *Journal of Homosexuality* 12(2):53–69.

Lyon, P., & Martin, D. (1970). The realities of lesbianism. *In* J. Cooke, C. Bunch-Weeks, & R. Morgan (Eds.), *The new woman*. Indianapolis: Bobbs-Merrill.

Maccoby, E. E. 1988. Gender as a social category. *Developmental Psychology* 26:755–65.

Maccoby, E. E. 1990. Gender and relationships. *American Psychologist* 45:513–20.

MacDonald, N. E., Wells, G. A., Fisher, W. A., Warren, W. K., King, Matthew A., Doherty, J. A., & Bowie, W. R. 1990. High risk STD/HIV behavior among college students. *Journal of the American Medical Association* 263(23):3155–59.

Mack, T. M., & Ross, R. K. 1989. Risks and benefits of long-term treatment with estrogens. *Scheiz Med. Wochenschr* 119:1811–20.

MacKinnon, C. 1984. Not a moral issue. *Yale Law and Policy Review* 2:321–45.

MacKinnon, C. 1985. Pornography, civil right, and speech: Commentary. *Harvard Civil Rights-Civil Liberties Law Review* 20:1–70.

MacLean, P. D. 1962. New findings relevant to the evolution of psychosexual functions of the brain. *Journal of Nervous and Mental Disease* 135:289–301.

Makepeace, J. M. 1986. Gender differences in courtship violence victimization. *Family Relations: Journal of Applied Family and Child Studies* 35:383–88.

Malamuth, N. M. 1978. Erotica, aggression and perceived appropriateness. Paper presented at the annual meeting of the American Psychological Association, Toronto.

Malamuth, N. M. 1981. Rape proclivity among males. *Journal of Social Issues* 37:138–57.

Malamuth, N. M. 1984. Aggression against women: Cultural and individual causes. *In* N. M. Malamuth & E. Donnerstein (Eds.), *Pornography and sexual aggression*. Orlando, FL: Academic Press.

Malamuth, N. M., & Ceniti, J. 1986. Repeated exposure to violent and nonviolent pornography: Likelihood of raping ratings and laboratory aggression against women. *Aggressive Behavior* 12:129–37.

Malamuth, N. M., & Check, J. V. 1980. Penile tumescence and perceptual responses to rape as a function of victim's perceived reactions. *Journal of Applied Social Psychology* 10:528–47.

Malamuth, N. M., & Check, J. V. 1981. Sexual arousal to rape depictions: Individual differences. *Journal of Abnormal Psychology* 92:55–67.

Malamuth, N. M., & Check, J. V. 1983. The effects of mass media exposure on acceptance of violence against women: A field experiment. *Journal of Research in Personality* 15:436–46.

Malamuth, N. M., & Check, J. V. 1985. The effects of aggressive pornography on beliefs in rape myths: Individual differences. *Journal of Research in Personality* 19:299–320.

Malamuth, N., Check, J. V., & Briere, J. 1986. Sexual arousal in response to aggression: Ideological, aggressive, and sexual correlates. *Journal of Personality and Social Psychology* 50: 330–40.

Malinowski, B. 1929. *The sexual life of savages in North-Western Melanesia*. New York: Halcyon House.

Malloy, T., & Wein, A. 1988, June. Erectile dysfunction: Effects of pharmacotherapy. *Medical Aspects of Human Sexuality:* 42–48.

Malyon, A. K. 1985. Paper presented at the annual meeting of the American Psychological Association, Los Angeles, CA.

Mandler, G. 1984. *Mind and body: Psychology of emotion and stress*. New York: W. W. Norton.

Marcus, S. 1966. *The other Victorians: A study of sexuality and pornography in mid-nineteenth century England*. New York: Basic Books.

Marshall, D. S. 1971, February. Too much in Mangaia. *Psychology Today* 4:43–44ff.

Marshall, D. S. 1972. Sexual behavior on Mangaia. *In* D. S. Marshall & R. C. Suggs (Eds.), *Human sexual behavior: Variations in the ethnographic spectrum*. Englewood Cliffs, NJ: Prentice-Hall.

Marshall, D. S., & Suggs, R. C. (Eds.). 1972. *Human sexual behavior: Variations in the ethnographic spectrum*. Englewood Cliffs, NJ: Prentice-Hall.

Marshall, W. A., & Tanner, J. M. 1969. Variations in the pattern of pubertal changes in girls. *Archives of Disease in Childhood* 44:291–303.

Marshall, W. A., & Tanner, J. M. 1970. Variations in the patterns of pubertal changes in boys. *Archives of Disease in Childhood* 45:13–23.

Martinson, F. M. 1973. *Infant and child sexuality: A sociological perspective*. St. Peter, MN: The Book Mark (Gustavus Adolphus College).

Maslow, A. 1954. *Motivation and personality*. New York: Harper & Row.

Maslow, A. H. 1968. *Toward a psychology of being*. 2nd ed. Princeton: Van Nostrand.

Mason, A., & Blankenship, V. 1987. Power and affiliation motivation, stress, and abuse in intimate relationships. *Journal of Personality and Social Psychology* 52:203–10.

Masson, J. 1984. *The assault on truth: Freud's suppression of the seduction theory*. New York: Farrar, Strauss & Giroux.

Masters, W. H., & Johnson, V. E. 1966. *Human sexual response*. Boston: Little, Brown.

Masters, W. H., & Johnson, V. E. 1970. *Human sexual inadequacy*. Boston: Little, Brown.

Masters, W. H., & Johnson, V. E. 1979. *Homosexuality in perspective*. Boston: Little, Brown.

Masters, W. H., Johnson, V. E., & Kolodny, R. C. 1986. *Masters and Johnson on sex and human loving*. Boston: Little, Brown.

Matek, O. 1988. Obscene phone callers. *Journal of Social Work and Human Sexuality* 7:113–30.

Mathes, E. W. 1975. The effects of physical attractiveness and anxiety on heterosexual attraction over a series of five encounters. *Journal of Marriage and the Family* 37:769–73.

Matteson, G. N., Armstrong, R., & Kimes, H. M. 1984. Physician education in human sexuality. *Journal of Family Practice* 19:683–84.

Maurus, M., Mitra, J., & Ploog, D. 1965. Cerebral representation of the clitoris in ovariectomised squirrel monkeys. *Experimental Neurology* 13:282–88.

Mazor, M. D. 1979, May. Barren couples. *Psychology Today* 12(12):101, 103–04, 107–08, 112.

McCabe, M. 1987. Desired and experienced levels of premarital affection and sexual intercourse during dating. *Journal of Sex Research* 23:23–33.

McCauley, E., & Ehrhardt, A. A. 1984. Follow-up of females with gender identity disorders. *Journal of Nervous and Mental Disease* 172:353–58.

McConaghy, N. 1970. Subjective and penile plethysmograph responses to aversion therapy for homosexuality: A follow-up study. *British Journal of Psychiatry* 117:555–60.

McConaghy, N., Proctor, D., & Barr, R. F. 1972. Subjective and penile plethysmography responses to aversion therapy for homosexuality: A partial replication. *Archives of Sexual Behavior* 2:65–78.

McConnell, J. V. 1977. *Understanding human behavior: An introduction to psychology*. 2nd ed. New York: Holt, Rinehart and Winston.

McCormick, E. P., Johnson, R. L., Friedman, H. L., & David, H. P. 1977. Psychosocial aspects of fertility regulation. *In* J. Money & H. Musaph (Eds.), *Handbook of sexology*. Amsterdam: Elsevier/North Holland.

McCormick, N. B., & Jesser, C. J. 1983. The courtship game: Power in the sexual encounter. *In* E. R. Allgeier & N. B. McCormick (Eds.), *Changing boundaries: Gender roles and sexual behavior*. Palo Alto, CA: Mayfield Publishing.

McDermott, M. J. 1979. *Rape victimization in 26 American cities*. Washington, D.C.: Criminal Justice Research Center (U.S. Government Printing Office).

McDonald, G. J. 1982. Individual differences in the coming out process for gay men: Implications for theoretical models. *Journal of Homosexuality* 8:47–60.

McElfresh, S. B. 1982. Conjugal power and legitimating norms: A new perspective on resource theory. Paper presented at the annual meeting of the American Psychological Association, Washington, D.C.

McFarlane, J., Martin, C. L., & Williams, T. M. 1988. Mood fluctuations: Women versus men and menstrual versus other cycles. *Psychology of Women Quarterly* 12:201–23.

McGovern, L., Stewart, R., & LoPiccolo, J. 1975. Secondary orgasmic dysfunction. I: Analysis and strategies for treatment. *Archives of Sexual Behavior* 4:265–75.

McGuire, L. S., Ryan, K. O., & Omenn, G. S. 1975. Congenital adrenal hyperplasia: II. Cognitive and behavioral studies. *Behavior Genetics* 5:175–88.

McIntyre, S. L., & Higgens, J. E. 1986. Parity and use-effectiveness with the contraceptive sponge. *American Journal of Obstetrics and Gynecology* 155:796–801.

McKinlay, J. B., McKinlay, S. M., & Brambilla, D. 1987. The relative contributions of endocrine changes and social circumstances to depression in mid-aged women. *Journal of Health and Social Behavior* 28:345–63.

McMullen, R. J. 1986. Youth prostitution: A balance of power? *International Journal of Offender Therapy and Comparative Criminology* 30:237–44.

McWhirter, D. P., & Mattison, A. M. 1984. *The male couple: How relationships develop*. Englewood Cliffs, NJ: Prentice-Hall.

Mead, M. 1928. *Coming of age in Samoa*. New York: Morrow.

Medea, A., & Thompson, K. 1974. *Against rape.* New York: Farrar, Straus & Giroux.

Medical Research International, Society for Assisted Reproductive Technology, & American Fertility Society. 1990. In vitro fertilization-embryo transfer in the United States: 1988 results from the IVF-ET Registry. *Fertility and Sterility* 53:13–20.

Meiselman, K. C. 1978. *Incest: A psychological study of causes and effects with treatment recommendations.* San Francisco: Jossey-Bass.

Menken, J., Trussell, J., & Larsen, U. 1986. Age and infertility. *Science* 233:1389–94.

Mermey, J. 1975, August. Serpent fat, crocodile dung, pomegranate halves, feathers. . . . *Ms.* 4(2):102.

Mernissi, F. 1975. *Beyond the veil: Male-female dynamics in a modern Muslim society.* New York: Wiley.

Mertz, G. J., Coombs, R. W., Ashley, R., Jourdan, J. et al. 1988. Transmission of genital herpes in couples with one symptomatic and one asymptomatic partner: A prospective study. *Journal of Infectious Disease* 157:1169–77.

Messe, M. R., & Geer, J. H. 1985. Voluntary vaginal musculature contractions as an enhancer of sexual arousal. *Archives of Sexual Behavior* 14:13–28.

Messenger, J. C. 1972. Sex and repression in an Irish folk community. *In* D. S. Marshall & R. C. Suggs (Eds.), *Human sexual behavior: Variations in the ethnographic spectrum.* Englewood Cliffs, NJ: Prentice-Hall.

Metzger, D. 1976. It is always the woman who is raped. *American Journal of Psychiatry* 133:405–08.

Meyer, J. P., & Pepper, S. 1977. Need compatibility and marital adjustment in young married couples. *Journal of Personality and Social Psychology* 35:331–42.

Mills, P. K., Beeson, W. L., Phillips, R. L., & Fraser, G. E. 1989. Prospective study of exogenous hormone use and breast cancer in Seventh-day Adventists. *Cancer* 64:591–97.

Mims, F. H., & Chang, A. S. 1984. Unwanted sexual experiences of young women. *Journal of Psychosocial Nursing and Mental Health Services* 22(6):7–14.

Minden, S. 1986, February. Planned obsolescence. (Book review of *Gendercide,* by Mary Ann Warren.) *Women's Review of Books* 3(5):13–14.

Miner, M. H., Marques, J. K., Day, D. M., & Nelson, C. S. 1989. Impact of relapse prevention in treating sex offenders: Preliminary findings. Paper presented at the annual meeting of the American Psychological Association, New Orleans, LA.

Mischel, W. 1966. A social-learning view of sex differences in behavior. *In* E. E. Maccoby (Ed.), *The development of sex differences.* Stanford: Stanford University Press.

Mischel, W. 1970. Sex-typing and socialization. *In* P. H. Mussen (Ed.), *Carmichael's manual of child psychology, Vol. 2.* New York: John Wiley & Sons.

Mischel, W., & Grusec, J. 1966. Determinants of the rehearsal and transmission of neutral and aversive behaviors. *Journal of Personality and Social Psychology* 3:197–205.

Mohr, J. C. 1978. *Abortion in America: The origins and evolution of national policy, 1800–1900.* New York: Oxford University Press.

Money, J. 1977. Paraphilias. *In* J. J. Money & H. Musaph (Eds.), *Handbook of sexology.* Amsterdam: Elsevier/North Holland.

Money, J. & Dalery, J. 1976. Iatrogenic homosexuality: gender identity in seven 46,XX chromosomal females with hyperadrenocortical hermaphroditism born with a penis, three reared as boys, four reared as girls. *Journal of Homosexuality* 1(4):357–71.

Money, J., & Ehrhardt, A. A. 1972. *Man and woman, boy and girl.* Baltimore: Johns Hopkins University Press.

Money, J., Hampson, J., & Hampson, J. 1955. An examination of some basic sexual concepts: The evidence of human hermaphrodism. *Bulletin of Johns Hopkins Hospital* 97:301–19.

Money, J., & Lewis, V. 1982. Homosexual/heterosexual status in boys at puberty: idiopathic adolescent gynecomastia and congenital virilizing adrenocorticism compared. *Psychoneuroendocrinology* 7:339–46.

Money, J., & Lewis, V. G. 1987. Bisexually concordant, heterosexually and homosexually discordant: A matched-pair comparison of male and female adrenogenital syndrome. *Psychiatry* 50:97–111.

Money, J., & Mathews, D. 1982. Prenatal exposure to virilizing progestins: An adult follow-up study of twelve women. *Archives of Sexual Behavior* 11:73–78.

Money, J., & Schwartz, M. 1977. Dating, romantic and nonromantic friendships, and sexuality in 17 early-treated adrenogenital females, aged 16–25. *In* P. A. Lee, L. P. Plotnick, A. A. Kowarski, & C. J. Migeon (Eds.), *Congenital adrenal hyperplasia.* Baltimore: University Park Press.

Money, J., Schwartz, M., & Lewis, V. A. 1984. Adult erotosexual status and fetal hormonal masculinization and demasculinization: 46,XX congenital virilizing adrenal hyperplasia and 46,XY androgen-insensitivity syndrome compared. *Psychoneuroendocrinology* 9:405–14.

Montagu, A. 1971. *Touching: The human significance of the skin.* New York: Columbia University Press.

Moore, B. E. 1961. Frigidity in women (panel report). *Journal of the American Psychoanalytic Association* 9:571–84.

Moore, K. A. 1989. *Facts at a glance.* Washington, D.C.: Child Trends, Inc.

Moore, K. A., Wenk, D., Hofferth, S. L., & Hayes, C. D. 1987. Statistical appendix: Trends in adolescent sexual and fertility behavior. *In* S. L. Hofferth & C. D. Hayes (Eds.), *Risking the future: Adolescent sexuality, pregnancy, and childbearing, Vol. 2.* Washington, D. C.: National Academy Press.

Moorman, J. E. 1987. The history and the future of the relationship between education and marriage. [Unpublished revision of a paper presented at the annual meeting of the Population Association of America, Boston, 1985.]

Morgan, R. 1978. *Going too far.* New York: Vintage Books.

Morin, S. F. 1977. Heterosexual bias in psychological research on lesbianism and male homosexuality. *American Psychologist* 32:629–37.

Morin, S. F., Taylor, K., & Kielman, S. 1975. Gay is beautiful at a distance. Paper presented at the annual meeting of the American Psychological Association, Chicago, IL.

Morosco, B. A. 1987. *The prosecution and defense of sex crimes.* New York: Mathew Bender.

Morris, J. 1974. *Conundrum.* New York: Harcourt Brace Jovanovich.

Morris, N. M., Udry, J. R., Khan-Dawood, F., & Dawood, M. Y. 1987. Marital sex frequency and midcycle female testosterone. *Archives of Sexual Behavior* 16:27–37.

Moser, C. 1979. An exploratory-descriptive study of a self-defined S/M (sadomasochistic) sample. (Unpublished manuscript.) San Francisco: Institute for the Advanced Study of Human Sexuality.

Mosher, D. L., & Anderson, R. D. 1986. Macho personality, sexual aggression, and reactions to guided imagery of realistic rape. *Journal of Research in Personality* 20:77–94.

Mosher, W. D., & Pratt, W. F. 1990. Contraceptive use in the United States, 1973–1988. *Advance Data From Vital and Health Statistics* 182. Hyattsville, MD: National Center for Health Statistics.

Mott, F. L., & Haurin, R. J. 1988. Linkages between sexual activity and alcohol and drug use among American adolescents. *Family Planning Perspectives* 20:128–36.

Mudge, D., & Younger, J. B. 1989. The effects of topical lidocaine on infant response to circumcision. *Journal of Nurse Midwifery* 34:335–40.

Muehlenhard, C. L., & Cook, S. W. 1988. Men's self-reports of unwanted sexual activity. *Journal of Sex Research* 24:58–72.

Muehlenhard, C. L., & Hollabaugh, L. C. 1988. Do women sometimes say no when they mean yes? The prevalence and correlates of women's token resistance to sex. *Journal of Personality and Social Psychology* 54:872–79.

Muehlenhard, C. L., & Linton, M. A. 1987. Date rape and sexual aggression in dating situations: Incidence and risk factors. *Journal of Counseling Psychology* 34:186–96.

Murdock, G. P. 1949. *Social structure.* New York: Macmillan.

Murstein, B. I. 1976. *Who will marry whom? Theories and research in marital choice.* New York: Springer.

Murstein, B. I. 1982. Marital choice. *In* B. B. Wolman (Ed.), *Handbook of developmental psychology.* Englewood Cliffs, NJ: Prentice-Hall.

Mussen, P. H., & Rutherford, E. 1963. Parent-child relations and parental personality in relation to young children's sex-role preferences. *Child Development* 34:589–607.

Mynatt, C. R., & Allgeier, E. R. 1990. Risk factors, self-attributions, and adjustment problems among victims of sexual coercion. *Journal of Applied Social Psychology* 20:130–53.

Narum, G. D., & Rodolfa, E. R. 1984. Sex therapy for the spinal cord injured client: Suggestions for professionals. *Professional Psychology: Research and Practice* 15:775–84.

National Academy of Sciences (Committee on Contraceptive Development and Committee on Population). 1990. *Developing new contraceptives: Obstacles and opportunities.* Washington, D.C.: National Academy Press.

National Gay and Lesbian Task Force. 1988. *Anti-gay violence, victimization and defamation in 1988.* Washington, D.C.: Author.

Nelson, C., Miner, M., Marques, J., Russell, K., & Achterkirchen, J. 1988. Relapse prevention: A cognitive-behavioral model for treatment of the rapist and child molester. *Journal of Social Work and Human Sexuality* 7:125–43.

Neugarten, B. L. 1967, December. A new look at menopause. *Psychology Today* 1:42–45ff.

Nevid, J. 1984. Sex differences in factors of romantic attraction. *Sex Roles* 11:401–11.

Newcomer, S. F., & Udry, J. R. 1985. Oral sex in an adolescent population. *Archives of Sexual Behavior* 14:41–46.

Newmark, J. J. 1984, January 10. A look at the obscene phone caller. *San Francisco Chronicle*.

Nida, S. A., & Williams, J. E. 1977. Sex-stereotyped traits, physical attractiveness, and interpersonal attraction. *Psychological Reports* 41(3, Pt. 2):1311–22.

Norton, G. R., & Jehu, D. 1984. The role of anxiety in sexual dysfunctions: A review. *Archives of Sexual Behavior* 13(2):165–83.

O'Neill, G., & O'Neill, N. 1972. *Open marriage: A new life style for couples*. New York: M. Evans.

Oberstone, A. V., & Sukoneck, H. 1976. Psychological adjustment and lifestyle of single lesbians and single heterosexual women. *Psychology of Women Quarterly* 1:172–88.

Offit, A. K. 1981. *Night thoughts: Reflections of a sex therapist*. New York: Congdon & Weed.

Offit, A. K. 1983. *The sexual self*. Rev. ed. New York: Congdon & Weed.

Olds, S. W. 1985. *The eternal garden: Seasons of our sexuality*. New York: Times Books (Random House).

Pagelow, M. D. 1984. *Family violence*. New York: Praeger.

Paige, C. 1987, February. Watch on the right: The amazing rise of Beverly LaHaye. *Ms.*: 24ff.

Paige, K. E. 1978, May. The ritual of circumcision. *Human Nature* 1(5):40–48.

Paige, K. E., & Paige, J. M. 1981. *The politics of reproductive ritual*. Berkeley, CA: University of California Press.

Palys, T. S. 1986. Testing the common wisdom: The social content of video pornography. *Canadian Psychology* 27:22–35.

Papini, D. R., Farmer, F. L., Clark, S. M., & Snell, W. E. 1988. An evaluation of adolescent patterns of sexual self-disclosure to parents and friends. *Journal of Adolescent Research* 3(3–4):387–401.

Parker, T. 1969. *The twisting lane: The hidden world of sex offenders*. Indianapolis: Bobbs-Merrill.

Parlee, M. B. 1974. Stereotypic beliefs about menstruation: A methodological note on the Moos Menstrual Distress Questionnaire and some new data. *Psychosomatic Medicine* 36:229–40.

Parlee, M. B. 1982. Changes in moods and activation levels during the menstrual cycle in experimentally naive subjects. *Psychology of Women Quarterly* 7:119–31.

Parrot, A., & Allen, S. 1984. Acquaintance rape: Seduction or crime? Paper presented at the eastern regional conference of the Society for the Scientific Study of Sex.

Pauly, I. B. 1985. Gender identity disorders. In M. Farber (Ed.), *Human sexuality: Psychosexual effects of disease*. New York: Macmillan.

Payn, N. 1980. Beyond orgasm. (Unpublished doctoral dissertation.) Berkeley, CA: University of California.

Payn, N., & Wakefield, J. 1982. The effect of group treatment of primary orgasmic dysfunction on the marital relationship. *Journal of Sex & Marital Therapy* 8:135–50.

Peck, M. S. 1978. *The road less traveled: A new psychology of love, traditional values and spiritual growth*. New York: Simon and Schuster (Touchstone).

Peel, J., & Potts, M. 1969. *Textbook of contraceptive practice*. Cambridge, England: Cambridge University Press.

Pelletier, L., & Herold, E. 1988. The relationship of age, sex guilt, and sexual experience with female sexual fantasies. *Journal of Sex Research* 24:250–56.

Peplau, L. A. 1984. Power in dating relationships. *In* J. Freedman (Ed.), *Women: A feminist perspective*. 3rd ed. Palo Alto, CA: Mayfield.

Peplau, L. A., & Gordon, S. L. 1983. The intimate relationships of lesbians and gay men. *In* E. R. Allgeier & N. B. McCormick (Eds.), *Changing boundaries: Gender roles and sexual behavior*. Palo Alto: Mayfield.

Peplau, L. A., Padesky, C., & Hamilton, M. 1982. Satisfaction in lesbian relationships. *Journal of Homosexuality* 8(2):23–35.

Peplau, L. A., Rubin, Z., & Hill, C. T. 1977. Sexual intimacy in dating relationships. *Journal of Social Issues* 33(2):86–109.

Perper, T., & Fox, V. S. 1980. Flirtation and pickup patterns in bars. Paper presented at the annual meeting of the Eastern Conference on Reproductive Behavior, New York, NY.

Perry, J. D., & Whipple, B. 1981. Pelvic muscle strength of female ejaculators: Evidence in support of a new theory of orgasm. *Journal of Sex Research* 17:22–37.

Persky, H., Lief, H. I., Strauss, D., Miller, W. R., & O'Brien, C. P. 1978. Plasma testosterone level and sexual behavior of couples. *Archives of Sexual Behavior* 7:157–73.

Peterson, J. L., & Marín, G. 1988. Issues in the prevention of AIDS among black and Hispanic men. *American Psychologist* 43:871–77.

Petty, R. E., & Mirels, H. L. 1981. Intimacy and scarcity of self-disclosure: Effects on interpersonal attraction for males and females. *Personality and Social Psychology Bulletin* 7:493–503.

Phelps, L., Wallace, D., & Waigandt, A. 1989. Impact of sexual assault: Post assault behavior and health status. Paper presented at the annual meeting of the American Psychological Association, New Orleans, LA.

Phoenix, C. H., Goy, R. W., & Resko, J. A. 1968. Psychosexual differentiation as a function of androgenic stimulation. *In* M. Diamond (Ed.), *Reproduction and sexual behavior.* Bloomington, IN: Indiana University Press.

Pietropinto, A., & Simenauer, J. 1977. *Beyond the male myth: What women want to know about men's sexuality.* New York: New American Library.

Pines, A., & Aronson, E. 1983. Antecedents, correlates, and consequences of sexual jealousy. *Journal of Personality* 51:108–36.

Pirog-Good, M. A., & Stets, J. E. (Eds.). 1989. *Violence in dating relationships: Emerging social issues.* New York: Praeger.

Pocs, O., Godow, A., Tolone, W. L., & Walsh, R. H. 1977, June. Is there sex after 40? *Psychology Today* 11(1):54–56, 87.

Pogrebin, L. C. 1980. *Growing up free: Raising your kids in the 80's.* New York: McGraw-Hill.

Pollack, S., & Vaughn, J. (Eds.). 1987. *Politics of the heart: A lesbian parenting anthology.* Ithaca, NY: Firebrand Books.

Pomeroy, W. B. 1972. *Dr. Kinsey and the Institute for Sex Research.* New York: Harper & Row.

Pope, K. S., & Bouhoutsos, J. C. 1986. *Sexual intimacy between therapists and patients.* New York: Praeger.

Pope, K. S., Levenson, H., & Schover, L. R. 1979. Sexual intimacy in psychology training: Results and implications of a national survey. *American Psychologist* 34:682–89.

Porter, F. L., Miller, R. H., & Marshall, R. E. 1986. Neonatal pain cries: Effect of circumcision on acoustic features and perceived urgency. *Child Development* 57:790–802.

Press, A., McDaniel, A., Raine, G., & Carroll, G. 1986, July 14. A government in the bedroom. *Newsweek:* 36–38.

Preston, K., & Stanley, K. 1987. "What's the worst thing . . . ?" Gender-directed insults. *Sex Roles* 17:209–19.

Preti, G., Cutler, W. B. et al. 1986. Human axillary secretions influence women's menstrual cycles: The role of donor extract from females. *Hormones and Behavior* 20:474–82.

Price, R. A., & Vandenberg, S. S. 1979. Matching for physical attractiveness. *Personality and Social Psychology Bulletin* 5:398–400.

Prince, V., & Bentler, P. M. 1972. Survey of 504 cases of transvestism. *Psychological Reports* 31:903–17.

Pruitt, D., & Rubin, J. Z. 1986. *Social conflict: Escalation, stalemate, and settlement.* New York: Random House.

Quinn, T. C., Connor, R. O., Glasser, D., Groseclose, S. L., Brathwaite, W. S. et al. 1990. The association of syphilis with risk of Human Immunodeficiency Virus infection in patients attending sexually transmitted disease clinics. *Archives of Internal Medicine* 150:1297–1302.

Quinsey, V. L., Chaplin, T. C., & Upfold, D. 1984. Sexual arousal to nonsexual violence and sadomasochistic themes among rapists and non-sex-offenders. *Journal of Consulting and Clinical Psychology* 52:651–57.

Rachman, S. 1966. Sexual fetishism: An experimental analogue. *Psychological Record* 16:293–96.

Rapaport, K., & Burkhart, B. R. 1984. Personality and attitudinal characteristics of sexually coercive college males. *Journal of Abnormal Psychology* 93:216–21.

Rasky, S. F. 1985, March 25. Those baffling trends in birth control. *San Francisco Chronicle.*

Reed, J. 1978. *From private vice to public virtue: The birth control movement and American society since 1983.* New York: Basic Books.

Reiss, A. J., Jr. 1961. The social integration of queers and peers. *Social Problems* 9(2):102–20.

Reiss, I. L. 1969. Premarital sexual standards. *In* C. B. Broderick & J. Bernard (Eds.), *The individual, sex, and society*. Baltimore: Johns Hopkins University Press.

Reiss, I. 1986. *Journey into sexuality: An exploratory voyage*. Englewood Cliffs, NJ.: Prentice-Hall.

Remis, R. S., Gurwith, M. J., Gurwith, D., Hargrett-Bean, N. T., & Layde, P. M. 1987. Risk factors for urinary tract infection. *American Journal of Epidemiology* 126:685–94.

Rentzel, L. 1972. *When all the laughter died in sorrow*. New York: Saturday Review Press.

Restak, R. M. 1979, December. The sex-change conspiracy. *Psychology Today* 13(7):20, 22, 24, 25.

Riche, M. 1988, November 23–26. Postmarital society. *American Demographics:* 60.

Richwald, G. A., Greenland, S., Gerber, M. M., Potik, R., Kersey, L., & Comas, M. A. 1989. Effectiveness of the cavity-rim cervical cap: Results of a large clinical study. *Obstetrics and Gynecology* 74(2):143–48.

Robbins, M., & Jensen, G. 1978. Multiple orgasm in males. *Journal of Sex Research* 14:21–26.

Roberts, E. J., & Gagnon, J. 1978. *Family life and sexual learning: A study of the role of parents in the sexual learning of children (Vol. 1)*. Cambridge, MA: Project on Human Sexual Development.

Robin, E. 1986. Hysterectomies and blood transfusions. *Stanford Magazine*, 14(3):20–21.

Robinson, P. 1976. *The modernization of sex*. New York: Harper & Row.

Rolker-Dolinsky, B. 1987. The influence of stress, neuroticism, and chronic self-destructiveness on premenstrual symptom change (Unpublished dissertation, State University of New York at Albany).

Rorvik, D. M., & Shettles, L. B. 1970. *Your baby's sex: Now you can choose*. New York: Dodd, Mead.

Rosebury, T. 1971. *Microbes and morals: The strange story of venereal disease*. New York: Viking Press.

Rosenberg, M. J., Rojanapithayakom, W., Feldblum, P. J. et al. 1987. Effect of contraceptive sponge on chlamydial infection, gonorrhea, and candidiasis. *Journal of the American Medical Association* 257:2308–12.

Rosenblatt, P. 1977. Needed research on commitment in marriage. *In* G. Levinger & H. L. Rausch (Eds.), *Close relationships: perspectives on the meaning of intimacy*. Amherst: University of Massachusetts Press.

Ross, M. (Ed.) 1988. Psychopathology and psychotherapy in homosexuality. *Journal of Homosexuality* 15(1–2). New York: Haworth Press.

Ross, M. W., & Need, J. A. 1989. Effects of adequacy of gender reassignment surgery on psychological adjustment: A follow-up of fourteen male-to-female patients. *Archives of Sexual Behavior* 18:145–53.

Rothman, E. K. 1984. *Hands and hearts: A history of courtship in America*. New York: Basic Books.

Roughan, P. A., & Kunst, L. 1981. Do pelvic floor exercises really improve orgasmic potential? *Journal of Sex and Marital Therapy* 7:223–29.

Rubenstein, C., & Shaver, P. 1982. *In search of intimacy*. New York: Delacorte.

Rubin, L. B. 1976. *Worlds of pain: Life in the working class family*. New York: Basic Books.

Rubin, L. B. 1983. *Intimate strangers: Men and women together*. New York: Harper & Row.

Rubin, R. T., Reinisch, J. M., & Haskett, R. F. 1981. Postnatal gonadal steroid effects on human behavior. *Science* 211:1318–24.

Rubin, Z. 1973. *Liking and loving: An invitation to social psychology*. New York: Holt, Rinehart and Winston.

Rubin, Z., Hill, C. T., Peplau, L. A., & Dunkel-Schetter, C. 1980. Self-disclosure in dating couples: Sex roles and the ethic of openness. *Journal of Marriage and the Family* 42:305–17.

Rubin, Z., Peplau, L. A., & Hill, C. 1981. Loving and leaving: Sex differences in romantic attachments. *Sex Roles* 7:821–35.

Rubin, J. Z., Provenzano, F. J., & Luria, Z. 1974. The eye of the beholder: Parents' views on sex of newborns. *American Journal of Orthopsychiatry* 44:512–19.

Ruble, D. N., & Brooks, J. 1977. Adolescents' attitudes about menstruation. Paper presented at the annual meeting of the Society for Research in Child Development, New Orleans, LA.

Rugoff, M. 1971. *Prudery and passion: Sexuality in Victorian America*. New York: G. P. Putnam's Sons.

Rush, F. 1980. *The best kept secret: Sexual abuse of children*. Englewood Cliffs, NJ: Prentice-Hall.

Russell, D. E. H. 1982. The prevalence and incidence of forcible rape and attempted rape of females. *Victimology: An International Journal* 7:81–93.

Russell, D. E. H. 1983. The incidence and prevalence of intrafamilial and extrafamilial sexual abuse of female children. *Child Abuse and Neglect* 7:133–46.

Russell, D. E. H. 1984. *Sexual exploitation: Rape, child sexual abuse, and workplace harassment.* Beverly Hills, CA: Sage.

Russell, D. E. H. 1986. *The secret trauma: Incest in the lives of girls and women.* Rev. ed. New York: Basic Books.

Russell, D. E. H. 1988. Pornography and rape: A causal model. *Political Psychology* 9:44–73.

Russell, D. E. H. 1990. *Rape in marriage.* Rev. ed. Bloomington: Indiana University Press.

Russell, D. E. H., & Howell, N. 1983. The prevalence of rape in the United States revisited. *Signs: Journal of Women in Culture and Society* 8:688–95.

Saftlas, A. F., Wolfe, J. N., Hoover, R. N., Brinton, L. A., Schairer, C., Salane, M., & Szklo, M. 1989. Mammographic parenchymal patterns as indicators of breast cancer risk. *American Journal of Epidemiology* 129:518–26.

Sagarin, E. 1976. Prison homosexuality and its effect on postprison sexual behavior. *Psychiatry* 39:245–57.

Saghir, M. T., & Robins, E. 1973. *Male and female homosexuality.* Baltimore: Williams & Wilkins.

Sanday, P. R. 1986. *In* R. Porter & S. Tomaselli (Eds.), *Rape.* New York: Basil Blackwell.

Sanger, M. 1938. *An autobiography.* New York: W. W. Norton.

Sarason, E. G., & Sarason, B. R. 1987. *Abnormal psychology.* 5th ed. Englewood Cliffs, NJ: Prentice-Hall.

Savitz, L., & Rosen, L. 1988. The sexuality of prostitutes: Sexual enjoyment reported by "streetwalkers." *Journal of Sex Research* 24:200–08.

Scanzoni, J. H., & Fox, G. L. 1980. Sex roles, family, and society: The 70s and beyond. *Journal of Marriage and the Family* 42:743–56.

Scanzoni, L., & Scanzoni, J. 1976. *Men, women, and change: A sociology of marriage and family.* New York: McGraw-Hill.

Schlesselman, J. J. 1989. Cancer of the breast and reproductive tract in relation to use of oral contraceptives. *Contraception* 40:1–38.

Schmidt, G. 1983a. Sexuality and relationships. *In* G. Arentewicz & G. Schmidt (Eds.), *The treatment of sexual disorders: Concepts and techniques of couple therapy* (trans. T. Todd). New York: Basic Books.

Schmidt, G., & Arentewicz, G. 1983. Etiology. *In* G. Arentewicz & G. Schmidt (Eds.), *The treatment of sexual disorders: Concepts and techniques of couple therapy* (trans. T. Todd). New York: Basic Books.

Schmidt, G., & Arentewicz, G. 1983b. Symptoms. *In* G. Arentewicz, & G. Schmidt (Eds.), *The treatment of sexual disorders* (trans. T. Todd). New York: Basic Books.

Schmidt, G., & Sigusch, V. 1973. Women's sexual arousal. *In* J. Zubin & J. Money (Eds.), *Contemporary sexual behavior: Critical issues in the 1970s.* Baltimore: Johns Hopkins University Press.

Schneider, H. K. 1971. Romantic love among the Turu. *In* D. S. Marshall & R. C. Suggs (Eds.), *Human sexual behavior: Variations in the ethnographic spectrum.* Englewood Cliffs, NJ: Prentice-Hall.

Schover, L. R. 1988a. *Sexuality & Cancer: For the woman who has cancer, and her partner.* Booklet published by the American Cancer Society.

Schover, L. R. 1988b. *Sexuality & Cancer: For the man who has cancer, and his partner.* Booklet published by the American Cancer Society.

Schover, L. R., & Jensen, S. B. 1988. *Sexuality and chronic illness: A comprehensive approach.* New York: Guilford Press.

Schwartz, M. F., & Masters, W. H. 1988. Integration of the addictions model into a comprehensive short-term treatment program for compulsive sexual behavior. Paper presented at the annual meeting of the Society for the Scientific Study of Sex, San Francisco, Ca.

Scott, C. S., Arthur, D., Panizo, M. I., & Owen, R. 1989. Menarche: The Black American experience. *Journal of Adolescent Health Care* 10:363–68.

Scott, J. E. 1985. Violence and erotic material: The relationship between adult entertainment and rape. Paper presented at the annual meeting of the American Association for the Advancement of Science, Los Angeles, CA.

Scott, J., & Cuvelier, S. 1987. Sexual violence in Playboy magazine: A longitudinal content analysis. *Journal of Sex Research* 28:534–39.

Scott, J. E., & Schwalm, L. A. 1988. Rape rates and the circulation rates of adult magazines. *Journal of Sex Research* 24:241–50.

Seaman, B. 1972. *Free and female.* Greenwich, CT: Fawcett.

Seaman, B., & Seaman, G. 1977. *Women and the crisis in sex hormones*. New York: Rawson Associates.

Seidner, A. L., Calhoun, K. S., & Kilpatrick, D. G. 1985. Childhood and/or adolescent sexual experiences: Predicting variability in subsequent adjustment. Paper presented at the annual meeting of the American Psychological Association, Los Angeles, CA.

Selden, I. 1979, February 4. Going all the way with contraceptive ads. *Los Angeles Times*.

Selkin, J. 1975, January. Rape. *Psychology Today* 8(8):70–76.

Semans, J. H. 1956. Premature ejaculation: A new approach. *Southern Medical Journal* 49:353–57.

Senn, C. Y., & Radtke, H. L. 1986. A comparison of women's reactions to violent pornography, non-violent pornography, and erotica. Paper presented at the annual meeting of the Canadian Psychological Association, Toronto.

Shabsigh, R., Fishman, I., & Scott, F. 1988. Evaluation of erectile impotence. *Urology* 32:83–90.

Shaul, S., Bogle, J., Hale-Harbaugh, J., & Norman, A. D. (Task force on the Concerns of Physically Disabled Women.) 1978. *Toward intimacy: Family planning and sexuality concerns of physically disabled women*. 2nd ed. New York: Human Sciences Press.

Shaver, P., & Hazan, C. 1987. Romantic love conceptualized as an attachment process. *Journal of Personality and Social Psychology* 52:511–24.

Shaw, J. 1989. The unnecessary penile implant. *Archives of Sexual Behavior* 18:455–60.

Shea, J. A., & Adams, G. R. 1984. Correlates of romantic attachment: A path analysis study. *Journal of Youth and Adolescence* 13:27–44.

Sheehy, G. 1973. *Hustling*. New York: Delacourte.

Sherfey, M. J. 1973. *The nature and evolution of human sexuality*. New York: Vintage.

Sherwin, B. B. 1988. A comparative analysis of the role of androgen in human male and female sexual behavior: Behavioral specificity, critical thresholds, and sensitivity. *Psychobiology*, 16:416–25.

Sherwin, B. B., & Gelfand, M. M. 1987. The role of androgen in the maintenance of sexual functioning in oophorectomized women. *Psychosomatic Medicine* 48:1176–90.

Shilts, R. 1984, May 10. Gay America enters the political mainstream. *San Francisco Chronicle*.

Shilts, R. 1989, August 30. Laws on prostitution don't help. *San Francisco Chronicle*: A4.

Sholty, M., Ephross, P., Plaut, S., Fischman, S., Charnas, J., & Cody, C. 1984. Female orgasmic experience: A subjective study. *Archives of Sexual Behavior* 13:155–64.

Shope, D. F. 1975. *Interpersonal sexuality*. Philadelphia, PA: W. B. Saunders.

Shostak, A. B., McLouth, G., & Seng, L. 1984. *Men and abortion: Losses, lessons, and love*. New York: Greenwood/Praeger.

Shotland, R. L. 1989. A model of the causes of date rape in developing and close relationships. *In* C. Hendrick (Ed.), *Close relationships*. [*Review of Personality and Social Psychology* 10.] Beverly Hills, CA: Sage.

Shrom, S. H., Lief, H. I., & Wein, A. J. 1979. Clinical profile of experience with 130 consecutive cases of impotent men. *Urology* 13:511–15.

Siegel, K., Bauman, L. J., Christ, G. H., & Krown, S. 1988. Patterns of change in sexual behavior among gay men in New York City. *Archives of Sexual Behavior* 17:481–97.

Siegel, R. 1982. Cocaine and sexual dysfunction. *Journal of Psychoactive Drugs* 14:71–74.

Sigall, H., & Landy, D. 1973. Radiating beauty: Effects of having a physically attractive partner on person perception. *Journal of Personality and Social Psychology* 28:218–24.

Silbert, M. H., & Pines, A. M. 1982. Victimization of street prostitutes. *Victimology* 7(1–4): 122–33.

Silbert, M. H., & Pines, A. M. 1983. Early sexual exploitation as an influence in prostitution. *Social Work* 28(4):285–98.

Silvestre, L., Dubois, C., Renault, M., Rezvani, Y., Baulieu, E. E., & Ulmann, A. 1990. Voluntary interruption of pregnancy with mifepristone (RU 486) and a prostaglandin analogue. A large-scale French experience [comment]. *New England Journal of Medicine* 322(10): 691–93.

Simenauer, J., & Carroll, D. 1982. *Singles: The new Americans*. New York: Simon and Schuster.

Simon, W., & Gagnon, J. H. (with the assistance of D. E. Carns). 1967. The lesbians: A preliminary overview. *In* J. H. Gagnon & W. Simon (Eds.), *Sexual deviance*. New York: Harper & Row.

Simon, W., & Gagnon, J. H. 1969. On psychosexual development. *In* D. A. Goslin (Ed.), *Handbook of socialization theory and research*. Chicago: Rand McNally.

Simon, W., & Gagnon, J. H. 1986. Sexual scripts: Permanence and change. *Archives of Sexual Behavior* 15:97–120.

Simons, G. L. 1973. *Sex and superstition*. London: Abelard-Schuman.

Simpson, J. A., Campbell, B., & Berscheid, E. 1986. The association between romantic love and marriage: Kephart (1967) twice revisited. *Personality and Social Psychology Bulletin* 12: 363–72.

Sinclair, A. H., Berta, P., Palmer, M. S., Hawkins, J. R. et al. 1990, July 19. A gene from the human sex-determining region encodes a protein with homology to a conserved DNA-binding motif. *Nature* 346:240–44.

Singer, J. L., & Switzer, E. 1980. *Mind-play: The creative uses of fantasy*. Englewood Cliffs, NJ: Prentice-Hall.

Slade, P. 1984. Premenstrual emotional changes in normal women: Fact or fiction. *Journal of Psychosomatic Research* 28:1–7.

Slater, P. E. 1973, November. Sexual adequacy in America. *Intellectual Digest* 4(3):17–20.

Slater, P. E. 1990. *The pursuit of loneliness*. 2nd ed. Boston: Beacon Press [First published in 1970.]

Slattery, M. L., Overall, J. C. J., Abbott, T. M., French, T. K. et al. 1989a. Sexual activity, contraception, genital infections, and cervical cancer: support for a sexually transmitted disease hypothesis. *American Journal of Epidemiology* 130:248–58.

Slattery, M. L., Robison, L. M., Schuman, K. L., French, T. K., Abbott, T. M. et al. 1989b. Cigarette smoking and exposure to passive smoke are risk factors for cervical cancer. *Journal of the American Medical Association*, 261:1593–98.

Smigel, K. 1990. Consensus on treatment of early stage breast cancer: Less surgery, more research. *Journal of the National Cancer Institute* 82:1180–81.

Smith, R. W. 1979. A social psychologist looks at scientific research on homosexuality. *In* V. Bullough (Ed.), *The frontiers of sex research*. Buffalo, NY: Prometheus Books.

Snyder, M., Berscheid, E., & Glick, P. 1985. Focusing on the exterior and the interior: Two investigations of the initiation of personal relationships. *Journal of Personality and Social Psychology* 48:1427–39.

Snyder, M., & Simpson, J. A. 1987. Orientations toward romantic relationships. *In* D. Perlman & S. Duck (Eds.), *Intimate relationships: Development, dynamics, and deterioration*. Newbury Park, CA: Sage Publications.

Snyder, M., Tanke, E., & Berscheid, E. 1977. Social perception and interpersonal behavior: On the self-fulfilling nature of social stereotypes. *Journal of Personality and Social Psychology* 35:656–66.

Sobata, A. E. 1984. Inhibition of bacterial adherence by cranberry juice: Potential use for the treatment of urinary tract infections. *Journal of Urology* 131:1013–16.

Sonenstein, F. L., Pleck, J. H., & Ku, L. C. 1989. Sexual activity, condom use and AIDS awareness among adolescent males. *Family Planning Perspectives* 21(4):152–58.

Sorenson, R. C. 1973. *Adolescent sexuality in contemporary America*. New York: World.

Sorenson, S. B., Stein, J. A., Siegel, J. M., Golding, J. M., & Burnam, M. A. 1987. The prevalence of adult sexual assault: The Los Angeles Epidemiologic Catchment Area study. *American Journal of Epidemiology* 127:1154–63.

Sorrenti-Little, L., Bagley, C., & Robertson, S. 1984. An operational definition of the long-term harmfulness of sexual relations with peers and adults by young children. *Canadian Children* 9:46–57.

Stall, R. D., Coates, T. J., & Hoff, C. 1988. Behavioral risk reduction for HIV infection among gay and bisexual men: A review of results from the United States. *American Psychologist* 43: 878–85.

Stannard, U. 1970. Adam's rib, or the woman within. *Trans-Action* 8(1):24–25.

Steege, J. F., Stout, A. L., & Carson, C. C. 1986. Patient satisfaction in Scott and small-carrion penile implant recipients: A study of 52 patients. *Archives of Sexual Behavior* 15:393–99.

Stein, M. L. 1974. *Lovers, friends, slaves . . . The nine male sexual types*. New York: Berkeley Publishing/G. P. Putnam's Sons.

Stein, M. L. 1977. Prostitution. *In* J. Money & H. Musaph (Eds.), *Handbook of sexology*. Amsterdam: Elsevier/North Holland.

Steinem, G. 1978, November. Erotica and pornography: A clear and present difference. *Ms.* 7(5):53–54, 75, 78.

Steinman, D. L., Wincze, J. P., Sakheim, D. K., Barlow, David H., & Mavissakalian, M. 1981. A comparison of male and female patterns of sexual arousal. *Archives of Sexual Behavior* 10:529–47.

Stephan, W., Berscheid, E., & Walster, E. 1971. Sexual arousal and heterosexual perception. *Journal of Personality and Social Psychology* 20:93–101.

Sternberg, R. J. 1985. A triangular theory of love. Paper presented at the annual meeting of the American Psychological Association, Los Angeles, CA.

Sternberg, R. J. 1988. *The triangle of love: Intimacy, passion, commitment.* New York: Basic Books.

Stets, J. E., & Straus, M. A. 1989. The marriage license as a hitting license: A comparison of assaults in dating, cohabiting, and married couples. *Journal of Family Violence* 4(2):161–80.

Stiller, R. 1974. *The love bugs: A natural history of the VDs.* Nashville and New York: Thomas Nelson.

Stock, W. E. 1983. The effects of violent pornography on women. Paper presented at the annual meeting of the American Psychological Association.

Stoller, R. J. 1979. *Sexual excitement: Dynamics of erotic life.* New York: Pantheon Books.

Storms, M. D. 1981. A theory of erotic orientation development. *Psychological Review* 88:340–53.

Strassberg, D. S., Kelly, M. P., Carroll, C., & Kircher, J. C. 1987. The psychophysiological nature of premature ejaculation. *Archives of Sexual Behavior* 16:327–36.

Straus, M., Gelles, R. J., & Steinmetz, S. K. 1981. *Behind closed doors: Violence in the American family.* New York: Doubleday.

Stretch, R. H., & Figley, C. R. 1980. Beauty and the boast: Predictors of interpersonal attraction in a dating experiment. *Psychology: A Quarterly Journal of Human Behavior* 17(1):35–43.

Strom, B. L., Collins, M., West, S. L., Kreisberg, J., & Weller, S. 1987. Sexual activity, contraceptive use, and other risk factors for symptomatic and asymptomatic bacteriuria: A case-control study. *Annals of Internal Medicine* 107:816–23.

Stuart, F., Hammond, C., & Pett, M. 1987. Inhibited sexual desire in women. *Archives of Sexual Behavior* 16:91–106.

Study Group of New York. 1983. *Children & SEX: The parents speak.* New York: Facts on File.

Sue, D. 1979. Erotic fantasies of college students during coitus. *Journal of Sex Research* 15: 299–305.

Sue, D., Sue, D., & Sue, S. 1990. *Understanding abnormal behavior.* 3rd ed. Boston: Houghton Mifflin.

Sulloway, F. J. 1979. *Freud: Biologist of the mind.* New York: Basic Books.

Surra, C. A., & Huston, T. L. 1987. Mate selection as a social transition. *In* D. Perlman & S. Duck (Eds.), *Intimate relationships: Development, dynamics, and deterioration.* Newbury Park, CA: Sage Publications.

Susset, J. G., Tessier, C. D., Wincze, J., Bansal, S., Malhotra, C., & Schwacha, M. G. 1989. Effect of yohimbine hydrochloride on erectile impotence: A double-blind study. *Journal of Urology* 141:1360–63.

Sutton-Smith, B., & Abrams, D. M. 1977. Psychosexual material in the stories told by children: The fucker. *In* R. Gemme & C. C. Wheeler (Eds.), *Progress in sexology.* New York: Plenum.

Sweet, E. 1988, March. A failed revolution. *Ms.:* 75–79.

Symanski, R. 1984. Prostitution in Nevada. *Annals of American Geographers* 64:359–77.

Tampax, Inc. 1981. *The Tampax report* (Conducted by Research & Forecasts, Inc.). Lake Success, NY.

Tanfer, K. 1987. Patterns of premarital cohabitation among never-married women in the United States. *Journal of Marriage and the Family* 49:483–97.

Tangri, S., Burt, M. R., & Johnson, L. B. 1982. Sexual harassment at work: Three explanatory models. *Journal of Social Issues* 38(4):33–44.

Tanner, J. M. 1962. *Growth at adolescence.* Oxford: Blackwell.

Tavris, C. 1974, June. The frozen world of the familiar stranger. [Interview with Stanley Milgram.] *Psychology Today* 8(1):70–73, 76–78, 80.

Tavris, C. (forthcoming). *The mismeasure of woman.* New York: Simon and Schuster.

Tavris, C., & Sadd, S. 1977. *The Redbook report on female sexuality.* New York: Dell.

Tavris, C., & Tiefer, L. (unpublished ms.). Bed time story.

Tavris, C., & Wade, C. 1984. *The longest war: Sex differences in perspective.* 2nd ed. San Diego: Harcourt Brace Jovanovich.

Tea, N. T., Castanier, M., Roger, M., & Scholler, R. 1975. Simultaneous radio-immunoassay of plasma progesterone and 17-hydroxyprogesterone normal values in children, in men, and in women throughout the menstrual cycle and in early pregnancy. *Journal of Steroid Biochemistry* 6:1509–16.

Teti, D., & Lamb, M. 1989. Socioeconomic and marital outcomes of adolescent marriage, adolescent childbirth, and their co-occurrence. *Journal of Marriage and the Family* 51:203–12.

Thibaut, J. W., & Kelley, H. H. 1959. *The social psychology of groups.* New York: Wiley.

Thomas, L. 1979. *The medusa and the snail: More notes of a biology watcher.* New York: Viking.

Thornburg, H., & Aras, Z. 1986. Physical characteristics of developing adolescents. *Journal of Adolescent Research* 1:47–78.

Thurber, J., & White, E. B. 1957. *Is sex necessary?* New York: Harper & Brothers. [First published in 1929.]

Tiefer, L. 1979. *Human Sexuality: Feelings and function.* New York: Harper & Row.

Tiefer, L. 1989. Applications of social constructionism to research on gender and sexuality. Paper presented at the annual meeting of the American Psychological Association, New Orleans, LA.

Tollison, C. D., & Adams, H. E. 1979. *Sexual disorders: Treatment, theory, research.* New York: Gardner Press.

Toniolo, P., Riboli, E., Protta, F., Charrel, M., & Cappa, A. P. 1989. Breast cancer and alcohol consumption: A case-control study in northern Italy. *Cancer Research* 49:5203–06.

Traupmann, J., & Hatfield, E. 1983. How important is marital fairness over the lifespan? *International Journal of Aging and Human Development* 17:89–101.

Trudel, G., & Saint-Laurent, S. 1983. A comparison between the effects of Kegel's exercises and a combination of sexual awareness relaxation and breathing on situational orgasmic dysfunction in women. *Journal of Sex and Marital Therapy* 9:204–09.

Trussell, J. 1988. Teenage pregnancy in the United States. *Family Planning Perspectives* 20:262–73.

Turkington, C. 1987, March. Sexual aggression 'widespread.' *APA Monitor:* 15.

Turner, B. F., & Adams, C. G. 1988. Reported change in preferred sexual activity over the adult years. *Journal of Sex Research* 25:289–303.

Tyler, D. C. 1988. Pain in the neonate. *Pre- & Peri-Natal Psychology Journal* 3:53–59.

U.S. Bureau of the Census. 1986. Household and family characteristics, March 1985. Washington, D.C.

U.S. Bureau of the Census. 1988. *Statistical abstract of the United States: 1989.* 108th ed. Washington, D.C.

U.S. Bureau of the Census. 1989. *Statistical abstract of the United States: 1990.* 109th ed. Washington, D.C.

U.S. Department of Health, Education, and Welfare. 1978. *Juvenile prostitution: A federal strategy for combating its causes and consequences.* (HEW Contract No. 105-77-2100.). Washington, D.C.: U.S. Government Printing Office.

U.S. Department of Justice (Federal Bureau of Investigation). 1985. *Uniform crime reports.* Washington, D.C.: U.S. Government Printing Office.

U.S. Department of Justice (Attorney General's Commission on Pornography). 1986. *Final report of the Attorney General's Commission on Pornography.* Washington, D.C.: U.S. Department of Justice.

U.S. Merit Systems Protection Board. 1981. *Sexual harassment in the Federal workplace. Is it a problem?* Washington, D.C.: U.S. Government Printing Office.

Underwager, R., Wakefield, H., Legrand, R., Bartz, C. S., & Erickson, J. 1986. The role of the psychologist in the assessment of cases of alleged sexual abuse of children. Paper presented at the annual meeting of the American Psychological Association, Washington, D.C.

Vance, E. B., & Wagner, N. N. 1977. Written descriptions of orgasm: A study of sex differences. *In* D. Byrne & L. A. Byrne (Eds.), *Exploring human sexuality.* New York: Thomas Y. Crowell.

Verhulst, J., & Heiman, J. R. 1988. A systems perspective on sexual desire. *In* S. R. Leiblum & R. C. Rosen (Eds.), *Sexual desire disorders.* New York: Guilford Press.

Vila, J., & Beech, H. R. 1980. Premenstrual symptomatology: An interaction hypothesis. *British Journal of Social and Clinical Psychology* 19:73–80.

Wade, C. 1985. Relaxing for romance. *American Health* 4:40–44.

Wade, C. 1988. Beyond birds and bees: What sex education leaves out. *Working Mother* 11:97–103.

Wakefield, J. C. 1987. The semantics of success: Do masturbation exercises lead to partner orgasm? *Journal of Sex & Marital Therapy* 13:3–14.

Wakefield, J. C. 1988. Female primary orgasmic dysfunction: Masters and Johnson versus DSM-III—R on diagnosis and incidence. *Journal of Sex Research* 24:363–77.

Walbroehl, G. S. 1984. Sexuality during pregnancy. *American Family Physician* 29:273–75.

Wallace, D. H., & Wehmer, G. 1972. Evaluation of visual erotica by sexual liberals and conservatives. *Journal of Sex Research* 8:147–53.

Wallis, C. 1984, August 27. Can science pick a child's sex? *Time:* 59.

Wallis, C. 1985, December 9. Children having children. *Time:* 78–90.

Walster, E., Aronson, V., Abrahams, D., & Rottmann, L. 1966. Importance of physical attractiveness in dating behavior. *Journal of Personality and Social Psychology* 4:508–16.

Walster, E., & Walster, G. 1978. *A new look at love.* Reading, MA: Addison-Wesley.

Walster, E., Walster, G. W., & Berscheid, E. 1978. *Equity: Theory and research.* Boston: Allyn & Bacon.

Walters, A. T. 1986. Heterosexual bias in psychological research on lesbianism and male homosexuality. *Journal of Homosexuality* 13:35–58.

Warren, M. A. 1985. *Gendercide.* Totowa, NJ: Rowman and Allanheld.

Warshaw, R. 1988. *I never called it rape: The Ms. report on recognizing, fighting and surviving date rape.* New York: Harper & Row.

Watson, R., & DeMeo, P. 1987. Premarital cohabitation vs. traditional courtship and subsequent marital adjustment: A replication and follow-up. *Family Relations* 36:193–97.

Weaver, C. 1986, December. Toxics and male infertility. *Public Citizen* 7:12–15, 23.

Weinberg, G. H. 1972. *Society and the healthy homosexual.* New York: St. Martin's Press.

Weinberg, M. S., & Williams, C. J. 1974. *Male homosexuals: Their problems and adaptations.* New York: Oxford University Press.

Weinberg, T. S. 1987. Sadomasochism in the United States: A review of recent sociological literature. *Journal of Sex Research* 23:50–69.

Weintraub, P. 1981, April. The brain: His and hers. *Discover:* 15, 17–20.

Weiss, R. W. 1973. *Loneliness: The experience of emotional and social isolation.* Cambridge, MA: Massachusetts Institute of Technology Press.

Wells, G. A., Fisher, W. A., Warren, W. K., King, M. A., Doherty, J. A., & Bowie, W. R. 1990. High risk STD/HIV behavior among college students. *Journal of the American Medical Association* 263:3155–59.

Westoff, C., Calot, G., & Foster, A. 1983. Teenage fertility in developed nations, 1971–1980. *International Family Planning Perspectives* 9:45–50.

Westoff, C. F., & Jones, E. F. 1977. Secularization of U.S. Catholic birth control practices. *Family Planning Perspectives* 9(5):203–07.

Whitam, F. L. 1977. The homosexual role: A reconsideration. *Journal of Sex Research* 13:1–11.

White, G. 1980. Physical attractiveness and courtship progress. *Journal of Personality and Social Psychology* 39:660–68.

White, S. E., & Reamy, K. 1982. Sexuality and pregnancy: A review. *Archives of Sexual Behavior* 5:429–44.

Whitley, B. E. 1988. College students' reasons for sexual intercourse: A sex role perspective. Paper presented at the annual meeting of the American Psychological Association, Atlanta, GA.

Wikler, N. 1982. Myth in the making: The status of women in the 80s. Speech presented to the Detroit Bar Association, May.

Wilbur, A. E. 1986. The contraceptive crisis. *Science Digest* 94(9):54–61, 84–85.

Williams, W. 1986. *The spirit and the flesh: Sexual diversity in American Indian culture.* Boston: Beacon Press.

Wilmoth, G., & Adelstein, D. 1988. Psychological sequelae of abortion and public policy. Paper presented at the annual meeting of the American Psychological Association, Atlanta, GA.

Wilson, E. O. 1975. *Sociobiology.* Cambridge, MA: Harvard University Press.

Wilson, G. T., & Lawson, D. M. 1978. Expectancies, alcohol, and sexual arousal in women. *Journal of Abnormal Psychology* 87:358–67.

Wilson, M. 1984. Female homosexuals' need for dominance and endurance. *Psychological Reports* 55:79–82.

Winch, R. F. 1958. *Mate-selection: A study of complementary needs.* New York: Harper & Row.

Wiswell, T. E., & Geschke, D. W. 1989. Risks from circumcision during the first month of life compared with those for uncircumcised boys. *Pediatrics* 83:1001–05.

Wiswell, T. E., Enzenauer, R. W., Holton, M. E., Cornish, J. D., & Hankins, C. T. 1987. Declining frequency of circumcision: Implications for changes in the absolute incidence and male to female sex ratio of urinary tract infections in early infancy. *Pediatrics* 79:338–42.

Wolchik, S. A., Spencer, S. L., & Lisi, I. S. 1983. Volunteer bias in research employing vaginal measures of sexual arousal. *Archives of Sexual Behavior* 12:399–408.

Wolfe, L. 1977, January 10. The coming baby boom. *New York Magazine.*

Wolner-Hanssen, P., Eschenbach, D. A., Paavonen, J., Kiviat, N., Stevens, C. et al. 1990. Decreased risk of symptomatic chlamydial pelvic inflammatory disease associated with oral contraceptive use. *Journal of the American Medical Association* 263:54–59.

Wolner-Hanssen, P., Eschenbach, D. A., Paavonen, J., Stevens, C. E., Kiviat, N. et al. 1990. Association between vaginal douching and acute pelvic inflammatory disease. *Journal of the American Medical Association* 263:1936–41.

Wood, C. S. 1979. *Human sickness and health: A biocultural view.* Palo Alto, CA: Mayfield Press.

Wyatt, G. 1985. The sexual abuse of Afro-American and white women in childhood. *Child Abuse and Neglect: The International Journal* 9:507–19.

Wyatt, G., Peters, S., & Guthrie, D. 1988. Kinsey revisited, Part I: Comparisons of the sexual socialization and sexual behavior of white women over 33 years. *Archives of Sexual Behavior* 17:201–39.

Yarber, W. L., & Whitehill, L. L. 1981. The relationship between parental affective orientation toward sexuality and responses to sex-related situations of preschool-age children. *Journal of Sex Education and Therapy* 7:36–39.

Yllo, K. 1983. Sexual equality and violence against wives in American states. *Journal of Comparative Family Studies* 14:67–86.

Young, R. C., Walton, L. A., Ellenberg, S. S., Homesley, H. D., Wilbanks, G. et al. 1990. Adjuvant therapy in stage I and stage II epithelial ovarian cancer. Results of two prospective randomized trials. *New England Journal of Medicine* 322:1021–27.

Young, W. C. 1961. The hormones and mating behavior. *In* W. C. Young (Ed.), *Sex and internal secretions (Vol. 2).* Baltimore, MD: Williams & Wilkins.

Young, W. C., Goy, R. W., & Phoenix, C. H. 1964. Hormones and sexual behavior. *Science* 143:212–18.

Zaslow, M. J., Pedersen, F. A., Cain, R. L., Suwalsky, J. T., & Kramer, E. L. 1985. Depressed mood in new fathers: Association with parent-infant interaction. *Genetic, Social, and General Psychology Monographs* 111(2):133, 135–50.

Zaviačič, M., Doležalová, S., Holomáň, I. K., Zaviačičová, A., Mikulecký, M., & Brázdil, V. 1988. Concentrations of fructose in female ejaculate and urine: A comparative biochemical study. *Journal of Sex Research* 24:319–21.

Zaviačič, M., Zaviačičová, A., Holomáň, I. K., & Molčan, J. 1988. Female urethral expulsions evoked by local digital stimulation of the G-spot: Differences in the response patterns. *Journal of Sex Research* 24:311–18.

Zeiss, A. M., Rosen, G. M., & Zeiss, R. A. 1978. Orgasm during intercourse: A treatment strategy for women. *In* J. LoPiccolo & L. LoPiccolo (Eds.), *Handbook of sex therapy.* New York: Plenum.

Zellman, G. L., & Goodchilds, J. D. 1983. Becoming sexual in adolescence. *In* E. R. Allgeier & N. B. McCormick (Eds.), *Changing boundaries: Gender roles and sexual behavior.* Palo Alto, CA: Mayfield Publishing.

Zelnik, M., & Kantner, J. F. 1977. Sexual and contraceptive experience of young unmarried women in the United States, 1976 and 1971. *Family Planning Perspectives* 9(2):55–71.

Zilbergeld, B. 1978. *Male sexuality.* New York: Bantam.

Zilbergeld, B., & Ellison, C. R. 1980. Desire discrepancies and arousal problems in sex therapy. *In* S. R. Leiblum & L. A. Pervin (Eds.), *Principles and practice of sex therapy.* New York: Guilford Press.

Zilbergeld, B., & Evans, M. 1980, August. The inadequacy of Masters and Johnson. *Psychology Today* 14(3):29–43.

Zilbergeld, B., & Hammond, D. 1988. The use of hypnosis in treating desire disorders. *In* S. Leiblum & R. Rosen (Eds.), *Sexual desire disorders.* New York: Guilford Press.

Zillman, D., & Bryant, J. 1982. Pornography, sexual callousness, and the trivialization of rape. *Journal of Communication* 32:10–21.

Zillman, D., & Bryant, J. 1984. Effects of massive exposure to pornography. *In* N. M. Malamuth & E. Donnerstein (Eds.), *Pornography and sexual aggression.* Orlando, FL: Academic Press.

Zillman, D., & Bryant, J. 1988. Pornography's impact on sexual satisfaction. *Journal of Applied Social Psychology* 18:438–53.

Zuger, B. 1989. Homosexuality in families of boys with early effeminate behavior: An epidemiological study. *Archives of Sexual Behavior* 18:155–66.

Zunzunegui, M. V., King, M. C., Coria, C. F., & Charlet, J. 1986. Male influences on cervical cancer risk. *American Journal of Epidemiology* 123:302–07.

Acknowledgments

•

The authors would like to thank the following for permission to reproduce material in this book.

Text

American Health Partners for "Relaxing for Romance" by Carole Wade from *American Health 4*, pp. 40–44. Copyright © 1985 American Health Partners.

Clyde and Susan Hendrick for adaptation from "A Theory and Method of Love" from *Journal of Personality and Social Psychology 50*, pp. 392–402. Copyright © 1986 Clyde and Susan Hendrick. Published with permission of the authors and the American Psychological Association.

Male Sexuality: A Guide to Sexual Fulfillment by Bernie Zilbergeld. Copyright © 1978 by Bernie Zilbergeld. Reprinted by permission of Little, Brown and Co.

Robert Gordis for excerpt from *Love and Sex* by Robert Gordis. Copyright © 1978 by Robert Gordis. Reprinted by permission of the author.

Plenum Publishers for extract from "Orgasm During Intercourse: A Treatment Strategy for Women" by Zeiss, A.M.; Rosen, G.M.; and Zeiss, R.A. (1978) from *Handbook of Sex Therapy*, edited by J. L. Piccolo and L. Piccolo. Copyright © 1978 by Plenum. Reprinted with permission of the publisher.

Simon and Schuster, Inc. for excerpts from a list of five distinct relationship categories from *Homosexualities: A Study of Diversity Among Men and Women* by Alan P. Bell and Martin S. Weinberg. Copyright © 1978 by Alan P. Bell and Martin S. Weinberg. Reprinted by permission of Simon and Schuster, Inc.

Tables

7–1   Irvington Publishers, Inc. for adaptation from "Contraceptive Methods: How Well Do They Work?" by Hatcher, Robert A.; Stewart, Felicia; Trussell, James; Kowal, Deborah et al. From *Contraceptive Technology 1990–1992* (15th rev. ed.) N.Y., Irvington (p. 134, Table 8–2). Reprinted by permission of the authors and publisher.

7–2   Irvington Publishers, Inc. for adaptation from "Putting Voluntary Risks into Perspective" by Hatcher et al, Copyright © 1990 Irvington Publishers Inc. from *Contraceptive Technology 1988–1989*, p. 146, Table 8–4.

8–1   Toni Falbo and Letitia Anne Peplau for table adapted from "Power Strategies in Intimate Relationships" from *Journal of Personality and Social Psychology*, *38*, pp. 618–628, Table 2. Copyright © 1980 by Toni Falbo and American Psychological Association. Reprinted by permission of the author and publisher.

10–1   Warner Books, Inc. for adaptation from "Sex Orientation Scale" from *The Transsexual Phenomenon* by Harry Benjamin. Copyright © 1966 by Warner Books. Reprinted with permission of the publisher.

14–2   Haworth Press for "Klein Sexual Orientation Grid" from *Sexual Orientation: A Multivariate Dynamic Process* by Klein, F; Sepekoff, B.; and Wolf, T.J. (1985). *Journal of Homosexuality II* (1/2), pp. 35–49. Copyright © 1985 by Haworth Press.

Photographs

Page **4** left: Oxford Scientific Films, Animals/Animals; right: Marty Stouffer Productions, Animals/Animals; **5** left: © M. Austerman, Animals/Animals; right: © Anup & Manoj Shaw, Animals/Animals; **7** © Mal Ent Inc.; **8** PPS Photographers, San Diego, CA.; **11** left: © Chad/Ehlers, International Stock Photo; right: © Henry H. Bagish, Anthro/Photo; **13** left: © Brent Winebrenner/International Stock Photo; middle: Owen Franken/Stock Boston; right: © Bob Firth/International Stock Photo; **15** Art Resource; **19** © Alex Webb/Magnum Photos; **23** © Steve McCurry/Magnum Photos; **33** COPYRIGHT 1987, G.B. Trudeau. Reprinted with permission of Universal Press Syndicate. All rights reserved; **35** Bridgeman/Art Resource; **39** Art Resource; **42** The Bettmann Archive; **44** The Bettmann Archive; **47** Culver Pictures; **49** Mary Evans Picture Library, London; **50** Billy Rose Theatre Collection, The New York Public Library at Lincoln Center, Astor, Lenox, and Tilden Foundation; **55** Philip Jones Griffiths/Magnum Photos; **56** Paul Steel/Stock Market; **67** John Caldwell; **70** The Bettmann Archive; **71** The Bettmann Archive; **75** UPI/Bettmann Newsphotos; **78** Culver Pictures; **82** The Bettmann Archive; **84** © Robert Levin 1981/Black Star; **88** The Bettmann Archive; **91** © Jules Feiffer; **132** © Alan Carey/The Image Works; **133** © Alan Carey/The Image Works; **146** © Willie L. Hill, Jr./Stock Boston; **154** © Eric Roth/The Picture Cube; **157** © Alan Carey/The Image Works; **159** Freer Gallery of Art, Washington, D.C.; **163** © Mark Wright/Photo Researchers; **164** The Library of the New York Botanical Garden, Bronx, New York; **165** © David Wells/The Image Works; **176** © Charles Gupton/Stock Boston; **185** © Stern/Black Star; **188** all: © Lennert Nilsson, *Behold Man*, Little, Brown & Company; **189** all: © Lennert Nilsson, *Behold Man*, Little, Brown & Company; **195** top: © Lennert Nilsson, *Behold Man*, Little, Brown & Company; bottom: © Bill Gallery/Stock Boston; **196** © Dario Perla/International Stock Photo; **210** © Lennert Nilsson, *Behold Man*, Little, Brown & Company; **212** © Lennert Nilsson, *Behold Man*, Little, Brown & Company; **214** ©Volker Hinz, Stern 1980/Blackstar; **227** The Bettmann Archive; **242** PPS Photographers, San Diego, CA.; **245** PPS Photographers, San Diego, CA.; **254** Pharmacists Planning Service, Inc.; **262** © L. Borshay/TIME Magazine; **279** Mel Calman, © Dist. Field Newspaper Syndicate; **282** © Peter Menzel/Stock Boston; **288** John Bateman; **289** © Robin Schwartz/International Stock Photo; **293** Art Resource; **295** © Alice Randell/Photo Researchers; **297** © 1987 United Feature Syndicate, Inc.; **298** © Chuck Fishman/Woodfin Camp & Associates; **299** © Marianne Goutary/Picture Cube; **300** Cathy COPYRIGHT, Cathy Guisewite. Reprinted with permission of Universal Press Syndicate. All rights reserved; **302** © Rae Russel/International Stock Photo; **310** © Richard Hutching/Photo Researchers; **318** John Caldwell; **327** L.L. Brown. Courtesy of The Institute of Psycho-Structural Balancing, San Diego, CA.; **344** Copyright 1986, John Caldwell; **354** © Bettye Lane; **358** © George W. Gardner; **363** © Joel Gordon; **366** © Ken Karp; **368** © Sepp Seitz 1979/Woodfin Camp & Associates; **374** Bloom County, Berke Breathed 1983, © The Washington Post; **385** © Frank Siteman/Stock Boston; **389** © Judy Gelles/Stock Boston; **392** © Paul Fortin 1980/Stock Boston; **397** Cathy COPYRIGHT, Cathy Guisewite. Reprinted with permission of Universal Press Syndicate. All rights reserved; **417** © Barbara Alper/Stock Boston; **421** © Steve Takatsuno/Picture Cube; **436** all: © Lennert Nilsson, *Behold Man*, Little, Brown & Company; **437** © Mimi Cotter/International Stock Photo; **438** all: Jean Claude Lejeune/Stock Boston; **442** © Chris Steel Perkins/Magnum Photos; **444** Judy S. Gelles/Stock Boston; **445** Barbara Rios/Photo Researchers; **452** all: Courtesy Dr. John Money from John and Anke A. Earhardt, *Man & Woman, Boy & Girl*, Baltimore, Johns Hopkins University Press; **454** © Hella Hammid/Photo Researchers; **458** Elizabeth Crews; **459** left: © Frostie 1981/Woodfin Camp & Associates; right: © Blevin McCurry/Magnum; **465** © Clemens/International Stock Photo; **477** © Sepp Seitz 1978/Woodfin Camp & Associates; **480** © Stephen Shames 1980/Woodfin Camp & Associates; **482** © Watriss-Baldwin 1980/Woodfin Camp & Associates; **484** © Stephen Shames 1981/Woodfin Camp & Associates; **487** © 1986 Planned Parenthood Federation of America; **489** Arthur Grace/Stock Boston; **490** Peter Sickles/Stock Boston; **491** © Robin Schwartz/International Stock Photo; **497** © Ira Berger 1978/Black Star; **499** top left, top right, bottom left: Katrina Thomas/Photo Researchers; bottom right: Stephanie Dinkins/Photo Researchers; **502** Photofest; **506** Opie © The New Yorker Magazine; **508** © 1984 Nancy Durrell McKenna/Photo Researchers; **514** Photofest; **522** © Chris Hardy; **526** Collection of The Library of Congress; **534** Peter Southwick/Stock Boston; **536** © Joel Gordon 1981; **541** Museum of Modern Art Film Stills Archive; **543** Eric A. Roth/Picture Cube; **544** © Rose Skytta/Jeroboam; **546** Ira Kirschenbaum/Stock Boston; **557** UPI/Bettmann Newsphotos; **569** Photofest; **573** Photofest; **578** UPI/Bettmann Newsphotos; **581** © Bettye Lane; **583** © Jim Anderson/Woodfin Camp & Associates; **585** Spencer Grant/Stock Boston; **589** Professional Photographic Services, Inc., San Diego, CA.; **591** © Cynthia Copple; **593** © Jerry

Abramowitz; **602** © 1984 Marvel Entertainment Group, Inc. All rights reserved; **612** © Joel Gordon 1979; **614** Wide World; **618** Cynthia Johnson/TIME Magazine; **621** © Nancy Durrell McKenna/Photo Researchers; **622** © David Harn/Magnum Photos; **635** © Jim Anderson 1981/Woodfin Camp & Associates; **637** © Leif Skoogfors/Woodfin Camp & Associates; **647** Centers for Disease Control; **650** National Library of Medicine; **651** Medical Stock Photo; **653** Medical Stock Photo; **654** left: Centers for Disease Control; right: Medical Stock Photo; **657** Jaye R. Phillips/Photo Cube; **658** Medical Stock Photo; **661** © Chris Hardy; **665** Collection of Dr. and Mrs. William F. Kaiser, Berkeley, CA.; **666** Centers for Disease Control; **668** World Health Organization; **669** Centers for Disease Control; **673** © Hazel Hankin; **676** © Pharmacists Planning Service, Inc.; **688** Medical Stock Photo; **690** © Peter G. Aitken/Photo Researchers; **694** Medical Stock Photo; **703** © Bill Bachman/Photo Researchers; **708** Elizabeth Crews; **711** © 1977 by N.E.A., Inc. Jim Berry; **712** Elizabeth Crews; **717** top left: Bruce Davidson/Magnum Photos; top right: M.B. Duda/Photo Researchers; middle left: Chester Higgins, Jr./Photo Researchers; center: Ellis Herwig/Photo Researchers; middle right: Chester Higgins, Jr./Photo Researchers; bottom left: © David Powers/Stock Boston; bottom right: © Chris Hardy.

Part Openers

Part I: Copyright 1989 Comstock; **Part II:** Robert Farber/The Image Bank; **Part III:** The Telegraph Colour Library/FPG; **Part IV:** Michael Salas/The Image Bank; **Part V:** © Daniel Forer/The Image Bank.

Name Index

•

Subject Index

•

A B C D E F G H I J
1 2 3 4 5 6 7 8 9 0